PRAISE FOR *THE COURAGE TO HEAL*

"This book advances the empowerment of survivors another major step—from breaking the silence to sharing recovery."

—Judith Herman, M.D., author of *Trauma and Recovery*

"*The Courage to Heal* is a wise and gentle book that should be read by all people trying to recover from having been sexually misused as a child, and by all friends, family members, and professionals with a genuine desire to understand both the experience of being a victim of sexual abuse and the arduous path to recovery. *The Courage to Heal* has helped countless survivors of sexual abuse in their efforts to confront the realities of their lives and to take charge of them in the present."

—Bessel A. van der Kolk, M.D., associate professor of psychiatry,
Harvard Medical School

"*The Courage to Heal* continues to be an invaluable resource for adults sexually abused as children. Ellen Bass and Laura Davis provide survivors with concrete and practical information about the healing process and its many challenges."

—Christine Courtois, clinical director of the Post-Traumatic Disorders Program
of the Psychiatric Institute of Washington, D.C., and author of
Recollections of Sexual Abuse: Treatment Principles and Guidelines

"With scrupulous care, balance, and a clear political vision, Ellen Bass and Laura Davis have written a groundbreaking book that will stand as a classic for many years to come. Clearly a labor of both love and commitment to the healing of tens of thousands of women still suffering the deep wounds of their experience, *The Courage to Heal* will find a wide, appreciative, and altered readership."

—Sandra Butler, author of *The Conspiracy of Silence*

ACCLAIM FROM SURVIVORS FOR *THE COURAGE TO HEAL*

"*The Courage to Heal* touched the deepest part of me, the part that has been walled off and silent for twenty-five years. You have spoken the words for me that I was unable to utter."

"When your book entered my life, it gave me the reassurance that one day I would be whole."

"Dealing with feelings that have been hidden, suppressed, and unacknowledged for fifty years is an awesome task, and your book is helping to make the process bearable and possible."

"If there was any one thing that helped me to believe in myself, and helped to reconstruct my life, it has been this book. *The Courage to Heal* has not spent a day on the bookshelf—I utilize it so often that it is a waste to put it away."

" 'Thank you' hardly seems like enough to say. You have changed the direction of my life in a *positive* way with as much impact as the incest changed my life in a negative way so many years ago."

"Thank you for helping me save my life and my sanity."

20TH ANNIVERSARY EDITION

The Courage to Heal

FOURTH EDITION

ALSO FROM ELLEN BASS AND LAURA DAVIS

Ellen Bass

The Human Line (poetry)

Mules of Love (poetry)

No More Masks! An Anthology of Poems by Women
(coeditor, with Florence Howe)

I Never Told Anyone:
Writing by Women Survivors of Child Sexual Abuse
(coeditor, with Louise Thornton)

Free Your Mind:
The Book for Gay, Lesbian, and Bisexual Youth—
and Their Allies (with Kate Kaufman)

I Like You to Make Jokes with Me, But I Don't Want You
to Touch Me (for children)

Laura Davis

The Courage to Heal Workbook:
For Women and Men Survivors of Child Sexual Abuse

Allies in Healing:
When the Person You Love Was Sexually Abused as a Child

Becoming the Parent You Want to Be:
a Sourcebook of Strategies for the First Five Years
(with Janis Keyser)

I Thought We'd Never Speak Again:
The Road from Estrangement to Reconciliation

The Last Frontier:
Is Reconciliation Possible After Sexual Abuse?
(available at www.lauradavis.net)

Ellen Bass and Laura Davis

Beginning to Heal:
A First Book for Survivors of Child Sexual Abuse

For current listings of foreign-language editions of both *The Courage to Heal* and *Beginning to Heal*, please visit www.ellenbass.com/books/php.

20TH ANNIVERSARY EDITION

The Courage to Heal

*A Guide for Women Survivors
of Child Sexual Abuse*

FOURTH EDITION

ELLEN BASS & LAURA DAVIS

COLLINS LIVING
An Imprint of HarperCollins Publishers

The names of some individuals have been changed. For more information, please see pages xxvii–xxviii and page 410.

This book is for informational purposes only and is not intended to be a substitute for appropriate psychotherapy or medical care. The publisher and the authors disclaim all liability that may arise as a result of using the information in this book.

The authors regret that they are unable to answer individual letters, e-mails, and phone calls. If you need resources, information, or support, please contact the many helpful organizations listed in the Resource Guide.

The Courage to Heal (1992) is available on audiocassette from HarperAudio, a division of HarperCollins Publishers.

Copyright acknowledgments precede the Index.

The first edition of this book was published in 1988 by Harper & Row, Publishers.

THE COURAGE TO HEAL, FOURTH EDITION. Copyright © 2008 by Ellen Bass and Laura Davis. All rights reserved. Printed in the United States of America. No part of this book may be used or reproduced in any manner whatsoever without written permission except in the case of brief quotations embodied in critical articles and review. For information, address HarperCollins Publishers, 10 East 53rd Street, New York, NY 10022.

HarperCollins books may be purchased for educational, business, or sales promotional use. For information, please write: Special Markets Department, HarperCollins Publishers, 10 East 53rd Street, New York, NY 10022.

FOURTH EDITION

Designed by Laura Kaeppel

Library of Congress Cataloging-in-Publication Data

Bass, Ellen.
    The courage to heal: a guide for women survivors of child sexual abuse: 20th anniversary edition/by Ellen Bass and Laura Davis.—4th ed.
        p. cm.
    Includes index.
    ISBN 978-0-06-128433-5
    1. Child sexual abuse—United States.   2. Women—United States—Psychology.
    3. Adult child abuse victims—United States.   I. Davis, Laura, 1956–   II. Title.
HQ72.U53B37 2008
616.85'8369—dc22   2008011616

08 09 10 11 12   OV/RRD   10 9 8 7 6 5 4 3 2 1

Contents

"Don't run away from it. Don't bury it. Don't try to produce a different reality getting all strung out on something, or eating your way through your feelings. Don't slash your wrists. Just deal with it, because it's going to keep coming back if you continue living anyway. It's painful, but you just have to keep going. It's just part of life, really."

—SOLEDAD

"Give as much commitment to healing as you did to surviving for the last ten or fifteen years."

—DORIANNE

"There's more than anger, more than sadness, more than terror. There's hope."

—EDITH HORNING

Preface to the
Twentieth-Anniversary Edition

When we began work on *The Courage to Heal* in 1984, the climate for survivors of child sexual abuse was dramatically different than it is today. There was little understanding about the process of healing from child sexual abuse. There were few therapists knowledgeable about treating abuse and almost no support groups. Incest was considered to be extremely rare. When survivors did disclose their abuse, they were most frequently met with denial, minimization, or blame.

Though an awareness of sexual abuse was dawning, little real help or hope was available for those who'd suffered from it. There was just a staggering need. We wrote *The Courage to Heal* to offer survivors practical, empowering firsthand information and to provide respectful, compassionate guidance through the healing process.

We chose to avoid academic language, psychological theories, and statistics. *The Courage to Heal* grew out of the women's movement, with its focus on empowering women both personally and politically. Women had begun confronting the reality of sexual and domestic violence, and in the tradition of speak-outs for rape victims, we believed in the power of women breaking silence and telling their own stories. By reading about other woman's experiences, survivors gained inspiration and strength. They learned they were not alone, they were not to blame, and that healing was possible.

In the decades since its publication, we've heard from thousands of survivors around the world describing what *The Courage to Heal* has meant to them:

> I've been in treatment since I was six. I've been in mental hospitals. I've been

given shock treatments. I've been on meds. I've seen counselors up the wazoo, but [your book] is the first real help I've ever received.

At times, I've simply sat holding your book knowing that at last someone understands how I feel inside.

If you had written *The Courage to Heal* only for me, it would have been worth every hour, every tear, every frustration, every effort you have put forth.

The Courage to Heal has saved my life—literally.

The Courage to Heal is, and has always been, in the process of evolution. Since its initial publication, we have regularly made changes—incorporating new material, adding information, and offering additional perspectives. We have responded to feedback from our readers; changes in the social and political climate for survivors; and the latest research on abuse, trauma, and healing. The book has been continually enriched by the determination of the pioneers, activists, therapists, and survivors who have passionately committed to their own healing, worked vigorously to stop child sexual abuse, provided essential services, and studied the most effective ways to heal trauma. We are grateful to their dedication and to everyone who has taken the time to share information, suggestions, and insights with us.

For this new twentieth-anniversary edition, we have revised *The Courage to Heal* extensively. Although the essentials of healing from child sexual abuse have remained the same, much has been discovered in the intervening years. This new knowledge has been integrated throughout *The Courage to Heal* to reflect both the complexities and the subtleties of the healing process as we understand it today.

The major changes in this edition are:

- An emphasis on self-care and pacing so that you don't become overwhelmed or retraumatized during the healing process
- An increased focus on the body's role in healing
- New research on trauma and the brain, traumatic amnesia, memory, and post-traumatic stress disorder (PTSD)
- The inclusion of additional healing tools, including imagery, meditation, spirituality, and body-centered practices
- New stories that reflect an even greater diversity of survivors and their experiences
- In-depth guidance to help you assess how you want to relate to your family now and over time
- New prose writings and poetry (all of the prose pieces are from survivors of child sexual abuse; most of the poems are written by survivors, as well, though some are not)
- The wisdom of survivors who have been healing for twenty years or more

• The removal of "Honoring the Truth,"* our 1994 response to the backlash against survivors of child sexual abuse, to make room for new stories and information about healing
• A thoroughly updated Resource Guide, reflecting the abundant books, organizations, films, and online resources now available

---

* You can read "Honoring the Truth" online at the Survivors Healing Center Web site: www.survivorshealing center.org/truth.

If you are new to *The Courage to Heal,* we want to emphasize a truth that will hold fast despite changing times: If you were sexually abused as a child, you can not only heal but also thrive. In the years since *The Courage to Heal* was first published, millions of survivors have succeeded in creating lives rich with meaning, joy, and self-acceptance. The rewards of healing are available to you, too.

—*Ellen Bass and Laura Davis, 2008*

Preface to the First Edition

ELLEN BASS

I first heard that children were abused in 1974, when a young woman in my creative writing workshop pulled a crumpled half-sheet of paper out of her jeans pocket. Her writing was so vague, so tentative, that I wasn't sure what she was trying to say, but I sensed that it was important. Gently, I encouraged her to write more. Slowly she revealed her story. In pieces, on bits of paper, she shared the pain of her father's assaults, and I listened.*

Shortly afterward, another woman told me her story. And then another. And another. There were no groups for survivors of child sexual abuse then. The word "survivor" was not yet in our vocabulary. But as they sensed that I could understand their stories, more and more women shared them with me. The psychologist Carl Rogers once said that when he worked through an issue in his life, it was as if telegrams were sent to his clients informing them that they could now bring that subject to therapy. Once I became aware of child sexual abuse, it was as if women knew that I was safe to talk to.

I was stunned by the number of women who had been sexually abused. I was deeply moved by the anguish they had endured. And I was equally impressed by their integrity, their ability to love and create through such devastation. I wanted people to know about this, about their strength and their beauty.

In 1978, three months after my first child was born, five women from my workshops

* This woman, Maggie Hoyal, went on to become a fine writer, and her story, "These Are the Things I Remember," is included in *I Never Told Anyone* (see p. 530 of the Resource Guide).

and I began collecting stories for *I Never Told Anyone: Writings by Women Survivors of Child Sexual Abuse.* By 1983, when it was published, I had learned a great deal about the healing process. One of the things I learned was that writing itself was healing.

I decided to offer a group for survivors and designed the I Never Told Anyone workshops. I tried to create an environment safe enough for women to face their own pain and anger so they could begin to heal. At the first workshop, I mainly listened. I wanted to learn what survivors needed to talk about, what they needed to hear. Women wrote about their experience of being sexually abused, and read what they had written to the group. The simple opportunity to share with other survivors was profoundly healing.

The women who came to the workshops had no historical reason to trust. As children they had learned that their trust would be taken advantage of. And yet in the groups, they trusted.

This book, like the workshops, is based on the premise that everyone wants to become whole, to fulfill their potential. That we all, like seedlings or tadpoles, intend to become our full selves and will do so if we are not thwarted. People don't need to be forced to grow. All we need is favorable circumstances: respect, love, honesty, and the space to explore.

Since I began the I Never Told Anyone workshops, I have worked with hundreds of survivors across the country. I've facilitated workshops for partners of survivors and offered training seminars for professionals who work with survivors. I have solidified my understanding of what it takes to heal from child sexual abuse. This is the knowledge I want to share with you here.

I am not academically educated as a psychologist. I have acquired counseling skills primarily through practice. Since 1970, when I began working as a counselor and group facilitator, I've had the opportunity to train with a number of excellent therapists. But none of what is presented here is based on psychological theories. The process described, the suggestions, the exercises, the analysis, the conclusions, all come from the experiences of survivors.

I am also the partner of a survivor. In the beginning of our relationship we struggled with issues of trust, intimacy, and sexuality common to many couples and exacerbated by the effects of sexual abuse. Now, several years later, the problems that caused us both such anguish are no longer wrenching. Sexual abuse no longer overshadows our relationship. I want to tell you this because when you are in the thick of the pain, it's hard to believe that it will ever change. Yet it does. And it does not take forever.

As my grandmother used to say, "No one gets cheated from trouble." I was not sexually abused as a child, but I too have had pain to heal from. In the three years since beginning this book, I have made major personal changes. I live in the same house, with the same family, doing the same work. But I am not the same. Inspired by the survivors I worked with, I followed their example. Slowly, repetitively, step-by-step, little by little, my old fears, my desperate places, my limiting ways of coping, have receded. After saying, "Healing is possible" to hundreds of survivors, it occurred to me that it was possible for me, too.

Sometimes people ask, "Don't you find it depressing always to be thinking about child sexual abuse?" But I don't think so much about the abuse. I think about the healing. The opportunity to be a part of women's healing feels a little like assisting at a birth. It's awesome to touch the miracle of life so closely. When women trust me with their most vulnerable, tender feelings, I am aware that I hold their spirit, for that moment, in my hands, and I am both honored and thrilled.

I want to see us all become whole—and not stop there. As we become capable of nurturing ourselves and living rich personal lives, we are enabled to act creatively in the world so that life can continue—the eucalyptus trees, the narcissus, the sunfish, the squirrels, seals, hummingbirds, our own children.

—*Ellen Bass, 1988*

LAURA DAVIS

I remember calling Ellen one day a few months after I'd first remembered the incest. I counted the rings—two, three, four—she had to be home! She had to be! Five, six, seven—if I didn't talk to her right now, I knew I couldn't last through the afternoon. Eight, nine, ten—well, maybe she was outside folding the laundry and was just slow getting to the phone. Eleven, twelve, thirteen—I cannot stand another moment of this pain. My heart hurts and I can't take anymore. Fourteen, fifteen . . .

"Hello, this is Ellen," she said, cheery and calm.

"Ellen, this is Laura. Look, you've got to tell me just one thing. Will I ever get through this? Is there ever an end? I can't take it anymore, and if you'll just tell me I can get to the other side, I'm sure I can last through the week." I was talking fast, my sentences piling up on each other.

"Hello, Laura. I'm glad you called." Her voice was smooth, reassuring. "And yes, you can make it. Healing is possible. You're already well on your way."

"Well on my way? How can you say that? I can't sleep, and when I do, it's all I dream about. I can't think about anything else. Every child I see on the street reminds me of incest. I can't make love, I can't eat, my whole body feels like a giant piece of rubber. I'm crying all the time. My whole life is flashbacks, going to therapy, and talking about incest. Half the time I don't even believe it happened, and the other half I'm sure it was my fault."

"It did happen, Laura. Look at what you're going through. Would anyone willingly choose to go through this torture? Why would you ever want to invent something this bad? You were just a little girl, Laura. He was what—seventy years old? You were a victim. You were innocent. You didn't do anything. It wasn't your fault."

Over and over, Ellen repeated those simple phrases: "It wasn't your fault. I believe you. Healing is possible. You're going to make it. You're going to be okay."

I expressed every doubt I could think of. Then I made up some new ones. I knew other survivors didn't make up this sort of thing, but I was the exception. I'd always been the exception, all my life.

"You can fight it all you want, Laura," she said finally, "but the door's been opened, and you're in the healing process whether you like it or not."

There was a long silence. Then I said, "Isn't there any way out?"

"The only way out is through, honey; I'm sorry."

I was quiet for a long time. "But it hurts, Ellen. It hurts so much."

"I know, Laura. I know. But there's a way through this stuff, and I know you're going to find it."

I wanted to write this book for probably the same reasons you are picking it up now—I felt a tremendous amount of pain in my life, and I wanted it to stop. Six months before I approached Ellen about collaborating, I had my first memories of being sexually abused by my grandfather when I was a child. Since that time, my life had fallen apart. My lover was leaving me. I was becoming increasingly estranged from my family. I was sure I was going crazy. I needed to understand what was happening to me. I needed to talk to other women who had been through it. Out of that need, my desire to write this book was born.

During the first year of our collaboration, it was my task to gather other women's stories. Ellen and I placed ads in papers, wrote to the women who'd come to her workshops, put out the call by word of mouth. I screened hundreds of calls and spent days on the phone listening to the stories of survivors, some of whom had never told anyone about their abuse before they read our ad, saw our poster.

Even though many of the women I interviewed had been actively healing for years, our conversations were never easy. One woman came to my house with a bag of food and ate from it for the whole three hours we talked. Another had to get stoned to tell me her story. A third burned sage and cedar, cleansing the room to make it safe. Sometimes the women cried. Sometimes we both did.

The honesty and courage of these women continually gave me hope. When I found it impossible to make love because of flashbacks, I'd ask a woman I was interviewing how she had healed her sexuality. When I started to wish I could shove the memories back where they came from, a woman would tell me that healing was the greatest miracle in her life.

As the months went by and the number of interviews grew, it became clear that there were tremendous similarities in the stories. The black ex-nun from Boston and the ambassador's daughter from Manila described the stages of their healing process the same way. A pattern started to emerge. What I was going through made sense.

As I moved along in my own healing, my relationship to the book changed. The acuteness of my own needs began to fade. It became increasingly important for me to communicate what I was learning. I began to talk more freely about the book with people I met. Within the first few minutes of any conversation, I'd be asked why I was writing it, and it would all be out on the table: "Because I'm a survivor myself."

Many people quickly changed the conversation or turned away. But an astonishing number responded with stories of their own: "It happened to me too." "My best friend says her swimming coach used to touch her." "My neighbor's kid reported her father just last week."

There are many phases involved in writing a book. For me, they have felt just like the stages of the healing process. With each new juncture I'd freeze, certain that I couldn't possibly jump over the next hurdle. I couldn't confront my family. I couldn't begin to write. Then I'd take that first terrifying step forward and be set in motion again.

Throughout the first year, I wrote nothing about my own experience as a survivor. Ellen began the first draft while I kept busy transcribing and editing the interviews. Underneath, I knew that this book was as much about my life as it was about theirs, but I successfully avoided the inevitable moment when I, too, would have to speak my truth.

I remember the day very clearly. It started with a sentence I came across in one of Ellen's drafts. I was lying on the floor of her living room, reading through "Disclosures and Confrontations" with a red marker in my hand. Ellen was explaining the fact that family members may be sympathetic when first told about sexual abuse, only to turn on the survivor later on. She had used me as her example:

When Laura told her mother about the incest, her mother's first reaction was to send her one of her favorite nightgowns, so that Laura would be comforted; but after she'd thought about it for a while, she called Laura back and she said . . .

After that, Ellen had left a blank. She'd forgotten the exact content of the call.

When I read what she had written, my breakfast curled up into a tight little ball in my stomach. I started to tremble, and then I started to sweat. Anxiety shot from my stomach straight through my head. The fact that I was writing a book about my experiences in healing from incest could no longer be denied, abstracted, placed in a vague never-never land. There was the sentence, clear as day. "This is about me! This is about my life. That's *my* mother she's talking about."

"You'll have to rewrite that part," Ellen said with studied casualness. "It'll be much better in the first person."

I picked up the manuscript, and I crossed out the "Lauras."

It wasn't easy to do it because I was holding my breath and my hand was shaking. Every time the word "Laura" appeared, I substituted the word "I." And whenever I saw the word "her," I put in "my." Then I finished the sentence. When I was done, it read:

When I called my mother and told her I had remembered the incest, her first reaction was to tell me she loved me and supported me. She had an old favorite nightgown. It was cotton, well loved and broken in. She said she was going to send it to me in the mail, so I'd have something that smelled like her, since she couldn't be with me to comfort me in person.

A week after the nightgown arrived, my mother called me at four in the morning, waking me out of a sound sleep. She was screaming: "I've been up all night, and you're going to be up all night too! My father would never have done anything like that! You're just making this up to destroy me! You've just jumped on the incest bandwagon. You've always been into the 'in' thing. It's all because you're a lesbian. You all hate men. You all hate your families. You just want to kill me! You couldn't have done anything worse if you'd shot me."

The words flew out in a torrent, filling the whole side margin and curving around into all the available space at the top of the page. They wavered before my eyes, a field of red. "I did it," I said to Ellen, my voice high and tight. "Wanna hear it?"

"Sure," she said. "What have you got?"

I read it to her. She pretended not to notice the tremor in my voice. "Sounds better," she said. "Sounds a whole lot better."

For days after I wrote those words, I lived in a state of raw, unparalleled terror. I became convinced that Ellen did not really want to write the book with me. It was clear the whole collaboration was going to fall through. There was a conspiracy against me. Every day my anxiety increased.

It wasn't until my friend Aurora, who is a very wise writer, invited me over for roast duck, fed me, soothed me, and listened to me, that I quieted down enough to hear her say, over and over, in a hundred different ways, "Yes, Laura, it seems that you and Ellen will have to talk, *but what about those sentences you wrote?*"

* * *

It's been my experience that every time the subject of incest comes up in any kind of personal way, I reexperience the terror I felt as a child being abused. It's the same terror I saw in the faces of the women I interviewed when we finally sat down, small talk and tea finished, and I nudged them, my voice gentle: "What happened to you?" It's the fear I've seen flash across the faces of other women who ask what my work is, and who cannot bear to speak to me once they've heard the answer. It's the terror that's silenced us.

This book has been a way for me to break silence. But it has been more than that. It has been a steady source of inspiration and amazement for the past two and a half years. It has taught me that it is possible to take something that hurt me so deeply and turn it around. I hope it teaches you the same.

—*Laura Davis, 1988*

And twenty years later:

LAURA DAVIS

Twenty-four years ago, when I was twenty-seven, I remembered the incest I experienced as a child. Six months later, Ellen Bass and I began working on *The Courage to Heal*. The writing of the book—which took more than three years—was so intertwined with my healing that it was hard for me to differentiate between the two. In the first five years after its publication, I traveled around the United States, speaking out about abuse and healing. The fact that I was a survivor of child sexual abuse was integral to my personal and professional identity.

Now, twenty years after its publication, I have had the opportunity to go back and revisit the ideas, stories, and perspective of *The Courage to Heal*—with two more decades of healing and life experience under my belt. Revising the book has been a rewarding and challenging process—intellectually, emotionally, and spiritually. Ellen and I have reread every sentence, deciding what to keep, what to add, and what to change, as we've sought out the best way to integrate what we have learned with the essential truths and stories that have always been the heartbeat of *The Courage to Heal*.

Just as our understanding of healing has evolved tremendously in twenty years, I, too, have gone through tremendous changes. I am the not the same young survivor I was then. When I read about her terror, anguish, shame, and pain, I can barely remember them. When I am reminded of her desperation and her despair, her feelings of alienation and isolation, her certainty that she was damaged beyond repair, I feel compassion for her, but I am not that same wounded woman anymore.

Twenty years ago, if you had asked me who I was, "incest survivor" would have been at the top of the list. Asked that same question today, I would reply: "I am a mother, a partner, a daughter, a teacher, an author, a grandmother, a community member, a spiritual seeker, and a friend."

It's not that my past has changed; my relationship to it has. And that slow transformation occurred not because I ignored my abuse or hoped it would go away but because I made an unwavering commitment to each and every step of the healing process. I am certain that it was my focus, determination, and courage—and the help of some incredible supporters along the way—that enabled me to heal deeply and ultimately, to move on.

My grandfather's abuse will always be part of my history, but it is no longer a headline in my life. The fact that I am a survivor is woven into the deep structure of my life, one of many influences that make me who I am today.

People sometimes ask me, "Are you healed?" My answer varies according to the day. I don't believe in absolute healing. I think human life is far too complex for that; I believe that challenges are an ongoing part of life, that there is no finish line. There is only growth, change, and the appreciation of what is available to us in the richness of every moment. The older I get, the fewer answers I have. Many things I was certain of twenty years ago, I am no longer sure of. I am much more interested in the journey than the destination.

Absolutely, I have experienced healing miracles along the way—the fact that I have a close relationship with my mother, from whom I was estranged for eight years, is one of them. The fact that I have a loving and functional family of my own is another.

It's not that the past doesn't come up to bite me—occasionally it does. At times when I feel particularly vulnerable, I recognize that things might have been different for me if my grandfather had not come to my bed. But the fact remains: I relate far more to the strengths I have gleaned from being a survivor than the residual deficits I still carry from being his victim.

My life is good and I am grateful for it. It is enough.

Although it saddens me that *The Courage to Heal* is still needed today, twenty years after it was first published, it has been powerful for me to revisit its pages. The experience has affected me deeply, making me reflect on my life and how far as a society we still have to go.

Ellen and I are honored to be able to offer you, once again, words of hope and tools to support your healing journey.

—*Laura Davis, 2008*

Introduction:
Healing Is Possible

"I know you're in a world of pain, but that pain will lessen. At the beginning you can't see this. You can only see your pain and you think it will never go away. But the nature of pain is that it changes—it changes like a sunset. At first, it's this intense red-orange in the sky, and then it starts getting softer and softer. The texture of pain changes as you work through it. And then one day, you wake up and realize that life isn't just about working through your incest; it's about living, too.

"When I was thirteen, I had a miscarriage with my brother's child. I tried to commit suicide because I was in so much pain. Now I am so grateful that I survived because I've had the glorious opportunity to become an adult in charge of my own destiny. My life is precious now. There are days when I walk out of the house and feel the sun on my face and realize that my body belongs to me and that no one is going to touch me if I don't want them to. I get to make the choices now. Knowing I'm in charge of my life is such freedom. For me, that's all that I need."

If you have been sexually abused, you are not alone. One out of three (or four) girls and one out of six boys are sexually abused by the time they reach the age of eighteen.* Sexual abuse happens to children of every class, culture, race, religion, and gender. Children are abused by fathers, stepfathers, brothers, mothers, aunts, uncles, grandparents, neighbors,

---

* Prevalence rates vary among studies; for an excellent discussion about the reasons for that variance, see www.jimhopper.com/male-ab. Several solid studies have shown one in three women were abused. See Diana E. Russell, "The Incidence and Prevalence of Intrafamiliar and Extrafamiliar Sexual Abuse of Female Children," *Child Abuse and Neglect* 7 (1983): 133–146. Others have shown one in four women and one in six men. See Shanta R. Dube, et al., "Long-term consequences of childhood sexual abuse by gender of victim," *American Journal of Preventive Medicine* 28 (2005): 430–438. For men see also David Lisak, Jim Hopper, and Pat Song, "Factors in the Cycle of Violence: Gender Rigidity and Emotional Constriction," *Journal of Traumatic Stress* 9 (1996): 721–743.

family friends, babysitters, teachers, and strangers. Although women abuse, the majority of abusers are heterosexual men.

All sexual abuse is damaging, and the trauma does not end when the abuse stops. If you were abused as a child, you are probably experiencing long-term effects that interfere with your day-to-day functioning.

However, it is possible to heal. It is even possible to thrive. Thriving means more than just an alleviation of symptoms, more than Band-Aids, more than functioning adequately. Thriving means enjoying a feeling of wholeness, satisfaction in your life and work, genuine love and trust in your relationships, pleasure in your body.

This book is about the healing process—what it takes, what it feels like, how it can transform your life.

People say that time heals all wounds, and to a certain extent that's true. Time will dull some of the pain, but deep healing doesn't happen unless you consciously choose it. Healing from child sexual abuse takes commitment and dedication. But if you are willing to work hard, if you are determined to make lasting changes in your life, if you are able to find good resources and skilled support, you can not only heal but also thrive. We believe in miracles and hard work.

GETTING SUPPORT

No matter how committed you are, it is extremely difficult to heal from child sexual abuse in isolation. Much of the damage experienced is the result of the secrecy and silence that surrounded the abuse. Trying to heal while perpetuating that lonely silence is nearly impossible.

It is essential that you have at least one other person with whom you can share your pain and your healing. That person may be another survivor, a member of a support group, or a counselor. He or she could be a nurturing partner or family member, or a sibling who was also abused. Ideally, you will have a combination of many resources. (For help in finding support, see "Overcoming Isolation," p. 30.)

WHAT READING THIS BOOK WILL BE LIKE

Since the first edition of this book was published, millions of survivors from all over the world have read *The Courage to Heal*. They tell us it that has opened new pathways to healing, reassured them that they weren't alone, and given them hope.

In response to reading *The Courage to Heal*, survivors have left abusive relationships, renewed their commitment to heal, or shared honestly with a friend, partner, or counselor for the first time. Some have had breakthroughs in their sexuality. Others have stopped blaming themselves.

Survivors have also reported feeling terror, fury, and anguish as they read. Others have connected with forgotten pockets of grief, shame, rage, and pain. Women have had nightmares, flashbacks, and new memories. One survivor, a recovering alcoholic, began

WAS I A VICTIM OF CHILD SEXUAL ABUSE?

When you were a young child or teenager, were you:

- Fondled, kissed, or held for an adult's sexual gratification?
- Forced to perform oral sex?
- Raped or otherwise penetrated?
- Made to watch sexual acts?
- Subjected to excessive talk about sex?
- Fondled or hurt genitally while being bathed?
- Subjected to unnecessary medical treatments that satisfied an adult's sexual needs?
- Shown sexual movies or other pornography?
- Made to pose for seductive or sexual photographs?
- Forced into child prostitution or pornography?
- Forced to take part in ritualized abuse in which you were physically, psychologically, or sexually tortured?

It is not easy to acknowledge that you were, in fact, abused. But that acknowledgment is the first step in healing.

---

to crave alcohol as she read. Many went back to therapy—or sought counseling for the first time. All said their lives were changed.

For you, reading this book may also be an intense and healing experience. As you begin to realize that your life makes sense and that you are not the only one who has suffered, you may experience a tremendous feeling of relief. But relief is not the only reaction you may have. If you have unfamiliar, uncomfortable, or disturbing feelings as you read, don't be alarmed. Strong feelings are part of the healing process.

If, on the other hand, you breeze through these chapters, you may not yet feel safe enough to confront these issues. Or you may be coping with the book the same way you coped with the abuse—by separating your intellect from your feelings. If that's the case, stop, take a break, talk to someone for support, and come back to it later. (We strongly recommend that you start by reading "Survival Skills for Healing," a chapter designed to help your develop skills and resources—both inner and outer—that will support you during the healing process.)

It's essential that you don't bear this book the way you bore the abuse: numb and alone. If you come to a part that feels overwhelming, the material in that section may be too difficult for you right now. Don't force yourself to read it. Try a different section instead.

It's also okay to put the book down—or to go slowly. Many people read *The Courage to Heal* a little at a time, taking weeks or even months in between sections. Many survivors have told us that they haven't been ready to read the book at all but have kept it on their bedside table so that they could simply read the title over and over again. They say that just having the book nearby feels healing.

Pace yourself so that you can stay present while you read. Pay attention to the thoughts, feelings, and sensations that arise. The idea of developing such a relationship with your inner world may be unfamiliar to you. As women, many of us have been taught to meet the needs of others and been told that focusing on ourselves is selfish. But healing requires a willingness to put yourself first.

One morning, when Ellen listened to her answering machine, there was a message that said, "I called to let you know that I really *am* healing. And this is the sweetest feeling I have ever known—to be whole."

You deserve this feeling.

About the Stories in This Book

"All suffering is bearable if it is seen as part of a story."

—Isak Dinesen

Since we began work on the first edition of *The Courage to Heal*, we have spoken with tens of thousands of survivors of child sexual abuse. Two hundred and fifty survivors volunteered to be interviewed for this book. Out of these, we talked to a hundred in depth, adding new narratives and new voices in every edition. We could not tell everyone's story in its entirety, but we have included portions of each woman's experience.

We have also included stories from former participants of Ellen's I Never Told Anyone workshops, as well as workshops we've offered for partners and for counselors. In this edition, we have also integrated some stories from survivors Laura interviewed for her books, *I Thought We'd Never Speak Again* and *The Last Frontier.* All of these survivors—and partners—generously gave us permission to include their experiences.

The survivors presented here represent a broad range of women. You will meet women who vary in terms of age, economic background, race, and sexual orientation. Some are in committed relationships, some are dating, others are single; there are mothers, grandmothers, and women without children; women who were abused under different circumstances and by a variety of perpetrators. You will read about survivors who are near the beginning of the healing process and others who have been actively healing for twenty years—and those at turning points all along the way. The approaches these women have taken to healing have been creative and diverse.

The quotes and stories throughout come

from survivors and partners of survivors. Most of the quotes are not identified by name. Each quote stands alone and represents one person's experience.

When we present a longer story, include someone more than once, or if a woman specifically asked to be identified, we do use names. We wanted to respect each person's right to choose whether she wanted to use her real name or a pseudonym. (For more on the use of pseudonyms, see "Names or Pseudonyms: The Right to Choose," p. 410.) When we share our own personal experiences, we identify ourselves by our first names.

Although we have written *The Courage to Heal* specifically for women, countless male survivors over the years have found it to be inspiring and beneficial. Since much of the healing process is universal, we hope that men will continue to use *The Courage to Heal*. We've also written two books for survivors since then— *The Courage to Heal Workbook* and *Beginning to Heal*. Both of these incorporate experiences by men. (First-person stories by male survivors are integrated into the "Survivors Speak Out" section of the Resource Guide on p. 530, and resources for male survivors can also be found in "For Male Survivors" on p. 539.)

Using the Writing Exercises

"There is no agony like bearing an untold story inside you."

—Zora Neale Hurston

For many years, Ellen led I Never Told Anyone workshops for adult survivors of child sexual abuse. Women came together in an environment of support, confidentiality, and safety to explore their feelings, mourn their violation, gather their strength, and celebrate their survival.

In the workshops, women were asked to write about being sexually abused as children. So often survivors have had their experiences denied, trivialized, or distorted. Writing is an important avenue for healing because it gives you the opportunity to tell your own story, to relay your history as you experienced it. You can say: This happened to me. It was that bad. It was the fault and responsibility of the adult. I was—and am—innocent.

By going back and writing about what happened, you also reexperience feelings and are able to grieve. You excavate the sites in which you've buried memory and pain, dread and fury. You relive your history, but this time with the compassionate support of your adult self.

WHY WRITING?

One handy thing about writing is that it's almost always available. At three in the morning, when you're alone or you don't want to wake your partner, when your friend's out of town, when your counselor's answering machine is on and even the cat is out prowling, your journal is there. It's quiet, cheap, and portable. A journal can help you figure out how you feel, what you think, what you need, what you want to say, how you want to handle a situation, just by writing it through.

ANYONE CAN USE WRITING

Using writing as a healing tool can be helpful whether or not you participate in an organized workshop with other people. You don't need to think of yourself as a writer or even like to write. You may have had a limited education. Perhaps you can't spell or you think you're a terrible writer.

Some survivors have special blocks associated with writing. If your mother read your private diary, if your father was an English teacher and always criticized your written work, if your best friend passed your intimate letters around the junior high school cafeteria, you may be wary of putting words on paper. But all of us have a deep need for self-expression. Yours may take forms other than writing, but if you'd like to try writing as one method of healing, even previous blocks need not stand in the way. Many women who have been reluctant to write have done these exercises—and benefited enormously.

TIME AND PLACE

Choose a time and place where you won't be interrupted. It's good to have at least twenty minutes of writing time for each exercise, though even ten minutes can produce deep and powerful results. Many survivors find it helpful to decide on a fixed ending time before they begin; it creates a container that makes it safer to write about their abuse.

Some women like to start with a ritual—you might light a candle, meditate or say a prayer, make a cup of tea, or just take a moment to sit quietly—and also end with one. These clear markers on either side of your writing time create safety and can help you reenter your daily life a little more easily.

Since writing about sexual abuse often brings up strong feelings, don't squeeze in your writing between picking the kids up from school and starting dinner. Make sure you give yourself some time afterward to absorb the impact of the writing.

If you feel shaken up by what you've written, you might want to finish your writing session with five or ten minutes of writing on a topic that reminds you of your resilience and strength, such as, "The Ground On Which I Stand" or "Things I'm Grateful For," or "What Gives Me Strength." Other women have found it useful to go on a short walk after writing or to do a grounding exercise (see "Exercises to Ground You" on p. 255) to anchor them more firmly in the present.

If you feel overwhelmed by what you've written or find yourself flooded with emotions from the past, refer to "Calming Down" (p. 35) for suggestions for calming yourself down and regaining your equilibrium.

BEING HEARD

Writing itself is very helpful, but sharing what you've written is important, too. After you write, read your writing to someone who will listen attentively and with compassion. (See "Breaking Silence" on p. 102.)

If there's no one you can read to right away, read out loud to yourself—at least you will be reading to one attentive listener. Just saying the words can make them more real. Often you don't feel the impact of what you've written until you speak the words out loud.

If you read your writing to someone who has no experience in listening to personal writing, tell that person what you need. You won't want them to criticize or judge what you have to say. You may want them to ask questions, to help you talk about it more, or to simply listen quietly. You may want comforting or you may not. People usually respond in more satisfying ways when you tell them what you need.

THE BASIC METHOD

Try to forget everything you've ever been told about writing. What you're going to do is a kind of free writing, or stream-of-consciousness writing. It's not about making art or getting a good grade or trying to make sense to someone else. Rather it's a way to short-circuit your censors to get to what you need to say.

Write without stopping. Go at a pace that's comfortable for you, and don't stop. If you get stuck or can't think of anything to say, you can write, "This is the stupidest exercise I ever heard of," or "I'm hungry—I wonder if time's up yet." One woman who was writing about her abuse stopped every few lines and wrote, "I cannot say any more," and then went on to say more. Giving herself permission to stop made it possible for her to continue telling her story.

You needn't use full sentences. You needn't spell or punctuate properly. It can be in English or in another language. Sometimes if another language was spoken when you were a child, you will remember or write more fluidly in that language. If you were abused before you learned to talk, your writing may sound childish or come out as baby talk.

Using Guided Imagery

Many survivors have found imagery to be a powerful healing tool. Using guided imagery can help you discover inner resources and deal with overwhelming feelings. These gentle techniques can help you calm down, create a safe place inside, and feel grounded in your body. You can use the same imagery over and over, strengthening your connection with this relaxed, safe feeling.

PREPARATION

It's necessary to listen to, rather than read, the guided imagery. You can ask a safe friend or a therapist to read the imagery to you or you can use a recorded version. Since the exercises in this book are ones you may want to listen to over and over again, having a tape or CD is a good idea.*

Whether the imagery is spoken in person or on tape, it's important that it be read slowly. Allow space between the sentences and phrases. Especially in the places indicated by an ellipsis (. . .), pause and take a few breaths. When you're listening to the guided imagery, you will need time to absorb the material and

---

* Belleruth Naparstek's excellent book *Invisible Heroes: Survivors of Trauma and How They Heal* (New York: Bantam, 2004) is full of useful information on therapies that include some aspect of imagery or meditation and also offers guided visualizations that many trauma survivors have found helpful in their healing. You can order the audio version of *Imagery to Heal Trauma* (which is included in "Getting in Touch with Your Feelings" on p. 222), as well as many others, at www.healthjourneys.com.

to allow any images to emerge. This is easiest to do when the pace is very slow, with pauses between ideas or sentences. A soft and gentle voice is best, providing the safety for you to go deeper. For some people, quiet music in the background can be helpful; for others it's distracting. Experiment to see what works best for you.

BASIC INSTRUCTIONS

Set aside a time when you won't be interrupted so that you can settle into an internal space. Close your eyes. If closing your eyes feels frightening or uncomfortable, it's okay to keep them open, allowing your gaze to be soft and easy.

Sometimes people worry if they aren't able to actually "see" anything during a guided imagery experience. But everyone's experience is different, and seeing clear images isn't essential for the imagery to be helpful. Don't worry about doing it "right" or having a particular outcome. Be receptive and simply allow what comes along. Using imagery is about being open to whatever arises.

Even if guided imagery doesn't feel effective for you the first few times, your experience may change with time and practice. You might find that there are times when nothing happens, times you feel more relaxed, times you fall asleep, and times when images, feelings, thoughts, stories, or memories emerge.

At the end of a session, be sure to leave a little time to transition back into your regular consciousness, rather than rushing off to your next responsibility. Sometimes people like to write or draw afterward to chronicle their experience.

THE EXERCISES

PART ONE

Taking Stock & Taking Care

Effects:
Recognizing the Damage

"People have said to me, 'Why are you dragging this up now?' Why? WHY? Because it has controlled every facet of my life. It has damaged me in every possible way. It has destroyed everything in my life that has been of value. It has prevented me from living a comfortable emotional life. It's prevented me from being able to love clearly. It took my children away from me. I haven't been able to succeed in the world. If I had a comfortable childhood, I could be anything today. I know that everything I don't deal with now is one more burden I have to carry for the rest of my life. I don't care if it happened 500 years ago! It's influenced me all that time, and it does matter. It matters very much."

—JENNIEROSE LAVENDER

The long-term effects of child sexual abuse can be so pervasive that it's sometimes hard to pinpoint exactly how the abuse affected you. It can permeate everything: your sense of self, intimate relationships, sexuality, parenting, work, even your sanity. As one survivor explained:

It's like those pictures I remember from *Highlights for Children* magazine. The bicycle was hidden in a tree, a banana was growing from someone's ear, and all the people were upside-down. The caption underneath said, "What's wrong with this picture?" But so many things were disturbed and out of place, it was often easier to say, "What's right with this picture?"

Many survivors have been too busy surviving to notice the ways they were hurt by the abuse. But you cannot heal until you acknowledge the impact of the abuse.

Because sexual abuse is just one of many

factors that shaped your development, it isn't always possible to isolate its effects from the other influences on your life. If you have trouble trusting people, is it because you were molested when you were nine, because your mother was an alcoholic, or because you were left alone for hours every day as a small child? It's the interplay of hundreds of factors that make us who we are today.

The way the abuse was handled when you were a child has a lot to do with its subsequent impact. If a child's disclosure is met with compassion and effective intervention, the healing begins immediately. But if no one noticed or responded to your pain, you were left feeling abandoned and alone. If you were blamed, were not believed, or suffered further trauma, the damage was compounded. And the ways you coped with the abuse might have created further problems.

Not all survivors are affected in the same way. You may do well in one area of your life but not in another. You may be competent at work and in parenting but have trouble with intimacy. Some women have a constant nagging feeling that something is wrong. For others, the damage is so pervasive that it feels as if nothing was spared:

> As far as I'm concerned, my whole life was stolen from me. I didn't get to be who I could have been. I didn't get the education I should have gotten when I was young. I married too early. I hid behind my husband. I didn't make contact with other people. I haven't had a rich life. It's not ever too late, but I didn't start working on this until I was thirty-eight, and not everything can be retrieved. And that makes me very angry.

The effects of child sexual abuse can be devastating, but they do not have to be permanent. As you read this chapter, you may rec-

---

These lists are not a diagnostic tool and are not intended to serve as a way to determine whether you've been sexually abused.

Reading about the range of effects that survivors of child sexual abuse experience can help you look honestly at the impact of abuse on your life today. Some of the effects of child sexual abuse are quite specific—such as intrusive images of the abuse while making love. Others are more general—such as low self-esteem or difficulty expressing feelings—and can be caused by a range of influences other than child sexual abuse. Physical and emotional abuse, as well as many other challenging life circumstances, can also lead to many of the difficulties listed here.

If you recognize your own problems in the following lists but are unsure whether you were sexually abused, don't rush to label yourself as a survivor before you're sure. Take care of yourself. Get support. Work on healing from the experiences you're certain of. And trust that over time your history will become clearer.

ognize, perhaps for the first time, some of the ways in which sexual abuse affects your life. Such recognition can be painful, but it is in fact part of the healing process.

HOW ABUSE AFFECTS SELF-ESTEEM

When children are respected and nurtured, they learn that they have value. They experience a foundation of safety from which they can take on new challenges. They develop competence and confidence. They feel good about who they are and who they are becoming.

Abuse interrupts this process of developing positive self-esteem. When children are abused, their boundaries, their right to say no, and their sense of control in the world are violated. They feel powerless.

If they tell someone about what is happening to them, they may be ignored or told that they made it up. Sometimes they are blamed. Their reality is denied or twisted, and they often end up feeling crazy. Rather than see the abuser or their parents as bad, they may come to believe that they are bad, that they did not deserve to be taken care of, and that they in fact deserved abuse. They feel isolated and alone.

Many abused children are told directly that they'll never succeed, that they're stupid, or that they're only good for sex. With messages like these, it's hard to believe in yourself.

Many survivors feel:

- Bad, dirty, or ashamed
- Powerless, like a victim
- Different from other people
- That there's something wrong deep down inside
- That if people really knew them, they'd leave

Some survivors:

- Hate themselves
- Feel immobilized or can't get motivated
- Are unable to protect themselves in dangerous situations
- Have experienced repeated victimization (rape, assault, battery) as adults
- Struggle with self-destructive feelings or feel suicidal

Often survivors have a hard time:

- Identifying their own needs
- Nurturing and taking care of themselves
- Feeling good
- Trusting their intuition
- Recognizing their own interests, talents, or goals

Some survivors:

- Are afraid to succeed
- Can't accomplish the things they set out to do

- Feel that they can never move forward in their lives
- Feel compelled to be perfect
- Use excessive work or achievements to compensate for feelings of inadequacy
- Forget whole chunks of their childhood

HOW ABUSE AFFECTS FEELINGS

When children are raised in a healthy environment, their emotions are respected. When they are sad, angry, or afraid, their parents or caretakers acknowledge their feelings, make room for safe expression, and offer comfort. Children raised in an emotionally supportive home are not talked out of their feelings or punished for them. Because of this, they learn that feelings are not dangerous. And their capacity to tolerate difficult feelings increases naturally as they grow up.

Abused children rarely have this kind of support. They cannot afford to feel the full extent of their terror, pain, shame, or rage; the agony would be devastating. They would not be able to do arithmetic with other second-graders, for example, if they acknowledged the depth of their sorrow and desolation.

Because their innocent love and trust are betrayed, abused children learn that they cannot rely on their feelings. And the feelings they do express may be disregarded or mocked.

If the adults around them are out of control, they get the message that feelings lead to violence. Anger means beatings or furniture hurled across the room.

Abused children often learn to block out their pain, because it is too devastating or because they do not want to give the abuser the satisfaction of seeing them cry. But since it's not possible to block emotions selectively, they may simply stop feeling.

On the other hand, they may feel overwhelmed with feelings, flooded with fear, grief, shame, and rage. All too often, they suffer with this distress alone, without a safe way to express their emotions and without consolation.

Often survivors find it difficult to:

- Recognize their feelings
- Differentiate between emotions
- Express feelings
- Calm down when they get upset

Many survivors feel:

- Disconnected, isolated, and alone
- A pervasive sense of shame
- Just a few feelings, rather than a full range of emotions
- Out of control with their rage or other feelings
- Confused
- Dead inside

Many survivors:

- Are prone to depression or despair
- Struggle with anxiety or have panic attacks
- Alternate between overwhelming anxiety, fear, or rage and being numb and shut down

- Feel agitated and on alert
- Have frequent nightmares
- Are afraid of their emotions
- Worry about going crazy
- Rarely feel pleasure, relaxation, or joy

HOW ABUSE AFFECTS THE BODY

Children learn about the world through their bodies. If they are protected and nurtured, they feel at home in their bodies. Living in their bodies is a source of pleasure, accomplishment, and satisfaction.

When children are sexually abused, they learn that the world, and their bodies, are not safe. Abused children experience pain, fear, and conflicting sensations of arousal. Often they leave their bodies to avoid these feelings—or numb themselves as best they can.

For abused children, the body is a place where frightening and painful things happen. They learn to always be on alert, to be ready for danger. Or they cut themselves off from their bodies and learn to ignore them, living mostly in their heads. For many survivors, the experience of trauma leaves a deep impression on the body.

Many survivors have a hard time:

- Appreciating and accepting their bodies
- Feeling at home in their skin
- Being fully present in their bodies

- Experiencing a full range of feelings in their bodies
- Experiencing their bodies as a unified whole

Some survivors:

- Have hurt themselves or abused their bodies
- Misuse or are addicted to alcohol or drugs
- Have eating disorders
- Have physical illnesses that may be connected to abuse
- Feel as though they sometimes leave their bodies
- Don't feel pleasure in physical activities such as dance, sports, or hiking

Often survivors:

- Aren't aware of the messages their bodies give them (hunger, fear, tiredness, pain)—or don't respond to these messages
- Mistrust or blame their bodies
- Feel numb or disconnected from physical sensations
- Startle easily and have a hard time calming down
- Are often on high alert for danger
- Are unable to relax or feel physically safe

HOW ABUSE AFFECTS THE CAPACITY FOR INTIMACY

The building blocks of intimacy—giving and receiving, loving and being loved—are learned in childhood. If children are given consistent caring and affection, they develop skills for establishing and maintaining nurturing relationships.

When children are abused, their innocence and trust are betrayed. If you were told, "Mommy's only touching you because she loves you," or "I'm doing this so you'll be a good wife to your husband someday," you grew up with confusing messages about the relationship between sex and love. And even if the abuser didn't say a word, the act of the abuse itself is a deep betrayal, seriously damaging your capacity to trust.

Many survivors find it difficult:

- To trust people
- To make close friends
- To create or maintain healthy relationships
- To give or receive nurturing
- To be affectionate
- To say no or set appropriate boundaries

Many survivors:

- Feel that they don't deserve love
- Are afraid of people
- Feel alienated or isolated

- Rarely feel connected to themselves or to others
- Get involved with people who are inappropriate or unavailable
- Don't know whom to trust or trust too readily
- Frequently feel betrayed or taken advantage of
- Have good friends but struggle in romantic or sexual relationships

Some survivors:

- Are unable to form lasting relationships
- Have trouble making commitments
- Shut down, get nervous, or panic when people get too close
- Cling to the people they care about
- Repeatedly test people to the point of sabotaging relationships
- Expect people to leave them
- Get involved with people who abuse them

HOW ABUSE AFFECTS SEXUALITY

When children are sexually abused, their natural sexual unfolding is stolen. They are introduced to sex on an adult's timetable, according to an adult's needs. They may not have a chance to explore naturally, to experience their own desires from the inside. Sexual arousal becomes linked to feelings of shame, disgust, pain, and humiliation. Pleasure is tainted as well. And desire (the abuser's desire) is dangerous, an out-of-control force used to hurt them.

Children often leave their bodies during sex with the abuser. They may numb themselves or disappear. They may disconnect from sexual feelings or experience arousal as confusing, bad, or shameful.

When abuse is coupled with affection, the need for nurturing can become linked with sex. Sometimes survivors don't know how to meet these needs in other ways.

Many survivors:

- Feel disconnected when they have sex
- Go through sex numb or in a panic
- Use sex to meet needs that aren't sexual
- Avoid sex or seek sex they really don't want
- Feel that their worth is primarily sexual
- Feel conflicted when they experience desire or sexual pleasure
- Need to control everything about sex to feel safe
- Experience flashbacks to the abuse while making love
- Feel confused about whether they want sex

Often survivors have trouble:

- Saying no to sex that they don't want
- Accepting nurturing or closeness that isn't sexual
- Staying present when making love

- Being emotionally close and sexual at the same time (or with the same person)

Some survivors:

- Think sex is disgusting or that they're disgusting for enjoying it
- Are turned on by violent, sadistic, or incestuous fantasies
- Engage in sex that repeats aspects of their abuse
- Have continued to be sexually abused
- Use sex as a way to exert power and control
- Have been sexually abusive to others

HOW ABUSE AFFECTS PARENTING

Our first lessons about being a parent come from our own families. If a child is nurtured and protected, that becomes her basic model for parenting.

But when children are abused by a family member, are not protected, or are not offered support when abuse is disclosed, they miss out on this healthy modeling. As a result, they sometimes end up repeating the same damaging patterns they grew up with. They abuse or neglect their own children or fail to protect them from abuse.

However, some survivors find that being clear about what they *don't* want to do as parents leads them to make different, more positive choices.

Sometimes, survivors feel too damaged or too busy coping with their own abuse to have children of their own. For women who wanted children, grieving this loss can be a painful part of the healing process.

Some survivors:

- Feel uncomfortable or frightened around children
- Are uncomfortable being affectionate with children
- Are confused about the line between appropriate and inappropriate touch
- Have been abusive or feared that they might be
- Have not adequately protected the children in their care
- Are overprotective, keeping their children from normal life experiences

Some survivors find it hard to:

- Set clear boundaries with children
- Balance their children's needs with their own
- Feel close or connected to their children

HOW ABUSE AFFECTS FAMILY RELATIONSHIPS

In a healthy family, there is respect and caring across the generations. Family members are affectionate and warm but not intrusive. Honest, respectful communication is the norm, and each member of the family has a secure, comfortable place in the fabric of the family.

When incest occurs, family relationships are distorted. The essential trust, sharing, and safety are missing, and in their place there is secrecy, isolation, and fear. If a family member abused you, you might have been made the family scapegoat, repeatedly told that you were crazy or bad. You might have felt isolated, cut off from nurturing contact with others.

Since alcoholism and other dysfunctional patterns often accompany sexual abuse, you might have had to cope with these problems as well. Adult responsibilities might have been forced on you at an early age.

If the abuse took place outside your family and you weren't adequately heard or responded to, you got the message that your pain wasn't important, that you couldn't rely on your family to listen to your feelings or protect you.

Many survivors:

- Have strained or difficult relationships with family members
- Feel crazy, invalidated, or depressed when they visit their families
- Have been rejected by their families
- Don't feel safe in their families
- Continue to deal with belittling, hostile, or abusive treatment
- Are alienated or completely estranged from family members

In many families in which there has been sexual abuse:

- The sexual abuse has not been talked about or acknowledged
- Incest is denied or minimized
- The survivor is told to "forgive and forget" or "let the past be in the past"
- The needs of the abuser are put ahead of the needs to the survivor
- The survivor becomes the family scapegoat; all of the family's problems are blamed on her
- Family members aren't supportive

In some families:

- Incest still goes on

YOU CAN HEAL FROM THE EFFECTS OF ABUSE

If you feel overwhelmed reading about the long-term effects of abuse, remember that you have already lived through the hardest part—the abuse itself. You have survived against formidable odds. The same abuse that undercut you has also provided you with many of the inner resources necessary for healing. One quality every survivor can be confident of having is strength. And with an understanding of what it takes to heal, that strength leads directly to determination. As one woman stated emphatically: "No one's gonna fuck with me no more."

WRITING EXERCISE: THE EFFECTS

(See the basic method for writing exercises on p. xxix.)

Write about the ways you're still affected by the abuse. What are you still carrying in terms of your feelings of self-worth, your relationships, your sexuality, your work? How is your life still pained, still limited?

Write about the strengths you've developed because of the abuse. Think of what it's taken for you to survive. What are the qualities that enabled you to make it? Perseverance? Flexibility? Self-sufficiency? Write about your strengths with pride.

Coping:
Honoring What You Did to Survive

"My whole life has pretty much been coping."

Coping is what you did to survive the trauma of being sexually abused. And it's what you do now to help you make it through each day.

Everyone copes differently. As a young survivor, you might have run away from home or turned to alcohol or drugs. You might have become a superachiever, excelling in school and taking care of your brothers and sisters at home. You might have blocked out huge parts of your past, withdrawn into yourself, or cut off your emotions. You might have used food to numb your feelings or sex as a way to prove your worth. Or you might have buried yourself in work. With limited resources for taking care of yourself, you survived using whatever means were available. Many survivors feel ashamed of

the ways they coped. You may find it difficult to admit some of the things you had to do to stay alive. It may be hard to acknowledge what it takes now for you to get up and face each day. As a child in terrible circumstances, you responded the best that you could—and you have continued to do so. The crucial thing is that you survived. It's important to honor your resourcefulness.

EVERYONE COPES

All of us use coping strategies to deal with overwhelming, painful, or stressful situations. Most of the strategies discussed in this chapter have been used, at one time or another, by people struggling to come to terms with a wide range of challenging circumstances. Some are more universal; others are more specific to survivors and may or may not apply to you.

You may discover that some of the ways you've coped have developed into strengths (being successful at work, becoming self-sufficient, having a quick sense of humor, being adaptable, responding well in a crisis). Others may have become self-defeating patterns (drug or alcohol abuse, compulsive eating, cutting yourself, emotional withdrawal). Most coping behaviors have both healthy and unhealthy aspects. Being independent, for instance, is a good quality, but taken to the extreme, it can keep you isolated.

Healing requires that you differentiate between the ways your coping mechanisms are beneficial and the ways they may be hurting you. Then you can celebrate your strengths while you start to change the patterns that no longer serve you.

CORE COPING STRATEGIES

DENIAL

Denial is turning your head the other way and pretending that whatever is happening isn't, or that what has happened didn't. It is a basic pattern in alcoholic families. It's almost universal where incest is concerned. "If I just ignore it long enough, it will go away."

It's often more bearable for a child to deny reality than to face the fact that the adults around her won't protect her and in fact may harm her.

One woman remembered the time a neighborhood boy told her that everyone knew that her father had been beating her the night before. They'd all heard her screaming. "I told him, 'Oh, that wasn't me. My father would never beat me.'"

Some survivors acknowledge that they were abused but deny that it had any effect. "I told my therapist I'd already dealt with it," one woman said. "He believed me."

MINIMIZING

Minimizing is pretending that whatever happened wasn't really that bad. It means saying, "My dad's a little pissed off," when in fact he just smashed an armchair to bits. Kids who live surrounded by abuse often believe that everyone else grows up the same way. Doesn't every father tuck his daughter into bed like that?

Yeah, I minimized it. "Hey, so your dad puts his prick in your mouth? What's the big deal? Hey!" Up until five years ago, people would say to me, "Were you from an abusive family?" and I'd say, "No!" After all, I didn't die. I was in the hospital with broken bones, but I didn't die. There was blood all over the place but at least I made it.

RATIONALIZING

Rationalizing is the way children explain away abuse. "Oh, she couldn't help it. She was drunk." Survivors invent reasons that excuse the abuser. "Four kids were just too much for her. No wonder she didn't take care of me." Rationalizing protects the abuser and buffers the survivor against the impact of her feelings:

> There's a part of me that always wants to figure out "Why the hell did he do it? What could have hurt this poor man so terribly that he would have to resort to these things?" That's a way of dramatizing his story instead of mine. It's a way of trying to forgive him, instead of allowing the real anger and fury I feel.

FORGETTING

Forgetting is one of the most common ways that children deal with sexual abuse. The human mind has a tremendous capacity to protect us from realities that are too painful for us to bear. Many children begin blocking out the abuse, *even as it is happening to them*:

> I had a visual image of a closet in my mind. I shoved everything that was happening to me into the back of that closet, and I closed the door.

This capacity to forget explains why many adult survivors are unaware of the fact that they were abused or remember only parts of their experience. (For an explanation of this phenomenon, see "Remembering," p. 70.)

Some survivors remember the abuse but forget the way they felt at the time. One woman, repeatedly molested throughout her childhood by her stepfather and her brother, said, "I had totally and completely repressed that it had even been uncomfortable."

PRESENTING A FAÇADE TO THE WORLD

One of the ways survivors cope with realities they cannot face, and the terrible shame they feel, is to cover over their real feelings with an acceptable façade. On the surface, there is a little girl having a good childhood, but underneath there's a child who's prone to nightmares and sees terrifying people hiding in the corner of the room.

Many survivors continue this pattern into adulthood. On the inside you feel evil and bad and know that something is very wrong, but on the outside you present a different front. Laura remembers:

> At twenty-one I was lying in my bed, unable to get up, watching the bugs march across my sheets, thinking I would either kill myself or go crazy. A half-hour later, I turned around and wrote my mother another cheery letter about how well I was doing. I was desperate to maintain the facade.

But the veneer is often very thin. A fifty-six-year-old psychotherapist explains the way she acted out the split in her life:

Growing up, I did everything super-right. I was an overachiever. I was an A student all through college. I was a Fulbright scholar in London. I was considered a huge success.

I developed a total false personality based on what you were supposed to be, and hid myself. My interpersonal relationships were exchanges of displays, nothing more. I got by because of money and status.

Underneath that false personality was a blankness, and underneath the blankness was a tremendous rage. I was sure that if I ever allowed my behavior to manifest any sign of the problems I had inside, everything would crumble entirely and I'd end up in an insane asylum or police lockup.

HUMOR

A tough sense of humor or biting wit can get you through hard times. As long as you keep people laughing, you maintain a certain protective distance. And as long as you keep laughing, you don't have to cry:

What My Father Told Me

BY DORIANNE LAUX

Always I have done what was asked.
Melmac dishes stacked on rag towels.
The slack of a vacuum cleaner cord
wound around my hand. Laundry
hung on a line.
There is much to do always, and I do it.
The iron resting in its frame, hot
in the shallow pan of summer
as the basins of his hands push
aside the book I am reading.
I do as I am told, hold his penis
like the garden hose, in this bedroom,
in that bathroom, over the toilet
or my bare stomach.

I do the chores, pull weeds out back,
finger stink-bug husks, snail carcasses,
pile dead grass in black bags. At night
his feet are safe on their pads, light
on the wall-to-wall as he takes
the hallway to my room.
His voice, the hiss of lawn sprinklers,
wet hush of sweat in his hollows,
the mucus still damp
in the corners of my eyes as I wake.

Summer ends. Schoolwork doesn't suit me.
My fingers unaccustomed to the slimness
of a pen, the delicate touch it takes
to uncoil the mind.
History. A dateline pinned to the wall.
Beneath each president's face, a quotation.
Pictures of buffalo and wheat fields,
a wagon train circled for the night,
my hand raised to ask the question,
Where did the children sleep?

Dorianne Laux, *Awake* (Spokane, WA: Eastern Washington University Press, 2007).

For years I used humor to deflect the pain and the shame I felt talking about incest. The humor was, of course, the gallows variety. It often pointed out the absurdity of the American Ideal, the family surrounded by a white picket fence—with blood dripping down the painted slats where the daughters had been sacrificially skewered. It was my way of telling the truth about something I wasn't sure anyone would believe if they hadn't lived through it.

Once I asked my therapist about my use of humor. It didn't seem right to laugh about these things. He told me, "Humor is only one way of dealing with tragedy. Other people destroy themselves or others, or they start fires or drink themselves to death. Of all the possible ways there are to deal with deep pain, you have chosen one that is fairly harmless and that affirms life with laughter. Not a bad choice. Not a bad choice at all."

DISSOCIATION

Children who are abused often disconnect from their bodies so that they will not feel what is being done to them. When an experience is too painful to endure, children emotionally and psychically separate from the experience. Because they cannot physically escape, they leave their bodies. As a result, survivors often describe watching the abuse happening, as if from a great distance:

It's like I actually rise up out of my body. I could feel myself sitting in a chair, and I could feel myself floating up out of my body. That's exactly what it's like—being suspended in midair. I know that my body is in the chair, but the rest of me is out of my body.

This process is called dissociation. While it is an excellent coping strategy for children, enabling them to endure unbearable situations, it can create problems for adult survivors. Dissociation often becomes a habit, and many survivors continue to dissociate, at least to some degree, whenever they feel threatened or scared:

A good part of the time, I'm not present in my body. It's as if inside, from my neck down, it's hollow, and there's this ladder, and depending on how things are going, I'm climbing up the ladder, and this little person that is me is sitting in my head, looking out through my eyes.

Others go somewhere they can't identify: "I can't tell you what happens when I leave my body, because I'm not there."*

---

* For more on dissociation, see "What We Know About Memory and Traumatic Amnesia" on p. 74, "Trauma and the Brain" on p. 242, and "From Splitting to Being in Your Body" on p. 253.

DISSOCIATIVE IDENTITY DISORDER (MULTIPLE PERSONALITIES)

When there is no way to physically escape the pain, terror, and despair of severe abuse, children sometimes create new selves—also known as alternate personalities—to separate from the abuse and to bear the burden. This may occur to such a degree that it meets criteria for the diagnosis of dissociative identify disorder (DID), formerly known as multiple personality disorder.*

Dissociating to this extent is a highly successful adaptation to otherwise intolerable pain. Even though finding out about the existence of separate personalities may be shocking, it's essential to remember that this ability—and these internal selves—enabled you to survive extreme trauma. The fact that you did is a miracle.

The problem is not primarily one of fixing yourself because you have this "disorder," but rather addressing and healing the trauma that made this way of coping necessary in the first place.

Sometimes it's difficult for survivors with DID to accept and appreciate all their inner selves. Some alternate personalities may appear hostile, weak, or in some other way be disturbing to you. You may wish you could get rid of them, but it's essential to remember that all of them—no matter how problematic they may seem to you now—played an important part in your survival. Every alternate personality developed to fill a need, and given the limitations of the situation, they fulfilled those roles in the best way they could. Everything you've done, even if it doesn't look like it makes sense now, has its own intrinsic logic, which is sane and rational.

Healing with multiple personalities is more complex than the healing process for survivors who have not separated into different selves. Each alternate personality holds part of the experience, each needs to be involved in the work of healing, and all need to learn to work together. However, there can be benefits, too. There is the potential for an internal system of support and collaboration that can be very valuable. Many survivors with multiple personalities have internal helpers, wise healers, and inner guides, as well as alternate personalities who are good at going to work, driving, and taking care of business even in the midst of crisis and chaos.

As a creative and highly intelligent way of coping with and surviving extreme abuse, the ability to create distinct selves is a formidable testimony to the resourcefulness of the human mind and spirit. As you learn to understand and respect the ways your mind has worked not only to keep you alive but also to preserve and enhance your strengths and capacities, you can offer yourself an attitude of acceptance, understanding, and honor.

---

* An increasing number of books and resources on dissociation are now available. We have many of these listed in the Resource Guide. See "Trauma, Memory, and the Brain" on p. 546. Diane Hugs, one of the women profiled in "Courageous Women," describes her experience with multiple personalities on p. 455.

SPACING OUT

Survivors have an uncanny capacity to space out and not be present. There are many ways to do this:

> I walked into walls and doors and furniture a lot, because I wasn't in my body, but a few bruises were a small price to pay for oblivion.

Whenever something scares her, one survivor finds an object in the room and stares at it—just as she did when she was being abused:

> I have total recall of the most intimate details of different rooms I've been in. I can't remember who I was talking to or what we were talking about, but I sure can tell you exactly what the window looked like!

Other survivors give the appearance of being present when they're not really there:

> I spent a lot of my life spacing out and disappearing. I pride myself on how slick I am. I have been known to sit there and be totally gone and then to come back and have no idea where I am in a conversation. I'll have been talking the whole time. And what's really weird is that most people don't even notice I'm gone!

The problem with this kind of distancing is that you not only cut yourself off from pain but miss the richness of life and human connection as well.

STRATEGIES TO PROTECT YOURSELF

AVOIDING PEOPLE

Survivors sometimes isolate themselves because they feel damaged and unlovable, undeserving of kindness, love, and concern. Or they may have never learned how to reach out, initiate a conversation, or establish a connection with another person. But human contact is a basic need. The lack of such relationships leads to loneliness, alienation, and despair:

> I knew I was different. Something was wrong with me and the other kids knew it. They could smell it on me and when kids sense a weakness . . . well, you know what happens. So I did everything I could to make myself stand out more. I wore my weirdness as a flag. When the other kids saw they couldn't get a rise out of me, they left me alone. My only friends were people I met online when I could pretend to be someone else. I can honestly say I've never had a real friend.

AVOIDING INTIMACY

If you don't let anyone get close to you, no one can hurt you. As one woman explained, "You can't be in an abusive relationship if you don't get in relationships." Another added, "I kept myself safe *and* alone."

Some survivors go to great lengths to limit intimacy. One woman said, "I can stop being friends with someone and never think twice about it." Another had relationships only with men who lived a great distance from her: "One of them was a plane ride away. The other one didn't have a car. That was really good."

Two Pictures of My Sister
BY DORIANNE LAUX

If an ordinary person is silent
it may be a tactical maneuver.
If a writer is silent, this is lying.
—JAROSLAV SEIFERT

The pose is stolen from Monroe, struck
in the sun's floodlight, eyes lowered,
a long-stemmed plastic rose between her
    teeth.
My cast off bathing suit hangs
in folds over her ribs, straps
cinched, pinned at the back of her neck.
Barefoot on the hot cement, knock-
    kneed,
comical if it weren't for the graceful
angles of her arms, her flesh soft
against the chipped stucco.

The other picture is in my head.
It is years later.
It is in color.
Blond hair curls away from the planes of
    her face
like wood shavings.
She wears a lemon yellow ruffled top,
    denim
cutoffs, her belly button squeezed to a slit
above the silver snap.

She stands against the hallway wall
while Dad shakes his belt in her face.
A strip of skin has been peeled
from her bare shoulder, there are snake
lines across her thighs, a perfect curl
around her long neck.
She looks through him
as if she could see behind his head.
She dares him.
Go on. Hit me again.
He lets the folded strap unravel to the
    floor.
Holds it by its tail. Bells the buckle
off her cheekbone.
She does not move or cry or even wince
as the welt blooms on her temple
like a flower opening frame by frame
in a nature film.
It lowers her eyelid with its violet petals
and as he walks away only her eyes
move, like the eyes of a portrait that follow
    you
around a museum room, her face
a stubborn moon that trails the car all night,
stays locked in the frame of the back
    window
no matter how many turns you take,
no matter how far you go.

Dorianne Laux, *Awake* (Spokane, WA: Eastern Washington University Press, 2007).

Some survivors avoid intimacy in less overt ways, seeming open and friendly on the surface but hiding real feelings inside. One survivor had a "Ten Official Secrets List" that she freely shared:

I'll tell people things about myself that seem too personal to share, but I don't really trust them or get close to them. They don't know what I feel inside. I hardly ever share that.

AVOIDING SEX

Many survivors go to great lengths to avoid sexual contact:

I intentionally married a man who was basically asexual. He was the three-times-a-year man, and he was absolutely perfect. When we wanted to get pregnant, I took my temperature. The conception of my children was as close to artificial insemination as you can get.

Others numb their bodies so that they no longer respond:

Part of the way I coped with the fact that some of the incest felt good was by saying, "It will never feel good. Sex will never feel good, because it felt good when it shouldn't have." So I don't ever feel. I don't pay attention to sex. I don't care about it and it doesn't make me feel anything. The other person is happy when it's done. And I can't wait until I'm

out of the situation so I don't have to do it again.

MAINTAINING CONTROL

Control is a theme that runs through the lives of many survivors:

I have a tremendous attachment to things going my way. It feels like I'm going to die if I don't get my way. There are a lot of small, everyday interactions that make me feel tremendously out of control.

Survivors often go to great lengths to keep their lives in order:

My shoes have to be put back in the same place at night. My room is always neat. When I come to work in the morning, I have this whole routine of putting the pen in a certain place, my keys in a certain place. Wherever I can maintain control, I do it, because there were so many places as a kid where I didn't have any control.

For many survivors, this need for control extends to people as well as to things. You may find it difficult to negotiate or compromise. An intense need for control can make it hard to see someone else's point of view, and accommodating someone else's preferences can feel extremely threatening.

HYPERVIGILANCE

As a child, tuning into every nuance of your environment may have saved you from being abused. Now, you may always need to be aware of where you are in a room. You sit where you can watch the entrance, making sure no one can sneak up behind you. You might also be hyperaware of people, always anticipating their needs and moods. One woman said she was a confirmed gossip for just this reason. If she kept track of what everyone was doing around her, no one could ever surprise her again.

CREATING CHAOS

Paradoxically, survivors sometimes maintain control over their environment by creating chaos. If your behavior is out of control, you force the people around you to drop what they're doing to respond to your latest crisis. In this way, you become the person calling the shots. As Laura's father used to say, "A family is a dictatorship run by its sickest member."

Like children of alcoholics, survivors are often good at both creating and resolving crises. One survivor, Jerilyn Munyon, explains:

They say that humans tend to gravitate toward what is comfortable, what they know. If this is true, then it explains why more often than not you find survivors in the midst of chaos. Not only are they familiar with it, they handle it beautifully. I could handle any extraordinary circumstance and in fact felt in my

element in those situations. But put me into the everyday world and I was very freaked out. I have always been hysterical in the midst of normalcy.

Before I found out that I was a survivor, I wondered why my life was filled with traumatic situations. Not only did I not have any middle ground, I was terrified at the thought of it. Whenever my life would calm down, I would start wishing for something major to happen so I could feel at home. While other people were looking for ways to put themselves on the edge, I could never get off it.

SAFETY AT ANY PRICE

One way to achieve control, or at least to attempt it, is to make choices that are secure and predictable. You take few risks, sacrificing opportunities for protection:

I married a man who would be stable, who wouldn't leave me, and above all, would not be intrusive. He was the rock. I didn't really have to do anything. I just clung to my husband. He was a high-status high achiever, and I shone in his glory for a long time. I lived in his protectorate for twenty-two years and that's how I survived.

SEEKING SAFETY IN RELIGION

Survivors sometimes seek safety and control by attaching to a belief system that has clearly defined rules and boundaries:

Searching for Security and Forgiveness: Marilyn's Story

I found some security in a born-again Baptist group when I was about fifteen. The evangelist talked about how bad we all were and how our sins could all be forgiven.

Everybody went to Bob Jones University with the pink and blue sidewalks, where the boys walked on the blue and the girls walked on the pink. We all wanted to go to Bob Jones. It was the ultimate. We were always out on the streets, evangelizing, handing out tracts, witnessing to all our friends.

Church was a release. It gave me the structure—if you do this and this, then you will be okay. There are formal dos and don'ts that you get from the pulpit, and then there are informal ones you get from your friends. You know which stores to buy your clothes in and which clothes to buy. You know which kinds of nightgowns to wear. You know which kinds of sexual activities with your husband are all right, which ones are not allowed. You all cook the same things. You raise your children in the same way. The point being that if you do those things, you're going to be all right.

I thoroughly believed that God intervened in the details of everything I did, including grocery shopping. I believed that as long as I was walking in the Light, nothing was going to happen to me that God wouldn't allow. I knew that if I couldn't make a decision, all I had to do was wait and God would tell me. I took no responsibility for my life—it was wrong for me to do so. What I had to do was find God's will in everything I did. I'd go to the store, and the sofa I had been looking at would be on sale, and it was God's will that I buy it.

I used to teach Bible studies for women. The teachings I lived by and taught for so many years were *Fascinating Womanhood* and *The Total Woman*. I just cringe when I think of those women, and I hope they have discarded what I taught them. One of them would be a little rebellious, and I would tell her she'd better knuckle under to her husband. I would quote scripture and verse.

I allowed no doubt. None. I just lapped those things up because they gave me great security. I knew I'd be forgiven for what a bad person I was.

ESCAPE BY ANY MEANS

As a child or an adolescent, you might have made attempts to run away from a home in which you were being abused. Or you might have escaped through sleep, books, or video games. Many adult survivors still read obsessively. One woman said, "I'd buy a junk novel and read it till I fell asleep, usually for a good thirty-six hours at a stretch." Others spend most of their lives in front of the TV or a computer screen.

If you couldn't bear to believe the abuse was really happening, you might have pretended something else was going on. Sometimes children create fantasies that explore their desire for power in a powerless situation. One woman dreamed of a little house she could live in all by herself, with locks on all the doors. Another spent her childhood dreaming of revenge:

> I'd watch *Perry Mason* to get ideas about how to kill my father. It was really the best of times. Every day I would get a new method. However the person was murdered on *Perry Mason* that day, I would go to bed that night, and that's how I would kill my father. One time on *Perry Mason* this guy killed his wife by knocking an electric fan into the bathtub. I imagined electrocuting him like that. I remember really vividly fantasizing about putting ground glass in the meatloaf. I was the cook. I thought about stabbing him, shooting him. Every night I killed him in another way.

Many survivors continue an intense fantasy life when they grow up:

> As an adult these changed to vindication fantasies, fantasies about having power in the world, revenge fantasies. I can work myself into a state of sobbing over something in a fantasy. I love fantasies about dying and everyone regretting all the wrongs they'd ever done to me. They're just an updated version of what I did as a kid. I can be lost in fantasy for hours. It's a lot safer to work things out in my head than to change things in the world.

Of course, imagination can be the source of a rich creative life. One teenager needed to escape so badly, she believed *Star Trek* was real.

When the series was taken off the air, she began to hear the voices of the characters in her head and started writing her own episodes. Today she is a successful science-fiction writer.

ADDICTIONS, COMPULSIONS, AND SELF-DESTRUCTIVE BEHAVIOR

Addictions are a common way to attempt to block out the memories and mute the pain of sexual abuse. If there had been safe people to turn to, you might have been able to develop other ways to handle your grief, shame, and rage. But if you didn't get the support and protection you needed, you had to find a way to manage by yourself.

You might have turned to drugs, alcohol, or food to numb your feelings. You might have become addicted to dangerous situations, crisis, or sex. (For more on overcoming addictions, see "From Addiction to Freedom," p. 260.)

Before I Remembered the Abuse: Sunny's Story

I started drinking with my mother in the afternoons after school. Her cocktail hour started with *Merv Griffin*. She was disabled, so when I came home from school, she'd say, "Make me a drink." And then one day she started to say, "Make us a drink." It wasn't until I was seventeen and went away to college that I started having blackouts and getting more serious about my drinking.

I never was a partygoer. I rarely went to bars. I did my drinking alone at home. I drank until I passed out, or until the bottle was empty. It was always the last time I was going to do it, so why not finish it off?

I did the same thing with eating. I wouldn't eat anything in the morning, because every day started out with me on a diet. I might go till two or three in the afternoon, and then I'd start eating. Instead of eating a meal like a normal person, I'd buy half a gallon of ice cream or a dozen doughnuts, and consume a huge quantity of food in a short period of time. It never tasted good. I just felt bad about myself, and the eating would make me feel worse. I'd feel horrible, that I'd failed. And then I'd say, "Well, I'll start tomorrow."

Before I went to AA and got sober, I felt that I was the only person in the world who felt the things I felt, who did the things I did, who lived the way I lived. I lived like a rat. I dressed normal, and I had a job, and I had a nice apartment, but I would go home on Friday, shut the drapes, lock the door, watch old movies and drink and eat.

I wouldn't ever watch anything current—like the news, or a parade, or a baseball game. Only old movies that were fantasies. Or soap operas. The characters were like my family. I especially liked the fact that they aired on holidays, because I could have Christmas and Thanksgiving with *All My Children.*

I would only get dressed to go to the store. There was a liquor store one block from the house and I would drive the one block. Sometimes I wouldn't even make it home. I'd have to stop the car and get into whatever it was that I had bought. Sometimes I wouldn't

even get dressed. I would put a coat over my nightgown and drive to the store.

I felt bad about living that way, but I tried not to think about my life. I knew there was something wrong with it, but I couldn't put my finger on it. I knew other people didn't live that way. I'd think that someday I'd do something about it. But not today.

I had no friends. I knew only a small handful of people. I remember thinking if I died, the first person to know it would be the landlady when I didn't pay my rent on the first of the month. There was really nobody in my life. No one I cared about. I was incredibly isolated. And I continued to feel that way until I went to Alcoholics Anonymous.

SEXUAL ADDICTION

While some survivors cope by avoiding sex, others use sex to meet all their needs, even ones that aren't sexual in nature. As one survivor said, "If you didn't want to have sex with me, I knew you didn't love me. Since I really needed to feel loved, I had sex with anyone who was willing to have me."

Like this woman, you may seek sex with strangers or have affairs that jeopardize a relationship that's important to you. You may be addicted to pornography, phone sex, Internet sex, or sex in circumstances that are humiliating, violent, dangerous, or reminiscent of the abuse. You may continue to be sexually abused or sexually abuse others. Whatever the habitual behavior, you may find it extremely difficult to stop, despite repeated attempts and good intentions:

I was married to a man I loved very much, but I couldn't stop having sex with other men. I picked up men in bars. I went to a sex club. It was all quick and anonymous. I told myself it had nothing to do with love, so it wasn't really a betrayal of my husband. Most of the time the sex itself wasn't even all that good. I just had to have it.

Of course my husband did find out. I got herpes and I had to tell him. It broke his heart and we tried to talk about it, but I had gone too far and it was too late to save our marriage.

ANOREXIA AND BULIMIA

Some young girls who were sexually abused develop anorexia and/or bulimia. In a family where the abuse is hidden and appearances are normal, anorexia or bulimia can sometimes be a cry for help. And for girls who've been pressured into sex they didn't want as children, growing into a woman's body can be terrifying. They think, "If this happened to me when I was a child, what will they do to me when I'm actually a woman?" Anorexia or bulimia can be one way girls try to say no, restrain their changing bodies, or assert control. One survivor recalls:

I had problems with anorexia for a long time, without understanding the cause, because in my case, it didn't seem to be about body image. When I was recovering from a recent surgery, still bandaged,

it finally came clear. Though there was food in the house, easily prepared, I was not eating; and I realized it was because post-surgery, as in post-abuse, I was damaged. Damaged women "are not good enough" to be fed. Understanding this, I could bring myself to cook and eat again.[*]

COMPULSIVE EATING

For many people, compulsive eating is a way to suppress emotions and avoid feeling pain. In addition, some survivors believe that being large will keep them from having to deal with sexual advances:

I've been overweight since I was nine. I remember exactly the day I started eating. It was the day my stepfather fingered me in front of other people. He took off my bathing suit and under the guise of drying me off, got his fingers inside of me. I felt completely exposed and I remember I started eating that day. And I really ballooned.

I frequently eat very consciously to gain weight to cover me, to protect me. When I lose weight, I feel totally exposed and naked. I can't stand it. There's a lot of heartache in being so overweight. It affects every part of your life, but I still need the protection.

---

* For more about anorexia and bulimia, see p. 262.

Another survivor said, "I kept eating so I wouldn't have to talk about what had happened. It just made sure my mouth was always full."*

EXCESSIVE BUSYNESS

One of the most common and accepted forms of compulsive behavior is busyness. Our culture rewards achievement and considers a frenetic pace of life normal. Still, many survivors take busyness to an extreme, using it as a way to avoid facing themselves, their feelings, or their past. One survivor, who lived her whole life according to the list she wrote first thing every morning, remarked, "I often mourn for a pace of life that I've never had."

Another survivor recalled:

They say, "If you need something done, give it to a busy person." That's me. I manage three kids' schedules and bake cookies for every bake sale. I'm the go-to person in church when a family is in crisis. I'm the first one there to comfort the bereaved or to visit a sick person in the hospital.

I get by on five or six hours of sleep a night. The rest of the time, I'm on the go, checking my PalmPilot and talking on my cell phone. Everyone thinks I'm great, but I know the truth: I'm running from any possibility of being with myself. I dread coming into contact with the ugliness and shame I know is pooled up inside. There's no way I'm stopping long enough to know what I feel inside— which is awful.

WORKAHOLISM

Many survivors feel an overwhelming need to achieve to make up for the badness that they feel is hidden inside. Excelling at work is valued in the high-achieving American culture, but when taken to excess, it can be a way to avoid an inner life or the possibility of intimacy with the people around you:

I became 100 percent work. I got into graduate school and just turned off to sharing or closeness with anyone. I was in a really intense MBA program, and I was determined to be perfect. If I wasn't at work with my job, I was working on school, which was supposed to get me further ahead in my job. It was all that mattered. It was the only place left where I could prove I was worth anything.

STEALING

Stealing is a totally absorbing activity that enables you to forget everything for a brief moment—including the abuse. It is a way to create distraction or excitement, to re-create

---

* Compulsive eating is not necessarily related to body size. Some large women are not overeaters, and some thin women binge compulsively. In U.S. culture, fat is a stigma, but we all have naturally different body sizes. Being large is not necessarily indicative of an emotional problem or a history or abuse. For more on compulsive eating, see "Eating Difficulties," p. 261.

the intense rush of adrenaline that you experienced when you were first abused. Stealing is also a way of defying authority, an attempt to take back what was stolen, to even the score. It can also be a cry for help. Sunny recalls:

> I worked at being a thief for a year and a half. When I first quit drinking, it was a way of coping. I didn't steal because I wanted the stuff—I got a terrific high from it. Unfortunately, it only lasted for about thirty seconds, and so I kept having to repeat the act.
>
> I embezzled from the company I worked for. I worked an insurance fraud that was grand larceny. And I shoplifted. I accumulated so much stuff that I started throwing it away. My car was full of loot. I never got caught.
>
> I stopped stealing five years ago on Christmas Day. I hadn't had one day where I hadn't stolen anything in a long time. All the stores were closed that day, so it seemed like a good day to begin. I finally called someone from AA and told her I had this problem. Just telling seemed to release me.

HURTING YOURSELF

SELF-MUTILATION

Self-mutilation is a way some survivors control their experience of pain. Instead of the abuser hurting you, you hurt yourself. Self-mutilation is a coping behavior people use for many complex reasons: to express anger and rage, to show on the outside how much pain they're in on the inside, to feel something when they're numb, or to reveal a need for help.

> I've wanted to hurt myself, to cause myself pain, and the way I usually think of doing that is cutting myself with a knife. It's a feeling that the pain inside is so bad, that if I cut myself, it'll come out. Lots of times I have images of putting my fists through glass, and I just think watching the blood go down the glass would make the pain go away somehow. It's like you're a balloon pushed full and you need to pop open a little. It seems like once you do it, it gets easier to do it again and again.[*]

YOU CAN CHANGE

It can be overwhelming to think about all the ways you've coped. But this recognition, though painful, is the first step in making positive changes.

When you were a child, you did not have many options. You did what you had to do to survive. Now you have more resources. You can change self-destructive patterns and let go of coping patterns that no longer work

---

[*] For a story in which one survivor deals with a pattern of self-mutilation, see "Michelle and Artemis" in "Courageous Women" on p. 467. For advice on stopping a pattern of self-mutilation, see "From Self-Injury to Self-Care," on p. 263.

for you. You can practice healthier responses, building on the positive ones you've developed, and create new habits to replace the ones you are leaving behind. This process isn't easy, and there are often setbacks along the way, but it is possible to make significant and meaningful changes in your life.

For each survivor, this journey will be unique. Everyone starts with a different set of opportunities and limitations. If you have coped in a way that gets positive recognition—by being supernurturing or successful in work—your options may be broader than if you have turned to drugs as a way to get by. If you are incarcerated in prison or a mental hospital, you clearly will not have the same range of choices. Your health, economic and social status, race, and education all influence your opportunities, but no matter what your situation, you can make better choices and change your life. ("Part Three: Changing Patterns" on p. 203 gives in-depth suggestions for changing specific areas of your life.)

The starting point for everyone, however, is to look at the ways you coped and to forgive yourself. You have no reason to be ashamed. You did the best that you could as a child under impossible circumstances. You have earned the name *survivor*. Now you are an adult with the power to make positive changes. From a place of self-acceptance and self-love, you can do so.

WRITING EXERCISE: COPING

(See the basic method for writing exercises on p. xxix.)

You've read about different ways that people have coped. Some of these you will identify with. There may be others not mentioned that have been recurring themes in your life. This is an opportunity for you to write about your experience of coping—how you've coped in the past, how you're coping today, and how these choices have affected your life. Write with as much detail as you can, always from the perspective of honoring what you did.

Survival Skills for Healing

"I survived the abuse, but sometimes I wonder if I can survive the healing process."

Healing is demanding work. It disrupts your old ways of coping; brings up deep pain, fear, and grief; and requires that you make profound changes in your life. When you are in the throes of healing from child sexual abuse, it is especially important to be kind to yourself. Yet a common side effect of child sexual abuse is insensitivity to our own needs and a lack of awareness about self-care, so one of the first challenges we face in the healing process is the need to develop a new survival skill: how to nurture ourselves.*

Often survivors ask Laura how far along they are in the healing process, and her re-

sponse to them is always the same. She asks them, "What are you doing to take care of yourself?" This is a better indicator of healing than how much therapy you've had, how many tears you've cried, or how many people you've told your incest story to.

Ask yourself: Am I gentle with myself when I make a mistake? Can I relax and take breaks from the intensity of healing? Am I able to do things I enjoy? Am I getting enough sleep and eating healthy food? Am I part of a community of people who love and support one another? Can I recognize the things that are going well in my life? Are there things I'm doing that I feel proud of? When you can answer yes to most of these questions or are making progress in that direction, you're well on your way to healing. However, if you are at the very beginning of

---

* Some of the suggestions for self-care and building a support system in this chapter were adapted from *The Courage to Heal Workbook* (New York: HarperCollins, 1990).

the healing process, you may not yet be able to say yes to a single question. Many survivors have been far too busy running, coping, and just getting by to consider how best to nurture themselves. But even if you're just starting out, you can take small steps toward self-care.

One way to begin is to take a gentle attitude toward the process of healing itself. Force doesn't promote healing; it impedes it. It's just as important to learn to relax, to laugh, to eat well, to sleep, and to enjoy everyday moments as it is to grapple with shame, to grieve, and to express outrage. You need quiet time for integration and gathering your strength. And of course, serenity is one of the goals of the healing process, a worthwhile prize in itself.

If you're at the beginning of the healing process and your life is full of painful emotions, memories, and crises, the idea of pacing yourself, taking breaks, or healing over time may seem irrelevant. You feel terrible now and want the pain to go away. But healing from sexual abuse is not a short-term proposition. It's a gradual process, rooted in small daily steps. You have to settle in for the long haul. You have to learn to live your life while you are healing.

OVERCOMING ISOLATION

If you are fortunate enough to be part of a supportive family or community, you have a safety net that will provide great comfort and be a source of strength. But many survivors are severely isolated. One woman, Krishnabai, recalled an experience that made her isolation glaringly obvious:

I got into a car accident. A drunken driver plowed into me. I went into the hospital and the doctor said, "Well, I think you're okay. But I don't want you to be alone for the night. Do you have a roommate?"

I said, "No."

And he said, "Do you have a friend you can call?"

I said, "No."

He said, "Do you have any family you can call?"

I said, "No."

And he looked at me with this incredible compassion and said, "Is there anyone there for you in your life?"

And I thought about it, and I said, "No."*

After a lifetime of loneliness, it can be hard to develop close relationships. Yet finding safe people and learning to trust is at the heart of the healing process. You already suffered the abuse alone. You don't have to heal in the same lonely isolation.

DEVELOPING A SUPPORT SYSTEM

A support system is a network of people who help you make it through life—and the demanding work of healing. They give you prac-

---

* For more of Krishnabai's story, see "Learning to Identify My Feelings: Krishnabai's Story" on p. 224.

tical support. They bring over a meal, provide care for your children, drive you to a doctor's appointment, or help you find a new place to live. They offer intellectual support, suggesting books and resources that might help you, talking over strategies and plans. They provide emotional support. They sit with you when you cry and comfort you when you feel down. And they give you spiritual support, inspiring you, giving you hope.

People in your support system trust your capacity to heal yourself. Rather than view you as someone who is damaged, they perceive you as a good person who's having a hard time right now. They recognize your potential and beauty even when you can't see it yourself. Above all, they like and respect you. By challenging your old ideas about yourself, your support people inspire you to grow. When you're around them, you should feel reassured, cared about, and listened to.

Now that you are healing, it's essential to structure your life so that you are in contact with people who respect you, understand you, and take you seriously. This is what you did not have as a child and what you need now.

Consider yourself valuable enough to be discriminating about the people you relate to. Although you are not always in a position to cut off contact completely with people who don't respect you (for example, a teacher in a required course), weed out the ones who have a pattern of being inconsiderate or unkind.*

ASSESS YOUR RELATIONSHIPS

Look at the relationships you already have. Who are the people you interact with each day, each week, each month? Consider roommates, relatives, friends, neighbors, coworkers, fellow students, acquaintances, people from your faith community, people you've met in 12-step meetings, counselors, and other helping professionals. Think about each person in turn and assess whether you could ask that person for a favor, confide in them, or safely share your feelings. Are there people who know you've been sexually abused and are supportive of your healing? Are there people whom you haven't told yet but who have demonstrated their thoughtfulness in other ways? Enlisting the understanding of people you're already close to is an important part of building a support system.†

If you're just beginning to reach out, start with just one person. Having even one person to confide in can radically change your experience.

LEARNING TO ASK FOR HELP

A support system is only effective when you use it. This may sound obvious, but it's not always easy to do. People who grew up in abusive families often believe that they have to do

---

* See "Learning to Trust" on p. 277 for more on this topic. For more on how to leave unsatisfying relationships, see "Separating" on p. 286.

† See "Breaking Silence" on p. 102 for more on how to tell people you think will be supportive.

everything themselves or that they deserve assistance only in a dire emergency. You may be afraid to ask for help because it means giving up control, depending on someone else, admitting "weakness," or risking rejection.

If you find yourself hesitant to reach out, consider whether you'd be willing to provide assistance to a friend in your position. If so, this may help you see that both the one who needs help and the one who gives it gain something valuable in the exchange. Often, there are people in your life who would like to help if they could. But if you don't tell them what you're going through and what you need, you deny them that opportunity.

Once you've acknowledged that you need—and deserve—help, you have to take the big leap and ask. Although there are times you may not get what you want, support sometimes shows up in unexpected ways and from unexpected sources:

My most comfortable style when I'm sad or upset is to withdraw. I have a loving husband and many good friends, but if I'm really in pain, I'm like an animal. I just want to crawl under a rock and lick my wounds. I come from a family where my mother and my sisters were all emotionally dramatic. There was no room for my feelings, so I learned to go inside. Slowly, I'm changing that. I'm sharing what I feel and the response has been wonderful. I never knew what nurturing was, but now that I'm opening up to it, I see that it's very sweet, very tender. It still amazes me when I actually allow someone to comfort me.

When you do ask for help, pay attention to the reactions you get. Your request may be treated respectfully or it may be criticized. If you consistently get negative responses, you may be asking the wrong person (someone who is too busy or who isn't interested in this kind of relationship with you) or you may be asking in the wrong way (not being direct or clear, not being specific enough, asking for too much at once). See what you can learn from your attempts and then try again.*

THE REWARDS OF GIVING

While this may be a time in your life when your needs are especially strong, don't forget that you have things of value to offer others. Sometimes when you're feeling especially vulnerable, sad, depressed, or hopeless, it can be a great relief to focus on someone else's needs. Attending to others reminds us of our strengths and validates our self-worth. When you help someone, you're temporarily lifted out of your own pain and into a meaningful connection with another person.

I started working in a soup kitchen one day a week and I could immediately feel myself looking forward to Thursdays. It was a few hours that I could just concentrate on chopping up chickens or potatoes. And the people who came to eat there were mostly regulars so I got to

---

* For more about building healthy relationships, see "Healthy Intimacy" on p. 271.

know them. There were no big expectations of me. After all, those folks weren't in such great shape either. I could just be in whatever state I was in—as long as I was getting the potato salad into the bowls, I was good enough.

Of course, if helping others has been a way you've avoided focusing on your own needs, it will be important not to continue this pattern. Your own healing needs to be the priority now.

THE VALUE OF COUNSELING

For many survivors, a skilled therapist is an integral part of their support system. A good counselor is a compassionate witness to your healing, knows the terrain, and can guide you through the process. By offering consistent support, encouragement, hope, information, and insight, a counselor provides a safe relationship within which you can grow. Laura explains:

When I couldn't believe in myself, when I didn't know if I could make it, my counselor believed in me. Week after week, she sat there, a loving witness to my pain and my progress. She loved me no matter what I did or said. For the first time in my life, I felt accepted as if I were valuable—not for what I did, but just for who I was. That was her greatest gift.

Your counselor should be someone who truly cares for you and consistently reflects your essential worth back to you:

When there has been real harm done by people who should have been trustworthy, there's a deep level of confusion about your own goodness, worth and value. Because the harm happened in relationship, it heals in relationship. A relationship with a therapist who's warm and loving and present is one of the places where deep healing can take place. I don't think I could have come to know my own goodness without having that reflected to me by my therapist, who really cared about me and made room for the horrible experiences I couldn't tolerate facing by myself. If I hadn't gotten good professional help, I don't think I would have stayed alive. Or if I had lived, I would have lived a very diminished potential.

A counselor provides a safe place to spill out the secrets and pain—and the hopes—that have been held inside. And in that sharing, a transformation takes place:

Some people think a therapist will try to fix them, like an auto mechanic—tinker here, adjust there, change a part—and this will feel disruptive and invasive and troubling. But if it's a good therapeutic relationship, it's not like that. Ultimately you do get healed, but in the places you need to be and in a way that feels right. It's comforting and it's a relief.

In a strong therapeutic relationship, a special kind of magic takes place. Feelings are reclaimed, ancient hurts resolve, lives are re-envisioned, and the future opens up with possibility. Therapy can be a powerful vehicle for change. (For guidance in finding a therapist and help assessing your current therapy, see "Working with a Counselor" on p. 45.)

DEALING WITH PANIC

Fear is a normal part of life—and of the healing process. The more you become familiar with it, the less distressing it will be. But in the beginning of the healing process, there may be times when you feel overwhelmed by fear.

Panic is fear that has spiraled out of control. You feel panic when you get scared by your own emotions and don't have the skills to calm yourself down or when you're trying like mad to suppress feelings or memories. Sometimes panic comes when the past intrudes into the present and it feels as if it's happening now.*

Although panic can seem to come out of the blue, there is always a trigger. Often it is a reminder of abuse that you aren't consciously aware of. Randi Taylor panicked whenever she stopped at a red light. The feeling of being boxed in and unable to move reminded her of the trapped feeling she had when she was molested.†

---

* For more about this phenomenon, see "New Feelings, Old Feelings" on p. 230.

† For more of Randi's story, see p. 462. Evie Malcolm, whose story is on p. 449, is another example of someone who overcame panic attacks in the course of her healing.

When you are in a state of panic, you are usually not aware of these connections. You simply feel out of control. Your heart is racing; your breathing speeds up. You may break into a sweat, want to run, or feel as if your body is going to explode. Even your vision can change. You might fear that you're going crazy. And not understanding what's happening only makes things worse.

Laura had her first major panic attack when she was twenty years old:

I was scared. I was scared about being scared, and the whole thing kept snowballing out of control. I was getting more and more terrified by the minute and I didn't know how to find the release valve. Somehow I had the sense to call my best friend. I remember telling her on the phone, "I feel like either I'll realize God, go insane, or kill myself." She gave me a priceless and simple piece of advice. It got me through that attack of panic and many other tight situations in the years that followed. "Breathe, Laura," she said. "Just breathe."

If you start to feel overwhelmed and panicky, breathe. Sit with the feeling. Often women think they have to do something quickly to get away from the feelings of terror and alarm, but this frenzy to escape can escalate your fear rather than relieve it. Don't rush into action. Instead, reassure yourself that this is just a feeling, powerful though it may be, and that feelings always change.

When you're extremely frightened, expressing your feelings can sometimes free you from your fear, but only if you're in a setting that's safe. A therapy group can be a good place to get in touch with deeply buried feelings. Driving home isn't. If you decide it isn't a good time to express or act on your feelings—or if expressing your feelings escalates your panic—take steps to calm yourself down.

CALMING DOWN

The most effective way to deal with panic is to catch it early. Once panic spirals out of control, it's more difficult to manage, but at least you can keep yourself focused in a positive direction so that you don't hurt yourself or others.

The important thing in calming down is to do whatever works for you, as long as it is safe, even if it seems silly or embarrassing. Through trial and error, you can develop a list of things that help. Try including activities that engage as many of the senses as possible (feeling, hearing, sight, taste, smell). And it's important to reach out to others, even if it's the last thing you want to do.

Because you don't think as clearly or creatively when you're in a panic, make a list in a calm moment and keep it handy. If it's all written out ahead of time, you only have to pick up your list, start at the top, and work your way down.

A sample list might look like this:

Things to Do When I'm Desperate
1. Breathe.
2. Look around at my environment. Acknowledge where I am and what is actually happening.
3. Put on a relaxation tape.*
4. Get in my rocking chair.
5. Call Natalie: 555–9887.
6. Call Vicki if Natalie's not home: 555–6632. Keep calling down my list of support people. [Put their names and numbers here.]
7. Pet my cat.
8. Take a hot bath.
9. Meditate.
10. Do a simple physical task such as sweeping the floor, washing dishes, cleaning the bathtub, or scrubbing the stove.
11. Run around the block three times.
12. Listen to soothing music.
13. Pray.
14. Write in my journal.
15. Draw, paint, work in clay, or make a collage.
16. Breathe.
17. Leave the house and do something safe that I enjoy.
18. Yell into my pillow.
19. Watch an old movie on TV or read a mystery novel.
20. Eat something healthy and comforting. (Name the food here and keep it on hand.)
21. Start again at the top.

Your list will be different and will probably change over time. If you get all the way to the bottom of your list and still don't feel better, you can start again at the top.

---

* For more on the benefits of guided relaxation and imagery, see "Using Guided Imagery" on p. xxxiii.

DON'T KILL YOURSELF

I've been very suicidal in the process of re-membering, to the point where I've had to say to myself, "You will not go to certain places because you couldn't resist the urge." I felt like the last things in my life that were important and gave me strength had been devastated. So there wasn't anything to look forward to. It's only been in the last few months that I've started to make plans again. Which means I've decided I want to live.

Sometimes you feel so bad, you want to die. The pain is so great, your feelings of self-loathing so strong, the fear so intense, or you are so weary of the battle that you really don't want to live. These are your authentic feelings, and it is important not to deny them. It is also essential not to act on them. It's okay to feel as devastated as you feel. It's just not okay to hurt your-self.*

We have lost far too many women al-ready. Far too many victims—both adults and children—have lacked adequate sup-port and, out of despair, have killed them-selves. We can't afford to lose more. We can't afford to lose you. You deserve to live.

Read the chapter on anger (see p. 136). You have been taught to turn that anger in-ward. When you feel so bad that you want to die, there's anger inside that you need to refocus toward the person or people who hurt you so badly as a child. As you get in touch with that anger, your fear and self-hatred will dissipate. You will want to sus-tain your life, not destroy it.

All of this takes time. In the meantime, don't kill yourself. Get help. If the first help isn't helpful, get other help. Don't give up. When you feel bad enough to want to die, it's hard to imagine that you could ever feel any other way. But you can. And will. As one survivor wrote in her journal:

I HATE LIFE! I hate myself! I hate what I do to myself. I want to crawl into the dark earth and cover myself up. I hate that I need to remember! That I need to go through the abuse over and over again in order to let it go and find life. Why should I want to live again? How do I know it won't just be more pain? How can any-one expect me to continue working toward something so unknown and intangible?

---

* Many of the women whose stories appear in the sec-tion "Courageous Women" (see p. 407) have felt sui-cidal at some point in their healing. Their words can reassure you that it's worth staying alive.

And yet I do. There is something inside me that must have incredible strength, because it has survived three major suicide attempts and lots of disillusioned and desperate times. And it's still there, keeping me going, making me work, urging me to remember and fight the guilt, to get angry, to cry, to feel, and share . . . and share . . . and share! Pushing me on toward that unknown which they call life.

If you start feeling suicidal or compelled to hurt yourself, get help right away. When you are struggling with suicidal feelings, it's important to have the support of a capable therapist. And make sure that you have the number of a suicide prevention hotline *before* you need it. Keep that number along with your therapist's number in an obvious and easily accessible place where you can find it even when you are very distressed.

It's also essential to make a no-suicide contract with your counselor. Work out the terms of the contract together so that it's very clear and you both can rely on it. For example, you promise to call your therapist if you are not certain that you can keep yourself safe. Then you agree to wait until she or he calls back, regardless of how long it takes. If a great deal of time goes by, call again because it's always possible that your message wasn't received. Your therapist promises to call back *as soon* as she gets the message. If you can't stay safe in the meantime, you agree that you will go to a hospital, call suicide prevention, or get other help while you wait for your therapist's call. This agreement, when both of you promise to keep it, provides a secure safety net. It also fosters trust and partnership in the alliance you are building together. If your therapist will not agree to such a contract, find another one as soon as possible.

The important thing to know is that the feelings will pass. You may think that the feelings will consume you, will be absolutely unbearable. But you can learn to wait them out. It's like a difficult childbirth. The laboring woman thinks that she can't handle another contraction, but she can. And then it passes.

Each time you are able to bear the pain of your feelings without hurting yourself, each time you are able to keep safe, to reach out for help, to befriend yourself through the anguish, you have built up a little more of the warrior spirit. You have fought the brainwashing of the abusers and won the battle. You have not let them destroy you.

CREATE A SAFE PLACE

It's a good idea to create a safe place in your home, somewhere you can go when you're scared. Your safe place might be a window seat on the stairway, your bed, or a favorite reading chair. Or it might be a hiding place where no one can find you. One woman spent the night sleeping in her closet on top of her shoes, something she'd done as a small child to comfort herself in a house where no place was safe.

Make a commitment to yourself that if you start to feel out of control and afraid of what you might do, you'll go to that place and stay there, breathing one breath at a time until the feeling passes. And make an agreement with yourself that as long as you're in that place, you won't hurt yourself or anyone else—you'll be safe.

If you are experiencing tremendous fear, anger, grief, or despair, you may doubt that you can live through even another minute, let alone the hours it may take for the feelings to subside or for you to get help. But Ellen advises survivors, "If you've tried everything you can think of and you still feel like you can't make it through the night, sit down in a chair and don't get back up. It might be the most miserable night of your life, but morning will come and you'll be alive without having hurt yourself."

CREATING A SAFE PLACE INSIDE

Guided Imagery by Amy Pine

Often when you've been traumatized, your body no longer feels like a safe place. It feels dangerous instead. So when you bring your awareness inside your body, you immediately want to jump right back out again. Learning to stay present and find safety in your body is an essential part of healing. This guided meditation is one way to begin. (For instructions on how to use it, read "Using Guided Imagery" on p. xxxiii.)

Make sure that you have the time and space to listen to the imagery without interruptions. . . . Find a position where your body can be comfortable and supported. . . . This may be sitting up in a chair, leaning back, lying down. . . . Whatever feels best in the moment. . . . Take a few minutes just to allow your body to settle, feeling the support of the surface beneath you. . . . Allow the weight of your body to be released, like grains of sand settling toward the earth. . . . Allow yourself to arrive at this very moment in this very place—nowhere else you have to go, nothing else that you have to do. . . . Notice your breathing. . . . There is nothing you need to do to change it, just simply watch and be aware. . . . Notice the sensation of your breath as it comes in through your nose, the way it travels down through the trachea and fills the lungs. . . . How the rib cage expands as you breathe in, how the back widens. . . . Notice your breath as you breathe out—how your body softens and empties, letting go. . . . Breathing in new oxygen that nourishes and fills you, breathing out what is no longer nourishing or needed. . . . Notice how the breath returns all on its own. . . . Take a minute to watch several complete rounds of breath. . . . Breathing in, breathing out, and the return. . . .

Allow yourself to imagine what it would be like to be in a place where you would feel completely safe . . . where you could let down your guard, your watchfulness . . . where your body could relax and soften with the complete confidence that you will be safe. . . . Whether or not you have known this feeling, you can imagine it now. . . . Where might this place be? Perhaps it is somewhere familiar to you. . . . Perhaps it is a place that you imagine. . . . It may be outdoors—the beach, next to a stream, a meadow filled with flowers, the forest. . . . Perhaps it is a place indoors—a cozy bedroom filled with pillows, a comforter, lacy curtains . . . perhaps a cabin in the woods that has been built for you alone, with everything you need inside. . . . It may be a place you know or have known. . . . Or perhaps it is a place that you are just now imagining into being . . . a magic bubble, an island in the sky. . . . Now look around—notice the colors, the objects, the temperature

of the air. . . . Are there sounds that you can hear? The trickle of a stream, soft music, chirping birds? What about smells? Flowers, fresh air?

What do you want to have with you in this space that brings you comfort, security, joy? Notice what it's like for your body and your whole self to relax and experience being in this place where you are guaranteed safety. . . . Do you like being alone there, or do you want to have a companion? Perhaps an animal friend, a hummingbird, plants, a spirit guide? This is a place that is completely your own creation, where everything can be exactly as you need it to be. . . . Notice what you are wanting and needing as you spend a few minutes inside of this safe space today. . . . Might you want a nap or a rest, to write in your journal, to take a stroll?

This place is accessible to you at any time. . . . You can return whenever you feel the need or whenever you want to. . . . It will be there inside you, available to you when you decide to take the time to return. . . .

Now, take a few easy breaths, anchoring your experience of comfort, safety, and well-being. . . . Take a moment to thank yourself and the space that you have created inside. . . . Gradually shift your awareness from the environment within yourself to your body resting upon the surfaces of support, finally opening your eyes and coming out into the environment outside of yourself as well. . . .

CHANGE YOUR ENVIRONMENT

Consciously changing your environment can sometimes bring you out of panic. This can be as simple as leaving your bedroom and walking into the kitchen to make tea. Or you can leave your house and take a walk down the block. You can go for a swim—or just take a bath or shower. Water can be very soothing. If you're out in nature, looking up at the stars or trees can give you a sense of perspective.

Sometimes the things that upset you are sensory reminders of past abuse. The smell of a certain cologne, the tone of someone's voice, the sound of corduroy pant legs rubbing together can trigger real anxiety:

> One day I was in the kitchen, getting more and more depressed. I started trying to calm myself down, telling myself, "Okay, you're doing fine. This'll pass. It always does." That didn't help at all. I'm beginning to know how to take care of myself, so I just went back to the basics. I reminded myself to breathe, asked myself when I'd eaten, started cutting up vegetables for dinner—and felt worse. Finally I noticed that the light in the kitchen was really dim. I turned on an overhead light and felt better right away. That kind of dim light always makes me feel terrible. It reminds me of the house I grew up in.

By becoming aware of your own triggers, you will be better equipped to respond when you encounter them.

SOME THINGS TO AVOID

Almost anything that works is fair game in dealing with panic, but there are a few things you should avoid whenever possible:

- Don't enter stressful or dangerous situations.
- Stay off the road.
- Don't abuse drugs or alcohol.
- Avoid making important decisions unless they are essential for your safety.
- Don't hurt yourself or anyone else.
- Avoid people who aren't safe or trustworthy.

AFTER YOU COME DOWN

When you're on the other side of a panic attack, relax and rest a bit. Such emotional intensity is exhausting, and you need to replenish your energy. When you feel balanced again, try to determine what triggered the panic. The following questions might help:

- What was the last thing you remember before you felt overwhelmed?
- Where were you? Who were you with?
- Was there anything disturbing that happened to you in the last day or two? (An upset at work? With a friend? Your partner? Did you get a disturbing phone call, letter, or e-mail?)
- Was there a glimmer of any other feeling before you lost touch with yourself? Is this something you've felt before?

- Are you under any unusual stresses? Time pressures? Deadlines? Money pressures?
- Were there thoughts that you quickly pushed away because they were uncomfortable? Were they old, familiar ones?
- Do any of these things remind you of your abuse in any way?

Sometimes questions like these can help you identify what led to the panic attack. It may take a series of episodes with similar dynamics before you can pinpoint the source, but it's worth the work. Once you discover the circumstances that trigger feelings of panic, self-hate, or despair, then you can anticipate them and deal with them more effectively.

THE IMPORTANCE OF SELF-CARE

Learning to nurture yourself is critical—not only in times of crisis. It's an important aspect of everyday life. Like many survivors, you may believe that you deserve to take care of yourself only when your life is absolutely falling apart (and maybe not even then). But this isn't so. With intention and practice, tending to your emotional needs can become a regular daily habit, like brushing your teeth.

Self-care is at the core of healing. It's a way that you can demonstrate love and respect for the child you were, the adult you are now, and the person you are becoming.

WHAT ABOUT MEDICATION?

Medication can't take the place of good therapy and the work necessary to heal. Unfortunately, survivors have often been misdiagnosed or given drugs they didn't want or need. Medication is frequently advised in place of the in-depth therapy necessary for healing. Insurance—even if you have it—often pays for only a limited number of therapy sessions—or only a small portion of the cost, making medication seem like the best, most affordable solution. Friends or family may also encourage the premature or excessive use of antidepressants and other drugs. As one survivor describes:

When my daughter tried to kill herself, we all got into therapy. The therapist wanted to instantly put me on medication because I was crying. I'm sorry I was feeling sad, but it seemed to me like crying was a normal thing for a person to do when they have a suicidal daughter and are dealing with sexual abuse. I'd worked hard to get to the point in my healing where I knew what sadness was. I'd worked hard to get to the point where I *could* cry. And now this therapist wanted to give me something to make it go away? That didn't make any sense to me.

Although it is not unusual for medication to be overprescribed, there are situations when it is genuinely helpful—and even lifesaving. Sometimes even though you are doing everything possible to work with your emotions, it isn't enough. If you are depressed, extremely anxious, feeling suicidal, unable to eat or sleep, or experiencing an emotional roller coaster that makes daily life unmanageable for an extended period of time, you might want to talk with a psychiatrist about whether medication could help you cope and make progress in your healing.

Hereditary factors as well as extreme early trauma can disrupt brain chemistry and neurological systems, causing a variety of effects. You may experience debilitating depression. You may be in an almost constant state of agitation or flooded with emotion, even when there's no immediate danger. You may find yourself overreacting to small upsets, unable to calm down even when the situation is resolved.*

Many people, including survivors of child sexual abuse, have found medication helpful in gaining some balance. There are a variety of drugs that may be beneficial to survivors, especially antidepressants such as SSRIs (selective serotonin reuptake inhibitors). Antianxiety agents and sleep medication have helped survivors through rough/difficult periods. Antipsychotics have been effective for survivors with psychotic symptoms such as auditory or visual hallucinations and paranoia. These medications—sometimes in very small doses—have made a huge difference for many survivors and allowed them to continue to function and to heal.

* See "Getting in Touch with Your Feelings" on p. 222 and "Trauma and the Brain" on p. 242 for more on this topic.

Some people need to take these medications for a long time. For others, a short period is sufficient to reset their emotional equilibrium. Afterward they are able to maintain their balance without medication.

Doctors, however, don't always steer people off medication once it has finished its usefulness, so you may have to bring up the possibility of getting off medication when you think it might be time. With psychiatric medications, though, it's extremely important not to quit cold turkey. Sudden withdrawal can lead to unexpected, potentially dangerous side effects, so if you are stopping a drug, do so under a doctor's supervision. It is also important to *start* taking medications only with a doctor's direct care and according to the doctor's recommended dosage. Don't try out your friend's drugs or begin taking any medication on your own. Medications are powerful and can be dangerous when not properly used or carefully monitored.

MISCONCEPTIONS ABOUT MEDICATION

Some survivors are reluctant to use medication because they fear that they will become dependent on drugs or that taking medication will create more problems in their lives than it solves. Others believe that it implies they are failures. Sometimes survivors worry that taking antidepressants or other medication will cut off their feelings, thus delaying their healing:

I was reluctant to take antidepressants. I thought it meant that I was weak.

But I just couldn't pull out of the pit. I was in weekly therapy, I exercised, I tried herbal remedies, but the fear just wouldn't let up. I could barely make it through the day and nights were worse. One day my therapist asked me, once again, if I wanted to try a low dose of antidepressants, and this time, I agreed. I couldn't believe the difference. I thought it would take away all my emotions. I expected to be like a zombie. But it just took the edge off so I could actually *do* the therapy, so I could actually work through the abuse.

It's important to bear in mind that all medications have benefits and risks. There are side effects that will be problematic for some people and insignificant for others. Find out all you can about any medication you're considering, and listen to yourself when it comes to side effects and effectiveness. No one knows your experience better than you.

Each person is unique, so what's right for one person is not necessarily right for another. But if you are suffering intensely over a significant period of time, you might want to talk to a psychiatrist to discuss possible options. Choose someone who is compassionate, whom you feel is trustworthy, and who has worked extensively with survivors who experience post-traumatic stress disorder (PTSD).* You want to make sure that your doctor is familiar with the latest research.

---

* For information about post-traumatic stress disorder, see "Trauma and the Brain" on p. 242.

LEARNING TO NURTURE YOURSELF

There are a million ways to nurture yourself. Choose those things that make you feel good and do them often. Nurturing yourself is not optional; it's an essential part of health. Weaving calm, soothing, and comforting activities into the daily fabric of your life furthers healing and is solid evidence of just how far you have come. You don't have to wait. You deserve to feel good.

"I love sushi. So I go out and have sushi."

"I love movies and I love to buy books. So I do a lot of both."

"I go away on the weekends to places I like."

"I set aside times in my week when I plan to come home and *not* think about incest. Or I go out with a friend and we agree not to talk about it."

"I get massages and take a lot of hot tubs."

"I've been exercising more."

"I surround myself with people with whom I can discuss the whole of my life, that I don't have to keep any secrets from. I worked very hard to get the secret out of my life. I need to be able to talk about it with the people in my life as easily as I can ask them what kind of coffee they want."

"I'm in a support group. I have close contact with the other group members. We talk every other day. And when one of us is feeling real bad, like wanting to hurt herself or something, we call. We support each other a real lot."

"I have affirmations all over my room. They say things like: 'I do not deserve to be hurt.' 'There's nothing wrong with my body.' 'I love myself.' 'I am gentle and patient with myself.' 'I am good.' 'I forgive myself.'"

"When I come out of a heavy therapy session, no matter what it feels like, I always buy myself flowers."

"I eat a good breakfast. I try to look after myself with food. It's the least I can do."

"I write."

"I make myself a big cup of tea and curl up with a book. Or I take a really hot bath with some nice bath oil, and stay in there with a book till the water gets cold."

"I've gotten clothes that are far more colorful and flattering. I went out last year and bought myself this absolutely gorgeous emerald green dress that was very fashionable. I look very good in it, and that was a real gift for myself. That was a real step for me, not to just buy it because it was on sale."

"Working in my garden is a wonderful healing metaphor for me. I'd never done anything like that before. When we bought our house, the garden was totally overgrown. I went out with pruning shears and cut back twenty loads of debris we took to the dump. Each time I turned over a shovelful of dirt or planted something new, it felt like I was doing that for myself."

"I try to get into nature and walk and hike and ski as often as I can."

Working with a Counselor

"One counselor said to me, 'You're at the center of your healing process. I'm just one of your tools.' I really liked that. That's the way healing should be."

—SAPHYRE

The support of a skilled counselor can be extremely helpful in your healing (see "The Value of Counseling" on p. 33). For survivors who were hurt by the people closest to them, one of the most valuable things about seeing a therapist may be that you have an opportunity to trust again.

For me the most important thing about therapy is that there is someone who will listen to you. Freely. He won't talk back or correct you or interrupt or tell you you're wrong or undermine you in more subtle ways. You can say anything you want, you can say the things closest to your heart, the things you may never have told anyone, and it's all right.

CHOOSING A COUNSELOR

Be willing to put effort into finding the right counselor. You don't have to go to the first person you see. Even if you are in crisis, don't commit yourself to a long-term therapy relationship until you feel confident that you've got the right person.

Ask for recommendations from friends, other survivors, or trusted family members. Shelters for battered women, rape crisis centers, parents' centers, and other women's programs are also likely places to get referrals.

You can save money and time by doing some preliminary screening on the phone. Counselors have different policies about this. Most will talk to you briefly on the phone for free.

Once you've narrowed down your choices, meet with the two or three you liked most. One woman went to six counselors, one each week, until she found the person she wanted to work with.

When you're evaluating potential counselors, here are some useful guidelines. Your prospective counselor:

- Should never minimize your experiences or your pain
- Should be knowledgeable about the healing process for adults who were sexually abused as children
- Should keep the focus on you, not on your abuser
- Should give you room to explore your own history without trying to define it for you
- Shouldn't push you to reconcile with or forgive the abuser
- Shouldn't be friends with you outside of counseling
- Shouldn't talk about his or her personal problems
- Shouldn't be sexual with you, now or ever in the future
- Should respect all of your feelings (grief, anger, rage, sadness, despair, joy)
- Shouldn't force you to do anything you don't want to do*

---

* The only exceptions to this are if you are actively suicidal or are threatening to hurt someone else. Also, if you disclose a situation in which a child is being abused, your therapist will be mandated to report that abuse, whether you want it reported or not. When faced with a mandatory report, many counselors will help you become strong enough to make the report yourself.

- Should encourage you to build a support system outside of therapy
- Should teach you skills for taking care of yourself
- Should be willing to discuss problems that occur in the therapy relationship
- Should be accountable for mistakes that he or she makes

Ask questions to get a sense of the counselor's attitudes, experience, and way of working. There may also be particular issues that matter to you. For instance, you may want someone familiar with alcoholism or with eating disorders. Many survivors prefer working with a woman because they feel safer, because a man molested them, or because they are more comfortable discussing intimate feelings with a woman. Other survivors have benefited from working with male therapists because they wanted a safe relationship in which they could learn to trust a man. You may also prefer a counselor of your race, economic background, sexual orientation, or religion:

As a nun I felt more comfortable going to a nun because we could talk about spiritual things. If you get the wrong counselor, they say, "Spiritual, smiritual. There is no God." My counselor was a nun herself. So I was able to join a group for incest and rape survivors that was made up of just nuns. That way we didn't have to talk about our marriage partners or our sexual partners. We all had the issue of being "good," and we had a lot of the same guilts. I would have been very nervous as a religious person to talk about sexual things in a secular group. I would have been very conscious of the fact that I was a nun, and that that was fascinating to people. This group was safe. We could focus on what was important.

Your needs may not be this specialized and your options may vary depending on where you live. But it's worth trying to find the best person for you.

Once you've talked to several counselors, compare the way you felt when you spoke with each of them. With whom did you feel the strongest connection? Where were you most at ease? Think about the way each person responded to your concerns. Compare their availability, philosophies, and fees.

When you're looking for a counselor, it's helpful to take the attitude that you are a consumer making an informed choice about the person you're hiring to work with you. Even though you're seeking counseling to fill an emotional need, being a consumer gives you certain rights: the right to determine the qualities you want in a therapist, the right to be treated with respect, the right to say no to any of the suggestions your therapist makes, the right to be satisfied with the services you're receiving, the right to freely discuss any problems that arise in therapy with your counselor, and the right to end a therapy relationship that isn't working for you.

IF YOU'VE BEEN AVOIDING COUNSELING

Although it's wise to choose carefully, don't insist on so many qualifications that no one can meet your criteria:

I kept picking counselors that I could easily get rid of. I went to see seven different counselors for either one or two sessions. I would go to great lengths to find people who worked far away from where I lived, so I could say, "Oh well, this is too far to drive."

I would pick nontraditional therapies because I didn't want to work on things. One time I picked a past-life counselor, and you know that wasn't what I needed to work on!

I'd make the initial appointment because I felt desperate. Within one or two visits, I wouldn't be quite that desperate, and so I'd quit.

Soledad wanted to see only a lesbian Chicana counselor who had worked with sexual abuse.* Since there was no one who met these specifications in her area, she could have talked herself out of therapy. But she decided getting help was more important. She compromised and found a skilled white, heterosexual woman who has effectively facilitated her healing.

---

* For more of Soledad's story, see p. 436.

WHAT DOES EFFECTIVE COUNSELING FEEL LIKE?

When you work with a good counselor, you should feel understood and supported. You should feel warmth and caring. And that should happen early in the therapy process.

However, you can't always judge whether you're with a good therapist by the way you feel in the moment. Some women experience counseling as a haven they can't wait to get to. Others dread every session and have to force themselves to go. One woman said, "There were times I was absolutely terrified of going to therapy. I don't know how I drove there, how I got out of my car, how I got through the door."

Counseling is not always comfortable, but you know you're with a good counselor if you develop more and more skills in taking care of yourself as time goes on. Even if there's an initial period of strong dependency, you should eventually become more independent. Gizelle's counselor was able to do this for her*:

> I really owe a lot to my counselor. When I was struggling time and again and would say, "Where do I go from here? What should I do?" he would say, "Trust your process. Trust yourself. *You* know." The greatest gift he's given me is belief in myself. He constantly reflected to me my own knowing and my own power, my own ability to heal. He never gave me the answers. *He* never did the healing. It's

---

* For more of Gizelle's story, see pp. 147 and 186.

very important to work with people who help you get back your power, who help you get back your trust in your body, in your instincts, in your gut, in your voice, in you.

Although your relationship with your therapist may be tremendously significant to you, it is essential that you not relinquish all of your power in the counseling relationship. Remember that you are at the center of your life and your healing. A good counselor is only one of the many resources you will use.

IF YOU FEEL THERE'S A PROBLEM

If you don't feel respected, valued, or understood or if your experience is being minimized or distorted, that's a sign that you're in bad therapy, or at least that there's a bad fit between you and the counselor. If you feel there is something wrong in the therapy relationship, or if you get upset or angry with your counselor, talk about it in your session. Afterward, you should feel you've been heard and understood. If your counselor discounts your feelings or responds defensively, then you're not getting the respect you are entitled to. Look elsewhere.

However, it's also important to recognize that your counselor may not be able to fulfill all of your needs. During some parts of the healing process, you may genuinely need support several times a day, for example. In an ideal world, that would be available to you, but realistically your counselor may not be able to provide all that you wish she could.

Also, some survivors have a self-defeating pattern of asking the impossible and then rejecting their counselor when they don't get what everything they want. It can sometimes be difficult to determine what is and isn't reasonable to ask for. And it can be challenging to identify your own role in creating a situation in which you feel betrayed yet again. If this is a pattern in your life—or if you suspect it might be—talk to your therapist about it. Sometimes meeting with a third person can be helpful in sorting through a complex or confusing relationship.

If a counselor ever wants to have a sexual relationship with you, get out right away.

FINDING YOUR OWN TRUTH

The foundation of good therapy is a respectful relationship in which the therapist provides a safe space, genuine caring, and support. Good therapists don't lead—they follow their clients into the difficult and painful places they need to go. In doing so, their clients are empowered to do their own healing work, to uncover their own history, to find their own truth. As Judith Herman,[*] author of *Trauma and Recovery*, explains, "Psychotherapy is a collaborative effort, not a form of totalitarian indoctrination."[†]

All therapists, even good ones, do sometimes make mistakes. In the past, these mistakes—relative to survivors—had more to do with minimizing and denying abuse than imagining it where it didn't exist. Even now, many therapists are reluctant to explore a history of abuse with their clients.[‡]

On the other hand, some therapists have concluded on their own that a client had been abused regardless of whether the person herself thought she had. This is irresponsible therapy and potentially dangerous for the client.

Remember, you are the expert on your own life. Sometimes the path to knowing your history is a gradual one, but try to be patient with the process and over time you will come to your best understanding of your past.[§]

---

[*] Judith Lewis Herman is associate clinical professor of psychiatry at the Harvard Medical School and author of *Father–Daughter Incest* and *Trauma and Recovery: The Aftermath of Violence—from Domestic Abuse to Political Terror*, both included in the Resource Guide.

[†] Herman, "Backtalk," p. 4.

[‡] This reluctance is often based on a fear of being sued. Faced with attacks on their professional judgment and the threat of legal action and ethics charges by irate parents, some therapists are finding themselves in conflict between protecting themselves and following the best interests of their clients.

[§] For more on the process of coming to your own truth, see "If Doubts Persist" on p. 100 and "Strategies for Working with Persistent Doubt" on p. 98.

Report the therapist to the appropriate licensing board. *It is never okay for therapists to have romantic or sexual involvements with their clients.**

If you have had a damaging experience with a counselor, you have a right to be angry, but don't let a negative therapy experience stop you from getting the help you need and deserve. Before you commit yourself to another counseling relationship, think about what you want; take your time and use the resources available to protect yourself in the future.

SUPPORT GROUPS

Being with other survivors is an important part of the healing process for many survivors. Group work is particularly useful for dealing with shame, isolation, secrecy, and self-esteem. Talking with other survivors is helpful for problem-solving also. There's likely to be at least one other woman in the room who has suggestions for dealing with whatever issue you're facing.

In groups, survivors get together at a regularly scheduled time specifically to support each other in their healing. Groups can be organized for a set number of weeks or they can be ongoing. Groups led by a trained facilitator or counselor usually have a weekly or monthly fee, but in some communities, there are groups

provided without charge. There are also free groups based on the 12-step model. Survivors of Incest Anonymous (SIA) and Incest Survivors Anonymous (ISA) are two such organizations that provide an opportunity to meet and share with other survivors.†

Being with survivors of child sexual abuse as they share their feelings, their struggles, and their triumphs allows you to reflect on your own experience from a different perspective. You see women who, in spite of their pain and problems, are strong, beautiful people with integrity. You can see that the abuse was not their fault, that they are not to blame. You can be outraged on their behalf and compassionate with their suffering—kindnesses you may not yet have extended to yourself. And as you realize that you are a lot like these other women— that you are one of them—you learn to see yourself in the same affirming light.

One survivor, Jennierose Lavender, explained the benefits she gained from being in a support group:

> When I joined a group with other survivors, it was the first time I ever felt connected with anybody. All my life I had felt alone. I had never trusted anyone. I had always isolated myself. All those years in therapy, I had just played psychi-

---

* If you have been abused by a therapist or other helping professional, see p. 551 of the Resource Guide for organizations and books that can validate your experience and support your healing.

† Hearing the stories of other survivors can sometimes be triggering. For some women, attending a group that doesn't have a trained facilitator who can help them process their feelings is not a safe enough situation. But for others, these groups offer valuable support. As with so much of the healing process, what's right for one person is not necessarily best for someone else. You're the best judge of what is helpful to you.

atrist with them. I told them the kinds of things I knew they wanted to hear. I never could talk about my fears or what was really bothering me.

But now I wasn't alone anymore. There were other people who had the same kind of symptoms I did, for the same kinds of reasons. I started to reach out and make friends. It was an incredible relief.

Working in a group is the only helpful therapy I've gotten in my whole life, and I've been in therapy since I was six years old. That's forty-one years. Being in a group is better than being with a therapist because other survivors really understand—they weren't *taught* to understand.

STANDARDS FOR A GOOD GROUP

A good support group should be a safe and respectful space in which each member is valued. Expectations should be clear, participants should share time and focus equitably, and no one should dominate or be excluded. You should feel accepted and able to speak honestly about your experience and your feelings. No one should ever feel that she needs to exaggerate either her abuse or her pain to deserve attention. Because survivors share extremely vulnerable parts of themselves, support groups are not appropriate places for confrontations and criticism. Instead, the focus should be on each woman's individual and unique healing journey.

A MUTUAL JOURNEY

When you entrust a counselor to witness and support your healing, you are allowing that person to see you, to know you, and to touch your life in a profound way. The counselor should consider it an honor and a privilege—and should extend to you the best of his or her skills, experience, and compassion. For your part, you offer the willingness to face your past and to work honestly with your best efforts. The result is a collaboration in which you are able to heal, to grow, and to create a rich and satisfying life. As one survivor expressed it:

A therapist once said to me, "Psychotherapy is looking your destiny in the face and saying 'NO!'" The people who abused me would have left me feeling worthless or going insane. In therapy, I got an outside, objective assessment, the chance to be heard, the chance to connect with supportive people and not be alone with fear or pain, or even joy.

I gained a sense of perspective that wasn't distorted. I found that the things I had been ridiculed for as a child were not indictments of me, but symptoms of abuse. I discovered that I was living in a situation where new rules apply: no one can hit or rape me and force me to suffer such brutality in silence.

But beyond that, I learned about human decency. I found out that the world is not only full of violent people, but that there are many or even more folks like me. For me therapy was a process of coming home, into the native land that had not been mine as a child. Therapy taught me that I felt bad about being an ugly duckling for so long because I was really a swan.

Counseling is not the only context in which such healing can take place. Many survivors do their healing work in other ways—through art, music, writing, outdoor adventures, spirituality, and activism, to name a few. Survivors draw their support from friends, partners, family members, and other survivors. But for many, counseling is at the core of their support system, providing a safe and supportive haven that makes growth and transformation a reality.

PART TWO

The Healing Process

An Overview

" 'Don't give up.' That's the most important thing in the beginning. There are people who have lived through it, and as trite and as stupid and as irrelevant as it sounds to you right now, you will not be in so much pain later. Even not so far in the future. If you made it this far, you've got some pretty good stuff in you. So just trust it. Don't give up on yourself."

Survivors are often troubled by how long and difficult the healing process is. One woman said, "I thought once I told someone what had happened to me, that would be the end of it. I wanted to get well, and of course it was going to happen overnight."

We live in a society of fast food, e-mail, and instant messaging. We are taught to expect results immediately. But deep change takes time.

The healing process is a continuum. It begins with survival, an awareness of the fact that you lived through the abuse and made it to today. Ultimately it leads to a rich and satisfying life, no longer programmed by the past. What happens in between is the subject of this book: the healing process.

There are recognizable stages that all survivors pass through. The next chapters will provide you with a map of those stages, enabling you to see where you are, what you've already accomplished, and what's yet before you.

We've presented the stages in a particular order, but you will probably not experience them that way. Few survivors finish stage 1 and then move on to stage 2. Healing is not linear. Rather, it is an integral part of life.

The healing process is more like a spiral than a straight line. You go through the same stages again and again, but traveling along the spiral, you experience them at a different level, with a different perspective. Each time, you have more inner resources and a wider range of options for how you respond. You might spend a year or two dealing intensely with your abuse. Then you might take a break and focus more on the present. A year or so later, changes in your life—a new relationship, the birth of a child, graduation from school, illness, being fired from a job, menopause, the death of a parent, a revictimization, or simply an inner urge—can stir up more unresolved memories and feelings, and you may focus on your healing again, embarking on a second or a third or a fourth round of discovery. With each new cycle, your capacity to feel, to recognize the impact of abuse on your life, and to make lasting changes grows stronger.

There is no one "right way" to move through the stages of the healing process. Each person's path will be unique, just as each person is unique. For some survivors, certain stages will be more prominent and require more time and attention than for others. The order in which you experience the stages may be different from what's presented here. And the meaning of each stage will be affected by your own life experience.

THE STAGES

Although most of these stages are necessary for everyone, some—the emergency stage, remembering, disclosing abuse to your family, and forgiveness—are not applicable to everyone.

The decision to heal. Once you recognize the effects of sexual abuse in your life, you need to make an active commitment to heal. Deep healing happens only when you choose it and are willing to change.

The emergency stage. Beginning to deal with memories and long-suppressed feelings can throw your life into turmoil. This is a time when emotional pain is intense, the old coping mechanisms are no longer intact, and it may be difficult to function at your usual level. Remember, this stage won't last forever.

Remembering. Many survivors suppress some or all memory of what was done to them as children. Those who do not forget the actual incidents may forget how they felt at the time or may not fully realize how much the experience has affected them. Remembering is the process of getting back both memory *and* feeling, and understanding the impact abuse has had on your life.

Believing it happened. Survivors often doubt their own perceptions. Accepting that the abuse really happened, and that it really hurt you, is a vital part of the healing process.

Breaking silence. Most survivors kept the abuse a secret in childhood. Telling a safe person about your history is a powerful healing force that can dispel the shame that often accompanies victimization.

Understanding that it wasn't your fault. Children usually believe that the abuse is their fault. Adult survivors must learn to place the blame where it belongs—directly on the shoulders of the abusers.

The child within. Many survivors have lost touch with their own innocence and vulnerability. Yet within each of us is a child—or several children of different ages—who were deeply hurt and need healing. Getting in touch with the child you once were can help you develop compassion for yourself.

Grieving. Most survivors haven't acknowledged or grieved for all of their losses. Grieving is a way to honor your pain, let go, and move more fully into your current life.

Anger. Anger is a powerful and liberating force that provides the energy needed to move through grief, pain, and despair. Directing your anger squarely at your abuser and at those who didn't protect you is pivotal to healing.

Disclosures and truth-telling. Talking about your abuse and its effects with the abuser or with family members can be empowering and transformative, but it is not right for everyone. Before taking this step, it is essential that you prepare carefully and wait until you have a strong foundation of healing and support.

Forgiveness? Forgiveness of the abuser is *not* an essential part of the healing process. The only essential forgiveness is for yourself.

Spirituality. Having the support of a spiritual connection can be a real asset in the healing process. Spirituality is a uniquely personal experience. You might find it through traditional religion, meditation, nature, working a 12-step program, or your support group.

Resolution and moving on. As you move through these stages again and again, you will achieve more and more integration. Your feelings and perspectives will start to stabilize. While you won't erase your history, it will truly become history, something that occurred in your past. You will make deep and lasting changes in your life. Having gained awareness, compassion, and power through healing, you will have the opportunity to work toward a better world.

The Decision to Heal

"If you enter into healing, be prepared to lose everything. Healing is a ravaging force to which nothing seems sacred or inviolate. As my original pain releases itself in healing, it rips to shreds the structures and foundations I built in weakness and ignorance. I am experiencing the bizarre miracle of reincarnating, more lucidly than at birth, in the same lifetime."

—ELY FULLER

The decision to heal from child sexual abuse is a powerful, life-affirming choice. It is a commitment that every survivor deserves to make. Although you may have already experienced some healing in your life—through the nurturing of close friends, the caring of an intimate partner, or the satisfaction of work you love—*deciding* to heal, making your own growth and recovery a priority, sets in motion a healing force that will bring to your life a richness and depth that you never dreamed possible:

For the first time I'm appreciating things like the birds and the flowers, the way the sun feels on my skin—you know, really simple things. I can read a good book. I can sit in the sun. I don't ever remember enjoying these things, even as a little kid. I've woken up. If this hadn't happened, I'd still be asleep. So for the first time, I feel alive. And you know, that's something to go for.

I am here now. I don't have my thoughts and feelings planned off into the future, or wasting away because of some memories. I am here right now. I am experiencing every bit of my life and I'm not wasting any of it.

This has given me the opportunity to look at me. I am emotionally more open. I've learned so much. It's not all bad. You do heal. And you do become stronger. I don't know what it would take to flatten me, but it would have to be something really big. I am, in fact, a survivor.

The commitment to heal arises from different life circumstances for every survivor. A young girl is mandated by the court to go to therapy after she turns her stepfather in for molesting her. A twenty-five-year-old woman gets married and suddenly finds that she can't maintain the intimacy she felt before her wedding. A mother starts to feel crazy when her daughter reaches the age she was when her own mother began abusing her. An older woman decides to heal at the funeral of her abuser.

Some women describe "bursting apart at the seams" or "hitting bottom" before they decide to heal. One woman didn't get help until she was hospitalized for anorexia: "I actively avoided getting a therapist for years. I didn't start dealing with it until I couldn't *not* deal with it."

Healing isn't always a matter of choice:

It was a compulsion. I think everybody has a compulsion to grow and to be whole. I think everybody has a compulsion to seek relief from pain.

A single interaction may be the impetus to embark on this journey. One survivor decided to heal because a friend told her, "I don't trust you. I never feel you're telling me the truth. I can't trust you with my feelings because I don't know what you're doing with them." The survivor was shocked—first, because it was true, and second, because she thought she'd done

a good job of faking it. "I felt she'd crawled inside my head and seen what was really there. She put words to what I'd been feeling all my life. So I went to therapy."

Another woman decided to heal when her younger sister killed herself. "She didn't make it. I had to understand what had happened to her and give myself the tools to make sure it couldn't happen to me."

One young survivor said she was motivated to heal because of a class assignment:

I was twenty years old. I was in a psych class doing a research project on the aftereffects of incest on survivors. Now, most people just wouldn't choose that kind of subject! But the stuff was pushing up from the inside. I wanted to annihilate my grandfather. I just wanted to castrate him by the time I finished this paper. I thought writing the paper would heal me from it, but my feelings were just erupting all over the place. By the time I presented the paper, I fell apart. I'd been contemplating therapy for a while, and a few days later I found a therapist.

A survivor who'd been a Carmelite nun described her decision to heal as a need to clarify her reasons for living in the convent. "I loved the convent, but somehow I distrusted my choice to be there. Until I worked out the sexual abuse, I felt I would never know if I was really choosing this life out of health, and out of all the good things that religious life should be chosen from. I wanted to believe that whatever I chose to do, I was doing it for all the right reasons."

to my friend, jerina
BY LUCILLE CLIFTON

listen,
when I found there was no safety
in my father's house
I knew there was none anywhere.
you are right about this,
how I nurtured my work
not my self, how I left the girl
wallowing in her own shame
and took on the flesh of my mother.
but listen,
the girl is rising in me,
not willing to be left to
the silent fingers in the dark,
and you are right,
she is asking for more than
most men are able to give,
but she means to have what she
has earned,
sweet sighs, safe houses,
hands she can trust.

Lucille Clifton, *Quilting: Poems 1987–1990*
(Rochester, NY: BOA Editions, 1991).

Many survivors have been motivated to heal by the courage of other survivors. Every time a survivor reveals her history to a friend, stands up in front of a group to tell her story, writes a book, or brings a lawsuit against abusers (or the institutions that allow abuse to occur), she inspires other survivors to break the silence. Many a woman has decided to heal after reading an article in the newspaper, watching a TV program, or hearing another survivor tell the truth about her life.

EVERYONE DESERVES TO HEAL

Everyone deserves to heal, and healing is possible for everyone. Yet many survivors believe that they are the exception. You may sincerely believe that others can heal but don't think it's possible for you. Or you may think that you don't deserve it.

There are many reasons for this. You may still be blaming yourself for the abuse. You may have felt discouraged for so long that you don't dare hope for anything good in life. Or you believe that you can't afford to take time for yourself that might interfere with family or other responsibilities.

There are additional circumstances that sometimes make it difficult to name your abuse and start healing. Age, race, and religious background all influence the decision to heal. Lack of money, physical, emotional and mental disabilities, and geographic isolation can all present daunting challenges. But everyone deserves to heal.*

---

* The "Courageous Women" section of this book is full of stories of women who overcame a wide variety of obstacles to commit to their healing. See p. 407.

It's Never Too Late: Barbara Hamilton's Story

Barbara Hamilton is sixty-five years old. Molested by her father in childhood, Barbara grew up, married, raised six children, and now has grandchildren and great-grandchildren of her own. Unknown to Barbara until a few years ago, when she started talking about her own molestation, some of her children and grandchildren were also molested, either by her father or other perpetrators. She talks about the difficulties older women have in making the commitment to heal.*

When you get older, especially as a woman, you deal with rejection on all sides. Society devalues you, and you fall right into that as a victim. Being a survivor ties right into that sense of isolation. It went underground for all those years I was raising my family, but as I got more and more alone, and as the insecurity in my life increased *because* I was an older woman, it all came back up. I had to realize that it hadn't been resolved. All I'd done is acknowledge that it happened. It hadn't really been touched. And I had fifty years of pushing it away.

Don't wait. Don't wait, because it won't go away. It always comes back, and it gets harder. But older woman deserve to heal, too. There must be thousands like me who are living under it just like I was. And though the focus of all the books is toward younger women, I don't think you're ever too old. You may be infirm. It may be too hard that way. You won't have the same experiences as a young person. As an older woman, you probably won't ever be able to confront your abuser. But it's worth it. I feel so much better about myself.

In spite of the horror, in spite of the tragedy, in spite of the weeks of sleepless nights, I'm finally alive. I'm not pretending. I feel real. I'm not playing charades anymore. I wouldn't go back to the way I was for anything. I'm really like a different person. I'm where I am, and I'm making the most of it. I *know* I'm courageous now. I found out I had it in me to face this. It's just not ever too late. Look what Grandma Moses did at ninety-five. There's still hope.

It's like going from black-and-white to color, and you never even knew you were in black-and-white. We all thought black-and-white was great all those years that all we had was black-and-white. Do you remember the first time you saw Technicolor? The first time you wore those 3-D glasses? Eventually you get to where life is Technicolor, and it's worth it.

If you say, "Why should I bother? I've coped this far," I'd say to you, "You *haven't* coped. You haven't even lived a fraction of yourself. You may be smothering an artist. You may be smothering all kinds of self-expression that needs to come out for your sake, and for others'. Why not give it a chance?"

---

* Barbara Hamilton has published her story in a compelling book, *The Hidden Legacy: Uncovering, Confronting, and Healing Three Generations of Incest.* See p. 532 of the Resource Guide. You can also read more of her story in "If Your Child Is Being Abused" on p. 345.

IT'S NOT EASY

While it is always worthwhile, healing is never easy. As Toni Morrison writes in her brilliant novel, *Beloved*: "Anything dead coming back to life hurts."

Choosing to work on abuse-related issues can raise questions you never planned to ask and give answers you didn't expect. Once you commit yourself to healing, your life will never be the same:

My therapist was not the kind of person who would lie to me. He would say, "I can't give you any guarantees. I don't know if you're going to feel better after you talk about this. You could feel a lot worse." And it was hard to make that leap, to decide that it didn't matter which way it went, that the leap itself was the important thing.

I was giving up a person who was really a very viable, powerful, self-reliant human being. There were a lot of positive things about those negative aspects of my personality. And I didn't want to give them up. Maybe it wasn't the best way of coping, but at least I was used to it. I felt incredibly vulnerable having to let go in order to make the room to create a new person. Into what void would I be thrown if I let go of this stuff? I felt like a raw muscle walking around for a long time.

You may wonder if it's worth it to take the risk. But as one survivor simply put it, "Taking that risk was the most promising choice I had."

Often the decision to heal wreaks havoc with friendships, marriages, and family relationships. It can be hard to function, to go to work, to study, to think, to smile. It can even be hard to sleep, to eat, or simply to stop crying:

If I'd known that anything could hurt this much or could be this sad, I never would have decided to heal. And at the same time you can't go back. You can't unremember. I spent so many years not hurting at all. It's like I don't have the coping mechanisms for hurting. I have the coping mechanisms for *not* hurting. And that's been real hard.

Sometimes the early stages of healing are so filled with crisis that women have a hard time accepting the fact that they made a choice at all. When Laura remembered her abuse and made her first call to a therapist, she made the decision to heal. But it didn't feel that way to her:

For a long time, I felt like a victim of the process. This was something I'd chosen? No way! Remembering the incest was something that had happened *to* me. The memories were like one of those plastic raincoats that come in a two-inch package. Once I opened them up, I could never fold them neatly back inside.

There are certain major decisions we make not really knowing where they will lead. As the French author André Gide said, "One does not discover new lands without consenting to lose sight of the shore for a very long time." Healing from sexual abuse is one of those instances when we have to let go of the shore:

> Though sometimes I want to crawl into a dark place and hide from reality, and other times I want to give up completely, I go on. I don't know where this "healing" will lead me. I live on other people's hopes. I live on other people's faith that life will get better. I continue to wonder whether it is worth it, but I go on. This, then, is healing.

Deciding to heal means opening up not only to past hurt but also to hope. For many survivors, hope has brought only disappointment.

Although it is terrifying to say yes to yourself, it is also a tremendous relief when you finally stop and confront your own demons. There is something about facing the thing you most fear that is strangely relieving. There is comfort in knowing that you don't have to pretend anymore, that you are going to do everything within your power to heal. As one survivor put it, "I know now that every time I accept my past and respect where I am in the present, I am giving myself a future."

The Thing Is
BY ELLEN BASS

The thing is
to love life, to love it even
when you have no stomach for it
and everything you've held dear
crumbles like burnt paper in your
    hands,
your throat filled with the silt of it.
When grief sits with you, its tropical
    heat
thickening the air, heavy as water
more fit for gills than lungs;
when grief weights you like your own
    flesh
only more of it, an obesity of grief,
you think, How can a body withstand
    this?
Then you hold life like a face
between your palms, a plain face,
no charming smile, no violet eyes,
and you say, yes, I will take you
I will love you, again.

Ellen Bass, *Mules of Love* (Rochester, NY: BOA Editions, 2002).

The Emergency Stage

"Remembering the rape triggered the worst period of the whole healing process. I felt like I was going to die. I couldn't take a breath without thinking about incest. In fact, it was a struggle to breathe a lot of the time. I had a few days where I just sat on the kitchen floor, rocking and holding myself. It felt like my body was inhabited by this thing that had happened in my childhood, that there wasn't a cell in my body that wasn't involved in it. The memories felt like they were invading me, the same way my uncle had invaded my body."

Many women go through a period when sexual abuse is literally all they can think about. You may find yourself talking about it obsessively with anyone who will listen, having uncontrollable flashbacks, crying all day long, or unable to go to work. Your life may be full of overwhelming crises. You may dream about your abuser or be afraid to sleep:

I just lost it completely. I wasn't eating. I wasn't sleeping. I did hold down a job at Winchell's Donuts. But I was afraid to stay in the house alone. I would go out in the middle of the night and hide somewhere, behind a Dumpster or something. I had terrible nightmares about my father. I was having all kinds of fantasies.

I'd hear the sound of my father's zipper coming down, the click of the buckle. Then I'd imagined all this blood. Physically, I was a mess. I had crabs. I hadn't bathed in a month. I was afraid of the shower.

When Laura had her first memories, the shock alone was enough to fixate her on incest for several years:

I hadn't had many real memories of my childhood, it was true, but I had created a picture I could brag about, of those early golden years. It's not that all those good things I remembered hadn't happened. It's just that I had somehow forgotten the fact that I had been sexually abused, too.

Breaking through my own denial, and trying to fit the new reality into the shattered framework of the old, was enough to catapult me into total crisis. I felt as if my whole foundation had been stolen from me. If this could have happened, then every assumption I had about life and my place in it was thrown up for question.

Women often describe the early stages of their healing as a variety of natural disasters: "It was like being lifted up in a twister." "It was like being caught in an avalanche." "It was a volcano erupting."

I felt like I was standing in a room, looking at the floor. I was shattered all over it, and I had to go through and pick up the pieces and put them back together. Look at each one and say, "This is me," put it on, and say, "This is where it goes." Or, "Nope, wrong place." Then I'd have to find the place where it really fit. I was picking up pieces of my life and looking at them, saying, "Do I want to keep this? Is it of any use to me anymore? When will the pain stop?"

The emergency stage is not something you choose, yet it must be ridden through to the other side. It cannot be ignored or pushed away through a force of will. As one survivor aptly remarked, "It's like learning a new word. Within days, you start seeing it in everything you read, and you never saw it before in your life."

The Emergency Stage: Catherine's Story

*In an Al-Anon group, Catherine first faced the fact that she had been sexually abused. It was at that point that the emergency stage kicked in with full force.**

I started feeling this uncontrollable sadness. The despair really had a chance to surface. It was like there were large six-foot-high letters in my living room every day when I woke up: *INCEST!* It was just so much in the forefront of my mind that I felt that everyone knew I was an incest victim. I thought I looked like one. I was sure everybody would know the real reason why I was such a creep. I was in constant fear of telling anyone that's what I was in therapy for, because I was so ashamed.

I had no energy to deal with other people or their problems. My reserves had been drained dry. I withdrew from my social time with acquaintances. I started to rely more on the people I felt were really true friends. I told them about my therapy and what I was discovering. The people I used to call up and say, "Hi. Let's go roller skating," I didn't bother to call anymore.

I had to find people who would sit with me no matter what I felt like. I had one friend who'd been beaten when she was a kid. I could call her up when I felt horrible, and she'd let me come over to just eat and watch TV. It

---

* For more of Catherine's story, see "Truth-Telling: Catherine's Story" on p. 161 and "Take a Break and Lighten Up" on p. 310.

was okay to go over there and feel shitty. She understood. She knew what was going on, but we only discussed it if I brought it up.

I also had to find a safe place to be alone. I went for walks in the woods. I ran a lot. I'd go for twenty- or thirty-mile bike rides. I spent a lot of time outdoors by myself. It felt a lot safer than being at home.

It was the most awkward feeling, to have to try out everything I'd been familiar with. I had to prove to myself that I could go to the store or drive my car, *and* be an incest victim, all at the same time. I had to spend time in my own house thinking, 'Now I know I'm an incest victim, and yes, I still live here, and yes, my cats still like me.' Outside, it all looked the same, but inside, it was just scrambled. I felt like I was in a vacuum for a whole year, and all that was in front of me were flashbacks and crying.

The only thing that saved me when I felt totally cut off from everything was that I had my therapist's phone number written many places, all over my house. I had it up on the mirror in the bathroom. I had it in my journal. I had it in books that I was reading. I'd stuff it in there on little pieces of paper. I just burned it in my memory, so at any time I could stop and call her. And many times, just making the call and getting her answering machine, and being able to leave a message in my real voice, in my cracking, crying voice, that I needed her to call me, let me know that I could reach out. It reminded me that there was actually something other than my pain and depression. There was actually somebody up on the ledge and I could reach out to her. I knew she would call me eventually, and I could hold out till then.

After about a year, something shifted for me. I was able to lift my head up a little bit and notice that the season had changed. I started to realize that even though I was an incest survivor, I could go on with my life. I could stop myself from thinking about it at times. It was a tremendous relief.

SURVIVING THE EMERGENCY STAGE

If the start of your healing feels turbulent and overwhelming, the important thing to remember is that the emergency stage is a natural part of the healing process, and it will get better. The nature of crisis is that it consumes you; while you are in it, it may be all you can see. But there will be a time when you will not think, eat, and dream sexual abuse twenty-four hours a day:

Sometimes when you look at your healing and the shit you went through, it's just so big. The pain can be enormous. You have to just put one foot in front of the other. Don't look at how big it is. Just put one foot in front of the other. And then when you look up, you're someplace else.

If you are in the emergency stage, that time will not come a moment too soon.

EASING THE INTENSITY OF THE EMERGENCY STAGE

Although entering into the process of healing from child sexual abuse means facing painful realities, there are ways to ease the impact of this challenging time. It's both helpful and wise to do all you can to take good care of yourself.

The work of healing should not be retraumatizing. If you find that the intensity of your feelings is unmanageable, try to pace the process. Full speed ahead is not always the most effective way to proceed. Although this isn't always in your control, sometimes you can back off from going deeper into your past and focus instead on self-care to build a stronger foundation. (See "Survival Skills for Healing" on p. 29.)

As poet Deena Metzger wrote, "We are in danger. There is time only to work slowly. There is no time not to love." One of the ways we can practice self-love is to be as kind to ourselves as possible as we heal, to listen to our needs and learn to take care of ourselves even in the hardest times.

SELF-CARE STRATEGIES FOR THE EMERGENCY STAGE

When things are particularly rough, here are some things that can help:

- **Know that you're not going crazy.** What you're going through is a recognized part of the healing process.

- **Find people you can talk to.** Don't try to bear it alone. (See "Breaking Silence" on p. 102 and "Developing a Support System" on p. 30.)

- **Get support from other survivors.** It's unlikely that anyone other than another survivor can listen as much as you'll need to talk.

- **Seek out skilled professional support.** (If you don't know where to look, see "Working with a Counselor" p. 45.)

- **Create a safe place in your home.** You need at least one place where you feel safe. (For suggestions, see "Create a Safe Place," p. 38.)

- **Accept where you are right now.** Don't make things worse by criticizing yourself for not being farther along on the journey.

- **Sit tight and ride out the storm.** Your decision-making capability is limited right now. The emergency stage is usually not a good time for making major life changes.

- **Get out of abusive situations.** If you're currently in an abusive relationship, take steps to get out of it (see "Recognizing Bad Relationships," p. 286).

- **Drop what isn't essential in your life.** Release the pressure any way you can. This isn't the time to take on difficult challenges, extra work, or more responsibilities. But if there are pleasurable activities that you enjoy and that nourish you, keep them up.

- **Watch your intake of drugs and alcohol.** Repeatedly numbing your feelings will only prolong the crisis.

- **Look for financial and material aid if you need it.** There may be government assistance you're eligible for, counseling offered through community groups, or just help from your friends (meals, a spare room, an old car or bike that isn't being used). Don't be ashamed if you need some extra help right now.
- **Don't hurt or try to kill yourself.** You deserve to live. If you start feeling suicidal or self-destructive, reach out. (And read "Don't Kill Yourself," p. 36.)
- **Remind yourself that you're brave.** This is a challenging, scary, difficult period. You don't have to do anything but live through it.
- **Remember to breathe.** Stay as connected to your body as you can. (See "Learning to Live in Your Body" on p. 247 for a variety of exercises to help you reconnect with your body.)
- **Spirituality can give you inspiration and strength.** Stay connected to spiritual beliefs that bring you comfort. (See "Spirituality" on p. 177 for more information.)
- **Consult with a doctor about medication, if necessary.** If you're doing everything you can to help yourself and you're still severely anxious, depressed, or unable to sleep, talk to a professional about the advisability of medication to help you through this crisis. (See "What About Medication?" on p. 41.)
- **This too shall pass.** Your experience tomorrow or next week or next year will not be the same as it is right now. (Pay special attention to "Why It's Been Worth It," p. 202.)

HEALING CRISES OVER TIME

Although you won't experience the same consistent intensity once the emergency stage is over, you may encounter other crisis periods in the course of your healing. Though these times can be very painful, we like to call them healing crises because they offer an opportunity for deep growth.

Some women have experienced so much trauma that they go through a prolonged emergency stage with only short breaks in intensity. Even though they are doing everything they can to heal, they still feel suicidal, self-destructive, or obsessed with abuse much of the time. If this is the case for you, it's important to make sure you have adequate support, including a capable counselor. You may also want to read "Trauma and the Brain" on p. 242 and "What About Medication?" on p. 41 to gain more insight into your situation. And remember, even the worst times won't last forever.

WHAT GAVE ME HOPE

"I had this vision one day of me at the end of the tunnel, and I could look out and I could see the blue sky. I was standing on this very thin ledge, not holding on to anything, just balancing there, and I had my arms spread out and I was going to fly."

"I was a nun in a contemplative order. Because I had lived that lifestyle, I knew that things took a long time. I was geared to an interior life. I knew that the process of becoming holy, of knowing God, was very slow. Day by day, I just knew I was growing closer to God. And I felt the same thing applied to dealing with the incest. I just trusted that something was happening, that there was a hidden growth going on."

"When I'm sure I'm about to be locked up as a crazy woman, the thing that gives me hope is remembering what my therapist kept saying to me, over and over: 'This is part of the change process.' I held on to that when there was really nothing else to hold on to: 'Oh, this is a recognized part of the change process.'"

"My friend Patricia gave me hope. She would basically talk me into wanting to live. She would tell me all the wonderful things there were about life in general, and I would believe her, because I loved her and I cared about her, and I knew she cared about me."

"My sister inspires me through her struggle. She had it a lot worse than I did. She went through absolute Nazi horror, and she is struggling to live. It's an amazing thing to see what people can live through, and still want to live."

"Reading gave me a lot of inspiration. I fell in love with the beauty of the human spirit through reading literature."

"Knowing another survivor who's been in a successful relationship for seven years gave me a lot of hope."

"My own inner strength gave me hope. I just won't quit. Period."

"Music. Spirituals have really helped me."

Remembering

"I've looked the memories in the face and smelled their breath. They can't hurt me anymore."

The experience of remembering abuse varies greatly from survivor to survivor. Many women have always remembered their abuse. They may have minimized its importance, denied its impact on their lives, or been numb to their feelings, but they have never forgotten the events themselves. One woman explained, "I could rattle off the facts of my abuse like a grocery list, but remembering the fear and terror and pain was another matter entirely."

Some women have blocked out entire segments of their childhood. For instance, they may not remember anything at all—or only the slightest fragments—before the age of seven. Other survivors have selective or partial memory. They remember some occurrences but not others:

I always knew that we had an incestuous relationship. I remember the first time I heard the word "incest," when I was seventeen. I hadn't known there was a word for it. I always remembered my father grabbing my breasts and kissing me.

I told my therapist, "I remember every miserable thing that happened to me." It seemed like I remembered so much, how could there be more? I didn't remember anything *but* abuse. But I didn't remember being raped, even though I knew I had been. I categorically told my therapist, "I don't want to remember being raped." We talked about the fact that I didn't want to remember that for months. Yet I knew my father had been my first lover.

Survivors sometimes remember physical or emotional abuse but not sexual abuse. Or they can recall the context in which the abuse took place but not the specific physical events. Others remember part of what happened—such as sitting in a bedroom crying, with the dresser pushed up against the door—but don't remember what happened to make them cry or why they barricaded themselves in. There are also survivors who don't remember anything about their abuse until the memories come crashing in:

I had clues all along, but I chose to ignore them. I concentrated on my goals, achievements, things I could make, do, produce. I didn't think about how I felt. How I felt was like a sewer—somewhere you wouldn't want to go. Then I got pregnant. It was an accident. I didn't love the man. I'd never loved anyone—I couldn't afford to. I thought about an abortion. It was the sensible thing. But I just couldn't.

I loved my baby so intensely, even before she was born, that I couldn't stop myself from feeling. The love was too strong to block out. And along with the love came the other feelings. All the feelings I'd kept buried—and the memories.

Remembering is a unique experience for every survivor. Although some survivors remember almost all of the abuse they experienced and others remember almost nothing, most fall somewhere in between. Whether you recall your abuse vividly or are just beginning to sense that something awful may have happened to you, you are engaged in a process of exploration and discovery that will ultimately help you know and understand more of your history.*

WHAT REMEMBERING IS LIKE

Remembering is different for every survivor. You may have numerous memories. Or you may have just one. You might have new images every day for weeks. Or you may experience your memories in clumps—several in a matter of days, then none for months. Sometimes survivors remember one abuser or a specific kind of abuse, only to remember, years later, another abuser or a different form of abuse.†

Remembering sexual abuse or any traumatic event is not like remembering ordinary, nonthreatening experiences. When traumatic memories return, they sometimes seem distant, like something you're observing from far away:

---

* Psychologist Christine Courtois commented on the difference between survivors who have always remembered and those who have forgotten part of their experience: "Those with access to memory usually wish to forget, repress, or minimize what they know. Those with absent, hazy, or fragmented memory are usually desperate to remember, until memory returns. Then they move to the position of survivors with memory: they want to forget." From "The Memory Retrieval Process in Incest Survivor Therapy," *Journal of Child Sexual Abuse* 1, no. 1 (1992): pp. 15–16.

† For an example of this, see Sheila O'Connell's story on p. 510.

The actual rape memories for me are like from the end of a tunnel. That's because I literally left my body at the scene. So I remember it from that perspective—there's some physical distance between me and what's going on. Those memories aren't as sharp in focus. It's like they happened in another dimension.

One woman said that her memories felt like a picture that gradually filled in:

When I had my first flashback, I remembered the sensation of being molested and I got a very clear image of the room. In fact, as the memory came back, I got more and more details of things in the room—there was a window here, and a dresser there, and always a person-size hole in the picture where my uncle should have been. He wasn't in the picture. I kind of started with the margins of the memory and then worked my way in.

Other times, memories come in bits and pieces.

I'd be driving home from my therapist's office, and I'd start having flashes of things—just segments, like bloody sheets, or taking a bath, or throwing away my nightgown. For a long time, I remembered all the things around being raped, but not the rape itself.

If memories come to you in fragments, you may find it hard to place them in chronological order. You may not know exactly when the abuse began, how old you were, or when it stopped. The process of understanding the fragments can be like putting together a jigsaw puzzle or being a detective.

Part of me felt like I was on the trail of a murder mystery, and I was going to solve it. I really enjoyed following all the clues. "Okay, I was looking at the clock. It was mid-afternoon. Why was it mid-afternoon? Where could my mother have been? Oh, I bet she was at . . ." Tracing down the clues to find out exactly what had happened was actually fun.

Ella is a survivor who remembered piecemeal. To make sense of her memories, she began to examine some of her own strange habits. She started to analyze certain compulsive behaviors, such as staring at the light fixture whenever she was having sex:

I'd be making love and would think, "Why would somebody lie here, when they're supposed to be having a pleasurable experience, and concentrate on a light fixture?" I remember every single lighting fixture in every single house we ever lived in! Why have I always been so obsessed with light under doors, and the interruption of light? That's a crazy thing for an adult woman to be obsessive about—that someone walks past and cracks the light. What's that about?

Ella realized that she was watching to see if her father's footsteps stopped outside her door at night. If they did, that meant he'd come in and molest her. Once Ella started to pay attention to these kinds of details, her memories began to fall into place.

Even though everything you remember may not be a literal representation of what happened, there is always an essential emotional truth to memory that can help us understand our experience. (For more information, see "The Essential Truth of Memory," p. 85.)

FLASHBACKS

Memories that were split off at the time of the abuse sometimes break through later in intrusive, overwhelming images, fragments, or feelings. Even though we may not be able to understand or tell the story of our abuse, we may be bombarded by feelings, body sensations, and visual images of terrifying scenes.

These intrusive memories, or flashbacks, can be so vivid that you feel as though the original experience is happening again *now*, rather than just being remembered. Flashbacks may be accompanied by the feelings you experienced at the time, or they may be stark and detached, like watching a movie about somebody else's life.

Frequently flashbacks are visual: "I saw this penis coming toward me," or "I couldn't see my mother's face, just the yellow nightgown she always wore." These memories can be very dramatic:

My husband was just beginning to initiate some lovemaking. I had a flash in my mind. The closest way I can describe it is that it was much like viewing slides in a slide show, when the slide goes by too fast, but slow enough to give you some part of the image. It was someone jamming his fingers up my vagina. It was very vivid, and enough of the feelings came sneaking in that I knew it wasn't a fantasy. There was an element of it that made me stop and take notice. I lay there and let it replay a couple of times.

I felt confused. I was aware that it was something that had happened to me. I even had a recollection of the pain. I scrambled around in my mind for an explanation. "Was that a rough lover I had?" Immediately I knew that wasn't the case. So I went back into the flash again. Each time I went back, I tried to open it up to see a little more. I didn't see his face, but I could sense an essence of my father.

But not everyone has visual recall. One woman was upset that she couldn't get any images. Her father had held her at knifepoint in the car, face down in the dark, and raped her. She had never *seen* anything. But she had *heard* him. And when she began to write the scene in Spanish, her native language, it all came back to her—his threats, his brutality, his violation.

Flashbacks can involve any of the senses. What you heard, saw, smelled, tasted, felt, or thought can return with such immediacy that you feel as if you are actually reliving the original experience.

WHAT WE KNOW ABOUT MEMORY AND TRAUMATIC AMNESIA

The fact that people can experience amnesia for traumatic events is beyond dispute.* It has been documented not only in cases of child sexual abuse but also among war veterans, battered women, prisoners of war, and others who have suffered severe ongoing trauma.†

To comprehend how someone can "not remember" traumatic events, it's useful to understand the process of dissociation. In situations of overwhelming pain, terror, and violence, when our minds cannot bear what we are forced to endure, we separate ourselves—or a part of ourselves—from the experience. We dissociate. Our consciousness splits, separating from what was unbearable. Survivors of child sexual abuse frequently report that they watched themselves being raped: "I left my body and looked down at myself from the corner of the ceiling."

Under these conditions, our brains do not function as they do under conventional circumstances. In fact, the entire physiology of the brain works differently.‡

When our minds are overstimulated like

---

* Judith Herman, *Trauma and Recovery,* 2nd ed. (New York: Basic Books, 1997); Daniel Brown, Alan W. Scheflin, & D. Corydon Hammond, *Memory, Trauma, Treatment and the Law* (New York: Norton, 1998); Bessel A. van der Kolk, *Psychological Trauma* (Washington, D.C.: American Psychiatric Press, 1987); James A. Chu, *Rebuilding Shattered Lives: The Responsible Treatment of Complex Post-Traumatic and Dissociative Disorders* (New York: Wiley, 1998); Jennifer J. Freyd and Anne P. DePrince, eds. *Trauma and Cognitive Science: A Meeting of Minds, Science, and Human Experience* (New York: Haworth, 2001); Christine Courtois, *Recollections of Sexual Abuse: Treatment Principles and Guidelines* (New York: Norton, 1999). The Resource Guide includes several other titles and Web resources on p. 546.

† Psychotherapist David Calof, who has worked with more than four hundred abuse survivors, explains: "What stood out in many of these cases . . . were symptoms common to other trauma victims, including survivors of such public horrors as the bombing of Dresden, the camps at Auschwitz, the massacred villages of Vietnam, Guatemala and Bosnia, the killing fields of Cambodia and the torture chambers of Brazil. Like survivors of these public traumas, my clients had dissociative symptoms, such as sleepwalking and memory disturbances, as well as signs of post-traumatic stress, such as flashbacks, sleep disturbances and nightmares. They wanted to be anonymous, or were socially withdrawn. They were depressed or had other mood disturbances. They often tended to minimize or rationalize painful

present realities, and they suffered from feelings of numbness, emptiness and unreality.

"Unlike the survivors of publicly acknowledged disasters, however, they did not know *why* they felt that way. Their memories of the traumas were often fragmented into bewildering mosaics or missing altogether. Often, they were veterans of intensely private wars that had taken place in barns, attics and suburban houses with the blinds drawn. Their wounds were never reported in newspapers or discussed with family members. There were rarely any witnesses other than the people who hurt them. . . . Their childhood rapes and beatings were encoded into memory in fragments, in a state of terror, when their hearts and minds were flooded with adrenaline. They didn't remember them the way one remembers a walk in the park, and they doubted the fragments they did recall." From "Facing the Truth About False Memory," *The Family Therapy Networker* 17, no. 5 (September/October 1993): pp. 40–41.

‡ See "Trauma and the Brain" on p. 242 for more.

this, we can become physiologically incapable of absorbing and storing information in a normal way. Instead, we may dissociate these experiences, splitting them off from conscious knowledge. Later fragments may return in the form of visual images, physical sensations, and intrusive feelings or thoughts.*

This is why survivors of child sexual abuse who dissociated at the time when they were abused may perceive and remember their experience only in bits and pieces—feelings, body sensations, sounds, smells, visual images—not in a coherent, chronological story that can easily be told.

TRAUMATIC AMNESIA AND SEXUAL ABUSE

Although survivors of publicly acknowledged disasters such as earthquakes, shipwrecks, war, or concentration camps sometimes have amnesia for some of the most painful aspects of their experience, they almost never forget that the entire event took place. For example, people who have been traumatized in a war know there was a war, even though they may not remember certain unbearable experiences during that war. Why then, might a survivor

of child sexual abuse have no memory of the abuse or only a fragmented memory?†

To begin with, earthquakes, wars, shipwrecks, and even concentration camps have names. When the room starts shaking, the walls buckle, and objects fall, we know what to call it. Even children too young to recognize the event as an earthquake have it named for them. An older person explains, "This is an earthquake. There may be aftershocks, little earthquakes, that follow." But after rape or sexual violation, it is unusual for the event to be explained accurately or named for the child: "You've just been sexually abused; the perpetrator had no right to do this to you; it's important that you get help." Thus, many children who are sexually abused do not have words for their experience.

Publicly acknowledged events are more likely to be remembered than events that are never discussed or that are denied or ignored. Yet even sexual abuse that has public confirmation is more likely to be forgotten than an earthquake because of other factors, such as shame. There is no shame or stigma associated with an earthquake. An earthquake is impersonal. If a person remembers being in an earthquake, it will not affect her sense of self-worth or self-esteem. She will not be blamed for the earthquake or told that she asked for it. Earthquake victims are not threatened with violent

---

* In dissociation, it is not only memory that can be affected. Any component of the self can be separated out. We can split off from bodily sensations, from the knowledge of what is taking place, from the meaning of the event, our feelings, or any other aspect that is normally integrated into our experience.

† In her book *Betrayal Trauma: The Logic of Forgetting Childhood Abuse* (Cambridge: Harvard University Press, 1996), Jennifer Freyd explores the issues of memory and amnesia when children are sexually abused by a trusted adult. See p. 547 of the Resource Guide.

consequences if they talk about what happened, as some abused children are. Also, survivors of child sexual abuse were, by definition, children when the abuse took place—often without any trusted adults to turn to even for sympathy. Except in families where siblings stuck together, these children frequently were isolated in their trauma—unlike soldiers in a war, who had a group to belong to and to bond with, and unlike concentration camp prisoners, who had at least some awareness of who was on their side and who was the enemy. For many abused children, the person who was supposed to be on their side *was* the enemy.

Traumatic amnesia enables the child to survive this terrible reality and makes it possible for her to continue to live with—and even love—the abuser, something essential to her continued survival.

We know that even survivors of recognized events such as wars or disasters can have amnesia for particularly painful aspects of their experience. When we consider the plight of an isolated child, unable to name her suffering, even to herself, unable to speak of it or to comprehend it—with no means of escape except in her mind—we can see why this process of burying the abuse might have been necessary to survive.

SENSE MEMORY

Often it is a particular touch, smell, or sound that triggers a memory. You might remember when you return to the town, the house, or the room where the abuse took place. Or when you smell a certain aftershave the abuser wore.

Thirty-five-year-old Ella says, "It's all real tactile, sensory things that have brought memories back. Textures. Sounds. The smell of my father's house. The smell of vodka on somebody."

Ella had a magic purple quilt when she was a little girl. Her grandmother made it for her. It was supposed to keep her safe—nothing bad could happen to her as long as she was under it. The quilt had been lost for many years, but when Ella finally got it back, at twenty-one, it triggered a whole series of memories.

THE BODY REMEMBERS

Psychiatrist Alice Miller writes, "The truth about our childhood is stored up in our body, and although we can repress it, we can never alter it. Our intellect can be deceived, our feelings manipulated, our perceptions confused, and our body tricked with medication. But someday the body will present its bill, for it is as incorruptible as a child who, still whole in spirit, will accept no compromises or excuses, and it will not stop tormenting us until we stop evading the truth."[*]

Memories are stored in our bodies—in sensations, feelings, and physical responses.

---

[*] Alice Miller, *Thou Shalt Not Be Aware: Society's Betrayal of the Child* (New York: Farrar, Straus and Giroux, 1998), p. 315.

Even if you don't know what took place, memory fragments of what you suffered can endure. You may be assailed by unexplained physical pain or sexual arousal, fear, confusion, or any other sensory aspect of the abuse. You may physically reexperience the terror, your body may clutch tight, or you may feel that you are suffocating and cannot breathe.

Touch often awakens memories. Women have had images come up while they were being massaged. You may freeze and see images from your past during sex. Your partner breathes in your ear just as your abuser once did, and it all comes spilling back:

Sometimes when we're making love, I feel like my head just starts to float away somewhere. I feel like I literally split off at my shoulders, and I get very lightheaded and dizzy. It's as if someone was blowing a fan down on top of my head. There's a lot of movement down past my hair. It's like rising up out of my head. I get really disoriented.

The other thing I experience is a lot of splitting right at the hips. My legs get very heavy and really solid. They just feel like dead weight, like logs. No energy is passing through them. Then I get real sick to my stomach, just violently ill. I find the minute I get nauseous, whatever it is is very close to me. And if I pay attention to it, I can see it, and move on.

TIMES WHEN MEMORIES SURFACE

Memories arise under many different circumstances. Three factors are usually present when survivors recall abuse that they have previously blocked out: distance from the original abuse, a life event that leads to the letting down of defenses, and an external situation that restimulates the memory.* Sometimes women remember abuse when there is sufficient safety for the memories and feelings to emerge—for example, when they're finally in a relationship that feels safe or when they move out of their parents' home.

Other times, difficult or painful events may precede remembering. You may experience a loss, such as divorce, retirement, menopause, or the death of a loved one and may feel as though everything in your life is unraveling. Medical treatment—a trip to the dentist, a gynecological exam, surgery, anesthesia, or other invasive medical procedures—can also jar loose buried feelings and images. A contemporary event that resembles the original abuse can sometimes trigger memories.

But memories don't always surface in dramatic ways. While visiting with a friend, one woman suddenly heard herself talking about being abused as a child for the first time. "It's as though I always knew it," she explained.

---

* Discussed by Karen Olio and William Cornell, "The Therapeutic Relationship as the Foundation for Treatment with Adult Survivors of Sexual Abuse," *Psychotherapy* 30 (3): 512–523 (1993). For a copy of this article go to http://kspope@kspope.com/memory/relationship.php. Also see Christine Courtois, *Healing the Incest Wound* (New York: W.W. Norton, 1988).

"It's just that I hadn't thought about it in twenty or thirty years."

Or, as Maya Angelou writes in the opening lines of *I Know Why the Caged Bird Sings*, "I hadn't so much forgot as I couldn't bring myself to remember."[*]

WHEN YOU BREAK AN ADDICTION

Many survivors remember their abuse once they get sober, quit drugs, or stop eating compulsively. These and other addictions can numb your feelings and block recollection of the abuse, but once you stop, the memories often surface. Anna Stevens, who was abused by her mother, explains:

> At the point I decided to put down drinking, I had to start feeling. The connection to the abuse was almost immediate. And I've watched other people come to AA and do the same thing. They have just enough time to get through the initial shakes, and you watch them start to go through the memories. And you know what's coming, but they don't.[†]

WHEN YOU BECOME A MOTHER

Mothers may remember their own abuse when they witness their children's vulnerability or when their children reach the age they were

---

[*] Maya Angelou, *I Know Why The Caged Bird Sings* (New York: Bantam, 1970), p. 1.

[†] For more of Anna's story, see p. 424.

WHILE MAKING LOVE
by Laura Davis

It was a sunny Sunday morning. We had not made love for a long time. We lay in bed, curled together like spoons. I was half asleep, half awake, feeling her warm weight curve into mine, her knees fitting smoothly against mine. Her musky breath touched me, warm and familiar on my neck, her fingertips gently searching my back, a question: "Can it be now? I want you."

I turned to face her, to study the green-gold eyes I loved. To wonder at this miracle woman who had crashed through all my defenses and disarmed me. She had made it all the way in and I trusted her. Finally, at twenty-eight, I felt safe in love. Before, I'd been a loner, too busy achieving, too busy living in my head, afraid of loving, a terror I could not name keeping me distant, just out of reach. There'd been other lovers, surely, others whom I dismissed when they got too close, others who skirted my edges. But she was the first who'd reached all the way through those walls. She was the one I'd dreamed of but never thought possible, the one whose soft presence beside me still surprised and awed me these slow weekend mornings. I was happy, happier than I'd ever been.

So to answer the question of her searching fingers, I looked up and smiled at her, inviting her caresses, and reached to stroke her face. She pressed her belly up against mine, and I felt the sudden jolt of passion flare skin to skin. "I love this woman," I thought. "And we have our whole lives to share it."

She was kissing me now, teasing and slow, waiting for me to answer, for me to rise, for me to catch the rush, like winds in a sail, to fly with her. "So far, so good," I thought, my tongue answering, responding, my body firm against hers, passion rising.

There was a gleam in her eyes. She'd been waiting for this for a long, long time. "I want you," she said, her fingers reaching in, her body on fire against me. "I want you."

And then I felt it. Subtle, unmistakable. Painfully familiar. A small spark of terror and then the screen. An impermeable wall suddenly cast between us, my body cut loose, my mind floating free. I tried to call myself back, but already it was too late. I was gone.

"Well, there's not enough eggs for waffles," I thought. "But there are those leftover baked potatoes. And they'd make great home fries." I closed my eyes, tried again to reel myself in. "C'mon, Laura. You want to be here. You want to do this. Get back in your body. C'mon! This is the woman you love!"

But it didn't work. My mind was already far above my body, spinning, dancing intricate loops. I felt totally out of control. My body lay on the bed beneath, still going through the motions. God, how I hated this! The old grief, this lack of presence, surged through me.

I slowed down my caresses, pulled my mouth away. I grew quiet, solitary. Looked back at her face, drawn tight and hard with disappointment. "I'm sorry, honey," I said after a moment. "I just can't." She looked stung, tears frozen in her eyes. We'd come so close.

This was not the first time I'd "disappeared." Nor the second. This was old, familiar territory, a vast chasm spreading between us, wider and wider the closer we got.

"Where the hell do you go?" she screamed at me then, months of patience suddenly giving way. "Where the hell are you? Just what is wrong with you anyway?"

Then silence. Her words reverberating, burrowing in, digging deep into my center. I felt them choking me. Nothing else was real. I didn't know where I was, who I was looking at. Her face wavered before me. I couldn't breathe. I stopped seeing. Stopped doing anything but feeling those questions probing deeper and deeper inside.

I must have looked stricken because her face softened then, and she held me, her eyes deep with concern and tender with love. "Breathe, honey," she said. "Go ahead and breathe."

That's all I remember. I know there were moments passing, quiet pensive moments. Something was happening to me. I could feel it—a tiny bubble of truth rising up from deep inside, a knowing coming from an unnamed core, the kind of knowing that pierces through years of fog and cannot be denied.

I started sobbing. Deep, wracking sobs that scared me and confused me, leaving me helpless and hurting, a child in pain. I had never cried like this. What was happening to me? Someone had hurt me very badly.

She stroked my forehead, peppered it with kisses. "Sweetheart, what is it?"

More sobs, more shaking. A terror, a truth, a knowledge too awful to utter, was finally breaking free. I did not recognize the words until they spilled from my lips. I knew I was going to say something, but I did not know what it would be.

"I was molested," I finally said, a tiny child's voice at last managing those three small words. As I heard them cut through the quiet of the sunny morning air, I knew that they were true. "I was molested."

when the abuse began. Sometimes they remember because their child is being abused. Dana was court-ordered to go for therapy when her three-year-old daughter, Christy, was molested. Dana first remembered her own abuse when she unconsciously substituted her own name for her daughter's:

I was in therapy talking about Christy, and instead of saying "Christy," I said "I." And I didn't even catch it. My therapist did. She had always suspected that I was abused too, but she hadn't said anything to me.

She told me what I had said, and I said, "I did? I said 'I'?" I hadn't even heard myself. It was really eerie.

What came out was that I was really dealing with Christy's molestation on a level of my own. The things that I was outraged at and that hurt me the most were things that had happened to me, not things that had happened to Christy. Part of the reason I fell apart and so much came back to me when I found out about Christy was because my husband was doing the same things to her that my father had done to me.[*]

AFTER A SIGNIFICANT DEATH

Many women are too scared to remember while their abusers are still alive. One woman said, "I couldn't afford to remember until both

my parents were dead, until there was nobody left to hurt me." A forty-seven-year-old woman first recalled her abuse a year and a half after her mother died: "Then I could no longer hurt my mother by telling her."

AFTER RETRAUMATIZATION

A shocking and deeply disturbing event such as a rape, a robbery, a serious accident, or the sudden death of a loved one can unearth long-buried memories. As one survivor describes:

I was a waitress at an all-night diner and I was robbed at gunpoint. There were two men and one held a gun to my back and told the manager to hand over the money or he'd shoot me. Fortunately he—the manager—kept his head and gave them the money and I wasn't harmed physically at all. I was incredibly shaken, of course. I didn't want to be alone. My boyfriend came over and I had a double scotch, but I still just shook and cried all night. I figured that was just normal and that it would just take me a little while to calm down. But that's not what happened. As the days and weeks went on, I got more—not less—upset. And then the memories started banging on the door.

Public events can also set off memories of childhood sexual abuse. Natural disasters, wars, a terrorist attack, or an epidemic such as AIDS that decimates an entire community can restimulate the trauma of child sexual abuse.

---

[*] For more of Dana's story, see "You've Got Two Choices" on p. 362 and "Breaking the Chain" on p. 347.

After Hurricane Katrina, one survivor from New Orleans was overwhelmed with images from her childhood:

I'd lost my home, my job, my whole city and pretty much all my possessions. I didn't have a pillow or a washcloth to my name. Not a can opener or a toothbrush. And everyone around me was devastated. We all knew people who had died.

On top of all that, I started having shooting pains in my vagina. I thought it was a bladder infection, but it wasn't. And then came images of my mother's face hovering over me, large and distorted and terrifying, and this feeling of horror and revulsion like nothing I'd ever known before. Actually I had known it before. Only too well.

MEDIA COVERAGE OF SEXUAL ABUSE

Jennierose, who remembered in her midforties, was sitting with her lover one night, watching a TV program about sexual offenders in prison. The therapist facilitating the group encouraged the offenders to talk about their own childhood experiences. Several of them remembered traumatic events.

In the middle of the program, Jennierose turned to her lover and said, "I wish there was a therapist like that I could go to, because I know there's something I'm not remembering." As soon as she spoke, Jennierose had a vision of the first time her father sodomized her, when she was four and a half and her mother had gone to the hospital to have another baby. "It was a totally detailed vision, to the point of seeing the rose-colored curtains blowing in the window."

Sobbing, Jennierose said to her lover, "I think I'm making something up." Her lover simply said, "Look at yourself! Look at yourself! Tell me you're making it up." And Jennierose couldn't. She knew she was telling the truth.

FEELING THE FEELINGS

Although remembering sometimes feels emotionally detached, when you remember with feeling, the helplessness, terror, and physical pain can be as real as any actual experience. Sexual arousal may also accompany your memories, and this may horrify you, but arousal is a natural response to sexual stimulation. You don't have to be ashamed.

You might recall feeling close; you might remember the pleasure of having the attention of someone you loved. Disgust and horror are not the only feelings that accompany memories. There is no *right* way to feel, but you must feel, even if it sends you reeling.

When I first remembered, I shut down emotionally right away. I climbed all the way up into my mind and forgot about the gut level. That's how I protected myself. For a long time it was just an intellectual exercise. "Oh, that's why I have trouble with men and authority. That's why I might not have remembered much about growing up." It took nine months after I first remembered for the feelings to start bubbling up.

I found myself slipping into the feelings I'd had during the abuse, that hadn't been safe to feel at the time. The first was this tremendous isolation. From there, I moved into absolute terror. I got in touch with how frightening the world is. It was the worst of the fear finally coming up. I felt like it was right at the top of my neck all the time, ready to come out in a scream.

I was right at the edge. I had an encounter with my boss, who said that my performance had been poor. I finally told him what had happened, which was really heavy—telling some male authority figure that you remembered incest in your family. He is a kind and caring person. The best he could do was back off and leave me alone.

I was then carrying around all this external pressure—my job was in jeopardy, my life was falling apart, and I was having all these feelings I didn't know what to do with. In order to keep myself in control, I started compulsively eating. Finally I decided I didn't want to go through this stuff by myself anymore. I got myself into therapy.

Having to experience the feelings is one of the roughest parts of remembering. "It pisses me off that I have to survive it twice, only this time with feelings," one woman said. "This time it's worse. I'm not so effective at dissociating anymore."

Another woman said, "I started off very butch about remembering. I kicked into my overachiever thing. I was going to lick this thing. I believed getting the pictures was what was important. I got a ton of memories, all on the intellectual level. It was kind of like I was going to 'do' incest, just like I might take up typing."

It was only after a year of therapy that this woman began to realize that *she* was the one who'd been abused. "I finally realized, I finally *felt*, that this was something that had happened to *me*, and that it had been damaging. I had to realize that just getting the memories was not going to make it go away. *This was about me!*"

LETTING MEMORIES IN

Few survivors feel that they have control over their memories. Most feel that the memories have control of them, that they do not choose the time and place that a new memory will emerge. You may be able to fight them off for a time, but the price—nightmares, headaches, exhaustion—is not worth staving off the inevitable.

Not everyone can tell when a memory is coming, but many survivors do get warnings, a certain physical sensation or feeling, that clues them in. Your stomach may get tight. You may sleep poorly or have frightening dreams. Or you may be warned in other ways:

I always know when they're coming. I get very tense. I get very scared. I get snappy at things that ordinarily wouldn't make me angry. I get sad. Usually it's anger and anxiety and fear that come first. And I have a choice. It's a real conscious choice. It's either I want it or I don't want it. And I said, "I don't want it," a lot. When I did that, I would just get sicker and sicker. I'd get more depressed. I'd get angry irrationally.

Now I don't say I don't want it. It's not worth it. My body seems to need to release it. The more I heal, the more I see these memories are literally stored in my body, and they've got to get out. Otherwise I'm going to carry them forever.

REMEMBERING OVER TIME

Sometimes when you've resolved one group of memories, another will make its way to the surface:

The more I worked on the abuse, the more I remembered. First I remembered my brother, and then my grandfather. About six months after that I remembered my father. And then about a year later, I remembered my mother. I remembered the "easiest" first and the "hardest" last. Even though it was traumatic for me to realize that everyone in my family

---

IF YOU THINK A MEMORY IS ON ITS WAY

- **Find a place where you will be safe.** If you're at work, try to get home. Go to the safe place in your home (see "Create a Safe Place," p. 38), or go to a close friend's home.
- **Don't fight it.** The best thing to do is to relax and let the memory come. Don't use drugs, alcohol, food, or other distractions to push it back down.
- **Remember, it's just a memory.** What you're experiencing is a memory of abuse that happened a long time ago. Your abuser is not really hurting you in the present, even if it feels that way. The memory is part of your healing, not an extension of the abuse.

- **Comfort yourself.** The return of memories is a stressful experience that can leave you feeling vulnerable. Take tender care of yourself.
- **Expect yourself to have a reaction.** Recovering memories can be a painful, draining experience. It may take you a while to recover. It's best to give yourself that time and not expect to bounce back right away.
- **Talk to someone.** Even if you prefer to be alone when you uncover a new memory, most people find it helpful to tell someone else about it afterward. For others, though, it feels best to stay with their own experience and wait until they're ready to share.

THE ESSENTIAL TRUTH OF MEMORY

Memories of child sexual abuse can be exceedingly accurate. In situations in which abusers are willing to relate their version of the events, the abuser's story often matches the survivor's memory. Also, when siblings or other family members share what they witnessed, there is often a striking correlation. When the abuser is outside the family, other victims of the same perpetrator frequently report similar abuse.

Yet we also know that memory is not 100 percent accurate. This is true of both ordinary and traumatic memory. Memories are not totally objective recordings of what took place and are likely to reflect some degree of distortion. It is inevitable that survivors remember the details of their abuse with some degree of inaccuracy. Time sequences may be mixed up, multiple incidents may be telescoped into a single incident, whole portions of incidents may be missing, and the events before and after may be blurred.

Sometimes the way you experienced the abuse leads to distortions. A common example is in the description of size. A small child may remember the abuser as being huge or the abuser's genitals as filling her whole field of vision. One survivor who was abused by a teacher remembered that the school was enormous, with extremely high ceilings and wide corridors. When she went back as an adult, she was shocked at how small it really was.

Another survivor originally thought she'd been penetrated with a lollipop. When she went back to her parents and told them what she was remembering, they reminded her that her pediatrician had sexually abused her during routine appointments. At the end of each visit, he'd given her a lollipop. Even though this woman had talked about the abuse as a child, and even though her parents had responded appropriately, she had forgotten the abuse entirely. It wasn't until she was an adult in therapy, trying to make sense of images of lollipops and flashes of vaginal pain that she started to remember.

Sometimes distortion in survivors' memories works as a shield against a more disturbing memory. One survivor thought that her babysitter had abused her. Later she discovered that it was actually her mother.

Another survivor described witnessing her father forcing oral sex on her adolescent sister. She remembered that after he'd finish with her sister, he'd come and kiss her goodnight and that "his kiss would hurt." But she felt sure that he didn't actually abuse her. Over time, however, she recovered the fuller memory that what hurt was not his kiss but his violation of her through oral sex.

Although inaccuracies may exist in your memory, you can still work with what you remember as an indication of what you felt. For example, one survivor related that she remembered her abuser putting a knife up her vagina. But she went on to explain that she didn't think that that was what actually happened. There was no blood, no scarring, and she had no memory of seeing a knife. She assumed that he penetrated her vagina—perhaps with a finger or his penis—and the feeling was so painful, so cutting, that she, in her child's mind, had no concept for it other than a knife.

The way these women worked with their memories is a good model. It's okay to shift your understanding of your childhood as you incorporate new information and learn more. Discovering, understanding, and integrating your past is an ongoing part of the healing process.

abused me, there was something reassuring about it. For a long time I'd felt worse than the initial memories should have made me feel, so remembering the rest of the abuse was actually one of the most grounding things to happen. My life suddenly made sense.*

The impact of new memories will shift over time. One woman who has been getting new memories for ten years says that remembering has become harder over time:

My first flood of memories came when I was twenty-five. The memories I get now are like fine-tuning—more details, more textures. Even though there was more of a feeling of shock and catharsis at first, remembering is harder now. I believe them now. It hurts more. I have the emotions to feel the impact. I can see how it's affected my life.

Laura also says that new memories are harder:

Just when I felt that my life was getting back to normal and I could put the incest aside, I had another flashback that was much more violent than the earlier pictures I'd seen. I was furious. I wanted to be finished. I didn't want to be starting in with incest again! And my resistance made the remembering a lot more difficult.

Other survivors say that memories have gotten easier to handle:

As I've come to terms with the fact that I was abused, new pictures, new incidents don't have the same impact. The battle of believing it happened is not one I have to fight each time another piece falls into place. Once I had a framework to fit new memories into, my recovery time got much faster. While my first memories overwhelmed me for weeks, now I might only cry for ten minutes or feel depressed for an hour. It's not that I don't have new memories. It's just that they don't devastate me anymore.

And new memories don't take anything away from the healing you've already done. Paradoxically, *you are already healing from the effects of things you have yet to remember.*

BUT I DON'T HAVE ANY MEMORIES

Sometimes when women say they feel that they were sexually abused but don't have any memories, they mean that they can't tell a cohesive narrative about the abuse. However, when these women begin to talk in detail about their childhoods, they frequently relate events that are covertly sexual or even blatantly abusive:

I remember the first time I told my therapist how my mother would give

---

* For another example of a survivor who remembered new abusers over time, see "Sheila O'Connell" on p. 510.

me enemas. She would lay me down on the bathroom mat and talk really sweet to me. She was usually abrupt, like we kids were in her way and she wished she didn't have to bother with us, but at enema time she'd turn all her attention on me, stroking me, telling me what a good girl I was. She'd rub my legs and my thighs and my buttocks, saying she just wanted to relax me.

When I told my therapist about this, she asked me how often it happened. I told her every day as soon as I got home from school. I'll never forget the look on her face. She didn't have to say a word.

You may not recall particular incidents such as the one this survivor describes, but you may discover that you know more than you think you do about the environment in which you grew up. Specific incidents of sexual abuse don't usually occur as isolated events in an otherwise healthy family. You may clearly remember times when you felt used, humiliated, undermined, manipulated, or smothered.

I've always remembered the violence— Dad beat Mom. It wasn't that often, but you never knew when it was going to happen. He was seething *all* the time. We kids would cower in the bed, covering our heads with pillows and singing TV jingles to drown out the noise. We were never allowed to have friends over. My sisters and I fought all the time. I was desperately lonely.

There is a pain—so utter—
BY EMILY DICKINSON

There is a pain—so utter—
It swallows substance up—
Then covers the Abyss with Trance—
So Memory can step
Around—across—upon it—
As one within a Swoon—
Goes safely—where an open eye—
Would drop Him—Bone by Bone.

Emily Dickinson, *The Poems of Emily Dickinson*, ed. by Thomas H. Johnson (Cambridge, MA: Belknap Press of Harvard University Press, 1983).

As you explore what you *do* know about your childhood, you will sometimes remember more. Other women never recall very much of what happened to them. There may be gaps and unknowns that become clear to you as your healing progresses, but it's also possible that there will be aspects of your experience you never fully remember. Fortunately, it's possible to heal from the effects of childhood abuse even if your memories are incomplete. One survivor explained:

There's a lot I'm pretty sure I'll never have straight. After all, it began before I can remember. I mean, there was never a time *before* the abuse. So a lot of it's blurred. And I honestly don't think it'll ever come into focus. But I've gotten clear on the essentials—what I need to know to do my healing work and get on with my life. I know the main cast of perpetrators. I know the extent of the damage. Maybe I'll get more bits and pieces as time goes on, but if I don't, it doesn't matter. The cards are on the table—which is a relief.

One thirty-eight-year-old survivor described her relationship with her father as emotionally incestuous. She has never had specific memories of any physical contact between them and for a long time was haunted by the fact that she couldn't come up with clear, concrete memories:

Do I want to know if something physical happened between my father and me? Really, I think you have to be strong enough to know. I think that our minds are wonderful in the way they protect us, and I think that when I'm strong enough to know, I'll know.

I obsessed for about a year on trying to remember, and then I got tired of sitting around talking about what I couldn't remember. I thought, "All right, let's act as if." It's like you come home and your home has been robbed and everything has been thrown in the middle of the room, and the window is open and the curtain is blowing in the wind, and the cat is gone. You know somebody robbed you, but you're never going to know who. So what are you going to do? Sit there and try to figure it out while your stuff lies around? No, you start to clean

it up. You put bars on the windows. You *assume* somebody was there. Somebody could come along and say, "Now, how do you know someone was there?" You don't know.

That's how I acted. I had the symptoms. I felt like there was something I just couldn't get to, that I couldn't remember yet. And my healing was blocked there.

But finally I got to the point where I realized, "If the specifics are not available to you, then go with what you've got."

I'm left with the damage. And that's why I relate to that story of the burglar. I'm owning the damage. I want to get better. I've been very ill as a result of the damage, and at some point I realized, "I'm thirty-eight years old. What am I going to do—wait twenty more years for memory?" I'd rather get better.

And then maybe the stronger I am, the more the memories will come back. Maybe I'm putting the cart before the horse. Maybe I've remembered as much as I'm able to remember without breaking down. I don't want to go insane. I want to be out in the world. Maybe I should go with that sense of protection. There is a survivor in here and she's pretty smart. So I'm working on healing myself.

Sometimes women don't have memories because no physical incidents of abuse took place. Instead, you may have been subjected to an environment of inappropriate boundaries, lewd looks, or behavior that was inappropriately romantic:

> My father made me his wife. After my mother died, he put me in her place. He'd send me bouquets of flowers addressed to "My darling," he'd bring me fancy chocolates, he'd dress me up. He even bought me a ring with a diamond chip. Everyone thought he was so devoted, so charming. But it was sick and it left me hopelessly confused. What little girl wouldn't lap up that attention? I worshipped him. But the underside of all that adoration was a kind of possession. It's affected every relationship I've ever been in.
>
> I was in therapy for three years, searching, expecting to uncover some rape or instance when he actually molested me. But he didn't do any of that. It was all emotional.

The process of coming to terms with your history is different for every survivor. If you remember very little of your abuse—or of your whole childhood—it may be hard to define your experience clearly. But if you are in deep pain, there is a reason for your distress. It may not be sexual abuse, but there's something for you to address. You're not crazy to be feeling so much pain.

Although the desire to know and name your experience may feel urgent, it often takes substantial time to explore your past. Try to be patient with yourself. It's better, in the long run, to acknowledge your uncertainty than to prematurely put a label on something you're not sure of. Don't rush. You can move forward in your healing in important ways, even if you don't know exactly what happened.

HONORING OUR MEMORIES

Poet Marge Piercy wrote, "Memory is the simplest form of prayer."[*] Memory is an integral part of our being, of our healing, of our social change, and even of our prayer. Our memories tell us where we've been and they help us to understand the totality of our experience. Even our painful memories have value. They are the record of what we've endured. Though our past may hold pain and suffering, healing allows us to emerge from that past with strength, joy, and hope for the future.

WRITING EXERCISE: I REMEMBER, I DON'T REMEMBER

(See the basic method for writing exercises on p. xxix.)

Write for ten minutes, beginning with the words *I remember*. You can write about any aspect of your childhood. When you run out of things to write, start a new sentence with the words *I remember*.

---

[*] Marge Piercy, "Black Mountain," in *Available Light* (New York: Knopf, 1988).

Surrender

BY MOLLY FISK

When the truth came to me,
slipped into my house in its white
robes, its face open as my face,
its heart obvious and trusting,
I stood calmly in the front hall
and did not move to bar the door.

When the truth laid its cool hand
on my sleeve and said,
Come with me, it's time, I went
quietly. She led me into the past,
through the backyards I once
knew, bedrooms and kitchens;
we sat in my father's car and talked.
I was shivering in my thin skin
and crying readily by this time:
    terrified,
furious. She offered her own
    consolation—
no false pats on the hand and no
    shoulder
to lean on, I had to learn to stand
    upright
or bend on my own. In her clear
    voice
the truth offered all she has to give us:
Herself, and the stern comfort
of belonging to this world.

Molly Fisk, *Listening to Winter* (Berkeley, CA: Roundhouse Press/Heyday Books, 2000).

Do the same thing, beginning with the words *I don't remember*. Continue for ten minutes without stopping, always coming back to the starting phrase *I don't remember*.

ART EXERCISE: CREATE A FLOOR PLAN

This exercise is a powerful way to evoke memories from childhood. Although it is a drawing exercise, you do not have to be an artist or be able to draw well to do it.

Using a large piece of newsprint or other drawing paper, a pencil, and some fine colored markers, draw a detailed floor plan of a home you lived in as a child. If you moved a lot, choose one place you lived that feels particularly significant to you. Don't worry about perspective, accuracy, or scale. If a room was more important, you can make it larger, or if it was less important, smaller. Your own childhood memory of the place is what matters. Feel free to include significant furniture or other objects. Note where people slept, ate, played, or fought, as well as significant events that happened in each room. Fill in as much detail as you can remember.

Your floor plan can include both the inside and the outside of the house. If you spent the majority of your time outdoors, your picture may be primarily focused there.

As you draw the floor plan, imagine the images, smells, sounds, voices, and events you associate with each room or area. Let memories and sensations run through you. Let yourself recall incidents that happened in each room.

Notice if there are any rooms that you can't reconstruct or any special places you went to be alone.

Spend up to an hour or more on your drawing. When you are done, you may want to share your floor plan with someone you trust.

Feel free to repeat this exercise for other places you have lived. This exercise can be particularly powerful when done in a group and then shared.

Believing It Happened

"Did it really happen? I'd like to tell you no. I'd like to deny it, but I just can't do that anymore. I've always had flashbacks; I've always seen bits and pieces of what happened. It was terrifying. I'd break into a sweat in the middle of sex. Sometimes even just taking a shower and washing my body, the revulsion was so strong, I'd have to hold on to the wall. But I didn't want to put it all together. I didn't want to know the story. It took me years to believe it happened. And although I'm healing now and life is better, there are times I wish I could go back to my denial that I had a happy family and parents who protected me."

To heal from child sexual abuse, you must face the fact that you were abused. Yet this is often difficult for survivors. When you've spent your life denying the reality of your abuse, when you don't want it to be true, or when your family repeatedly calls you crazy or a liar, it can be exceedingly difficult to hold on to the validity of your experience or even believe in your right to search for the truth of your past.

Yet this is a most crucial right for survivors, for all people: the freedom to explore and understand your history. You know more about your life than anyone else—you lived it. No author, book, therapist, or family member can tell you whether you were abused or if your memories are valid. You are the expert on your own life.

Some survivors have no trouble believing that they were abused. Corroboration can make it easier to accept the truth. You may have a sister or brother who talks about it with you. A mother who said, "But honey, we had to stay with him." Physical scars from a rape at age four. A doctor's report. Court testimony. An abuser who says, "Yes, I did it." A neighbor who remembers. Another child you told.

What cemented it for me was when I told my mother what I remembered. I watched her face go blank, like she was in shock, and then she said, "That's your old room on the farm in Kentucky."

Other times, unfortunately, memories are validated through the discovery that the person who abused you is currently abusing another child.* Sometimes this tragic turn of events is the only thing that finally brings families to acknowledge that the adult survivor is telling the truth. As one survivor described:

I'd told my mother. I'd told my brothers. And my sisters-in-law. I'd screamed at them to keep my niece and nephews away from my father. They thought I was a raving lunatic. My mother believed me for about two weeks and then she collapsed. She couldn't face it. And nobody did anything. Now it's too late. The kids have all been abused and finally, everyone believes me.

But sometimes even when survivors have confirmation of their abuse, they still struggle to believe it happened. For many survivors, denial has been a way of life. You may have grown up in a family where many things were hidden, not just abuse. You may have learned by example to numb your feelings, to dissociate from painful or confusing experiences, to ignore troubling realities. These long-standing patterns don't just go away, even when there's clear proof of abuse.

And for many survivors, such proof is not available, nor is support or validation from family members. Yet even if your memories are incomplete, even if your family insists nothing ever happened, you still have the right to explore your own history, name your experience, and come to terms with what happened to you.

THE ROLE OF DENIAL

Survivors sometimes go to great lengths to deny their memories. One woman convinced herself that it was all a dream. Another dismissed her memories by saying, "Oh, it's just a past life." When Laura was flooded with her first pictures of the actual abuse, she did not want to believe what she saw:

I did not want to believe with a passion. Even as part of me recognized the truth, another part fought to deny what I had seen. There were times when I would rather have viewed myself as crazy than acknowledge what had happened to me.

I had come from a wonderful family. *I* couldn't have been raped as a child. *I* couldn't have been molested by the

---

* See *The Hidden Legacy: Uncovering, Confronting, and Healing Three Generations of Incest* by Barbara Small Hamilton (Fort Bragg, CA: Cypress House, 1992) for an illustration of how unacknowledged sexual abuse can devastate an entire family. Some of the survivors always remembered the abuse (including the author), others regained memories as they healed, and some continue to have memory gaps.

grandfather I had revered and loved. I remembered all the wonderful things he did. That he had abused me was out of the question! It couldn't be!

This type of denial might seem surprising, but in reality it is a self-protective way to deal with traumatic pain. Denial gives you a respite when you cannot bear to align yourself with that small, wounded child for another minute. It allows you to go to work, to make breakfast for your kids. It is a survival skill that enables you to set a pace you can handle.

Moving in and out of denial is a natural part of the healing process. Often in the beginning stages, belief in your memories comes and goes. One woman explained:

It's like being in a fog and the clouds go away. I'd have a memory. I'd relive the experience. Then I'd know it was true. "That was real. I don't want it to be true. But it happened." Then as soon as I said that, I'd deny it: "But I love my father. He couldn't have done that." But there'd be these little things inside that would say, "But what about the mysterious bladder infections I had when I was eight? He never could look me in the eye when I was in the hospital."

A dramatic example of this touch-and-go belief in memories occurred in one of Ellen's workshops. During a writing exercise, one woman wrote about the abuse she experienced when she was very young. When she read it aloud to the group, she experienced a complete regression, sobbing, stuttering, and shaking as she relived the experience. Everyone in the group was deeply moved.

Later that day, the same woman asked, "Do you think I really could have been abused? Maybe I was just acting." Another woman in the group turned to her and said, "Could you have acted joy and happiness as convincingly? If you're such a great actress, why do you only act out the same scene again and again?"

It is natural to have periodic doubts about your experience. And sometimes the doubt is there because the events in question did not occur. But even women who *were* sexually abused often wonder if the abuse really happened. For many survivors, some degree of doubt is a normal part of the healing process. (For more on dealing with persistent doubts, see "If Doubts Persist" on p. 100.)

FIRST LIGHT

by Aurora Levins Morales

This is an excerpt from a longer, unfinished piece. The character, a nine-year-old girl, has just been raped by her uncle.

She lay on the narrow bed in the very early morning light and felt herself dying. She kept herself very still until she could feel nothing at all, and then she knew the process was complete. She was dead. Now, she knew, came the washing of the corpse, and this one needed it. The monster that had killed her had left blood on her. It was a strange thing, being killed in your own bed like that, in such an ordinary place. Nothing looked different, but it was all unfamiliar. Like the kind of bad dream where after you wake up, for a few minutes the clothes draped over the chair still look like a wolf and you're afraid to move.

Only she couldn't remember waking up after this dream. The events were seamless. She had paid close attention, but the only waking she remembered was when the door opened and the monster came in her room.

So it must be real. As she thought this, she felt the cold in her body deepen. Because what if they insisted it was a dream? Insisted she was still alive? What if they made her walk and talk and go to school and eat, when really she was dead? What if they told her it was just pretend?

Suddenly, small and clear, like a picture on a very tiny far-away television screen, she remembered the afternoon with her aunt Luisa. They had been playing that she was a wicked witch and her aunt was the evil creature who tagged along. In the middle of the game her aunt got tired and said she wasn't an evil creature at all. Disappointed that the game was ending so soon, she had insisted, "You *are*, you *are*, you *really* are!" Aunt Luisa had made her sit down on the floor for a serious talk, and her face—long and stretched tight around the eyes and mouth—had scared her.

"It's okay to play and make up stories, but you mustn't believe in what you make up. You have to know the difference between real and pretend. Otherwise people think you're crazy." Then she whispered, "And maybe they'd be right!"

Now her aunt was in the hospital and all anyone would say was that she didn't feel well.

So if this was just a dream and she couldn't tell the difference, then maybe she was crazy. But even if she wasn't, even if the monster was real, what if no one believed her? They would think she was crazy anyway, and put her in a loony bin. She imagined a loony bin. It had smooth white sides like the bin her mother kept onions in, and the crazy people were dropped in with tweezers and lay in a heap on the bottom of it. She would hate that. It would be much better to pretend, to go along with them and act alive.

The first thing was to wash. When you washed a dead person, later people went to look at them and said, "She looks just like herself," "She looks like she's only sleeping." She would pretend she was only sleeping from now on, and she would look like herself.

It was growing lighter now. She could see the blood on her thigh, but none of it was on the bed yet. She got up quietly and went to the bathroom, closing the door gently so as not to wake up her grandmother. Using wet toilet paper she began to wash herself between the legs, and being dead, it hardly hurt at all.

Aurora Levins Morales has published several books, including *Remedios: Stories of Earth and Iron from the History of Puertorriquenas* (Cambridge, MA: South End Press, 2001); *Medicine Stories: History, Culture, and the Politics of Integrity* (Cambridge, MA: South End Press, 1998); and (with Rosario Morales) *Getting Home Alive* (Ithaca, NY: Firebrand, 1986).

LOOK AT YOUR LIFE

One practical way to learn more about what took place in the past is to look at your life now. Your feelings, your responses and interactions, hold clues to your history. You may find that as you face and work through the trauma of abuse, your behavior changes in healthy ways:

The hardest part was accepting and believing that it really happened. Being in the group really helped. I was able to see other people who had gone through sexual abuse, and my symptoms were similar. I have all the classic symptoms of sexual abuse—feeling suicidal, running away, a high pain tolerance, spacing out, not being able to succeed at anything, denial, always being isolated.

Another thing that helped me believe it was watching my own behavior change. Like my paranoia going away. I used to think the Mafia was out to get me, and that someone was going to set fire to a place I was in. When I remembered the incest, I realized those were threats my father had made. He used to lock me in the cedar closet and sodomize me. Then he'd threaten to set fire to it. He said if I ever told anyone, the Mafia would come and get me. As soon as I made those connections, my paranoia went away.

LEARNING TO RECOGNIZE ABUSE

Some survivors grow up in families where abuse is such a part of their daily lives that they believe that what happened to them is normal:

> I remember sitting on the stoop with my friend Stephanie when we were about nine. She asked me why my arm was black and blue from the elbow to the shoulder, and I told her. She said, "You mean your father hits you?" She was incredulous.
>
> So was I, when I said, "You mean your father *doesn't*?" It wasn't until that moment that I recognized that what went on in our apartment was not normal. Although I've forgotten much—most—of my childhood, I remember those couple of sentences as if they had been spoken last week. Or today.*

Part of healing involves learning what to expect in a healthy family. As one survivor explained:

> I would talk with my therapist about what people had done to me in my family. And she would say to me, "That's abuse. It's terrible that that happened to you." And I was shocked, because I thought I'd had a normal childhood. I only knew it was abuse because other people would mirror it back to me. I would walk around saying, "My family abused me." I had to say it a lot to really believe it. My first year and a half was spent just accepting the fact that I had been abused.

Sometimes, even when we know what happened, we still don't want to identify it as sexual abuse because of our loyalty to the people involved:

> I knew my brother had forced himself on me. I knew it happened more than once, but I didn't want to call it abuse—for sure—not sexual abuse. He got it so much worse from our father than I ever did—the beatings, the humiliation. Now I was going to call him a child molester? He was only a kid himself. And now he was grown up, having lots of troubles of his own. How could I lay one more thing on him? But it wasn't until I could name it for myself that I could begin to heal.

BELIEVING IT MATTERED

Sometimes women have no doubts about the actual events that took place but play down their significance. Over the years, many women showed up at Ellen's survivor workshops afraid that their abuse wasn't bad enough for them to be allowed to participate. They said things such as "It wasn't incest—it was just a friend of

---

* For another powerful example of this, see Kyos on p. 457 in "Courageous Women."

the family" or "I was fourteen and it only happened once" or "He just showed me movies" or "It was with my sister. She was only two years older than me."

Such statements show the gross extent to which abuse is minimized in our society.

The fact that someone else has suffered from abuse more severe than your own does not lessen your suffering. Comparisons of pain are simply not useful.

There are many ways to de-emphasize sexual abuse. A particularly offensive one is to claim that if a man didn't force his penis into some opening of your body, you weren't really violated. This is not true. The severity of abuse should not be defined in terms of male genitals. Violation is determined by your experience as a child—your body, your feelings, your spirit. The precise physical acts are not always the most damaging aspects of abuse. Although forcible rape is physically excruciating to a small child, many kinds of sexual abuse are not physically painful. They do not leave visible scars.

Some abuse is not even physical. Your father may have stood in the bathroom doorway, making suggestive remarks or simply leering when you entered to use the toilet. Your uncle may have walked around naked, calling attention to his penis, talking about his sexual exploits, questioning you about your body. Your tennis coach may have badgered you into telling him exactly what you did with your boyfriend. There are many ways to be violated.

There is also abuse on the psychological level. You had the feeling your mother was aware of your physical presence every minute of the day, no matter how quiet and unobtru-sive you were. Your neighbor watched your changing body with an intrusive interest. Your father took you out on romantic dates and wrote you love letters.

Nor is frequency of abuse what's at issue. Betrayal takes only a minute. A father can slip his fingers into his daughter's underpants in thirty seconds. After that the world is not the same.

Believing It Mattered: Vicki's Story

*Many women believe that their abuse doesn't count because it happened only once. But as the following story shows, all abuse is harmful.**

There was always a creepy feeling in my house of my father being really inappropriate. He'd be too affectionate, too close. He was always kissing me too long. It got worse when I was a teenager. He had a more difficult time containing himself. My girlfriends felt weird around him and he was really hostile to my boyfriends.

My father only molested me once, when I was twelve years old. I was asleep in bed. He came into my room and lay down next to me. He put his hand down my pajamas and started playing with my vagina. It woke me up. I turned away from him. I pretended I was turning over in my sleep. He must have gotten frightened that I would wake up, and

---

* For more of Vicki's story, see "It Brought Us Closer Together: Vicki's Story" on p. 166 and "Vicki Malloy" on p. 487.

he left. I remember watching his shadow outside the door. He never did it again.

Before he molested me, I felt very free in my body. I felt wonderful. I was coming into the height of puberty. I was outgoing and friendly. I had boyfriends. Everything was awakening. And my first intimate sexual experience was with my father. He was the first man ever to touch my genitals.

It was very upsetting and confusing to me. I loved my father. We had a really strong relationship. After he molested me, I went into a deep depression. I shut off communicating with the outside world. It was like this veil just came down, and that was it. It took me until I was twenty-two to even realize something was wrong. I've had to find out what my real personality was underneath.

I never forgot what happened. It sort of went underground. I didn't think about it a lot, but it's had long-lasting effects. I've had a really difficult time getting close to my lovers. I need a disproportionate amount of control in relationships.

I've been estranged from my father for the last five years, ever since I confronted him. Our relationship has basically fallen apart.

I never compared what happened to me to what other people went through because I really felt the hell inside myself. I knew it was wreaking havoc in my life and in the lives of my lovers. You don't have to have it happen over and over to know "This is really terrible." It doesn't take much for a child to feel the devastation of a parent crossing over those boundaries.

If I was talking to someone and she said, "Oh well, he just fondled me a little bit. It's not such a big deal," I'd ask, "When you connect with another human being in a deep way, how does it make you feel? Does it make you feel scared? Like closing down? Or like being completely one with that person?" Really check it out with yourself. In the deepest part of you, how are you connecting with people? Then reassess if you were affected.

It counts if it keeps you from being close to another person. It counts if it's devastated your life, if you're missing a part of yourself. Even if it only happened once, it counts.

STRATEGIES FOR WORKING WITH PERSISTENT DOUBT

Have patience toward all that is unresolved in your heart and . . . try to love the questions themselves.

—RAINER MARIA RILKE[*]

- **Look at the times doubts arise.** If doubts come up when you visit your hometown, or right after you talk to parents or siblings who don't believe you, it's likely your doubts are related to these influences. If they persist even when you're calm and centered, there may be more reason to think you may have at least part of your story wrong. Yet even if you find that

---

[*] Rainer Maria Rilke, *Letters to a Young Poet* (New York: Random House, 1984).

some of the things you believed are not true, it doesn't mean that all of your memories are unreliable. It's possible to be mistaken about one incident while remembering other events accurately. (See "The Essential Truth of Memory" on p. 69 for more about this topic.)

- **Know that there's a reason for your pain.** If you're experiencing the level of anguish common to survivors of sexual abuse, there is some legitimate reason for that distress. It may not be sexual abuse, but there's something there for you to identify and address. You're not crazy to be feeling so much pain.

- **Heal from the things you are certain of.** For example, if you're sure you were beaten as a child but you're not certain if there was any sexual abuse, focus on healing from what you know. You'll be making progress in your healing even if you aren't yet sure whether other events took place.

- **It's okay if you're not sure.** Although you may feel under pressure (from yourself or others) to know exactly what happened, it may take time for you to discover the truth. Give yourself that time. It's okay to not know everything yet—or ever.

- **Don't affirm anything you're not ready to affirm.** If you're not sure whether you were sexually abused, don't rush to a conclusion. You may need time and space to figure it out for yourself. People who pressure you either way are not helping you. Talk instead with people who will hear your questions, respect your struggle to know, and encourage you to take the time to find out. Minimize your contact with those who insist it be one way or the other.

- **Assess your own therapeutic relationships.** If you're in therapy, talk about your doubts with your therapist. Your therapist should be supportive and open to your questioning. He or she shouldn't pressure you to decide what you think is true or try to force answers on you as you explore your history.

  If you're in group therapy, you should feel that there's room for you to share your own experience, as it happened, without embellishing it in any way. You should never feel that you have to stretch the truth in order to be accepted or acknowledged. Whatever your childhood experience, it should be respected and taken seriously. If you're not certain about what happened, there shouldn't be pressure for you to identify yourself as a survivor prematurely.

  If you never really thought you were abused and your therapist insisted that you were, or if you thought you had to make up a story and now you don't know if it's true, you're going to need sophisticated and capable help. A consultation with a second therapist can often help clarify the situation. Make sure that you choose someone who doesn't have an investment either in validating your memories or in proving that you were misled. Work with someone who can keep an open mind until your true history becomes clear.*

- **Hold off on confronting your abuser or disclosing the abuse to family members who are likely to be extremely upset.** Don't talk with your family about the abuse until you're ready. If you're uncertain about what happened, if you're still sorting through possibilities, it's usually best to postpone talking to your family about the abuse. Wait until you're clear and then assess whether talking to them is in your best interests.†

- **Remember, you can trust yourself.** Above all, trust your own sense of who you are and what your experiences have been. If the healing process is about anything, it's about learning to trust yourself, your feelings, your reality.

---

* For an example of a therapist who remained open to the possibility that memories may or may not have literally happened, see "Sheila O'Connell" on p. 510. Also, read the section "Finding Your Own Truth," p. 49, in "Working with a Counselor."
† For an in-depth discussion of this subject, see "Disclosures and Truth-Telling" on p. 157.

You are the best judge of what happened to you. Continue to value your own knowing, even if that changes as you discover more.

IF DOUBTS PERSIST

For some survivors, disturbing doubts about their abuse persist for a long time. One survivor grew up in a family where her reality was so severely tampered with, it's no wonder she has trouble trusting her perceptions:

> At night, before I went to sleep, my mother would tell me that what went on during the day when I was awake was really a dream. And that what happened in my sleep, that was real. She turned reality and dreams, awake and asleep, exactly opposite.

This is an extreme example, but some distortion of the truth is common in families where sexual abuse takes place. If you've grown up unsure of what to believe, if your perceptions haven't matched what you were told, you may find it particularly hard to trust your own reality when it comes to sexual abuse.

However, consistent doubt can also be an indication that you're on the wrong track. If you're genuinely unsure about what happened to you, don't rush yourself—or allow anyone to rush you—into giving it a label. Take your time. Explore your history, your feelings, your concerns. Trust yourself. Eventually you will come to a fuller understanding of your experience.

BELIEVING DOESN'T HAPPEN ALL AT ONCE

Even when you know the facts are true, you may still, at a deep emotional level, have trouble believing it happened. Believing doesn't usually happen all of a sudden—it's a gradual awakening:

At first, I had regular doubts that the abuse had happened at all. Once I became more steady, I still thought of it as something that had happened to someone very far away from me. Over time, I've been able to incorporate it more into the texture of my life. I include it when I tell people about my life. I talk about it freely, much as I would the fact that my family went to museums a lot when I was a kid. It's no longer a shameful secret, separate from the rest of who I am. I used to feel I had this good childhood, and then off to the side was this horrible, shameful abuse. But now I know there was only one child and she lived through it all.

Breaking Silence

"What would happen if one woman told the truth about her life? The world would split open."

—MURIEL RUKEYSER, FROM "KATHE KOLLWITZ"*

Everyone has the right to tell the truth about her life. Although most survivors have been taught to keep abuse a secret, this silence is not in your best interests. The sexual molestation of children and the resulting shame thrive in an atmosphere of silence. As one survivor explained, "Incest is not a taboo. Talking about it is a taboo."

Speaking out is a powerful step toward personal liberation, healing, and social change. Yet it is something many survivors find difficult:

I feel very lonely and isolated. I've always had so much to say, and I've never said it. What's hindered me the most is being so skilled at being silent.

HOW SURVIVORS ARE SILENCED

The first time you tried to talk about your abuse, you might still have been a child. Under ideal circumstances, you would have been believed, protected, and assured that the abuse wasn't your fault. You would have been given age-appropriate counseling or placed in a support group with other children. If the abuser were a family member, he or she would have been the one taken out of the home, not you.

One young survivor describes the compassionate, effective support she received when she told her mother about being abused:

I was a star player on the Junior Varsity basketball team and I really loved my

---

* Muriel Rukeyser, *The Speed of Darkness* (New York: Random House, 1968).

Putting Away My Bras
BY FRANNIE LINDSAY

They are clean and papery gray and the
    lace, if
there is any lace, is torn, and the
    atrophied straps
are hitched tight in their plastic pincers.
The underwire on one
pokes up, no wonder the fire-
red itch on my rib. They are scentless
and warm from the dryer. Once they
    were pretty,
I bought them because I wished I were
    pretty.
Now the hooks grab and ravel
my socks. My bras are nothing at all

like my father's exact-fitting hand
    during beauty
pageants on TV. We sat on the couch
in his musty study and watched them;
he asked me why I couldn't
look like that, he dangled his arm over
my shoulder's ledge, he touched
    me and I
made believe he did not. I tried
his drink and chit-chatted with him,
and my mother, and each of us picked
    the girl
we liked best, my tit staring into his
    palm.

Frannie Lindsay, *Lamb* (Florence, MA: Perugia, 2006).

coach. All the girls did. He was a great coach. The abuse started when he was driving me home from night games. For several months I couldn't tell anyone. I stopped eating and my grades went to hell. I wanted to tell my parents, but I knew how angry they'd be. I was afraid they'd go after him and that it would ruin his life and all the girls on the team would hate me.

Then one night, my mother and I got into a fight about some outfit I wanted to wear and I just blurted it out. The first thing she did was comfort me. It was such a relief to finally get the secret out.

We did go to the police and in the end, it was the right thing to do. We found out he'd been doing this to lots of the girls, for years, and a few of us took him to court. It wasn't easy, but I was proud that I helped protect other girls.

This young woman received prompt, skilled, and sympathetic help, so her original trauma was not compounded by further mistreatment. Unfortunately, many survivors do not have the benefit of such a positive reaction. Instead, they are blamed, ignored, attacked, or called liars.

Defensive reactions are more likely if the security or status of the family is threatened by the disclosure. Parents are more likely to be supportive when the abuser is a stranger, a teacher, a coach, or a minister rather than a relative. When a brother, father, aunt, or grandmother is implicated, families often close ranks and deny the abuse, leaving the survivor outside the family circle.

Defensive responses can be extremely hostile.

You might have been accused of "asking for it" or called "a little whore." If your brother was sent away to a treatment center, if your parents divorced, or if your father was sent to jail, you might have been blamed for breaking up the marriage, separating your family, or ruining a "happy home."

Many children never tell at all. They are silenced while the abuse is still going on. Abusers say things such as, "It would kill your mother if she knew" or "I'll kill you if you tell." Even if the abuser did not overtly threaten you, being overpowered is an implicit threat that your very existence is in danger.

Sometimes telling leads to further abuse. One child confided in her best friend. That girl told her father, who asked for the details. He then took both girls into the garage and did to them all the things he'd just heard about.

If your case was taken to court, you might have been subjected to brutal testimony procedures, grilled by insensitive defense attorneys, or repeatedly forced to face your abuser. Although progress has been made over the years in meeting the special needs of child witnesses, the court process can still be a difficult, and at times traumatic, experience for children.*

Children not slapped with an actively cruel response are often met with devastating silence or told never to speak of it again. Families often go on as if nothing happened. Some-times parents avoid talking about the abuse because they believe it's best for the child. They don't think they should remind the child of her painful experience and want to help her move on. Sometimes they don't know how to bring up the subject or what to say. But never talking about the abuse can give children the message that their experience is too horrible for words—and, by implication, that *they* are too horrible.

In these and myriad other ways, children learn that there is no one they can trust, that sharing leads not to help but to harm or neglect, and that it's not safe to tell the truth. In other words, they learn shame, secrecy, and silence.

TELLING: IT TAKES A LEAP OF FAITH

Telling is transformative. When you let someone know what you have lived through and that person hears you with respect and genuine caring, you begin a process of change essential to healing.

The first person I told about my abuse was my friend, Kate. I told her one day when we were walking home from a movie. There'd been a scene of a rape attempt and it had really upset me. I hadn't planned to say anything, but I was sick and tired of always filtering myself, always thinking before I spoke. I thought, "Hell, why can't I just say whatever I

---

* See "Janel Robinson" on p. 444 for an example of a young survivor who was further traumatized by her experiences in court and in the foster care system.

have to say?" And I told her about my grandfather abusing me.

When I think of it now, it kind of stuns me. How I just blurted it out. And how kind she was. She looked at me with such a simple tenderness and said, "Oh, Jessie. Oh, I'm so sorry." After all those years, it was amazing how much those few kind words meant to me.

Other survivors first share their story in a support group. When you tell your story to a group of other survivors, you no longer feel so different or alone. You know you're under- stood because you've been listening to other survivors' stories and you understand them. You learn that you're important, worthwhile, and lovable because you feel the compassion of the other women as they listen and respond to you. And you experience release because there is relief in the telling:

> When I talked about the incest with my counselor, it stayed almost as big a secret as when I hadn't told anyone. Going to group and speaking to all those people was important. It was a real coming out.

After telling in a group, you may feel as though being a survivor, with all its difficul- ties, is not all bad. The strength, resilience, and courage of survivors are powerful and ad- mirable qualities. As one woman said, "We're a beautiful, courageous bunch of women—and I'm proud to be one."

THERE ARE MANY WAYS TO TELL YOUR STORY

Some abuse happened at a time before you had the language for what was hap- pening or was so traumatic that your brain stored the experience in images and physical sensations rather than in words. As a result, you may have no words with which to capture your ex- perience. You may not be able to relate your story as an uninterrupted narrative with a beginning, middle, and end. In this case, you may find it more effective to tell your story through dance, move- ment, drawing, writing, or other creative forms, where you can communicate using imagery, metaphors, and symbolic language.

TELLING ISN'T ALWAYS EASY

Not everyone feels better after telling. Some- times, even when you get a supportive, com- passionate response, you still feel as if you've done something terribly wrong—that you've broken the rules or that something awful is going to happen. Some survivors feel terri- fied when they finally speak the truth. Others doubt themselves or feel crazy. These reactions can be confusing, particularly when your dis- closure has been met with respect and support.

WHY TELLING IS TRANSFORMATIVE

"The victim who articulates the situation of the victim is no longer a victim; he or she is a threat."
—JAMES BALDWIN

- You move through the guilt and secrecy that keep you isolated.
- You move through denial and acknowledge the truth of your abuse.
- You make it possible to get understanding and help.
- You get more in touch with your feelings.
- You get a chance to see your experience (and yourself) through the compassionate eyes of a supporter.
- You make space in relationships for the kind of intimacy that comes from honesty.
- You establish yourself as a person in the present who is dealing with the abuse in her past.
- You join a courageous community of women who are no longer willing to suffer in silence.
- You help end child sexual abuse by breaking the silence in which it thrives.
- You reclaim your voice.
- You become a model for other survivors.
- You (eventually) feel proud and strong.

It may help to understand that distress after telling can be triggered by past threats and conditioning, rather than by the positive reactions you are receiving in the present. Cassondra recalls:

I first talked about my incest in a 12-step meeting sixteen years ago, yet even today, every time I open my mouth and tell my story, I still have to work to get past my fear that my brother is going to find me and kill me. To a certain extent, every time I tell my story, I have to tell myself, "It's okay. This is my truth and I need to work on it in order to live."*

Catherine was in a therapy group when she first told about her abuse:

I had to get up and talk about what my parents had done to me, and why it was hard for me to grow up in my family. I remember being in the group and crying, and saying, "I can't tell this to you. My parents are going to get me if I say this to you!" It was horrible. People encouraged me to tell my story, and I finally did.

When it was over I went home and laid in my bed, and literally waited to die. I had never told anybody before. I knew my parents would find out that I had told on them, and would get me.

And that's when I decided I was going

---

* You can read more of Cassondra Espinoza's story on p. 492.

to become a person who could talk, instead of being a person who had to keep secrets.[*]

Telling can also be difficult because it makes our childhood experiences more real. When we verbalize the truth that we have carried in silence and hear ourselves say the actual words—"I was abused," "My teacher raped me after school," or "My mother touched my vagina in the bath"—it becomes much harder to deny what happened or to pretend it didn't matter. Once the experience is shared, it exists differently in the world. Even if we just tell one other person, our history and our suffering have moved from the private realm to a public one and we can never minimize them or make them disappear in quite the same way again.

But telling your story, describing the details of what was done to you, can also bring you back into the pain and terror you experienced at the time of the abuse. Rather than feeling relief in sharing your story, you may feel overwhelmed and retraumatized.

If you feel extremely anxious and triggered when you tell your story, it may be wise to back off and focus more on building your support system and developing your skills for self-nurturing and self-care.[†] Or you may want to experiment with other ways to "talk" about your abuse—using art, writing, movement, or imagery. With a less direct approach, you may find the experience of sharing your story less distressing and more manageable.

BUT THEY'LL USE IT AGAINST US

Survivors of groups who have faced racism, discrimination, or oppression face particular challenges in speaking out about their abuse. In some cultures, the silence around sexual violence is so complete that there is no language for abuse. In others, a disclosure of abuse can lead the survivor and her entire extended family to be ostracized from the community they depend on. Many survivors fear that their disclosure to an outsider will reinforce negative stereotypes about their race, religion or ethnic group, and thus they keep the abuse a secret to maintain a united front. Breaking silence about violence in the family can feel like a betrayal of the culture as a whole. (The first-person survivor stories in the section "Courageous Women" include many examples of brave women who have found the courage to speak out in spite of these obstacles.)[‡]

---

[*] For more of Catherine's story see "The Emergency Stage: Catherine's Story" on p. 65, "Truth-Telling: Catherine's Story" on p. 161, and "Working It Out With My Lover" on p. 309.

[†] The chapter "Survival Skills for Healing" on p. 29 includes a wide variety of ways—both internal and external—that you can develop a stable system of support for the healing process.

[‡] See "Cassondra Espinoza" on p. 492, "Soledad" on p. 436, "Kyos Featherdancing" on p. 457, "Sachiko O'Brien" on p. 430, and "Rifat Masoud" on p. 476.

I Can't Betray My People:
Rachel's Story

Rachel Bat Or lives in Oakland, California. She works with abuse survivors, helping them reclaim their strength. Born to Jewish parents who survived the Holocaust, Rachel was abused by all four members of her family—her mother, father, brother, and grandfather. Through the course of her own healing and her work with other survivors, Rachel has seen a reluctance on the part of many Jewish women to break silence, acknowledge that they were abused, and therefore to commit to healing.

Compared to many of our parents' lives of poverty or escape from anti-Semitic countries, whatever happens to us gets played down. As long as we have a roof over our heads, we have clothes and food, then nothing that happens to us can be as bad, because they lived with rats, in incredible poverty, the families often separated in traveling to America. And so, no matter how awful we feel inside of us, we feel we can't say that out loud because our parents had it so much worse.

Then the stereotypes of Jewish women are that we're loud and pushy and that the men are gentle and hardworking. And so we're taught to feel sorry for the men and blame the women. So if the men—our fathers or brothers—are abusing us, there isn't that instantaneous hatred, because they're so exalted in the religious teachings and the culture. So it's very hard for us to hold on to that anger.

And then there's the myth that Jewish men are not alcoholics or batterers. So if our family is different, that can't be admitted.

BREAKING THE SILENCE: ABUSE BY WOMEN

Although the majority of sexual abuse is committed by heterosexual men, women also abuse children. Both girls and boys have been abused by their mothers, aunts, grandmothers, or sisters, as well as by teachers, nuns, coaches, older girls, or babysitters. Like abuse by male perpetrators, women's abuse can be overtly sexual or violent and it can also be subtle and covert. Frequently, abuse by mothers begins when the child is very young, sometimes masked in cuddling or daily caretaking. In some families, the father is also sexually abusive, either separately or in conjunction with the mother, creating a devastating double jeopardy for the child.

Despite this reality, the fact that women sexually abuse continues to be minimized, dismissed, and denied. Women (and especially mothers) are supposed to be nurturing; they should be the protectors, not the abusers. So when survivors of mother-daughter incest (or other abuse by women) tell their stories, they frequently face shock and disbelief. It can be hard for them to get the validation and support they deserve.

This unwillingness to acknowledge women as offenders has slowly started to break down, but many women still find themselves discounted when they share their history:

I find that when I tell my story, a lot of people are uncomfortable. People have all these squirmy reactions. It's almost as if they don't quite believe it. I can't just tell my story—I have to tell my story and then explain it.

People like to think in categories. So when you talk about women as sexual abusers, it blows a lot of myths: Women aren't sexual. Women are gentle. Women are passive. How could a woman do that to a child?

But people need to hear it. They need to hear, "I'm an incest survivor, and it was my mother." Women do abuse, and if it's not put out there, the healing can't happen.

Although abuse by men is much more prevalent, it is essential not to discount the pain and betrayal experienced by survivors abused by women. The gender of the abuser shouldn't add to anyone's isolation or the burden they carry.

THE IMPACT OF MOTHER–DAUGHTER INCEST

Most of the issues explored in this book apply equally to all survivors, but there are some additional problems faced by women abused by their mothers.

Feelings of worthlessness can be heightened for survivors of mother–daughter incest. As human beings, we're biologically and emotionally dependent on our mothers' care. When mothers are abusive, survivors often feel responsible and are particularly hard on themselves:

I was sure I was rotten at my core because not even my mother could love me. Everywhere in nature, mothers protect their young, yet my mother turned on me and used me for her own gratification.

Since small children usually bond most closely with their mothers, abuse by mothers can leave children with a pervasive lack of trust in intimate relationships. When a mother abuses her child, normal, healthy boundaries are violated so severely that it can be impossible for a survivor to distinguish between her own needs and desires and those of her mother:

For a while I didn't know where my mother left off and I began. I thought she had a psychic hold on me. I was convinced she knew every thought I had. It was like she was in my body—that she was evil and I was possessed. I've had a real fear that if I look at the stuff I don't like about myself, it would be my mother inside of me.

Also, when a girl is abused by her mother, her role model for womanhood is someone she doesn't want to emulate. As an adolescent, she may have a hard time maturing, watching her body grow to resemble that of her abuser:

For a long, long time, I didn't call myself a woman. When I left home at eighteen, I continued to call myself a girl because I couldn't stomach the associations with "woman," which meant being sexual. My mother was a woman, but I was a girl. If being a woman meant being like her, that's not what I wanted. It took a long time for me to get rid of that self-hate.

(For more on healing from abuse by mothers, see Anna Stevens's story on p. 424 and "Abuse by Women" on p. 549 of the Resource Guide.)

The next thing is, "What will the neighbors say? We're Jewish." Because we have to protect our religion from being criticized, we ignore whatever happens in our family. If there are any problems, it's the whole religion that gets looked on, not just our family. We know that. It's not some myth.

And then there's the last thing that puts us in a real quandary: There's the us/them dichotomy. If we do tell about whatever happens to us, it's usually to the "them," someone who's not Jewish, who's outside the family, who doesn't respect our family, and so we lose the "us" security. It's hard to go to a "them." And maybe we can muster our courage and do that, but then we lose any of the benefits we do get from being an "us."

THE LEVELS OF TELLING

There are many levels of telling, ranging from the first time you dare broach the subject to when you have told so many times and in so many ways that you can talk about it naturally, as just another part of your life. Each time you tell is a different experience. Telling your therapist or your support group, telling your partner or a new lover, telling a friend, telling publicly, telling in writing will all feel different.

Jude Brister, a coeditor of *I Never Told Anyone*, said that each time she talked about her abuse, she put more distance between herself and the pain. The more she talked about it, the less she identified herself as a victim. She saw herself instead as a strong, capable adult.

Ella, another survivor who has told her experiences many times, describes her process in detail:

For me there were at least three different levels of telling. The first was telling the story and not feeling anything. Telling it as a third-party story. Saying "I" but not really meaning it happened to me. At that point I still didn't really believe it happened. And part of that telling was that I was really angry. It was a way to get back at them. Like "I'm going to tell on you." It's kind of like "I couldn't get anybody mad at you then, but watch this!"

Then there was a really painful, scared level of telling. The tone of my voice changed and I looked like I was seven years old. My language was more simple. And it hurt. That's the place I discovered my feelings. And usually people got sad when they heard it that way. They felt sorry for me. The people I told that way included my therapist, my close friend, people in caretaker positions, paid or unpaid. It included the people in my support group. I told not like a victim, but like a little kid that hurt.

The last way I've told has to do with stepping back and seeing the bigger picture. I looked at family dynamics and got the rest of the story. I saw what happened and why it happened. I put the abuse through a sieve and was able to see parts of it I couldn't see when I was only hurt or angry.

So I went from anger to pain to a fixing. In Hebrew there's a word, *tikun,* that means a fixing, a healing. That way of telling was a *tikun.*

CHOOSING SOMEONE TO TELL

If you are in counseling or a support group where you feel safe, that's an excellent place to begin to talk about your abuse. Telling for the first time can feel scary, and it helps to be in a context where you know someone will listen compassionately.*

Telling your partner, lover, or close friends is also important. You need to let the people around you know why you are sometimes sad, angry, upset, preoccupied, or want to be alone. Your friends need to understand why you may not trust them readily. Your lover needs to know why you may have difficulty with sex, why you cling or withdraw. There is a lot of work involved in building healthy relationships, and you need the people in your life as allies. Although it is not necessary—or even appropriate—to tell every single person you meet, it is important that you share with the people you want to be close to.

I don't run around telling every soul I meet that I'm an incest victim, because

I don't want that to be my definition, but I went through a period of time when it was just about like that. That was the first thing I would tell people, almost anybody. "Did you know I was an incest victim?" "Oh really, thank you for sharing that." It's like any movement, whether it's black power or gay rights, you need time to try that identity on and claim it. I needed to do that, but that need has faded over time. Now I just do what I feel like doing. If I feel like telling someone, I do. If I don't, I don't.

For some women, telling goes even further. They see breaking the silence as a political choice, a necessity. Dorianne Laux, who has run workshops on sexual abuse for teenagers and has given readings of and published her poetry about incest extensively, explains:

So many women still feel they have to hide the fact that they were molested. I can just see it in their bodies, that they're real frightened that somebody might find out. Well, I don't like that. I don't have to be frightened that somebody's going to find out.

I always use my first and last name when I talk about incest. It's a political statement for me. I don't have anything to be ashamed of. I don't have to be anonymous. Even though it could affect my life in some way, it shouldn't. It should affect *his* life.

And the whole idea of the secret is perpetuated when I keep my name out of it. Incest doesn't need to be hidden.

---

* If you don't feel safe enough with your counselor or support group to talk about these issues, read "Working with a Counselor," on p. 45, to determine whether your counselor is a safe person for you to tell and it's just hard for you to trust, or whether you would do well to seek a different counselor.

It needs the exact opposite. People need to come out and say, "My name is so-and-so, this happened to me, and I'm angry about it."

Also, I'm a fairly well-adjusted person, and I make a good role model for the young people I work with. So speaking out and saying who I am is real important to me.*

HOW TO TELL

Talking about your abuse with a skilled counselor or group of survivors needs no planning. They should be able to hear you however you get the words out. But if you are telling friends or family for the first time, it's best to make the circumstances as favorable as possible. (This applies only to telling family members you expect to be supportive. If you're planning to tell people who may find this information upsetting and are likely to react with anger, disbelief, or blame, see "Disclosures and Truth-Telling" on p. 149.)

You can maximize the likelihood of a positive response by choosing wisely. When you're considering talking to someone, ask yourself the following questions:

- Does this person care for and respect me?

- Does this person have my well-being in mind?
- Is this someone I've been able to share my feelings with before?
- Do I trust this person?
- Do I usually feel safe with this person?
- Is this person reasonably comfortable talking about personal issues?

If you can answer yes to all of these questions, you're choosing someone who's likely to be supportive.

Tell your friend (lover, partner, cousin) that there's something personal and vulnerable that you want to share and ask if this is a good time to talk. Suggest that if it isn't, you could make it another time. By asking, you ensure that your friend has time to pay attention. You also give that person a chance to either postpone the talk or prepare to listen.

If there are certain responses that you want or don't want, say so. You may want your cousin to listen but not to give a lot of advice. You may want to be asked questions, or you may want to be listened to silently. You may want to be held or you may not want to be touched at all. Often people want to support you but don't know how (or how to ask). A good friend will welcome your guidance.

If you want what you say to be kept confidential, say so. Although it is important to break silence, do so at your own pace, with people *you* choose.

---

* For more of Dorianne's story, see "I'm Awake Now: Dorianne's Story" on p. 329. Several of Dorianne's poems appear in this book. See "What My Father Told Me" on p. 15, "Two Pictures of My Sister" on p. 19, "Girl Child" on p. 131, and "The Lovers" on p. 330.

WHEN CHILDREN MOLEST

Sometimes children who are sexually abused molest other children.* When children mimic and repeat what was done to them, this is called abuse-reactive behavior.† Sometimes these victims are too young to understand that what they're doing is wrong and can harm the other child.

Most children who act out sexually with children feel enormous guilt and shame. As they grow older and are able to comprehend that they victimized another child, they may be filled with remorse. They may also be afraid of becoming sex offenders themselves.‡ And

___

* For advice on how to respond to normal sexual exploration and play between children, see "Sex Play Between Children" on p. 341.

† Some abuse-reactive children have not been sexually abused, but may have been exposed to pornography, watched graphic sex in movies or on TV, or have accidentally witnessed adults having sex.

‡ Most abuse-reactive children do not go on to become sex offenders, yet without intervention, some do. Today, there are compassionate, effective resources for both juveniles and adults who have sexually abused in the past or are currently abusing but want to stop. If you are acting out sexually with children or feel tempted to, it is essential that you seek help *now* so you

as adults, they often suffer with the burden of their shameful secret long after they have disclosed and worked to heal from their own sexual abuse.

Acknowledging that you have acted out sexually with other children can be difficult and painful, but it is essential to your healing. Although abusing another child is a serious and damaging act, you were a child acting out the consequences of your own abuse or sexual overstimulation.

It's unreasonable to expect children to be able to understand the impact of their actions. If there are ways in which you can be accountable now, it's important to do what you can. Beyond that, your work is to understand that your behavior was also a result of the abuse you suffered, to develop compassion for the child you were, and to work toward forgiving yourself.

___

can deal with these impulses and stop hurting children. Support is available that will not judge or shame you. Look for a therapist who is experienced working with perpetrators and does so compassionately. There are opportunities for your own healing and recovery. Take advantage of them now. See "Stop It Now!" on p. 528; "The Safer Society Foundation, Inc." on p. 527; and "Generation Five" on p. 528 for resources and referrals. For books, see "When Children Molest" on p. 578 of the Resource Guide.

FINDING ALLIES

Listening to the truth of someone's life is a privilege and an honor. When you tell someone your history, he or she should receive it as such. But because this is not always the case, you need to be prepared for possible negative responses.

Some people may be threatened. Others may go blank or be shocked. If any of the people you tell were abused themselves, all their defenses may ring in alarm. Some may be horrified or not believe you initially. Some may be incredibly crass or insensitive. One woman waited until after she had had three children to finally tell her husband about the incest. His response: "You mean I wasn't the first one?"

Other people have been titillated by the stories of survivors and have asked for "details." In a society where the sexual abuse of children has been eroticized, this is not surprising.

Although you may occasionally encounter a hostile, insensitive, or insulting response, it is still important to tell. There is a weeding out that goes on in relationships when you start to share who you really are and how you genuinely feel. You may find that some relationships cannot stand up to this challenge, and you will grieve for them, along with your other losses. Or you may choose to continue the relationship on a more superficial level rather than abandoning it altogether.

Although it is likely that you will get some unsatisfying responses, it is also likely that you will get some supportive, sympathetic ones, as Laura described:

> When I first remembered my abuse, I was overwhelmed. I stopped calling my friends and when they called me, I was distant and preoccupied. Karen, my closest friend, was hurt and angry. She was about to write me off totally. Finally, I told her about the abuse. Once she knew what was going on, she was wonderful. She became my most devoted supporter.

It is important that you have some relationships in which you can be your whole self—with your history, your pain, your grief, and your anger—and the only way to create those is to share honestly about yourself. When you are met in that honesty, then you feel real intimacy.

Remember, although you may not get a positive response when you first tell someone about being sexually abused, very often people will become supportive over time. Don't assume that someone's first reaction is a permanent attitude. It's common for people to need some time to assimilate difficult information, so you may want to keep the door open to further dialogue.

WHEN TELLING FEELS LIKE A MISTAKE

Sometimes when you tell someone that you were sexually abused, the other person's reaction makes you wish you hadn't shared the information. The encounter may leave you feeling confused, disappointed, shocked, devastated, or abandoned. You may be flooded with shame, frustration, rage, or a combination of disturbing emotions. You may play the scene over and over in your mind, wondering what you might have said or done differently.

In the aftermath of a difficult, disappointing experience like this, it's useful to take stock and see what you can learn for the future. Rather than blaming yourself, this is an opportunity to become more aware. Ask yourself:

- What motivated me to tell this person?
- Did I do my best to assess the relationship beforehand?
- Might I have gotten a better response if I'd told earlier in the relationship

or after I'd gotten to know the person better first?

- Did I choose a time that was conducive for deep conversation?
- Were there red flags that I was ignoring?
- Was there a point where I should have stopped the conversation but instead I continued, hoping things would improve?
- What can I learn from this experience?

There's an old saying that wisdom comes from experience and experience comes from making mistakes. So be gentle with yourself. This is how we all learn.

Ultimately, though, even if you choose carefully, on the basis of your best knowledge and instincts, no one's response is ever completely predictable. Taking stock of what you might have done differently can teach you valuable lessons, but it's equally important not to take responsibility for someone else's reactions. If the person you confided in didn't listen well or respond respectfully, that's the other person's shortcoming, not yours.

WRITING EXERCISE: THE FIRST SILENCE YOU BREAK IS TO YOURSELF

(See the basic method for writing exercises on p. *xxix*.)

Many women have found it very difficult to tell people that they were sexually abused. When they do tell, it is often in very generalized terms: "I was molested by my brother"; "I was raped when I was ten." Rarely do they share the details, partly because it's hard to tell even the general facts and partly because they want to spare the listeners. They don't want to impose.

But the tight statement "My stepfather abused me" is not the way you live with the abuse or experience flashbacks. That's not indicative of the creepy feelings you get when something triggers your memory. What you remember are the details: the way the light fell on the stairway, the pajamas you were wearing, the smell of liquor on his breath, the feel of the gravel between your shoulder blades when you were thrown down, the terrifying chuckle, the sound of the TV downstairs.

Write about your experience of being sexually abused as a child. When you write, include as many sensory details as you can—what you actually saw, heard, smelled, tasted, felt.

If your abuse covers too much time and too many abusers to write it all in half an hour, just write what you can. Don't worry about which experience to start with. Begin with what feels most accessible or what you feel you most need to deal with. This is an exercise you can do over and over again.

If you don't remember a lot of the details of what happened to you, write about what you do remember. Re-create the context in which the abuse happened, even if you don't remember the specifics of the abuse. Describe where you lived as a child. What was going on in your family, in your neighborhood, in your life? Some women think they don't remember, when actually they remember quite a lot. But since the picture isn't in sequence and isn't totally filled in, they don't feel they have permission to call what they know "remembering." Start with what you have. When you use that fully, you may find that you get more.

If there's something you feel that you absolutely can't write, then at least write that there's something you can't or won't write. That way you leave a marker for yourself; you acknowledge that there's a difficult place.

If you go off on tangents, don't pull yourself back too abruptly. Sometimes what may look irrelevant leads us to something more essential. Although you want to stay with the subject, do so with loose reins.

There is no one right way to do this exercise. Your writing may be linear, telling your story in chronological order. It may be a wash of feelings and sensations. Or it may be like a patchwork, piecing together scattered bits and pieces. As with all the writing exercises, try not to judge or censor. Don't feel that you should conform to any standard, and don't compare your writing with others. This is an opportunity to uncover and heal, not to perform or to meet anyone's expectations—not even your own.

I Give Thanks for the Sky

BY TERESA STRONG

Teresa Strong's poetic response to "The First Silence You Break is to Yourself" is vivid and deeply moving. We hope it inspires you to tell your own story.

It's morning twilight, gray world, dreamworld, non-world time. I'm asleep, or at least I think I am. I'm dreaming, or maybe I'm crazy like my grandmother. I'm sleeping in the back room and hear my grandfather (and know he's *not* really my grandfather) coming in. He sits down beside the bed I used to sleep in—the one my niece sleeps in now. (Get her *OUT* of the fucking bed. It should be burned and chopped and destroyed. No one should sleep in that bed.)

He sits down beside the bed and starts easing me from sleep by rubbing his hand over me on top of the covers (the whole world is asleep), and under the covers and under my nightgown and over and all around me. And his touch is soft and he strokes and I don't know what is going on but it feels like a charge, like Life going through me. And it feels good to be touched and sometimes I pretend to be asleep and sometimes I am asleep and he just keeps touching and stroking and gliding and then somewhere in the tingling and feeling like Life going through me flashes *DANGER! DANGER! DANGER! STOP!* And that's when he starts moving faster and he's not stroking or touching anymore. He's grabbing and rubbing and holding me down and leaning over me.

And all I see are cold steel balls where his eyes used to be. And he's over me and all I can see from the corner of my eye is the sky and a leaf. I hold on to them.

That's the sky. I know that's sky. That's a piece of the sky, and that's a leaf. I know that's a leaf. And I'm clinging to the sky with my eye and he's whispering in my ear. "Oh Honey, see how much you like this and the best is yet to come."

I hear his zipper unzip. My body is jerking and writhing under him. *I* say it's because I'm trying to get away and he's almost giggling (these are the only times I see him smile big smiles), telling me how much I love this. His touch isn't a human touch anymore. He just presses and grabs. And then his penis is in front of my face and I know I'm either dreaming, crazy, or about to die, and my only hope is to hold on to the sky. And I do.

That's the sky and that's a leaf and he shoves his penis in my mouth. I die looking at the sky and he pushes and shoves and it feels like the roof of my mouth has to split open soon. And it feels like he's all the way down my throat. I can't breathe! I can't breathe! I need to throw up! *WHERE* is the sky? *WHERE* is the leaf? I can't see anything. I'm going to be sick. I want to *DIE*. I leave my body. I hide in my forehead and then in the sky. My throat is burning. He comes half in my throat, half in my face. I gasp for breath. He holds my jaw shut and I lose sight of the sky. I *HAVE* to see the sky—it's my only hope of getting out of here alive.

Sometimes he wipes my face clean and sometimes he forces me to eat it. Sometimes he grins and sometimes he strokes me for a long time. Sometimes I completely lose sight of the sky and pass out. And when I wake up to the sounds of breakfast being prepared, the world is ordinary and fine.

As time goes on he doesn't bother to stroke or hold or touch me. I'm not even there. But each time before he leaves, he leans down, his nose brushing against my ear, and whispers, "Just remember, Honey, nothing happened." And being eager to please, I remember perfectly.

Once I ask my mother to let me sleep in a different room and she refuses because I'm now four and a big girl. My grandfather's story changes. Sometimes he tells me that if I tell, everyone will know I'm crazy and I'll be sent away. But, unlike my grandmother, he'll make sure I never come back. He also tells me that because I like this so much (and here he'll stroke me again like he hasn't for a long time and I do like the touch), if anyone finds out I'll really be in trouble because only whores/bad girls/crazy people like being touched like this. And besides, he tells me, we come to his home every year on my father's vacation.

So when early morning comes I pretend to be asleep as long as I can until he shakes me awake. And when I can't do that I look for the sky. And I keep the secrets that I like being touched and that I'm crazy. I fool people by getting good grades so no one knows I'm crazy. And I don't let anyone touch me, so they don't know I like it. And I hold on to the sky.

FACING RITUALIZED ABUSE

Ritualized abuse is severe physical, sexual, and psychological abuse involving the use of rituals and carried out by members of a group. The abuse is premeditated and may include sadistic torture, illusion, mind control, and the use of drugs, as well as sexual abuse. Because the ritual elements are so extreme, ritualized abuse can seem unbelievable, even to its victims.

It is understandable that as a society and as individuals, we are reluctant to face such atrocities, but our inability to believe is what leaves victims vulnerable and survivors bereft of compassion—or even acknowledgment.

Elie Wiesel, renowned author and survivor of the Holocaust, was interviewed by Oprah Winfrey. In response to her exclamation of how "unbelievable" his experiences were, Wiesel responded, "The enemy counted on the disbelief of the world."*

Although stories of ritualized abuse are horrifying in their cruelty, they are not implausible considering the documented crimes we hear about every day. In the newspaper we read of babies abused so severely that they have died, children murdered by their parents, children used in the production of pornography or forced into prostitution or sexual slavery. We read of hate crimes that include both torture and murder committed by groups of otherwise ordinary people. Though it is staggering to recognize what human beings are capable of, it is important that we not turn away from survivors of ritualized abuse.

This does not mean that every detail of a survivor's account of being abused in a ritualized way is accurate. One survivor, for example, told her therapist that while she was being abused, a woman was killed. Her therapist had no way of knowing what literally took place, but she knew this survivor was telling her story as best she could. As this woman was able to face more of her history, she recovered enough information to determine that while she was being abused, her perpetrators had shown a snuff film in which a woman was indeed murdered. In her child's mind—in this ordeal of extreme pain and terror—the images on the screen seemed to be happening in the room.

Alterations like this are due, in part, to the nature of memory, especially in situations of extreme terror.† But the perpetrators may also deliberately create such distortions. Illusion may be used in ritualized abuse to terrify, silence, or otherwise control the victim, as well as to lessen a survivor's credibility should she seek help. For example, one survivor reported that she had been told she was going to be operated on and a bomb would be put in her stomach. She was threatened that if she ever told anyone about what had been done to her, the bomb would go off, killing her. They told her that if she even thought about telling, she'd feel sick to her stomach, nauseous. Then she was drugged, superficially cut, and when she woke up, she saw blood and believed she had been operated on.

Such tactics, used by perpetrators, make some degree of distortion almost inevitable. However, this does not lessen the ordeal of the survivor, the essential truth of her disclosure, or the heinousness of the abuse.

None of us wants to believe such shocking stories, but we must struggle with our disbelief in order to offer needed support. There are some

---

* *Oprah*, July 16, 1993.

† For more about distortion and traumatic memory, see "What We Know About Memory and Traumatic Amnesia" on p. 74 and "The Essential Truth of Memory" on p. 85.

adult survivors of ritualized abuse who bear the long-term damage in their bodies—so much so that doctors who treat them now are at first stymied and then appalled by the residual damage. And of course the emotional, mental, and spiritual devastation is profound.[*]

It is painful—devastating—to face this reality. But unless we face it, we allow it to continue. The Talmud asks: "To look away from evil: Is this not the sin of all good people?"

[*] See Sheila O'Connell's story on p. 510.

Bearing Witness
BY ELLEN BASS

For Jacki Phoenix

> If you have lived it, then
> it seems I must hear it.
> —HOLLY NEAR

When the long-fingered leaves of the sycamore
flutter in the wind, spiky
seed balls swinging, and a child throws his aqua
lunch bag over the school yard railing, the last thing,
the very last thing you want to think about
is what happens to children when they're crushed
like grain in the worn mortar of the cruel.
We weep at tragedy, a baby sailing
through the windshield like a cabbage, a shoe.
The young remnants of war, arms sheared and eyeless,
they lie like eggs on the rescue center's bare floor.
But we draw a line at the sadistic,
as if our yellow plastic tape would keep harm
confined. We don't want to know
what generations of terror do to the young
who are fed like cloth
under the machine's relentless needle.
In the paper, we'll read about the ordinary neighbor
who chopped up boys; at the movies we pay
to shoot up that adrenaline rush—
and the spent aftermath, relief
like a long-awaited piss.

But face to face with the living prey,
we turn away, rev the motor, as though
we've seen a ghost—which, in a way, we have:
one who wanders the world,
tugging on sleeves, trying to find the road home.
And if we stop, all our fears
will come to pass. The knowledge of evil
will coat us like grease
from a long shift at the griddle. Our sweat
will smell like the sweat of the victims.
And this is why you do it—listen
at the outskirts of what our species
has accomplished, listen until the world is flat
again, and you are standing on its edge.
This is why you hold them in your arms, allowing
their snot to smear your skin, their sour
breath to mist your face. You listen
to slash the membrane that divides us, to plant
the hard shiny seed of yourself
in the common earth. You crank
open the rusty hinge of your heart
like an old beach umbrella. Because God
is not a flash of diamond light. God is
the kicked child, the child
who rocks alone in the basement,
the one fucked so many times
she does not know her name, her mind
burning like a star.

Ellen Bass, *Mules of Love* (Rochester, NY: BOA Editions, 2002).

Understanding That It Wasn't Your Fault

"I know I was only five years old, but I was an extremely intelligent five-year-old. I should have been able to figure out a way to escape."

Children often believe that they are to blame for being sexually abused. Many adult survivors continue to hold this belief. Although large numbers of children and adolescents are abused, it is never the fault of any of them. Yet there are many reasons why survivors assume that blame.

Some survivors were told explicitly that it was their fault. Your father said, "You're a bad, nasty, dirty girl. That's why I'm doing this." Your brother told you, "You really want this to happen. I know you do." Your teacher said, "You're such a sexy little girl. I just can't help myself."

You might have been punished when someone did find out. If you said anything, you might have been told that you made up horrible lies. Or the subject was never discussed, giving you the message that it was too terrible to talk about.

Your religion might have told you that you were a sinner, unclean, damned to hell. You might have become convinced you were unlovable, even to God. One woman said: "That little incested girl inside of me is still waiting for the lightning to strike because I told people what happened to me. If I say, 'I think it was my dad,' I'll burn up in hellfire."

One small child was even begged by her abuser to stop him. He kept telling her how wrong it was and that she must not let him do it ever again—and then he'd force her once more:

I felt I was really evil. It's almost like those child-devil movies, like Damian. Inside this innocent little child is this evil seed. I used to think that just my presence made people feel bad and made bad things happen. I used to think that if only I did something, then everything would change. If only I got straight A's, then my dad would stop touching me. I felt I could control things by my behavior. No one around me seemed to be controlling anything. I still have this really warped sense of what I can do with my presence or my actions.

There are also less obvious reasons why survivors blame themselves. It is a stark and terrifying realization for a child to see how vulnerable and powerless she actually is. Thinking that you were bad, that you had some influence on how you were treated, gave a sense of control, though illusory. And perceiving yourself as bad allowed for the future possibility that you could become good and thus, things could improve.

In truth, nothing you did caused the abuse; nothing within your power could have stopped it. Your world was an unsafe place where the adults who abused you were untrustworthy and out of control, where your well-being, and sometimes your very life, was in danger. This perspective, though realistic, is more distressing for many children than thinking that they were bad and somehow responsible for the abuse.

Children need to believe in the goodness of their primary caregivers. Even if your parents were negligent, drunk, violent, or sexually abusive, as a dependent child, you still needed to see them in the best possible light. It was easier to blame yourself than to face the stark reality that they were not the safe, reliable people you wanted and needed them to be.

Recognizing that you were not to blame means accepting the fact that the person who abused you—someone you might have loved and trusted—didn't have your best interests at heart. In one workshop, a woman blamed herself because at the age of twelve she said no, and her father stopped. "Why couldn't I have done that right away, at four, when he started?" she chastised herself. "I *did* have the power to stop him."

Another woman answered her: "I said no and my father never stopped. I fought and kicked and screamed no. But abusers don't stop because you say no. They stop when they're ready to stop. By the time you were twelve your father was ready to stop. Maybe he only liked small children. You had less control than you think."

Women blame themselves because they took money, gifts, or special privileges. But if you were able to get some small thing back, you should instead give yourself credit. At ten, one woman was given a bicycle by her abuser. At the time, she felt confused and guilty about accepting this gift from him, but she'd wanted the bike for a very long time. On it, she was able to ride away from her house, out to the woods, and there feel the safety of the trees. As an adult looking back, this woman blamed herself for having taken the bicycle. Instead, she should be commended for taking what she could get in that wasteland.

Bubba Esther, 1888
BY RUTH WHITMAN

She was still upset,
she wanted to tell me,
she kept remembering
his terrible hands:

how she came, a young girl
of seventeen, a freckled
fairskinned Jew from Kovno
to Hamburg with her uncle
and stayed in an old house
and waited while he bought
the steamship tickets
so they could sail to America

and how he came into her room
sat down on the bed, touched
her waist, took her by the
breast, said for a kiss
she could have her ticket,
her skirts were rumpled, her
petticoat torn, his teeth were
broken, his breath full of
onions, she was ashamed

still ashamed, lying
eighty years later
in the hospital bed,
trying to tell me,
trembling, weeping with anger

Ruth Whitman, *Permanent Address: New Poems 1973–1980* (Farmington, ME: Alice James Books, 1980).

BUT I WANTED TO BE CLOSE

Many survivors hold particularly shameful feelings if they needed attention and affection and did not fight off sexual advances because of those needs, or if they sought out that affection. The closeness may have felt good to you. You may have adored your abuser. You may have loved feeling like Grandpa's special little girl. Women say, "I'm the one who asked for a back rub," or "I kept going back," or "I climbed into bed with her."

But you were not wrong. Every child needs attention. Every child needs affection. If these are not offered in healthy, nonsexual ways, children will take them in whatever ways they can, because they are essential needs.

BUT IT FELT GOOD

Although some women felt only pain or numbness when they were abused, others experienced sensual or sexual pleasure, arousal, and orgasm. Even though your experience of abuse might have been confusing, frightening, or devastating, you might also have experienced some degree of pleasurable feelings. For many, this aspect of the abuse is one of the most difficult to deal with:

Some of it felt good, and ugh! It's still hard for me to talk about it. When I think back on some of the times I was close to my mother in a sexual way, where I was getting turned on, there's a lot of shame there. It feels real yucko! It feels really embarrassing.

Another woman was gang-raped as a teenager and had an orgasm. "For a long time I thought it was a cruel joke that God had made my body that way. I forgot what had happened because of the shame of having liked it." When she first remembered the rape, this woman spent a night frantically skimming *Voices in the Night* from cover to cover to see if anyone else had had an orgasm while being abused.* She urgently needed to know that she wasn't the only one.

It is important to recognize that it is natural to have sexual feelings, and that even if you had sexual responses to the abuse and those sensations felt good, it still doesn't mean that you were responsible in any way.

Our bodies are created to respond to stimulation. When we are touched sexually, our whole physiology is designed to give us pleasure. These are natural bodily reactions over which we do not have control. When we eat a sandwich, our stomachs digest the sandwich. We can't stop our stomachs from digesting the sandwich. In a similar way, when we're stimulated sexually, we can't always stop our bodies from responding.

The girl or woman who is sexually abused and experiences orgasm does not want to be abused. The fact that she responds sexually is not a statement that sexual pleasure is bad. And—very important—it is not a betrayal of

---

* Toni McNaron and Yarrow Morgan, eds., *Voices in the Night: Women Speaking About Incest* (San Francisco: Cleis, 1982).

her body. Her body did what bodies are supposed to do. You were betrayed not by your body but by the adults who abused you. For Saphyre, it's taken a lot of self-love to overcome the shame:

I had to realize I didn't get off because I liked it but because I have a female body that is made to experience passion. My body responded to touch. That was all. And they had no right to mess with that. That anger helped me get over the shame.

BUT I WAS OLDER

Whether you were a small child or a teenager at the time of the abuse, you deserved to be treated with respect by your parents and other adults in your life. *Abuse is abuse no matter how old you were when it happened.* Yet many survivors who were abused when they were older have a difficult time accepting that it wasn't their fault. As one woman explained:

I was fifteen and I'd already been having sex with my boyfriend. It's not like I was a little kid. I knew exactly what my uncle was doing. That first time, he even told me that he hadn't wanted to approach me while I was still a virgin. But now that I was having sex, he said there'd be no harm in us "having a little fun." I was disgusted. And I knew better. Why did I let it happen?

There are many reasons a teen or young adult may not be able to stop sexual abuse. The abuser might have terrorized you all your life with threats, beatings, or violent rages and as a result, you were too frightened to try to resist. The abuser might have overpowered you physically. Or he might have tricked or manipulated you with his superior command of language. Or you might have grown up in a culture in which older people are revered, honored, and never questioned. Saying no was simply not something you could have done.

If the abuser was someone you loved very much, a father who worked hard to take care of you, taught you to throw a baseball, and read you bedtime stories, you might have been so shocked, confused, and distressed when he came to your bed that you froze or didn't say anything. And if the abuser cried or told you his troubles, you might have been afraid of hurting his feelings or believed that it was your duty to take care of him.

Teenagers and young adults do not have the same power and perspective as older people. Nor do they have years of experience that might help them confront such a devastating situation. And even if you had put up a fight, there's no guarantee that your resistance would have changed anything.

NO MATTER WHAT, THE ADULT IS ALWAYS TO BLAME

It is unfair to expect children to be able to protect themselves. Children do a lot of testing. They test limits. They test attitudes. This is their job. They develop a sense of what the world is all about through this testing. And it is *always* the responsibility of adults to behave with respect toward children.

Even if a sixteen-year-old girl walks into her living room naked and throws herself on her father, he is still not justified in touching her sexually. A responsible father would say, "There seems to be a problem here." He would tell her to put clothes on; he'd discuss it with her, get professional help if necessary. Regardless of age or circumstance, there is never an excuse for sexual abuse. It is absolutely the responsibility of adults not to be sexual with children.

IF THE ABUSE CONTINUED INTO ADULTHOOD

In some cases, the abuse began when you were young and continued into adulthood. Yet even in this situation, you are not to blame. When children are abused, their capacity to say no and set limits is severely damaged. There is no magic age when you suddenly become a responsible, cooperative partner in sexual abuse. Even if your father is still having sex with you when you are thirty, it is not your fault. You may be an adult in age, but you are still responding from the perspective of a small, powerless child.

Mary spent her childhood being regularly abused by her stepfather and brothers. When she was twenty-one she went on a weekend trip with her twenty-two-year-old brother and some of his friends. The two were asked to share a room. "I spent the night sleeping on the bathroom floor, because my brother would not leave me alone. He begged to make love with

I Was Abused by My Younger Brother: Meera's Story

Survivors who were abused by other children often have a particularly difficult time believing that their abuse mattered. Yet when the offender is another child, the impact can be just as painful, terrifying, and severe as abuse by an adult. And sometimes even a younger child can abuse an older child. Power, not age, is the critical factor. In this story, Meera's brother, though two years younger, was the oldest born son in a South Asian family, and as such was endowed with an authority that allowed him to overpower his sister.

I was born in New Orleans. My father was a Sikh from India; my mother was Scottish and Cajun, from the South. I was the oldest child and had a brother two years younger. In both Indian and Southern culture, the oldest-born son is dominant. Decisions about my brother's education and life were always primary and mine were secondary. I always put my brother's needs first. That was the message in my family. My brother was treated like a god. That gave him the license to emotionally and physically abuse me, and later to sexually abuse me.

The abuse started when I was seven and my brother was five. It stopped when I was eleven. He would lie on top of me and start humping me. He'd hold me down, pull down my underwear, and try to put his penis inside of me.

For years, I doubted myself. I'd say, Was that a real experience? Can I trust myself? Can I really have a perpetrator who was two years younger? I went through mental somersaults around it. I'd ask myself, How much did he weigh? Was he really stronger than me? Why didn't I push him off of me? Why did I just lay here?

One therapist I went to reinforced my doubts. She dismissed what had happened: "It was just child's play. All children do that." That's when I thought, "Maybe it wasn't really abuse. Maybe I enjoyed it. Maybe I was a participant and not a victim."

At one point, I found an old Super 8 movie of my brother forcing his tongue in my mouth. He did it for a long time and the person taking the movie didn't intervene; they just kept taking the movie. Seeing it, I felt a huge sense of relief—and a huge sense of disgust. It gave me proof that my memories were real.

A couple of years later, I went to a different therapist who validated my experience. She helped me answer the question "How does someone two years younger abuse you?" by explaining who I was as a cultural being. She talked about how much power the men in my family had. She talked about the racism coming toward our family and my father's violence toward my mother. She put everything in context and helped me see that there were cultural patterns that allowed child sexual abuse to happen.

That's when it finally clicked for me. My brother had power in the family way beyond his years and I had been taught to submit and be passive. It had nothing to do with size. It had to do with who could say yes and who could say no in our family. It wouldn't have mattered if my brother were four years younger than me. I still couldn't have said no to him.

* For more of Meera's story, see "Staying Connected to My Family: Meera's Story" on p. 360 and "My Faith Has Given Me Strength: Meera's Story" on p. 183.

me. He kept grabbing at me. Finally I locked myself in the bathroom."

For a long time, Mary felt guilty about what had happened. He was her brother. He was only a year older than she was. She was an adult and should have known better. She should never have agreed to go on the trip in the first place. It was all her fault.

It wasn't until Mary went to therapy that she began to accept the real facts of the matter. "What happened when I was twenty-one was exactly the same thing as being eight years old and having to take a bath with my father."

If your boundaries have always been violated, then it is unfair to expect yourself to be able to set them all of a sudden. You don't become assertive and powerful just because you grow up and leave home. No matter what age you are, no matter what relationship you have with the abuser, if someone with more power is pressuring you into a sexual relationship, you are being abused.

If you are still in an abusive situation, it is essential that you get the support you need to protect yourself, set boundaries, and say no to further violation. You have the right to relationships that honor you as a human being, where you feel seen, respected, and acknowledged. It is an important part of your healing to end relationships that abuse you in any way.

OVERCOMING SHAME

A key sign of healing is that your shame becomes less. Instead of looking at somebody's watch while you tell them what happened, you can look at their face. And then eventually you can look in their eyes and tell them, without feeling they can see what a creep you are. You can just look at someone, tell them, and say, "And I'm okay," without having to ask, "Right? I am okay, aren't I?"

There are many ways to overcome shame. The most powerful is simply talking about your abuse. Shame exists in an environment of secrecy. When you begin to freely speak the truth about your life, your sense of shame will diminish.

> You know how they say, "Speak the truth and the truth shall set you free." Well that's how it really is. I'm not in a cage anymore. I have no bars. The best part is there are no more secrets. And it's the secrets that kill you. It's not the poison and the hate that kill you; it's keeping secrets. Because you live in fear that someone will find out. Secrets destroy people, and they destroy them unnecessarily. It's like being reborn when you shed the secret, because you have no more fear.

JOIN A SURVIVORS' GROUP

Being in a group with other survivors is a powerful way to vanquish shame. When you hear other women talk about their abuse and can see their strength and beauty, and when you see those same women listen to your story with respect, you begin to view yourself as a proud survivor rather than as a conspiring victim. As one woman said, "When your counselor says, 'It wasn't your fault,' that's one thing. But when you have eight people saying it to you, it's a lot more powerful."

SPEAK OUT IN PUBLIC

Speaking publicly—doing outreach to other survivors, working on child assault or rape-prevention programs—is a potent way to transform shame into a feeling of personal effectiveness and power.* For Jennierose, who'd been a prostitute and a thief in her twenties, speaking out was a way to let go of shame, once and for all:

> After I'd been working with the incest for a while, I felt the need to help other people. I did it by going out talking to kids in school, and talking to professional training groups. One of the training programs I did was for police officers. All these years, I'd been sure that people still thought that I was a prostitute. And that was twenty years ago! I stood up before all those cops and I said, "I'm not a thief. And I'm not a prostitute." It was one of the most rewarding moments of my whole life. I faced the enemy.

LOOK TO THE CHILDREN

Spending time with children can provide you with convincing evidence that the abuse wasn't your fault. Children help you remember how small and powerless you actually were. One mother said:

Watching my daughter grow up gave me a sense of "How could anyone do that to a kid?" that I couldn't get just in relation to myself. I had been able to rationalize the mistreatment of kids for a long time. But when I saw how little power she had, how small she was when I put her to bed, I got a real picture of how small and vulnerable *I* had been. I got it in my heart that abuse was not okay. And that I had not been responsible for what had happened to me. I started to forgive myself.

At the workshops she does for teenagers on child sexual abuse, this woman passes around a picture of herself at the age of three. "I tell them, 'This is the child that my father was having sex with, the one with the rubber pants and the little lace-up shoes.' I always show that picture to let the kids know it wasn't my fault."

Even if you don't have children of your own, you can still find opportunities to observe children. The next time you're near a schoolyard, a mall, or a place where kids hang out, look around for kids who are the age you were when your abuse began. Watch the way they interact. Listen to the pitch of their voices. Look at their actual size. Do you honestly think one of those children deserves to be abused?

If you still believe that the abuse was your fault, you have lost touch with the simplicity of a child's longing to share love. One woman told the following story:

> When my daughter was about six, we were riding in the car on our way to visit friends and she told me she wanted to

---

* Many of the women who contributed their stories to *The Courage to Heal* have been involved in activism as an outgrowth of their healing. For two examples, see "Rifat Masoud" on p. 476 and "Sachiko O'Brien" on p. 430.

be my lover. I knew her concept of lover was somewhat fuzzy, but she had enough idea to feel she wanted that. I responded gently that it wasn't possible. She quickly added, "I know I'm too small, but when I'm grown up."

"No," I explained. "Even when you grow up, I'll still be your Mom and you'll still be my daughter. We have a special relationship that will never change. We can never be lovers, but we will always love each other in our own special way."

"Yes," she assented, "that will never change." Then, as we got out of the car she turned to me. "Mom, don't say anything to them about what we talked about, okay?"

I took her hand as we walked to the house. "Of course not."

This is the innocent love that abusers exploit.

The Minks

BY TOI DERRICOTTE

In the backyard of our house on Norwood,
there were five hundred steel cages lined up,
each with a wooden box
roofed with tar paper;
inside, two stories, with straw
for a bed. Sometimes the minks would pace
back and forth wildly, looking for a way out;
or else they'd hide in their wooden houses,
    even when
we'd put the offering of raw horse meat on
    their trays, as if
they knew they were beautiful
and wanted to deprive us.
In spring the placid kits
drank with glazed eyes.
Sometimes the mothers would go mad
and snap their necks.
My uncle would lift the roof like a god
who might lift our roof, look down on us
and take us out to safety.
Sometimes one would escape.
He would go down on his hands and knees,
aiming a flashlight like
a bullet of light, hoping to catch
the orange gold of its eyes.
He wore huge boots, gloves
so thick their little teeth couldn't bite
    through.
"They're wild," he'd say. "Never trust them."
Each afternoon when I put the scoop of raw
    meat rich
with eggs and vitamins on their trays,
I'd call to each a greeting.
Their small thin faces would follow as if
    slightly curious.
In fall they went out in a van, returning
sorted, matched, their skins hanging down
    on huge metal
hangers, pinned by their mouths.
My uncle would take them out when
    company came
and drape them over his arm—the sweetest
    cargo.
He'd blow down the pelts softly
and the hairs would part for his breath
and show the shining underlife which, like
the shining of the soul, gives us each
character and beauty.

Toi Derricotte, *Captivity* (Pittsburgh: University of Pittsburgh Press, 1989).

The Child Within

"When I first heard people talk about forgiving the child within, I raised my left eyebrow and thought, 'California.' There was no little girl inside of me. And if there was one, she was too weak and helpless for me to want to know her. She was the one who'd gotten me into this. She was a troublemaker and I wanted nothing to do with her."

Healing from sexual abuse requires that we find compassion for the vulnerable child inside each of us who was hurt, betrayed, and abandoned. When we talk about "the child within," we are talking about forming a loving, respectful relationship with the person you once were: as a baby, as a toddler, as a school child, as a teenager. Developing empathy for these inner children is an essential part of healing.*

---

* For survivors with dissociative identity disorder (formerly called multiple personality disorder), the idea of the "child within" or "children within" is much more complex than what we discuss here. Survivors who have dissociated as a way to survive the abuse may have child parts that have split off into separate selves, alternate personalities each holding different attributes and pieces of their history. Working with these child alters is a much more complex process that requires the support of a skilled therapist.

Many survivors struggle with the child within. Too often, women blame her, resent her, or ignore her completely. Survivors sometimes hate themselves for having been small, for having needed affection, for having "let themselves be abused."

You may feel split, caught in a real schism. There is the "you" that's out in the "real" world, and then there's the child inside you who is still a frightened victim: "I felt like all my successes had been one big fake, because I ignored the little child who never got over it, and who lives her life in humiliation and pain because of it." This survivor saw herself as a

---

For more about this, see "Dissociative Identity Disorder" on p. 17.

successful career woman, carrying a briefcase and walking out the door to work. Beside her she pictured a little child whining over and over, "You can't go to work! You have to stay home and take care of me."

For a long time the briefcase-carrying woman could respond in only one way: "I can't stand being around you. I hate your guts, and I don't want to sit and look at your sad little face all day!"

Yet as long as you ignore that child's frozen pain, you won't feel whole:

Coming to terms with the little girl was really hard. I had to see all along that I'd had the enemy in the wrong place. And when I started to see what she had to deal with, and how well she did, I began to see how amazing it was that she survived. It took me a long time to accept and love her, but I finally was able to start cutting her some slack.

I WAS ONLY A CHILD

If you find it difficult to accept or identify with the child within, there are good reasons you feel that way. Your survival depended on covering up her vulnerability. Even acknowledging the fact that you once *were* a child can be threatening. It means remembering a time when you did not have the power to protect yourself. It means remembering your shame, vulnerability, and pain.

One woman had a terrible time accepting the fact that the incest was something that had happened to *her*. Even after years of therapy, she, like many survivors, couldn't remember being a child at all. It wasn't until her therapist asked her to bring in pictures of herself at various ages that she began to realize that *she* was the same person as that child who'd been molested. "See," her therapist would say, pointing to the photos, "*this is you*. This is something that happened to you. Do you see that this child is only *this* tall? Can you see that this child is you?"

Survivors who are mothers often say that it was their children's vulnerability that finally enabled them to have compassion for the child they once were. Laura's reconnection to the inner child came about in a similar way:

I have always loved children, but for months after I remembered the incest, it was too painful to be around them. I'd see them playing or running down the streets, little girls flipping up their skirts and showing white cotton panties, and I'd cringe inside. "They're too vulnerable," I'd think. "They're too little."

I spent Halloween at my friend's house, just a few months after I had my first memories. I'd fled the trick-or-treaters in my neighborhood. It still hurt too much to see those innocent little faces. They'd say, "Trick or treat," and all I could think was, "Who's going to ruin you?" Every child seemed like a target.

The doorbell rang. My friend asked me to get it. I opened the door to a mother and a little girl. The girl was dressed as an angel, in a flowing white dress with gold trim. She had straight

Girl Child
BY DORIANNE LAUX

Shouldn't she be in bed, you think,
as she slaps her hands on the rocks
of your bare knees, climbs you like
a fence, one sweaty palm the size
of a pocket watch, warm, a little
sticky, pressed to your cheek.
It's painful to look into her face,
this strange child touching you
as if she knows you and trusts you,
sent here to say whatever
hardened you all those years ago
was not your fault, though when you
look into her eyes you see how it was,
how it will always be, someone
touching her back.

Dorianne Laux, *Facts About the Moon* (New York:
W.W. Norton, 2006).

blond hair cut in a pageboy. Set on her head was a halo made of aluminum foil and a bent wire hanger. I asked her how old she was. "Five and a half!" she answered proudly.

I couldn't take my eyes off her. She looked exactly like I had when I was her age. It was like looking in a mirror back twenty-five years. I just stared at her, until her mother put a protective arm around her shoulder, and glared at me. I gave the girl a Snickers bar and turned away. I shut the door slowly and sat down in the living room, dazed.

All I could think was, "That's how small I was! I was that little when he forced himself on me. How could he have done that?" I felt tears of outrage and grief. I had been innocent! There was nothing I could have done to protect myself. None of it had been my fault. "I was only a child," I screamed into the empty living room, the sudden reality of a child of five flooding through me.

MAKING CONTACT

Not having that little girl in your life means that you have lost something. You have not had access to her softness, to her sense of trust and wonder. When you hate the child within, you hate a part of yourself. It is only in taking care of her that you can really learn to nurture yourself. Although you may start with feelings of mistrust and ambivalence, part of healing is accepting her as an integral part of you:

I had to make a real commitment to the child inside myself. I had to say, "What do you need today? What can I do to make you feel safe? No, I'm not going to just tell you to go away." I had to make a literal commitment to do that. I had to say, "Okay, you need for me not to talk to so many people about what's going on." Or, "Okay, today you need for me to take five minutes at lunchtime to talk to you."

Getting to Know the Child
by Eleanor

When I communicated how dependent I feel on being fat to keep me safe from men, my therapist asked me to imagine what it would take for the little girl inside of me to feel safe. When I closed my eyes, I saw myself as a young girl walking down the road, with a machine gun, a shoulder sash full of bullets, a couple of grenades, and a knife in my cowgirl boots. My therapist noted that my child believes she has to take care of herself, whereas it is my job to become the kind of adult who can protect her from harm. That way she won't have to do it herself with excessive body weight and other defenses.

In a later fantasy, I approached the little girl to tell her that I would keep her safe. She was playing in a sandbox with toy soldiers and tanks. She had on khaki shorts, a T-shirt, and an army helmet. She never looked at me. In utter sarcasm, she said, "Yeah, right." But she believed me. When she knew that I knew she believed me, she said, "But don't think this means I'm going to put on a dress or be nice to company." I told her not to worry, she doesn't have to do anything to get my protection.

Later the same day, she let me see tiny glimpses of her, sometimes tough, sometimes vulnerable, soft, feminine, pretty, scared. Once when I approached her, she was in her jeans and T-shirt, with a camouflage army cap on. Long, soft tendrils of her beautiful hair had escaped her hat and were falling along her back and shoulders. I asked her if there was anything I could do for her.

Without a moment's delay she answered, "Well, you could stop stuffing me with food!"

"What do you mean?" I asked, shocked. "It's you who demand all that stuff."

She made a loud smack with her tongue. "Somebody has to be the adult around here, you know. Just because I ask you for it doesn't mean you have to give it to me. You don't let your son eat all that junk, no matter how he acts to try to get it. Don't you love me as much as you love him? What's the matter with you anyway?"

I am so delighted with her. She's intimidating too, though. I told her that I'd think about what she's saying but that I don't have any magic solutions and she's going to have to be patient while I learn to parent her. She seems satisfied with that. She doesn't trust adults, but she thinks I'm a lot better than most grown-ups. She likes me. Maybe not full-out, but she does like me. She has seen me parent my son and she trusts me to proceed with integrity. I'm educable, she has decided.

She's such a smart, alive, spunky little thing. If she thinks I can do it, I can do it. She's an excellent judge of character. I'm hopeful. I have a new chance. I begin now.

It was wonderful, because suddenly I felt a real loyalty to this child. I began to feel that I wanted her to be a part of me. I wanted to help her feel all right. And I had never felt that before. What I had felt was "Get this fucking brat out of my way and let me get on with my life!"

Coming into an intimate relationship with the child means hearing the depth of her pain, helping her face her terror, comforting her in the night. This will not be easy. But embracing the child inside is not all painful.

One woman asked her husband to read her children's books at night before going to sleep. Another sat down before she went to bed and wrote a letter to the child within. "I'd tell her all these nice things. And then I'd get up and read it in the morning."

Your job is to listen to the child, give her pleasure, and let her show you what she needs to heal. As Gizelle explained:

My child had been silenced for forty years. I began to hear her crying out in me. She needed someone to listen to her. "Someone has to listen to me. No one's ever listened to me. No one's ever believed me." That was her first need— to be listened to—if she was going to heal.

I began to listen to her and honor her, to nurture her and do nice things for her. She'd been deeply wounded and I needed to be her mother. And so I began to respond to that child: whether she needed to wear soft clothes or eat an ice cream cone or watch *I Love Lucy* or sit in

the flowers. She knew what she needed to heal.

And this is what I'm discovering more and more. She will guide me. She's the one who's been wounded. She knows if she needs to be held. There may be times she just needs to have her hair brushed. She *knows*, and I do as much as I can. I hold myself. I stroke myself. I rock. I comfort the child that was wounded.

It was very important during that time to be with people who knew, who understood, who could support me. They helped me do the comforting. I had to be gentle with myself. My child had been so abused. She didn't need to be whipped to heal.*

WRITING EXERCISE: THE CHILD WITHIN

(See the basic method for writing exercises on p. xxix.)

This is a chance to talk to the child within. If you're capable of loving and comforting the child within, express the compassion that you feel toward her. You can do this by writing a letter directly to her. Or you can engage in a written dialogue, first writing as the adult and

---

* For more of Gizelle's story, see "My Outrage Comes From Love: Gizelle's Story" on p. 147 and "There's a Great Deal of Magic in This Healing Process: Gizelle's Story" on p. 186.

then as the child responding. You may find it helpful to place a childhood photo of yourself in front of you as you write.

If you don't yet feel any connection, allegiance, or tenderness toward the child yet, start with how you honestly feel. You can't write, "I love you, I'll take care of you," if that's a lie. Start with: "I'm willing to sit down and write to you even though I'm not quite sure you exist" or "I don't know how to love you." Any point of contact is a start. You can't have a loving relationship until you take the first step.

Another way to get in touch with your inner child is to write a dialogue using your dominant hand (your right hand if you're right-handed; your left if you're left-handed) for your adult self and your other hand for the child's responses. Writing with the nondominant hand is slow and childlike and can help evoke the feelings and voice of the child.

With your dominant hand and in your own adult voice, ask the child a question, such as "What do you need right now?" or "How can I take care of you?" Or "Can you tell me a little about yourself?" Then, switching your pen (or crayon or marker) to the other hand, respond in the voice of the child. When it feels like the child has had her say, switch back to the other hand and respond as your adult self. Go back and forth, changing hands, until you feel finished. This can be an effective way to open up a dialogue with your inner child.

If you feel totally alienated from the child within, imagine another child the age you were during your abuse. Try writing to her instead.

This is a good exercise to do more than once, particularly if you're not starting from a place of compassion. Eventually you'll be able to tell the child that she's not to blame, that she's innocent, and that you'll protect her.

Moon

BY BILLY COLLINS

The moon is full tonight
an illustration for sheet music,
an image in Matthew Arnold
glimmering on the English Channel,
or a ghost over a smoldering battlefield
in one of the history plays.

It's as full as it was
in that poem by Coleridge
where he carries his year-old son
into the orchard behind the
    cottage
and turns the baby's face to the sky
to see for the first time
the earth's bright companion,
something amazing to make his crying
    seem small.

And if you wanted to follow this
    example,
tonight would be the night

to carry some tiny creature outside
and introduce him to the moon.

And if your house has no child,
you can always gather into your arms
the sleeping infant of yourself,
as I have done tonight,
and carry him outdoors,
all limp in his tattered blanket,
making sure to steady his lolling head
with the palm of your hand.

And while the wind ruffles the pear trees
in the corner of the orchard
and dark roses wave against a stone wall,
you can turn him on your shoulder
and walk in circles on the lawn
drunk with the light.
You can lift him up into the sky,
your eyes nearly as wide as his,
as the moon climbs high into the night.

Billy Collins, *Picnic, Lightning* (Pittsburgh: University of Pittsburgh Press, 1998).

Grieving

"Sometimes I think I'm going to die from the sadness. Not that anyone ever died from crying for two hours, but it sure feels like it."

An essential part of healing from child sexual abuse is to express and share your feelings. When you were young, you could not do this. To fully feel the agony, the terror, and fury, without any support, would have been too much to bear. And so you suppressed those feelings. But you have not gotten rid of them.

To release these painful feelings and to move forward in your life, it is necessary, paradoxically, to return to the experience you had as a child—to grieve, this time with the support of a caring person and the support of your adult self.

What you need to heal is not fancy or esoteric. It is remarkably simple, though for many survivors it has been hard to find. You need the safety and support that enable you to go back to the source of your pain, to feel the feelings you had to repress or deny, to be heard, to be comforted, and to learn to comfort yourself.

And in this way, a transformation takes place. Once you have felt an emotion, known it and lived in it, shared it, acted it, given it full expression, the feeling begins to transform. The way to move beyond grief and pain is to experience them fully, to honor them, to express them with someone else, thus assimilating into your adult life what happened to you as a child.

YOU HAVE A LOT TO GRIEVE FOR

As a survivor of child sexual abuse, you have a lot to grieve for. You grieve for your violation, abandonment, shame, and fear. You grieve for your losses in the past and in the present, for the harm that was done to you, the wounding you now must heal, the time and energy it takes, the money it costs, the relationships ruined, the pleasures missed. You grieve for the opportunities lost while you were too busy coping.

Sometimes the losses are extremely personal. An older woman recalls:

I don't remember ever being a virgin. It wasn't fair. Everybody else got to be one. It has always really hurt me. I still have a real anger that that was taken away. Nobody asked. It was just gone. I didn't have that to give. I know that's just "The American Dream," but I heard that dream the same as any other woman did. Whether it's important now or not, it was to me.

If you maintained the fantasy that your childhood was "happy," then you must grieve for the illusion you're giving up. If the person who abused you was a parent who was supposed to love and protect you, you must recognize the depth of the betrayal you suffered.

GRIEVING FOR LOST INNOCENCE

As a survivor of child sexual abuse, you must grieve for the shattered image of a world that is just, where children are cared for, where people respect each other. You must mourn your lost innocence, your belief that it's safe to trust. And sometimes, you must even grieve for a part of yourself that didn't make it:

I went down to see the children inside me. The first one I noticed just sat on the curb in my abdomen. She'd sit there with her head in her hand, looking very sad, or she'd be jumping up and down, being manic. Then there was one in my heart who would sit in a room behind a door. She'd open the door and peek out, and then shut the door, 'cause she got scared. Then there was the one who was dead. I'd been waiting for her to wake up. And one day I was lying in bed crying, and I said, "Okay, it's time for you to wake up," but she was dead. I sobbed and mourned that a part of me had died. The part of me that had really wanted to believe in the good of the family and the good of everyone just died.

Some survivors mourn not just for themselves but also for the abuse that was done to the people who abused them, for the generations of victims continuing to perpetuate abuse. A woman who was abused by her mother explains:

There was a lot of grief, lots of tears realizing I didn't have the kind of family I thought everybody else had. It really hurt. It still hurts. It comes in waves. Those kinds of tears go real deep. It's a sadness for what I didn't have; it's also a sadness for my mother. It hurts that she's so sick. It hurts that she never realized her beauty, and still doesn't. Because she had so much self-hate, she had to abuse me. For a long time I was angry about that, but then there was a stage of grieving for her because she *is* beautiful, she is loving; it's just that her sick side is overwhelming to her.

When My Father Was Beating Me[*]

BY TOI DERRICOTTE

I'd hear my mother in the kitchen preparing dinner. I'd hear the spoons hitting the mixing bowl, the clatter of silver falling into the drawer. I'd hear the pot lids clink and rattle. The normality of the sound was startling; it seemed louder than usual, as if she weren't ashamed, as if she were making a point. Perhaps the house was cut in two by a membrane, and, though her sounds could come to my ears, my screams and cries and whimpers, his demands and humiliations, the sounds of his hands hitting my body, couldn't pierce back the other way. I learned to stretch time and space so I could think what she was thinking. I learned to hear things far away, to live in a thought that could expand itself even until now: What Einstein said is true—everything slows down the farther you get from your mother.

It seemed as if she wanted it, that either I was taking her place, or maybe she thought I deserved it. Maybe there was an overload of violence in the universe, a short in a wire that had to spill its electricity, and she was glad, this time, she hadn't felt it.

Maybe there was some arcane connection between her and my father's hand, his arm let loose and flying, maybe she was in command, making him hit, telling her side of the story—that I was evil, that I had to be beaten, not just for the crime I had committed, but for the crime of who I was: hungry, trying, in every way, to get through barriers set up for my own good. "You're tearing me apart, you're driving me crazy," my mother would scream.

Sometimes I saw the world from her perspective: she *was* beautiful and pitiful and overwhelmed, she was also some blood-sucking witch—not a whole being—able to stretch and contort herself like a cry, something that hated and was flexible. She wanted to beat me in the same way my father did, but she knew she couldn't, because I'd fight back, I'd cry that cry that made her go crazy. "You can't manipulate your father the way you can manipulate me." She meant it as a compliment for herself, as if she loved me more.

They wanted a stillness, a lack of person, place, agony swallowed. They wanted me to die, or, not to die, to exist with a terrible pain, but have it sewn up—as if they could reach into my ribs, crack them open, put a handful of suffering in there and stitch it back, as if my body had a pocket, a black pocket they could stick a thought in that they couldn't stand.

I would fold, collapse like a marionette. (I beat my dolls for years, pounded and pounded and nobody seemed to notice.) "Just keep trying," my father'd say just before he'd strike me. And I did. I kept trying to be beaten.

Serving the dinner plates with her face bland, as if it were virtuous not to take sides, serving the beautiful food that she had cooked all day—her great gift—to say, *I've given everything I could, I've got nothing left.* Often when my father would hit me she'd say, as if he and I were man and wife, "I'm not going to come between the two of you. You two have to work this out for yourselves." He'd give me a warning. "Wipe that look off your face or I'll knock it off. Dry up," he'd scream, "and eat."

---

[*] Toi Derricotte, *Tender* (Pittsburgh: University of Pittsburgh Press, 1997).

COMING TO TERMS WITH THE WAY THINGS ARE

Part of grieving is replacing the unconditional love you held for your family as a child with a realistic assessment. On the one hand, your childhood might have been completely awful. On the other hand, there might have been a lot of good times mixed in with the abuse. If you also have feelings of love for your abuser, you must reconcile that love with the fact that he or she abused you.

GRIEVING FOR THE MOTHER YOU WISH YOU HAD

For many women—abused by grandfathers, fathers, brothers, or people outside the family—the deepest hurt they experience is with their mothers. Of all relationships, the mother–child bond is the most primal, where most of us experience our first and deepest sense of love, nurturing, and protection. If your mother didn't recognize that you were being abused, if you tried to tell her and she didn't listen, or if she knew but didn't act in your defense and protect you, you may be left with profound grief:

The primal impulse a mother has to protect her young is universal. You always hear stories about the mother who lifts a car off her three-year-old who is pinned beneath it. You read stories in the paper about mothers who can't swim saving their children from drown-ing. This fierce protectiveness of mothers willing to give up their own lives to save their children is legendary. Yet my mother looked the other way. She refused to see what was going on right before her eyes. This has been absolutely the hardest thing for me to deal with—my mother's betrayal. Over and over, I've asked myself, "What was so horribly wrong with me that my mother didn't save me?"*

GRIEVING FOR THE LOSS OF FAMILY

If the abuse has made it impossible to continue a relationship with your family, you may grieve for the fact that you don't have an extended family. If you have children, you may feel sad that they don't have the benefit of grandparents, aunts and uncles, or cousins. And if the abuse or its long-term effects made it impossible for you to have children of your own, you may have to grieve that loss as well:

Once I left my parents' home, I only wanted to wipe out the past. I spent twenty years blotto, drunk or high. You name it, I took it. Pills, tequila, crank, heroin. I was married to oblivion. After my 3rd DUI, I got sober, and the first thing that came up was what my mother had done to me. Over the next year, I

---

* If your mother was your abuser, see "Breaking the Silence: Abuse by Women" on p. 108.

tried to kill myself three times—the last time I carried a red folding chair to the Bay Bridge so I could climb over the guardrail.

Luckily, a cop got to me first and I ended up in a psych ward. It was a good place with good people. I owe my life to them. While I was in the hospital, I decided to live, but the next few years were hell. It took five more years for me to gain any real stability and by that time, I was 45. I didn't have a career. I could barely make a living. I didn't know the first thing about relationships. At a time when most of my peers were raising kids—or having grandchildren—I was starting my adult life from scratch.

I've had to face that there are a lot of things that are never going to happen for me, and one of them is having children of my own. The fact that that choice was taken away from me is one of the saddest things I'm dealing with now.

Grieving for My Grandfather: Rae's Story

Rae Luskin is a forty-seven-year-old artist whose grandfather was both her mentor and her perpetrator. A big part of Rae's healing has been reconciling her love for him with his betrayal.

My grandfather was an artist. I felt like he was the only one who really understood me in my whole family. He always asked me what I thought and felt. He was always there for me. He truly loved me.

When I was eight or nine, he'd have me and my sister over to his art studio. He'd have one of us paint at the easel and the other one would be over on the couch with him, and he'd fondle us. Then he'd have us switch. This went on for years. Finally when I was thirteen, I stood up to him and it stopped.

That was really hard for me. I lost the one person who had been in my corner. I still saw my grandfather periodically at family gatherings, but we didn't talk or interact much.

When I was thirty-three, my grandfather committed suicide. I was devastated. On one hand I was totally relieved—there was this sense of freedom. But on the other hand, I needed to find a way to say goodbye, a way to say to him, "This is what you did to me, and this is how it affected my life."

I had a shiva service at my house.* We said prayers. I dialogued with him. I wrote him a couple of letters. I told him what he'd meant in my life—the good and the bad. I told him how confused I'd been because I loved him so thoroughly and hated him at the same time. I told him how what he did affected my life—the idea that what brings me joy and pure love—my art—is so interwoven with his sickness. I stopped painting for twelve years because of him. And I wanted him to know that. Then I burned the letters and said a prayer and a blessing for me.

For years I felt guilty about still loving my grandfather after what he did to me, but I don't any longer. When I think about him

---

* Shiva is the traditional seven-day period of mourning the dead that is observed by Jewish families.

now, I see him as a very loving, giving person who really knew me. But he was also a very sick man, and I feel compassion for him now. My grandfather gave me the gift of creativity. He encouraged me as an artist, and he was the only one to do that. I hate what he did to me, but I feel at peace with him now.

BURIED GRIEF

You may feel foolish crying over events that happened so long ago, but grief waits for expression. When you do not allow yourself to express your grief, it festers. Buried grief poisons, limiting your capacity for joy, for spontaneity, for life. It can limit your vitality, make you sick, and decrease your capacity for love.

Sometimes the sadness feels so big and the losses so great that you fear that your grief will never end, that it will overrun your life and keep you from functioning—and it might at first. But grief comes in waves. If you give it time and expression, the intensity of your grief will eventually lessen, the waves of grief will ebb and flow.

Grief has its own rhythms. You can't say, "Okay, I'm going to grieve now." Rather you must allow room for those feelings when they arise. Grief needs space. You can only really grieve when you give yourself time, security, and permission:

After I had been in therapy for several months my whole self began to respond to that environment, within which I could allow my feelings. There were weeks I entered the building, went up the stairs, checked in with the receptionist, all with a smile on my face and cheerfulness in my step. Then I'd enter the office, my therapist would close the door, and before she'd even get to her chair, I'd be crying. Deep within me I held those feelings, waiting until I knew there would be time and compassion.

TAKE THE TIME TO MOURN

In order to make room for your grief, take this period of mourning as seriously as if someone close to you had died. One survivor, whose abusive parents were still alive, spent a month dressed in black. Another wrote a eulogy for her abuser. Rituals such as these can be powerful channels for grief:

I wrote a divorce decree from my mother, because I kept having these dreams of wanting to cut the umbilical cord and her not letting me. I just couldn't figure out how to separate from her. We weren't talking. We weren't seeing each other, but I was still feeling too connected.

You may not be drawn to create a ritual or ceremony. Instead, you may simply cry a lot. As one woman put it: "I hadn't cried in years. It's only recently that that's been restored. I'm not sure I'm happy about it. It's like Niagara Falls at times."

Some survivors experience a long, deep sadness. Give yourself the space you need to mourn for all you've suffered, all you've lost. This can be difficult in a culture that exhorts us to be happy, but try to be patient with your feelings. Allow yourself to release the emotions you have struggled all your life to contain. Grieving can be a great relief.

WRITING EXERCISE: GRIEVING

(See the basic method for writing exercises on p. xxix).

Write about what you've lost, what was taken, what was destroyed. Write about the extent of the damage. Write about the things you need to grieve for. This is a chance to give voice to your pain, and to write about how you feel about your loss.

SEXUAL ABUSE, PREGNANCY, AND ABORTION

Many survivors have become pregnant as a result of sexual abuse. Some girls have given birth to their babies and raised them themselves,[*] some have relinquished their babies for adoption, and others have had abortions—often arranged by their family or by the abuser himself.[†] Each outcome carries its own kind of suffering.

In this story, Janne Gonzales shows how long-lasting the trauma of these early abortions can be.

Medical History
BY JANNE GONZALES

I go through doctors quickly. When their touch becomes familiar I stop seeing them—because I'd rather be touched by a stranger. I've heard my new doctor is kind, patient; I wonder how long I can keep distance between us—keep her from knowing me too well. I arrive for my first appointment and the receptionist hands me a medical history questionnaire. With familiar trepidation, I take a pencil and find a seat toward the back of the waiting room. My heart pounds.

Height, weight, medications, reason for visit. Have you now, or have you had in the past, any of the following? Hepatitis, high blood pressure, allergies, asthma, ulcer, pelvic infection, etc. I go down the list, checking too many boxes.

Next is the women-only section. Date of last menstrual period. Number of pregnancies? I

---

[*] See Eva Smith's story in "Courageous Women" on p. 418.

[†] For other examples of incest resulting in pregnancy, see "Lorraine Williams" on p. 482 and "Cassondra Espinoza" on p. 492.

hesitate, and write "four." Number of live births? "zero." Miscarriages? "zero." Abortions? I look over my shoulder, inhale slowly, and write "four." Dates of the above? 1970, 1971, 1973.

I cover the questionnaire with an insurance form and hand it to the receptionist, hoping she won't examine the papers. What do I think is going to happen? As if she could tell anything by reading my history.

My name is called and I follow the nurse to the exam room. She takes my blood pressure. I joke, trying to add levity to what looks like a tedious day for her. She hands me one of those dreadful paper gowns. "The doctor will be with you shortly." I undress, remembering the embarrassment and anxiety I've experienced in many rooms like this. The gown rips as I pull it on.

The doctor enters, donning a white coat and stethoscope, all that distinguishes her from anybody's daughter. She's much younger than I am. Causing me, at 39, to feel old.

She reviews my history, asks predictable questions, turns the page. "Four pregnancies?" she asks. I nod. "*All* abortions?" I nod again, hoping she'll stop asking; go to the next section. "How old were you when you had these abortions?" Nonchalantly, too quickly, I answer; "Thirteen, twice at fourteen, and seventeen."

This is the moment I want to be over. I hope she assumes I was promiscuous as a teenager. I hope she won't remember that abortions were illegal in 1970. That would require an explanation. And I don't want to explain. Not in this too-small ridiculous paper outfit. Not here, not now.

And what would I tell her? The truth? That I got pregnant because my father was having sex with me? The first time he tried I was nine. When I was thirteen it became a regular thing—something I could count on—like the diarrhea I had each morning after first period English.

The doctor is still looking at me. I'm not sure if she's going to ask another question or turn the page.

I don't want to explain how the abortions happened. There are no records of them. My father is a doctor. He knew what to do. He knew who to contact. My father told his colleague I was promiscuous and he understood. With my father's standing in the community, this had to be taken care of. My mother didn't know; no one knew. My father caught it early. He knew when I missed my period, and noticed when my breasts swelled. Fathers aren't supposed to know when their thirteen-year-old daughters are menstruating, or how their breasts feel. But my father knew.

After the third pregnancy he got concerned. This couldn't keep happening. (Of course, he would never stop coming to my room—something he did almost every night from the time I was three.) So he solved the problem. He switched to sodomy. What a compromise. What a solution. No more pregnancies.

Not until I was seventeen. I was to leave home permanently within a few months and he must have panicked. So he started again. And I got pregnant *again*. That is especially shameful to me; I was almost an adult and should have been able to refuse him. But I couldn't. I knew what he was capable of doing to me if I resisted him, even a tiny bit, so he kept on. But soon I moved out. And it stopped for good.

My doctor glances at my history again and back at me. She seems distracted. Distracted is good. She raises her eyebrows and asks, "So, what brings you here today?" I dare not show my relief, and hurriedly explain that my cold has hung on; I have a fever; maybe I need antibiotics?

"Lie back, and I'll listen to your chest," she says, reaching for her stethoscope. I breathe deeply, a stray tear falling from my cheek, as she listens to my pounding heart.

Anger

"When I'm angry, it's because I know I'm worth being angry about."

—SHAMA

Anger is a natural response to abuse. But it's unlikely that you were able to experience, express, or act on your outrage when you were abused. You might not even have known that you had a right to those feelings. Rather than be angry with the person or people who abused you, you might have denied your anger or turned it on yourself.

Anger turned inward can lead to depression and self-destructive behavior. You might have wanted to hurt or kill yourself. You may criticize yourself relentlessly or feel that you're essentially bad. Or you may stuff your anger down with food, drown it with alcohol, stifle it with drugs, or make yourself ill. As poet Adrienne Rich writes: "Most women have not been able to touch this anger, except to drive it inward like a rusted nail.*

Lorraine Williams recalls what happened when she couldn't express her anger:

I'm albino and I get severe sunburn whenever I'm exposed to the sun. As a kid, I'd get really pissed about what was happening at home. But you weren't allowed to get angry at my house. So rather than say anything, I'd purposefully go out on a sunny day without a hat or any other protection. I'd come home blistered and with a fever.†

Having been taught to blame yourself, you stay angry at the child you once were—the child who was vulnerable, who was injured, who was unable to protect herself, who needed affection and attention, who experienced sex-

---

* Adrienne Rich, "Disloyal to Civilization," in *Lies, Secrets, and Silence* (New York: W.W. Norton, 1979), p. 309.

† For more of Lorraine's story, see "Lorraine Williams" on p. 482 of "Courageous Women."

ual arousal or orgasm. But this child did nothing wrong. She does not deserve your anger.

On the other hand, some survivors have been angry their whole lives. They grew up in families or circumstances so pitted against each other that they learned early to fight for survival. Anger was a continual armoring for battle. And sometimes the line between anger and violence blurred:

I saw men and women angry and rageful when I was growing up. Both of my parents, and other relatives, too. I remember my mom slapping the shit out of this woman in the bar because the woman said, "We don't allow dirty Mexicans in this bar." But then my parents would turn it on each other, and on us. Anger, violence, and self-defense are all mixed up for me.

LASHING OUT

Some survivors have turned their anger against partners and lovers, friends, coworkers, and children, lashing out destructively. You may find yourself pushing your child against the wall or punching your lover when you get mad:

I had a lot of physically abusive relationships. I didn't know how not to fight. My first impulse when I got angry was this [she smacks one hand hard on the other], because that's what I saw growing up. Whenever I started to get upset with someone, I would literally feel the adrenaline running up and down my arms. My muscles would get really tight, my fists would clench, and I would break out into a sweat. I'd be ready to smack the person around. I'd want to fight.

If violence has been part of your life and you find yourself acting out your anger in abusive ways, you need to get help right away. It's okay to be angry, but it's not okay to be violent. (For help dealing with anger that is out of control, see "Learning to Live Without Violence" on p. 232.)

If you don't fight physically, you may pick verbal fights or look for things to criticize. You mean to tell your son to do his homework and you find yourself yelling or calling him names. Your husband forgets to change the oil and you tell him he's a stupid idiot. Even though it isn't physically violent, verbal abuse can be just as destructive.

I went through a lot of years of feeling really pissed at everybody. I wanted to strike out at everyone and lay the blame somewhere. I alienated everybody who ever tried to be close to me. I drove them away from me with my rage and my criticism, but that was fine with me because I didn't trust anyone anyway. I didn't want to be close.

DIRECTING YOUR ANGER WHERE IT BELONGS

Anger doesn't have to be suppressed or destructive. Instead, it can be a healthy response to violation and a powerful, healing energy. It is transformative to direct your anger accurately and appropriately at those who violated you. You must release yourself from any responsibility for what was done to you, placing it clearly on the abuser:

I had a hard time directing the anger at my dad. My therapist would say, "Well, how did you feel when your dad picked you up and threw you against the wall?"

And I'd say, "Well, I pretty much felt like he was an asshole."

And my therapist would say, "Hmmm."

One time, after years of therapy, when he asked me something about my father, I was holding this pencil, and I just threw it across the room and said, "That bastard!"

It was the first time I was ever clearly angry with him. Sure, I'd been mad at my dad. But it was directed in all the wrong directions. This was the first time in all those years that I was just mad at him, period, without laughing about it, without being sarcastic or defensive. Just full on, "That shit!"

FEAR OF ANGER

Many survivors are afraid to get angry because their past experiences with anger were harmful. As one survivor put it, "I don't get the difference between anger and violence yet. When I hear loud noises, I think they're coming after me." In your family, you might have witnessed anger that was destructive and out of control. But your own anger need not be either. You can channel your anger in ways that you feel good about and respect.

Even women with no history of violence are often afraid of getting angry because they think it will consume them. They sense that their anger is deep and fear that if they tap it, they'll be submerged in anger forever, becoming bitter and hostile. Or they're afraid that if they allow themselves to get angry, they'd be capable of hurting or killing someone:

I know the anger is there. I'm too scared to let myself experience it. I'm scared that I won't be gentle with myself, that I'll turn the anger on myself. I'm so used to watching other people hurt people. I don't want to be a perpetrator. I don't know how to discharge my anger in a way that's safe.

It is rare for women to violently act out their anger toward the people who abused them as children. For women with no history of violence, the fear that you might suddenly become violent is usually unrealistic.

Anger is a feeling, and feelings themselves do not violate anyone. It's important to make the distinction between the experience of feeling angry and the expression of that anger. When you acknowledge your anger, then you have the freedom to choose if and how you want to express it. Anger does not have to be an uncontrolled, uncontrollable phenomenon. As you accept your anger and become familiar with it, you can direct it to meet your needs—like an experienced rider controlling a powerful horse.

ANGER AND LOVE

Another aspect of anger that is often misunderstood, and thus keeps women from releasing their dammed emotions, is the relationship between anger and love. Anger and love are not incompatible. Most of us have been angry, at one time or another, with everyone we love and live closely with. We are often angriest with the people we love the most because the pain of their betrayal is the greatest. Yet when you've been abused by someone you loved, with whom you shared good experiences, it can be difficult to admit your anger for fear that it will eradicate the positive aspects of that relationship—or even your entire childhood.

But getting angry doesn't negate what was good in your life. You can be furious about the abuse and still hold onto things from your childhood that nourished you. Paradoxically, when you give your anger full expression, it often clears the space to recognize and appreciate the aspects of your childhood—or even of the abuser—that you might have liked or loved. What you forfeit is only your illusion of the abuser as innocent.

My Outrage Comes From Love: Gizelle's Story

Gizelle was born in Newton, Massachusetts, the second of four girls in an Italian Catholic family.* Her father was a surgeon at a prominent New England hospital. Gizelle was dressed in Saks Fifth Avenue clothes, took ballet and piano lessons, and was sent to private schools and expensive colleges.

Gizelle has suffered much of her life with disabling illness. Shortly before sharing her story, Gizelle had made the connection between the violent rape she experienced at her father's hands, at age three, and the emotional and physical problems she has had all her life.†

I had to learn to honor all my feelings, especially the anger and the outrage. I was outraged not only against my father but against all of the men who are doing this.

This friend of mine said, "You know that you created this because you are the creator of your universe and your soul set this energy in motion. So take responsibility for it and stop mewling and whining and bellyaching about it. Just forgive and go on."

And I got *so* pissed! I was just choked with anger. When you're feeling anger, you need to honor that. If you try to get to the forgiveness before you deal with the anger, you're going to fuck the whole thing up. You have to work from where you are in your belly, not from where you think you should be in your head.

I go through real revenge periods. I

---

* Gizelle wanted to use her own name but couldn't for legal reasons. Of her pseudonym, Gizelle says, "The name I have chosen belongs to a Canadian friend, a woman who is making her own healing journey from sexual abuse. Her story and mine are not the same; however, I have chosen

her name (with her permission) so that I can honor yet another brave and beautiful woman. This lessens the pain of having my own name deleted." For more about this, see "Names or Pseudonyms: The Right to Choose" on p. 410.

† For more of Gizelle's story, see "Making Contact" on p. 131 and "There's a Great Deal of Magic in This Healing Process: Gizelle's Story" on p. 186.

imagine walking into my parents' house with a shotgun aimed right at my father's balls. "Okay, Dad. Don't move an inch. Not one step, you sucker. I'm gonna take 'em off one at a time. And I'm gonna take my sweet time about it, too!"

But at the same time, I believe that the only way to stop abuse is to come from a consciousness of love and forgiveness. Hate cannot be stopped with hate. Abuse cannot be stopped with abuse. That does not mean you don't stop the people who are doing this, or that you stop prosecuting them. But you do it from a place of love. If I didn't feel love for the child in me who had been raped, I would not have this outrage.

Sometimes I sit here and feel such compassion for my father, I weep. Other times I see myself taking a gun and shooting his balls off. I am letting it all come right on through. And the more I allow all of it to come up, the more I find myself moving toward love. The more I block the rage, the more I stay stuck. And so for me they're both right there. I reconcile it by saying I trust the process. I trust the validity of my outrage. The outrage is because I honor and value and love life.

THE DESIRE FOR REVENGE

At some point in facing their abuse, many survivors go through a period of wanting to get back at the people who hurt them so terribly. Giving yourself permission to visualize revenge can be a satisfying outlet for your anger. But it's important not to act on violent fantasies:

WORKING THROUGH MOTHER BLAME

Although our culture usually criticizes women for being angry, it does not hesitate to direct anger toward women, and specifically mothers. This is evident when a mother is blamed for her husband's abuse of their child.

Fathers often blame their wives for the fact that they abused their daughters. They cite their wives' failure to meet their needs for companionship or sex. They refer to her drinking, illness, affairs, working nights, or being otherwise unavailable. "And so," the father pleads, holding up his hands in a gesture of helplessness, "I turned to my daughter."

This is preposterous. It is never anyone else's fault when a man abuses a child. Regardless of how inadequate a woman may be as a wife or mother, no behavior on her part is license for a man to sexually abuse a child.

The role of mothers in father–daughter incest has traditionally been misunderstood and misrepresented. It has been assumed that the mother knew the abuse was going on—and that if she didn't, it was because she didn't want to know. Mothers have been labeled collusive, contributing, weak, passive, withholding, and inattentive. Certainly some mothers have been. Mothers have looked the other way, failed to leave abusive men, and repeatedly chosen their husbands over their daughters. And some mothers have actively participated in the abuse of their children. More than one survivor has described literally being handed over for sex by her mother.

But not all mothers of abused children are irresponsible. Some genuinely didn't know the abuse was going on. Sometimes even a mother's best efforts are insufficient to stop it. Mothers have lost custody cases, been dismissed as vindictive, paranoid, or unfit by judges and social workers. In states where joint custody is the norm, they have been forced into shared custody arrangements with abusive men.

Women who find themselves in these situations face formidable odds and terrible choices. Some mothers have gone underground with their children to shield them from abusive fathers. While these children have been protected from further abuse, they have had to face the ordeal of hiding their identities and at times, living life on the run. Other mothers have gone to jail rather than comply with court orders to hand over their children, leaving their children bereft of both parents.[*] Sometimes there aren't any good choices in a legal system that still does not adequately protect children.

***

[*] See "If Your Child Is Abused," on p. 577 of the Resource Guide.

You Have a Right to Hold Your Mother Responsible

Despite these realities, you still have a right to be angry if *you* weren't protected. If your mother did not listen when you tried to tell her, did not leave an abusive or alcoholic man, did not offer the warmth, attention, or understanding that you needed, you have a right to hold her responsible.

Yet you might find this difficult. You may identify so much with your mother's oppression that you minimize or negate your own. You may feel close to your mother because you were both victims, and you may worry that acknowledging your anger will threaten that bond. But if your mother didn't protect you, looked the other way, set you up, or blamed you, she was complicit in the abuse. It is necessary to acknowledge this and to get in touch with your anger at what she did or failed to do. This is not only your right; it is essential for your healing. However, unless your mother was your abuser, you must not direct *all* of your anger toward her.[*] The abuser *always* holds the ultimate responsibility for sexual abuse and thus deserves your legitimate anger.

***

[*] For a discussion of abuse by mothers see "Breaking the Silence: Abuse by Women" on p. 108.

What I say to myself is, "Wait a minute. I don't want to go to prison. I don't want the cops to come." I grew up with the cops coming. I don't want to go back to jail for being violent.

If you meet violence with violence, you stoop to the level of your abuser. You have to decide if you want to perpetuate more abusive behavior or if you want to break the cycle. As Soledad put it, "I've learned to respect human life."*

There are nonviolent means of retribution that can be powerful tools both for healing and for social change. Some survivors have spoken out publicly about their abuse. Others have pursued legal resolution through the criminal justice system or sought restitution from their abusers in civil court.†

One woman found it satisfying to send her abuser the following telegram:

> YOU HAVE WONDERED WHY I DON'T WANT TO BE IN TOUCH WITH YOU ANYMORE. NOW I KNOW WHY, AND I HAVE PEOPLE WATCHING YOU. IF YOU EVER MOLEST ANOTHER LITTLE GIRL, EVEN LOOK AT HER IN THE WRONG WAY, I WILL TAKE YOU TO COURT AND WIN.

BARBARA LITTLEFORD

---

* For more of Soledad's story, see p. 436 in "Courageous Women."

† See "Legal Resources for Survivors of Child Sexual Abuse" on p. 529 of the Resource Guide.

> YOUR MESSAGE WAS DELIVERED BY TELEPHONE AT 2:19 PM PST ON 1/21 AND WAS ACCEPTED BY JACK.
>
> THANK YOU FOR USING OUR SERVICE. WESTERN UNION

Some survivors feel that revenge is not in their hands. One woman, a devout Christian, said simply, "God will take care of him. It's not my job." Another woman said that she couldn't do anything to her father that was worse than what he was doing to himself. He was dying of testicular cancer.

And often the best revenge is living well.

ANGER-RELEASE WORK

For many survivors, it is empowering to release anger in physical ways. Pounding pillows, yelling, and tearing up newspaper are safe expressions of long-held rage. As one survivor describes:

I felt incredible anger, but I never allowed anger my whole life. It was really a difficult thing to let out. One day my therapist got up out of her chair, and she said, "Your father's in that chair." And she handed me a rolled-up towel and she said, "I want you to hit your father."

It took me a long time to psych myself into doing that, but once I started, I couldn't stop. I pounded and screamed

SAFETY GUIDELINES FOR ANGER-RELEASE WORK

For anger-release work to be safe, there must be clear safety guidelines:

- Don't hurt yourself or anyone else.
- Don't destroy any property that you haven't specifically designated as appropriate (for example, old dishes to break).
- You can imagine the object of your anger to be your abuser or anyone else you're angry at—except yourself. Even if you feel angry with yourself, don't imagine the pillows you hit or the paper you shred to be yourself.

until I couldn't move anymore. It was such a relief and an important turning point for me.

Eva Smith arranged a satisfying outlet for her anger[*]:

I had a friend who made ceramic things, and if they were cracked or whatever, he'd set them aside for me. I'd come around at midnight. I'd go around the back and throw them against the fence. It was a miracle no one called the police because I'd be out there throwing stuff.

[*] For more on Eva's story, see "Eva Smith" on p. 418 of "Courageous Women."

Another woman got together with one of her siblings and they came up with an innovative form of self-expression: "My brother and I sledgehammered the old family kitchen table, where we'd both experienced so much violence. It was great."

Although expressing anger physically like this can be incredibly liberating, it's not right for everyone. The purpose of this kind of anger work is to move bottled-up energy through and out, leaving you with a sense of release and peace. But for some survivors, exercises like these just keep recycling the rage, creating more and more agitation and distress. It's important to learn about yourself so that you come to know what is and isn't helpful for you.

If you aren't sure whether anger-release exercises will be useful for you, experiment in a small way and then check in with yourself to see how you feel. Ask yourself: Do I feel lighter? Is there more room inside? Does it feel good to set the burden of this old rage down? Do I feel calmer after doing this? Or do I feel even more upset than when I began? Am I more angry? More agitated?

Anger is a powerful tool, but it has its limits. Screaming, pounding on pillows, expressing anger in large, physical ways can create freedom or it can throw fuel on the fire. By paying attention to your own experience, you can learn what does and what doesn't help you to heal.

For some survivors, simply acknowledging their anger in a clear way is enough: "Father Michael took advantage of me. He robbed me of my childhood, and I'm angry about it." Saying these words out loud to a sympathetic listener—or simply writing them in your journal—can be an effective way to express your anger.

POSITIVE EXPRESSIONS OF ANGER

- Speak out publicly about child sexual abuse.
- Write a letter to your abuser or to the person or people who didn't protect you. This is not a letter to send but a chance to get your feelings out.[*]
- Pound on the bed with a tennis racket.
- Shred newspapers or break old dishes.
- Take a course in martial arts.
- Scream. Choose a place where it's okay to make that much noise or scream into a pillow to muffle the sound.
- Organize a survivors' march.
- Dance an anger dance.
- Work to change laws that continue protecting abusers.

---

[*] If you want guidance in how to actually communicate with your abuser or family members, see "Disclosures and Truth-Telling" on p. 157 for a thorough discussion of this topic.

THE POWER OF ANGER: THREE STORIES

Barbara Hamilton, a sixty-five-year-old survivor who has written a book about her abuse and her healing, describes the first time she really got in touch with her anger.[*]

> I went racing back and got a hold of my therapist before she left. I started to rage and the whole mental health department of Napa heard me, because I raised the roof. Everything came up. All the obscenities and everything were connected. The male assaults of me and my kids all went together. I had been intellectually angry with my father before, but this time I just blew. I just screamed my fury all over the place. I threw my glasses against the wall. I was just beside myself. I can't say that it felt good, but it was a turning point. It was so clear where the rage was coming from. It was the beginning of me not blaming myself.

If you've suppressed your anger for many years, it can be explosive. But even torrential anger doesn't have to be dangerous. Mary McGrath was able to trust her anger with striking results:

---

[*] Barbara Smith Hamilton, *The Hidden Legacy: Uncovering, Confronting, and Healing Three Generations of Incest.* (Fort Bragg, CA: Cypress House, 1993). See p. 532 of the Resource Guide. For more of Barbara's story in this book, see "It's Never Too Late: Barbara Hamilton's Story" on p. 61.

I did some rage work with Elisabeth Kübler-Ross. She has people work in a large group with telephone books and rubber hoses. Doing the actual rage work wasn't scary. In fact, it was very exciting. It's such a safe environment with so much love, you have the feeling you can do or say anything. It's okay if you bash in your stepfather's face with a rubber hose. I remember thinking, "This isn't so bad. This isn't going to kill anybody." Every once in a while I'd stop, look around the room, and think, "No way, that didn't come from me!" I had totally shredded a Denver phone book, just obliterated it, and still more to come. I'd have to catch my breath or blow my nose, and I remember looking at the devastation and thinking, "My God! That was all inside!" I was flabbergasted at how much rage there was.

After all that release, I started having powerful dreams. In one, I was lying in bed as a teenager. I felt my stepdad was in the room. I'd always thought if I could only scream, I could stop it. And in the dream, I did. I literally did. I let out a piercing, bloodcurdling scream. I was able to scream and stop it.

Edith Horning's experience clearly illustrates the dramatic healing effects of anger:

I had my therapist on one side of me, and a man I was very close to on the other. My therapist had me imagine I was in the balcony of a movie theater, and that quite far away my father was up on a tiny movie screen. I did this scenario where I imagined him coming closer, getting larger and larger, and as he did, the people on either side of me encouraged me to stop him, to do whatever I had to do to make him powerless. They encouraged me to say no. It took me two or three tries before I could get the nerve to shout. Suddenly I got this tremendous surge of feeling from inside. I screamed, "No! You get back! Just stop it!" And in my mind, I could see my father getting smaller and smaller and smaller. And I pounded on him until he was really tiny, just a shrimp.

That's when my father stopped being more powerful than I was. That's when I stopped protecting my mother or father. I no longer felt sorry for them. They made choices as they went along, just like I have. And when you make the choices, you pay the price. I did. They are. And that's the way it is.

THE LIMITS OF ANGER

Our anger helps us recognize injustice, gives us strength, and counteracts fear and self-destructive behavior. Many survivors would have succumbed to despair and killed themselves were it not for their anger. Yet anger, if it is your primary emotion, can be a defense. When you maintain a constant state of anger, your experience of life becomes one-dimensional and you avoid having to feel more vulnerable emotions such as grief, fear, shame, hopelessness, and terror.

It does not feel good to live in a perpetual state of anger and turmoil. What you once experienced as exhilaration—finally getting to express your outrage—can sometimes become a habitual pattern that is exhausting and debilitating:

> My mother's abuse devastated my whole life. I fled from her as soon as I turned sixteen. Life on the streets wasn't much better, and I blamed her for that, too. For years, I was full of rage toward for what she had done to me. That was my M.O. for years: rage at Mom.
>
> At 40, I was diagnosed with hypertension and my doctor suggested that maybe all my rage had something to do with it. All those years, I thought my anger was punishing my mother, but it was punishing me more. I wasn't even talking to my mother; I hadn't talked to her in years. She wasn't the one living with my anger; I was.

Anger can also keep you enmeshed with the person you're angry with in a way that you never intended. Although you may desperately want to get that person out of your life, your active rage can keep the connection alive:

> For years I hated my father with a passion that knew no bounds, and for years that anger was a powerful healing force in my life. It motivated me to build a new life for myself because I didn't want my father to have the satisfaction of destroying me. But eventually, as my life got better and better, I realized that my rage was like a cord connecting me to the one person in the world I most wanted to leave behind. After that, I stopped feeding the fire.

It's not healthy to deny your anger, but it's also not healthy to live permanently bound up in your rage. The nature of feelings is to ebb and flow. Eventually your anger will take its place as just one of a wide range of emotions, rather than a constant companion.

SUPPORTIVE ANGER

In the introduction to *I Never Told Anyone,* Ellen wrote about her experience as a child being protected by her mother's anger when a deliveryman tried to molest her[*]:

> My mother got furious at him. Then she fired him. She cared about me. Not the deliveryman. She didn't tell me to take his feelings or his bad past experiences into consideration. She didn't care if he had trouble getting another job. She cared about me. I internalized the mes-

---

[*] Ellen Bass and Louise Thornton, eds. (See p. 530 of the Resource Guide.)

sage that I was important, worthy of protection, worthy of her outrage.

This kind of fierce, protective anger is powerfully supportive. Although counselors are traditionally trained not to show more emotion than their clients and parents are warned not to "overreact" when their children are abused, someone else's anger can be directly healing. Ellen has seen this frequently in her work:

> The women with whom I've been privileged to work have felt the power of my fury and it has been a shelter, a spark, a breath of fresh air, a model, an exciting if scary possibility, an affirmation.

ANGER AS AN ORDINARY PART OF LIFE

As you become more familiar with your anger, it can become a part of everyday life. When it's not so pent up, anger can stop being a dangerous monster and take its place as one of many feelings:

> I'm learning that I can let people know when I'm angry without it being this terrible traumatic thing. I can say, "No, that upsets me," without feeling like the world is going to end.

Anger can be so safe that even children aren't scared by it. In Ellen's family, they have an enormous stuffed frog that a friend bought for two dollars at a garage sale:

> When one of us gets really angry, we stomp all over it. Even as a very small child, my daughter would explain, "It's okay to beat up Big Frog because he's not alive. It doesn't really hurt him." And at times when I was crabby she would encourage me: "Go get Big Frog, Mom. You can yell all you want. There's nobody here but me and you, and I don't mind."

ANGER INTO ACTION

> Our task, of course, is to transmute the anger that is affliction into the anger that is determination to bring about change. I think in fact that one could give that as a definition of revolution.
>
> —BARBARA DEMING, "ON ANGER"*

In Ellen's story about her mother protecting her from the deliveryman, her mother experienced her anger, expressed her anger, and then acted on her anger. She fired the deliveryman. She threatened to tell his wife if he ever spoke

---

* Barbara Deming, "On Anger," in *We Are All Part of One Another: A Barbara Deming Reader,* edited by Jane Meyerding (Philadelphia: New Society Publishers, 1984), p. 213.

to Ellen again. She demonstrated her power to take action. This part is critical.

Action, using the anger as a motivating force, is a vital part of healing. If you listen to what your anger is telling you, if you allow it to be a guide, then it becomes a valuable resource moving you toward positive change.

Women's anger has inspired them to cut ties with abusers, never again to have to endure pinches, inappropriate jokes, or drunken advances while they try to chew their Thanksgiving turkey. Women's anger has catalyzed them to quit jobs with domineering bosses, to divorce battering husbands, and to break addictions to drugs and alcohol. Focusing anger precisely—onto the abuser and away from yourself—clears the way for self-acceptance, self-nurturance, and positive action in the world.

WRITING EXERCISE: ANGER

(See the basic method for writing exercises on p. xxix.)

Write a letter to your abuser. Do not be reasonable. This is not a letter to send. Write exactly what you want to say without thinking about possible repercussions. Be as blunt and hurt and angry as you want to be. Express your longing. Express your grief. Express your rage, your hurt, your humanity. Say it all. Let it be a cleansing.

You can write this letter more than once. You might have had more than one abuser. Your feelings about your abuser may change over time. You may want to write to a nonprotective parent or other person as well.

Disclosures and Truth-Telling

"Telling my father how his abuse changed my life was the hardest day of my adult life. It was the hardest thing I'd ever chosen to do. But it was more than worth it. When I walked out of that room I was trembling and exhausted, but I felt lighter than air. Talk about carrying a burden. I had no idea how much fear I'd been carrying."

It is essential to talk to sympathetic people about your abuse. Stepping out of isolation and sharing the pain you have carried alone is an essential part of healing. (This topic is discussed in depth in "Breaking Silence" on p. 102.) Eventually, you may also decide to speak about your abuse—and its repercussions—with the people who abused you or didn't protect you. You may also choose to tell family members who have strong ties to the abuser. These difficult disclosures can be an important part of reclaiming your power, but if they are undertaken too soon or without adequate preparation, they can be overwhelming and may even derail your healing process.

Unlike most other parts of recovery, confronting the abuser or telling your story to family members who may respond negatively is not an essential part of the healing process. Rather, it is an individual choice that is best made after you have established a solid foundation.*

During the first stages of healing, your

---

* We thank Mary Jo Barrett, director of the Center for Contextual Change in the Chicago area, for her innovative work with families and for sharing her insights and experience with us. Mary Jo Barrett initiated the use of the word *conversation* rather than *confrontation*, thus providing a more neutral ground for families to meet on as they worked to heal from the damage of child sexual abuse. The Center for Contextual Change provides psychotherapy for individuals and families and mediation for families struggling with their relationships in the aftermath of sexual abuse. To learn more, visit www.centerforcontextual change.org or call 847-676-4447.

primary need is for safety and support. If you talk about what you're going through to the abuser or to family members who are unlikely to be understanding *before* you've established adequate groundwork, you may be thrown into a level of emotional upheaval you're not capable of handling. You may disturb the fragile equilibrium you've barely established. You will almost certainly be distracted into focusing on the abuser or your family rather than keeping your concentration on your own healing.

Wait until you have worked through the early challenges of the healing process and are firmly grounded before considering a difficult disclosure.

WHAT TO DO IN THE MEANTIME

It's important to make a conscious choice about how you want to relate—or not relate—to the abuser or other family members in the early stages of healing. If you don't normally interact very much, you may be able to navigate infrequent contact without revealing that you're in a process of recovery from childhood sexual abuse. But if you see each other often or have a close relationship, it may not be possible to act as though nothing has changed. If you do not feel ready to broach the topic of abuse, you may need to reduce the time you spend together or temporarily pull back from the relationship to give yourself the space you need to heal.

You don't have to explain the reasons for this separation. Many survivors have found it workable to simply say that they need some time apart to deal with issues in their own lives. Depending on your relationship with your family, your relatives may or may not press for more information. If they do, and this produces a stressful or awkward situation, it's still likely to be less problematic than bringing up the topic of the abuse before you're ready:

I wasn't ready to confront my father. But my parents live only an hour away and we saw each other a lot. I expected that everyone in the family would give me a pretty hard time for pulling back. I was shocked at how little anyone said when I told them I needed time away to deal with some things.

It was almost two years before I was ready to talk to them. As it turns out, it's a good thing I waited. My father was vehement in his denial and my mother was cruel. That's the only word I can use to describe her. If I'd opened up right away, I'd have been devastated.*

MAKING THE CHOICE

The process of thinking through whether to disclose abuse is as important as the disclosure itself. This period of preparation is an opportunity for internal discovery. Take the time you need to explore your thoughts and feelings

---

* For more on healing separations, see "The Benefits of a Healing Separation" on p. 356.

thoroughly. Make your decision in the context of your overall goals for healing. Ask yourself:

- What is my priority in my healing process right now?
- Will a truth-telling conversation help me to meet these goals? Why or why not?
- Whom do I want to talk to? Why?
- What do I hope to gain from this encounter? What are my motives?
- Are my expectations realistic?
- What are the risks involved? Am I willing to take those risks?
- Can I realistically imagine both the worst and the best possible outcomes? Could I live with either one?
- Have I prepared adequately?
- Am I stable and grounded enough to handle whatever reaction I get?
- Do I have a solid enough support system to back me up before, during, and afterward?
- How might things change if I wait?

BUT HE'LL COME AND GET ME

It is natural to be frightened when you consider broaching the subject of abuse with people whose responses are unpredictable. Some of your fears may be realistic. Others may be based on the fact that you are still looking at your abuser or family members from the perspective of a child.

You may fear that your abuser will further hurt you if you speak out about the abuse. One woman was sure that her father would appear on her front steps and try to kill her. In actuality, he hid from her after that, avoiding her totally. *He* was scared of *her*. You may not realize it, but you hold a lot of power when you tell the truth.

Of course, there are some instances where there is genuine danger. In those cases it is essential that you take measures for your safety. You need to set up adequate protection for yourself so that the encounter does not lead to further assault. For example, you may want to meet only in a public place; withhold your present physical address, e-mail address, or phone number; or have an ally along. And if the abuser is too violent or unpredictable, the wisest course is not to interact at all.

IF THE ABUSER WASN'T A FAMILY MEMBER

If the person who abused you was not a family member, you may find it easier to initiate a disclosure purely for the opportunity to say what you have to say rather than with a longing for acknowledgment or an apology. Your family is also less likely to find it threatening to be supportive. Obviously it is easier for a mother to find out that a neighbor or a youth group leader abused her daughter than it is to hear that her husband, father, or son hurt her child.

Whatever your situation, it is important not to minimize the effects the process can have on you. One woman, who'd been abused by one of her teachers, found herself shaking and unable to sleep all night just from looking up the man's name in the phone book. Breaking the taboo of silence is never something to take lightly. It can shake your whole world.

THE TRUTH-TELLING CONVERSATION

In a truth-telling conversation, you clearly and directly tell someone about your abuse: what happened, how it hurt you, and how you feel about it today. You speak about the impact and meaning it has had in your life. You ask the other person not to interrupt until you've finished speaking.

In addition to these essentials, you can also ask for what you want. For example, you may want the abuser to admit what he or she has done. You may want your experience acknowledged. You may want an apology or a willingness to make amends. You may want the abuser to read certain books about sexual abuse or to go into therapy. It is not common for the abuser to make major psychological changes as the result of your requests, so it's usually more effective to ask for specific behaviors rather than a shift in attitude. It's also easier to see whether you're getting what you've asked for if you've been concrete. For example, survivors have insisted that abusers no longer hug them, make comments about their bodies, or drop by without calling first.

However, even if you ask for what you want clearly and directly, you may not get it. You can control what you say and do, but you can't control the response you receive. So it's best to keep the focus on yourself and what is within your power. Many survivors find it more satisfying to say what they have to say without asking for any acknowledgment. In this way, you affirm that you are the authority on your own experience and that you don't need anyone else to validate it.

PREPARING TO SPEAK IS HEALING IN ITSELF

Survivors often feel that the work of preparation is as useful to them as the actual encounter—and sometimes more so. In planning for a truth-telling conversation, it's important to remember that this experience is for your healing. You choose the timing, you initiate the meeting, you set the dialogue in motion. Although you can't control the results, you have a great deal of power over what you do and how you do it.

It's essential to have clear expectations and goals. This is your chance to say your truth, to remain in charge, to stay grounded, and to set any necessary limits or boundaries for a continuing relationship, if there's going to be one. Regardless of the outcome, you want to leave this experience feeling empowered.

MAKING A PLAN

It may feel strange to set out a concrete plan for something that is so emotionally charged, but that's precisely why you need one. Your plan will give you a framework to lean on if you start to feel out of control. Things may not go exactly according to your design, since you're dealing with people who have their own feelings, thoughts, and agendas, but it's very helpful to think through various potential reactions and come up with strategies for handling each one.

It's useful to practice saying what you want to say and responding to different reactions. You can role-play possible scenarios in therapy or with supportive friends.

Walk through each step of the meeting, from beginning to end. What do you want to say? How do you want to say it? You can write out the points you want to get across and memorize them or bring the paper with you to read. And make sure your preparation includes a strategy for taking care of yourself.

Where, when, and how the meeting takes place is of primary importance. Usually it's more satisfying to talk in person, but in some situations you might decide it's better to write a letter or call on the phone. As with all challenging or emotional communication, it's best to avoid e-mail, where the temptation to dash off a hasty reply is sometimes too great to resist—and your communication can be forwarded with the click of a button.

If at all possible, involve a skilled therapist in the planning as well as in the meeting itself. A capable facilitator can help authentic communication take place. A counselor can not only support you but also help the abuser or family members feel safe enough to listen and respond more honestly. And if the person you are confronting continues to act in disturbing ways, there's immeasurable value in having a witness to observe what happened, validate your perceptions, and to confirm dynamics you have been living with your whole life.

Truth-Telling: Catherine's Story

Catherine is a twenty-eight-year-old West Coast radio producer. She grew up in a rural Midwestern town, the child of alcoholic parents. Her father was a doctor, her mother a psychiatric nurse. Catherine was abused by her father from early childhood and began to remember the abuse a year before this confrontation with her parents.

Catherine's story illustrates some of the difficulties that arise when you disclose abuse without a plan, before you are ready. After the initial call with her parents, Catherine's therapist helped her prepare for a second conversation with her parents, this time in person, with her therapist there as a facilitator and ally. At this meeting, Catherine was much more prepared.*

I was beginning to want to tell one of my parents. My mother called one weekend. She said she'd been worried about me; she knew I'd been depressed. She was concerned that I had been avoiding the family. She asked me what was wrong.

I had just gotten out of bed, and I thought, "Well, I might as well do it now." So I just

---

* For more of Catherine's story, see "The Emergency Stage: Catherine's Story" on p. 65 and "Working It Out With My Lover: Catherine's Story" on p. 309.

said, "I'm an incest victim, and I think it was Dad." Then I said to myself, "Oh my God! Why did you say that? You're half asleep! What have you gotten yourself into?"

I could hear my mom choking on the other end of the phone. It was awful. She cried while I told her the story. I cried also.

At first she was very comforting. The first thing she said was, "I believe you 100 percent. You were a trustworthy child. Mothers usually side with the fathers in this kind of thing, and I'm not going to do that."

A couple of days later, I got a letter in which she asked me how she could possibly go on living with him. Her attitude began to shift from that point on. And now she denies it even happened.

TALKING TO MY FATHER

I had asked her not to tell my father. I said I wanted to be able to tell him in my own time. But she told him everything and he called up a week later, extremely angry, demanding, "What's this incest shit you're talking about?"

At that moment, I decided to tell him the whole story and we spent the next two hours on the phone, screaming at each other about whether or not it had been him, why I hadn't said anything before, and why I hadn't been able to remember. He said it was just like me to accuse him. He said he'd never touched me in my life. He demanded that I come up with proof and that I meet with him. I said I didn't know whether I wanted to meet with him at this time, and that when I did, it would be on my time and on my turf. Turning him down

and maintaining my own power was really hard. I'm proud I did it.

FAMILY THERAPY

Some time later, I asked my mother and father to do a family therapy session with me. I met with them for two hours. We both drove about a hundred miles to get there. There was a very tense scene while we waited for my therapist to get there, a lot of suspicious glances between us.

Once we got in the session, my therapist introduced the topic. She said we were here to talk about my feelings about having been abused. She said we had to walk a fine line between honesty and kindness and if we were to err, we would err on the side of honesty. She said the session would dwell on the bad things that had happened, but that didn't mean there hadn't been good in our family life.

Then she turned it over to me. My goal was to show my parents how hurt I was, to cry in front of them, and to tell them what had happened. It was hard for me to let myself be vulnerable to people who I felt had a lot of hatred for me.

My worst fear was that my parents were going to come off being the sweetest, nicest, most rational people, who never could have abused anyone, and that my therapist would know what a liar I was. Within five minutes they played out their whole relationship right in front of her—yelling, screaming, running all their usual numbers. It was a relief to have someone else see what had gone on my whole life.

The thing that changed for me the most since that family session was my level of hope that they would ever change. It dropped dramatically to about minus ten. Part of the session, I think, was to destroy the hope that maybe they really weren't the people who had done this to me.

Listening to them, and watching them during the session, I saw how abusive they were. And that perception has certainly changed how I went about dealing with them. It helped me to focus on my own work, not to drag them into it, because they certainly weren't out to help me.

WHY I'M GLAD I DID IT

I'm really glad I told my parents. It was one of the most unpleasant things I've ever done in my life. But the freedom of telling the truth to the people who abused you is really amazing. It feels rotten before you do it, it feels rotten while you're doing it, and it feels rotten after you've done it, but at least it's not hanging over your head anymore.

I would like to tell people who are considering doing a confrontation about the attitude I took in my family session which really helped me, and which was absolutely terrifying for me. I would recommend it for anyone who is afraid they might waffle and not say everything that they have to say. Just think that they're going to die the minute you end the session. I pictured them dead, and me wringing my hands, saying, "Why? Oh, why didn't I tell them?" It really helped me to be bold and to say the worst, and to say it in a way that didn't protect them.

STAYING CENTERED AND GETTING SUPPORT

Dealing with abusers or close family members can activate childhood insecurities and throw you back into old coping patterns. Therefore it is important that you provide yourself with ample support. You need people who can offer a contemporary mirror, remind you of who you are now, and affirm that your experience makes sense. Simply hearing someone validate that your father is flirting with you or that your mother constantly contradicts you can be a great relief.

Another practical aid in staying centered is to keep a record of your interactions. If you write letters, keep copies. Make notes after phone conversations. Keep a journal. If you decide to travel to meet with your family, bring something with you that reminds you of your current life: photographs, your pillow, a favorite memento or a present given to you by a friend. You can also call home for reality checks while you're away or, better yet, bring a trusted friend along. Be careful about whom you pick, though. Choose someone who won't get drawn into family dynamics. Be clear with that person about your expectations. For instance, you may want them simply to be there and bear witness, rather than entering into the conversation. Make sure that they are reliable and capable of supporting you through the process.

All of this preparation, however, doesn't mean that you won't feel scared. Even when you've waited until you have a strong foundation and have planned thoroughly, you still may feel terror when it comes to breaking old silences. As one survivor put it, "I could plan till I was purple, but when I finally made that call, it was like jumping off a cliff. When you pick up that phone, you just don't know what's going to happen at the other end."

I Had Been Silent for So Long: Patricia's Story

Patricia Robinson was the youngest of four in a wealthy, prominent family. Patricia was largely raised by governesses, flew first-class around the world, and learned to keep her family's secrets. Beneath the lavish exterior of their lives, Patricia's father was an alcoholic who sexually abused his daughters, and her mother was a prescription-drug addict who spent years being secretly shuttled in and out of mental institutions. Patricia's brother, five years her senior, also molested her throughout her childhood.

It wasn't until she was in her fifties and her parents were dead that Patricia was finally ready to disclose the abuse to her siblings. She was terrified to do so, but she felt determined. And because singing and songwriting were important parts of her healing, she did it with a song.*

Music has always been a big part of my life. I think I would have died or committed suicide if I hadn't had music. Being able to sing and write songs was a gentle route through

my history and back into myself. It was the thread that carried me through my recovery.

As I neared fifty, I wrote a song about the incest with my father. I didn't intend to write it—it just came out. When I brought the song to my therapist, she encouraged me to send it to my family.

It took me months to get up the guts to do it because I was breaking all of the family taboos. I was afraid if I told that my whole world would come crashing down. I worried that my brother might go crazy—he was in pretty precarious shape mentally. I thought I was risking whatever tenuous relationships I'd built up with my siblings over the years. I was sure I was going to lose everything when I sent those tapes out in the mail. But I did it anyway.

With each tape, I sent a letter that said I'd been suffering over this for many years, and that I needed to have it out in the open with what was left of my family. I said I was scared to death that everybody was going to disown me and tell me it didn't happen. But no one did.

Being able to share the incest with the primary players in my life—my siblings—took an enormous load off of me. Sending out the song broke the silence at a big level and opened the door to our reconciliation.

Because we were brought up as stiff-upper-lip, upper-crust Bostonians, none of us had ever gotten down in the dirt about anything. Writing the song allowed me to get graphic. Instead of just saying, "I was abused," I said what it looked like, what it smelled like, what it felt like. The song was bodily and real, and it enabled all of us to stop skating on the surface, and to get really specific about our

---

* For more of Patricia's story, see "You May Feel Compassion or Forgiveness" on p. 173 and "Healing With My Siblings: Patricia's Story" on p. 371.

memories. It opened the door for all of my siblings to say the truth, to say, "This is what happened to me."

BEING REALISTIC

It is impossible to predict the response you will get when you first broach the abuse with the abuser or with family members. Sometimes the abuser will acknowledge his or her actions, show remorse, and want to do whatever it takes to make amends. A parent who didn't protect you may be horrified to hear what happened and offer to do anything possible to support you now. These outcomes, though the most coveted, are not the most common. Instead, you may be met with defensive or aggressive reactions. And often there's a mix of both understanding and hostility.

It's important to be realistic about the reactions you might get. If someone has abused you in the past, that person is unlikely to be sensitive to your needs now. Although you may receive some sympathetic responses, the disclosure of abuse frequently disrupts a family system of denial. Family members may find the exposure so threatening that they deny what happened, blame the survivor, or minimize the abuse. One woman, whose grandfather violently attacked her while she was playing cops and robbers in the basement, told her mother about the abuse. Her mother retorted, "You wanted it. What else would you have been doing playing in the basement? You must have been looking for sex."

This kind of irrational or hostile reaction is not uncommon. If your mother knew that you were being abused and didn't take steps to protect you, it is unlikely that she will be understanding now, unless she has made some significant personal changes.

Sometimes the people you want to talk to are family members who have also been abused. If they have repressed the abuse or are reluctant to think about it, they may be extremely upset by your disclosure. Unearthing their long-buried feelings can be so threatening, or can imply such drastic changes, that members of your family may reject you altogether rather than deal with the abuse. Therefore it is essential that you approach a disclosure focused on yourself, what *you* want or need to say, how *you* want to handle the situation, rather than on any response you may hope for.

You should never proceed naively expecting that finally, now that you are speaking out, you will get everything you didn't get as a child, or that if you tell in the "right" way, you'll get the support and love you're entitled to. Yet many survivors hope, secretly or openly, for just such a response. You need to be very clear about this so that you don't set yourself up for another betrayal. When you confront the abuser or disclose your abuse, you are deciding to give up the illusion of a "loving mother" or a "happy family" in order to acknowledge the reality do

If, on the other hand, your parent, other relative, or even the abuser genuinely listens to you, extends compassion, and is willing to support you, then you have the real benefit of that relationship. Although this is not something that you can count on, the odds of greater understanding and a healthier relationship do increase when you prepare thoroughly and enter a truth-telling conversation with thoughtfulness and clear goals.

It Brought Us Closer Together: Vicki's Story

The way I told my mother that my father had abused me was during a therapy session I arranged with her therapist. I'd set it up that way because she was the hardest person for me to tell. I called her up and said, "Mom, I have something really important I want to talk with you about. Is it okay if I fly down and go to your therapist with you? It would probably be a lot easier."

Her first reaction was, "Are you okay?"

And I said, "Yeah, I'm okay." She told me to go ahead and call her therapist. So I did. I told her therapist what I wanted to do and we set up an appointment two weeks later. I talked to my mother a few times during that period. She never once said, "Tell me what it is! You're driving me crazy." But she was terrified.

I flew down and she picked me up at the airport. In the car, on our way to the session, she said, "I want to ask you two questions. Are you dying of some terrible disease?" I thought my heart would break. Her second question was "Are you in very deep trouble?"

I said, "Neither one of those."

She said, "I feel better now."

When I finally told her that my father had abused me, her reaction was what I'd always wanted the whole time I was growing up. She looked at me and said, "I'm so sorry."

She reached toward me and just held me, like a mother holds a child who's been hurt. It wasn't thought out. It was genuine. She just came toward me with raw emotion. Twenty years flashed in front of me. I said, "My God, why did I wait so long to tell her?" She was totally sympathetic.

She had no denial whatsoever. And it wasn't until halfway through the session that she started in on what a bad mother she must have been. Then she got fiercely angry at my father. She wanted to go over to his house and shoot his brains out. She wanted to kill him. I loved it.

Telling her has brought us much closer together. We're much more honest with each other now.*

THE WORLD DOESN'T FALL APART

Our feelings about our families are often complex and paradoxical. Many survivors don't feel just one emotion about the person who abused them or about other family members. You may passionately want to tell the truth about your life *and* simultaneously be terrified to speak out. You may be afraid that your family will fall apart *and* may be filled with anger that you need to express. You may deeply love the person who abused you or a parent who

---

* For more of Vicki's story, see "Believing It Mattered: Vicki's Story" on p. 96 and "Vicki Malloy" on p. 487.

didn't protect you *and* hate that person at the same time. There is no shortage of mixed feelings when it comes to our families.

Celia is a poet. As she began to write about the incest that she experienced, she was afraid that her words would destroy her family. Like many abused children, she had grown up with an unrealistic sense of her own power. "I had this ridiculous feeling that any little thing that I said or did could blow the whole world apart and destroy all of its inhabitants. What I had to realize was that my family stayed intact through all those years of incest. Me opening my mouth and talking about it now was not going to break those bonds."

When Celia finally began to read her work in public, her mother was afraid that Celia would end their relationship. But Celia chose to keep visiting her family. "In doing so," Celia explained, "I was saying to my mother, 'I don't have to only hate you. I don't have to only love you. I can do both.' I was setting an example that these things can be talked about and the world doesn't fall apart."

AFTER A TRUTH-TELLING CONVERSATION

The immediate aftermath of a difficult disclosure can feel horrible, great, or anything in between. Sometimes, even when things go well, survivors feel grief, fear, or disappointment mixed in with the relief. Women often fear that their words will cause a cataclysm: their mother will go insane, their father will attack them, the priest will kill himself. It is very rare for such reactions to occur; it is far more likely that very little will change. Whole families—and institutions—may pretend nothing was ever said.

Over time, too, the reactions you get may shift. When you first tell a relative that you were abused, it's likely to be a shock. But sometimes a negative or lukewarm reception will change to real support once people have had some time to work through their initial feelings. In other cases, your family may initially be sympathetic, and then, when the implications sink in, may withdraw all support.

Sometimes, one family member will empathize and another will reject you. Alicia wrote to her parents and told them that her uncle had abused her:

My mother wrote back, accusing me of being spiteful. She must have used the word "abuse" twelve times in two pages. It was over and over again, how *I* was abusing *her*. It was clear that *she* wanted to be the abused child in this interaction.

My father, on the other hand, was wonderful. And this was his brother we were talking about. He said, "I don't feel defensive for Steve. What I feel is for the little girl, and I just want to pat her on the head and say, 'There, there.'" It was just the perfect response. There was no question at all that he believed me. I know I was really lucky.

I went to visit them a couple of months after I sent the letter. He and I were alone in the car together, and at one point he said, "Can I ask you something about the incest?"

And I said, "Yeah." I expected him to ask me factual things.

All he wanted to know was, "Are you going to be okay? Is there an end point in sight?"

It was so moving. He didn't care about his brother. He didn't say, "Are you sure?" He just wanted to know I was going to be okay, and then he wanted to know how he could help. He offered to help me pin down factual stuff. He said he'd find out when my uncle was and wasn't in the country, to help me get external timetables. My dad actually sat down and helped me figure out how and when it could have happened.

All he said to me about my mother was, "We feel very differently about this. Don't assume we have the same reaction."

With difficult disclosures, you never know what's going to happen. There are as many different outcomes as there are survivors. And often, interactions with abusers and family members include mixed results: exhilaration *and* despair, hope *and* disappointment, tragic moments, absurd moments, and sometimes even comic ones.

Whatever the outcome of a difficult disclosure, it's common to feel some sense of relief mixed in with your other emotions. There is no longer a secret in the air. There is no longer hiding. If you don't want to trim the Christmas tree, share Chinese New Year, or attend a cousin's wedding because you will be expected to interact with the abuser, you don't have to lie about it.

After the initial encounter, there are many possibilities as to how your relationships with the abuser and your family might progress. In the immediate aftermath, you may need time to assimilate the experience—and they might need time, too. Sometimes it's possible to plan a series of talks so that everyone has a chance to think over what's been said and then get together again. Other survivors don't want any contact at all—for a long time or at least for a little while. Still others feel that there's potential to rebuild the relationships and are ready to take the first steps.

Whatever you decide, it's good to be aware that what's right for you now may not be permanent. One of life's truths is that things change. Over time, you may feel differently about the kind of connection you want with the abuser or with particular family members—and what's possible in your relationships may change over the course of your lifetime. (See "Relating to Your Family Now—and Over Time" on p. 352 for an in-depth treatment of this subject.)

IF YOU CHOOSE NOT TO DISCLOSE

Choosing not to disclose your abuse to family members or to speak about it directly with the abuser is a reasonable option if the choice is made after thinking it over carefully, rather than because of an unexamined fear. There are many reasons for not bringing up the abuse you experienced at this time (or ever). You may be in actual danger. You might not have enough support to back you up. You might not want to take on the additional stress. You may not feel clear enough about what you want to say. You may not be far enough along in your healing. You may not be ready to risk a total break with your family. You may have already made a complete break with your family. You may have a limited but acceptable level of interaction now and don't want to disrupt what's working well enough. Or perhaps you just don't want to be discounted or once again told that you're crazy:

The thing about confronting my abuser is that I don't think it would be very satisfying. He's a real reality manipulator. He's been married a whole bunch of times, and each time he gets a divorce, he justifies it by saying how crazy his wife is, using all this medical terminology. I decided I didn't want to hear that crap turned on me.

If it doesn't feel right, don't allow yourself to be pressured—and don't pressure yourself—into a discussion about the abuse with your abuser or family members. You can heal without it.

PROTECTING OTHER CHILDREN

Whether the abuser is a family member, a neighbor, or someone who works professionally with children, protecting children in the present and future is an important consideration. Child sexual abuse thrives in a climate where people let the past be past and hope for the best. As adults, we all have a responsibility to children—to speak out, to warn parents of children the abuser has access to, to alert supervisors in camps, schools, and recreation programs, to confront the church officials and the governing boards of synagogues to let children know that we will listen if they need to talk. We have heard countless stories of survivors who didn't think the abuser would hurt anyone else, only to find he had also molested nieces, nephews, neighbors, or their own children.

It can be extremely difficult to weigh your need to focus on your own healing against the pressing obligation to protect children at risk. If you think that someone who abused you may be abusing other children now, enlist the help of a capable therapist to help you assess your particular circumstances and decide how best to protect the children involved and also take care of yourself.*

---

* StopItNow! at (888) PREVENT can help you if you are in this position. They are professional, caring, and supportive. Also helpful is Childhelp National Child Abuse Hotline, at (800) 4-A-Child. See "Organizations that Provide Resources or Direct Services to Survivors" on p. 526 and "Hotlines" on p. 525 of the Resource Guide for more about these organizations.

WHAT IF THEY'RE DEAD OR GONE?

Sometimes you don't have the option of talking to your abuser or to family members. The abuser might have been a stranger or might be someone you no longer know. Or the abuser might be dead. Survivors often have mixed feelings about this situation. On one hand, you may be disappointed or furious that you don't have the opportunity for either confrontation or reconciliation. On the other hand, you may feel tremendous relief that you don't have to go through this ordeal, that you don't have to carry around the hope that someday (if you're good enough, wait long enough, pray enough) things will change.

If the abuser or other significant people are no longer around, you still need to deal with your own unresolved feelings. Even without a direct confrontation, you can experience the satisfaction and catharsis of truth-telling. There are many symbolic ways to face your abuser and assert your truth. You can write your abuser a letter and not mail it. You can write in your journal or make a painting about your abuse. You can donate money to an organization that helps survivors. You can design your own ritual:

I buried my uncle and sent him out to sea. It was a ritual Indians do. I chanted and I cried about it. I put him and all the things he had done to me into this litter box and visualized him going away. I took a picture of him and burned it.

There are many ways to creatively speak your truth and express your feelings in a therapy setting. Psychodrama is a particularly useful tool for acting out a confrontation. In psychodrama, you choose group members to take the parts of people in your life. You tell them what these people are like and what they might say, so that they can respond to you in character. Then you set and enact a scene with them. Psychodrama can feel very realistic, and it is an effective tool for resolution when real-life meetings are impossible or too difficult.

THE POWER OF SPEAKING TRUTH

There's enormous power in speaking your truth. As poet Audre Lorde wrote, "Your silence will not protect you." Although there are risks in speaking out, there are dangers in staying silent as well. While it is important to establish a strong foundation before you enter into a truth-telling conversation or difficult disclosure, never doubt your right to tell the truth about your life.

Forgiveness?

"I would never in a million years forgive my father. He had a choice. He made a choice. I've had choices in my life that were just as difficult. Sometimes I've failed. But for the most part I try very hard not to. And I don't think he tried one bit. I think he gave in every single time to his impulses."

When we talk about the stages of the healing process, the question is inevitably raised: What about forgiveness?

Many survivors try desperately to forgive the abuser. They despair that they can't heal without it. But it is *not* necessary to forgive the abuser in order to heal from child sexual abuse. The only person you have to forgive is *yourself*. Forgiving your abuser or the members of your family who didn't protect you is not a required part of the healing process. It is not the path to healing or the final reward.

Although it is necessary eventually to come to some resolution—to make peace with your past and move on—whether this resolution encompasses forgiveness is a personal matter. For many survivors, forgiveness is out of the question:

Forgiveness? I have my doubts. Acceptance, maybe, but not forgiveness. Acceptance of who he was and what happened to me. Because there's no way of changing that. But I can't forgive him. He robbed me of twenty years of my life.

Other survivors experience forgiveness as something that arises naturally after a long, committed process of healing. One survivor who was abused by her mother recalls:

After the grieving and the anger and the loss, somehow came forgiveness. It's not okay what she did; I can't excuse her, but I forgive her from my heart. I've let go of the anger and by doing that I'm not carrying it on my back as much. Forgiving her is a way of healing myself.

IT'S NOT THE SAME AS FORGIVING A FRIEND

Forgiving a heinous crime such as child sexual abuse is not the same as forgiving a friend. When a friend inadvertently hurts our feelings and apologizes, we forgive her. We no longer blame her. The relationship is mended. We are reconciled and we continue with trust and respect, without residual anger between us. This kind of forgiveness—giving up anger and pardoning the abuser, restoring a relationship of trust—is not a requirement in healing from sexual abuse:

Certain things are unforgivable. My father raped me when I was five years old. And that is not something I can ever forgive. However, I have come to understand my father's life—what happened to him when he was a child, and later as a soldier in war. As an adult, I can finally recognize the circumstances in which he lost himself. Now he is an old man and he is dying. I am a grown woman, and to a large extent, I have overcome the effects of what he did to me. I no longer feel like his victim. I accept who he is now, and we have a relationship. But I will never forgive him for what he took from me.

BUT THEY HAD A BAD CHILDHOOD

Laura remembers her mother coming home from her job as a social worker and telling stories about all the crazy, misguided people she worked with:

She'd take us to Burger Chef, and over the french fries she'd tell us a particularly juicy story about a sixteen-year-old murderer or a fifteen-year-old rapist. We'd always look up from our Cokes and ask the same question: "But why, Mom? Why would somebody do something like that?" My mother's answer never varied. She'd pick up her double hamburger and say, "They had a bad childhood."

While it's true that many abusers were abused as children and that sexual abuse is often repeated in families, generation after generation, these facts alone are not enough to excuse the horrible things adults do to children. Although many women and men have been abused, the vast majority of them have not become abusers. Regardless of childhood pain, there is no justification for abusing children, as this survivor so clearly and simply states:

Bastard. He took my soul, and I don't give a shit that it might have happened to him. It happened to me, and I didn't do it to my kids! That excuse is bullshit.

"OH, HONEY, JUST FORGIVE AND FORGET"

It is never helpful to tell a survivor of child sexual abuse that she needs to forgive the person who abused her. This advice minimizes and denies the validity of her feelings. Yet the issue of forgiveness is one that is pressed on survivors again and again.

People may urge you to forgive for a variety of reasons. They may believe that you'll feel better if you forgive. They may assume that forgiveness will speed your healing process and free you to live in the present. They may be uncomfortable with intense feelings of anger and grief or may not want to face the harsh realities of child sexual abuse. Their religion may teach that forgiveness is essential. Yet even if the people around you believe that they have your best interests at heart, you should not let anyone talk you into trading your honest feelings for the "higher good" of forgiveness.

In fact, trying to force forgiveness can be dangerous. We've seen many instances where survivors have been urged to forgive before they've had a chance to grieve or express their anger. In trying to comply, they have turned their anger inward, becoming seriously depressed or even suicidal.

When you begin to heal, it's important to focus on what happened to you and what it has meant in your life. *Trying* to forgive can get in the way of doing this important, necessary work.

If you have strong religious beliefs, you may feel it is your duty to forgive.[*] But you are not more moral or spiritually evolved if you forgive. If there is such a thing as divine forgiveness, it's God's job, not yours. If compassion and forgiveness arise naturally, they can be a powerful part of your healing, but not if they're forced—or rushed—because you think you should feel them:

Healing depends a lot on being able to forgive yourself, not on being able to forgive your molester. I don't think any time spent trying to forgive your molester is worthwhile time spent. You don't try to forgive Hitler. You don't sit around and work on that. There are a lot of other things to be doing with a life.

Forgiveness of yourself is what's important, and when you start to feel it, it naturally extends itself to other people in the world. That's what forgiveness is really about.

YOU MAY FEEL COMPASSION OR FORGIVENESS

As you move through the healing process, you may feel compassion for those who have hurt

---

[*] For an excellent analysis of the role Christian forgiveness plays in healing from child sexual abuse, read *Sexual Violence: The Sin Revisited* by Marie Fortune (Cleveland, OH: Pilgrim Press, 2005). The author combines a theological perspective with a feminist analysis of sexual violence. (See the "Religious Issues" section on p. 553 of the Resource Guide.)

you or failed to protect you. Some women feel both compassion and forgiveness; others experience compassion but don't forgive their abusers. And most of those who say they have forgiven do not believe that this pardons the abuser. Part of healing is being true to your own feelings and experience.

Sometimes forgiveness for the abuser grows out of the compassion you now hold toward yourself. Other times it comes because you have begun to view someone in a different way. One woman came to forgive her mother, who failed to protect her, as she gained more perspective on her mother's position in the family:

My mother was no more empowered than any of us. She was very much the victim. There's a picture that stays in my mind of my mother standing in the hallway with all of us kids when my father was in the bathroom, beating one of my brothers, and we're all crying and saying, "Daddy, Daddy! Daddy!" And my mother's saying, "Don, don't! Oh, Don, don't!" And she's right there crying with us. And to me she was as much a part of the helplessness as we were. I really believe she did the best she could do. It wasn't very good, but it was the best she could do.

Another survivor, Patricia, began to feel empathy for her brother after years of feeling disgusted by him. Her feelings of compassion arose naturally after two decades of healing, largely because he was willing to be accountable:

In the beginning, everyone said I should forgive my brother. But I've seen people just glide over the whole thing and say that they've forgiven when they really haven't. For me forgiveness means going through all the feelings. I've wrestled with this for twenty years and gone to the bottom of the pit myself, and gradually my response to my brother has shifted.

My brother has apologized a lot, and at this point, he's beating himself up about it more than I could ever possibly beat him up. He lives like a hermit and has been in and out of mental hospitals.

There was a time when I'd look at him and want to puke, but when I look at him now, I feel my heart open.*

Forgiveness sometimes arises spontaneously when you least expect it. One woman, who was abused by all four members of her family, swore she would never forgive them. She'd written them off and gone on with her own life. Months later, she had an impulse to go to temple for Yom Kippur. Yom Kippur is the Jewish Day of Atonement, when Jews let go of the wrongs they have done to others and the wrongs others have done to them. Without trying to, or expecting to, this woman suddenly started sobbing and, much to her surprise, found herself not only deeply forgiv-

---

* For more of Patricia's story, see "I Had Been Silent for So Long: Patricia's Story" on p. 164 and "Healing With My Siblings: Patricia's Story" on p. 371.

ing herself but forgiving her family as well. She recalls, "From that day on, my life was mine. For the first time in my life, I had an experience of being separate from them."

Many survivors describe similar feelings, saying that forgiveness released the abuser's hold on them and opened new doors of healing:

A lot of the intensity in my feelings is gone since I've forgiven him. I don't wake up feeling like if I had his picture I'd throw daggers at it. In fact, I have been able to see him in dreams again after not being able to visualize his face for years. I was able to say, "Your face no longer scares me. Your name no longer puts me in fear."

Another survivor, who was abused by her brother-in-law, made it clear that her forgiveness was not about absolving him:

When I forgave him, I wasn't saying, "It's okay you were a scumbag." I wasn't pardoning him or wiping the slate clean. But I was letting go of hating and vilifying him; I was letting go of my desire for vengeance.

It was as if I was saying to him, "We're gonna see this in a different light from now on. Even if we never speak to each other, I'm going to know that it didn't end the last time you molested me. I'm going to know that it ended here, with me giving up my hatred for you." I'd carried the pain for twenty-three years.

Now, I was the one who got to change the ending.

If you do ultimately come to a place of forgiveness, you don't have to take any particular actions as result. Forgiveness is a private experience, not a public event. Whether you choose to tell someone that you have forgiven him or her is up to you. Feelings of forgiveness can be communicated, but they can also be held quietly inside.

THE ONLY ESSENTIAL FORGIVENESS IS FOR YOURSELF

There are myriad ways to find resolution around child sexual abuse, and each survivor needs to chart her own way. Although for some survivors that course includes forgiveness, for others it does not.

You have the right to your honest feelings and convictions. No one else has lived through your abuse. No one else is in a position to tell you how to feel or think about it.

Ultimately, the only person you must forgive is yourself. If you are still blaming yourself or feeling ashamed of the things you've done to cope, it's time to forgive yourself, to stop blaming the child who was vulnerable, the child who felt pleasure, the child who survived as best she could. As one woman said, "I've had to forgive my genitals for responding. I've had to forgive myself for not being able to second-guess my father and avoid the abuse."

It's time to forgive yourself for anything you're still feeling guilty about, anything you're still holding yourself responsible for.* It wasn't your fault that you couldn't protect yourself. It wasn't your fault that you needed attention and affection. It wasn't your fault that you were pretty, precocious, smart, or any other quality the abuser might have used as an excuse.

You must also forgive yourself for the limitations you've lived with as an adult or for repeating your victimization. You must forgive yourself for needing the time to heal now. And you must give yourself all the kindness and compassion you can, so that you can direct your attention and energy toward your own healing. *This* forgiveness is what's essential.

---

* A small percentage of people who were sexually abused go on to abuse others. If you have abused anyone, the process of coming to terms with what you did and reaching a place of self-forgiveness will be very different—and more complex—than forgiving yourself for your own victimization or the things you did to cope with it. Confronting the ways in which you have been abusive may be the hardest thing you must face, but this too is an essential part of healing. See "When Children Molest" on p. 113 and "If You've Been Abusive" on p. 347.

Spirituality

"There was some voice in me that just said, 'You'll get there.' And I took hope and courage from the voice inside of me. Somehow, I felt sure there was a process and that I was going to get to the end of it. And I believe that was my spirituality."

A spiritual connection can provide strength and hope during hard times. It can remind you of all that is good and beautiful in a world that also contains much violence and suffering. Spirituality offers a way to hold your experience and the process of healing in a larger perspective. One survivor describes how her belief in the indestructible nature of what is most sacred sustained her through both her abuse and her healing:

My core belief is that love, touch, and sexuality are sacred. With abuse someone could harm me, even greatly, but they could not access my soul. That is mine to give and only at my will. Through the long, difficult healing journey, it helped to know that the innermost part of me was untouched and that an abuser could never touch that. I don't know how I came to have this spiritual belief. I think I was born with it, and for that I am very grateful.

Everyone's spirituality is unique and personal. You may be a member of a traditional religion and belong to a church, temple, or mosque. You may have a personal belief in God or a higher power. You may be on a 12-step journey. You may practice a discipline of prayer or meditation. Maybe you feel at peace in nature, watching the ocean roll in, looking out over a vast prairie, or walking in the desert. When you are truly intimate with another human being, when you are uplifted through singing, when you look at a child and feel wonder, you are in touch with something larger than yourself.

There is a life force that makes things grow, that makes thunderstorms and mountain ranges and perfect avocados. The fact that a baby is born, learns to roll over, then sit up, and then crawl, is a miracle of life. There's a part of everything living that wants to become itself—the tadpole into the frog, the chrysalis into the butterfly, a person emerging into her wholeness.

As the Jewish holy book, the Talmud, says, "Every blade of grass has its angel that bends over it and whispers, 'Grow, grow.' "

Spirituality is staying in touch with the part of you that is choosing to heal, that wants to be healthy, integrated, fully alive. The kernel that is already whole can lead the way through the healing process.

One survivor experienced a spiritual epiphany in the moment of being violated. In that time of pain and terror, she heard something true and deep about her own worth:

> Spirituality was not a word I even knew or understood until my twenties. Before I even knew this word, I knew rape. Before I even knew the word for rape, before I had acquired the education and fortitude to call my rapists what they are and were, before all of this, there was a moment . . . a moment within the first violation where I became aware, primally aware, that I was more than my body, more than the body raping me. I became aware as though being told a secret by a voice way inside my head, that I was someone who was important, that I mattered for reasons that might never be uttered to me by another soul in my lifetime. I became aware that no one might ever save me, defend me, believe me. Within that life of the walking dead, within the unbearable existence of the aftermath of abuse, the one thing that kept me alive was the voice in my head telling me that even if I died, even if I died while being raped, after being raped, I would have been important . . . more important than I would ever know. This voice was born the first day I was raped and speaks to me every day since then. . . . Some days I can barely hear this voice above the din of my own recriminations and the deep pull to let my own pain take me and die, but she persists. I do not know where she came from. But I am very glad she has journeyed to here with me. Her name, I believe, is Spirit.

A BREAK IN THE CLOUDS

Laura once spent a couple of years in Ketchikan, Alaska, the rain capital of North America, where annual precipitation averages thirteen feet a year. "It was always raining. We were on an island and it was gray and stormy and overcast all the time. I'd forget what the sun even felt like. But every time I flew out of there, I'd have the most incredible experience. The plane would take off. As usual, it would be raining. But seconds later, we'd break through the cloud cover into the most brilliant sunlight. It had always been there. It's just that I couldn't see it from the ground."

It's the same with healing. That person you want to become is already with you; you just can't always see her. If you stay focused on how far you have to go, rather than turning around to see how far you've already come, you stay caught in the storm and forget that the sun is just overhead. You lose your sense of perspective. Getting in touch with the stillness inside is a way to gain it back, a way to remember that you are more than just the abused child crying out in pain. It's not that you transcend your abuse or get rid of the "bad" parts of yourself—rather, you enlarge yourself to include everything. You start to see a self greater than the struggle. As therapist and author Alice Miller expresses so well, "The human spirit is virtually indestructible, and its ability to rise from the ashes remains as long as the body draws breath."*

KEEPING THE FAITH

One way we lose perspective is by focusing exclusively on our problems, our process, and our pain. While some preoccupation with sexual abuse is inevitable and in fact helpful, beyond a certain point it becomes self-defeating. Obsession can be a defense against feeling the pain, shame, and fear you're still burdened

---

* Alice Miller has written a number of brilliant books on abuse, trauma, and healing. See p. 535 of the Resource Guide for more.

with. It comes from a lack of conviction that you've already set the healing process in motion through your own hard work and determination. You think you have to be vigilant at every moment. But that doesn't work.

If you have an injury and you press on the wound, insisting that it heal *now*, it will not heal. But if you take care of it and then direct your attention somewhere else, healing naturally takes place.

Breakthroughs often happen that way. You work and you work, and then suddenly, when you stop trying, you grow. But letting go takes faith. You have to trust your capacity to heal yourself. Each time you do, you move forward just a little farther. You gain confidence that you're going to be all right.

If you have an established religious path, faith will probably play a strong part in your healing. Mary, a survivor who spent several years as a nun, told the following story:

I had this picture of Jesus. And I used it like you'd use a candle, to center me to pray. And I looked at this picture, and I said, 'It's too much! No more. You have to make this stop. My heart cannot bear any more pain. They say you don't push a person beyond, but I'm telling you, this is it. This is as much as I can bear.' And somehow that particular moment of anguish passed, and I felt less burdened.

Another survivor, who has explored many religious paths and found great solace in a 12-step program, put it this way:

Faith has been a thread to sanity. God has held my hand through each and every stage of my healing. Being connected to God gave me a sense of hope that I would be okay and that there was going to be something different in my life.

At times, when I felt like I was going crazy, the only thing that felt constant and solid in my life was this belief that there was someone who cared about me, someone who was going to hold my hand and walk me through. It's my personal relationship with my higher power that keeps me going every day—my walk of faith.

Even without a belief in God, you can develop a sustaining spiritual connection. As one survivor explains:

I am an atheist but find great happiness in my human connections. I consider myself a humanist—I gain understanding from being open to other humans. Collective human intelligence is my higher power.

Whether you have a traditional concept of a God, believe there is a life spirit coursing through us all, or simply trust your own intuition, having faith in something more powerful and constant than your shifting emotions can be a great comfort as you heal.

AN INTRODUCTION TO MINDFULNESS MEDITATION

Many survivors have found meditation to be an important component of their healing process. The meditation we present here is rooted in the body and teaches you to pay attention to—and stay with—sensations and feelings as they arise.[*]

This basic introduction to Vipassana, or mindfulness meditation, is from Radical Acceptance: Embracing Your Life with the Heart of a Buddha, *an excellent book by therapist and meditation teacher Tara Brach.*[†]

Find a sitting position that allows you to be alert—spine erect but not rigid—and also relaxed.[‡] Close your eyes and rest your hands in an easy, effortless way. Allow your awareness to scan through your body and, wherever possible, soften and release obvious areas of physical tension.

Because we so easily get lost in thoughts, Vipassana begins with attention to the breath. Using the breath as the primary anchor of mindfulness helps quiet

---

[*] If you are interested in using meditation for therapeutic purposes, classes are offered in many cities through meditation and yoga centers. Also, hospitals and community colleges frequently offer mindfulness-based stress-reduction classes, which teach the basics of meditation. See http://umassmed.edu/cfm/mbsr for an international listing of classes.

[†] Tara Brach, *Radical Acceptance: Embracing Your Life with the Heart of a Buddha* (New York: Bantam, 2003), p. 46.

[‡] If sitting is difficult or painful for any reason, it's fine to lie down or use any other comfortable position.

the mind so that you can be awake to the changing stream of life that moves through you.

Take a few very full breaths, and then allow your breath to be natural. Notice where you most easily detect the breath. You might feel it as it flows in and out of your nose; you might feel the touch of the breath around your nostrils or on your upper lip; or perhaps you feel the movement of your chest or the rising and falling of your abdomen. Bring your attention to the sensations of breathing in one of these areas, perhaps where you feel them most distinctly.

There is no need to control the breath, to grasp or fixate on it. There is no "right" way of breathing. With a relaxed awareness, discover what the breath is really like as a changing experience of sensations.

You will find that the mind naturally drifts off into thoughts. Thoughts are not the enemy, and you do not need to clear your mind of thoughts. Rather, you are developing the capacity to recognize when thoughts are happening without getting lost in the story line. When you become aware of thinking, you might use a soft and friendly mental note: "Thinking, thinking." Then, without any judgment, gently return to the immediacy of the breath. Let the breath be home base, a place of full presence. While you might notice other experiences—the sounds of passing cars, feelings of being warm or cool, sensations of hunger—they can be in the background without drawing you away.

If any particular sensations become strong and call your attention, allow those sensations, instead of the breath, to become the primary object of mindfulness. You might feel heat or chills, tingling, aching, twisting, stabbing, vibrating. With a soft, open awareness just feel the sensations as they are. Are they pleasant or unpleasant? As you fully attend to them, do they become more intense or dissipate? Notice how they change. When the sensations are no longer a strong experience, return to mindfulness of breathing. Or if the sensations are so unpleasant that you are unable to regard them with any balance or equanimity, feel free to rest your attention again in the breath.

In a similar way, you can bring mindfulness to strong emotions—fear, sadness, happiness, excitement, grief. Meet each experience with a kind and clear presence, neither clinging to nor resisting what is happening. What does this emotion feel like as sensations in the body? Where do you feel it most strongly? Is it static or moving? How big is it? Are your thoughts agitated and vivid? Are they repetitive and dull? Does your mind feel contracted or open? As you pay attention, notice how the emotion changes. Does it become more intense or weaken? Does it change into a different state? Anger to grief? Happiness to peace? When the emotion is no longer compelling, turn your attention back to the breath. If the emotion feels overwhelming for you, or if you are confused about where to place your attention, relax and come home to your breath.

SPIRITUALITY IS NOT ESCAPE

Spirituality, however, is not a shortcut through any of the stages of the healing process. It is not an alternative to feeling your anger, working through the pain, or fully acknowledging the damage done.

Some religious doctrines and spiritual practices encourage you to focus on God, forgive the abuser, and "transcend" your feelings. Although it can be tempting to try to rise above your emotions, this isn't a realistic path to healing from child sexual abuse. We need our feelings in order to heal.

Sheila, whose spirituality has been integral to her healing, recalls:

> When I first started to meditate, there was a real subtle way that I was using that to get away from my suffering. I was trying to bypass the pain to get to a different place so I could feel better. But it wasn't real change; it wasn't real transformation, because as soon as I stopped, all that stuff was still there, carried in my body, waiting for me.*

No matter how much faith you have, it's not going to bring you deep healing unless you roll up your sleeves and do your share. Having a relationship with God doesn't mean that He—or She—does all the work, as Mary explains:

---

* For more of Sheila's story, see "Sheila O'Connell" on p. 510.

I really believe I received the grace of God to do this work and to stick with it. I've always believed I've been blessed with a strong mind to survive what I survived. I *chose* to go back to therapy week after week. I *chose* the grace. I could have not gone back and just said, "I'd rather suffer this quiet way I've always suffered." But then I had the grace to choose. I'll give God 65 percent and my guts 35 percent.

Religious faith and spirituality are not substitutes for healing. Rather they are enrichments to healing, sources from which you can draw comfort, strength, patience, and inspiration.

TAPPING THE LOVE

Everyone healing from sexual abuse has a tremendous need for love and support. Many women feel they're working at a deficit, trying to make up for the love and security that they missed out on as children. A spiritual connection is one way to connect with a deep source of love:

> Like most incest survivors, I have kind of a bottomless pit of need inside me. I no longer believe human beings alone can fill it. Nobody can give that sort of thing. If there's a source of love in the universe that can fill that, it's not another person.

My Faith Has Given Me Strength: Meera's Story

Meera is a survivor whose religion is an integral part of her healing. The fact that Sikhs honor the strength and power of women has been an ongoing inspiration to her.*

I grew up doing yoga, chanting and mantras. My religion taught me that women are valuable and that it is my responsibility to do *seva* (service) for people who are hurting. Even though my family didn't always live up to these values, the philosophy sunk in really deep in me.

I wear a bracelet called a *kara* on my arm. Every Sikh wears one. It's made of

* For more of Meera's story, see "I Was Abused By My Younger Brother: Meera's Story" on p. 125 and "Staying Connected to My Family: Meera's Story" on p. 360.

steel, the strongest metal. It represents the strength of my connection to God and to other people.

To me, being a Sikh means being a warrior—not a warrior that takes people down, but a warrior that lifts people up, builds beloved community, that has keen eyes that can see where help is needed.

I have applied these Sikh principles to my healing. When I was having flashbacks or when my self-esteem was in the toilet, I'd look at my *kara* and it would remind me of my strength and that I could heal.

Sikhs believe that Nirvana comes in this lifetime, not in the next. My actions in this life are what matter most. Knowing that helped me get out of bed, go see my therapist, do what I needed to do to heal. To be a good Sikh means I have to save myself so I can help others and make the world safer for all people.

"I don't have to say the hole will never be filled," one survivor explained. "Love doesn't only come from the two people who raised me. I can parent me. Other people can love me. God can love me."

With this love comes a feeling of belonging, a sense of safety, a deeper faith in your capacity to heal. And this love is not dependent on specific people. It's a relationship within yourself that no one can take away.

FINDING OUT WHAT YOU ALREADY KNOW

When you're about to make a decision and a friend says, "Sleep on it," what that really means is to let the implications settle down past your conscious mind. It often works. You may go to sleep unresolved about what to do and wake up with a clear idea about the course of action to take.

Finding a place of stillness, of calm inside, gives you a neutral place in which you can stay centered and watch the rest of the action. This enables you to see what's essential, to let other things fall away.

There's comfort in that space—a place to lay down your burdens for a time. A place you can go for reassurance before diving into the fight once more. Like an oasis. A place of nourishment and regeneration—what a baby feels at its mother's breast, what it feels like to be held and comforted when you're scared.

TURNING IT OVER

For some survivors, a spiritual perspective enables them let go of the tight control they've maintained over every aspect of their lives:

> I've been a control freak all my life, and that need to micromanage everything connects directly back to my abuse. If I could control things—whether it was my spouse, my kids, my work, my environment, my eating—then maybe I could keep from feeling abandoned and betrayed again. But controlling doesn't work. It keeps people at a distance and limits me from exploring new opportunities. Besides, control is a sham. You can't control what comes your way in life. None of us can.
>
> Yet for more than fifty years, I tried my damnedest to control every single aspect of my life. For me, the deepest part of my healing has been about giving up control. It's been about surrender, or as they say in the 12-steps, "turning it over." Frankly, I can't believe I'm saying that, because for years "surrender" was a dirty word to me, synonymous with that little girl lying on the bed being abused. But this kind of surrender is different. It is a willingness to meet life as it comes. It's rooted in faith that there are forces greater than myself at work and that everything is not up to me. Life became so much more rich and interesting when I set down the reins. And I think this is a journey that is going to continue for the rest of my life.

WHEN YOU'VE BEEN HURT BY RELIGION

Though a source of strength and comfort for many, the words *spirituality* and *religion* do not have a positive association for many survivors. You may remember forced processions to church or the hypocrisy of piety in an abuser who molested you. You might have lost faith in a God who didn't protect you:

> I was in a very conservative religious group for twenty years. For a long time I thought Jesus could heal me. When I was thirty-eight, I went to hypnotherapy as a last resort to cure the intense migraines I was having. That's when I started remembering the sexual abuse. And the first thing I thought was, "What kind of God have I been believing in?"
>
> A little girl had been beaten and raped and no God did anything about it. I got

real angry. So I went to my minister and he gave me this cock-and-bull story about how God wasn't responsible. It was all man's badness. He told me I shouldn't be angry at God.

The more I remembered, the more I realized that God didn't care for me at all. If He didn't care for me, He wasn't who I thought He was. And who was He?

It's been an incredible loss. The spiritual side of me, which had been nurtured all my life, doesn't have a place to go. It's been very painful. I lost my sense of roots, my sense of purpose. All my friends in the church rejected me. I haven't been able to find a God I can believe in.

Survivors abused by a minister, priest, rabbi, or other religious leader may struggle with confusion and alienation or may feel abandoned by God.* As one survivor recalls:

My family was extremely religious. I loved going to Church and all the rituals of the Catholic Mass. I was particularly close to Father John. He praised my piety and offered to give me private catechism lessons. My parents were delighted, and they sent me off on my bicycle each afternoon to study with him. They had no idea what actually happened in that back room.

---

* There are now many excellent resources available for survivors who've been abused by clergy members and for those struggling with religious concerns. In the Resource Guide, see "Abuse by Clergy" on p. 552 and "Religious Issues" on p. 553.

Father John told me that I would burn in hell forever for what I was making him do. So I never told anyone and kept it bottled up inside. On the outside, I continued to act the devout child.

But eventually it caught up with me. As a teenager, I hated God and left the church. My parents didn't understand. They tried to talk to me about it, and I just told them that God was dead.

Now I'm a confirmed agnostic, but I long for the simple connection I had with God before Father John touched me. But I'll never set foot in a church again.

I've learned to find God in other things, but it's not the same. Father John not only took my innocence, he shattered my faith.

For survivors hurt in this way, it can take a lifetime to find their way back to a spiritual connection that has meaning for them, if that way can be found at all. One woman, abused by a priest, left the Catholic church and spent some time exploring Judaism, but it wasn't until she began attending 12-step meetings that her spirituality came alive:

I learned to create a relationship with God within myself. I recognized that God is within me and within everyone I meet. God does not belong to me or to any religion. It's tapping into a life force that simultaneously encompasses the horror of death and the joy of life.

I can have access to that connection to the universe, of which I am an infinitesimal piece of dust, anytime: when things

are wonderful, when things are not wonderful, when I'm in pain, when I'm in joy.
When I pray now, my prayers have come
alive because I am connecting with an
energy that existed long before anybody
tried to contain it in a belief system.

There's a Great Deal of Magic in This Healing Process: Gizelle's Story

*Gizelle is a forty-two-year-old survivor who has
suffered from physical and emotional illness for
much of her life. She survived a major suicide
attempt, and her commitment to live is strong
now. Spirituality has played a major role in her
healing.*[*]

When I get into a crisis now, instead of saying, "Oh my God, I'm never going to heal,"
I see that it's like layers, and the more I work
with it, the more they keep coming around.
And even though it's like, "But I was feeling
good two days ago and now I'm shaking and
crying and can't sleep," I'm beginning to see
that I'm not coming back to the same place,
I'm coming back at a different level. It's a
circling, an up and down, and I have to be
with it, ride it, and trust it. When I reach the
next level where the tears are, where the fear
is, where the tiredness is, I have to trust in
my life energy—that I am where I need to be.
And by being there as fully as I possibly can,
I move to the next step.

I feel there's a great deal of magic involved in this healing process. And what
I mean by magic is that the old ways of
healing, that have been lost, are waking up.
I'm awakening in my cells a lot of that old
knowledge. It comes from the earth, from
the spirit of the earth. It's the knowledge
of women who have healed through the
centuries. It's very mysterious and it's very
in our gut. It doesn't come from books.
It doesn't come from medicine. It doesn't
channel through churches or through yoga
teachers or through anything like that. It's
ancient traditions that were passed down
from mother to daughter until they were
lost through witch hunts and the systematic
elimination of women healers.

This knowledge connects with the capacity to heal the rift that has the world in crisis.
It's the healing power of mother earth. It's
been taken away and lost. And She's coming
back through us now.

Sometimes when I think that one man can
molest thirty children, I feel hopeless. When
I get in that space, I have to get in contact
with the power of the Mother. She could
line up a hundred bleeding women and Her
power could touch each of those women and
they could heal. Only She is more powerful
than the forces of destruction and death.

To me, She is the sweetest, force, the most
gentle healing force there is. She's so sweet,
it's almost too much to take; it's almost
unbearable. And She's very powerful. This is
the kind of healing force that heals so gently.
It's like a feather. And I feel very strongly that
She is what's needed to heal me and to heal
all the destruction upon this earth.

---

* For more of Gizelle's story, see "My Outrage Comes
from Love: Gizelle's Story" on p. 147.

GRACIAS A LA VIDA

The work of healing is arduous and painful. But eventually you emerge into a place where you can feel the beauty in life and the beauty in your own life, without denying any of the pain. And over time, the joy deepens:

> I like to think this is my last day on earth. If this was my last breath, what would be important to me? I think of the song *"Gracias a la Vida,"* which is about the simple things in life. That song says, "Thank you for the alphabet. Thank you for words. Thanks for being able to hear music. Thanks for being able to see." Taking time each day to notice the simple things I have to be grateful for has been one of the most healing things for me. Let today be enough. For peace of mind, I have to stop all my doing and be content with the simple things.

Resolution and Moving On

"I feel like I'm home free. I still have a lot of work to do, but I know it can be done. I know what the tools are and I know how to use them. When I talk about the incest now, a lot of it is about the healing and the success and the joy."

—SAPHYRE

Jean Williams, an incest survivor and the adult child of an alcoholic, has worked on healing from child sexual abuse for many years. Recently she had an experience that dramatically shifted her focus:

I went to live in Mexico for a few months, and I really learned a lot by living in another culture. When I came back here my mail was full of circulars and fliers about human growth workshops and self-improvement programs. And I thought, "My God! I don't want to improve myself anymore. I don't want to go to therapy anymore. I'm good enough the way I am! For eleven years, I've been improving myself. It's time to realize *I'm already there.*" I want to do things because I enjoy them, not because I'm going to fix myself in some way. I *am* healed. I'm whole. I'm ready to go.

Moving on is a tricky business for survivors. It cannot be rushed. It cannot be pressured from the outside. And there will be pressure. From the moment you first speak up, people will tell you to forget it, to "let the past be the past." But moving on to please someone else will not help you.

Most survivors reach points in their healing where they want to "move on" simply because recovery is such a painful process. But if you're motivated by the fact that you don't want to face your rage, your shame, your abusers, or your vulnerability, moving on is an escape, not a liberation.

Authentic resolution is a natural result of going through each step of the healing process:

> Knowing I'm not against the wall means I can get up in the morning, look in the mirror, and not have to say, "Oh God, incest again!" It's being able to brush my teeth and get through half my breakfast before I remember. Or I went to a movie and laughed through the whole thing, and didn't think about abuse one time.

Moving on has to be an inside job, as this survivor explains:

> I got to a point where I said to myself, "Reacting to my past, and healing from it, has taken up so much of my life and energy, I don't want to put energy into it anymore. I want to move forward. I want to enjoy the rest of my life as much as I can."
>
> It was a realization that grew organically out of my own hard work and commitment to the healing process. I had to come to it on my own. Someone else coming up and saying, "Get over it," never would have worked.
>
> And getting there took time. You can't convince yourself "I'm over it" until you're ready. I had to earn it. I did years of therapy to clean out the wounds so they could heal. I couldn't just slap a Band-Aid on the infected wound and

hope it would go away. I had to face the pain and then face it some more. It was the hardest thing I've ever done, but also the most rewarding. And now I'm ready to move on. From deep inside, I know it's time.

STABILIZING

Resolution comes when your feelings and perspectives begin to stabilize. The emotional roller coaster evens out. You see that your life is more than just a reaction to abuse:

> You can look at my life and say there've been some real tragedies, and there have been, but there've also been some exquisitely beautiful times. To me those far outweigh the others.

One survivor, whose childhood had good times mixed in with the abuse, sat down with a calculator and figured out the number of minutes she actually remembered being abused as a child. She multiplied this number by five, figuring there was probably a lot she'd forgotten. Then she took that total and compared it to the total number of minutes in her childhood. The nonabused hours far outweighed the abusive ones. "It helped me realize that there were other, more positive forces that had shaped me as a child. I had other things I could draw on."

Seeing your abuse from a different vantage point sometimes gives you a new perspective that contributes to moving on:

In trying to understand what happened to my family, I began doing genealogical research. I started putting together things I didn't know about or that my family didn't talk about. It made such a difference to put things into perspective. The families on both sides are troubled. What happened to me and my brothers and sisters didn't happen in a vacuum. My mother was also abused as a child. My father was an orphan and was physically abused in all his foster homes. The research I did made everything that happened make sense. And along the way, I made wonderful little discoveries—like the fact that my grandmother was a flapper during the 1920s. I found this wonderful picture of her with the beads and the dress and the hat.*

Another survivor remembers:

When I was young, I saw my whole childhood as a personal attack. But the more healing I did and the more that I talked to other people with similar issues, the less personal it became. It became less about someone doing something to me for a reason, and more that I simply got in the way of forces that were beyond my control. I saw that I wasn't being singled out by the universe to suffer like that. That kind of abuse isn't about one person. It wasn't about just me. It was the results of generations of abuse cy-

cling down to me. The older I've gotten, the more I can see it as just part of the human condition. It wasn't fun, and it still has its effects sometimes, but it also forged in me a very strong character.

Moving on means affirming the strengths you've developed. You recognize your own resiliency and drive to be healthy. You stand up for what you know to be true. You face your demons and come out alive. And finally, you make the changes you can, letting go of the things that aren't in your power to change.

Learning to Live With A Broken Heart: Anna's Story

Anna is a sixty-year-old therapist who was sexually abused by her father, a man she deeply loved. He died when Anna was twelve, leaving her bereft and confused, alone with an extremely controlling mother. With the perspective of time, Anna says it was her relationship with her mother that was by far the more damaging. It is a relationship she has spent a lifetime trying to resolve.†

I was estranged from my mother for twenty years. I spent years raging at her and decades running away from my pain. Now I have reconciled with her, but the reconcili-

---

* For more of Pauline's story, see "Pauline Szumska" on p. 502 of "Courageous Women."

† This story first appeared in Laura Davis's book, *I Thought We'd Never Speak Again: The Road from Estrangement to Reconciliation* (New York: HarperCollins, 2002), p. 216.

ation I've experienced is more inside myself than it is a real heart-to-heart reconciliation with her. I accept who she is and what her limitations are. I don't rule out the possibility of a deeper, more reciprocal relationship with her, but I'm not naïve about her limitations. I am going to see her in a couple of weeks, and she is quite ill, and you never can tell what surprises people will come up with when they know they're facing death. There are always wild cards. But I'm not holding my breath waiting for some kind of dramatic change. I accept things the way they are.

Morning Meditation
BY LEE WHITMAN-RAYMOND

This morning my clothes are strangers
I take a sweater, green and white squares
from the shelf
pull on jeans oddly loose
startle to see my hand veined and rough
not chubby not
gripping the blanket tightly
Rain sighs down
foreign rhythms from the radio
cinnamon tea
hand on my belly grateful for
dry shelter warm clothes
sea glass palely glinting on the sill

most of all glad
that you can no longer draw breath
out of my lungs to fill your own

I have grown to have deep compassion for my mother and for her pain. She's living alone. Her health is failing and she's going blind. She's contemplating suicide. She's old and frail and she won't be here a whole lot longer. I feel compassion for her life. I feel compassion for her end. She won't be surrounded by loved ones. She will kill herself quietly one night and not wake up.

I don't expect my mother to ever say, "I'm sorry I took my rage out on you." "I'm sorry I didn't mother you the way you needed to be mothered." She'd have to have a pretty profound spiritual epiphany for her to ever say those things. I never stop believing it's a possibility, but I don't expect it or even hope for it. But that's okay with me. I think part of healing and reconciling is living with a broken heart.

Part of what we all run away from is feeling how much our hearts have been broken by the people who've harmed us. Underneath the anger and the rage and the drugs and the sex and the wild lives that we lived is a small child with a broken heart. And I've gotten to the point where I'm much more comfortable feeling that broken heart in relation to my mother. I expect that when I see her this time we will talk about her suicide and then I'll just sit there with a broken heart, because I'll never have a mother the way I wanted one.

It is one of those wounds that has shaped me, and it has made me as fine a therapist and a mother as I am. It's like a subtle limp. There's no cosmetic surgery that takes those kinds of scars away. I will always have the imprint of her as my mother, but what I choose to do with that is my business.

LETTING GO OF THE DAMAGE

There may be times in the healing process when sexual abuse is all you see, times when you lose touch with the fact that *you are investing all of this time and energy in healing so that you can move on to something else in life.* There may even be a part of you that doesn't want to get through it.

Survivors often complain about how long it takes to heal, but there is an identity in being a committed survivor of sexual abuse. That identity has been closely linked to your survival, and it can be hard to give up.

A lot of people get stuck in that rage and that hatred and that fear. But I realized I didn't have to hang on to it. I started to think of it like a big wad of mucus that I had to cough up. I decided, "Okay, I've had enough of walking around like I'd like to brutalize everyone who looks at me wrong. I don't have to feel like that anymore." Then I thought, "How would I like to feel?"

I wanted to feel safe in the world. I wanted to feel powerful. And so I focused on what was working in my life, in the ways I was taking power in real-life situations.

I stopped sitting there picking open wounds, saying, "If I only pick deep enough, I can see some real blood and gore here." I started to function like I didn't have to carry around that baggage anymore. There was a point where I simply stopped carrying the bags.

Every now and then the porter brings it up to me and says, "Here's your baggage, ma'am." And I open it up and go through it again. And then I say, "I've seen enough of you for now. I want to go on with my life again." And life feels much better. It's a tremendous relief to stop suffering all the time.

And it's not a question of denial. It was an organic change. It wasn't like there was a road sign that said, "Leaving Guilt. Entering New Zone of Healing." It was almost like looking in a mirror after you get out of the shower, and it's all fogged over, and as the moisture begins to dry up, you see more of yourself. Things just got clearer.

I began to relate more to the person I was becoming, rather than the person I had been. When I leave that baggage over to one side and step into that new self, I recognize her. She's not a facade. She's real. She's the person I was before I ever got abused.

REASSURING THE CHILD

One thing that can make moving on difficult is the feeling that you are somehow betraying the child who was injured. If you have had to struggle to get in touch with your childhood pain, you may be surprised by a reluctance to let it go. Evie Malcolm explains:

Emotionally, for me, and I'm not defending this, letting go of the damage would mean abandoning that eleven-year-old girl who's still alive in me, who nobody was there for, who wasn't listened to. If I get better, if the bruise heals, then there's going to be no sign of it, and it'll be as if she never got heard. And that would be an incredible disloyalty, a betrayal of that little girl.

So I'm trying to get myself healed and over the symptoms of the damage without denying that it happened. This is the intellectual "me" talking. This is not the eleven-year-old girl. She doesn't want to let go. It's an emotional feeling. And emotions are very powerful. You can have all the right intellectual thoughts, and emotionally you can be very childlike. And the fearful child in me doesn't want to be forgotten. So I have to reassure her that my getting better doesn't mean I'm abandoning her or denying her pain.*

There is no need to leave the child behind. Rather, by healing, you are creating a safe, healthy place where she can thrive.

FEELING CONNECTED

As you reach the stage of resolution and moving on, your earlier feelings of isolation and separation give way to an increased sense of belonging. Rather than believing that there is something terribly wrong with you, you begin to feel like an integral part of the larger human community. This sense of connection, which tethers you to the world around you, is your birthright. As Laura recalls:

I spent the first thirty years of my life feeling like I was behind a thick glass wall that separated me from all of the real people in the world. I could watch them through the glass going about their lives—eating together, making love, playing with their children, running, crying, laughing, praying, even paying their bills—but no matter what I did, I could never cross that wall. I could see what I was missing, but I wasn't one of them. I didn't belong in their world. No matter how much I longed to cross through that barrier and become real, I never could. I don't think there are any words for that kind of isolation, and I felt that way for years.

Feeling connected to my feelings, to my heart, to my children, to my therapist, to my friends, to the people who love me, and to the earth, has been the core of my healing for two decades now. I have taught myself how to feel and how to love, how to listen and how to be present. There is no glass wall separating me from the rest of the world now.

---

* For more of Evie's story, see "Evie Malcolm" on p. 449.

LEARNING TO LIVE IN YOUR BODY

As you reach the place of resolution and moving on, you grow increasingly comfortable staying present in your body. Rather than dissociating whenever a painful feeling or uncomfortable sensation arises, you learn to recognize and understand the feelings, signals, and sensations in your body. You feel physically alive and start seeing your body as a source of pleasure and wisdom rather than as a repository for pain. As one survivor recalls:

For years, I wasn't aware of my body. Only the strongest of sensations—running hard, having sex, or getting hurt—would make me pay attention. The rest of the time, I lived so far outside of my body, it was as if I was on Pluto. I floated through life, feeling disconnected.

Once, when I was upset, a friend was trying to comfort me. She was holding my hand and touching me. I could see what she was doing but I could hardly feel the sensation. She loved and cared about me, but I couldn't take it in because I wasn't there. That's when I realized what I was missing. And that's when I made a deep commitment to become embodied.

Being separate from my body robbed me of a lot of my life. Learning how to breathe, how to feel my feet on the ground, and how to be physically present have been essential parts of my healing. Now I feel more. I remember things more fully. And I feel a deeper sense of happiness. It's like walking in clear sunlight after years of walking through the fog. Where there used to be vagueness, there's now connection. I feel alive in a whole new way.

INTEGRATION

A big part of moving on is integration. You see yourself as whole, not compartmentalized—your body, your sexuality, your feelings, and your intellect as interconnected parts of a whole. You start to accept the gray, the paradox, the complexity that makes us all human:

The last thing someone from our kind of family can do is learn to accept paradox. It's not black and white. It's not all neat. It's not all going to work out perfect. Learning to hold paradox is a real sign of healing to me. It's been very hard for me to accept that I'll still feel bad. I thought when you were healed everything felt good, but it's not true. You still feel shitty, though not all the time. I wanted to select certain things—humor, warmth, love, fun—I didn't want to feel scared, angry, or any "negative feelings." But they're all part of being human.

Integration means gaining perspective on growth over a lifetime. Susan King found a wonderful image for her healing journey:

I think of a Russian nesting doll my sister had. It fascinated me. A brightly painted wooden doll. I could twist her apart at the waist, and there was another smaller doll inside her. And another inside that, and another, down to a tiny diapered baby. And each Susan inside me has other little Susans inside her, and I am, at this moment, inside a wiser gray-haired Susan that is yet to be. Like the Russian doll, I am round—and complete.

COMING TO TERMS WITH ABUSERS AND FAMILY MEMBERS

Coming to terms with your family and the abuser is an ongoing part of the healing process. What this looks like varies greatly from survivor to survivor, depending on whether the

Reconciliation
BY CHERYL MARIE WADE

Thirty-seven years of denying my father's sexual abuse has taken a toll: massive deterioration of all my joint tissue. I use an electric wheelchair for mobility and my almost boneless fingers are as fragile as a cat-mauled wing. The medical establishment calls this rheumatoid arthritis. I call it my body's eloquent expression of my incest story.

I wheel my chair through Mojave sands
until I sink
There I sit
sun baking my spongy bones
so brittle
that when I stand
instead of feeling shin
push into ankle
ankle press
into heel
heel slam into a shoe of nails
my pelvic bones
snap
and I fall
slow motion

onto the warm
warm grains
I am bleached
white
nothing but a heap
of white sprigs
He comes
with his little girl
Holding her hand
he guides
her eyes to the lizard
a flicker of iridescent pink
but her interest is the white twig
at her feet
She bends and with a small
perfect hand
lifts what once had been
my aching finger
Look Daddy
a treasure
He leans down to admire her find
She puts it in the pocket of his plaid shirt
and the two of them walk on
My skull
opens wide
swallows the desert
and sings hosanna to the dry dry air.

abuser was a family member, how your family reacted at the time of the abuse (as well as now), and a multitude of other factors.

When your family is supportive from the beginning, your relationship with them will most likely be much easier than when your disclosure of abuse is met with hostility or denial. Naturally, it is far more difficult to reconcile your love and loyalty toward your family if you simultaneously have feelings of disappointment and betrayal. Coming to a place of resolution with your family, whether it involves separation or reconciliation (or a combination of both), is a process that evolves over a lifetime.*

When you reach the stage of resolution and moving on, you have arrived at a point where you are at peace with where things stand—at least for now. In most cases, this will mean that you've disclosed the abuse and dealt with the results. You might or might not have confronted the abuser, but you are at peace with the choices you have made. You might have created a healing separation from your family, become comfortable with a superficial and limited relationship, or achieved healing with some family members. The question of how to relate to your family or your abuser is no longer uppermost in your mind. You have followed a course of action that makes sense for you and you accept the outcome.

Most importantly, you are no longer fantasizing that your family members will magically be transformed into the mother, father, sister, or brother you wish they were. You give up trying to get an acknowledgment, a confession, an apology, or anything from them that they are not able or willing to give. You accept the reality of who they are—and their limitations—and you no longer think you have the power to change them.

When you reach this point with your family or your abuser, the effect is often transformative. When you stop longing for rescue from unlikely sources, you open the way to realistic riches in your life. It's as though all the energy you'd been funneling into that old longing is suddenly released and you are catapulted into the present. Your identification with the abuse and its effects is greatly diminished, and you are freed to enjoy a new and much more satisfying relationship with yourself and with the world.

It's taken me a long time to integrate the fact that people who were supposed to love me and care about me could have molested me and made my life miserable, and then deny that to my face. To try to squeeze that reality into the happy American home scene that's in my head has been very hard.

But it's worth it because it's a quantum shift in my perception of the universe. It's put me back on the track of creating my own life. As long as I held on to those fantasies and ideas that never were and never will be, it really limited me. As long as where I came from was clouded, it was very hard for me to take steps in another direction. If I hadn't come to terms with the reality of my family, the only option I would have had was to repeat it all over again.

---

* For more about resolving relationships with family, see "Relating to Your Family Now—and Over Time" on p. 352.

Little Things
BY SHARON OLDS

After she's gone to camp, in the early
evening I clear our girl's breakfast dishes
from the rosewood table, and find a small
crystallized pool of maple syrup, the
grains standing there, round, in the night, I
rub it with my fingertip
as if I could read it, this raised dot of
amber sugar, and this time
when I think of my father, I wonder why
I think of my father, of the beautiful
    blood-red
glass in his hand, or his black hair
    gleaming like a
broken-open coal. I think I learned to
love the little things about him
because of all the big things
I could not love, no one could, it would be
    wrong to.
So when I fix on this tiny image of resin
or sweep together with the heel of my
    hand a
pile of my son's sunburn peels like
insect wings, where I peeled his back the
    night before camp,
I am doing something I learned early to do, I
    am
paying attention to small beauties,
whatever I have—as if it were our duty to
find things to love, to bind ourselves to this
    world.

Sharon Olds, *The Gold Cell* (New York: Alfred A. Knopf, 1988).

LETTING GO OF CRISIS

It's easy to get used to the tangible anguish and turmoil of healing. Being in constant crisis means that you don't have to look at the changes you need to make in your own life. Those survivors who are accustomed to crisis know just how hard giving it up can be:

I'm an intensity junkie. I feel a letdown whenever I come to the end of a particular cycle of intensity. What am I going to cry and throw scenes about now? What am I going to obsess about now? What is going to lend my life that particular tinge of stormy skies and *Wuthering Heights*?

I see it as almost a chemical addiction. I became addicted to my own sense of drama and adrenaline. Letting go of the need for intensity has been a process of slowly weaning myself. I've gotten to a point where I've actually experienced bits of just plain contentment, and I notice it, and I enjoy it.

Giving up this level of stress can be a major milestone in your healing. At first, you may be excited, proud of yourself. Yet after the initial victory, you may also feel hollowed out inside. You have cleared space so that new things can grow, but at the same time you may enter an unsettling limbo.

It may take some time before you begin to get the first inklings of who you are becoming. Those empty in-between times can be unsettling and scary, but you will regain your bearings. You will come through, in fact, more solid than ever before.

LIFE IN THE PRESENT

When you let go of the need for crisis, you make room for the rich and varied texture of ordinary living. You discover new, less stressful sources of excitement—challenging work projects, creative ventures, or greater depths of intimacy.

Part of resolution is learning to balance the excitement in your life with quiet, peaceful times. With practice, you can find contentment in small things—listening to music, cooking dinner, taking walks. From a calm place, you can assess what you want and take steps to get there.

If you don't yet know what you want in your life, this is a good time to explore possibilities. Make a list of things you've dreamed of doing or becoming. This kind of self-discovery is something no one can take away from you. It is more rewarding than any crisis. And as you leave the effects of the past behind, the future becomes open possibility.

I lived a hard life on the streets. I was in and out of mental institutions. I don't know what's going to happen now. So much has changed, and I'm seeing myself differently. I am forty-seven years old, and there are not a lot of options at forty-seven like there are at fifteen. But I'm not closing any doors. I'm opening up a lot of doors, in fact.

HOW HEALED DO I HAVE TO BE?

Healing is not about eternal struggle, the kind where you push the boulder up the hill, only to have it roll back down on top of you. There is a point when you will stop feeling like a victim, either of the abuse or of healing itself.

Recently Ellen was talking to a young woman who has been in therapy for the past two years, actively working on her healing. Because the work was so demanding, she cut back on many other activities early in the process in order to devote her full energies to healing. Gradually, as she became able to handle both the healing work and more commitments, she added school, a part-time job, and a lover to her life.

Now this woman had the opportunity to move to another city, join her lover there, and enter a school program that she very much wanted to be in. "But," she said to Ellen, "I think maybe I should wait until I'm all better. I'm not finished with therapy. How healed do I have to be to do what I want?"

Ellen laughed and told her to go. Part of healing is doing what you want to do, those things that will give you both fulfillment and pleasure. You don't have to wait.

THERE IS NO END OF THE LINE

There is no such thing as absolute healing. You never completely "get over" child sexual abuse.

Issues will continue to emerge from time to time, but they won't have the same power, intensity, or ability to wreak havoc on your life. You will enter each new round of healing with more skills, better support, and a greater sense of perspective. Sheila, who has been actively healing for more than twenty years, put it this way:

These days, I'm dealing with the after-effects of the abuse in a more subtle way—feeling when I shut down and what that costs me. I still have memories emerge from time to time, but it's much more rare—maybe one a year. I still get more vulnerable around Halloween or Easter, times when the rituals would happen. It's not as bad as it used to be, but it's still there. It's not like those things never happened or that the impact is never there, but even when I'm in the throes of it, it doesn't touch me in the same way.*

The abuse happened. You never erase your history. It affected you in profound ways. That will never change. But you *can* reach a place of resolution.

I don't know if I will ever be completely healed. It's like there was a wound and it healed over but it was still infected in there. It needed to be lanced and cleaned out so that good healthy scar tissue could grow over it. I knew that once that scar tissue grew, it wouldn't be very pleasant to look at, but it wouldn't hurt anymore. It would be raised, and you would know it was there, but you could touch it and it wouldn't be painful. And I think that's how it is. I have scars, but they don't hurt. They're cleaned out now.

That doesn't mean every scar is. I'm sure there are still some I will discover as the years go by. That's one thing you can say about people like us, there's always going to be something that comes up. I don't think I will ever be completely healed, because it really cut to the core of my trust in the world. I don't believe in complete transcendence. I think people are too complex for that.

Part of coming to resolution is an acceptance that the healing process will continue throughout your life. As one woman recalls:

There were times when I thought I was through the whole healing process. About fifteen of those times! I'd say to myself, "Now I've done incest. Now I'm through." I understand, finally, that you never really get to the end.

Accepting that fact, paradoxically, is essential to moving on. One survivor spent years resisting and hating herself every time the incest resurfaced in a new way:

Finally, I had to realize it was part of me. It's not something I can get rid of. The way

---

* For more of Sheila's story, see "Sheila O'Connell" on p. 510.

I work with it will change, but I think it will always be there. If I'm going to really love myself totally, then I had to love all of me, and this is part of who I am.

Many survivors make the decision to heal out of pain, shame, and terror, and at the outset the work frequently feels like a burden. But by the time you reach the stage of resolution and moving on, you come to an appreciation of the deep healing you have done. You recognize that healing has brought you more than just the alleviation of pain. You may, in fact, see your healing as the beginning of lifelong growth. As one survivor put it, "I have no intention of stopping. I fully intend to grow until I die."

A BROADER COMMITMENT

As you heal, as you feel more nourished, balanced, and whole, you will have more energy available to direct as you wish. When you don't have to struggle just to cope day to day, you have strength and resources available for creative, life-affirming pursuits.

What really amazes me is that survivors can be out in the world completely functional using maybe 20 percent of their capacity. Can you imagine what we'll be able to do when we let the other 80 percent out? If we were able to recover, stop the abuse, and heal everyone, the world we live in would be so phenomenal.

If you think of all the ways in which you have been stunted, all the energy you have consumed simply to keep hanging on by your fingernails, all that you might have created or accomplished or simply enjoyed had you not had to stagger under the burden of abuse, you may have a formidable list.

If you multiply that times the number of other women similarly struggling—not only now but also back through the decades and centuries—the result is awesome.

Now, imagine all women healed—and all that energy no longer used for mere survival but made available for creativity, nurturing relationships, working for peace and equality. The effect on the world would be monumental.

We have never in recorded history lived in a time when women were, as a whole, empowered. We can only begin to imagine the riches.

HEALING MOVES OUT FROM THE CENTER

Your first allegiance must always be to yourself. If you race out to do good deeds without attending to your own needs, it's easy to create more problems than you solve. For too long, women have been expected to sacrifice themselves while they helped everybody else.

It's a little like using oxygen masks on an airplane. If you're traveling with small children, the flight attendant tells you to secure your own mask first, and then to assist the child. Your initial reaction might be to help your child first, but if you pass out while trying to get the child's mask on, no one survives. When you ensure your own stability first, then you can help others, and everyone can be safe.

Although your responsibility toward healing begins with yourself, it does not stop there. Child sexual abuse originates from the same fear, pain, hatred, selfishness, greed, and ignorance that lead people to abuse and assault in other ways. These attitudes are woven into the very fabric of our society and oppress on a large scale. We get rape, war, poverty, inhumane working conditions, and the contamination of our environment.

As you affirm your own worth, your own integrity, you become increasingly capable of taking positive, life-affirming action in the world in a multitude of ways.*

It is you—you who know something about both justice and injustice, about abuse and respect, about suffering and about healing—who have the clarity, courage, and compassion to contribute to the quality, and the very continuation, of life.

And remember, every individual act of healing is already a contribution toward healing the world.

---

* Many of the women who contributed their stories to *The Courage to Heal* have become activists as a natural outgrowth of their healing. For two examples, see "Rifat Masoud" on p. 476 and "Sachiko O'Brien" on p. 430. There are many organizations working to end child sexual abuse that would welcome your involvement. In the Resource Guide, you'll find them in "Activism and Public Policy" (p. 528) in "If Your Child Is Abused," and among the subcategories in "Special Topics" (p. 577).

WHY IT'S BEEN WORTH IT

"I feel like Rip Van Winkle sometimes, like I'm just waking up. Things like crying—I find myself crying now. I had given it up when I was eight. Or laughing. Giggling. Rough-housing with my kids and having it be safe. Playing. Getting angry at somebody I love. Telling the truth. Feeling something in the moment it's actually happening, instead of five minutes later, five years later, always *later*. Taking risks I never would have taken before. Just kind of waking up. It's a silly metaphor, but it's what flowers do. They just come out."

"Solitude has become important to me. I used to feel terribly lonely. I don't have to be lonely anymore."

"I'm not afraid of people like I used to be. I have a phone list that's incredible, and I really talk to these people. A lot of the bar-riers I've always put up between myself and other people are gone."

"These are the ways I've turned things that have damaged me into things that work. They're survival tools, and I've sharpened them up to use in real life. I'm proud of them."

"I feel life more intensely. Pain, but good things, too. I can take a walk in the park and be really upset, and I can still see how beautiful everything is."

"I feel more peaceful. I feel like I'm normal now. Like I don't have to carry around this burden anymore."

"I'm thriving as opposed to surviving. There's all the difference in the world in how I look at life. I like myself so much bet-ter. And I'm happy most of the time. I'm more completely myself almost all the time. In fact, I am myself all the time."

PART THREE

Changing Patterns

The Process of Change

"For a long time I felt like damaged goods. I was obsessed with the question 'What is wrong with me?' But I just kept doing the work. A part of me knew that I was not locked into anything. My cells replace themselves completely every seven years. How could I still be damaged goods? Of course I could change."

—SAPHYRE

When you first remember your abuse or acknowledge its effects, you may feel tremendous relief. Finally there is a reason for your problems. There is someone, and something, to blame. But eventually you realize that things are not that simple—or fair. As one survivor said: "My grandfather was dead and gone and I was still alive with the same problems I'd always had. I had to face the fact that if I wanted a different life, I was going to have to do something about it."

One woman went to ten years of incest-related therapy before she realized she was the one responsible for changing her own life:

I had to go from dealing with the incest an hour a week in therapy to dealing with it in my real life. I realized I had to stop talking at forty dollars an hour* and start doing. It's a lot cheaper to fix yourself on your own time than to depend on an hour a week to get better. I could talk therapy with anyone who had the lingo, but I had to realize I wasn't taking care of myself in real life.

I decided to change my life and take responsibility for what was happening to me. I started asking myself questions like "What did I do to immobilize myself? Why did I stay in an abusive relationship?"

And then I started taking care of my own life. I *changed* my relationship. I

---

* This woman was interviewed in the mid-1980s when $40 was considered a lot of money for therapy. Now, it sounds like quite a deal!

changed my job. I *changed* my home. I started taking care of business! I filed a suit against my ex-lover for assault. I got money back that I had loaned out. I fought a custody battle against my ex-husband. I started getting angry. I started to cry. I've really changed. I *look* different. I *sound* different. I changed my life intentionally.

You may feel resentful or angry that you have to deal with problems that you didn't create. The fact that you are left with the damage is not fair. But recognizing that you are now responsible for your own life represents a significant leap in maturity.

HOW TO CHANGE

The basic steps to making changes are:

- **Become aware of the behavior you want to change.**
- **Examine the reasons you developed that behavior to begin with.** When do you first remember feeling or acting that way? What was going on then? Try to understand why you needed that behavior.
- **Have compassion for what you've done in the past.** Even if you didn't make the wisest, healthiest choices, you took the options you saw at the time. And now you're making better choices. Focus on that.
- **Keep doing your own work.** Deep, lasting change comes about only when we continue to work through the grief, anger, fear, and shame that underlie many of our life choices.
- **Find new ways to meet your needs.** Although every change doesn't expose an unmet need, many do. By taking such needs seriously and finding new ways to meet them, you make it possible to maintain healthy behavior.
- **The best way to change old, destructive patterns is to replace them with something else.** Rather than trying "not to do" something, you give yourself a positive message instead. For example, in AA, people are advised to "Pick up the phone instead of a drink."
- **Get support.** Your ability to make changes is directly affected by your environment and the people you spend time with. People who are working to grow in their own lives will support you with encouragement and by example. People who are still living out the patterns you're trying to break will continually suck you back in. Respect the power of influence.
- **Most change happens gradually.** Although sometimes you can soar, making changes is usually a plodding process that doesn't look very heroic or exciting. Sometimes change happens so slowly, you don't even notice it's happening. Yet those small, daily steps lead to real change and a more rewarding life.
- **Be persistent.** Most of the changes we make in our lives require repetition. If not smoking *one* cigarette were sufficient, it wouldn't be so hard to quit smoking.

OBSTACLES TO CHANGE

We do not change in a vacuum. Your new choices will have repercussions on those around you. Your determination to change can sometimes be threatening to people in your life because it means they will have to change, too. Even though it's change for the better, people don't always willingly make the commitment to healthier living.

A forty-six-year-old survivor described the way her second husband responded when she got into therapy: "I made change after change after change. John was terrified. What happened to the woman he married? I looked like a little widow lady with three kids. All of a sudden, I wasn't. I was this woman who was just taking off."

Change requires support and community. If you do not get it from the people closest to you, you will need to seek it elsewhere, whether through new friends, a counselor, or a group of other survivors.*

ACKNOWLEDGING FEAR

It helps to name your fears. Naming things gives them less of a hold. One woman, who suffered from continual depression and immobility, made a list of what she would have to face in life if she actually healed. Her list was extensive. She'd have to face the possibility of success—or failure—in her career. She'd have to risk greater intimacy with her

lover. She'd have to stop blaming her family for her problems and would have to give up their image of her (that she was a loser). She'd lose her identity as a sick person, as a victim. She'd have to learn to deal with her deep grief instead of masking it with hopelessness and anxiety. She'd have to attract people on her own merits, not because they felt sorry for her. When she looked over her list, she could see why she was afraid.

FEAR DOESN'T HAVE TO STOP YOU

Often fear accompanies the unfamiliar and exciting leaps we take in life. It's the feeling that makes your knees shake the first time you sing in public, when you apply for a job you really want, or when you confront the person who abused you. When you do something new and challenging, you need that energy. It's adrenaline. Often women feel this kind of fear when they are taking absolutely the right steps for themselves. It can help if you recognize that this feeling may not be purely fear. It may also contain excitement, exhilaration, hope, and uncertainty about new endeavors.

Fear doesn't have to stop you. Even if you're afraid, you can still go ahead and make the changes you want. You just do it anyway. You do it afraid. You do it nervously, awkwardly. You shake or sweat. You are not graceful or composed, but you do it. This is the definition of courage.

---

* See "Developing a Support System" on p. 30.

Autobiography in Five Short Chapters

BY PORTIA NELSON

I

I walk down the street.
　There is a deep hole in the sidewalk.
　I fall in
　I am lost . . . I am helpless
　　It isn't my fault.
It takes forever to find a way out.

II

I walk down the same street,
　There is a deep hole in the sidewalk.
　I pretend I don't see it.
　I fall in again.
I can't believe I am in the same place.
　　But it isn't my fault.
It still takes a long time to get out.

III

I walk down the same street
　There is a deep hole in the sidewalk.
　I see it is there.
　I still fall in . . . it's a habit.
　　My eyes are open.
　　I know where I am.
It is my fault.
I get out immediately.

IV

I walk down the same street.
　There is a deep hole in the sidewalk.
　I walk around it.

V

I walk down another street.

Portia Nelson, *There's a Hole in My Sidewalk: The Romance of Self-Discovery* (Hillsboro, OR: Beyond Words Publishing, 1994).

THE PATTERN FIGHTS BACK

A pattern is any habitual way of behaving. By its nature it is deeply entrenched, set by repetition, and brings a familiar result. Even if that result is not ultimately what you want, predictability is part of its grip. Patterns usually start unconsciously as a way of coping when your options are limited. They serve you, but at a cost.

Patterns have a life of their own, and their will to live is very strong. They fight back with a vengeance when faced with annihilation. Once you recognize a pattern and make the commitment to break it, it often escalates, as Laura recalls:

> I decided I wanted to be more present in my life, that I no longer wanted to space out every time a strong feeling surfaced. But the pattern fought back with a frenzy. Things got much worse than they had ever been. I was spaced out all the time. Then just when I thought that I would never, ever get through it, it broke. I'd earned the scary miracle of being able to stay present.

Another woman, who'd had a long series of abusive intimate relationships, worked toward changing this pattern. But just as the pattern was about to give way, she said, "I had a three-week affair in which I replayed every screwed-up relationship I ever had. I went through all my patterns in real rapid motion. It was like a Charlie Chaplin movie."

It's important that you not give up at this critical point. It's likely the "I can't stand it anymore" feeling means you're close to the change you're working so hard to achieve.

THE SPACE BETWEEN THE OLD AND THE NEW

Change is fraught with uncertainty. Even if you know you are making room for something better, there's still loss—the loss of the known, the loss of a familiar habit, the loss of the good qualities in people you may be leaving behind. This can be a painful and awkward time for you, a kind of limbo when you have let go of the old but have not yet established the new. One woman, who was letting go of several friendships that revolved around drinking, talked about her way to ease the pain of this difficult transition:

> When I feel lonely, I find that several things help me—telling someone how I'm feeling, knowing that the feelings will pass, and remembering a parable an old friend told me once: it's only when you have an empty cup that it can get filled with fresh, life-giving water.

A LITTLE SELF-LOVE GOES A LONG WAY

Be kind to yourself. Be patient. Babies do not go from crawling to walking in a single day. We are not impatient or angry when they tot-ter and fall. In fact, we delight in their first forays, even when they end in a plop.

Forgiving yourself when you backslide, being gentle with yourself, may be a pattern-breaker in itself. One survivor related how her attitude toward herself has softened over time:

> When I slip into an old pattern, I see it almost as if I'm putting on a pair of shoes that don't fit anymore. I've put them on again, and here I am trying to tap-dance, and it's not working. At first I'd whip myself: "Why did you put those stupid shoes on again?" I'd get really despondent that I'd never change.
>
> As I've gotten further along in my healing, I've been able to be gentler with myself: "Oh God, I slipped again." I'll congratulate myself on recognizing it so quickly, and then I'll ask myself, "What happened this time to trigger it?" Instead of beating myself up, I tell myself I'll take care of myself the next time and I figure out ways to do that.

GIVE YOURSELF CREDIT

Often people are acutely aware of how difficult something is before they do it. You are scared, you vacillate, you collect all your strength and courage, and somehow you manage to do what you set out to do. Then, as soon as it's over, you jump in with "Okay, what's next?" Or worse, you frown at yourself and say, "I don't know why I had to make such a big deal out of that. It wasn't much."

It was much. And you need to acknowledge that.

One woman, who was working with Ellen, was upset with herself for being in a relationship with a man she really didn't care for. Afraid she'd never find anyone else who wanted her, afraid to be lonely, she hung in. Now and then she'd try to work up her courage to break off with him, but each time she'd waver and stay. Finally, after many months, she ended the relationship. That week in counseling she talked about other things for most of the session and then mentioned that she had broken up with this man. In the same sentence she went on to say that she was feeling bad about herself because she was still ambivalent and wondered if she should go back.

"Wait," Ellen interrupted. "You broke up with him?"

"Yes, but I don't feel strong about it. I've—"

Ellen interrupted again. "But you broke up. Even if you decide at some time that you want to go back, you still did this thing that you really wanted to do and were very afraid to do. You did it! You don't even give it a sentence of its own."

Finally this woman slowed down enough to experience her achievement. She was willing to hear that many people feel unsettled when they act in unfamiliar ways, even if those ways are in their best interests.

CELEBRATE

When you accomplish a goal, when you make a change you have worked hard to make, celebrate. A celebration can be anything that feels right to you, from raucous to serious. Eat lobster. Buy a lovely card and mail it to yourself. Light a candle. Go out dancing. Do what's special for you.

WRITING EXERCISE: CHANGING PATTERNS

(See the basic method for writing exercises on p. xxix.)

Take some time to assess how far you've come in your healing. Are you at the beginning, or have you made some progress? What have you accomplished already? What do you have to be proud of? What obstacles have you broken through? What small (and large) successes have you achieved? Even just making the decision to heal is a major step. Give yourself credit. In detail.

You've already done a lot of work—and there's still more to do. What are your goals for your healing now? What are some ways you may be able to work toward these goals? Write about the things you still need to do to move ahead in your personal life. These can be general, such as "I need to be more compassionate with myself," or as specific as "I need to go back to school so that I can do work that's meaningful to me."

Change

BY ELLEN BASS

This is where I yank the old roots
from my chest, like the tomatoes
we let grow until December, stalks
thick as saplings.

This is the moment when the ancient fears
race like thoroughbreds, asking for more
and more rein. And I, the driver,
for some reason they know nothing of
strain to hold them back.

Terror grips me like a virus
and I sweat, fevered,
trying to burn it out.

This fear is invisible. All you can see
is a woman going about her ordinary day,
drinking tea, taking herself to the movies,
reading in bed. If victorious
I will look exactly the same.

Yet I am hoisting a car from mud ruts
half a century deep. I am hacking
a clearing through the fallen slash
of my heart. Without laser precision,
with only the primitive knife of need, I cut
and splice the circuitry of my brain.
I change.

Self-Esteem and Trusting Yourself

"I remember saying in fits of depression, 'You think I'm a good person, but I'm not. I'm a bad person.' Deep inside, under all this cheerleader, straight-A bullshit, there is this little kernel, this bad seed, that's forced me to become perfect on the outside. Because if I keep pretending that I'm good, it will make up for the awful person I really am."

Self-esteem is a central issue for many survivors. When children are abused, they are harmed at a core level. And one of the areas hardest hit is their developing sense of self-respect and self-worth. This lack of self-esteem often continues into adulthood. You may experience it as a constant feeling of worthlessness, a nagging voice that tells you that you didn't do enough, that you didn't do it right, or that if you did, it was a fluke—that next time, you'll screw up. At the most basic level, you may believe that you don't deserve anything good in your life.

Your feelings about yourself may fluctuate wildly. You may feel okay about yourself most of the time, self-critical feelings lying dormant until you have some kind of setback—a loss, a period of change, an argument with someone you love. Then you suddenly lose touch with the good things about yourself and fall into a pit of self-loathing and despair. The self-love you've nurtured so carefully evaporates like mist.

Feelings of self-hatred can erupt seemingly out of the blue. A small interaction can trigger an avalanche of self-doubt and uncertainty. You get one problem wrong on an exam and you say to yourself, "I'm a stupid idiot." You make a well-thought-out decision to leave a job where you're underpaid and treated badly, and instead of feeling proud, you're sure no one will ever hire you again. Even though you are taking care of yourself, you somehow end up feeling wrong and defective—again.

Self-esteem is experienced in the moment, and your feelings about yourself will fluctuate as you move through the healing process. When you're first facing your grief and anger or struggling with the impact of abuse on your life, you may feel worse than you felt before. Often shame, powerlessness, and self-hatred are bottled up with memories of abuse, and as the memories come through, these feelings do, too.

Yet healing isn't only about pain. It's about learning to love yourself. As you move from feeling like a victim to being a proud survivor, you will have glimmers of hope, self-respect, and satisfaction. Those are natural by-products of healing.

INTERNALIZED MESSAGES

When you were abused, it's likely that you were given the message, directly or indirectly, that the abuse was your fault. You might have been told you were bad or stupid. You might have been humiliated or called a liar. Many survivors were told that they would never amount to anything. You may still be receiving this message. One survivor whose poem was published in a local newspaper sent a copy of it to her mother. Her mother replied, "It was just beginner's luck. You'll never write another one."

Another woman, elected homecoming queen in high school, had such a distorted image of herself that she was convinced her friends had chosen her only because they pitied her.

Even if you weren't given such messages directly, the very fact that you were abused taught you that you were powerless, alone, not worthy of protection or love. If you were ignored or neglected, your basic value was denied. You learned that you were undeserving, unable to have an impact in the world.

When your worth is negated often enough, you begin to believe there's something wrong with you. As a result of these childhood messages, you may believe that you're unlovable, that nothing you do matters, or even that you don't deserve to live. As Ellen says, "Survivors were programmed to self-destruct. You learned to put yourself down so effectively that the abusers don't even have to be around anymore to do it. They can go off and play golf while you do yourself in."

This self-destructiveness often is at war with the positive, sustaining self-concept you are trying to build:

I have often felt like two different people. Wednesday I was going to buy a gun to kill myself. The gun store closed at 6:00. We had a sales meeting at work, which I didn't go to because I figured it was going to take me a half hour to get to the store from downtown.

All day I'd been going through this bullshit with the gun, but I'd also made this list of things that make me feel good. And then on my way to the store, I decided I didn't really want to buy the gun. So I bought a teddy bear instead. I made an appointment for a massage. And I bought myself a ticket to a show I really wanted to see.

A lot of times there's two people operating. There's this person inside who's really striving to be healthy. And then there's this other person who's been beaten so much, she just takes up where my father left off.

CHANGING INTERNALIZED MESSAGES

At the beginning of your healing, you may experience negative messages constantly. But as time goes by and your basic self-image starts to shift, these messages will come less frequently. They will stand out more distinctly against a background of basically liking yourself.

While you may think such thoughts come without cause, they are usually sparked by something. Each time you feel bad about yourself, try to isolate the thought or event that set off the feeling. At first this won't be easy, but with practice you will be able to identify the source. Ask yourself:

- When did I start feeling this way?
- Did I have a disturbing conversation with someone? Receive an upsetting phone call, e-mail, or letter?
- Did something scare me or make me angry?
- Is there a reason I'm feeling particularly vulnerable right now?

Once you find the event or thought that started this feeling, ask yourself, "Is this feeling familiar?" Search back to find the first time you felt that way, the first time you were told that particular lie. What was the context? Who told you that you were selfish? Who implied you were in the way?

Allow yourself to feel the pain and shame of the child you once were. Allow your compassion for her, your anger at those who hurt her, and any other feelings to rise. Recognizing and expressing these feelings helps to release the grip of negative internalized messages. You feel like this not because it's true but because you were conditioned to feel this way.

SETTING LIMITS AND BOUNDARIES

The capacity to set limits is essential to feeling good about yourself. Many survivors have not known how to define their own time, to protect their bodies, to put themselves first, to say no.

> I've always given my time over to whoever asked for it because I didn't think it was mine to deal with. When I was little, if anybody wanted anything from me, they took it. I have poor boundaries. It makes me ridiculously easy to get along with. I'll do anything anyone asks me to do. If you do that, everybody likes you. And it's very important for me to be liked.

Although learning to say no is difficult, it is a relief to stop doing what you don't want to do. By setting limits, you protect yourself and give yourself freedom at the same time. As you say no to other people, you start to say yes to yourself.

But saying no isn't easy. As women, we've been taught to please others, to put their needs first.

> I went to a workshop on dating. We were paired up and told to ask each other out on an imaginary date. Those of us being asked were instructed to say no. We were supposed to turn down the invitation. But when the women reported back to the group, a surprising number had said yes anyway. One even offered to cook dinner.

Watch for situations in your life in which you want to say no. Start with what's easiest and build up to the harder ones. When a friend wants you to go out to lunch but you've set aside time to play the piano (and playing is what you *really* want to do), say no. When your six-year-old asks you to get her the milk, tell her she's capable of getting it herself and that you're sure she can do a good job of it.

If you've never (or hardly ever) said no, your first attempts may feel awkward or even rude. When you feel that you don't have the right to say no, or when you're new at it, you may add cumbersome explanations or refuse more strongly than necessary. Yet saying no doesn't have to be loud or hostile. As you feel more secure in your ability to set clear boundaries, you'll be able to decline with a simple statement: "No, I don't want to." "No thanks." "No, I'd rather not."

If you've been taking care of other people and saying yes all your life, you may encoun-

ter some resistance when you start to say no. People may say you were nicer before, that they prefer the "old" you. On the other hand, you may find that your honesty and clarity are respected by friends, who are glad that you are finally taking care of yourself.*

TRUSTING YOURSELF

When children are abused, it's threatening for them to trust their own perceptions. It was unbearable to acknowledge that the neighbor who pushed you on the swings and gave you birthday presents also made you touch his penis. It was too terrifying to admit that your mother, who went to work to support you and stayed up late to make you a dollhouse, had a scary smile on her face when she touched your genitals. So you pretended they weren't doing these things or that these things were really all right. The lengths to which children go to distort their perceptions are striking.

> When my father would come into my room at night, I would think, "That's not my father. That's an alien being." I'd look at these people doing these things to me and think, "Invaders have taken over their bodies." And these invaders were doing things to me. The original was still out there somewhere and why wouldn't they come back? I'd think, "Daddy, why

---

* Learning to say no and set boundaries is something that you can learn physically in your body. See "Exercises to Ground You" on p. 255.

42 WAYS TO SAY NO (OR BUY TIME UNTIL YOU CAN)

by Margot Silk Forrest, author of
*A Short Course in Kindness**

A lot of us have difficulty saying no. This list, offered with compassion and a little humor, will help you get comfortable with turning people down, refusing to answer nosy or offensive questions, asking people to stop doing something you don't like, and telling others you disagree with them.

As you develop your "no" muscles, see if you can shift from saying, "I can't" to forthrightly saying, "I won't." Also try exchanging "I don't want you to" to "Don't!" You will feel vastly more empowered—and have more time for self-kindness and kindness to others when you do.

When Someone Asks You to Do Something for Them or With Them:

1. The enthusiastic (polite/helpful/etc.) part of me would like to say yes, but the rest of me is overcommitted (more realistic/unwilling/etc.).
2. I don't know. I'll have to think that over.
3. I wish I could help you out, but I'm over-extended/overcommitted right now.
4. I'm going to pass. I'm really trying to slow down my pace these days.
5. That's something I'll have to think about.
6. I don't have my calendar with me, but I can call and let you know tomorrow.
7. Sorry, I'm already booked.
8. No, I can't make it after all. But it was nice of you to ask.
9. I'll think it over.
10. Thanks, but I'm way too tired.
11. No, that's not really my thing.
12. Don't hold your breath!
13. I have an appointment that day/night. *(And you don't have to say what it is!)*
14. That's not for me, thanks.
15. Oh, that sounds interesting. Let me think about it and get back to you.
16. I'm not sure if I'm free that day/night. Let me check and call you tomorrow.
17. Sorry, but my schedule is too full right now.
18. The part of me that wants to make you happy wants to say yes, but the rest of me won the vote. I'll pass.
19. Thanks, but I don't think I will.
20. That's not really something I enjoy.
21. That doesn't work for me.
22. That doesn't fit for me.
23. When you want to have some fun saying no, try one of these:
   • Not in this lifetime! Forget it! Dream on!

---

* Margot Silk Forrest, *A Short Course in Kindness* (San Luis Obispo, CA: L.M. Press, 2002). This wonderful book about love and self-care can be ordered at www. lmpress.com.

- You must be kidding! Not in a million years!
- Are you out of your tiny little mind?

When Someone Does, Asks, or Says Something Invasive:

24. I'm not comfortable with that.
25. I'd like to ask you not to _____.
26. I'd like you to stop _____.
27. Please stop doing that. I don't like it.
28. I'm uncomfortable right now with what you're saying/doing.
29. That's not something I talk about except with family.
30. Let's talk about something else.
31. I want to keep that to myself.
32. That's my business.
33. I'm surprised you think you have a right to that information.
34. I don't feel like talking about it.
35. And you are asking me this because . . . ? (Try saying this one with a look of utter disbelief.)
36. Sorry, that's not something I talk about.
37. I never answer questions like that.

When Someone Says Something You Disagree With:

38. I see it differently than you do.
39. We certainly don't agree about that.
40. I have a different point of view.
41. My experience of _____ is somewhat different.
42. I hear what you are saying, but I don't agree with it.

did you let those aliens take your body over?"

If the significant adults in your life told you that your experiences didn't really happen, or that they happened in ways radically different from how you perceived them, you probably became confused and distressed, unsure what was real.

A father can stroke his daughter's breast and explain it away by saying, "I'm just tucking you in." A daughter can tell her mother that her stepfather touched her in a funny way. The mother can respond, "Oh, honey, that was just a dream."

Family members aren't the only ones to perpetuate this invalidation. Many young girls try to tell teachers, counselors, ministers, or other adults, only to have them say, "You must be mistaken. Your Uncle Jimmy is a deacon in the church." Survivors have gone to therapists for help and been told, "You should be over that by now," or "It was just your sister; all kids play doctor."

It can also be terrifying to trust your inner voice if you're afraid of what it will tell you. One survivor explained: "My greatest fear is that if I listen to my insides, I will become crazy like my mom. She's often said to me, 'You have the same kind of powers I do.' So the message is if I listen to my insides, I will really become off the wall. If I listen to my inner voice, I will drift into my own inner world, which is really crazy."

Although there are many reasons why it's difficult to have faith in your own perceptions, it is possible to develop the capacity to trust your inner voice.

THE INNER VOICE

Within all of us, there is a wise, authentic inner voice that can tell us how we feel. If it's been covered over or if you don't have much practice listening to that voice, it may be very small, just a pipsqueak. Yet it is there. And the more you listen and act on it, the stronger and clearer that voice will grow.

In child assault prevention programs, children are taught to identify the voice inside that warns them that something isn't right. They refer to this intuition as the *uh-oh* feeling. With encouragement, children easily recognize this feeling as danger—*uh-oh, something's wrong here.*

Everyone experiences her inner voice differently. You may have bad dreams. You may get headaches. You may become exhausted. You may have a sudden urge to binge on cookies. Or you may notice you've cleaned the house twice in two days. The important thing is not what you experience but that you recognize it as a message.

Ellen discovered a few years ago that every time she was about to make a poor decision for herself, she'd get a tight, anxious feeling in her stomach:

> Looking back, I could see that that simple physical warning had been there throughout my life, but I'd never before given it a hearing. I'd never stopped and said, hey, what is this squeamish feeling in my stomach telling me? Once I began to listen and to respect this feeling, I began making much better decisions for myself. Now, whenever I feel it, I stop what I'm doing and take a minute to trace where the feeling originated. This information has been immensely valuable.

CREATING A POSITIVE SELF-IMAGE

Learning to love and accept yourself—your strengths, weaknesses, personality traits, and basic nature—is a capacity that grows over a lifetime. Here are some things you can do to take positive steps in that direction.

DO THINGS YOU'RE PROUD OF

It's impossible to feel good about yourself if you are doing things that you aren't proud of. If you are gambling compulsively, not spending enough time with your children, or avoiding therapy, you're not going to feel self-respect. Your self-esteem will improve when you work to change problematic behaviors and start acting in ways you feel good about.

ACCENTUATE THE POSITIVE

If you're used to seeing yourself as ineffective or worthless, you may not notice the wonderful things about yourself. Try making a list of all the things you do well. Include everything. "I make perfect fried eggs. I can whistle on pitch. I'm good at untying knots." Make another list of the things you like about yourself: "I like that I'm a good listener. I like my feet. I like my stubborn determination." Read your list to yourself when you're feeling self-critical. Find an appreciative friend and read it aloud. Or ask friends what they like about you. Listen and take notes.

TAKE IN THE GOOD THINGS THAT PEOPLE SAY ABOUT YOU

As you begin to surround yourself with people who genuinely like and respect you, you will hear more and more positive things about yourself. At first, the simple genuine appreciation of who you are can be so unfamiliar that you don't even notice it.

Ellen had grown to like one of her clients very much. One day, when this woman was feeling bad about not having a lover or many close friends, Ellen reassured her that as she began to feel better about herself, she would connect more deeply with others. "You're a likable person," Ellen told her. "I like you."

The woman continued talking as though Ellen hadn't said anything. "Did you hear me say, 'I like you'?" Ellen asked.

The woman looked at Ellen quizzically. "No."

"Well, let's try it again," Ellen said. "I like you."

"You're different. I pay you to like me," the woman protested.

"No," Ellen responded. "You pay me to help you, to support you in your healing, to care

about who you become. You can't pay me to like you. I just happen to feel that way."

The woman looked at Ellen again and nodded, taking it in just a little.

Train yourself to hear the positive things people reflect back to you. They shouldn't go to waste.*

VISUALIZATION

Visualizing yourself as you want to be is another effective way to move toward your goals. You can imagine various scenes that show you as a more capable, powerful person: you may be brilliantly arguing a case in front of a jury, receiving your black belt in karate, or simply walking along the street with your back straight and your head held high. You can visualize yourself in a healthy relationship or having fun. You can imagine whole scenarios. One woman who felt as if she was dirty, as if she was covered with shit, imagined scraping off all the shit and throwing it back at her abuser. Afterward, she reported feeling great.

FIND A TASK

If you're sinking into the quicksand of self-hatred and desperation, it can help to get planted in the present by taking on some manageable task that

---

* For the basics on building a support system of people who are kind, respectful, and loving toward you, see "Developing a Support System" on p. 30.

you can handle competently. You might want to clean house, cook a pot of soup, or plant some flowers. Ellen says that when she feels miserable, accomplishing something helps:

> I often go to my desk and answer mail, pay bills, clear the mass of papers that accumulate. Throwing things out always helps. And doing dishes—the warm water and the clarity of the task. After doing such routine tasks, I may not feel great, but at least I can feel good that I got something done.

DO SOMETHING FOR SOMEONE ELSE

Helping someone else can be gratifying. Extending kindness, offering assistance to a friend, and volunteering with an organization that feeds the hungry or works to stop child sexual abuse are all rewarding activities that allow you to see yourself as an active, useful person in the world.

TAKE BREAKS

Although a time of intense involvement in the healing process is often inevitable, as well as useful, it's good to stop occasionally and appreciate how far you've come. If you feel discouraged that you still have the same basic problems, you need to remind yourself that this is only a partial assessment. In reality, the severity of your problems may have lessened, and the way you handle them may be radically different.

Taking breaks can help you see that you are more than a reaction to abuse. Acknowledging the other parts of your life affirms that you are a complex, multifaceted person and that even if abuse issues loom over much of your life, they still do not gobble up every bit of it.

LIVE FOR YOURSELF

We all have the right to make the choices in life that we believe will bring us satisfaction. We have the right to determine our own values, lifestyle, and priorities. Try approaching your life from the inside, according to your own values and what's important to you, rather than in response to other people's expectations.

Thinking for yourself and making your own decisions can be frightening. Letting go of other people's expectations (or their approval) can leave you feeling empty for a time. And yet, seeing yourself as an independent adult who can stand up for your own choices frees you to accept yourself as you are.

Eva, a survivor and former battered wife, recalls:

> I used to feel like nothing I said counted, that people wouldn't listen to me. I didn't like myself. I think I went out of my way to find things that happened in my life that reinforced the things my ex-husband said about me, that I believed about myself. It took a long time for me to acquire the characteristic of being my own woman, of not letting other people dominate me and dominate my ideas.

All those things have changed tremendously. I'm more confident about who I am now. There were parts of me I liked when I was young. Now I've reclaimed them. I have a certain boldness. I was the boldest woman I knew. There was a time when I was afraid of what people would say, and now I don't give a damn. I'm gonna be who I am and if other people can't hang, that's their tough luck.*

---

* For more of Eva's story, see "Eva Smith" on p. 418.

Writing Exercise:
What I'm Grateful For:
A Letter of Thanks to Myself

*Cassondra Espinoza wrote this letter to herself as an exercise in her Latina survivors' group. In it, she thanks herself for her dedication to healing and everything she has done to be able to have a functional, fulfilling life. This "Letter of Thanks to Myself" is a powerful writing exercise that can highlight all that you've accomplished on your healing journey.**

Dear Cassondra,

When you tried to kill yourself at 13 because of the pain, but couldn't, you then made a pact with yourself to find a better life when you grew up and were finally able to leave the madhouse you called "home."

Thank you, thank you for having the courage to open your eyes wide and not live in denial. You were sexually abused, but because you worked hard, now we have a good life. Because you felt all the pain, got therapy, went to 12-step, did your journaling, called someone when you needed support, we are alive and living large. Because we got help, we are not nearly as afraid of new people and experiences. We can travel. We can have a good (really good) sexuality. We don't hurt ourselves anymore. We don't overdo with alcohol or sugar. We can have an intimate relationship, and best of all, we can feel.

There is no empty hole. There is no more losing time. Feelings the feelings may be tough, but even the hard feelings are better than the emptiness used to be.

Thank you for learning to take care of our body, for not being afraid to look good. Thank you for learning how to figure out when something (a situation) or someone is bad for us. Thank you for learning about boundaries and being able to say NO!

Thank you for knowing that feelings aren't going to kill you, that they will change, lessen, and there are do-overs. It's okay to make mistakes and say you're sorry when necessary, especially to yourself.

Thank you for learning how to be a good mom. Thank you for struggling through the hard times and not giving up. Thank you for keeping a positive outlook on life and learning how to start trusting people, relationships, and a higher power.

---

* You can read Cassondra Espinoza's story on p. 492 of "Courageous Women."

Getting in Touch With Your Feelings

"For a long time, I thought I didn't feel. I had ignored my own internal cues for so long that I was sure I didn't have any feelings to be in touch with. I thought of feelings as some mystical thing I had to concoct, rather than as an already functioning part of me that I had to uncover. Any feelings I did have were something separate from me that I had to hurry up and get over, so I could shift back into the safety of neutral—being numb and in control."

We have feelings all the time, whether we're consciously aware of them or not. Feelings arise in response to everything that happens in our lives. A threat makes us fearful. When someone injures us, we feel hurt and angry. When we are safe and our needs are met, we feel content. These are natural responses. We may not always have the ability to recognize and understand our feelings, but they are there.

When you were a child, your feelings of love and trust were betrayed. Your fear, pain, rage, and shame were too great for you to experience fully and continue to function, so you suppressed your feelings in order to survive:

Certain feelings just went under. I stopped having them at a really young age. I stopped having physical sensations. You could beat me and it literally didn't hurt. By the time I was thirteen, I no longer felt angry. And once I stopped feeling anger, I never felt love either. What I lived with most was boredom, which is really not a feeling but a lack of feeling. All the highs and lows were taken out.

Or, conversely, you may have lived with certain emotions so long and so intensely that you've gotten stuck in those feelings:

I walked around leaking sadness most of my life. Almost anything could make me cry. I'd cry at phone commercials—reach out and touch someone. I drove my husband crazy. We couldn't have even the smallest disagreement without me crying. I didn't *want* to cry. I'd try hard not to, but it was like an underground spring that just kept seeping up.

You may feel as though you've spent your whole life steeped in sadness, rage, or loneliness or that you struggle, even now, with constant anxiety, fear, or depression. Or you may find that you fluctuate between extremes: feeling flooded by overwhelming emotions and then shut down and numb inside.*

If you have often felt overwhelmed by your emotions, it can seem especially frightening to get in touch with the feelings that arise during the healing process. But experiencing our full range of feelings is important. Emotions are useful messengers that give us insight and the ability to make wise choices. Feelings, even painful ones, are allies. They tell us what's going on inside and often guide us in responding to the situations in our lives.

There are times in the healing process, however, when you may be inundated with feelings and you need a respite from their intensity. In these situations, it is more important to use the skills you have—or are learning—for self-soothing and calming down. Even though getting in touch with your feelings is necessary, there are times when regaining your equilibrium and sense of balance take precedence. (For more on taking care of yourself

and calming down, see "Dealing with Panic" on p. 34).

FEELINGS ARE A PACKAGE DEAL

When you open up to your feelings, you don't get to pick and choose. They're a package deal. One of Ellen's clients had been abused by her father over the course of many years. When she and Ellen began working together, she said she felt numb; she wanted to have feelings. After a few months, she was crying through every session, crying at home, crying when she went out with friends. One day she came in, started crying, and then laughed, "Well, I sure got what I asked for."

Yes. She was feeling. And the way feelings work is that you can't feel selectively. When you allow yourself to feel, you feel what there is to feel. For this woman, there was a great deal of pain and sadness. And after that, a lot of anger. And some fear. But slipped in among these difficult feelings were pride, hope, pleasure, self-respect, and a growing contentment.

To feel, you have to be open to the full spectrum of feelings:

When I first started to grapple with the concept of feeling—and in the beginning it *was* only a concept—I ranked all the possible emotions in two lists: good feelings and bad feelings. Every time I had a feeling, I'd think, "Is this a bad feeling or a good feeling? Is this a feeling I can allow myself to have?" Then I'd

* For more on feeling overwhelmed by your emotions, see "Trauma and the Brain" on p. 242.

either feel it or suppress it. It's been hard for me to accept that there is no right or wrong to feeling.

The more you can accept your feelings without judgment, the easier it will be for you to experience them, work with them, and learn from them.*

YOU FEEL IN YOUR BODY

Getting in touch with feelings requires that you live inside your body and pay attention to the sensations that are there. Feelings are just that—things that you feel in your body: tightening in your throat, trembling, clutching in your stomach, shortness of breath, moistness behind your eyes, moistness between your legs, warmth in your chest, tingling in your hands, fullness in your heart.

If you have ignored your body for a long time, tuning in to these sensations may seem scary, strange, or unfamiliar. Or you may be able to objectively report the sensations you feel in your body but not know what they mean.

When children are very small they don't have the conceptual ability to say, "I feel scared." They might say, "I feel yucky in my stomach." When adults give that sensation a

name, the child learns to connect the feeling with the emotion.

If no one paid attention to what you felt and you never learned to name your feelings, you will be starting at the beginning, teaching yourself to read the messages that your body gives you.†

Learning to Identify My Feelings: Krishnabai's Story

Krishnabai is thirty-five years old. She does workshops for survivors and works as a consultant. Growing up, she says, "I had no feeling of being part of a family. It was like being a member of a boardinghouse. Although I was close to my father, I had no relationship whatsoever with my mother."

When she was nine, Krishnabai was sexually abused one time by her great-uncle. The sexual abuse made already existing problems much worse.

Krishnabai was psychotically depressed for most of the first twenty-five years of her life. Then she made the decision to live and began a long journey toward healing.‡

I was working in a hospital and I was terribly depressed. I decided to kill myself that night by hanging myself with the telephone cord,

---

* Throughout *The Courage to Heal* there is support for dealing with your feelings. See the chapters "The Emergency Stage" on p. 64, "Grieving" on p. 136, "Anger" on p. 144, and "Learning to Live in Your Body" on p. 247 for more on the role emotions play in the healing process.

† Emotions and the body are integrally related. You can read more about the relationship between the two in the chapter "Learning to Live in Your Body" on p. 247.

‡ For more of Krishnabai's story, see "Overcoming Isolation" on p. 30.

and just then, my coworker called to check in with me. She talked to me for two hours on the phone, and then came and got me. She said, "I think you need to see somebody."

I went to this psychiatrist at the hospital where I worked, and I said, "Look, I need help, and I don't know how to get it." And so she agreed to take me on. And then in the process of unfolding me, she kind of went, "Oh, my God! We've got this person on our staff!"

She listened to me for maybe five sessions and she said, "Something is really wrong here. You've never experienced connection. You've never experienced happiness in your life. I think there's something going on with you biologically and I want to try some drugs on you." Well, I had nothing to lose.

She put me on a drug that was brand new at that time. One day a few weeks later, I woke up and felt really weird. It was about four in the afternoon. I'd worked the night before. I called her up and I said, "I don't know what's going on, but I feel really weird." And I kept talking, and she got really excited. And she said, "You've got to come right over here."

So I went over and she said to me, "You're starting to have feelings! I can't believe it! It's working! These are emotions you're feeling! This is what everybody has. Your TV is going from black-and-white to color and you don't understand because you've never seen color before."

We spent the next six months in therapy with her saying, "This is sadness. This is happiness." She described different feelings to me and helped put them in a framework that I could understand. I was like a baby looking out at the world and beginning to understand

things for the first time. And my life really started to change.

When I got access to my feelings, the psychotic episodes dropped down a whole lot. Some kind of pressure was released. I started to have more energy. I was hungry to explore the world.

LEARNING TO PAY ATTENTION

All of us feel in different ways, with different levels of intensity. Getting to know your feelings is part of getting to know yourself as a unique person.

Many survivors have spent their lives racing to stay just one step ahead of their feelings. Slow down enough to ask yourself, "How do I feel?" Whenever you notice yourself gliding on automatic pilot, stop and check in with your body. Are you in your body? What sensations are going on? What might those sensations be telling you?

Pay attention to your behavior also. If you are acting inappropriately, slamming around the kitchen or crying at something small, you may be having a feeling you haven't yet acknowledged. Laura remembers:

When I first started to pay attention to my feelings, the thing I felt most often was the sensation that I was lost in a dense fog. Or I'd be overwhelmed by things like boredom, confusion, desperation, hopelessness, or anxiety. What I gradually learned was that these were not actually emotions but lids I kept on my emotions. As soon as I'd have a glimmer of the raw feeling, I'd throw a big thick blanket over it to cover it up. If I scratched beneath the boredom, there was usually anger. Anxiety covered up terror. Hopelessness and depression were rage turned inward. And so on.

If you have habitually covered your feelings, this may take place so quickly and automatically that you don't even have a chance to notice the initial emotion. When you begin to feel happy, you slide into anxiety. When you're angry, you immediately hate yourself. These patterns are different for everyone, but if you are overwhelmed by states such as depression, confusion, guilt, or a general feeling of anxiety, there's probably a more specific emotion underneath.

Sometimes it's a thought pattern that takes over when you start to feel something. If you catch yourself in an old, self-critical line of thinking, it probably has a feeling underneath. Thoughts like "I'll never change" or "People don't like me" often indicate buried feelings. As a child you couldn't afford to say, "I hate my father; I want to kill him," so you turned your anger on yourself, finding a hundred reasons why you were bad, why the abuse was your fault. By this time it's like a rut in a dirt road. Hundreds of cars drive on the road. Each car travels the same path, until it becomes automatic for the tires to follow the tracks. The same is true for thoughts. If you've had a lifetime of practice diverting the first glimmer of anger into "I'm bad," you need to explore the feelings underneath that habit, consciously changing the track. (For more on changing negative thought patterns, see "Internalized Messages" on p. 213.)

FEAR OF FEELING

Many survivors are afraid that if they open up their feelings, they'll suddenly go out of control:

I was terrified of my anger. I knew that if I didn't laugh about what had happened to me, I'd go stark raving mad and kill everybody who was in my way.

Although you may indeed be very angry or very sad for a long time, those feelings don't have to be overwhelming.

As I've allowed myself to feel a little at a time, I learned that the valve to feelings was neither totally open nor totally shut—totally overwhelming or totally suppressed. I could feel bad without wanting to kill myself. I could be scared without being terrified. There was a whole range of gradations. Once I stopped trying to rein my emotions in, I had more control than I thought.

When you've repressed feelings for a long time, it's natural to be wary. But having strong feelings doesn't mean that you'll be unable to control yourself. Deep sobbing or pounding pillows furiously does not mean you've gone crazy. In fact, actively expressing intense feelings in a safe, structured way makes it less likely that you'll explode. Very few murderers kill their victims after coming out of a pillow-pounding session with their counselor or support group.

HONORING FEELINGS

When you first become conscious of the emotions that move through you, all you have to do is be aware: "I'm feeling a feeling." If you're sad, let yourself feel sad—without worrying, panicking, or needing to take any action. It's okay just to feel sad. Your feelings aren't dangerous. They're not things you have to get rid of.

> The more I felt, the easier it got. Feeling became less and less scary. Even though I lost my capacity to just put things aside and I felt a lot of pain, my main feeling was one of relief. I found that the fear of feeling and the stress of suppressing my feelings were more painful than the feelings themselves. Some of the feelings—especially the old ones I had to relive—were just as awful as I thought they'd be, but they didn't last forever.

Feelings simply arise, but when you're not used to them, having an emotion you can't tie to a concrete event can be frightening. While it's reassuring to understand why you feel a certain way or where that feeling originates, that's not always possible. Even if you don't figure it out, the feeling still counts.

Valuing and believing your feelings takes time. But eventually you will stop seeing feelings as something separate from yourself:

> I've integrated emotions into my life. I no longer have to take time out to feel. If I'm walking down the street and I feel sad, I can start crying. I don't have to wait until I get home and plan the time to do it. My emotions are a part of who I am; they're not split off from my body. I don't have to make a date to feel my emotions anymore.

FEELINGS CHANGE

It's the nature of feelings to ebb and flow, to change. You can be furious one hour, sad the next, full of love an hour later. Pain turns into rage, and rage into relief. If feelings are not jammed up, they shift with a natural rhythm that matches your experience in the world. Paradoxically, the best way to move through a feeling is to feel it fully. When you accept a feeling, it often transforms.

When you're working with long-denied feelings, the transitions won't happen as quickly as they will with contemporary feelings, but all feelings, if you allow yourself to experience them naturally, will eventually change.

EXERCISES FOR GETTING IN TOUCH WITH YOUR FEELINGS

The next two exercises, from *Learning to Live Without Violence* by Daniel Sonkin and Michael Durphy, can be helpful in beginning to identify feelings.*

Feeling vs. Thinking

People commonly confuse feelings with thinking or observation. For example:

"I feel it was unfair."

"I feel you are going to leave me."

These statements are "I feel-thinking" statements rather than "I feel-emotion" statements. A good test for whether a statement is an "I feel-thinking" statement is to replace "I feel" with "I think." If it makes sense, then it is probably more of a thinking statement or observation than a feeling statement. If we change the above "I feel-thinking" statements to "I feel-emotion" statements, they might read:

"I feel hurt by what you did."

"I feel afraid that you might leave me."

What Are Feelings?

Here is a list of feeling words. Say them out loud. Try out different tones of voice for each word, or say it louder or softer. Pay attention to your feelings as you say each word. What sensations does it stir up? How does your body feel? Do some words fit you, but not others? Add any other words that especially describe you. When you are finished, choose the three words that you respond to most strongly.

excited	frustrated	hurt	grateful
tender	anxious	jealous	vulnerable
sad	contented	loving	numb
lonely	depressed	frightened	elated
edgy	ashamed	happy	timid
isolated	despairing	relieved	angry

Use Your Mind

If you can't readily identify a feeling, your intellect can sometimes help. Say to yourself, "My lover just left me and I don't feel anything. What would someone else be feeling in this situation? What have I learned from books, movies, and friends about the feelings that might be common in this circumstance? Could it be relief? Anger? Grief? Could that be what this knot in my throat is about?"

Draw Your Feelings

Amy Pine, a creative-arts therapist in Santa Cruz, California, suggests trying to draw a feeling that you have. Use color, shape, texture, degree of pressure, space, and literal pictures to help you express this feeling. Stick figures are also fine. Then draw the way you want to feel. Share these drawings with someone. What do they represent? What do you notice when you look at them? Then draw a third picture that takes elements of the first through a transition that brings it to the second. What had to happen to connect them? How did you do it? Is there any correlation with what you might do in your life?

---

* Daniel Jay Sonkin and Michael Durphy, *Learning to Live Without Violence*, updated edition (Volcano, CA: Volcano Press, 1997).

GET SUPPORT FOR FEELING

If your feelings were denied or criticized in childhood, it may take a while before you feel safe enough to express your feelings. Many women first experience this safety with a counselor:

> One day my therapist said to me, "I won't leave you no matter what you do." Before the session was over I got angry at her for the first time.

Being with people who respect your feelings and who are in touch with their own can also speed the learning process:

> At first I didn't know how to have feelings by myself. I'd be numb until I saw my lover, my therapist, or a really good friend. They would draw me out, help me figure out what I was feeling. When they held or talked to me, I would squeak out a few tears or have a quiet moment of anger. I needed comforting and permission from someone else to be able to feel.

Although it's good to have loving, supportive people around when you start to connect with your feelings, over time you'll feel safe enough to open up by yourself. In your mind or out loud, you can tell yourself the comforting things others have told you: "It's okay to cry." "You have a right to your anger." By calling on the part of yourself that is able to nurture and stand up for you, you provide a wise and kind mother for the frightened, hurt, or angry child within. You can stroke your own hair, rock yourself in a rocking chair, make yourself a cup of warm milk and honey, or set out pillows to punch. You become your own catalyst, midwife, permission-giver.

COMMUNICATING YOUR FEELINGS

Once you start to feel your feelings, you still may have a hard time expressing them:

> My facial expressions didn't match what I said. I was always grinning. I might be down in the dumps, three feet depressed, but I kept smiling no matter what, so the outside world wouldn't know how much pain I was in, couldn't guess my secret. That way, they wouldn't fuck with me.

Or as Laura recalls:

> All my life I've had this problem. I'd be overwhelmed with feeling and no one would believe me because it didn't show. A big expression of heartfelt grief for me would be several tears rolling down my cheeks. I'd be suicidal, sure I was going crazy, and my friends would maybe think I had a little something bothering me—a flea bite maybe? For a long time I thought something was wrong with me, that I had to become dramatic in the way I expressed my feelings before they counted. I wasn't really angry unless I tore up phone books with my bare hands. Being happy without ecstatic leaps in the air didn't count.

There's no single way to show emotion. Everyone has her own individual style. But it's important to be able to express what you feel in a way that's satisfying and that communicates.

Certain ways of expressing feelings increase the likelihood that you will be heard. If you say, "I'm upset. When you are late and you haven't called, I worry. Please call me next time," you'll probably get a better response than if you say, "You're the most thoughtless person I've ever met. You never care about my feelings."

Timing is important too. If you have something to say that's important or vulnerable, don't undermine yourself by picking a time that is not conducive to real listening. Give yourself—and your friend—the benefit of a fair start.

NEW FEELINGS, OLD FEELINGS

As you move through the healing process, there will be times that you will be simultaneously dealing with buried feelings from the past *and* feelings that arise in your current life. Frequently, contemporary feelings trigger older, deeper feelings. Grief over a friend's death can bring up feelings of sadness over the losses from your childhood. Frustration with your child's lack of cooperation spills into old rage about having no control over your life. Despair about the end of a marriage or losses associated with aging lead you back to old feelings of abandonment and hopelessness.

When you operate unconsciously out of buried emotions, life can feel out of control. Whenever your reaction seems out of proportion to any given situation, there's a good chance that you've tapped into the past. The first step is to recognize it:

When my feelings are over the top, I've learned to ask myself if I might be tapping into old feelings. It's rare that something in the present—by itself—is going to make me feel like my life is worthless. So when I start feeling like I'm a failure or that no one will ever love me, it's a signal that I may be feeling old feelings from my hellhole of a childhood. It's the old well I'm drawing the bucket up from. If I listen hard, I can hear the rusty chains clanking. Just recognizing that is a real relief. It's almost like waking from a bad dream. My life is not horrible now; I'm not a hopeless wreck of a person.

As you work with the shame, fear, grief, anger, and other deep emotions that survivors often feel, it will get easier to identify which are old feelings you've carried forever and which are responses to something in your current life.

For example, if you find yourself slapping your children, yelling at your coworkers, or being furious at your partner for the small trespasses of daily life, you are probably reacting from the past. Although your anger may be set off by contemporary events, you may be responding more strongly or more swiftly because of old rage left over from childhood. When the two blur, you tend to overreact, behaving in ways that cause problems for you and may be abusive to others.

As soon as you become aware that your feelings are more intense than the present circumstances warrant, take a break. Excuse yourself from the situation and try to separate the old from the new. (This is true for other feelings as well, such as feeling rejected, abandoned, humiliated, or hurt.) This will give you the opportunity to work directly with your feelings from the past rather than layering childhood pain over your current situation.

Understanding the root of your emotions will make your feelings more manageable. The rush of mixed-up feelings will start to subside, and you'll be able to respond more appropriately to your present experience.

WHEN YOU CAN'T GET RELIEF

If you've been working through the healing process for an extended period of time, have good support and a capable therapist, and you're still suffering with depression, anxiety, or other debilitating emotions that are making it difficult for you to function, it's a good idea to consider whether there are any physiological or other problems that might be contributing to your distress. Conditions such as thyroid imbalance, hormonal imbalance, diabetes, bipolar disorder, depression, and many other biochemical disorders can have a powerful effect on our emotions. A good physician or psychiatrist who is familiar with post-traumatic stress disorder may be able to help you assess your situation and determine whether medica-

tion—for either the short or long term—might be useful. (See "What About Medication?" on p. 41.)

POSITIVE FEELINGS CAN BE SCARY, TOO

Over time, as you heal, your positive feelings will increase. Happiness, excitement, satisfaction, love, security, and hope will appear more frequently. Although these are "good" feelings, you may not be comfortable with them at first.

For many survivors, positive feelings are scary. As a child, happiness often signaled a disaster about to occur. If you were playing with your friends when your brother called you over and molested you, if you were sleeping peacefully when your mother abused you, if you were having Sunday dinner at your grandparents' when you were taken by surprise and humiliated, you learned that happiness was not to be trusted. Or if you pretended to be happy when you were suffering inside, happiness may feel like a sham to you still.

Even the idea that you might, someday, feel good can be threatening. One woman said she dared not hope. As a child she hoped day after day that her father might come home cheerful, might be nice to her, might stop abusing her. And day after day, she was disappointed. Finally, out of self-preservation, she gave up hope.

Sometimes peace and contentment are the most disconcerting feelings of all. Calm may be so totally unfamiliar that you don't know how to relax and enjoy it. Unexpected good feelings can be hard to come to terms with:

> I'd been unhappy all my life. When I remembered the incest, I finally knew why, but I was *still* unhappy. Healing was a terrifying and painful experience and my life was as full of struggle and heartache as it had always been. Several years after I started therapy, I began to feel happy. I was stunned. I hadn't realized that the point of all this work on myself was to feel good. I thought it was just one more struggle in a long line of struggles. It took a while before I got used to the idea that my life had changed, that I felt happy, that I was actually content.

FEELING GOOD IS NOT A BETRAYAL

Feeling good can seem like a betrayal to the hurt child within. You may think—consciously or unconsciously—that if you feel good, that means the abuse has been forgotten, minimized, or condoned. But this is not true. Your history will always be what it was. The abuse will have been as wrong and as horrible as it was. You and those who love you will not forget the significance of the abuse, even if you feel good now.

You don't have to spend the rest of your life in pain to honor the hurt child and to validate her suffering. That hurt child is a part of *you*.

LEARNING TO LIVE WITHOUT VIOLENCE

Violence is a way to assert power over others. It's effective in the short run but at too great a cost. You cannot heal from the effects of child sexual abuse while continuing to perpetrate abuse on others. If you're in a situation where you are hurting your children, battering your partner, or being verbally or physically abusive in any way, you need to stop now and get help. (And if you are currently in a relationship where you are being abused, there are women's shelters in most communities that can support you in protecting yourself and your children.)*

Learning to Live Without Violence[†] by Daniel Jay Sonkin and Michael Durphy, gives sound, practical guidelines for changing abusive patterns of expressing anger. Although it is directed toward men, it is useful for women as well. The following material is drawn from their outstanding work:

RECOGNIZING YOUR OWN ANGER

There is a difference between anger and violence. Anger is an emotion, and violence is one of the behaviors that can express that emotion. Some people don't know they're angry until they explode. Identifying your own anger cues can help you control your

---

* The phone number for the National Domestic Violence Hotline is listed in the Resource Guide on p. 525 under "Hotlines." See "Domestic Violence, Rape, and Sexual Harassment" on p. 563 of the Resource Guide for further resources and referrals.

† Daniel Jay Sonkin and Michael Durphy, *Learning to Live Without Violence*, Updated edition (Volcano, CA: Volcano Press, 1997).

violence. (You can modify these questions to learn to identify other emotions as well, such as sadness or fear.)

Body Signals

- How does your body feel when you are angry?
- Are the muscles tense in your neck, arms, legs, face?
- Do you sweat or get cold?
- Do you breathe deeper, faster, lighter, slower?
- Do you get a headache? A stomachache?

Behavioral Signs

How do you behave when you're feeling angry? Do you:

- Get mean? Blame others?
- Act extra nice?
- Start laughing?
- Become sarcastic?
- Withdraw?
- Shut down?
- Break commitments? Arrive late or leave early?
- Have difficulty eating or sleeping? Eat or sleep more?

Time-Outs

Time-outs are a basic tool for controlling violence. They provide a structure that allows you to break abusive patterns. Time-outs not only stop the violence but also help to rebuild trust. The rules are simple:

- **When you feel yourself beginning to get angry, say, "I'm beginning to feel angry. I need to take time out."** In this way, you communicate directly. You take responsibility for your own feelings and assure the other person that you're committed to avoiding violence.
- **Leave for an agreed-upon period amount of time, such as an hour.**
- **Don't drink, take drugs, or drive.**
- **Do something physical.** Take a walk, go for a run, or ride a bike. Exercise will help discharge some of the tension in your body.
- **Come back at the agreed-upon time.** If you live up to your agreement, it will build trust.
- **Check in and ask the person you were angry with if they want to discuss the situation.** If you both agree, talk about what made you angry and why you needed the time out. If it's still hard to discuss, come back to it later.

Alcohol and Drugs

Alcohol and drugs do not cause violence. However, if you already have a problem with violence, they can make it worse. Alcohol and many drugs suppress feelings. You may be less aware that you are getting angry, and thus less able to take a time-out or direct your anger appropriately. Your ability to control violent impulses may also be lessened. If alcohol and drugs are a problem in your life, it is essential that you deal with your substance abuse or addiction if you want to stop your violent behavior.

And you deserve to experience all the joy and happiness possible.*

YOU DESERVE TO FEEL GOOD

Being liked, loved, and appreciated has felt threatening for many survivors. Visibility is a kind of exposure. Appreciation can bring up feelings of shame. The contrast between someone's high opinion of you and your own self-hatred can be intolerable. And feeling positive about yourself—feeling worthy, deserving, and proud—may seem fantastically out of reach. But again, these feelings are so pleasant that you'll find it's worth getting used to them.

When someone pays you a compliment, try saying, "Thank you," instead of immediately rattling off a list of your faults. If you receive a present, say: "This makes me feel really good." If you get a raise, say: "I like being acknowledged for my work."

Curiosity and the desire to try new things are often stifled in survivors. Healing makes room for these new feelings to emerge.

Learning to tolerate feeling good is one of the nicest parts of healing. Once you get started, you may find that you want to do it a lot. Take all the opportunities that come your way. A quiet moment drinking tea in the morning. Reading your child a bedtime story. A call from a friend just to say hello. An omelet that turned out perfect. The feeling of a warm breeze on bare skin. Notice these things. Take

the risk of admitting that you feel good—first for a moment, then for longer.

Although you've had a lot of pain in your life, you have a multitude of opportunities for wonderful feelings as well. Take them. You deserve to feel good.

The Guest House
BY RUMI
translated by Coleman Barks

This being human is a guest house.
Every morning a new arrival.

A joy, a depression, a meanness,
some momentary awareness comes
as an unexpected visitor.

Welcome and entertain them all!
Even if they're a crowd of sorrows,
who violently sweep your house
empty of its furniture,
still, treat each guest honorably.
He may be clearing you out
for some new delight.

The dark thought, the shame, the malice,
meet them at the door laughing,
and invite them in.

Be grateful for whoever comes,
because each has been sent
as a guide from beyond.

Coleman Barks, *Rumi: Selected Poems* ([originally published as *The Essential Rumi*] New York: Penguin, 2004), p. 109.

---

* See "Reassuring the Child" on p. 192 for more on allowing yourself to feel good.

WRITING EXERCISE: WRITE ABOUT YOUR FEELINGS

Buddhist teacher Ajahn Sumedho* talks about learning to become a witness to your own feelings. Rather than saying, "I'm angry," he suggests saying, "Anger feels like this. . . ." Instead of saying, "I'm happy," try saying instead, "Happiness feels like this. . . ." Instead of saying, "I feel ashamed," try, "Shame feels like this. . . ." Witnessing your feelings in this way can be helpful if you find yourself frequently beset by a particular emotion and want to understand the role it plays in your life. And if you find it difficult to identify or differentiate between feelings, this exercise can be a way to explore the nature of the feeling itself.

Go back to the list of words in the "What Are Feelings?" exercise on page 228. Identify the emotions that you frequently experience. If there are other feelings that you feel regularly, add them to the list. Now choose one that you are willing to explore. Then, at the top of a sheet of paper, write the sentence: "_____ feels like this," filling in the blank with the emotion you have chosen. Then, using the guidelines for free writing on page xxix, write for ten minutes without stopping about that feeling or state of mind. Whenever you run out of things to say, return to the original phrase, "Shame feels like this . . ." or "Gratitude feels like this . . ." or "Betrayal feels like this. . . ."

---

* Ajahn Sumedho teaches in the Theravadin Thai Forest tradition of Buddhism.

A sample response might start like this:

Fear feels like this: a giant vice, slowly, inexorably closing in on my chest. It is getting harder and harder to breathe, but there is no way for me to stop the pressure. Fear feels like this: the sound of heavy footsteps stopping outside my door on a stifling summer night. I know the door will open soon. Fear feels like this: standing in front of the class with everyone staring at me. I know I am there for a reason, but my mind is blank and I have nothing to say. Fear feels like this: I am sitting at the kitchen table folding yellow towels. The light changes and I am transported back to another kitchen from long ago. I hear my mother's voice on the front stoop. I know instantly that she is loud, sloppy, and drunk. I should call someone to come and help me, but there is no one to call, and besides, what would I say? As I hear the key in the lock, I shrink back into my body and go very far away. Fear feels like this: . . ."

Continue writing until the ten minutes are up. Afterward, it's helpful to read what you've written aloud to yourself or to a supportive person. Then try doing the exercise again using a different emotion.

FURTHER PRACTICES

IMAGERY TO HEAL TRAUMA*
by Belleruth Naparstek,
from *Invisible Heroes*

This powerful imagery is designed to heal trauma, layer by layer, by taking you on a safely guided journey into your own broken heart—and then deeper still—into your core that is still beautiful and whole. This visualization is intense, and we suggest that you become familiar and comfortable with the imagery "Creating a Safe Place Inside" on p. 38 before moving on to this one.

Once you have recorded "Imagery to Heal Trauma," you can listen to it repeatedly. Some survivors prefer to ease into it gradually, listening for a few minutes each day, adding a little more each time. (See the instructions for using guided imagery on p. xxxiii before you begin.)

To begin with, position yourself as comfortably as you can, shifting your weight so that your body feels well supported . . . and gently allowing your eyelids to close, if that's comfortable . . . and arranging it so that your head, neck, and spine are straight. . . .

And now, breathing in as fully as you comfortably can . . . and breathing out, completely and easily . . . and with the next in-breath, imagining that you're sending the warm energy of your breath to any part of your body that's sore or tense or tight . . . and releasing the tension with the exhale. . . . So you can feel your breath going to all the tight, tense places . . . warming and loosening and softening them . . . and then, gathering up the tension and breathing it out . . . so that more and more, you can feel relaxed and comfortable, watching the cleansing action of your breath. . . .

And any unwelcome thoughts that come to mind . . . those too can be noted, and acknowledged, and sent out with the breath . . . so that for just a moment, your mind is empty . . . for just a split second, it is free and clear space . . . and you are blessed with stillness. . . .

And any emotions you might be feeling inside . . . those too can be noticed and sent out with the breath . . . so that your emotional self can be still and quiet . . . like a lake with no ripples. . . .

And now . . . see if you can turn your attention inward for a moment . . . to see how your body is feeling . . . noticing where it might feel tight or tense, achy, or sore . . . and where it feels loose and comfortable and open . . . so you're moving your awareness down into your body . . . taking a moment to pay attention

---

* A beautiful version of this guided visualization, with music, was released as a CD by Health Journeys in 1999, and can be downloaded or ordered online from www.healthjourneys.com. The text was published in *Invisible Heroes* (New York: Bantam, 2004), an outstanding book on healing from trauma.

to how it's feeling . . . noticing any sensations in your head . . . your neck . . . your shoulders . . . your arms . . . and hands . . . inside your chest . . . down your back . . . inside your belly . . . down your hips and bottom . . . your legs . . . and in your feet . . . just taking a moment to check in with your body . . . your oldest friend . . . your steadiest companion. . . .

Still aware of your breathing, in and out . . . slow and steady . . . and now . . . taking an extra moment to focus on your heart . . . connecting to the powerful rhythms of your heart . . . sensing how it pulses life and strength, all through your body . . . strong and steady. . . .

And just becoming aware of how it feels right now, all around and through your heart . . . because it changes from moment to moment . . . and maybe you're aware of some tightness around your heart . . . some fluttery feelings . . . or an ache inside . . . or a heavy sensation . . . perhaps it feels hard around your heart . . . or it might feel exposed and vulnerable . . . you might sense deep pockets of sorrow tucked away inside . . . but whatever you notice, you're continuing to breathe deeply and easily . . . curious but detached . . . noticed what's there with the neutral eye of a camera. . . . no praise, no blame. . . .

You slowly become aware of a warm and gentle presence beside you . . . very comforting . . . maybe this someone or something is familiar . . . or maybe not . . . but clearly is radiating love and protection and support . . . and you somehow know that this visitor knows you in a deep and true way . . . that this presence accepts you as you are and carries great comfort and care. . . .

And maybe with a soft touch on your shoulder . . . your guide invites you to come along so that together you can explore your own broken heart . . . the gentlest invitation . . . to see if you are willing . . . and somehow, together, you magically enter the weary landscape of your own heart . . . perhaps slipping in through a torn or jagged place . . . to have a look around . . . for the sake of your own healing . . . and so you enter your heart. . . .

And it may seem harsh and dark and cold inside at first, as you look around here in this topmost layer. . . .

Because you're making your way through crumpled piles of shattered dreams . . . ragged heaps of lost innocence . . . and your guide is at your side, comforting and encouraging you to continue . . . gently pointing out crusty outcroppings of old guilt and self-blame . . . acknowledging with you the chill wind of loneliness that howls through this place . . . helping you move through smoky slag heaps, crackling and steaming with helpless anger . . . gently guiding you around sticky tar pits of shame . . . pointing out the heavy quicksand of self-pity. . . .

And showing you startling geysers of terror, suddenly bursting Forth at unexpected times . . . announced by a loud crack as they break through the surface . . . and then gone as inexplicably as they appear . . . and so you walk together . . . gently exploring the territory of your own pain . . . continuing to breathe deeply and easily . . . always aware of the comforting presence by your side. . . .

Imagery to Heal Trauma (*cont.*)

And you notice that you can explore this dismal landscape with steady courage . . . like the survivor that you are . . . even though it's not pretty . . . but somehow you know that even in this ravaged, lonely place, there is great power here . . . that treasures are buried deep in the debris. . . .

And your guide looks at you with the wise and loving eyes and says, "You can't make this place go away, but your courage in exploring it will change it in time . . . and there are gifts for you here, where you'd least expect to find them" . . . and leaning down, picks up a luminous object from under the rubble . . . and gives it to you for safekeeping . . . and it might feel warm in your hands . . . a perfect fit as you wrap your fingers around it . . . and continue along your way. . . .

Noticing a golden light glowing up from the ground some distance away . . . and walking toward it, you slowly approach what looks to be a glowing cave or hollow . . . with a hazy, golden light filtering out from it . . . and you can see that this is a tunnel, but like no other, because it glows . . . leading down in into an older, deeper part of your heart . . . and so the two of you enter . . . continuing to breathe deeply and easily . . . moving along the glowing pathway . . . deeper and deeper . . . sensing a sweet peace in the soft, golden air that gently billows all around you . . . and so you travel together . . . down into the deep center of your heart. . . .

Until you emerge into an exquisite landscape . . . a place pulsing with its own peaceful, stunning beauty . . . awash in light and color . . . with air that sings with healing energy . . . dancing gently on your skin . . . and you're captivated by the breathtaking radiance and splendor of this place . . . buoyed and held by the sweet magic all around you. . . .

Aware that somehow this place is familiar to you . . . you know this place . . . and slowly you remember that this is your oldest home . . . the part of you that can never be destroyed . . . the exquisite core of who you really are. . . .

And you can inhale the beauty of this place with deep, full breaths . . . breathing it in and letting its healing energy permeate every part of you . . . sending soft waves of comfort and peace all through your body. . . .

Your companion smiles . . . and with a gesture calls forth a gentle parade of guardians and allies . . . sweet spirits . . . magical beings . . . animal helpers . . . guardian angels . . . teachers and guides . . . powerful ancestors . . . old and dear friends . . . sweet singers and dancers . . . some familiar, some not . . . but all smiling and nodding . . . gently approaching, one by one. . . .

And you can see that they are holding out to you, with great tenderness and respect, the shattered pieces of your heart . . . delicate, sparkling shards and slivers . . . lost or left along the way . . . separated from you at times of great fear and anguish . . . but now, in this place, in the deepest, oldest, truest part of you . . . they are tenderly offered back . . . still pulsing with life and power. . . .

And you know that you can take back whatever you wish . . . whatever you're ready for . . . no more, no less . . . so you can stand at full strength . . . your full self and much more . . . more wisdom, more power . . . more compassion, for yourself and others . . . more awareness of the invisible support, all around you . . . and you might tentatively accept one or two pieces . . . to see how it feels to have them back. . . .

And suddenly you are certain . . . you know with your whole being. . . . that you are healing . . . that you will continue to heal . . . that a time is coming when you will accept your sorrow, dismiss your shame, release your anger, forgive yourself, reclaim your strength, and express your gifts. . . .

And so, whenever it's time to say good-bye, you thank your visitors . . . and watch them depart . . . and you and your guide make your way back up through the tunnel lit with golden light . . . step by step, together . . . until, closer to the surface, you reach the darker, cooler landscape of your pain . . . although perhaps it looks a little different now . . . not quite as dismal or heavy or dark. . . .

And as your departing steps crunch through the debris . . . you might notice other luminous treasures twinkling at you from the rubble . . . and you may pick one or two up . . . or you may decide to come back for them later . . . because perhaps you have all you can carry for now. . . .

And so . . . together . . . the two of you come back out of your heart . . . and your guide, with a look of great tenderness, gently touches the center of your chest . . . and you can feel the soft warmth of it fill your heart . . . spill over into your chest . . . fill your whole torso . . . your shoulders, neck, and head . . . move into your arms and legs, hands, and feet . . . until your whole body is filled with warmth. . . .

And with a bow, your visitor withdraws for now . . . and you're peaceful and easy, knowing that you can invoke more assistance whenever you wish . . . to further the work you have already done. . . .

And so . . . breathing deeply and easily . . . very aware of your hands and your feet . . . the support beneath your body . . . your breath in your belly . . . you can very softly open your eyes . . . becoming aware of how good it feels to stretch and move again, after being still for so long. . . .

And knowing in a deep place that you are better for this. . . .

And so you are. . . .

COMPASSION MEDITATION

This meditation, taken from the Buddhist tradition,* is normally an advanced practice, reserved for experienced meditators. But survivors of child sexual abuse, including those who are new to meditation, have found it to be sustaining in hard times. Because it opens you to the full intensity of your feelings and the feelings of others, use care if you experiment with this practice. It's usually best to wait until you are well grounded in your healing and to begin with short periods of meditation. As with any exercise, if you find this distressing or overwhelming, stop and turn to the ideas for calming down that you've established as part of your survival skills (See "Dealing with Panic" on p. 34).

This is a practice you can do either sitting in meditation or at any time in your life when you encounter strong feelings.

In Meditation:

To begin, sit in a comfortable position, cross-legged or on a chair with your spine straight. If for any reason you can't sit this way, it's fine to be in another position. Ellen has a good friend, a quadriplegic, who meditates in a wheelchair tipped back, so whatever position works for you will be fine.

Spend a few minutes just sitting and bringing your awareness to your breath. You can pay attention to your breath as you breathe in and out. Or you can pay attention only to the out breath. You'll notice that your mind will wander into thoughts, and when you realize that's happened, gently say to yourself, "Thinking," and then bring your attention back to your breath. It's common for our minds to spend a great deal of the time wandering, so don't worry that you're doing something wrong if you need to bring your attention back over and over again. It's a little like training a puppy; kindness and persistence are essential.

When you're ready, invite in one of the strong feelings that you've been experiencing in the healing process. As you begin to feel this emotion, say to yourself, "Other people feel this, too." Just this first step of realizing that you are not alone in this feeling can be comforting. It's not only you who are suffering this way. You're not isolated from the rest of humanity. This feeling that you're having (rage, longing, depression, grief, alienation) is part of the human experience. Many survivors feel relief simply in widening their perspective to remember that this is a human emotion that has been felt by people throughout time.

If you'd like to continue, the next step is to use your breath to experience this feeling more fully and to offer compassion to yourself and others who are experiencing this same feeling. As you inhale, imagine yourself breathing in whatever it is that you feel: anger, shame,

---

* This is a variation on Tonglen practice as taught by Pema Chödrön and other teachers in the Shambhala tradition of Buddhism. For more about Pema Chödrön's books and recordings, see p. 556 of the Resource Guide.

isolation, fear, sadness, or any other feeling. You can breathe in the feeling in any way that is vivid for you: You can feel the sensation of the feeling in your body; you can picture it as a color, as a temperature, as an image. Breathe in your feeling and the feelings of everyone else in the world who is experiencing what you are.

Then, when you exhale, exhale compassion, comfort, or any other kindness or relief to yourself and to all the others. Make your in breath and your out breath the same length of time so that you are equally balanced between experiencing the feeling and offering comfort.

Do this until you're ready to stop. It may be just a few breaths or you may continue for ten or fifteen minutes. Then end with a short time of just sitting with your breath, as at the start.

On the spot, in your life:

You can use this practice on the spot in your life as well as in a formal meditation session. Whenever a strong feeling arises, the first step is to stop and simply feel the feeling. Emotions are a combination of actual feelings in our bodies and the thoughts that go with them. In this practice, pay attention to the feeling in your body and interrupt the story line of the thoughts. It isn't as easy to do as it might sound, because most of us are very attached to our story lines, even when they cause us much suffering. But interrupting the thoughts that we habitually tell ourselves about our feelings has a powerful effect. It allows us to experience just the actual physical feeling in our bodies without the trappings we've layered over it.

As with the sitting meditation practice, use your breath to work with these feelings. As you inhale, imagine yourself breathing in your feeling and the feelings of everyone else in the world who feels this way, too. On the exhale, send compassion or comfort to yourself and to everyone else.

This practice allows you to connect with powerful feelings and to discover connection and spaciousness within even the most painful feelings. You are not trying to transcend the feelings or push them away. Instead you open yourself to the feelings as part of the human experience. And within that opening, there is often some kind of shift in the old patterns, some room for the feelings to keep changing, and a deep connection with others.

Trauma and the Brain

"There are so many things that have sent me into a panic over the years—relationships, sex, anyone getting too close—but also simple things: shopping in big stores, getting my hair cut, certain foods. The list is endless and strange. But it's not strange, I now find out. All these things are connected, in one way or another, to the abuse. And when I'm confronted with something that throws me back there, I have all the symptoms—my heart starts racing. I sweat. I feel like I can't breathe."

We have learned a tremendous amount about the physical and emotional effects of trauma.* Although there are important differences between child sexual abuse and other kinds of trauma, there are also many similarities. If you have been sexually abused as a child, you have a lot in common with people who have gone through other types of traumatic experiences—an orphan living in a war zone, a shopkeeper held up in a robbery, a driver in a head-on collision, a veteran struggling with memories of war. In some cases, the trauma is linked to a one-time event; in others, the experience is severe and ongoing. But in every instance, victims suffer a devastating combination of terror, helplessness, and loss of control.

When people are confronted with a traumatic event, their bodies have an immediate physiological reaction. Every species has this biologically driven response to dire threats of harm or annihilation. The instant a threat is perceived, your brain reacts, sending signals to the pituitary and adrenal glands to release a flood of stress hormones. These hormones—among them, adrenaline, cortisol, and norepi-

---

* Some of the pioneers in the field of the body–mind connection in trauma and healing are Bessel van der Kolk, Judith Herman, Babette Rothschild, Robert Scaer, Peter Levine, and Belleruth Naparstek. We would also like to acknowledge the many somatics innovators who developed the field, including Wilhelm Reich, Marion Rosen, Thomas Hanna, Richard Strozzi Heckler, Joseph Heller, and Ron Kurtz.

nephrine—make you hyperalert, preparing you to either fight or flee. This fight-or-flight response is extremely useful when survival is at stake: The heart beats faster, blood pressure rises, breathing speeds up, and the entire body prepares for action, while nonessential functions—such as hunger, sleepiness, and digestion—shut down. Once the threatening event passes, normal functions are reactivated and the body returns to normal. People often become suddenly aware that they are exhausted, hungry, or in physical pain.

A third biological response to danger is the freeze response. In nature, when fight or flight would be futile, animals instinctively collapse and become inert. They look as if they are "playing dead." This reflex releases more chemicals—pain-killing endorphins and opioids—that take the animal from a state of extreme energy to complete immobility. Tense muscles instantly relax and breathing and heartbeat slow to barely perceptible. If the animal survives, it immediately begins to discharge the built-up chemicals through intense shaking and trembling, heavy breathing, and sweating. Ultimately animals return to a state of equilibrium and leave the encounter fully recovered, carrying no residual trauma.

DISSOCIATION: A SURVIVAL SKILL THAT MAKES SENSE

In human beings, dissociation is the mind state that accompanies the freeze response. With the help of the pain-killing biochemicals that have suddenly been released, we disconnect from what is happening to us. Our capacity to feel—both physically and emotionally—shuts down and we distance ourselves from the pain and terror we would ordinarily experience. Dissociation is an extremely effective survival mechanism, shielding us from the full impact of traumatic events. But the trauma itself is not processed or healed. In most cases, it is stored, not as a usual memory that fades and distorts over time, but as a nonverbal body memory, which is much harder to identify and process through thinking and talking. This is why we are not able to change our reactions to traumatic events just by "thinking them through."

THE BEGINNINGS OF POST-TRAUMATIC STRESS DISORDER

When humans freeze or dissociate, we are deluged with the same hormones as animals under attack. Once the danger has passed, we can sometimes use the same natural recovery mechanisms. We can shake, move, cry, yell, and breathe deeply, processes that sometimes help eliminate the chemicals our bodies have produced, just as animals do. And when we have the support of a caring person or community, we can receive comfort, thus meeting our need for understanding and connection.

But when children are sexually abused, they are rarely in a situation with optimum conditions for recovery. Instead, silence, secrecy, and isolation are the norm. Sometimes children are prevented even from crying out. And far too often the abuse is a recurring event, without time for recovery before the next assault.

In the weeks and months after a traumatic event, trauma survivors often experience an acute stress reaction that can incorporate an array of troubling symptoms, including nightmares, flashbacks, trouble concentrating, intrusive thoughts, insomnia, an increased startle reflex, panic, depression, numbness, mental confusion, sudden explosions of rage, and alienation. The world no longer feels like a safe place.

For many people, these reactions last a few weeks or months and then gradually subside. But for others, the symptoms persist, eventually developing into post-traumatic stress disorder, or PTSD. Survivors of child sexual abuse—especially incest—are at increased risk because they experienced many of the dynamics that make long-term PTSD more likely: the trauma (or threat of trauma) was repeated and of long duration, they were children when the abuse occurred, they experienced great helplessness and betrayal, they believed the abuse was their fault, and, most significantly, they used dissociation as a way to escape. Although dissociation is an important protection, it is a factor that is correlated with the later development of PTSD.

Post-traumatic symptoms can grow stronger and become more entrenched over time. Or they can go underground and reemerge years, or even decades, later at a time of increased vulnerability—when a life event acts as a stimulus and triggers the post-traumatic reaction.

THE EFFECTS OF POST-TRAUMATIC STRESS DISORDER OVER TIME

People with PTSD continue to cycle through rounds of distress. Memories of the trauma remain stored in the amygdala and the hypothalamus—the primitive, instinctual parts of the brain that are concerned with survival. These areas of the brain (also called the "old" brain) can only react; they are not able to think, reason, plan, or compare. The old brain responds instantly to danger, overriding the thinking parts of the brain. This ability to react immediately—without thinking—can save our lives, but at a cost.

The old brain deeply imprints information related to danger and survival, and since it does not have the capacity to integrate the experience of trauma and cannot differentiate the past from the present, it continues to react as if you are still in danger. Whenever you experience anything that is reminiscent of the initial trauma, the amygdala and the highly attuned structures surrounding it are activated, triggering a new cascade of stress chemicals.

For survivors of child sexual abuse, smelling a particular cologne, seeing the shadow of a man at sunset, sensing a sudden movement out of the corner of the eye, or being touched in a particular way can set off an intense alarm reaction in which the initial panic, helplessness, and terror are reexperienced in the present. (For more about this phenomenon, see "Remembering" on p. 70, "Working with Triggers" on p. 312, and "Flashbacks with a Partner" on p. 306.)

As time goes on, PTSD symptoms can become more ingrained, and for some people, traumatic memories grow more intrusive. Survivors often vacillate between a state of hypervigilance, in which all of the body's distress signals are on "red alert," and the opposite, shutting down completely. Over the years, survivors of child sexual abuse may feel increasingly numb, agitated, or a combination of the two.

Fortunately it is possible to gradually move the trauma that has been locked in the old brain to the higher, reasoning part of the brain that holds our language centers—the cerebral cortex. Unlike the old brain, the cerebral cortex has the capacity to integrate new information and to change. Once trauma memories are integrated into this more advanced part of the brain through tools such as imagery, the creative arts, and body-based therapies—along with psychotherapy—survivors of abuse learn, on the deepest level, that the abuse happened in the past and that it is over.

As a result, automatic stress responses and other PTSD symptoms can be significantly reduced and, in some cases, eliminated altogether.

WORKING WITH POST-TRAUMATIC STRESS DISORDER

Survivors of child sexual abuse have found many of the following approaches helpful in working with PTSD symptoms:

- **Develop skills in self-soothing and self-care.** Learning to pace yourself and become grounded in your body can minimize triggers and bring comfort when PTSD symptoms arise. Deep breathing, progressive relaxation, and prayer are among the practices that survivors have found helpful. (See "Dealing with Panic" on p. 34.)

- **Work with things that trigger you.** Recognizing the things that trigger you is important. If you understand why you feel alarmed or terrorized, your reaction will be less frightening to you. In the early stages of healing, you will want to avoid some triggers. As you move through the healing process, you'll be able to understand your triggers better and learn how to manage them, rather than trying to avoid them altogether. (See "Working with Triggers" on p. 312 and "From Splitting to Being in Your Body" on p. 253.)

- **Address the trauma in an integrated way: mind, body, and spirit.** There are many healing approaches that can help you discharge tension that was stored physiologically at the time of the trauma, reduce the body's automatic reactions, and teach you to use the body's resources in healing. (See "Body-Based Therapies and Groups" on p. 542 of the Resource Guide.)

- **Use guided imagery and meditation.** These techniques have been powerful tools for many survivors in managing distressing symptoms and in healing from PTSD. (See "Using Guided Imagery" on p. xxxiii as well as the guided imageries "Creating a Safe Place Inside" on p. 38 and "Imagery to Heal Trauma" on p. 236.)

• **Consider medication.** Medication has helped some survivors struggling with the effects of PTSD. Some medications have proven effective in alleviating the symptoms of PTSD. Others have found acupuncture, homeopathy, herbal remedies, and other alternative healing practices helpful. (See "What About Medication?" on p. 41.)

These techniques—along with the long-term in-depth work of healing—help many people get relief from PTSD, either entirely or through a lessening of intensity. But for some survivors, even when they are doing everything they can to heal, some symptoms persist. The impact of severe, ongoing trauma is not something you can control completely. But you can learn how to work with your circumstances and manage the effects so that you don't feel at the mercy of overwhelming emotions.

Learning to Live in Your Body[*]

"What I've had to tell myself again and again is 'Trust yourself.' When my body tells me to stop, I stop. When my body tells me to go, I go. I used to push myself beyond my limits, and I'd always get sick. Now I've learned to listen so I don't have to go to that point. I trust myself because I'm my own greatest healer. Even the best therapist can't help me heal unless I listen to my body."

Children initially learn about themselves and the world through their bodies. Hunger, fear, love, acceptance, rejection, support, nurturing, terror, pride, mastery, humiliation, anger—all began with sensation on the body level. As a child, your body was the means through which you learned your first lessons about trust, intimacy, protection, and nourishment.

When you were abused, your body and your psyche were invaded. You were taught through direct experience that your body, rather than being your home, was a dangerous place where terrible things could happen. Gizelle, who was violently raped by her father, recalls:

---

* We wish to acknowledge Staci K. Haines, somatic therapist and author of *Healing Sex: A Mind–Body Approach to Healing Sexual Trauma* (originally published as *The Survivor's Guide to Sex*) for her generous assistance in revising and expanding this chapter for the twentieth-anniversary edition of *The Courage to Heal*. Her groundbreaking work assisted us greatly in integrating new information about the impact of trauma on the mind and body.

Somatics works with the mind, body, and spirit as a whole. It approaches the body as an essential place of change, learning and transformation. When we reconnect the vast intelligence of the body with the mind and spirit, powerful change and healing are available. The Greek root of *somatics* means "the living body in its wholeness." For more information see www.somaticsandtrauma.org.

In earlier editions of this chapter, we relied heavily on the expertise and advice of Amy Pine, creative-arts therapist and cofounder, with Ellen Bass, of Survivors Healing Center in Santa Cruz, California. Amy played an integral role in our original concept of this chapter.

I felt caught, trapped in my body. That continued into adulthood. I never heard any messages from my body. I would be really sick and I'd stagger around and go to work. I made a lifetime dedication of not listening to my body, because if I had, I would have had to hear that I had been raped, and I couldn't do that and survive.

Like Gizelle, you may have cut yourself off from your body—from its knowledge, sensations, and feelings, from its riches and its wisdom. You protected yourself as best you could—but at a terrible price. Most of the problems survivors experience with their bodies—dissociation, numbing, and addictions, to name a few—arise from this attempt to find safety by leaving their bodies behind.

Some survivors are so estranged from their bodies that they don't know how to relate to them at all:

I had to start with the very basic question, "What is my body?" Is it a bunch of unrelated parts—arms, legs, head, torso, and feet? Is it my organs, muscles, bones, and DNA? Is it the part of me that runs marathons, but has two left feet on the dance floor? Or is it how I look? Most of my life I've viewed my body as a necessary evil—a receptacle that needs sleep and demands food, a thing that carries around my brain. Now that I was healing, it began to dawn on me, "Was it actually possible that my body was *me* and not something separate from me?"

Like this woman, many survivors live disembodied lives, existing solely in their heads. Rachel Bat Or recalls her relationship to her body before she began to heal:

If someone said, "What do you feel in your arm?" I would have had no idea what they were even talking about. If I touched it, I felt my arm with my hand. But I couldn't get inside of it. I could only touch the skin from the outside. I couldn't have felt my heart beating. I couldn't experience anything from inside my body, because *I* wasn't inside my body.

But when we don't live inside our bodies, we miss the crucial information our bodies continually offer us. By habitually cutting ourselves off from our feelings—of discomfort, pleasure, anger, or even relaxation—we disconnect from ourselves a little more each day. We deaden ourselves and grow numb, and in doing so, we lose access to the innate healing power of the body. Our world becomes smaller and less vibrant, and we often don't even know what we're missing.

Although you may have become estranged from your body for good reasons, a big part of healing is re-integrating yourself into your body. Being embodied means learning to live within your own skin, staying present, and getting to know your body, not as a place of pain but as an integrated source of wisdom, strength, and healing. Your body can become a powerful ally, leading you to a place of greater vitality and wholeness.

THE RELATIONSHIP BETWEEN BODY, MIND, AND SPIRIT

There has been a revolution in our understanding of the relationship between body, mind, and spirit. We have learned that our minds and bodies are not separate entities; rather, they are interconnected parts of one unified organism. Research in neuropsychology and brain chemistry has taught us that our physiology plays a central role in surviving trauma (see "Trauma and the Brain" on p. 242). Innovative approaches toward healing have shown us how working directly with the body can be instrumental in resolving trauma as well. Changes you make on the body level can profoundly affect your thinking and your emotional responses and can actually create new pathways in your brain, dramatically increasing your capacity to heal trauma and to change old, habitual patterns of behavior.

THE IMPORTANCE OF WORKING WITH THE BODY

Talking about your abuse and sharing your experiences and feelings verbally is an important part of the healing process. But this release must happen in your body as well. You were abused on many levels, and your healing must take place on many levels as well.* One survivor recalls:

---

* For an in-depth story of a survivor who did substantial healing on a body level, see "Sheila O'Connell" on p. 510.

I didn't feel associated with my body for many years. I was all mental until my mid-thirties. After ten years of bodywork, I've brought my center down out of my head. Now I know my body is as much a part of me as my head or my heart.

There is only so far we can go in our healing if we don't include the body. For example, when you are having sex with your lover, you know that he is not your father, but that understanding alone isn't enough to stop you from flinching when he reaches out to touch you. Or you may understand theoretically why you should set limits, but you may not be able to do so until you learn to create boundaries on a physical level.

Author and teacher of somatics Staci Haines remembers the huge changes that occurred once she started incorporating her body more fully into her healing process:

The abuse seemed to pour out of my body. The more I reconnected with my body, the clearer I became about what trauma was stored where. My thighs retained rage. Moving my thighs and kicking my legs allowed me to begin expressing my anger. My chest held much of the deep grief. Where my body had been pinned or frozen during the abuse, I now began to move. How many times had I wanted to push someone off of me and couldn't? I learned how to let my arms and body do that. The relief was incredible. The process was painful. I was coming back to me. I started to identify my body, not only as a shell that housed my "self," but

USING THE EXERCISES IN THIS CHAPTER

It's important that you go slowly and get support as you begin to work with these exercises. The safety of a class, a bodywork session, or a therapist trained to work with the body can be extremely beneficial. If you are practicing these exercises on your own, the following suggestions can be helpful.

- **Expect resistance.** When you've been sexually abused and have learned to survive by leaving your body, it makes sense that you might find the prospect of working with your body frightening. Rather than fighting it, acknowledge your resistance for what it is—a leftover survival mechanism.

- **Remind yourself why you are choosing to do this work.** You might say to yourself, "I am doing this body scan to be more present with myself so that I can be more present with other people and build more intimacy in my life." Or "I am trying this boundary exercise so I can learn where I stop and other people begin." Or "I am doing this grounding exercise so that I can feel safe when something scares me."

- **Check in with yourself.** Ask yourself, "What could make me feel safe enough to do this exercise?" Then try to provide those conditions for yourself.

- **Take small steps.** If an exercise seems daunting, skip it for now. Start with something that feels more manageable. Or set a kitchen timer for ten minutes—knowing that there's a definite end time can help you feel safer.

- **Trust yourself and know your limits.** Doing more is not necessarily better. Forcing yourself to complete an exercise when it no longer feels good can be retraumatizing. Stop when you need to stop, even if you aren't "finished."

- **Take time afterwards to integrate the exercise.** Don't try one of these exercises right before you have to rush off to work or pick up your child from school. Give yourself time afterward to reflect on your experience, to write or to talk about it with a trusted person.

- **If you find it too difficult to do these exercises on your own, look for a class, a workshop, a trained bodyworker or a body-oriented therapist.** See p. 542 of the Resource Guide for suggestions.

as a source of wisdom and inspiration. My body actually knew things about the healing process that I didn't. In the thawing out, I got to live inside myself again.*

---

* Staci K. Haines, *Healing Sex: A Mind-Body Approach to Healing Sexual Trauma* ([originally published as *The Survivor's Guide to Sex*] San Francisco: Cleis Press, 2007).

Yet making your body central to your healing can be challenging. Survivors often feel great resistance when they begin to inhabit their bodies. When you bring your consciousness back into your body, feelings of fear, rage, loneliness, and hopelessness—as well as the physical sensations of being abused—can return with startling clarity. You may also fear entering your body because you're afraid you'll discover something terrible about yourself.

But healing on the body level is invaluable. As you begin to address and alter the survival mechanisms that are still in place in your body, you will no longer automatically respond as if you are still being abused.

Healing holistically, with your body fully engaged, also lets you know on a deeper level that the abuse is truly in the past. This powerful awareness—that the abuse is over and that you can never be hurt in the same way—can bring you a new level of possibility and freedom.

FROM HATING YOUR BODY TO LOVING YOUR BODY

Sexual abuse is an assault on our bodies. Yet many survivors blame their bodies rather than the abuser. You may blame your body for responding, for being attractive, for being womanly, for being small, for being large, for being vulnerable, for being susceptible to stimulation and pleasure, even for feeling anything. *But you were not abused because of your body; you were abused because of your perpetrator.*

Learning to love your body is a major element of healing. Here are some suggestions for learning to feel better about your body:

- **Start with what you can appreciate.** Begin with what you can genuinely appreciate about your body. Examples might be: "My body is strong and healthy and serves me well." "I am thankful that my legs take me wherever I want to go." "My hands are competent and can do many things, such as hold my baby, type, make egg rolls, and dig in my garden. I am grateful for such good hands." "I have a well-shaped head. My short hair looks good on me."

- **Look in the mirror.** One way to counteract the distorted messages that you received is to look in the mirror—and really look. Take time for yourself when you won't be interrupted. Look at your face and also at your body. Look as if you were an artist, a painter. Don't look in order to criticize. Look simply in order to be introduced, to make the acquaintance of your body, to see this body in which you live. This time look with *your* eyes, not through the eyes of the abuser, the society, the lover, the mother, the judge. Look to see, not to judge. Do this for five minutes a day and then write about the experience.

- **Draw yourself.** Another way to shift your image of your body is to draw it. Artemis is an artist (her story is on p. 467). While she was remembering her abuse, she created an extensive series of self-portraits. "At first, the agony was drawn all over them, but bit by bit, they became softer. In the beginning, the lines were hard and black and angular, but then I would force myself

EXERCISES TO HELP YOU RELAX*

Tense and relax. Lie on your back or in any other comfortable position. Make sure your clothing isn't constricting in any way. Take off your shoes; undo your belt. Take a few deep slow breaths and release the air. Starting at your feet, focus your attention there and feel any tension in your feet. With your next natural exhalation, let the tension go, and let your feet relax. Next, move to your ankles. Notice any tension there. As you exhale, release any tightness. Continue the same exercise, working your way up your body—feet, ankles, calves, thighs, buttocks, genitals, stomach, chest, back, shoulders, arms, hands, neck, face, head—until your body becomes more and more relaxed. This is wonderful just before sleep.

Belly breathing. When you're scared or are starting to panic, your breath becomes shallow and uneven and catches high up in your chest. To belly-breathe, lie on your back and place one hand on your stomach, one hand on your chest. If the hand on your chest is the one moving up and down, you're breathing from your chest. Practice sending your breath deeper into your belly, until the hand on your stomach begins to rise and fall. Consciously blow the air out of your mouth, and let your belly refill with air. If lying on your back is uncomfortable or frightening, you can do this exercise while sitting in a chair, standing up, or in any other position that's comfortable for you.

_____

* These exercises were contributed by Amy Pine.

---

to sit in front of a mirror and draw my own body nude, and try to draw it with all the sensual softness of a female body. I would use charcoal, which is very soft, and I'd keep drawing until I could draw my body very soft and very sensuous. And I learned to love my body through that."

- **Nurture yourself.** Treating your body with care is another way to love yourself. Relax in baths, soak in hot tubs, or take saunas. Use bath oil, body lotion, powder.

Just paying attention to your body while you wash can make a difference. One woman learned to feel more sensual this way: "My therapist suggested that when I take a shower in the morning, not to treat myself like I'm scrubbing the kitchen table—that I take some pleasure in my body, to feel the curves of my body with the soap and water."

You can buy yourself warm socks, cozy pajamas, flannel sheets, silk underwear—whatever feels good. You can also wear things that are soothing to areas of your body that have been particularly traumatized. One woman, who survived being strangled, felt especially tense and vulnerable in her neck. Wearing soft, lovely scarves was a way she took care of herself. She liked the feeling of the extra warmth and gentle protection.

FROM SPLITTING TO BEING IN YOUR BODY

Children often deal with the unbearable experience of sexual abuse by emotionally and psychically distancing from the abuse while it is happening.* Although dissociation is an intelligent, miraculous, and effective coping mechanism for the child, it can become habitual in adult survivors, so that every time you experience uncomfortable feelings and sensations (anger, sexual arousal, fear, etc.), you automatically "check out" and leave your body, even though you may not be in any real danger. The problem is that you may be leaving your body at times when you clearly don't want to—like when you're having sex with someone you want to be with or when you need to stand your ground in your life now.

When you habitually dissociate, you also miss a great deal of joy, because life is lived and experienced and enjoyed through the body.

A crucial part of healing from child sexual abuse is learning to stay present in your body, to tolerate the full range of sensations and feelings you find there. In *Healing Sex: A Mind–Body Approach to Healing Sexual Trauma*, Staci K. Haines† offers practical steps to reduce dissociation and become more present—both during sex and in the rest of your life:

LEARN ABOUT YOUR PATTERNS OF DISSOCIATION

- **Become familiar with the way you dissociate.** Pay attention to how it feels when you "leave." Do you get lost in racing thoughts? Feel as if you're floating above yourself looking down at the action? As if you exit out of the top of your head? Or does your mind suddenly go blank?
- **Notice how your body feels when you dissociate.** Check in with your body. Where do you feel sensations, and what are they like? Does your breath become shallow? Do you feel cut off at the hips? What places feel tight, numb, or frozen?
- **Learn to recognize the signs of dissociation.** Often, right before you dissociate, there are warning signs that it is about to happen. You may find yourself feeling spacey or tense, your hands might tingle or sweat, you may feel like crying, or you may have thoughts such as "I'll never amount to anything

---

* For more on dissociation see "Dissociation" on p. 16, "What We Know About Memory and Traumatic Amnesia" on p. 74, and "Trauma and the Brain" on p. 242.

† The ideas and exercises in this section are drawn from *Healing Sex: A Mind–Body Approach to Healing Sexual Trauma* ([originally published as *The Survivor's Guide to Sex*] San Francisco: Cleis Press, 2007).

anyway" or "What's the use?"* Becoming familiar with these cues makes it possible for you to choose to stay embodied rather than go away.

- **Notice what triggered you.** Usually you dissociate to get away from uncomfortable feelings or sensations. See if you can trace back to what was happening right before you went away. Was someone angry with you? Did you feel angry? Turned on? Scared? Threatened? Ashamed?

When you become aware of the feelings that trigger your dissociation, you can gradually learn to tolerate those emotions in your body. As you practice staying present, you will find that your feelings and sensations are not unbearable and that they do not last forever. Rather, they continuously change.†

TO COME BACK INTO YOUR BODY

- **Choose to return.** Setting a clear intention that you want to stay in your body—and feel what there is to feel—is a powerful step toward being more present.
- **Pay attention to your surroundings.** Look around at where you are and who you're with. Notice the temperature around you and the feeling of the air on your skin. Feel the ground under your feet. Listen to the sounds in the room. Extend your senses out into the world around you.

- **Pay attention to sensations in your body now.** Feeling the sensations occurring in your body in the moment is the fastest way to reenter your body because sensations always happen in the present. Body sensations include things such as temperature (Are you feeling more warm or cool and where?), pressure (Where do you feel more relaxed? Where do you feel more tense?), and movement (Can you feel your breath moving in and out of your lungs, your nose or mouth? Can you feel your heartbeat or a muscle twitch?) Sensations are the key to staying in your body and getting in touch with your feelings.

- **Learn to recognize how emotions manifest in your body.** What does anger feel like in your body? Where do you feel it? How about fear? Shame? Pleasure? To become more present, you need to learn to stay with the feelings that once sent you into dissociation.

Sometimes, tuning into the physical sensations underneath our emotions makes it possible to stay with painful or difficult feelings longer. Rather than thinking, "Uh-oh . . . fear . . . I'm out of here," pay attention to the tightening in your throat or the clenching of your belly. By focusing on these sensations, you will be less likely to automatically split when strong feelings arise.

---

* See "Internalized Messages" on p. 213 for more on this subject.
† To experience this in your own body, you may want to try "An Introduction to Mindfulness Meditation" on p. 180.

- **Explore other techniques that help you get back in your body.** Invite yourself back into your body. Drop your breath deeper in your belly. Move. Try swinging your arms or shaking your legs. Notice any places that are numb or feel dead to you, and stroke, pat, or rub them, reminding yourself, "This is my arm," or "This is my belly. It belongs to me."
- **Reach out.** Dissociation can be lonely. Telling someone what's going on can help to bring you back. You can also make an agreement with close friends to ask you what's happening when they notice that your attention seems to be wandering.
- **Get support dealing with material that arises as you become more present.** Unprocessed reactions, memories, and trauma are stored in the body, and as you become more present, challenging emotions—as well as further memories of the abuse—may emerge. Although this may be painful, it is a positive step in your healing because the trauma is "thawing" out of you and you are becoming more present. Even though you may understand this intellectually, your old survival mechanisms may scream in alarm and urge you to get away from the "bad" feelings by dissociating. This is a time to be extra gentle with yourself. And get the support you need to stay with the feelings, sensations, and memories that are arising.

EXERCISES TO GROUND YOU*

Feel your connection to the earth. Imagine that you are a tree sending your roots deep into the earth. Imagine these roots reaching down through your legs, through the bottom of your feet, into the earth, all the way to its center, where they're firmly planted.

Another way to feel connected with the earth is to go for a walk. Find a place where you can walk on the earth itself, on grass or dirt—a country road, a park, a playground, the beach. Walking, with or without shoes, can be very grounding and centering.

Push with a partner. Stand facing a partner and place your hands together, palm to palm. At a signal of "go," push against each other as hard as you can. Take turns trying to back each other up to the end of the room (or yard). (Make sure that there are no obstacles behind you.) Either person can stop the exercise if he or she feels uncomfortable. Afterward, check your body and see what you notice. Discuss your reactions. Try the same exercise back-to-back. This should be done in a spirit of support rather than competition, the goal being for each person to feel solid and grounded.

---

* These exercises were contributed by Amy Pine.

FROM NUMBNESS TO FEELING

Numbness is another way not to feel. Like dissociation, numbing physical sensations was a sensible and effective defense at the time of the abuse. You blocked out pain, as well as conflicting sensations of arousal. But numbing no longer serves your needs.

Here are some ways to wake up and feel more in your body:

- **Pay attention to physical sensations.** Watching your breathing is a good place to start. Just allowing yourself to feel the breath entering and leaving your body—the air through your nostrils, your chest, and your abdomen expanding and contracting, and the other small sensory components of breathing—can bring your body back to life. (See "An Introduction to Mindfulness Meditation" on p. 172 for instructions to one basic breathing practice.)

  Extend this awareness of detail to any common activity: walking, brushing your teeth, petting the cat, drinking a glass of water. Starting with the less threatening physical experiences, you can pay attention to how your body feels. You can register cold and hot, texture, thirst, taste, pressure, tingling, the pumping of your heart.

- **Nurturing touch.** Self-massage is a wonderful way to become aware of body feelings, to release tension, and just to feel good. Try giving yourself a foot or neck massage.

  You can also seek safe, nonsexual touch from others. Everyone needs touch. You can talk forever, but some wounds are in a place more primal than words.

  You can receive safe touch from friends who are comfortable holding or stroking you in nonsexual ways. Take time to establish beforehand that the touch will be strictly nonsexual, and agree to let each other know if something doesn't feel right or if you want to stop.

  If you haven't received a massage from a sensitive, skilled practitioner, this can be a powerful way to wake up your body. Be sure to find someone who is trustworthy so that there's no chance of inappropriate touch.

  If you tell your massage practitioner that you are healing from child sexual abuse, you may feel more free to cry, to stop the massage, or just to breathe into your feelings. You can set limits, saying you don't want to be touched in a certain way or in a particular place. Although it may feel awkward at first, stating your needs directly is a mature way to take care of yourself.

  Massage sometimes releases intense feelings. Some women have felt overwhelmed either during or after a massage, especially if they aren't accustomed to the vulnerability of being touched deeply. If you're planning a massage for the first time, you may want to start with a foot massage or just neck and shoulders. You may also want to arrange a session with your counselor or a supportive friend shortly afterward, so that you will have a chance to talk about your feelings.

If you start to go numb when someone else is touching you or when you touch yourself, stop and try to isolate your thoughts or feelings at the moment the numbness started. Talk about your feelings or write them down. It's important not to continue the touching while you are numb. That's what happened during the abuse, and it won't help to repeat that same pattern.

- **Body-oriented therapies.** Understanding the relationship between the brain, body, and trauma is groundbreaking because it allows us to develop more relevant tools and interventions for healing. A number of therapies integrate our growing awareness of trauma's impact on mind, body, and spirit. Somatic therapies use a combination of talk, therapeutic touch, and somatic practices. Therapeutic bodywork is touch or movement specifically designed to open up the stuck, frozen places in your body and to help you process the traumatic memories and feelings that may be stored there.*

---

* Some practitioners are standard therapists trained in body-oriented modalities and others are body-workers trained to work with trauma. It's best to choose a practitioner who is skilled in both somatics and trauma. See "Body-Based Therapies and Groups" on p. 542 of the Resource Guide.

- **Movement that integrates body, mind, and spirit.** Yoga, tai chi, chi gong, martial arts, and some forms of dance can help you feel present, powerful, and safe in your body. Sports such as tennis, bicycling, swimming, and running are also ways to feel more connected to your body. As you participate in these activities, focus on staying in your body rather than performing or trying to "look good." Our bodies change based on what we practice.

FROM IGNORING YOUR BODY TO LISTENING TO YOUR BODY

Many survivors have decided that their bodies are more trouble than they're worth and have chosen to ignore them. Ignoring body needs includes going to work when you're sick, neglecting to put on a sweater when you're cold, or waiting to pee until you've finished just one more task.

This kind of negligence can have serious consequences. A former deputy sheriff, who had to retire early because of a back injury, describes the events that led up to her disability:

I never was in touch with my body. The reason I ended up having back surgery is because I completely ignored serious symptoms for six months.

I had a doctor. I had medical coverage. There was nothing keeping me from the doctor except that I didn't want it to be true, because I had something else I wanted to do at that time, and as far as I was concerned, my back was betraying me. I wanted to go to school and I wanted to graduate. And I did.

It wasn't until years later that I realized I believed my body had betrayed me by having pleasurable feelings when my brothers were abusing me. Therefore

---

EXERCISES TO HELP YOU BE MORE PRESENT*

Do a full-body scan. This exercise helps you practice living inside your body and teaches you to tolerate more of your own sensations and emotions. Start at your head and feel the sensations that are there. Notice temperature, pressure, and movement in and on your head. Don't watch yourself from the outside. Instead, really feel what is happening inside your head and on your scalp right now. Notice how your jaws and eyes feel. Pay attention to your ears, your cheeks, your eyes, your lips.

Now bring your focus to the sensations in your neck and shoulders. Pay attention to the surface of your skin as well as deeper inside—your muscles, tendons, and bones. Continue all the way through your body— move down your arms, through your wrists and hands and fingers, throughout your chest and your inner organs, down through your hips and genitals, thighs, knees, shins, and feet.

Notice the sensations that are pleasant or neutral and the ones you wish would go away. Notice times that you want to distance yourself from either pleasant or unpleasant sensations. Both are sources of significant information about your body.

If you come to places where you cannot feel anything or feel empty or numb, it may mean that trauma is held in that spot. In the past, this might have been a place where it was important for you not to feel. This can also be valuable information to work with.

If you don't have time for a full-body scan, try noticing the sensations in your body for five minutes each morning.

If you do this exercise on a regular basis, you will notice fluctuations in the sensations you feel and your ability to stay with them. As time goes on, you will grow more comfortable in your body and gradually be able to feel more.

Practice being present with a partner. Sit or stand with your feet solidly planted on the floor. Make eye contact with a partner and really see her. Don't space out. Squeeze your partner's hands if your attention starts to waver. Simply be there together, with the partner mirroring (following and imitating) your breathing pattern as it changes. Talk about how you feel as you do this exercise. Notice any changes.

---

* The Body Scan exercise was contributed by Staci K. Haines. The Being Present with a Partner exercise was contributed by Amy Pine.

I hated my body, and if it did anything I didn't want it to do, like be hungry at an inappropriate time or be in pain at a time that was inconvenient to me, I would simply ignore it. And I did that to the point of nerve damage in my leg and a ruptured disk.

Listening to body messages is not only critical for maintaining physical health but also necessary for being in touch with your feelings and your needs. Our bodies are our essential connection to life. To listen to your body, you have to be willing to feel. Although sometimes this means being willing to bear difficult feelings, it also means being willing to take the time to feel good. If you're used to ignoring your body, this can be a radical yet pleasant change:

I always took a shower the very last thing at night before sleep. Showers for me are a total pleasure. Unless something very serious is bothering me, I feel relaxed afterwards. But even if I needed a shower earlier in the day, even if I was tense, chilled, or irritable, I wouldn't take one until I had done all my work.

One evening, around seven o'clock, I decided to take a shower even though I still had a lot of homework to do that night. I showered, put on pajamas and a robe, made myself a cup of tea, and sat down to study. It was so pleasant. I was warm, relaxed, and productive. Feeling good wasn't incompatible with working. And feeling good didn't always have to come last on my list.

THE VALUE OF EXERCISE

Our bodies are designed for motion. You don't have to be a marathon runner or an Olympic swimmer to enjoy moving. Even simple walking is good exercise. Moving stimulates your circulation, massages your internal organs, stretches and strengthens your muscles, and energizes you. Exercise is also a great way to discharge tension, work through emotional blocks, release anger, and gain self-esteem.

As Jayne Lacey relates, "I swam again today. It feels so good to be back in the water, to be pushing my body to get strength. I look at it as being in training for my life."

If you're not accustomed to exercising, choose an activity you think you might enjoy, and start with just a little. It's more inviting to start small and work up than it is to set unreasonable goals, strain muscles, exhaust yourself, and give up. Exercise is not another ordeal to be endured. Rather it is a healthy part of living in your body.

You may also want to join a class or find a running buddy. Many people enjoy physical activity more if it's not "just" exercise. You may like playing golf, digging in the garden, or walking to work and back. Having support for undertaking a new activity—and using your body in a new way—can provide essential encouragement.

FROM ILLNESS TO A HEALTHIER BODY

Some survivors were abused in ways that have left them with physical illnesses. For others, the ways they coped led to illness. Because trauma puts great stress on the body, many medical conditions, including migraines, autoimmune disorders, asthma, arthritis, pelvic disorders, urinary tract infections, and problems with sexual organs sometimes have origins in early trauma and stress. An area of your body that was injured may develop problems later—such as pain in your jaw if you were orally raped. You may also experience more subtle problems such as chronic tiredness, or susceptibility to colds and flu.

Of course, all illness does not necessarily stem from abuse. People who were not sexually abused develop arthritis, and the incidence of immunity disorders is increasing dramatically in the whole population. Some schools of alternative healing "blame the victim" by insisting that any physical illness is a result of an emotional attitude and claim that if the patient would only work through the emotions, she would no longer be sick. This is simplistic, false, and damaging.

Yet there sometimes is an emotional component to illness. If you are suffering from an illness that you suspect has its roots in your abuse, recognizing its origins gives you a chance to work with those aspects.*

There are many alternative means of healing available today that work on both the physical

and the emotional levels. Acupuncture, chiropractic treatment, homeopathy, biofeedback, therapeutic bodywork, and visualization all can be valuable. If you are under the care of a physician, you may want to discuss some of these possibilities. Doctors are becoming increasingly open to the benefits of less conventional treatments. Sometimes you can design a treatment plan that uses both traditional and nontraditional methods.

FROM ADDICTION TO FREEDOM

Addictions have not only a physical component but also an emotional one. For survivors, the roots of addiction often lie in the desire to escape from painful emotions or the need to push down memories that are too overwhelming to face. When you are besieged by pain, terror, grief, and anguish, it makes sense that you might want to avoid those feelings. And addictions give you a way out; when you are in the grip of your compulsion, nothing else exists. Alcohol, drugs, compulsive sex, overwork, gambling, and other addictions help you numb out, feel alive, find relief, or gain a sense of control, no matter how illusory or fleeting it may be. It is not surprising that so many survivors struggle with serious addictions.

But addictions can also destroy your body, tear down your self-esteem, interfere with relationships, delay your healing, and sometimes kill you. You must be honest with

---

* Read David Clarke's *They Can't Find Anything Wrong! 7 Keys to Understanding, Treating and Healing Stress Illness* (Boulder, CO: Sentient, 2007) and Nellie A. Radomsky's *Lost Voices: Women, Chronic Pain, and Abuse* (Binghamton, NY: Haworth Press, 1995) for information on illnesses related to early childhood trauma as well as other stresses. See the section "The Body's Role in Healing," which begins on p. 541 of the Resource Guide, for details.

yourself about the extent of your problem, identify the purpose it serves, and recognize it as both a survival tool and a self-destructive pattern.

To free yourself from an addiction, you will need a lot of support—and the commitment to address the deep underlying issues that might have contributed to the addiction.

ALCOHOLISM AND DRUG ADDICTION

Many survivors are addicted to alcohol or drugs. Drugs and alcohol are temporarily effective ways to numb feelings, suppress memories, and escape from pain. Yet healing requires that you safely learn how to feel again.

Breaking addictions is very difficult to do in isolation. Alcoholics Anonymous (AA) and Narcotics Anonymous (NA) are extremely effective in helping people deal with their addictions to alcohol and drugs. They have 24-hour hotlines in almost every city in the country (and the world), many meetings at a wide variety of places and times, and people (recovering addicts and alcoholics) who will help anyone who picks up the phone or goes to a meeting. Both AA and NA are nonjudgmental and completely free. Twelve-step programs have helped millions become clean and sober and reclaim their lives.*

---

* To find a group in your area or to learn more about these programs, go to www.aa.org, www.na.org, or www.12step .org or look in your local telephone book.

EATING DIFFICULTIES

Before we begin to talk about problems with eating, it is essential to say that there is no ideal size or shape for a woman's body. Some of us are tall, some are short; some are angular, some are rounded; some are small, some are large; some are firm, some are soft. And none of these qualities are better or worse in themselves.

American culture sends out a strong message that women should look a certain way. That way has numerous characteristics, ranging from light-colored skin to long eyelashes, and one of its most relentlessly pushed characteristics is thinness. The mass media praises thinness and condemns large women. This is oppressive to anyone who isn't slim. We don't want to perpetuate that standard. What we are talking about are problems with eating—how we eat or don't eat, and what that means to us. We are not talking about body size.

COMPULSIVE EATING

Survivors eat compulsively for many reasons. Some women binge to numb their feelings. While you are totally involved with eating, shoveling spoonful after spoonful of ice cream into your mouth, other pains, fears, and hungers recede. Compulsive eating is an escape. Although you may hate yourself in an hour, you get relief in the moment.

If you are hurting, eating compulsively may be the only way you know to nurture yourself. You need to be held, you need time alone, you need more fulfilling work. But you're not accustomed to recognizing these needs and responding to them, so you eat. You give yourself food as a substitute for other needs.

Some women overeat for protection. Our culture perpetuates the myth that large women are less sexually desirable. Some women do experience less sexual attention when they are large and thus feel less vulnerable. Also, children are small, and when you were a child, you were abused, so now you may feel safer in a large body. However, size alone cannot protect you. Women of every size experience sexual advances—and sexual assault.

Although body size is not necessarily related to how or how much you eat, some women purposely eat large quantities of food to make themselves larger. One survivor decided in her late teens that the only way to avoid sexual abuse was to get fat. She didn't like sweets very much, but she forced herself to eat them—and everything else—until she got to be a size that she thought was large enough to be unattractive.

Look at why you eat the way you do. What does it give you? What needs does it meet? Don't condemn yourself for having tried to meet those needs through food. Instead, begin to honor them in healthier ways.

If you eat to be larger so that you'll feel safe or have more power in the world, think of other ways you might gain that same protection or power. If you eat to avoid unwanted advances, it's essential to learn to say no. "No" is simple and direct. Practice saying it frequently. In most situations, a firm "no" will protect you at least as well as eating, and usually better.*

---

* See "Setting Limits and Boundaries" on p. 214.

ANOREXIA AND BULIMIA

Anorexia and bulimia thrive in our culture, which exalts thinness and despises fat. Girls and women internalize this attitude and are terrified of being large. Sexual abuse compounds the problem.

Many girls who have been sexually abused begin developing anorexia when they go through puberty. They may falsely believe that if they don't grow breasts, develop full hips, and become curvy, they won't be attractive, and then no one will force them into being sexual. For these girls, it feels especially frightening to become women. They think, "If this is what happened to me when I was a child, what's going to happen when I'm a woman?"

Anorexia, like compulsive eating, is an attempt to protect yourself and to assert control. By strictly controlling what you do and don't take into your body, you are trying to regain the power that was taken from you as a child.

Not eating, or eating too little to sustain health, is also a way of saying no to life. If life has given you abuse, fear, pain, and humiliation, this attitude is understandable. With anorexia, you are not instantly killing yourself, but you eat only enough not to die. And sometimes not even that.

Bulimia is a pattern of eating and throwing up, or bingeing and throwing up. You might have begun this pattern because you didn't want to gain weight or because you felt a compulsion to vomit that you've never understood.

Bulimia, like anorexia, is an attempt to control what happens to your body. Throwing up is a way of saying no. As children, many survivors had fingers, penises, and objects shoved into their body openings. You might have had a penis shoved into your mouth. You might have gagged or vomited. If you're still vomiting, you may be still trying to get those things out of your body.

The problem, of course, is that food is actually nourishing to you. And repetitive throwing up robs your body of important nutrients and damages your teeth and digestive system. Ultimately, it can kill you. It is essential that you establish the ability to say no in other ways.

In a workshop for survivors who also had eating problems, one woman made a dramatic breakthrough in her struggles with bulimia As Ellen describes:

> After one survivor read her writing, some painful and humiliating memories began to surface. She felt a strong urge to vomit. If this had been a woman who rarely vomited, I would have grabbed a bowl and told her to feel free. Vomiting, if we do it *very* rarely, can be a cathartic release. But since this woman was bulimic, vomiting would have been just one more repetition of a self-destructive behavior. Instead, I encouraged her to get that penis out of her mouth another way. She was terrified and shaking, recoiling into a small childlike bundle. But with encouragement, she gradually sat up and began to say no. Bit by bit she got louder, until she was pounding the pillow in front of her with passionate force, screaming, "NO! Get that out of me! You can't put anything in me that I don't

want! NO. NO. NO!" She screamed and pounded to exhaustion and then leaned back. Sweating, trembling, and smiling, she looked at us and said, "That felt a lot better than throwing up."

Anorexia and bulimia are dangerous, life-threatening patterns. If you're caught in either one, you need immediate skilled help so that you can sustain your body while you heal your emotions and your spirit.

FROM SELF-INJURY TO SELF-CARE

Many survivors have hurt themselves physically—carving into their bodies with knives, burning themselves with cigarettes, or repeatedly harming themselves. It is natural that survivors struggle with self-injury. As children they were indoctrinated to abuse, and now they continue the pattern themselves, never having known other choices.[*]

Self-injury provides an intense feeling of relief and release. It is also an attempt at control, a type of punishment, a means of expressing anger, and a way to have feelings. Hurting yourself is a way to re-create the abusive situation, producing a familiar result.

One woman suffered from severe nighttime attacks of terror and vaginal pain. When she could stand it no longer, she would insert objects into her vagina, causing herself pain. Im-

---

[*] Read "Michelle and Artemis" on p. 467 for an example of a woman struggling with self-injury.

EXERCISES TO ACCESS THE WISDOM OF THE BODY*

Listen to your body. Pick a body part and spend five to ten minutes allowing that part to move in any way it wants. The rest of your body may join in, but keep your primary focus on your chosen part. There is no right or wrong way to do this—the movement can be very small, almost still, and silent. It can also be large or connected to a sound. You can choose a toe, a hand, wrist, eyes, mouth, or pelvis—any part. Give your attention to what the movement feels like or has to say to you.

Another way to do this exercise is to give the various parts of your body a voice; allow them to talk. For example, the stomach might say, "I'm all knotted up. I've been tense for the past week. I'm sick of everything!" You can ask that part of your body

questions to get more information. For example, "What are you sick of?" Allow the stomach to answer. If you don't know for sure, take a guess. Give yourself permission to improvise. See what comes out.

This is also a good exercise to do with another person. Have a friend or counselor ask the questions and you answer them, speaking in the voice of your body part.

Use movement to explore themes in your life. Choose a theme that is relevant in your life—being open/closed, strong/weak, hiding/reaching out, depression/elation, centered/off-centered. Ask a partner to sit with you as a witness while you explore this theme through movement. You don't have to be a dancer—everyone moves. Afterward, talk about it together, sharing your feelings and observations. (The witness should be careful not to interpret the mover's experience.)

* These exercises were contributed by Amy Pine.

mediately afterward, she would feel relief and fall asleep.

At first glance this might seem incomprehensible, but like other coping mechanisms, it had its own intrinsic logic. When this woman was a child, she went to bed every night terrified that this would be one of the nights when her father would abuse her. She would lie sleepless until he did come in—and torture her by putting objects in her vagina or by burning her. Only after he had left could she sleep, knowing that her agony was over for that night.

This woman had no explanation for her actions. She only knew that after the pain came relief and sleep, states of being she was able to achieve no other way. Once she began to understand the connection to her childhood abuse, she took the first steps in stopping this self-destructive compulsion.

Self-injury is not always obvious. One survivor hid it under the guise of accidents:

One of the only ways for me to get attention and be taken care of was to be sick or injured. I intentionally injured myself playing sports. Later, when I worked as a contractor, I'd slice my hand. Because of my work, there was always a reason for the injuries. I was not a wrist slasher. One thing about me, I'm subtle to the max. But these things were clearly intentional.

Self-injury can be a source of great shame and humiliation, but it is important to talk about it because, like child sexual abuse, it grows worse in a climate of secrecy.

To stop harming yourself you need to get help. A skilled counselor can provide essential support. It's no longer necessary to hurt yourself. You deserve kindness both from others and from yourself:

To keep from cutting myself, I write affirmations. I do it right on my wrist. I'll write things like "I love myself," "I will not hurt myself," "I am good," "It's okay to be in pain. It's okay to say it." There was a while I'd change it every day. And then I tell people about what I want to do. I tell my group members. I tell my therapist.

One survivor went so far as to write loving messages all over her body. As a child she had carved "help" into her arm. Now, wanting to make peace with her body, she gently wrote love notes to all her body parts.

Once you decide that hurting yourself is no longer an option, you need to find healthier ways to gain that feeling of release. Stopping a pattern of self-injury requires that you express feelings directly in a safe way. If you are angry, refocus your anger where it belongs—at the person or people who abused you (see "Anger"

on p. 136). If you hurt yourself when you're scared, practice responding to feelings of fear in a different way (see "Dealing with Panic" on p. 34).*

FROM VICTIM TO VICTOR: THE IMPORTANCE OF SELF-DEFENSE

All women are potentially the targets of violence. Even if you use good judgment, have solid self-defense skills, and firmly believe that you have the right to protect yourself, you are not immune to assault.

Survivors of child sexual abuse are sometimes even more vulnerable. If you are unable to identify your own feelings or accurately gauge other people's intentions, you may not recognize danger. If you space out or dissociate, you may be oblivious to warning signs, and it will be harder for you to take effective action. If no one was there to help you as a child, you might hesitate to ask for help to prevent an assault—or might not persist if the first person you turn to isn't responsive. And if you've been indoctrinated into false belief that you deserve abuse—or that abuse is inevitable—you will be less likely to act in your own defense.

To feel comfortable and relaxed in your body, you need to know that you can protect

---

* Some good resources for healing from self-injury are: Tracy Alderman, *The Scarred Soul: Understanding & Ending Self-Inflicted Violence* (Oakland, CA: New Harbinger, 1997) and Ruta Mazelis, ed. *The Cutting Edge: A Newsletter for People Living with Self-Inflicted Violence* (Baltimore, MD: Sidran Institute Press).

EXERCISES FOR LEARNING TO SET BOUNDARIES*

Feel the edge of your body. Take a few moments to consciously acknowledge and appreciate the way your body is held inside your skin. Think about what a magnificent job the skin does of containing and protecting the muscles, veins, arteries, organs, bones, blood, etc. that make up the inside of you. As you are thinking these thoughts, touch your body with your hands. Feel the shape of yourself, no matter what it is, with the mind-set of recognition, curiosity, and gratitude. Notice how your skin is the edge of who you are physically, how it holds and defines you. What would you be like without it? This is your physical body boundary, and it can teach you a lot about other kinds of boundaries as well.

Learn to set physical boundaries with a partner. To effectively set boundaries with another person, you must first become aware of your own needs and level of comfort regarding physical distance and closeness. It's helpful to practice this exercise with several different partners, some of whom you know and trust more than others but all of whom will be safe and respectful.

Stand at the opposite end of a room from your partner. Decide which of you will be the leader. The leader controls the exercise, and the follower does what the leader asks. If you like, you can do the exercise a second time, switching roles.

Begin by bringing your awareness into your body, noticing the sensations, feelings, and thoughts going on inside you. Then, when you feel ready, indicate that you want your partner to move toward you slowly. This exercise is best done in silence, so direct your partner through hand signals rather than words.

Maintain an awareness of how you feel and what you are thinking as your partner moves closer. Tune into your breath, the levels of tension in your body, and how your feelings, thoughts, and body sensations change with greater or lesser proximity. At any point, you can use hand signals to tell your partner to slow down, to speed up, to stop, or to back up.

Take the time to explore what feels comfortable and uncomfortable, safe and unsafe. Explore the following questions:

- When do you want your partner to come closer? Move further away? Stay still?
- Is there a distance that feels the safest and most comfortable to you?
- If you ask your partner to come closer than your ideal comfortable distance, how do you feel?
- What signals tell you that you've overstepped your comfort zone?
- How does it feel to send someone back? Do you worry that you might hurt your partner's feelings or think that your partner will be mad at you?
- Is there a distance when you begin to feel lonely?
- Are your reactions what you'd expect, or are you surprised?

When you feel that you've explored long enough, take a few minutes to talk about your experience or write about it. If you'd like, let your partner be the leader and see what it's like to play the other role.†

---

† For more about learning to say no and set boundaries, see "Setting Limits and Boundaries" on p. 214 and "Setting Limits" on p. 283.

---

* These exercises were contributed by Amy Pine.

yourself. Usually the ability to say no firmly and to move out of a threatening situation is enough to keep you safe. But sometimes an assailant will not be deterred by words alone. Then you need to use additional self-defense skills—shouting, yelling, running, kicking, hitting, making use of your wits and intuition. Most women in our society are not encouraged to be fierce on their own behalf. But you have the right and responsibility to take care of yourself.

There are many forms of self-defense that help you increase your determination to fight back against assault and gain the confidence to do so.* Most rapists and assailants will be frightened away by a vigorous show of opposition, even if your skills are less than perfect.

Seventeen-year-old Marcia told the following story shortly after she took a KIDPOWER self-defense workshop:

I was closing the store where I work. This is a peaceful, safe neighborhood, so I decided to take the trash to the Dump-ster, even though it was late at night. A man was standing outside smoking a cigarette. He smiled and looked down. But when I got to the Dumpster, he was suddenly behind me. He grabbed me and threw me to the ground. Everything was in slow motion. He started dragging me towards the alley. I knew it was now or never. I twisted away from him, pulled up my leg, and kicked him hard.

I heard him yell and felt his grip loosen. I rolled away from him and ran for the back door of the store. As soon as I got in, I locked the door and yelled to my coworkers to lock the other doors.

That night I gave a composite drawing to the police and they caught him very soon after. He was wanted for having committed a number of sexual assaults and is now in jail. The skills I'd learned made it possible for me to stay calm and react quickly and effectively. Who knows what would have happened if I hadn't kicked him and I'd panicked instead?

Of course, there are some situations in which no amount of practice or good judgment are enough to protect you. But if you have basic self-defense training and feel powerful and entitled, you are much more likely to think clearly and be able to keep yourself safe.†

---

* Physical self-defense is most effective and empowering when it is taught in the context of other personal safety skills, including boundary-setting, conflict resolution, and advocacy. In choosing a self-defense program, look for teachers who are committed to creating an emotionally and physically safe environment, are respectful of their students, adapt what they do to meet individual needs, teach that fighting is a last resort, and take a hands-on approach. Ellen Bass is the founding board president of KIDPOWER TEENPOWER FULLPOWER International, a nonprofit organization that provides high-quality self-defense training to adults as well as children and teens. The KIDPOWER method creates an opportunity for each student to be successful in practicing each skill in a way that is relevant for her or his age, ability, culture, and life situation. See p. 526 of the Resource Guide.

† Training in self-defense actually makes a physical fight less likely because you learn skills to prevent a threat from turning into a physical attack, such as moving away, setting a strong boundary, yelling, and getting help.

As an added benefit, you will be teaching your body a new set of responses to replace automatic patterns such as freezing and dissociation.

Learning to protect yourself is an important component of taking back your power. And age, health, or disabilities don't necessarily have to stop you. We know of an eighty-year-old woman in a wheelchair who scared a young rapist so with her spirited defense that he jumped out the window.

YOUR BODY AS A PLACE OF SAFETY, YOUR BODY AS YOUR HOME

There are many aspects of healing that bring great rewards, but perhaps none is more fundamental or personal as healing at the body level. When we reclaim our bodies, we gain access to the most direct knowledge of our lives—our immediate physical experience. When our bodies are our own again, we have a safe home in the world. And when we truly inhabit our bodies, we are empowered.

Finally Free From Terror: Claire's Story

Claire is a survivor who works as a somatic therapist. Working on the body level has been an essential part of her healing.

For many years, the only way I related to my body was how it appeared to other people. I was constantly aware of how men perceived my body. When I would walk down the street, having a man look me up and down was what I expected. I hated the attention, yet I was ruled by it at the same time. I was hyperobsessed with how I looked but completely ignorant about how I felt in my body.

My body was something I made to do things, but I could never get it to do what I wanted it to do. It was a constant struggle. I saw my body as a pain in the ass.

One day, when I was nineteen, I was sitting on the floor in a room full of people, wearing a skirt. I looked down at my legs and thought, "These are my legs." I had the startling realization that I had never really noticed my legs before and that they didn't seem connected to me. In fact, I had never really looked at my body and thought of it as mine. It was first time I realized there might be something wrong—that I might be estranged from my body.

I raced mountain bikes in my twenties, but I felt like a robot. I had no concept of how I felt or what I looked like when I was riding. One day, one of my teammates said to me, "You ride really gracefully." His comment threw me, because I had no concept of my body in space. In fact, I had no direct experience of my own body.

HEALING IN MY BODY

When I first started dealing with the incest, I did nine years of talk therapy. I was terrified of my body because I knew there were memories in it. I'd always sensed that intuitively, but when I first heard the term "body memories," that confirmed it. It took all those years of talk therapy for me to feel safe enough to go into my body.

When I was in grad school, a friend invited me to go to a Five Rhythms dance class. It's a form of ecstatic dance where you go inside your body and move according to five different rhythms. The instructions were to go with whatever movement came out; there were no guidelines about how it should look.

I went back every week for a year. It was the first time I ever consciously made contact with what was happening inside my body and allowed it to be expressed freely. It was terrifying and incredibly exciting at the same time. I began a journey that helped me answer the questions "What does this body do? What does it feel? How can I express myself authentically through my body?"

I had so many pivotal experiences in that class. I developed a relationship with all the parts of my body—suddenly I knew what my toes were feeling, and I'd never known that before. It was amazing for me to look in the mirror and watch my body move. I began to see beauty in whatever it was that I was expressing. It was the first time I ever felt really good in my body, outside of having sex, and it was just with myself.

Sometimes when I was dancing, images of the abuse would come up. I learned I didn't have to push them away—that it was safe to stay with them, to move through them—that I would come out the other side.

I became absolutely passionate about healing my body. Over the course of the next several years, I explored many avenues of working at a body level.

THE MEMORIES AND TRAUMA HAVE LEFT MY BODY

In talk therapy, I went through memories, looked at the patterns in my behavior, confronted family members, and got in touch with my inner child. These were all big, important changes. But it was through the dancing and body-centered therapy that I became a healed person. It feels as if the memories and trauma have left my body.

Before I did the bodywork, my predominant feeling was to be on alert. For most of my life I lived with terror all the time. I thought that was normal. I never felt safe in the world; I was always waiting for something bad to happen. Everyone who walked by me was a threat. If I went on a run, I'd always carry pepper spray and wait for someone to jump out at me. Now I run in the woods alone and I am not afraid. I feel both joyful and safe. The best way I can put it is that I am free of terror. Being embodied is a lack of terror. I don't feel like a victim anymore.

My ability to be congruent from the inside out has grown tremendously. I am present in a way I never was before. I'd never trusted my body to give the right cues, but now I do. I know that they will lead me in a good direction.

My enjoyment of life has increased dramatically. I feel as if I was living in a one-dimensional world before and now I experience the world in a three-dimensional way. I can't imagine going back to not having my senses fully open, experiencing the world.

I now have a loving, generous, compassionate relationship with my body—because my body *is* me. There is no separation between me and my body anymore. I don't see my mind as separate from my body or my heart.

Healthy Intimacy

"I have beautiful things and people in my present. I have beginning friendships with women who understand from inside what I'm going through, unlike the friends I had a few years ago. I have a lover who supports me in my healing, who is not afraid or enraged to see me, and sometimes be with me, in the hellish place I must go in my deeper remembering. I do not have to lie to them. I do not have to keep up appearances for them, I do not have to regain perspective (their perspective). I am not alone."

—ELY FULLER

Intimacy is a bond between two people that is based on trust, respect, love, and the ability to share deeply. When you are truly intimate with someone else, it is safe to be fully yourself. You are seen, and known, accepted, and understood. You experience the give-and-take of caring.

You can have intimate relationships with lovers, partners, friends, children, or other family members. Most survivors have trouble with some, if not all, of these close relationships. If handling things alone and taking care of yourself was what you had to do as a child, it may feel unfamiliar and frightening to be in a close, committed relationship. Many survivors describe intimacy as suffocating or invasive.

They feel claustrophobic when someone gets close. Learning to tolerate intimacy, to feel both close and safe, is often a challenge.

One survivor, Saphyre, had no real closeness in her life for many years:

I had nobody who cared about me, nobody who touched me, or who I touched emotionally. I didn't know how to be emotional. I'd go into total anxiety if there was a hint of connection with anybody. It's hard to explain how severe that is. It's really a critical problem. People die from it. I think "shy" has got to be the biggest euphemism for pain.

On the other hand, you may cling to those you love, unable to tolerate a healthy level of independence:

> I want to be more independent, but the old pattern of needing to be connected at the hip is strong. If I go visit a friend, I call my husband all evening long. I'll call once to check to see if the baby fell asleep. Then I'll call to see if he needs me to pick up anything from the store on my way home. Then I call to tell him what time I'll be home. I'll ask if he returned his mother's call. My clinging annoys the hell out of my husband and it irritates my friend, but I can't seem to help myself. What I say I want to do and what I do are still miles apart.

Your issue may not be one of needing constant connection. You may simply find yourself too absorbed in your own problems to be able to participate in a reciprocal relationship:

> I needed relationships with people who would allow me to be close when I needed to be close, and in another world when I needed that. Since I needed to be close a lot less of the time than I needed to be in my own world, I never got what I needed. I ached for it. I can remember feeling like I would do anything in the world to have the kind of friend who would just put their arms around me and hold me and love me and care, without me having to give anything back. Some nights I would cry all night long, just wishing for that.

Many survivors run into particular problems with intimacy when they are romantically or sexually involved. Physical closeness may be threatening or confusing to you. You may not know how to give or receive nurturing. You may sabotage relationships or repeatedly find yourself in relationships where your basic needs are not being met.

These may seem like insurmountable problems, but it is possible to teach yourself the necessary skills to have real love in your life. The capacity for intimacy lives inside you. As a child, you started out with a healthy desire to trust and to be close, but it was stolen from you.

Healing is the process of getting it back.

FORMING HEALTHY ATTACHMENTS

In a healthy family, babies and children form deep attachments to their parents and other family members. But in families where sexual abuse occurs, the ingredients for strong bonding are often missing. As a result, many survivors have a hard time sustaining an ongoing feeling of connection with the people in their lives.

One woman, who worked with Ellen, couldn't really grasp that they were in a meaningful relationship for many months. As Ellen recalls, "Week after week she'd come into counseling and look at me as though I were a stranger. We'd have to start over again each time. Finally, I suggested that we meet twice a week and that's when we began to get some traction. She just couldn't hold the continuity of our relationship for an entire week."

Many survivors find it hard to comprehend that they matter to other people. They feel as if they don't really make a difference in other people's lives or that if they died or disappeared, no one would care:

I didn't realize how important I was to other people until I tried to kill myself. That's a horrible way to find out, but when I woke up in that hospital bed my husband was there, my aunt was there, my brother was there. They were all furious at me and I couldn't understand why. They were crying and telling me how angry they were. And that's when I got it. I wasn't an isolated, unconnected speck, I was part of this web of people and what I did affected them. I mattered.

You *do* matter, and it's a real indication of healing to realize that you are important to other people and they are important to you:

For the first few years of my marriage, I'd just go off without telling my husband what I was doing or when I'd be back. When he got mad, I thought he was trying to control me. It took a long time for me to understand that he was worried. He'd be thinking maybe I had a car accident; he wanted to know that I was okay. Here we were married, loving each other, having sex, everything, but I still didn't really get it that I mattered to him.

If being close is not easy or familiar to you, you can practice with friends, partners, safe family members, and other support people. If you don't have such people in your life (and even if you do), you can learn a tremendous amount about intimacy with a capable counselor. A counselor can provide you with the safety, unconditional love, and structured dependability that allow you to risk sending out those first tendrils of connection.*

Another way to begin to open your heart is by loving a pet. Animals offer a simple, uncomplicated relationship:

I was starved for love and touch, but every relationship I'd been in quickly became a disaster, so I decided to go to the SPCA. There was an adorable litter of puppies and I thought I'd take one, but then an older dog, a shepherd, caught my eye. We looked at each other and I knew she was the one. It was like we'd both been hurt and needed someone to love. Ginger has been with me for six months now and I don't know how I ever lived without her. In the evenings, we lie on the floor together and I stroke her and we both relax. I look in her eyes and I can feel the love being communicated back and forth. It's as tangible as if it were a two-way river. Someday I may be able to love a person like that. I hope so. But Ginger will always be my first love.

Everyone deserves closeness and meaningful relationships. Begin where you are, take small steps, and slowly open your heart. As you experience the benefits of caring and being

---

* For more on the benefits of counseling, see "The Value of Counseling" on p. 33.

cared for, you will gradually be able to take greater risks and love more.

FEAR OF LOVE

Opening our hearts to love may be the most wondrous feeling in the world, but it can be difficult to trust if we were betrayed as children. If the people who said they loved you also abused or neglected you, it can feel terrifying to love again:

> I had a hard time telling anyone I loved them. My father, you see, was always gentle and loving to me. He always told me, "I love you. I love you in a way I can't love your mother." He'd say that to me while he was doing these horrible things to me. So I've had real fears of saying, "I love you."

Committed love can be even more frightening. The child inside you still equates commitment with being locked into a situation where there's no escape. So as you get closer to someone, you may become paralyzed by all your old defenses and memories:

> There was a point, right around the time Joe and I decided to get married, where I just decided that the relationship wasn't giving me anything I wanted, and that I should start from scratch with somebody else. It was terror about the intimacy. I had assumed that people wouldn't come through for me for so long. And here he was coming through for me, and what went along with that was a price tag of intimacy. I had to open up. I no longer had an excuse. There were no wrong actions on his part that I could blame for the lack of intimacy. So I had to let go of my defenses. I was absolutely terrified.

Another woman recalls:

> When my therapist started telling me that she loved me, I hated her for it. I screamed at her. I wouldn't talk to her. For her to tell me she loved me meant that she was going to leave me or abuse me. That was all that I could believe about it. It wasn't until she kept sitting there, week after week, saying, "But I love you" with this complete open heart that I stopped being so terrified and let it in.

Try talking to people close to you about what love and commitment mean to them. And if the word *love* sticks in your throat, try saying how you feel in your own words: "I am so glad I know you." "You make me feel special." "I get happy just thinking of you." One woman who refused to use the word *love* told her new boyfriend, "I'm in serious like with you."

Love is a terribly misused word.[*] Eileen, a workshop participant, began to feel hopeful when she discovered there was more to love than she had experienced as a child:

> I felt a lot of sadness when I realized that "love" was not what I was getting when

---

[*] See "But Honey, I Love You," p. 356.

I was a kid. The funny part is that the awareness comes as a tremendous relief. It gives me the opportunity to say, "Well, if that wasn't love, maybe it's not love that I'm terrified of." Hence the new beginning . . .

A WORKING RELATIONSHIP

By its very nature, intimacy isn't something you can do alone. Intimacy assumes a relationship, and a relationship means risk. The other half of any relationship is a person you can't control. But being hurt or disappointed by someone you love now can never be as devastating as it was when you were a child. Broken trust hurts, but it doesn't have to annihilate you. You can recover. You are building a more complete self to fall back on.

To develop a working relationship, you don't have to marry someone or become lovers. You can learn a tremendous amount about intimacy with a friend. There are many varieties of relationship, each with its own kind of closeness.

If you already have a regular lover, committed partner, or close friend, those are natural places to take new risks with intimacy. But first, you want to be sure that the relationship you're in is a safe place to explore. To assess the quality of a relationship, ask yourself the following questions:

- Do I respect this person? Does this person respect me?
- Is this a person I can usually communicate with?
- Do we both try to listen and work through conflicts? Is there give-and-take? Do we both compromise?
- Can I be honest? Can I show my real feelings?
- Do we both take some responsibility for the relationship's successes and problems?
- Is there room for me to grow and change in this relationship?

If you can answer most of these questions with a yes, it's likely that you have a solid working relationship. If you aren't sure of the answers, the relationship may be new or you may not be asking enough of the relationship to know what is or isn't possible. If you answered no most of the time, it's unlikely that this will be a relationship in which you'll be able to practice deeper levels of healthy intimacy (see "Recognizing Bad Relationships," p. 286).

THE IMPACT OF CHANGE ON RELATIONSHIPS

When one person changes in a relationship or a family, the whole equilibrium shifts. Although people sometimes appreciate the changes you make, frequently they do not. Instead, you may encounter reactions of anger, dismay, passive-aggressive behavior, and outright complaints:

As I got more in touch with my needs and my rights, I got more assertive. And of course, I brought it all right home to my relationship. Like with anything, when we get a new skill or a new tool we almost bludgeon people with it until we're comfortable enough to back off and relax. So I said, "I'm not going to whimper through life. I'm going to start having some expectations of my own."

And my partner said, "I liked you better before you were in therapy. You used to want to please me all the time. I don't get my way now, and I don't like it."

I got very assertive and she got very angry. Her feeling was "Okay, take care of yourself, but this is ridiculous!" And my feeling was that I was barely taking care of myself.

As you heal, you will change and your loved ones will be challenged to change with you if you are to create healthy, meaningful relationships. This is often stressful, but if both of you are committed to growing personally, you will be more likely to see new behaviors as positive and to welcome—or at least tolerate—them.

My lover has had to change a lot for our relationship to work. But mostly they've been changes he wanted to make anyway. He knew he needed to be more independent, less desperate about sex, less tense in general. The fact that I needed him to be that way just pushed him to move a little faster than he would have done otherwise.

Your growth makes demands on the people close to you. Sometimes relationships can't withstand the strain—and you grow apart. Other times, the changes you make will be beneficial to both you and to your partner, and to your evolving relationship—even if you have to go through a rocky adjustment period first.

CALCULATED RISKS

Learning to be intimate is rewarding, but it is not always comfortable. As one woman said, "I kept myself safe, but I also kept myself alone." Becoming intimate means peeling back the layers of protection to let someone in. It means going to the place where you're comfortable, and then taking one step more. One step, not twenty.

Instead of spilling out all your innermost thoughts, say, "I'm frightened" one time. Instead of moving in with your boyfriend, try spending the weekend together. It's the little steps that have staying power.

There's no fixed goal and no urgency. Intimacy is experienced in the moment as part of a changing, fluid relationship. Learning to be intimate is a process, involving mistakes, small successes, and backsliding.

A calculated risk is different from a reckless leap. It's not wise to shut your eyes and lunge forward, hoping that things will work out magically. You start an affair with a married man, positive he'll leave his wife. You get pregnant, hoping a baby will save a faltering relationship. You tell a new friend your deepest secrets a week after you've met. Abandoning all caution rarely pays off.

Calculated risks are different—you weigh your chances and step out onto the ice only when you're relatively sure it's solid. With intimacy, nothing is 100 percent certain, but with forethought and a responsive partner, you maximize your chances for communication, increased closeness, and satisfaction.

LEARNING TO TRUST

Survivors tend to see trust as an absolute, either not trusting at all or trusting completely. You may bounce between the two, not trusting until you are so hungry for contact that you throw your trust at the first likely target. Since most people can't handle that kind of desperation, you end up disappointed, exploited, or abandoned, thus proving your original belief—that people aren't trustworthy.

Before you can trust anyone else, you have to learn to trust yourself (see "Trusting Yourself," on p. 215). If you know that you can rely on yourself, you won't fling your trust out indiscriminately in the hope that someone will take care of you. That kind of absolute dependence is what a child needs from its parents. It's not what two mature adults feel for each other.

I've come up against the issue of trust again and again. The more I love myself, the more that allows me to love someone else. And the loving is getting stronger than the fear.

It's also important to have realistic expectations. Sometimes survivors sabotage their own efforts at intimacy without meaning to.

You may misjudge the nature of a relationship, considering someone a reliable friend, while they see you only as a pleasant acquaintance. Or, you may feel let down because your friend agreed to support you, but didn't do it exactly as you imagined. Sometimes survivors feel betrayed so easily that all their experiences reaffirm their original belief that no one can be trusted.

In a healthy relationship, the level of trust varies according to what's actually happening between you and the other person. You experience gradations of trust, periodically assessing whether your needs are getting met, whether you're growing in the ways you want to grow. And if you see that the relationship warrants it, you open up more. Trust accrues over time. It's earned.

EXPERIMENT WITH TRUST

As you come to trust yourself, you build a foundation for trusting someone else. You can always go back to not trusting if you want to, but at least give it a try. The basic premise of this experiment is that under some circumstances, and with some people, trust is safe. Given that, try trusting in small doses.

Choose simple situations that give you a good chance of success. Instead of saying, "I trust that you'll never betray me in any way," ask your partner to make dinner for you on a night you work late. Trust a woman in your support group to hold you in a nonsexual way for five minutes. Or call a friend when you're feeling sad and ask if she'll spend a little time listening to you.

Say that you are experimenting with trust and that this is important to you. Then, ask if the person is willing and able to do what you've requested. Make sure you leave room for them to say no if it's not possible or if it's not what they want to commit to.

If this person comes through for you (or if they are kind, even though they can't help at that time), let that information enter the tally. Maybe trusting is not as dangerous as it was when you were a child.

If you end up feeling let down, try to analyze what happened. This is a learning experience. Ask yourself:

- How long did I know this person? Did we have good communication?
- What did I ask for? Was it more than the relationship was ready for?
- Did I say that this was important to me? Did I make my expectations clear? Was there room for him/her to freely say yes or no?
- Were there any elements in the interchange that paralleled my original abuse?
- Was the person I chose truly untrustworthy, or were there other factors I should consider? For example, if someone is going through difficulties in her own life or has complex issues of her own in this arena, that could make it hard for her to respond well to you. Sometimes people can be trustworthy in some arenas but won't be able to come through for you when their difficulties dovetail with yours.

Use the insight that you gain from these questions to learn more about assessing when to trust. Then try again. Jerilyn Munyon is one survivor who learned to trust through this kind of trial and error:

I didn't know how to trust—not others, not myself, not the world. I always thought trust was something you either had or you didn't, like a talent. It took me a while to figure out that trust is a skill, a skill that even I could learn. I really didn't know what trust felt like or how to get it, but I did know I wanted and needed it. For a long time I either couldn't trust or I'd trust the wrong person, or the right person for the wrong thing.

Eventually, as I found out more about myself and accepted myself more, took more responsibility for myself, I began to see that I could actually make choices that would affect the outcome of situations. I hadn't known there were right—or at least better—times, people, and places for trusting. I had learned from my conditioning that I had to take everything that came along, good or bad. That was a lie. It was true when I was three and had no choice, but now I was in my thirties and for the first time, I really began to take my life in hand and make some choices. At first they were pretty mixed, but as time has passed I find that my choices get better.

The Attic
BY MARIE HOWE

Praise to my older brother, the seventeen-
     year old boy, who lived
in the attic with me an exiled prince
     grown hard in his confinement,

bitter, bent to his evening task building
     the imaginary building
on the drawing board they'd given him in
     school. His tools gleam

under the desk lamp. He is as hard as the
     pencil he holds,
drawing the line straight along the ruler.

Tower prince, young king, praise to the boy
who has willed his blood to cool and his
     heart to slow. He's building

a structure with so many doors it's finally
     quiet,
so that when our father climbs heavily up
     the attic stairs, he doesn't

at first hear him pass down the narrow
     hall. My brother is rebuilding
the foundation. He lifts the clear plastic of
     one page

to look more closely at the plumbing,
—he barely hears the springs of my bed
     when my father sits down—

he's imagining where the boiler might go,
     because
where it is now isn't working. Not until
     I've slammed the door behind

the man stumbling down the stairs again
does my brother look up from where he's
     working. I know it hurts him

to rise, to knock on my door and come in.
     And when he draws his skinny arm
around my shaking shoulders,

I don't know if he knows he's building a
     world where I can one day
love a man—he sits there without saying
     anything.

Praise him.
I know he can hardly bear to touch me.

Marie Howe, *What the Living Do* (New York: Norton, 1997).

TESTING

It's healthy to do some testing in a new relationship, but many survivors carry this to extremes. You may taunt your partner, waiting to see if he hits you. You may sleep with your husband's best friend to see if your husband will get disgusted and leave. One woman never shows up for the first three dates. If someone makes it to the fourth date, she'll begin to consider him a potential friend.

> In the early months of the relationship I'm in now, I can't think of anything I didn't do to test Malcolm. After three years it's just starting to ease up, because he's stuck it through. He's passed the major tests.

It's legitimate to test people to see if they're trustworthy or if they can meet your needs, but if you find yourself excessively testing your friends or lovers, you may be reenacting the familiar betrayals of your childhood. If you set up tests that no one could possibly pass, then you're not testing. You're saying good-bye.

Instead, try designing tests that are fair: "I'm going to wait and see if you really take care of the kids two afternoons a week like you promised," or "I have something I want to tell you about and I want you to just listen and not give me advice. Are you willing to do that?"

Discuss your needs with your friend, lover, or spouse to make sure that you've set up reasonable assessment points.

CONFUSING THE PAST WITH THE PRESENT

You may have a husband, partner, or friend who genuinely loves and respects you, but you don't experience it that way because you expect relationships to be abusive:

> I was very frightened of being abused again. And it didn't take much for me to think someone was being abusive, either. Until you get clear, you judge men from the standpoint of what you've learned in life, right? My experience was that 95 percent of men are abusers. So all I had to figure out was, "How do they do their abuse? Is it physical, mental, or emotional?"

Of course if someone *is* abusing you, you need to get out of that situation (see "Recognizing Bad Relationships" on p. 286). But if you only *imagine* you're being abused, you must learn to make the distinction between the people who care about you now and your abuser.

One way to break this identification is to create reality checks for yourself:

- My father never listened to what was important to me. Bill usually listens.
- My mother always said things were going to change and nothing ever did. With Maureen, although we've still got a way to go, our relationship *has* changed.

Reinforce these distinctions so that you don't confuse the people in your life now with your abuser.

DON'T COME NEAR ME

It is common for survivors to create and maintain distance between themselves and the people they love. When you feel threatened by closeness, you pull away. You criticize the other person because you're scared and want a reason to leave. Or you stay present in your body, while your mind is whirring a million miles away.

I knew I was going to get a divorce. No matter how hard I tried, this just wasn't going to work. I didn't want to be close to him, period. I just wanted out. And that statement, "I just wanted out," is a direct result of the child abuse. The way I kept myself safe all through my childhood was by getting out. I got out of the house. I got out of the bedroom. I got out of the basement. I spent half my childhood in the orchards, up a tree, over with the horses, anywhere that was out, away from people. I only felt safe when I was alone. There was no safety with people. Not ever.

Sometimes creating distance is a healthy thing to do. It's important to be able to separate from someone you're close to, so that you can nurture other aspects of your life and keep your relationship in perspective. Being close,

then returning to yourself, and then being close again is a natural cycle in a healthy relationship. Withdrawing every time you feel uncomfortable is a problem.

Notice when and why you pull back, and in each situation assess whether it's what you really want to be doing, whether it's appropriate, or whether it's a carryover from childhood that is no longer useful. If you decide you do want to be more separate, practice taking time for yourself in healthy ways. Picking a fight or having an affair is not a good way to create independence.

If you decide that what you really want is to be close and not to withdraw, you will have to force yourself to reach out, even if your natural habit is to pull back. Instead of saying, "I'm leaving you; this will never work," try to talk about what is upsetting to you, your feelings, your fears. The key to greater intimacy is honest expression.

If you need to build in a cushion of safety, strike little bargains with yourself—"I'll let myself be close tonight, but tomorrow night is just for me to be by myself."

If the distancing you do is in your head, triggers may be harder to pinpoint. Watch where and when your thoughts stray. Enlist the help of the people close to you. Ask them to watch for the telltale signs—a lack of focus in your eyes, a drop in your voice, a feeling that you're just not around anymore. If you're caught, or if you catch yourself, stop and look at the reasons why you withdrew when you did (see "Dissociation" p. 16).

FEAR OF BEING ALONE

Many survivors didn't get the nurturing they needed in childhood. Or they may have been smothered, not allowed an age-appropriate level of independence. Now you may find yourself clinging, afraid to be alone:

> Every time I meet a new guy I think he's the one. It feels so good to have someone hold me, call me, sound excited to talk to me. I fall in love immediately and tell my friends. I introduce him to my kids. I'm convinced that my lonely nights are over. And then, it falls apart. My last boyfriend got engaged a week after he left me. It was so humiliating. I had to go back and tell all my friends what had happened. I just kept asking myself what I did wrong. I just wanted to be loved.

It took a long time for this woman to learn to hold herself back from plunging into relationships without any real assessment. She explains, "Even now, holding back feels unnatural, but it's necessary if I don't want to keep making a fool of myself with men who aren't right for me."

MERGING

Merging is a state of extreme dependency. Without a strong sense of identity, you can confuse your thoughts, feelings, and needs with those of others, until it's hard to tell where you stop and the other person begins:

> My former husband and I were so desperate for intimacy that we totally fell into each other's lives. We capitalized on the things we genuinely had in common and denied our real differences. We wore the same style clothes, went on the same health food diets, and read the same books. We used to make a joke that you could tell us apart because I was the one in the green sweater.

If you are afraid to be alone, this kind of closeness is seductive. But it can also be damaging. If you can't tell yourself apart from someone else, you are liable to sacrifice your own ideas, feelings, and needs. You forfeit authenticity to maintain the illusion of oneness.

One survivor explained her process of moving away from this kind of dependency:

> Healing has been a process of giving back what does not belong to me and reclaiming what was eclipsed in its shadow. Unraveling the differences between intimacy and merging has been at the heart of my journey. As a young adult, all of my close relationships were an attempt at symbiosis. To love well meant faithfully abandoning myself to soothe the other. The triumphs filled me with hope that together we could make up for what we lacked alone, but they also strengthened the desperation and resentment that grew out of being unable to care for myself. The failures confirmed

that I was unlovable and could drive me deep into despair and hopelessness, but it was in those unbearable moments that I began to learn to turn towards myself.

A strong relationship is made up of two people sharing together. For that you need an independent self.

Overcoming unhealthy dependency is much the same process two-year-olds go through in learning to play on their own. The toddler will spend a few minutes with a toy and then run back to the living room to make sure her mother is still there. Reassured by a pat or a smile, she ventures out again, until a few minutes later she needs to see her mother again. Learning to feel secure while spending time alone requires much the same thing: practice, positive reinforcement, and more practice.

Take time alone in small increments, doing things you actively enjoy. Ask your friend or partner to say encouraging things: "I'll still be here when you get back" or "I'm proud of you."

Planning ahead is a big help, too. You can arrange to have dinner with your husband after spending the day by yourself.

You can also find nourishment in a wide variety of places: nature, creativity, pets. If you spread out the ways you take care of yourself, you will be less reliant on any one person.

SETTING LIMITS

Survivors often have trouble setting limits in relationships, because they didn't learn about healthy boundaries as children. You may do all the giving. Maybe you've never questioned this arrangement or you believe that you don't have the right to say no. But if you are part of a relationship, you deserve to participate in making decisions and to share in the power. In healthy relationships both people contribute to making it work. You don't have to sacrifice yourself to merit love. If you haven't had much practice setting limits, start with something small: "I don't want you to call me after 11:00, because my roommates are sleeping." Or, "If you use up the milk, please replace it."

Once you've had some practice, you can move on to something bigger. For example, if you work all day and then cook the family dinner every night, and you no longer want sole responsibility for that job, talk it over with your family. You might say: "I don't want to do all the cooking anymore. I'd like you to prepare dinner one night a week." Discuss possible solutions and try to come to something that feels workable.

The fact that someone doesn't like a limit that you set doesn't mean that you have to back down. When Tuesday night rolls around, if no one is making any moves toward cooking, you might go out for a walk or take an apple and go to another room and read.

Your family may grumble. Even loudly. But they won't starve. Your oldest son might discover that he has a flair for cooking. And you might find that you like setting limits. [For more ideas on how to say no, see "42 Ways to Say No (or Buy Time Until You Can)" on p. 216.]

DEALING WITH CONFLICT

Conflict is threatening to many women, and especially to survivors. If you grew up in an environment where disagreements exploded into violence or were suppressed entirely, you may not know how to deal with conflict in a healthy way. You might freeze, withdraw, or try to manipulate the situation to meet your needs without a direct confrontation. You may be afraid that if you assert yourself, you'll be abandoned. You may fear getting hurt or hurting someone else. Or you may escalate a small disagreement into a war in which you say or do things you really don't mean.

Some survivors find conflict so frightening that they can't tolerate it at all:

I had a lot of love and closeness with my friends, but any time there was conflict, I would get completely worked up and upset to the point where it became unmanageable, to the point where I burned out certain relationships.

But conflict is normal—and inevitable. It's a basic part of intimacy. As Ellen's mother used to say, "If two people always agree, one of them is superfluous."

Talking directly, with respect for both yourself and the other person, is a healthy way to air problems. Try to share your feelings as soon as you recognize them so that you don't store up a backlog of resentments and disappointments. Say how you feel and what you want. Then listen to your friend or partner without interrupting.

To keep a conflict from spiraling out of control, you can decide beforehand on some basic guidelines, such as no violence and no name-calling. You can agree to stick with the present issue and not trash the relationship as a whole. Agreements like these can help you feel safer.

Until now, I've had trouble sharing when it had to do with anger. I think, in a sense, anger is the ultimate intimacy. If you can feel safe enough to express anger with a significant person in your life, then you've got a real measure of intimacy. My relationship now is the first one where I've felt free to do that.

Not all conflicts involve anger. Sometimes you simply see things differently or have different desires and need to work out a compromise that's acceptable to both of you. Either way, it's important to hear each other's perspective. If this isn't happening naturally, set a timer so that each of you can talk for five minutes while the other really listens. Then repeat back what the other person said, until you can do so to their satisfaction. Or try reversing roles— pretend that you're the other person and say what you think he or she is feeling.

In most situations there's usually more than one solution that can meet both people's needs. It's not necessary to back down from what's important to you or to invalidate the other person's needs. Listening, sharing your concerns, and negotiating respectfully are skills you can learn.* As you resolve conflicts

---

* There are a number of excellent books on discussing difficult issues and resolving conflicts. We recommend

in ways that you feel good about, you build trust.

GIVING AND RECEIVING

Two important aspects of intimacy are giving and receiving. For some people, giving may be more difficult; for others, receiving is. Learn by practicing. If you have been unable to give, start by giving something that's easy for you—perhaps a compliment or a favorite food.

As time goes on, work up to offering things that are harder. You may find it relatively easy to give on your own terms—what you want to give, when you want to give it. Children often pick out presents, for instance, that reflect their own interests rather than those of the recipient. But as an adult, you need to work toward being able to give people what *they* need, when *they* need it. Your husband may want you to accompany him to an important event that you find boring, rather than have you cook him a special meal. Your friend might need to talk to you even though you want to treat him to the movies.

Receiving feels wonderful once you get used to it. But first you must acknowledge how scary it is to be open. If, when you were a child, there were strings attached to getting what you

Difficult Conversations: How to Discuss What Matters Most by Douglas Stone, Bruce Patton, Sheila Heen, and Roger Fisher of the Harvard Negotiation Project (New York: Penguin Books, 2000) and *Nonviolent Communication: A Language of Life: Create Your Life, Your Relationships, and Your World in Harmony with Your Values* by Marshall B. Rosenberg (Encinitas, CA: PuddleDancer Press, 2003).

needed, you learned that help was either unavailable or unsafe. But now, receiving doesn't have to mean owing something back.

Start asking for at least one thing you want every day. It can be as small as "Would you make me a cup of tea?"

Tell the people close to you that you're experimenting with asking for what you want, that you're learning to receive. You never know—your spouse might spontaneously put love notes in your lunch bag. Your roommate might buy you flowers on her way home from work.

In healthy relationships, there is a balance to giving and receiving. If you've always leaned heavily one way, you will need to focus more on the other aspect, but eventually, as you feel safer, both giving and receiving will develop a relaxed natural rhythm.

IN TIMES OF CRISIS

During certain crucial periods when healing from child sexual abuse demands all your attention, you may be unable to give anything. You may be so self-absorbed that you become temporarily unable to meet (or even pay attention to) other people's needs.

This kind of self-absorption is a natural side effect of engrossing emotional work, but you can't focus only on yourself all the time and expect to maintain intimate relationships. Make the effort to keep relationships reciprocal.

If you can't give quality attention, at least apologize. Acknowledge that you can't do more just yet but that you intend to be more present and available as soon as you can. Express your appreciation for your friend's loyalty in continuing to love you even when you can't offer much back. Then see if there's something small you *can* do. Perhaps you can wash your partner's laundry even while you're obsessed with your own thoughts. If you can't give fully, give what you can.

Generally, the deeper a foundation you have with someone, the more the relationship is able to withstand trying times. Sometimes a healing crisis actually helps a relationship grow in depth and commitment. But even with a solid bond, the demands of healing can still be hard on your partner and friends. (See "For Partners," p. 386, for more on working through hard times.)

RECOGNIZING BAD RELATIONSHIPS

We all have the tendency to repeat childhood patterns. For survivors, this often means leaving a family situation that was unsupportive, distant, or abusive only to get involved with a partner who embodies those same qualities:

I'd be talking to a man I was in a relationship with and suddenly I'd hear him talking to me like my father or acting like my ex-husband, who abused me. It wouldn't be obvious until a month or two into the relationship, but then one thing would happen and it would all click into place. I picked men like my father over and over again.

If you are in an abusive relationship, it's essential that you don't deny the situation, hope it will magically get better, or expect the other person to change. The only power you have is to change yourself. You can act. You can develop alternative support networks. You can advocate on your own behalf in the present. And if you make all the changes you can and still are being abused or treated disrespectfully, it's time to consider leaving the relationship.* It is better not to be in a relationship at all than to be in one that links closeness to betrayal, abandonment, and violation.

SEPARATING

Separating from an abusive, violent, or disrespectful relationship can be extremely difficult. Sometimes the very fact that the relationship has never met your needs makes it even harder to leave. You've been trying to make it work for so long, it's frightening and foreign to think of doing something different. And you may have compelling reasons for staying, such as financial dependence, young children, or your reluctance to give up hope. You may have a strong conviction that families should stay together. Or you may still love your partner very much, despite the fact that the relationship is unsafe or unhealthy for you. Sometimes women take on the mission of rescuing a partner or repeat-

---

* Seal Press has published a number of excellent step-by-step guidebooks for women on getting out of abusive relationships. We recommend them highly. (See the "Domestic Violence, Rape, and Sexual Harassment" section on p. 563 of the Resource Guide for more information.)

ing a pattern of caretaking or negative relationships from the past. All this plays a part in keeping you where you are.

The first step in giving up an unhealthy relationship is to honestly assess what's going on, how *you* feel in the relationship. Ask yourself how much of the time you're living in the future, waiting for things to get better or for your partner to change. Also be willing to hear feedback from people who love and know you as an individual, separate from your relationship.

Start to do things on your own: Take a class. Get involved in a project, go on a short vacation alone—even just taking one whole day off to spend time away by yourself can be an empowering way to begin. Independent activities give you a chance to become more comfortable on your own and help you to gain a clearer perspective on your feelings and your situation.

No relationship is perfect and many relationships go through difficult periods, but staying in a relationship that is abusive, unhealthy, or fundamentally unfulfilling is not in your best interests. This is true of friendships as well as marriages and romantic relationships. Although leaving may be hard, over time this decision can open the door to more rewarding intimacy and greater contentment. One woman recalls:

I wasn't happy in my relationship, but I didn't think about that. We'd made a life together. We remodeled the kitchen. We both were crazy about our dogs. I wished there were more sexual intimacy. We only had sex once or twice a year. I wished we could talk about things that interested me more. I love to read, I'm a news junkie, but she really wasn't interested. She went to work, came home, ate dinner, and watched TV. That was about it. I never really felt connected to her, but it would never have occurred to me to leave. The relationship ended only because she left me for another woman. At the time I was devastated and thought my life was ruined, but it was the best thing that ever could have happened to me. Shortly afterward I met a woman who was much, much better for me. She was smart, spirited, funny, passionate and generous with her love.

EXPLORING NEW RELATIONSHIPS

Sometimes there's a period of transition between the old and the new. You know what you *don't* want, without knowing what you *do* want. A woman in her midfifties said:

I realize I need to know more about men. I really don't know much about them. My father was so distant and so abusive. My uncles were distant. My husband was distant. And I didn't get along with my son, naturally. I don't have any models from my past of what it's like to be warm and friendly with a nice man. So I've been working on developing that. And it's funny, my perception of men is changing—they're seeming nicer all of a sudden!

Try looking at new relationships as places to practice intimacy. We have all been conditioned to judge relationships on the basis of their length—a good relationship is one that lasts forever and everything else is a failure. But relationships can be worthwhile even if they are short or don't give you everything you need. If a relationship provides a context in which you can practice communication, trust, and the give-and-take of caring, then you have a healthy basis for growth and intimacy.

ARE WE HAVING FUN YET?

A women's band in Santa Cruz, California, used to sing a song about relationships. The chorus is:

Work on it, work on it,
*I don't wanna work on it.**

Whenever they played it in concert, the audience roared. We can all recognize the feeling of having worked at relationships to the point of overkill. If you add to that the work of healing from child sexual abuse—and then

* From "Work On It" by Wicked Stance.

throw in laundry, your mother who just moved in, and your demanding boss, life can be overwhelming. When you're running on empty, trying to catch up, fun is often the first thing to go. But that's a mistake.

If you see your partner only when you crawl into bed, exhausted, at the end of the day, you're both liable to forget what brought you together to begin with. If you talk only about sexual abuse when you go out with your friend Carol, Carol may stop calling. And even if you're fortunate enough to have friends and lovers who stick by you, you'll be missing out on pleasurable times together.

If healthy relationships are important to you, structure your life to allow for quality time with the people you love. Laura did this quite successfully with a friend who is also a survivor:

When we first met, we'd get together and spend the whole evening talking about heavy, depressing things. After a few months, it wasn't so exciting to see each other. So we decided to make a change. We made a contract to do something fun once a month. Last month I took her on the carousel in Golden Gate Park. This month we're going bowling.

Fun is not an optional part of the healing process. It's one of its chief rewards.

Reclaiming Your Sexuality

"For years I thought of sex as a way you hurt people. And for me, it wasn't just the abuse. As a young woman, I was enraged about the objectification of women that I experienced every day. I hated anything to do with sex and sexuality. Gradually, as I went through my healing process, that started to change. Now I love sex and think it's wonderful and empowering. For me, sex is now connected to spirituality and health and joy. But it's taken a long time and a lot of effort to get there."

The perspective on sexuality that is presented here applies to both heterosexual and lesbian women. Although there are some differences in the difficulties these groups face, they are far outweighed by the similarities.

We use the word "lover" in this chapter to describe any sexual partner. This includes someone you are casually dating, someone you are deeply committed or married to, and any relationship in between. Healing takes place on many levels, and whether you are celibate, dating, or in a committed partnership, you can heal sexually. (If you are the partner of a survivor, see "For Partners" on p. 386.)

Survivors are not alone in needing to heal sexually. Almost from birth, girls are given mixed messages about their sexuality. They are alternately told to hide it, deny it, repress it, use it, flaunt it, or give it away. Sex is promoted as a means of power, seduction, and exchange. As a result, many women grow up with conflicts around sex. For women who were abused, these problems are compounded.

Many survivors feel particularly vulnerable, damaged, confused, or stuck when it comes to sex. For some women, these problems connect directly to the abuse. If your softball coach pinched your breasts in the locker room, you may not want your lover touching your breasts today. If your mother abused you in the morning before school, you may be repelled by the idea of sex when you first wake up.

Your problems may not be tied to specific acts of abuse. You may avoid sex because you're unable to stay present when you make love or because you feel an overall terror when you're in a sexual situation:

I'm fifty-three and I've never married. I have close friends, but as soon as somebody wants to be sexual with me, I get absolutely terrified. I've had sex twice in my life, not counting my uncle. The first time the guy couldn't penetrate me. With the second guy, I felt disgusting and dirty and couldn't wait for it to end. I never wanted to see him again. I feel really, really angry—not about the rape, but about my life! I'm fifty-three years old and I don't even know what it's like to have somebody be intimate with me, to have sex that I love.

As an abused child, your sexual feelings were wired directly into fear. Every time you felt aroused, you also felt afraid. Now you may not be able to become aroused without fear. Or you might be scared of the painful feelings that come up when you are sexual:

It seems to me that the memories are stored at the same level the passion is. If I don't make love, I don't connect with them. But whenever I open myself to feelings of passion, the memories are right there. It's like opening Pandora's box.

You might be afraid of being hurt or hurting someone else:

There's some kind of connection between passion and anger for me. As soon as I start feeling passionate, anger gets involved, and I get afraid of being aggressive in a hurtful way. So when I start feeling passionate, I shut right down, because I'm afraid of hurting my partner.

If you were abused by a man and your lover is male, you may be alarmed by this fact alone:

There were times in the process that I would forget he was Joe and react to him as "generic Man." He had never hurt me in any of those ways, but I would confuse his identity completely. We'd be lying in bed at night. I'd be trying to go to sleep, and I'd have to get up because I felt, "I can't lie here with this male body. It's too terrifying."

You may avoid sex because you don't want anyone that close to you, because you believe you'll be suffocated by such intimacy. You may be afraid of losing control, feeling overwhelmed, or losing touch with yourself or your own boundaries.

On the other hand, you may have responded to the abuse by going in the opposite direction—wanting sex all the time:

After my divorce, I was really into frantic fucking. I think that what I felt was some kind of release, some feeling of being held or comforted. But it was so fleeting I had to keep doing it over and over again.

You may find yourself using sex to meet all kinds of needs. When you want closeness, intimacy, or communication, when you want to feel you are loved and worthwhile and cared for, when you're unhappy, disappointed, or angry, you ask for sex instead:

Anyone who ever loved me had a sexual relationship with me. So if you didn't make a pass at me, you didn't love me.

It makes sense that survivors, who received all their attention and affection sexually as children, now sexualize even nonsexual needs. Sometimes this compulsive drive for sex leads survivors into situations that are hurtful, dangerous, or not in their best interests:

Sex was like an addiction for me. It was the only way I was sure I was close to someone. I didn't trust relationships unless they were sexual. I had sex with just about everyone I knew. It was the only way I could be sure that they loved me.

THE RELATIONSHIP BETWEEN SEX AND LOVE

Although many survivors manifest difficulties sexually, the more basic issue is often trust. As one survivor put it, "It's difficult to talk about sex without talking about intimacy. That's one of the problems."

I've always had the physical and the emotional separate, so I can always fuck men. I like to call it that because I like to call things what they are. I always knew I wasn't making love to them.

If your abuser was someone you loved and trusted, then sex, love, trust, and betrayal became linked in profound ways. Many abused women can maintain sexual relationships with some satisfaction until they fall deeply in love. Then the bottom drops out and their fear becomes overwhelming. Sex is okay when they keep their feelings out of it. But sex with deep feeling brings back all the ancient pain. It is too much like the original abuse:

The image I have of my husband is that he reached through some sort of window in my life and pulled me out. He was being nonjudgmental. He loved me unconditionally. Here was love coming at me without any expectations. We were really good friends. We got along well. I liked his temperament.

After we met, I went into a two-month anxiety attack. My stomach was always in knots. The closer we got emotionally and the more vulnerable we were to each other, the less I could be present when we were making love. There were points when the sexuality was very present, but then we were communicating less. I felt that if I gave all of myself over, I'd lose myself and I wouldn't be able to get me back. So I kept parts of myself inaccessible.

Some women don't remember the abuse until they are in a loving, trusting relationship. They need that much security to be able to experience the memories.

I met my husband eight months after my father died. I'd never had a constructive, positive relationship before. He was someone I'd really been waiting for. And it was about a year later that I had my first memory.

Understanding these patterns is essential. Then you can stop breaking up as soon as relationships become meaningful. You can see your difficulties as signs that you are in an important relationship in which you have a special opportunity to restore your trust and inner security.

YOU DESERVE TO FEEL GOOD

Sexual intimacy and erotic pleasure can be deeply joyous and gratifying experiences, but they often raise conflicting feelings for survivors:

I'm afraid of feeling too much pleasure in my body. Do I really deserve it? I'm afraid if I feel that much, I'll burst open, that my body can't contain that much pleasure. It can contain that much pain, but can it contain that much pleasure?

Although many survivors experienced only pain or numbness when they were abused, others felt sexual arousal or orgasm. Because these good feelings were entwined with fear, confusion, shame, and betrayal, they grew up feeling that sexual pleasure was bad. As one woman said, "It hasn't been until recently that I even thought of putting the words 'sex' and 'pleasure' together."

Some survivors do not feel any pleasurable sensations when they make love. Others have orgasms but feel tremendous guilt about enjoying sex. And some feel conflict or distress: "Pleasure doesn't feel like pleasure to me. I want to throw up every time I have an orgasm. I feel disgusted, and all I can think about is my uncle."

It was a terrible violation that your body's natural responses were exploited. However, sexual pleasure in itself is not bad. You can make choices about where, when, how, and with whom you want to be sexual, and within those choices, you can give yourself permission to feel pleasure. Sexual feelings are not inherently dangerous or destructive. Like fire, their qualities and effects depend very much on who is using them and to what purpose.

SEXUAL HEALING IS POSSIBLE

Your sexual problems, like the abuse itself, were forced on you. Fortunately, it is possible to experience your sexuality in a dramatically different way:

For a long time I felt like a sexual failure, like I was damaged beyond repair. Yet something in me wouldn't give up. And

ON BEING A LESBIAN AND A SURVIVOR

I've heard forever and ever, "Oh, you're a dyke because your daddy did this to you." It's a comment that makes me mad. It's a way that people take choices away from me. Maybe if I was a murderer, you could say that was connected to the incest. If there were going to be a correlation, it would be between the incest and my capacity for violence or hatred, not with my capacity for love.

If you are a lesbian, what you are trying to heal from is the destructive effects of having been sexually abused, not the fact that you're a lesbian:

I had believed that I was a lesbian because I had been so badly abused by my father. I thought maybe it was a point of being stuck in my emotional growth. I thought that until I met a lesbian who came from a happy home, who had never been abused in any way. She was well balanced. Her family accepted that she was a lesbian. She never had any problems with it, and that's when I realized my lesbianism didn't have to have a cause. It's got nothing to do with what happened to me.

It is true that being abused by men has influenced some women to relate sexually and emotionally to women rather than men. However, many heterosexual women were abused by men, and most continue to choose men as their sexual partners. If abuse were the determining factor in sexual preference, the lesbian population would be far greater.

I'm a lesbian because I love women, not because I hate men. I'm not a separatist. I have a male child who I think is terrific. There are men in my life I care a great deal for.

Being a lesbian is a perfectly healthy way to be, not another effect of abuse to be overcome.

If You're Not Sure

If you're not sure about your sexual orientation, give yourself some time for things to settle. It's okay not to know, or to be in transition.

If you haven't been in touch with yourself sexually—because you've been dissociating, pretending, or not very conscious—it may take some time to find out what your true responses are.

Sexual orientation is a continuum, like a bell curve. Many people have the potential to be bisexual, able to feel attraction for either gender. A small percentage of people are exclusively heterosexual or homosexual. Some lesbians say they were born that way; others feel that it was a choice.

However, if you hope that becoming a lesbian will magically solve all your problems with sex and intimacy, this isn't likely to be the case. While becoming a lesbian may make some things possible for you that weren't possible before, it's not a panacea. Regardless of your sexual orientation, it's still necessary to do the work of healing from child sexual abuse.

it just amazes me. Problems that seemed insurmountable five years ago, I can hardly relate to anymore. I haven't had a flashback in years. And now I regularly initiate sex. I can actually say I like sex. No, in fact, I love it. I'm not afraid of my passion anymore. It's an exciting part of my relationship.

Although it is ultimately rewarding, reclaiming your sexuality is slow, painstaking work. As you allow yourself to remember and open up to buried feelings, you may find that making love is even harder than before. You may question your wisdom in trying to heal, wondering if it wouldn't have been better to just stick with your old ways of getting by. But you deserve more.

A TIME-OUT FROM SEX

Healing sexually is not usually the first challenge that survivors undertake when they begin healing from abuse. If you're in the emergency stage, struggling with overwhelming emotions, or establishing basic safety and self-care, it's not likely that you'll have the energy or inner resources necessary to address the complex challenge of sexual healing.

If sex feels like a battleground for you right now or if other aspects of your healing are demanding all of your attention, consider taking a time-out from sex. This isn't necessary for every survivor, but time away from sex can be a clarifying beginning. If you experience fear, disgust, or a lack of desire for sex, or if you have been unable to say no to sex, a vacation from

sex is an opportunity to set your own boundaries and to get to know your body without the pressure of sex. If you have been sexual in addictive or abusive ways, taking a break offers a chance to examine and understand your behavior. It is up to you to say how long this time of celibacy should last. You may want a month, a few months, a year, or even longer.

LEARN TO SAY NO

Around the age of two, children learn to say no. They practice it all the time. They are asserting themselves, making it clear that although some things are okay with them, not everything is, and they are going to make sure they have some say about it. Toddlers often go though a period when they say no to almost everything. This is healthy. Unless you can say no clearly and effectively, your yes is meaningless. To heal sexually, you must learn to say no to unwanted sex. It is important to make a commitment to yourself that you will never again grit your teeth and endure it when you really don't want sex. Every time you have sex when you genuinely don't want to, you add another layer of abuse, repeat the pattern of victimization, and thus delay your healing.

THERE'S MORE TO LIFE THAN SEX

One woman said that she wanted to say no to sex not only with lovers but also with herself. She established a hands-off policy that applied even to touching herself, recognizing that she needed a break from any kind of sexual stimulation.

Many survivors were given the message that they were good only for sex. All of your other qualities and skills, needs, and aspirations, were minimized while sex was emphasized. By allowing sex to recede for a time, by saying no to the pressure of it, the problems of it, and even the pleasure of it, you can begin to recognize that there is more to life, and to your worth, than sex.

If you are in a relationship, an extended period of celibacy can cause a lot of strain. You may need to consider compromises to include your lover's needs. (See "Be Creative" on p. 309, "You're Not in This Alone" on p. 307, and "Creative Intimacy" on p. 400.) But it is important not to deny your own needs in the process. If you absolutely need more time without sex and you push yourself to have sex when it's not right for you, it won't do your relationship much good in the long run and it will certainly not help your healing.

START WITH YOURSELF

When you are ready and want to begin the process of being sexual again, start slowly and with awareness. Many women find that they are their own best lovers in these early stages. As one woman said, "If I can't have sex with myself, there's no point trying to do it with anybody else."

If you've never been comfortable touching yourself, you are not alone. Many of us have been told that masturbation is wrong, dirty, and shameful. Although you are supposed to enjoy it when your lover touches you, you are not supposed to touch yourself. This attitude is not in your best interests. Who has more right to your body than you?

Many survivors carry revulsion for their bodies. Some were told directly that they, or their genitals, were disgusting. One woman hates her right hand because her grandfather forced her to masturbate him with that hand. For others the whole experience of abuse was so sickening that everything connected with it still carries that feeling.

But your body is not hateful. It is rich and marvelous. And it belongs to you.

EXPLORING SEX ALONE

Many survivors have approached masturbation, like sex, from a disconnected place. One woman explained: "Using my vibrator doesn't have anything to do with sex or intimacy. It has to do with tension and it's about release. It doesn't take that long. If I turn it on high it takes even less time."

Another woman said she would start out with a good warm feeling, be unable to come to orgasm, and keep frantically masturbating just to have a climax. "It's as if I become the rapist. I don't even enjoy it anymore. It's the angry, compulsive part of myself."

If you avoid touching yourself altogether, masturbate compulsively, or have always experienced masturbation as quick stimulation and release, take some time to be with yourself in a relaxed, attentive way. Run a hot bath, light candles, listen to soothing or sultry music. Put clean sheets on the bed, light incense, place fresh flowers in your bedroom, take your time. Maybe you'd like to smooth oil or lotion on your body. Feel your skin, your muscles. Don't start out by touching yourself genitally. Stroke your arm or another more neutral part of your body. See what kind of touch feels good to you, what you like. Many women have gone through sex numb or in a panic, never taking time to notice how touch actually feels. Maybe on the first date with yourself you'll only touch one shoulder. That's fine. There's no rush. Make another date. Touch the other shoulder.

Over time you can allow yourself more and more feelings, more sensation. Whatever you feel is fine. When you're ready, but not too quickly, you can touch your breasts, your vulva, your clitoris, your vagina. Perhaps you will feel sexual arousal, perhaps not. The object here is not to do it fast and be done. The object is not orgasm. It's to feel your feelings, to give yourself pleasure, to know your body. Stop anytime you want. Notice, when you want to stop, what it is that made you uncomfortable. Stay in your body. Stay aware.

If you find yourself spacing out—thinking about what you're going to wear tomorrow or about a report that's due at the office—stop. Slow down, back up, breathe back into your body. Do whatever helps you reconnect with yourself. Sex is about connection—in this case, your connection with yourself.*

I consciously try to connect my whole body. I have this meditation I do, even in the middle of making love. I imagine my body filling up with fluid or light. I imagine it coming all the way up from my feet and washing over me. Somehow that circular thing helps me feel like I'm all in one piece.†

FLASHBACKS

If you have flashbacks to the original abuse while touching yourself, don't panic. Flashbacks can be an opportunity to understand your experience as a child and can yield valuable information and insight. (For more about flashbacks, see "Remembering" on p. 70 and "Flashbacks with a Partner" on p. 306.)

If you get upset, open your eyes and ground yourself in the present. Tell yourself that touching yourself here and now is not abuse even though it may bring back memories of abuse. Tell yourself that touching yourself in a loving way is your right, that you deserve touch, you deserve pleasure. It is neither harmful nor shameful nor wrong. This is fine. This is healing. And you deserve it. (For more on dealing with flashbacks and triggers, see "Working with Triggers" on p. 312.)

---

* *Sex for One* by Betty Dodson is a wonderful sex-positive guide to masturbation. See the "Sexuality" section on p. 567 of the Resource Guide.

† For more on this topic, see "From Splitting to Being in Your Body" on p. 253.

ORGASMS

For women who have difficulty having orgasms, it can be helpful to take some time deliberately avoiding orgasm when you touch yourself sexually. You might set aside a period of time to masturbate as often as you want, but rather than having orgasms (or trying to), allow the sexual energy to build and then contain it, holding it in your body. If you get close to an orgasm, back off a little, lessen the stimulation, and let the energy subside. In this kind of touching there's no prescribed time to end. You stop when you want to.

Touching yourself without striving for an orgasm can be a tremendous relief. There's no longer any pressure to "achieve" orgasm. There's nothing to strive for, nowhere to rush to, no "trying." Instead, there's a spaciousness to experience whatever feelings arise, to become aware of the gradations of arousal as you feel them, to stay in the moment, to experience pleasure, and to get to know your own responses as they are, rather than as you think they should be. This exploration can clear some of the obstacles to experiencing orgasms. It can also be very exciting. (This is effective with a partner, too. In that case, neither of you has an orgasm.)

While the point of this exercise is to take the pressure off, you may instead feel it's putting pressure on. One woman had a hard time not having an orgasm because when she was a child, an orgasm signaled the end of that particular episode of abuse. "For me, sex without an orgasm is incredibly threatening because the sex becomes endless. I panic when there's no clear end in sight."

If you've never had an orgasm, see the books on sex listed in the Resource Guide for some excellent suggestions for becoming orgasmic. If you've never used a vibrator, we suggest you try one (see p. 568 for mail-order sources).

Some women say that their orgasms have changed as they worked out their sexual abuse issues. Old blockages were loosened and stored emotions released, allowing room for a fuller body experience.

EXPLORING SEX WITH A PARTNER

How long you explore your sexuality alone is up to you. No one can tell you how much time you need. Let your body and your feelings tell you when you're ready. If you have a lover and have taken a break from sex, it is essential that you don't start again solely because you feel pressured. Making love for the wrong reasons will backfire on both you and your relationship.

WHAT'S YOUR MOTIVATION?

Be honest with yourself about your motivation for wanting to work on sexuality at this time.* You might make a list of the things you want to change about your sexuality. Then make a list of the reasons you're willing to do so. In one column list why you want to change for

---

* This concept is drawn from the work of JoAnn Loulan, author of *Lesbian Sex*. See the "Sexuality" section on p. 568 of the Resource Guide.

yourself, and in another, why you want to change for your lover.

Although it's often hard for survivors to separate their needs and desires from those of others, it's essential that you have your own reasons for beginning to make love. Such reasons might be "I feel that I'm missing out on an important part of life," "I want to feel pleasure," "I don't want my past to rule me," or "I want to experience an intimate sexual relationship."

Lasting changes are made only when we have a deep desire to change within ourselves. At first you may be motivated by your acute awareness of your lover's impatience or your fear of losing the relationship, but eventually you must come to see sexual healing as something you're doing for yourself. If you force yourself to be sexual before you're actually ready, it's likely you'll experience struggle and disappointment but little growth.

> When my memories first came up, I turned off sexually right away. I told my lover I wanted to take a few months off from sex. He refused. I didn't want to lose him, so I backed down. We struggled over sex for six more months. He got more and more angry. I withdrew more and more. Finally we broke up over it. Those last six months were devastating. If I'd followed my own intuition and just held firm to my no, the relationship might have ended, but I wouldn't have felt like such a hopeless failure.

If it becomes clear that you're not ready to tackle your sexuality, and you're doing it solely because of the outside pressures, then this isn't the right time for you to focus on sexual healing. As a child you engaged in sex because someone else wanted you to. It is essential that you break this pattern. Sex is for you first, and there is no sense forcing yourself through a deep and painful process of change if you don't want it for yourself. It's okay if you're not ready yet. Focus on other aspects of your healing. There is more to life than sex.

WHAT IS SEX, ANYWAY?

Making love while healing from child sexual abuse will probably not fit the description in a popular romance novel: You fall into your lover's arms, your clothes magically drop away, you have no need to talk about fears or discomforts, and you come together in a burst of spontaneous passion.

Before you start sharing sex with a partner, it's important to reenvision lovemaking. Too often sex is seen as a series of events that take place in a prescribed order. Survivors often go through the motions either not feeling at all, not liking what they do feel, or absolutely panic-stricken. You (and your lover) must give up the idea that sex is a series of events: first you kiss, then you touch, then you get genital, then you have orgasms, then you go to sleep. Instead, try looking at sex as an experience in loving, loving both yourself and another person—sex as an experience of honesty, pleasure, and intimacy. It starts, it changes, and eventually it's over. But other than that, anything can happen.

USES OF THE EROTIC: THE EROTIC AS POWER
by Audre Lorde

Another important way in which the erotic connection functions is the open and fearless underlining of my capacity for joy. In the way my body stretches to music and opens into response, hearkening to its deepest rhythms, so every level upon which I sense also opens to the erotically satisfying experience, whether it is dancing, building a bookcase, writing a poem, examining an idea.

That self-connection shared is a measure of the joy which I know myself to be capable of feeling, a reminder of my capacity for feeling. And that deep and irreplaceable knowledge of my capacity for joy comes to demand from all of my life that it be lived within the knowledge that such satisfaction is possible, and does not have to be called marriage, nor god, nor an afterlife.

This is one reason why the erotic is so feared, and so often relegated to the bedroom alone, when it is recognized at all. For once we begin to feel deeply all the aspects of our lives, we begin to demand from ourselves and from our lives' pursuits that they feel in accordance with that joy which we know ourselves to be capable of.

Our erotic knowledge empowers us, becomes a lens through which we scrutinize all aspects of our existence, forcing ourselves to evaluate those aspects honestly in terms of their relative meaning within our lives. And this is a grave responsibility, projected from within each of us, not to settle for the convenient, the shoddy, the conventionally expected, nor the merely safe.

During World War II, we bought sealed plastic packets of white, uncolored margarine, with a tiny, intense pellet of yellow coloring perched like a topaz just inside the clear skin of the bag. We would leave the margarine out for a while to soften, and then we would pinch the little pellet to break it inside the bag, releasing the rich yellowness into the soft pale mass of margarine. Then taking it carefully between our fingers, we would knead it gently back and forth, over and over, until the color had spread throughout the whole pound bag of margarine, leaving it thoroughly colored.

I find the erotic such a kernel within myself. When released from its intense and constrained pellet, it flows through and colors my life with a kind of energy that heightens and sensitizes and strengthens all my experience.

Audre Lorde, *Sister Outsider* (Berkeley, CA: Crossing Press, 1984).

IF YOU'RE STARTING A NEW RELATIONSHIP

You may feel especially burdened at the beginning of a new relationship by your problems with sex. One woman said it was actually harder to start new relationships the further along she got in her healing:

The more aware I am of the problems I face sexually, the less confident I feel with someone new. In the old days, when I was out of my body, things were much easier. If I was scared or disconnected, I never knew about it and neither did my lovers. Now I can't fake it anymore. Even though I'm more healed, the ways I'm damaged are a lot more visible. Couples who've been together for years have a hard time with this stuff. How can I expect a new person to deal with it? Sometimes I feel like I'm giving my relationships a death sentence before they even start.

It's helpful to remember that everyone comes into a new relationship carrying unresolved problems. No one is perfect. While it's true that you might have a difficult time having an orgasm or you might experience flashbacks, your lover might have a hard time with other things, like talking about feelings. Everyone has difficulties they need to work out. Focus on your strengths. The person who is falling in love with you is noticing your good qualities. Pay attention. Those qualities are just as much a part of you as your problems.

Going slow can help if you're afraid your problems with sex will overwhelm a new lover. If you have sex right away and then shut down, there's less of a foundation to support your relationship through the tough times. But if you get to know each other first, without sex, you will have a basis of friendship to help sustain you.

Couples often use immediate sex as a way to obscure the fact that they are starting a relationship with someone they barely know. Opening up to a new person can be terrifying. Passionate sex creates a comforting sense of closeness and connection. But sex alone is not a lasting or substantial basis for intimacy. The fact that you need to go slow may seem to be a hindrance now, but it can actually be an asset. When you're forced to develop trust and closeness before leaping into sex, it gives you and your potential lover the opportunity to build a solid foundation.

Try some old-fashioned courtship. Go out for a few dates where you only stare at each other with lingering looks. Let the excitement (and the trust) build. When you're ready to touch each other, start with some hand-holding, a few good-night kisses, and then ease into some heavy petting. And when you're ready to make love, acknowledge that you're ready. Savor every moment.

One couple designed a lovemaking ceremony. They knew they were going to have sex, but they took the time to acknowledge the rising passion between them. They talked about their feelings for each other, about their hopes and expectations for the relationship. They lit candles and proceeded very slowly, honoring the specialness and vulnerability of the moment. In doing so, they were able to ease each other's fears, build trust, and celebrate the beauty of coming together.

TALK TO YOUR LOVER

Lay the groundwork first: Whether you are talking to a new or an old lover, there are certain things you can do to make difficult conversations about sex easier:

- **Think about what you want to say ahead of time.**
- **Practice.** Role-play the situation with your counselor or a friend. Imagine different ways that your lover might react. Think through how you might respond to each one.
- **Work with your own feelings.** Deal with your own fears outside of the relationship so that you don't overwhelm your lover.
- **Talk out of bed.** You're both less vulnerable with your clothes on. It's easier to listen and talk on more neutral ground.
- **Pick the time carefully.** Don't initiate this conversation when your lover is on the way to work or otherwise preoccupied.
- **Don't bring up the subject as a way to push your lover away.** The goal of this conversation is to make you closer.
- **And remember, you're worth it.** You deserve loving support, an ally in your healing.

Talking to a new lover: With the proliferation of highly contagious and potentially life-threatening sexually transmitted diseases, it is absolutely essential that you talk with a new lover before having sex. Although these conversations are awkward and difficult, there is an up side: They open the door for talking frankly about sex. You can slide a little information about sexual abuse right in there next to the herpes.

Be direct and straightforward. Keep it simple. Give your lover an idea of what to expect from you sexually. If you're scared or uncertain or want to go slowly, say so. Explain your limits. If you've made a commitment to yourself never to make love when you don't want to or to stop when you have a flashback, let your lover know this. Tell your lover what you need. Give as much information as is necessary so that you don't feel alienated or need to fake it.

Women have said, "But I don't know him/her well enough to talk about things like that." If you don't know your lover well enough to talk, consider getting acquainted first. As one survivor said:

You shouldn't be sexual with someone that you can't talk to, because that's a pattern. If you're in a relationship where you can't say no, then you're sleeping with Daddy.

At the same time, don't overwhelm your lover with more history or detail than is appropriate. Don't make things sound horrendous if they're not. Remember to say that you're actively healing, and that things will change over time. Set the basis for talking if problems come up.

Dialogue is a two-way street. The fact that you are being open gives your lover a valuable opportunity to talk about his or her sexual fears, needs, and wants. Honest communication may not burden your lover at all; it may be a welcome relief from the assumption that satisfying sexual intimacy should just magically happen.

Talking in an established relationship: If you've never shared what you really experience during sex, your lover may be stunned when you first start talking. If you admit you've been faking it, don't feel desire, or are often disgusted by sex, your lover is likely to take it personally, think you've fallen out of love, feel responsible for your sexual problems, or become furious that you didn't say anything before.

Although you risk a negative reaction in being honest, you also stand the chance of gaining your strongest supporter. Lovers often feel relieved, having sensed all along that something was wrong. They may grieve for your pain and become allies in your healing. Honestly confronting problems deepens intimacy.

Whatever your lover's reaction (which may shift over time), healing requires that you stop pretending and tell the truth about your experience.

Pillow talk: Communication doesn't always have to be heavy or serious. You can talk sweet talk, make jokes and laugh, or just share your feelings as you're going along.

When I was in the hardest part of healing, I had a boyfriend who talked a lot when we had sex. I'd never been with anyone who said a word before except some very explicit stuff, but he would kind of keep a running commentary—how my skin felt, how beautiful I was, how much he loved me—really sweet things. I couldn't say a lot back, but I did manage to squeak out a few things, especially if he'd ask me a direct question. And though I couldn't really let him know the effect this had on me—and maybe didn't even know it myself—looking back I can see how much safety and comfort it gave me. It was like we were in an ongoing conversation that helped me stay very much rooted in the present.

Talking during sex helps many women feel connected and reassured:

I've always needed to talk, to hear a voice during lovemaking, but I think men can get thrown by this. I'd sometimes ask for a glass of juice or an extra blanket, just to make contact.

You may feel uncomfortable asking to talk directly, but the need to connect is a real and valid one. Talking is another way of making love.

TAKE YOUR TIME

In exploring sexually with a lover, it's important to remember that you can stop anytime. Give yourself the freedom to take breaks, to do only what feels good, and to go slowly enough so that you can feel.

If you get scared, tell your lover. This gives your lover the chance to slow down and connect with you, to offer comfort, to learn more about what scared you. At that point you may be ready to continue making love or you may not.

If your lover does something that makes you uncomfortable, say so. If you start to make connections between the way you respond now and what happened to you as a child, let your lover know. These realizations are an essential part of healing:

I always pee a little when I am very aroused. One time when this happened, I suddenly realized that when my brother molested me, peeing was my only line of defense. I used to think it might save me from making love. When I remembered all of this, I had to say to my lover, "I need to stop." And then we talked about it.

FIND YOUR OWN PACE

When you were abused, you either had sexuality thrust on you before you were ready or you were exploited in the process of coming into your sexuality. If sex still feels overwhelming, it can be helpful to give yourself the opportunity to explore at your own pace.

Perhaps certain sexual acts feel okay, while others don't; some places you may be comfortable being touched and some you may not. Tell your lover. Just because you say yes to one thing, it doesn't mean that you're saying yes to everything. And just because you say yes once, it doesn't mean that you have to say yes every time.

Try proceeding slowly and from your own inner promptings. Don't kiss until you feel the desire to kiss in your lips. Don't pull someone closer until your body yearns for that. As Kyos tells us, the results can be quite nice:

I started a sexual relationship with a friend who is a survivor. When we touch, there's space for me to explore, to learn about touch. It's okay for me to be whoever I am and for her to be whoever she is. It's like reclaiming the child on a sexual level. I learn by doing.

Whatever I feel when she touches me is the important thing, not how it matches some sexual idea. We're not there to get off on each other. We're there because we love each other. If I start sobbing right before I come, that's okay. If I suddenly get angry, that's okay. If I have a flashback, that's okay. It doesn't matter. It's in the safety to stay in the present moment with whatever is happening that the healing takes place.

Sexuality is not a problem anymore. It's an exciting process. We're exploring our passion together. Once I realized that my sexuality was my power, I was able to embrace it. I'm looking forward to a lot of fun practice for the rest of my life.*

Talk. Share. Experience the level of closeness and touch that you can handle now. You can feel good with someone even if you don't sail through sex, even if you don't "finish." There *is* no finish, no goal except intimacy, honesty, and pleasure.

---

* For more of Kyos's story, see p. 457.

STAYING PRESENT

To me, making love is a duet in solos. It's nice that someone's there with me, but I'm not there with them. I'm there as an observer. I'm there all by myself, and I don't like it, and it's scary. I have a flight reaction: "I *have* to get out of here." And the more someone likes me, the more they're turned on to me, the more scared I get and the faster I'm out of my body. I start looking up and making patterns out of the cracks on the ceiling.

I would make love with my husband and be totally detached. I'd look over his shoulder and watch the football game: "Oh, it looks like they made another ten yards." I'd find as many ways as I could to space out during The Act. I'd look out the window and think, "God, aren't you done *yet?*" I don't remember much about it. I just wasn't there. And the thing I find incredible is that I so rarely got caught, that I could be in this relationship and I'd be the only one who knew I wasn't there. *Don't you know I'm gone? Can't you even see that I'm not here anymore?*

If you find yourself spacing out while you're making love, stop or slow down. Talk to your lover. Look your lover in the eyes. Say your lover's name. One woman kept a jar of potpourri on her night table and stopped to smell it when she felt herself drifting. That strong sensory jolt helped her stay present.

But don't keep going through the motions while you are disconnected from your feelings.

The Split
BY ALICE ANDERSON

This is how it happens. You are just out of the
   shower maybe
in the afternoon when your lover comes up behind you and kisses you

on the shoulder. You turn, kiss back. And you
   even remind yourself,
during that first heavy breath or fall to the
   bed—I am not

going to close my eyes. But you cannot help
   yourself and you
close your eyes, forgetting your promise, and
   you see him.

A figure, moving form, enormous shadow appearing somewhere
between your eyelids and the air. There he is
   above you

and for a moment you are happy about it,
   amazed to feel again
what it is to be that small. How exquisite your
   tiny fingers,

how fragile the bones of your wrists. You see
   how easily
your thigh fits in a hand, your chin in a mouth,
   your buttocks

in the crook of a hip—how easy it is then to be
   filled.
This is real to you: this is what you turn sex into.

You feel your knees pushed open with thick
   warm thumbs and
you can feel your knees are skinned and then
   you see them

getting skinned, you see yourself somewhere beyond that shadow.
You see your white skates on the drive, the slope of the tar,

and into this vision you escape. Leave. Cease to exist.
You are gone from the place of the thin bed and the blue panties

caught around an ankle. Someone else has taken your place.
You then are on the driveway and your cat is in the flowerbed

and your mother looks out the kitchen window at you in your
good dress which you are not supposed to wear with skates.

You skate in circles and watch the sky, picking shapes
out of clouds—turtle, clipper ship, heart, hand.

Your mother tells you *Watch where you are going young lady.*
And even before you skin your knees you feel something

slowly rising in your throat, the way the cream lifts every time
from the milk in the glass bottles that arrive on Sundays,

no matter how many times your mother shakes it up for you.
It rises in you like that—thick and lukewarm as your father's skin.

The taste inches up but you keep skating, try to make the circles

perfect and small, try to smell the beefsteaks on the barbeque

in the side yard where your father calls over the fence
to the neighbor, saying *This is the life.* But when you hear

his voice it is enough to send you down. You fall.
Your knees are skinned and full of rocks but you're almost

you again, panties wrapped around an ankle, undershirt pushed up.
You hear your breathing and his breathing. You're hot.

Your eyes are open again, staring at something they
don't even see. And when finally it happens you realize

that it isn't your father filling you this time, he is
only making you fall. It hits you that you've done it again:

this shrinking into someone, then somewhere else. It is always
the same. You cannot control it. You never learned to skate.

You are there in your grown up bed with your lover and you have
just made love and he says *Isn't sex amazing* and you say *Yes.*

Alice Anderson, *Human Nature* (New York: New York University Press, 1994).

Even though you may be scared, awkward, or embarrassed, come back. Give yourself—and your lover—the respect of honest communication.

FLASHBACKS WITH A PARTNER

I had flashbacks making love. Frequently. One time the light was a certain way in the room. My lover got up to go to the bathroom. I looked up and she was standing in the doorway. I knew it was her. But what I saw was my father standing in the doorway watching my brother molest me. It didn't matter that I knew it was my lover. It *was* my father. It *was* my brother.

If you find yourself bombarded by flashbacks, talking helps. One woman and her husband developed the code word "ghosts," which she would say whenever she had a flashback. This would alert him that they were no longer in present time, and he could then respond appropriately.

Sometimes you may want to stay with the flashback and open it up, so you can gain information about the past. Other times, you will choose to stay in the present. At those times, you can say to your lover, "I want to stay here, with you. I don't want to go back to the past. Help me stay here. Talk to me. Call my name. Remind me who you are."

One woman had a lover who helped her stay in the present just by saying, "Open your eyes, Edith. Open your eyes." When she opened her eyes, she saw him, saw her own room, and was able to slip into the present, away from the flashbacks.

You have a right to feel good in your present experience, even if it means regular reality checks to remind yourself that the abuser is no longer in your bed. Even if you start off with, "Sex? Uh-oh," you can talk to yourself and say, "No. Now sex is fun. This is James. This is not my cousin."*

WE HAVE TO DO IT MY WAY

One common element among survivors is the need to control the sexual experience, sometimes to the extent of managing every detail. You may feel comfortable only if you are in certain positions, if the lights are on, if you initiate, if it's morning, if it's *not* morning, and so on. Although this is limiting and sometimes difficult for your lover, it may be essential for you. You need to set your boundaries. You need to be in an environment in which you can feel secure enough to relax. In short, you need control:

Sex is the act of being out of control. It's wonderful, but it terrifies me to give up control. It's the approach that stops me. I have to stop and think, "Do I want this to be happening? Or is it because someone is approaching me and I'm letting it happen?" If I initiate it's much easier. Then I'm the one feeling sexual, I *know* I'm feeling sexual, and I'm pretty sure I'm not being molested.

---

* For more, see "Working with Triggers" on p. 312.

Recognizing and fulfilling your need for control, without criticizing yourself, gives you power:

It was very threatening for me just to have a male reaching out and touching me. The fact that someone was coming to me wanting something was hard. Our therapist suggested that he ask my permission before he touches me. We did that for a while, and then it felt less like an attack. It allowed me to make the differentiation: "This isn't my father coming after me. This is my husband."

As you feel more able to be both sexual and protected, you will find that some of the elements you once needed to control are no longer as critical.

YOU'RE NOT IN THIS ALONE

While there may be short periods when you need to exercise total control over sex, ultimately you have to engage in some give-and-take with your lover.

One day, our therapist asked Roger, "How do you feel when Karen's not re-

---

STRATEGIES FOR WORKING WITH SEXUAL FEAR

- **Go slow.** Back off to whatever is more comfortable.

- **Find a place in the middle.** Many survivors fluctuate between extremes—shutting down totally or trying for complete sexual abandon.

- **Stay in the present.** Pay attention to the sensation of touch. Open your eyes.

- **Listen to your fear.** What is it trying to tell you? Is there something unsafe in your current environment? Or is this an old fear you want to overcome?

- **Find ways other than sex to connect deeply to yourself.** If you start to confront painful feelings and memories in other settings (such as therapy), sex will no longer be the only access point for connecting deeply with yourself, and you will gradually break the connection between passion, letting go, intensity, and abuse.

- **Check in with your lover.** If you're afraid that your lover might experience the intensity of your desire or passion as coercive, talk to him or her. (Your lover may enjoy your passion.)

- **Push yourself a little.** If you want to make love and you're afraid, push yourself a little. Stay in touch with yourself and your partner. Communicate like crazy. Be prepared for a lot of feelings.

- **Stop if you need to.** Sometimes the gap between what you *want* to experience and what you *are* experiencing gets too wide. If your terror is too great, take a break. Find another way to be close.

sponding to you, when she's closed off?" And he started talking about being flat-out terrified. To hear him talk about being terrified that our relationship was going to end made me stop and realize that I wasn't the only one who was going through terrible, awful feelings. Here was another human being, who I loved very deeply, who was bleeding, and some of that was a wound I had inflicted by being so wrapped up in myself.

While there may be stages in your healing when you are oblivious to the needs and feelings of anyone but yourself, the fact is that your pain—and your healing—affects everyone close to you. Nowhere is this more apparent than in the realm of sexuality. Lovers are often confused, hurt, frustrated, and furious with the sexual changes survivors go through.

While you'd probably like an all-giving, totally understanding, completely patient lover while healing sexually, this is not realistic. Even the most supportive lover has personal feelings and needs. Although you can't force yourself to be sexual, you do have to make room for your lover's feelings, as fully as you possibly can. This is essential if you want the relationship to survive.

Here are some things you can do to be more responsive to your lover's needs and feelings:

- **Be willing to listen.** Although it's essential that your lover have other people to talk to, you need to hear your lover's feelings at least some of the time.

- **Validate your lover's feelings.** Your lover has a right to have needs, to be hurt, angry, or frustrated. You would probably be, too, if the situation were reversed.

- **Put yourself in your lover's shoes.** If you can't imagine being upset about not having sex, think of something important to you—like communication—and imagine how you'd feel if your lover wouldn't talk to you and wasn't sure when he or she might feel like it.

- **Don't condemn your lover for wanting sex.** The fact that right now you see sex as a problem or a threat doesn't mean it is. Your lover's desire is a healthy, vital part of life.

- **Don't blame your lover.** This is all the abuser's fault, remember?

- **Be as consistent as you can.** At times this may be impossible, but it helps if you keep your limits as clear and consistent as possible, so your lover doesn't feel like a puppet on a string.

- **Communicate.** Let your lover know what's going on.

- **Let your lover know that you're committed to changes over time**. Say it a lot. Reassure your lover that you want your sex life to change.

- **Say the good things.** If you'd like to be able to make love, if you find your lover attractive, say so—*frequently*.

- **Give as much as you possibly can.** Then stretch just a little bit more. If you can't give sex, then give something as close to sex as you can. (See

"Be Creative" below for some suggestions.)

- **Take breaks from dealing with sex.** Don't forget—there's more to life, and to your relationship, than sex.

BE CREATIVE

There may be times when your lover wants to make love and you don't. You have the right to say no, and it's important that you feel able to. But saying no every time isn't a viable practice if you want to have a sexual relationship.

If you do not want to make love, you might be willing to suggest alternatives: a massage, kissing and cuddling, sharing a bath, an intimate talk. Although these don't meet the specific desire for sex, they can fulfill the longing for closeness and intimacy. Many lovers will appreciate being able to share in *some* way rather than being totally shut out. You may find yourself welcoming the closeness as well, once you know that the touching is within safe, nonsexual boundaries. Often when survivors say no to sex, they are so enmeshed in their own guilt that they push their lovers further away. Finding other ways to be close is an opportunity to build intimacy and trust instead.

Variations on mutually involved sex can help ease the process of working through sexual difficulties. Sometimes you may not want to be touched sexually—you don't want that stimulation or intrusion. But you may be comfortable touching your lover. Or you may not want to touch your lover but you would be open to being touched. Other times you may not want to give or receive but would feel fine about holding your lover while he or she masturbates:

> There were a lot of times I just couldn't feel my libido at all. No desire. Zilch. But my husband was being so patient with me and I knew how much he wanted sex, so often I'd be with him while he masturbated. I'd hold him and kiss him. I felt safe doing that and it helped me feel a lot less guilty. At least I was doing something and he really appreciated it. And sometimes, watching him get aroused, I'd actually get turned on and touch myself or ask him to touch me afterward.

If you expand your preconceptions a bit, often more is possible than you thought.

Working It Out with My Lover: Catherine's Story

A lot of times what I wanted to do sexually and what I could do were light-years apart. I wanted to maintain a pleasant, fun, playful sexual relationship with Barbara. At the same time, our lovemaking became tense, nearly impossible, and finally impossible. It became burdened with so much meaning. If she didn't get off, I couldn't just chalk it up to one time and see that it wasn't so important. It was "Because I'm an incest victim, you don't like making love to me anymore." *Everything* was my fault. I blamed myself for all our sexual problems. I was hyperaware of every little change in our usual routine.

She had to reassure me constantly. I needed her to validate my decision to look at incest material, that it was worth going through a period of changed sexuality in order for me to be able to integrate what had happened in my life. She needed patience and more patience.

I needed a lot of affection that wasn't sexual. I needed a lot of verbal expressions of love so all the pressure wasn't sexual. I needed to know she didn't love me only because I fulfilled her sexual needs. I needed to know she wanted the person inside the body, not just my body. I needed reassurance that I was still the person she wanted to be with. I needed to know she wasn't eager for me to get over it.

We decided that if sex felt bad to either one of us, we would stop. I felt, "Phew! Now I don't have to do that anymore." I started saying no all the time. Barbara got furious: "You're *always* saying no! You're always the one that doesn't want it! What am I doing wrong? I'm sick of you going through your goddamn incest stuff! I'm not your Dad! I'm not your Mom! I'm not the people who hurt you!" That would just make it worse. I'd feel like I was a terrible person.

That started to turn around when I said, "Look, it's not my fault. I know you're angry. I'm angry too. I want there to be sexuality. Yes, you're angry. But go deal with it somewhere else. And if you can't take it, leave!" We had to start from scratch, rebuilding our sexual relationship from zero. It's scary. But we're doing it. And it's been worth it.*

TAKE A BREAK AND LIGHTEN UP

Sometimes as you work to change sexually, the process seems grim. You're fed up with "trying to do it." Words like *spontaneity* and *enjoyment* sound foreign. This is when it helps if you can dig out your sense of humor and lighten up:

Sometimes we take on this real hard-working approach to making love, so sincere and serious and lacking in spontaneity. We focus in a very narrow way. We don't laugh. We don't tickle. We don't play. It's very cut-and-dried. And that can be terribly boring and frustrating. What we're trying to do now is consciously lessen that, to be more playful in bed, to just have fun.

---

* For more of Catherine's story, see "The Emergency Stage: Catherine's Story" on p. 65, and "Truth-Telling: Catherine's Story" on p. 161.

YOUR LOVER CAN BE YOUR ROLE MODEL

If sex is an exciting, rich part of life for your lover, free of conflicts and problems, you can hold this not as a threat to your limitations, but as a vision of what sex can be:

Making love was special for her. She wanted to know how to please me. She had so much patience. It was new. People really feel this way about sex? My God! I'd never seen anyone that passionate. I watched her for a year and a half. Eventually I decided I wanted to learn to be that free. That's what it was—freedom. So I slowly started to say, "It's okay."

She would do or say something, and I'd say, "Oh, that's nasty!"

And she'd say, "That's not nasty. It's a lie. Who told you that?"

I'd say, "Yeah, it's not nasty," but in my mind I was still saying, "That's nasty!"

Eventually I got to the point where I could say, "Well, maybe it's not *that* nasty." I started to relax.

SEE YOURSELVES AS ALLIES

Lovers can become allies, united in solving a difficult and painful problem, rather than adversaries blaming themselves or each other. When your needs and the needs of your lover differ, it does not mean that either of you is wrong or to blame. It is helpful if you can see yourselves as caring partners facing a mutual challenge.

MAKING ROOM FOR DESIRE

There is no set amount of sexual desire that is "normal." Some people have sexual feelings many times in a day, others once a week, once a month, or once a year. And most people experience changes in their level of desire. These fluctuations can result from stress, accompany feelings of grief or depression, or coincide with major life changes such as giving birth, nursing a baby, illness, the death of someone close to you, the use of medication, new sobriety, or menopause. Such shifts are a natural part of life.

Survivors often experience a lack of desire as a direct result of their abuse. Your lack of desire might be a defense against unwanted sex, a sign of sexual fear, a symptom of being disconnected from your body, or a reaction to the fact that you see desire as dangerous:

I've never had a sexual desire. It's amazing that someone can have screwed as often as I have, and as many as I have, and in as many places as I have, and had no desire. People ask, "Well, why did you do it?" I did it to get rid of them. I thought it was appropriate to sleep with your husband. I had a multitude of reasons, and one of them was never because I wanted to.

WORKING WITH TRIGGERS

In her indispensable book, Healing Sex: A Mind-Body Approach to Healing Sexual Trauma *(originally published as* The Survivor's Guide to Sex),* *Staci K. Haines explores the concept that triggers are a rich source of information to be embraced and explored. In this adapted excerpt, Haines suggests that instead of trying to avoid triggers, survivors welcome them as opportunities for healing.*

Triggers are automatic responses connected to your past sexual abuse that can suddenly rush into the present. Certain acts, smells, words—perhaps even a tone of voice—can bring up images and feelings from the past. While the pain, anger, or confusion can seem to be a response to something that is happening today, it is really a fragment of visual, emotional, or body memory making its way to the surface.[†]

Triggers often recur until that piece of memory or trauma is processed and released. In this way, they act as flags to alert you to aspects of healing that need to be addressed. Attending to and healing *through* your triggers helps you unpack the baggage of sexual abuse from your sexuality.

---

* Staci K. Haines, *Healing Sex: A Mind-Body Approach to Healing Sexual Trauma*, originally published as *The Survivor's Guide to Sex* (San Francisco: Cleis Press, 2007).

† For an in-depth discussion of memory, see "Remembering" on p. 70.

Trying to Avoid Triggers

Most survivors hate triggers. They can be painful, annoying, and devastating, and they interrupt otherwise good experiences. Because of this, many survivors try to avoid the things that trigger them as much as possible. They try to organize their lives, and especially their sex lives, to avoid stirring up uncomfortable and often painful feelings. Eventually, people can build a narrow life entirely motivated by avoiding triggers.

But the harder you work to circumvent them, the bigger and more powerful triggers seem to become, while the space for *you* becomes smaller. Avoidance also leaves all the land mines of sexual abuse in place, so the terrain of your life continues to feel dangerous and untrustworthy. When triggers are taken on, felt, and processed, they shrink or transform altogether. What was once a trigger becomes a completed part of your history. You become more powerful than what happened to you.

Trigger Plans and Tools

Here are some simple steps to take when you are triggered in a sexual situation. These tools can be used in both partner sex and masturbation. It's a good idea to review these steps before you need them in a sexual situation.

- **Notice.** Begin by noticing when you are triggered. This can be the biggest step.

What is triggering you? What sensations are you feeling in your body?

- **Stop and breathe.** Stop, pause, and breathe. Assess the situation. What are you feeling? What's going on? What do you need?

- **Choose.** Once you have noticed your trigger and paused, there are numerous options for handling it. Check in with what you need right now and what will be best for your ongoing healing process. If, in the past, you have tended to stop being sexual, try something different. Take a break and then re-engage sexually. Or change what you are doing, but remain in contact with yourself and your partner. Or move toward the trigger to work with it. Taking new risks is important. It expands your options and lets you learn to do what was previously not possible.

- **Engage.** Continue to be present with yourself and your partner. Communicate your choice and talk it over. Then, engage. Keep bringing yourself to the experience, whether you have chosen to go into the trigger, to continue being sexual, or to get up and do something else. Stay connected to yourself, your body, and your partner as much as possible. This is a process of retraining your body. You don't have to go away or disappear. If your first choice doesn't work for you, feel free to change your mind and make a different choice.

- **Don't blame your partner.** If you are engaging in partner sex, there is a tendency to blame your partner for the feelings of discomfort, fear, or aversion that may emerge. Instead, ask yourself, "How can my partner be an ally to me now, instead of an enemy?"

Many Choices

Building a repertoire of choices allows you to practice different approaches at different times. You may be best supported in your healing process by stopping sex altogether in one encounter and by continuing in another. Here are a number of options:

- **Go into the trigger.** You can choose to keep your attention on the visual, auditory, or bodily sensations that have been triggered. The intention here is to move into, feel, remember, release, and complete the stored memory or trauma. You may experience grief, anger, fear, or any other emotion connected to the abuse. Keep breathing and let these feelings emerge and be released.

- **If you are with your partner, share what is happening and how you feel.** If you are shaking, crying, or laughing,

Working With Triggers (*cont.*)

do it fully. If you need to express anger, yell into a pillow, hit the bed, or twist a towel as hard as you can. (For more on safe ways to express intense emotions, see "Anger-Release Work" on p. 150.)

- **If you are experiencing a memory of abuse, tell your partner as much as you can about it.** When you are able, make eye contact. Connect with your partner's support in the present. Communicate your needs as much as possible. And remember, this can be an intense experience for your partner as well.

- **If you are alone while you go through this process, talk to a trusted person afterward.** Tell someone what you went through. This step is essential to take you out of isolation and rebuild connection.

- **Watch from a distance.** Another approach to being with a trigger is to watch it from a distance, while remaining rooted in the present. This can be useful with a trigger you've already processed or one you're working with but don't want to process fully right now. Noticing objects in the room or sounds in the environment will help you remain rooted in the present. Feel your body—your weight on the bed or your back pressed up against the wall. Remind yourself that you are here in the present. Breathe. From the present, attend to the trigger or memory. Acknowledge it by speaking about it out loud or writing it down.

- **Move.** Get up and move. Walk around, stretch, breathe, and relax your body. Make sounds or shake your body to "shake off" the trigger. Moving can bring you to a present and settled place from which you can return to being sexual.

- **Take care of the child.** You can approach a trigger as if it were a small child who is afraid and upset. Treat the trigger as you would a real child who interrupted you while you were having sex. Stop being sexual for the moment and attend to your inner child. What does she need? Pick her up and comfort her; sit down and rock her. Explain to her that sex is for grown-ups, not for kids. Once you have taken care of her, put her back to bed. You can then return to sex if you so chose.

- **Let's make a deal.** Engaging in internal negotiations with triggers is another approach. You can "talk to" triggers as if they were parts of you that could communicate. You can ask the triggered part of yourself what it needs and how you might provide that. Often the trigger is a cry for love and attention. You can negotiate to take care of that triggered part of you at a later date. If that seems agreeable, make a specific date and time when you will check in with yourself again and attend to the trigger. Keep your commitment.

- **Change sexual activities.** Changing positions or sexual activities, turning on the light, or adjusting your environment can shift a trigger. If you feel uncomfortable with what you are doing, communicate this to your partner and adjust accordingly. This can add to your sexual play and does not need to be a distraction that ends the encounter.

- **Take a walk.** You can also choose to change activities altogether. You can choose something that is still sensual or erotic, such as massage with no genital contact or a shared bath. Or you can take a break from sex altogether. Take a walk, listen to music, go to the movies, pet your dog—anything you like. Whatever your choice, practice being embodied and present with yourself and your partner.

- **Return to the present.** Pause and breathe. Orient yourself to the pres-

ent by noticing objects, sounds, smells, temperatures, and sensations. Remind yourself where you are, whom you are with, and that what you are doing is consensual. Review the reasons you like to be sexual and how expressing yourself sexually benefits you. Return to the present and continue to be sexual.

- **Say no to repeating triggers.** If a recurring image or trigger appears after you have thoroughly processed it, you can tell it, "No, you are no longer welcome here. Do not come back." You can decide now who is allowed in your inner space. This is a process of setting internal boundaries. Turn away the image or trigger each time it appears, until it doesn't return again.

Triggers Don't Have to Last Forever

You need not assume that because a particular sex act triggers you now, it always will. Once you have released the trauma from the area of your body where the trigger is stored and processed the experience emotionally, the trigger will usually fade.

As you work with your triggers, you will increasingly be able to choose your sexual expression on the basis of your own authentic desires rather than on the limits induced by childhood sexual abuse.

You may never have had the chance to feel your own desire. When children are forced to be sexual at an early age, their natural sexual feelings don't have a chance to emerge. This pattern often continues into adulthood:

When I began to get in touch with the earliest abuse, I could no longer feel desire of my own, only desire called up by the needs and desires of someone else, in this case my lover. This was so terrifying that I would space out, feel pain, or fear, or just not want to make love in the first place. I wanted loving and affectionate and sometimes sensual closeness, but I wanted these to have their own integrity and not just be a prelude to sex.

As a child, you experienced the desire of your abuser as being out of control. You were forced to comply with your abuser's needs. Desire was a weapon used against you, so today you may be threatened by your own desire, afraid it too might be abusive:

I got to a point where I allowed myself to get very turned on when I was making love. I was being very aggressive and in touch with my passion. I was on top of my lover, and all of a sudden I had this creepy feeling that I'd become the abuser. I just froze and turned off right away. The next thing I knew, I started having flashbacks of being raped as a child. It was horrible. I didn't have a sexual feeling for months afterward.

The fact that you have flashbacks or painful feelings while making love may eliminate your desire for sex. People want to have sex because it makes them feel good, connected, and whole. If sex for you dredges up pain, grief, and anguish, it makes sense that you experience a lack of desire.

If you never (or rarely) experience sexual desire, taking a break from sex can give you room to see whether those feelings emerge naturally when you are not feeling pressure to perform for somebody else. One woman who'd opted for a period of celibacy said she was feeling sexual desire for the first time in her life, but added that the feelings began to arise in an embarrassing way:

Recently, I've just started to have sexual feelings like "God, I'd really like to make love with my therapist." God, am I attracted to her! I've told her. We talk about it. She's the keynote speaker in my sexual fantasies.

BROADEN YOUR CONCEPT OF DESIRE

In her book *Lesbian Sex*, JoAnn Loulan has creatively reshaped traditional concepts of desire in a way that is enlightening for heterosexual women as well as lesbians.* Loulan says desire can be felt on an intellectual, emotional, or physical level. Intellectual desire is a decision that you want to make love. Emotional desire is wanting to make love with someone because you feel close to them. Physical desire is a spe-

---

* See the "Sexuality" section on p. 567 of the Resource Guide.

cific feeling in your body that says you want to make love. These three types of desire can exist together or separately. All three are valid.

Loulan suggests making a list of things that the culture defines as desire (being turned on by your lover's naked body, wanting sex whenever you can get it, and so on). Then make a list of what desire is for you. Compare the two. It's likely there'll be differences. That's because the cultural stereotypes don't have much to do with people's real feelings. What's important to focus on is your own internal experience of desire.

If you let go of the expectations you have for yourself and broaden your concept of desire, you may find that you have more sexual feelings than you thought:

Sex for me used to be what I did when I went into the bedroom with my husband. Now everything can be a turn-on. Like ice cream. I'm not talking about wanting sex ten times a day. It's how I respond to things, visually and tactilely. I'm much more in touch with my senses now. Life is so much more of a turn-on now.

WILLINGNESS

One of the most pervasive myths about sexuality is that you have to start with desire or excitement to enjoy making love. Loulan exploded this myth in her revised version of the female sexual response cycle. Previous models of women's sexual response cycle cite either desire or excitement as the necessary starting point for sex.

In this model, the sexual response cycle begins with neither of these. It begins with the willingness to have sex. Willingness simply means that you are willing to enter into the sexual realm with yourself or another person and to be open to what you might find there. Willingness is an attitude. It doesn't commit you to anything more than beginning.

The concept of willingness as a legitimate entry point for sexual activity makes sex much more accessible to women who don't experience a high level of desire. It means you can have sex even if you're not feeling physical arousal, excitement, or desire of any kind. This is a radical and liberating approach to female sexuality.

The reasons you are willing may vary. For example, you might be willing because you want the physical pleasure sex brings, because you know you will enjoy it once you get started, because you want that depth of intimacy with your lover, because you want to work on sexual issues with your lover, or because you want to practice making love to yourself.

For many women, the idea of willingness is a tremendous relief. Instead of asking yourself, "Do I want sex?" or "What's wrong with me that I don't feel desire?" you can ask instead, "Am I willing to begin?" The concept of willingness gives you the permission to explore sexually from exactly where you are. Instead of trying to generate desire out of nowhere, you can simply say, "Yes, I'm willing to try."

EXPANDED PLEASURE

Willingness can lead to any of the other stages in the sexual cycle—shutting down, desire, excitement, engorgement, orgasm, or the final stage, pleasure. In this view of women's sexual response, pleasure is not dependent on orgasm,

LEVELS OF SEXUAL INTERACTION

Wendy Maltz, therapist and author of the groundbreaking book *The Sexual Healing Journey,** has created a Hierarchy of Sexual Interaction that provides a useful way of evaluating sexual behavior within the context of relationships. Sexual energy is recognized as a natural force that can be channeled in either destructive or life-affirming ways. Maltz's model presents six levels of sexual interaction: three negative levels (impersonal, abusive, and violent) and three positive levels (role fulfillment, making love, and authentic sexual intimacy). This way of looking at sex makes clear the need for communication, safety, and trust and points to authentic sexual intimacy as a peak experience in human relationships.

Certain conditions determine the nature of sexual interaction—whether it is experienced as healthy or hurtful. Conditions such as consent, equality, respect, trust, and safety lead to healthy interactions, while dishonesty, disregard for physical safety, domination, objectification, and shame lead to negative interactions.

Within this model, we don't judge specific sexual behaviors. Instead, we look at the context in which a sexual behavior takes place—and the consequences of that behavior. Sexual energy can unite a couple in a dance of tenderness and passion, heightening their self-awareness and strengthening their connection and commitment to each other. Or, if used in a violent act such as rape or humiliation, sexual energy can shatter trust and destroy one's sense of self-worth and safety. And of course there is a great range in between these extremes.

---

* Wendy Maltz, *The Sexual Healing Journey: A Guide for Survivors of Sexual Abuse*, revised edition (New York: Quill, 2001). There is also a wealth of information on Wendy Maltz's Web site at www.healthysex.com.

POSITIVE AND NEGATIVE DIRECTIONS IN THE MALTZ HIERARCHY OF SEXUAL INTERACTION

Sexual energy is a benign, natural force which can be channeled in either positive or negative directions. Below are two different sets of qualities each corresponding with a different direction. The negative qualities increase and intensify as one travels downward, and positive qualities increase and intensify as one travels upward.

POSITIVE DIRECTION

➕

life-affirming celebration
healthy bonding
connectedness
creative expression
emotional intimacy
enhanced self-esteem
open communication
mutual respect
trust
sense of equality
consent
safety
caring

GROUND ZERO:
Influx of drives, hormones, and sexual energy

emotional isolation
risk and danger
dishonesty and shame
impulsive, compulsive
betrayal of trust
imbalance of power
coercion and fear
dislike of partner
silencing of inner reality
pain and injury
limited options
disintegration of relationship
destruction of body and soul

➖

NEGATIVE DIRECTION

physical excitement, or arousal. Rather, it is a unique experience determined solely by the woman involved.

You may experience pleasure because you took the time to touch yourself in a loving way or because you were willing to engage in sexual activity after a long period of celibacy. Or you may feel satisfaction because you took good care of yourself when memories of your abuse came up. All these are reasons to feel good. If you expand the acceptable reasons for getting into sex and widen your expectations of what you can get out of it, your pleasurable experiences may increase considerably.

WHEN YOU ALWAYS WANT SEX

While many survivors' sexual difficulties have to do with not wanting sex, others want sex all the time and try to use it to meet all needs, including nonsexual ones:

I've noticed that whenever I felt lonely or scared or had a need to connect with my husband, I would immediately interpret it as a sexual need, even though it was clearly an emotional need. I wanted to be made love to all the time. I was very seductive, trying to get sex I really didn't want at all. I would feel real stormy and out of control and freaked out if I couldn't get it. It felt like a powerful way to behave, but it really came from a distorted sense of my own desires.

It is possible to stop using sex to meet all your needs. Begin by paying attention to how you feel when you want sex. Ask yourself if what you feel is a desire for sex specifically or whether it might be one or more other needs that you habitually try to meet through sex. Try to assess exactly what you want. Is it closeness, intimacy, relaxation, approval, validation, power, the gratification of pleasing someone, distraction from worries or problems, security, good feelings in your body?

In *Getting Free*,* Ginny NiCarthy breaks sexuality down into five components: affection, sensuality, eroticism, intimacy, and romance. Of the five, eroticism (which she defines as "orgasm and the explicitly sexual arousal and tension associated with it") is the only need that can't be approached in ways other than sex itself.

If your pattern is to try to fill a wide variety of needs sexually, it will be challenging (but ultimately rewarding) to try other approaches. Sometimes just cuddling will actually give you more of what you want than sex. Sometimes an honest talk is more satisfying. Sometimes you'll feel better swimming, dancing, going to a concert, or painting a picture. The idea here isn't to stop enjoying sex but to broaden your repertoire of ways to meet your needs, thereby giving you more freedom and creativity.

---

* Ginny NiCarthy, *Getting Free: You Can End Abuse and Take Back Your Life*, 4th edition (Emeryville, CA: Seal Press, 2004). See the "Domestic Violence, Rape, and Sexual Harassment" section on p. 563 of the Resource Guide.

It is also a clear message to yourself that you are more than just a sexual being. Although sex can be a wonderful and amazing part of life, it is only one part. You are a whole person, of many aspects, and you deserve to have access to them all.

SEX THAT RESEMBLES ABUSE

Many survivors engage in sex that repeats some aspect of their victimization. Some have married abusive lovers or had sex with lovers in contexts that ranged from disrespectful to humiliating to dangerous. Some survivors compulsively masturbate, rely on violent por-

---

LOOKING AT TROUBLING SEXUAL BEHAVIORS

In *The Sexual Healing Journey,** Wendy Maltz helps survivors get clear on abuse-related sexual behaviors that they may want to change. These questions, adapted from her suggestions, provide a useful starting point in determining whether you want to continue using particular fantasies or engaging in specific behaviors:

- Does this behavior recreate aspects of the abuse? If so, how?

- Does this behavior reenact the relationship dynamics I was exposed to in the abuse? If so, how?

- Does this behavior reflect a false or negative view about myself as a sexual person?

- Does this behavior hurt me or have the potential to hurt me? If so, how?

- Does this behavior hurt others or have the potential to hurt others? If so, how?

- What are the positive and negative consequences of this behavior for me?

- Do I engage in this behavior in a compulsive or addictive way? Do I find myself engaging in it even when I don't really want to?

- Why might I want to stop this behavior? (Could it lead to my losing an important relationship? Having an unwanted pregnancy? Being subjected to violence? Developing or passing on sexually transmitted disease? Being accused or convicted of a crime? Suffering years of loneliness and remorse?)

- What part of me wants to continue it, and why?

- Am I willing to do the deep healing work required to address the underlying basis for this behavior?

---

* Wendy Maltz, *The Sexual Healing Journey: A Guide for Survivors of Sexual Abuse*, revised edition (New York: Quill, 2001). There is also a wealth of information on Wendy Maltz's Web site at www.healthysex.com.

nography, engage in unsafe sex, or allow others unlimited access to their bodies. They have sex that leaves them feeling disconnected, violated, exploited, used, or disempowered.

One woman, who worked as a prostitute for five years, recalls:

> After I left my second husband and my children, I came to California and within three weeks hooked up with a very violent pimp who turned me out on the streets. They were very abusive years. When I look back, it's hard for me to understand how I did that to myself. *I didn't know I didn't have to.* It was too close to my childhood.
>
> Women say they're on the streets by choice, but it's not really a choice.
>
> I'd been set up for it. My father was abusive and he would pay me for sex. He would give me something afterwards that I wanted, something he hadn't let me have before. He taught me, "That's all you deserve. That's all you're good for." Being out on the streets was just a continuation of the same pattern.

WHEN VIOLENCE AND SEX ARE LINKED

For many women abused in violent circumstances, the connection between sex and violence is strong:

> When I was little, my mother would start yelling and screaming and throwing things from one end of the room to the other. And what that usually meant was that I could count on my father being in my room later. So there was a connection established between violent scenes and sex. And that's been repetitive in my adult life. It's the "break up to make up" syndrome. Sex is always better after a fight. That feels really familiar. I know when I was beat up by my last lover, one of the things that really frightened me was that when I was on the floor and she was kicking me, I flashed back on my mother. I had no idea who was hitting me. My lover pulled me up by the hair, and I knew at that very moment that it could only end in two ways. One was me taking the door to the right, which was outside. Or I could take the door to the left, which was to the bedroom.

Changing this pattern is essential to creating a healthy sexuality. If you are in a relationship where violence and sex are linked, you will need to break the connection between the two. Or you may need to leave the relationship altogether (see "Recognizing Bad Relationships" on p. 278).

FANTASIES THAT INCLUDE ABUSE

Many survivors can feel sexually aroused or have orgasms only if sex incorporates some aspect of the abuse they experienced as children. One woman could climax only if she imagined her father's face. One could come only if she was stimulated the way same way her mother had touched her clitoris when she was a child.

Others have orgasms only if they imagine being bound or raped or if they fantasize being the abuser themselves. One survivor described masturbating while reading incest literature: "For weeks on end I compulsively read about incest—*If I Should Die Before I Wake* in one hand and my vibrator in the other."

Most women feel ashamed to admit they have such feelings or fantasies. A fifty-six-year-old psychotherapist, who was tortured with enemas when she was a child, explains:

I felt grossed out by my own sexuality. At times I've felt that my sexuality was grotesque and that it was sick and that it would land me in the hospital. When other people bring up the grosser details of their sexual abuse, I'm fascinated. Everything else just pales and I go right straight to it like a starving dog.

I have tremendous sadomasochistic fantasies which are just beginning to come out after seven and a half years of therapy. That's because of the intense shame. I have hospital fantasies, concentration camp fantasies, slicing people's bodies up fantasies. So naturally I had to keep my sexuality, my life energy, bottled up, because I felt so ashamed and terrified of where that stuff would take me.

When the fantasies first came up in therapy, I experienced a lot of destructive rage at myself. I wanted to kill myself. I was so horrified that those were the things that turned me on. I just wonder if that isn't really the hard core, the pivot of this whole thing—the shame and horror and utter self-despair about being

turned on by terribly abusive, sadistic situations.

If you share this woman's experience, you are not to blame. You did not create these fantasies out of nothing. They were forced on you just as intrusively as those hands, penises, or leers were forced on you during the original abuse.

The context in which we first experience sex affects us deeply. Often there is a kind of imprinting in which all the things that are going on at the same time become woven together. So if you experienced violation, humiliation, and fear at the same time as you experienced arousal and pleasurable genital feelings, these elements twisted together, leaving you with emotional and physical legacies that link pleasure with pain, love with humiliation, desire with an imbalance of power. Shame, secrecy, danger, and the forbidden feel thrilling.

A TRULY CHOSEN SEXUALITY

If you can become aroused only by imagining (or acting out) fantasies of violence, rape, incest, or humiliation, and you want to change these linkages, it is possible to unhook the connection between pain and humiliation and sexual excitement. It is possible to overcome your conditioning and create an authentic sexuality that does not rely on images derived from your abuse or fantasies that you want to leave behind.

Making these changes, however, is difficult. It is hard to relinquish strong, ingrained behaviors that have been linked to feelings of arousal, power, and control, particularly when these behaviors have become habitual or compulsive. Reliable methods for getting turned on or having orgasms are hard to give up. To stop a persistent pattern of sexual arousal, a strong intention is essential, but wanting to stop is not enough. The only way to break your dependence on unwanted patterns of arousal is to commit to deep healing work that deals with the core wound beneath the compulsion. If you do that, over time you can alter these patterns and experience your sexuality in a new and truly chosen way.

Changing the Tapes:
Saphyre's Story

When Saphyre started working on incest, her only way of getting turned on was through rape and sadomasochistic fantasies. After years of acting them out, she decided that she wanted to get rid of them.

I don't believe we're born with our sexuality that way. I knew I had to start from a place of not feeling guilty about the fantasies, in the same way that I stopped feeling guilty about the incest. They were both coming from the same place. Letting go of the guilt was really important. But I wanted to take it further than that. I wanted to stop having them.

I started masturbating more, paying attention to exactly what the core feeling was that made me come. The characters could change, the costumes could change, but what was the core feeling? It was "I'm totally overcome by passion. I'll do anything you want." It was the only way I knew how to deal with my passion. I couldn't afford to take responsibility for it without being overpowered.

I kept working with those fantasies until I could really identify that feeling. The next step was learning to isolate the orgasm, the passion, the intensity, from the fantasy. I had to undo the programming. It was hard to separate the two. I didn't have any support. I was doing this in isolation. I didn't know what the outcome would be, and I wasn't even sure of what I was doing, but I wasn't about to wait till someone came along and told me what to do. I had the belief that I could change.

It helped for me to feel that I *deserved* to have passionate feelings, and that they didn't have to be linked to those fantasies. I came to the point where I really understood that they weren't *my* fantasies. They'd been imposed on me through the abuse. Once I separated the fantasy from the feeling, I'd consciously impose other powerful images on that feeling. And gradually, I began to be able to have orgasms without thinking about the SM, without picturing my father doing something to me. I reprogrammed myself and could have the same intensity of feeling.

SEXUAL HEALING OVER TIME

Sex does not hold equal meaning for everyone. How much you want sex and how much sex you want varies greatly from person to person. As you heal, your genuine level of desire and your authentic attitude toward sex will become clearer, no longer obscured by abuse. For some survivors, sex will be an extremely significant part of their lives. For others, it will be of lesser or little importance.

What you experience sexually today is not necessarily what you'll experience in a year or two. A terrible problem now may seem like a minor annoyance later on. Or sex may get easier for a time, and then hard again, when you hit a deeper layer.

Sex may also have a lot to do with the level of intimacy in your relationship, the dynamics in the relationship, even the particular lover you have. Adrienne has had several lovers since she started working on sexual abuse issues, and her experience with each one was dramatically different:

Before I met Alan, I'd had lots of lovers. The sex wasn't fantastic, but I enjoyed myself, and it was never a big issue. But Alan was the first man I really fell for, and somehow the combination of love and sex did me in. I started to have a hard time with sex, and since sex was really important to Alan, he got more and more upset. He pressured me a lot and the pressure just shut me down entirely. It got so bad, we broke up. I felt like a failure.

After Alan, I was afraid to get involved with anyone. I felt like I wasn't good enough, that something was really wrong with me. But then I met Lance, and after being friends for a while, we

became lovers. I'd warned him about my problems, but he didn't seem to care. Lance was a wonderful lover and never pressured me, and the sex was great between us. He gave me lots of room to explore and let me control the whole thing. I did a lot of healing with him, and left the relationship feeling good about my sexuality.

I thought I had this sex thing licked then, so when I got involved with John, I didn't even tell him. We got into it hot and heavy, and I opened up to feelings of passion I'd never allowed before, and then, boom! Two months later I started having new memories. And sex was the furthest thing from my mind. It was bad. I thought I was finished with all this stuff. But there it was again. At least I didn't hate myself this time. I had a better idea of what to do.

Your experience of sex can change within a single relationship as well. With a new lover, there's often a passionate rush that obscures problems. But as the relationship settles, sexual issues may need attention again. As you risk more emotional intimacy, you may start to shut down sexually. Or you may find that as your trust grows and deepens, you heal on a deep body level, surpassing even your own expectations.

Because it takes a long time to heal sexually, you may wonder whether you're making progress. But even though the process has ups and downs, you are headed in the right direction. If you are putting steady, consistent effort into developing a fulfilling sexuality, have patience:

WHEN SEXUAL HEALING HASN'T WORKED

Sometimes survivors choose celibacy for positive reasons, such as a desire to focus on other parts of their life or to make a spiritual commitment. Other times, they stop having sex because it's too frightening, painful, demanding, or just not worth the difficulties of attempting a sexual relationship. Other survivors have not chosen celibacy; they have tried hard to heal sexually, but haven't been able to establish a healthy, satisfying sex life—or any sex life at all. Pammy explains:

I have been celibate for 13 years now—whether this is "by choice" or not would have to depend upon one's definition of that phrase—because I have never been able to enjoy sex. I've done countless sexuality workshops. I've read a million books and chapters of books. I've watched videos. I've been in support groups. Back when I was still trying with partners, I did all the partner stuff you're supposed to do. I took every imaginable type of bath, lit every possible kind of candle, tried every invented form of bodywork and exercise, explored my body in every way known to womankind. Play therapy. Artwork. You name it. And at this point what I can say is that while most areas of my life have improved appreciably after 25 years of healing work, including 10 years in which I focused on virtually nothing else, my relationship with sex has not.

I said as much in a 12-step survivor meeting the other evening, with four other survivors in the room—all middle-aged or older—each with years of healing behind her. They were all 12-step types who ordinarily wouldn't even *dream* of cross-talking but they ended up doing precisely that. After I said my spiel, they all said, one after the other, completely out of turn, "Ditto!" "Ditto!" "Ditto!" "Ditto!" And then we all laughed to keep from crying and cried to keep from laughing. Two of them are in long-term marriages. One is fairly recently separated. The other one is long-term single like me. But "ditto." Sex? Feh.

Let's face it, for some of us it's like we got a leg blasted off. No amount of communicating or loving touch will ever bring a leg back once it's gone. I ain't dead yet, and maybe I'll still experience a miracle around my sexuality. But at this point, the best way I can think of it is as a phantom limb. The loss is so enormous I don't even have the words for it.

This is a subject that is often passed over in books on healing, and survivors themselves sometimes hesitate to speak of it because they feel ashamed, as if they should have been able to move forward in this primary area of life, and that there is something wrong with them because they haven't. It can be very hard to admit that you have not succeeded in something you've tried very hard to do—and that has meant so much to you.

But silence only leaves us feeling more ashamed and isolated. Deena, who's been married for twenty years, makes that abundantly clear.

Be Careful What You Wish For: Deena's Story

I've healed in so many aspects of my life, but my sexuality . . . I don't even know where I am with that.

When I was in the throes of dealing with my incest twenty years ago, my fiancé left me because I couldn't function sexually. I'd space out, I was having flashbacks all the time. I'd have to stop each time we got into it and of course I wanted to control everything. He couldn't take it and he left. I was devastated and I blamed myself. Now, of course, I can see he had his own problems, but at the time I felt he was perfectly justified in leaving.

Over the next few years I alternated between celibacy and trying to make things work with new lovers. It was a disaster and I had to face my failures again and again. I prayed desperately to meet someone who would love me, yet not make any sexual demands. I wanted to be loved without having to show up sexually.

And you know what? My prayers were answered. I met Steven. We fell in love and got married. He came from a terrible family, too. He wasn't a survivor, but he had his own brand of sexual trauma. I knew right from the start that Steven was the last person in the world who was going to pressure me sexually. He was safe. He was loyal. He wanted children. And he did love me. He couldn't always show it, but he loved me.

We have three kids and we do the whole family thing really well. But we're 20 years into our marriage and we live like roommates. It's been like that for years. It's hard to admit it, because I feel so ashamed, but I live in a celibate marriage. I guess you can say, be careful what you wish for.

SEX WAS NEVER OUR STRONG SUIT

Sex was never our strong suit. Oh there was hot and heavy action the first few months, but then the struggles set in—and they've never stopped. I can't tell you how many couples' therapists we've gone to, how many workshops we've attended, and nothing has ever changed. Sex has always been a minefield for us, and when you live near a minefield, you eventually stop going there. I can't tell you how many miserable nights I've spent, lying next to him, devastated at another failed attempt at sex. Nights like that I'd remember what Marilyn

French once said: "Marriage is lonelier than solitude."

Eventually, Steve and I gave up on sex. We never talked about it. We just stopped trying. Whether he's shut down or I am, I couldn't tell you. I spent years raging and blaming him, but that got tiring after a while. Maybe this whole situation—miserable as it is—serves me just as well.

For years, I thought of leaving Steve, but when you've been married as long as we have, marriage is a lot more than just a love relationship between two people—it's the interrelationship of all the people who rely on us to be together. I don't believe in divorce. I've thought about it for years, and I've come to the conclusion that I don't want to break up my family in the hopes that I might meet someone with whom I could heal and thrive sexually. At this point in my life, I'd just be trading in one set of problems for another. The way I look at it is—everyone has troubles in life. I think I'll stick with my own. And who knows—maybe this is just the best I can do.

Sometimes I feel philosophical about the whole thing and focus on all the things I have to be grateful for, but other times, I feel such despair, I can't tell you. I know there's this whole part of life I'm missing out on—a passionate woman inside of me who is growing old without ever having a chance to express herself.

I'm getting to the age where I'm learning to accept that not everything can be healed and that everything doesn't work out in the end. I focus on appreciating what I have—except on the days when I can't. Those can be really hard days. But they're just part of life. Maybe a bright sexual future is just not in the cards for me this time around. My work right now is to accept that, rather than to fight it.

Don't Blame Yourself

Child sexual abuse is a profound violation—and because the means of violation are sexual, it is inevitable that there will be a strong impact on sexuality. For many survivors, it is possible to heal and to create a deeply gratifying sexuality. For many others, though some limitations and difficulties remain, sex is still a positive and welcome aspect of their lives. But for some survivors, the impact of sexual abuse is too destructive to overcome.

Like everything in the healing process—and in life—though you may feel that your inability to heal sexually is permanent, you may find, in the future, that it isn't. As Pammy says, it would be a miracle. But this wouldn't be the first miracle we've seen in healing from child sexual abuse.

If you have tried to heal sexually and it hasn't happened the way you hoped it would, this doesn't mean that you have failed. Even your sincere attempts are a feat worthy of admiration—you were willing to try in the face of all that might have stopped you. The shame in this situation belongs not to you but to the abuser.

I've had to learn to accept myself. I know I've had experiences that maybe made me a little different, and that might have made my sexual appetite more, might have made my sexual appetite less, it might have made my sexual appetite different, but so what! It's me! Let me enjoy who I am! I feel that within every woman there are a thousand and one women, and it's okay to let each one of them out. The partner will just have to deal. That's all there is to it. Sexuality is not just about getting up and humping every night. It's about exploring who you are and not being afraid of that.

Healing requires work and time, but the rewards are worth it. As one survivor enthusiastically proclaims:

Honest to God, I have a fantastic sex life. Oh honey! When you can say you have an absolutely fucking awesome sex life, that's when you know all your hard work has been for something good.

Although sex was used against you in bitter ways, you can take steps toward reclaiming your sexuality and shape it to reflect your own deepest values.

Sex can be a powerful surge toward creation, like writing a song or choreographing a dance. All of these require absolute attention and presence; all have that great intensity; all bring something new into existence. If you choose to share that opening with a lover, it's a risk, a thrill, and a deep affirmation of trust. You affirm vitality, joy, connection. Your passion becomes a passion for life.

Even without a lover, reclaiming your sexuality is worth it. One older survivor went through a long period of struggle before she realized why:

I don't expect I'll ever be in that kind of relationship again. And just thinking about having a sexual feeling makes me practically want to kill myself. But there's a way I've been looking at it recently— that sex is a part of life, part of being alive. It's a kind of life energy. And even if all I ever do is just feel the feelings in my own body, even if I never act on them, it's still worth it. Can you understand? It's like saying yes to life, yes to being alive.

I'm Awake Now: Dorianne's Story

Dorianne Laux says she began writing poetry "to save my life." The author of four volumes of poetry, she teaches at North Carolina State University in Raleigh where she lives with her husband, poet Joseph Millar. She began her journey of healing sexually more than thirty years ago.[*]

When I was a child, sex was forced on me. It was out of my control. So when I came

---

[*] Dorianne's books include *What We Carry*, a finalist for the National Book Critics Circle Award, and *Facts About the Moon*, winner of the Oregon Book Award. She is co-author of *The Poet's Companion: A Guide to the Pleasures of Writing Poetry*. Several of Dorianne's poems appear in this book. See "What My Father Told Me" on p. 15, "Two Pictures of My Sister" on p. 19, "Girl Child" on p. 131, and "The Lovers" on p. 330. For more of her story, see "Choosing Someone to Tell" on p. 111.

of age and began having sex by choice, I wanted to be the one in control. One way I did that was to create a sexuality that was extreme. I created so much intensity around sex: clawing, grappling, screaming, that it was almost cinematic, and therefore unreal, allowing me to escape the true reality of it.

What I learned is that the reality of sex comes when you're actually communicating, talking, asking questions, taking your time, and are aware of your surroundings and the person you're with—their identity and their vulnerabilities.

My early years of sex weren't like that; it was more hallucinatory, an out-of-body

---

The Lovers

BY DORIANNE LAUX

She is about to come. This time,
they are sitting up, joined below the belly,
feet cupped like sleek hands praying
at the base of each other's spines.
And when something lifts within her
toward a light she's sure, once again,
she can't bear, she opens her eyes
and sees his face is turned away,
one arm behind him, hand splayed
palm down on the mattress, to brace himself
so he can lever his hips, touch
with the bright tip the innermost spot.
And when she finds she *can't* bear it—
not his beautiful neck, stretched and corded,
not his hair fallen to one side like beach grass,
not the curved wing of his ear, washed thin
with daylight, deep pink of the inner body.
What she can't bear is that she can't see his face,
not that she thinks this exactly—she is rocking
and breathing—it's more her body's thought,
opening, as it is, into its own sheer truth.
So that when her hand lifts of its own volition

and slaps him, twice on the chest,
on that pad of muscled flesh just above the nipple,
slaps him twice, fast, like a nursing child
trying to get a mother's attention,
she's startled by the sound,
though when he turns his face to hers—
which is what her body wants, his eyes
pulled open, as if she had bitten—
she does reach out and bite him, on the shoulder,
not hard, but with the power infants have
over those who have borne them, tied as they are
to the body, and so, tied to the pleasure,
the exquisite pain of this world.
And when she lifts her face he sees
where she's gone, knows she can't speak,
is traveling toward something essential,
toward the core of her need, so he simply
watches, steadily, with an animal calm
as she arches and screams, watches the face that,
if she could see it, she would never let him see.

Dorianne Laux, *What We Carry* (Rochester, NY: BOA Editions, 1994).

experience. I wasn't there for a lot of it. I paid attention to the extremity of it and not the subtleties. I didn't do a whole lot of reflection, either. I was like your worst nightmare of a man. It was all very quick: *I got what I want. See you later.* Now I linger.

SEXUAL HEALING CAME NATURALLY

Much of my sexual healing came naturally. It wasn't something I set out to do. The more I became familiar with who I was, with my own value and the value of the people I was with, the less I was able to depend on what I used to do sexually in the past. It didn't work any longer because I was stopped short by my awareness that allowing another human being to enter my body was a sacred act.

I've had many sexual partners and I never ever had anyone who was anything less than kind or understanding. All along the way, they've been caring in different ways depending on where I was in the process. In the beginning they were compassionate when I'd cry or get frightened or want them to stop.

I've had men respond with outrage for what had happened to me, as well as with a deep concern for me, and they were very vocal about not wanting to add to my suffering or have me suffer inadvertently at their hands. They showed incredible patience and kindness.

As time went on, I didn't want to discuss it with my partners anymore. I felt I knew enough about it that I didn't need to engage them or ask for their understanding because

I had my own. I was able to give myself the comfort and patience I needed. I didn't need to bother them or interrupt their thoughts with it.

SPEAKING OUT ABOUT SEX

I consciously began talking about sexuality in my everyday life, in my teaching, and in my poetry. Sex became just one of the things that I did in my life's journey, one thing I did in a day's interaction in the world. Sex is an important part of my life, but it's just a part of my life. In a way it lost some of its specialness, but what I've gained is integration.

Writing poems about my sexuality is one way of reclaiming it for myself. I find a good deal of comfort and grounding in writing about sexuality. It's also a way to make a political statement about the place of sexuality in our ordinary female lives. Yes, we clean the house, go to work, eat dinner, have sex, brush our teeth. Or maybe we brush our teeth before we have sex. Either way, it's an integrated activity that lives inside our daily adult lives and there's no fear or shame attached to it.

I'm awake now and participate in sex, rather than being a victim of my father's abuse. I've turned the tables, balanced the scales. In line with that, I also notice a number of my sex poems are about me being the aggressor, the one who instigates, the powerful observer, the witness, the stronger one. These poems grew out of my experiences, but they also helped me to attend more closely to those experiences.

I think that you can actually change your patterns of thinking and feeling using this method. It has certainly worked for me. I once thought I would never stop having nightmares about my father, but they did stop. I believe I've rerouted my brain and those old pathways shriveled up from lack of use. I shifted my focus and my focus shifted me. What I share with my husband now is built upon the work of the past, but has everything to do with the relationship we enjoy in the present.

Children and Parenting

"My kids gave me hope. My kids would laugh, be crazy and stupid, and pull me out of it: 'Okay, back to the future.' Feeling totally responsible for these kids has really been an incentive to get better. I wouldn't have made it without them. I wanted them to have a responsible adult taking care of them, to be able to say, 'This is where it stops. This is the end of it.'"

*P*arents are not the only adults who have nurturing family relationships with children. Many of the concepts in this chapter also apply to extended family and to friends who are chosen family.

Being around children can be an inspiring, rewarding part of life. That's just as true for survivors as it is for everyone else. Yet for survivors, relationships with children offer some special benefits. Children can teach you that the abuse wasn't your fault. They can help you get in touch with the child within. They can motivate you to heal, to keep on keeping on. They offer you an opportunity to have a positive experience of family life. For thirty-five-year-old Ella, having children has been an integral part of her healing:

I nurture them and I get it back. They love me, and you can't coerce that out of a kid. You can coerce sex out of kids, but you can't coerce something as pure as love. That's what keeps me going all the time. I look at my kids and know that I really *am* a survivor. Being able to parent gives me a perspective on how well I really am. Just the way they are shows me that I'm okay. It makes me feel that I'm a real winner. I can have anything I want. I can do absolutely anything. Being around them shows me that all the time.

But being close to children can also bring up unresolved feelings, restimulate difficult memories, put you face-to-face with the ways you're like your parents, or remind you of your own vulnerability in ways that may be painful to recognize.

THE CHALLENGES OF BEING A PARENT

Most survivors face basically the same problems as anyone else in trying to be a good parent. With infants, there's the lack of sleep, the twenty-four-hour-a-dayness of it, the necessity of putting another person's needs before your own. With toddlers, there's constant movement and a strong will opposing your own. As children grow, their needs change and you must make decisions constantly about matters both small and large—how late they should be allowed to stay up, how old they should be to ride the bus alone, what to do when your thirteen-year-old comes home drunk from a party.

Many survivors function very well as parents. Though they may be having a hard time in other areas of their lives, they find that they are able to be nurturing and stable in relationship to their children.

When she became a mother, Laura discovered that being sexually abused had less impact on her parenting than she thought it might:

Having kids was the best thing I ever did. I kept expecting a lot to come up because of my own abuse—memories, being overprotective, confusion about boundaries—but it never really did. There are lots of ways I've been challenged and had to grow as a parent, but

very few of them have had to with the fact that I was sexually abused.

Many women who were abused, neglected, or have had poor parenting become capable mothers themselves. The fact that they had poor role models doesn't stop them from doing well with their own kids. In fact, their difficult histories sometimes give them a reference point from which to make healthy decisions. As one mother put it: "I knew what I didn't want to do. When in doubt, I did the opposite of what they did with me."

Another survivor explained her approach:

I parent my kids very intentionally. I knew what kinds of things kids needed, that I didn't get—things like good touching, good physical contact, talking to them like real people—but I didn't know how to provide them. I had to teach myself to do those things. I watched how a couple of good families worked. I did a lot of reading. I actively fantasized about what a good family would be like. Initially it was awkward, but now it feels natural.

Being a parent is one of the most complex and demanding jobs anyone can undertake. Under the best circumstances, it's hard. If you have to teach yourself from scratch, it's even harder:

I wasn't sure of myself and what I was doing with my boys. I didn't have a memory of the right things to use as a base in my parenting. The base I had was of the wrong things, the things not to do. So I couldn't go with what I *felt* was right; I had to do what I *thought* was right. I had to be awake all the time to make sure I didn't hurt my kids. I had to be very aware.

If you're unsure of yourself, you can read books, talk to people whose parenting you respect, take a parenting class, or start a parent's support group.* Other parents, who listen, share their own experiences, and offer suggestions, can be an invaluable source of support and guidance. Laura and Ellen, and their respective partners, were members of a mothers' group that met monthly for many years. As Ellen explained:

Whenever my partner and I were unsure how to handle a difficult situation, or one of my kids wanted permission to do something and my partner thought one way and I thought another, we asked the Moms for advice. The collective wisdom of that dozen women was formidable. We rarely bothered to argue over parenting questions anymore after that. Instead, when in doubt, we simply "took it to the Moms."

Making mistakes and trying out new approaches is a natural part of parenting. As your children grow, you grow, too. While it's not easy, learning to become a good parent—in your own estimation—is a rich and rewarding experience:

Parenting is something I conquered. At first I thought I would be a wonderful parent and that I could undo all the wrongs my parents had done to me. And then I realized that was an absolute farce. And I was able to really pull out and say to myself, "You can do it. It's not going to be as easy as you thought it was, but you can just plod through it, day after day, and have little tiny victories along the way." That's real affirming to me as a human being, that I was able to do a right thing. I committed to it, and I was actually able to carry it through.

While most of the issues you will deal with as a mother are issues you share in common with all parents, there may be some questions that are more specifically linked to being a survivor of child sexual abuse. The rest of this chapter addresses some of these specific challenges.

TALKING TO CHILDREN ABOUT YOUR ABUSE

Children are very perceptive. If you are angry, distracted, or in crisis, they will sense it. Pretending nothing is wrong will only make them feel crazy and confused. Without facts, children draw their own conclusions, generally assuming that they are the cause of the problem.

---

* If you are the parent of young children, we recommend *Becoming the Parent You Want to Be* by Laura Davis and Janis Keyser (New York: Broadway Books, 1996). Also see "Parenting" on p. 571 of the Resource Guide.

If you are going through a hard time, let your children know they're not to blame.

Whether to talk to your children about your abuse is a personal—and often difficult—decision. You need to use your best judgment about whether an honest conversation would be helpful or harmful to them. If you feel unsure, you may want to consult with a counselor or other parents. Sometimes just talking over your concerns and feelings can help you know your own mind.

If you decide to tell your children about your own abuse, talk to them in ways that are appropriate to their age. They do not need detailed descriptions. Instead, make a general statement that reassures them and speaks to *their* needs: "I was hurt by my father when I was a little girl. That's why I've been going to so many meetings and crying a lot. I want you to know that if I seem sad, it doesn't have anything to do with you. I'm getting help now so I can feel better."

If your children want to know more, they will ask. Answer questions honestly, but provide only the information you think they need at the time instead of overwhelming them with aspects of the abuse they might not want to hear or be able to deal with.

If you're not comfortable answering certain questions, communicate that in a respectful way, such as, "I'm not ready to talk about it more now, but I really did want to tell you a little about how I've been feeling, so you won't think my upset has anything to do with you. When I'm ready, I'll answer more of your questions."

It was important to Cassondra to talk to all her children about her abuse:

When the abuse finally came out, I said, "No more lies. No more hiding." I told my kids what had happened to me in terms that they could understand at the time. I told them, "We can't go see your grandpa and grandma no more." And they asked, "Why not? How come I can't see all my cousins?" My son grew up with them. He didn't understand why he couldn't see any of his family anymore, except for his dad's side. That's when I started telling them my truth. Where's Mom on Monday night? She's at her group where she talks about hard issues.*

A mother of five grown children describes the impact of her disclosure on her family:

I told my kids about the incest when I was working at the rape crisis center. My kids were surprised and supportive and then mixed up in their feelings toward their grandfather. "I can't believe he did that." Or, "He's real nice to me." And they've continued to be mixed in their feelings toward him.

Two of my daughters live in the same town as him and he takes them out to breakfast. They know all about the incest. They say, "Granddaddy's been good to us. We don't like what he did, but we're willing to see him." So they visit him, and at the same time they've been understanding about why I don't.

If your children say that they don't want to hear any more about your abuse or your heal-

---

* For more of Cassondra's story see "Cassondra Espinoza" on p. 492 of "Courageous Women."

ing, respect their boundaries. It's best to tell them the basics and then take your cues from them.

As with all important issues, abuse and its effects aren't things you can bring up once and be done with. Talking with your children is an ongoing process, part of creating a family environment of openness and sharing.

SETTING BOUNDARIES

If your own boundaries were violated as a child, you may have difficulty maintaining appropriate boundaries with your children now, or you may be confused about what is appropriate:

When I had my children, I experienced real bonding for the first time—a physical, sexual, emotional bond with these babies. It was just overpowering and I was scared to death that I was going to engulf them. For years it frightened me.

Clear emotional boundaries enable you to experience yourself as separate from your children. You realize that they don't think and feel as you do, nor should they. Their interests and needs are different from yours and don't necessarily reflect on you. Assuming your own individuality and allowing your children theirs is respectful and healthy.

It's not appropriate to use your children as confidants or to look to them for sympathy or advice. Your emotional intimacy with them should be to meet *their* needs, not yours. If you're unsure about your emotional boundar-

ies with your children, pay attention to their responses. If your children are pushing you away, let them move out from you a little more. Be available if they want to come close but don't clutch them to you.

One single mother describes her progress in maintaining healthy emotional boundaries with her teenage son:

I make conscious decisions about how much of my feelings to share with my son, and how. It's tempting to never share anything because I'm afraid of saying too much. That's what my mother did with me and I felt overwhelmed by the intensity of her emotions. I certainly don't want to repeat that, but I know that not sharing anything isn't right either. What kind of a message does it give if your child never sees you react with feeling to events in your life?

So I carefully say just a little from time to time. I say such and such happened at work and I'm really disappointed. Or maybe a guy I've been dating has dumped me and I tell my son that my feelings are hurt. I sometimes feel like I'm in a play, saying the right lines of a mother—and sometimes my words sound stilted. But I don't get hung up on that. I feel like I'm doing a pretty good job, all things considered.

SEXUAL BOUNDARIES

Many survivors feel uncomfortable, confused, or worried when engaging in daily caretaking routines with young children—diapering, bathing, and dressing. This discomfort falls into several different categories. You may take pleasure in your child's physical closeness and wonder if it's okay to feel that way, or a heightened awareness of your children's vulnerability during these activities may bring up feelings of fear or even anger. Painful memories of the ways abuse was woven into your physical care when you were a child may arise, or you may feel the actual impulse to hurt or abuse your own child in the way you were abused, or in another way.

It's important to differentiate between these responses so that you can determine whether your feelings are in the normal range or if you've crossed (or could cross) a line that would put your children in danger. You need to talk about your concerns and address your fears and confusion, so you can get the information, support, and help you need.

Yet this can be an extremely scary thing to do. Even in a survivor support group or with a counselor, broaching this subject—with all its inherent confusion and shame—can still feel like breaking a terrible taboo. You may feel like you're the only survivor who has ever had to struggle with these concerns, but you're not. Many survivors worry that they will act inappropriately with children or be unable to set proper limits:

> I have to be constantly aware of my boundaries. Whenever I'm being physical and affectionate with a little kid, I have to think, "Is this okay? Am I crossing over his boundaries? Is this getting into anything sexual?"

If you've been abused and your own boundaries were violated, these are natural fears. But once you are actively engaged in healing, it is extremely unlikely that you will start abusing children if you haven't already done so. (If you have been abusive to children, read "If You've Been Abusive" on p. 347.) If you continue to be afraid, see a counselor to determine if there's a real danger or if you're just scared. Being scared is okay. And common. Acting out isn't.

What's Normal, What Isn't

It is normal for parents to have sensual feelings toward their children. Taking pleasure in physical closeness to your children—the softness of their skin, their sweet smell, their generous shows of affection—is a natural part of mothering. Caretaking, especially of small children, is very physical, and it's not unusual for mothers to feel an occasional sexual response. But being sexually aroused by your child can feel extremely frightening to a survivor of child sexual abuse.

If these erotic feelings are fleeting and are neither consistent nor compelling, they're probably within a normal range. If, however, sexual desire for your children is strong or persistent, or if you are feeling any temptation to act on these impulses, it's essential that you get help. Make an appointment with a therapist or another professional immediately.

Don't act on these feelings. And don't talk about them with your child. Talking about your sexual feelings for a child is sexual abuse.

It Is Always Your Job to Set the Limits

Children test limits, sexually as well as in other areas. They experiment with boundaries regarding intimacy, closeness, and physical affection. They might try to touch you in sexual areas or try to get you to touch them. If your child is testing you in these ways, set limits firmly while staying affectionate:

When my son was eight he kept trying to French-kiss me. I guess he saw me kissing my lover and was interested. Also, on TV there's plenty of all that and it's made to look pretty exciting. I had to tell him over and over that he couldn't do that with me. I said I knew he was really curious and wanted to try it out but that he'd have to wait until he was older and then experiment with someone his own age. He was incredibly persistent until finally I insisted he stop asking. He even cried and begged, "If you let me do it just once, I promise I'll never ask again." I told him absolutely no, but said he could ask for something else—he could have three wishes. He asked for a roll of Scotch tape, a lullaby at bedtime, and Play-Doh.

This story illustrates the innocence of a child's "sexual desires" and underlines the need for the adult to be clear about what is and isn't appropriate physical contact between parent and child.

HEALTHY TOUCH

Children have a right to say no to touch, even if it's yours. Let your children know that their bodies are their own and that no one should touch them without permission. Unless you're sure your child wants a hug, ask, "Can I give you a hug?" Or say, "Tell Uncle Fred good night," instead of "Give Uncle Fred a kiss." These are ways of giving a child control. Affection should meet their needs, not the needs of the adults around them.

On the other hand, don't be so cautious that you deny children their basic need for physical affection:

I don't touch people, and I don't like being touched. When it came to my kids, I had to make a conscious decision that they were going to get the benefit of the physical contact that I didn't get. Once I decided they would, I had to say, "Okay, who's going to do it?" And it looked like it had to be me. So that became part of my healing, having these babies and touching them.

As you learn to nurture yourself, you will find that you are better able to give to your children. As you begin to trust your capacity to set appropriate boundaries, you will feel more comfortable giving them the warm, safe touching they need. And you'll be able to experience the pleasure of being close, too.

Sometimes at night when I'm reading to my daughter before bed or kissing her good night, I'm so touched by how good she feels. Snuggled up soft against me, with that sweet child smell. I love the physical closeness of mothering.

PROTECTING YOUR CHILDREN

If a survivor hasn't remembered her abuse or acknowledged its effects, she may not be able to recognize signs that her children are in danger or respond effectively. One woman, who'd forgotten her own abuse, described an incident that happened to her daughter when she was six:

A young man in church started paying attention to her and of course she ate it up. He'd come over to the house and ask to take her out on rides. They'd go to his house and he'd take pictures of her. We always let her go with him. This went on every day. Then we'd see the pictures. She'd be up a tree, her dress pulled up, her panties exposed, in a very seductive pose. I'd feel uncomfortable looking at the pictures, *but my husband and I knew absolutely nothing about child molesting.*

It wasn't until a friend called to say he was doing it with her daughter, too, that we went to a deacon in the church to put a stop to it.

When survivors are faced with the fact that their children are in danger or are being abused, they sometimes freeze and are unable to act:

When I heard that my brother had molested one of my girls, I blanked out. I was a total zombie. It was like I was back in bed as a nine-year-old. It was like trying to run in a dream. I could hear myself saying, "He did? Isn't that terrible?" My daughter was screaming at me, "You've got to do something!" And I didn't know what to do. All I knew how to do was avoid.

It's essential to do your own emotional healing so that blocked memories or fears don't obscure your vision or keep you from acting on your child's behalf. As difficult as it is to break lifelong patterns of ignoring, denying, and hiding, this is what is required of us as parents.

OVERPROTECTION

Overprotection is an exaggeration of the healthy desire to keep children safe. If you're afraid, especially if you're unaware of the source of your fears, it's easy to become obsessive:

I always scrutinized anyone I left my children with. If just a hair was out of place, I wanted to know about it. I wouldn't leave my kids if I could help it. I never let my husband bathe my kids. I didn't think then that I didn't trust him, but I clearly didn't. All this was before I remembered anything. I never knew why I took all those precautions. I just did.

You may try to keep your children safe by limiting their activities and keeping them near you, but children should have the mobility and freedom appropriate for their age. You need to overcome your fears, not pass them on.

> I remember going through this thing about my daughter wearing shorts and trying not to let her do that. Luckily I have this friend who is like my brother, and he told me how unreal I was being about this whole thing. He said, "Now we know you have a certain amount of things that bother you. Do you want to give her a trip about her own sexuality because you won't let her wear those shorts?" He's really helped me keep on track with my children on little things like that.

If you're uncertain about the limits you're setting, talk with other people. Getting feedback from a variety of parents (and maybe a professional as well) can be a useful way to gauge whether you're being overprotective. Ultimately, you may not draw the line in the same place, but hearing their views can help you become clearer about your own.

Although wanting to protect your children is a natural desire, you need to distinguish what you can protect them from and what you can't. No matter how careful you are, you cannot regulate every aspect of your child's life. Children spend time in situations and with people you cannot control. For this reason, it is essential that you teach your children personal safety skills. You must prepare them as best you can, take a deep breath, and let them go.

TEACHING CHILDREN SAFETY SKILLS

Parents sometimes hesitate to talk to their children about sexual abuse because they don't want to frighten them. But in reality, children are aware of danger. With the extensive coverage of sexual abuse in the media and the faces of missing children appearing daily on milk cartons, children are already afraid. And fear does not help children to be powerful. You were scared when you were a child, and fear did not save you from being abused.

Teaching children personal safety skills will replace their fear with self-confidence. Some excellent books and programs are described under "Safe, Strong, and Free" in the Resource Guide.*

Children need to know that they have choices, that they can say no, and that they are capable of protecting themselves in a variety of ways.

> When my daughter was little, I told her that she should tell me if she ever felt funny about the way anyone talked to her or touched her, and that she had a right to her own body. I told her no one should ever touch her body in a way that was uncomfortable, even her mom or dad.

---

* See "Safe, Strong, and Free" on p. 571 of the Resource Guide.

SEX PLAY BETWEEN CHILDREN

It's normal for children to engage in some sex play with their peers. Many parents feel uncomfortable and embarrassed when they discover such play and feel unsure how to respond. For survivors, this can be a particularly confusing arena. You may worry that your child is being abused or is being abusive to another child. * *And it may be particularly difficult for you to determine what constitutes healthy, appropriate sex play between children.*

These guidelines, adapted from Laura Davis's book Becoming the Parent You Want to Be: A Sourcebook of Strategies for the First Five Years,† *describe ways to respond when young children are engaged in mutual sex exploration and play.*

Parents are often at a loss when they find their child playing doctor or engaging in sex play with another child. Many parents freeze or panic. They immediately think of adult sex or molestation, making it difficult for them to recognize what children are actually trying to explore.

When dealing with sex play between children, there are a few basic goals to keep in mind. Children need to learn about safety, setting limits, family rules, and rules about what's socially appropriate. Also, children's curiosity needs to be respected.

Your experiences, perspective, and values will all influence how you feel about your children's sex play. In some families, such explorations are accepted openly. In others, sex play between children is not allowed. Regardless of whether you allow the play or not, here are some guidelines that can help you achieve these goals:

- **Respect children's curiosity.** Whether you allow the play or not, respect your children's curiosity. Say something like "Looks like you're interested in each other's bottoms, but I'd like you to put on your pants now" or "Seems like you're curious about what your vulvas look like. It's okay with me for you to look, if it's okay with each of you."

- **Find out more about what the children are actually doing.** Ask questions. "Looks like you're really curious about each other's bodies. What have you found out?" Or "I see you're under the blanket. Is this a special game you're playing? Tell me about it."

- **Keep communicating.** When children know that they can talk to us, we're better able to help them if they're

---

* See "When Children Molest" on p. 113 for information on situations where one child is sexually abusing another.

† Laura Davis and Janis Keyser, *Becoming the Parent You Want to Be: A Sourcebook of Strategies for the First Five Years* (New York: Broadway Books, 1996).

struggling with confusing information or a hurtful situation.

- **Establish some limits and safeguards.** Tell children what is and isn't allowed: "You can only *look* at your friend's body," or "You can only explore your body with *your* hands. No one else is allowed to do that."

- **Teach children to ask permission.** Say, "Your friend has to ask you before he touches any part of your body" or "Anyone gets to say no to any part of the play they don't like."

- **Work with kids on saying no.** Say, "It looks like this game is okay with you now. How would you tell Sandra if you didn't want to play this game anymore?" or "Roberto, is this a game you still want to play, or would you like to play something else instead?"

- **Know the children who are involved.** Sex play can become problematic if one of the children has been sexually abused or had an unhealthy experience. This may lead that child to bring a different level of knowledge or intensity to the play. Children who've been hurt around sex often try to come to terms with violation through play. They might try out some things with another child that are unsafe or inappropriate.

- **Know the other family.** Another thing that is crucial to consider is the other family's level of comfort. Parents should communicate with each other about what is allowed.

- **Be on the lookout for any power imbalance.** Children sometimes do things they're uncomfortable with just because they're fascinated with an older child, or a child might go along because she's afraid of losing the friendship.

- **Sex play is unlikely to be the first time you'd see such a power imbalance in the relationship.** It's a dynamic that would probably show up in other areas first. Ask yourself, "Can each child say no in other aspects of this friendship?" If one of the children consistently gives in, that's a red flag that there might be a problem during sex play too. It's important to help children deal with the power imbalance in all areas of their relationship.

- **Give children other play options.** Sometimes children will get into a pattern of "doctor play," "marriage play," or some other kind of sex play with a particular friend. If you're concerned about children being stuck in that kind of play, structure some other activities when those children get together.

YOUR CHILDREN SHOULD KNOW

This information is taken from Your Children Should Know *by Flora Colao and Tamar Hosansky, an excellent resource for teaching children how to feel both safe and empowered.*

To teach children the skills to protect themselves, we must talk frankly. Personal safety strategies can be presented in the same manner as fire and traffic safety—with straightforward, practical information and explanations.

Self-defense is anything that enables children to escape dangerous situations. It can be crossing the street if being followed, not answering questions over the telephone, refusing to open the door to a stranger, saying no, screaming and yelling, making a scene, calling for help, running away, talking calmly to an attacker, pretending to cooperate with an attacker, or physically resisting an assault. It is a state of mind and body that allows children to feel comfortable and secure. It's the belief that their own safety is more important than the feelings of the assailant. And it's the knowledge that they're in control of their own well-being.

Children need to be given rights over their bodies and feelings in order to prevent abuse effectively. The following rights are crucial.

A Child's Bill of Personal Safety Rights

1. The right to trust one's instincts and funny feelings.

2. The right to privacy.

3. The right to say no to unwanted touch or affection.

4. The right to question adult authority and to say no to adult demands and requests.

5. The right to lie and not answer questions.

6. The right to refuse gifts.

7. The right to be rude or unhelpful.

8. The right to run, scream, and make a scene.

9. The right to bite, hit, or kick.

10. The right to ask for help.

When introducing these rights to children, be simple and concrete, using language they can understand. Encourage children to think for themselves by using imaginative or what-if games, role-playing, fantasies, or incidents from your own childhood. Always acknowledge the children's contribution, thus helping them to develop the ability to do spontaneous problem solving in unexpected situations.

And she did have an incident happen to her. She and a girlfriend were playing outside, and a man offered them some candy and asked them to get into the car. As it turned out, they both ran in the house and told me. Later the police came. They identified the man, and he was indeed a child molester they'd been looking for for a couple of months. So they were instrumental in getting him caught and sent to jail.

I made sure they were very proud of what they had done, of how strong and brave they had been. I told them they had saved a lot of other kids, and that they were the heroines of the block. My daughter still talks about it, about how she did the right thing. She helps other kids now. She's very strong.

DEALING WITH YOUR FAMILY OF ORIGIN OR YOUR ABUSER

If you were abused by a family member, it's essential that you protect your child from possible abuse by that person. It's your responsibility to make decisions that keep your child safe. Other considerations—such as maintaining family ties, providing an extended family for your child, not hurting people's feelings, not wanting to make waves, guilt—are all secondary to your child's safety.

Many a survivor has been certain that her abuser only was interested in abusing her and

would never abuse her child—only to find out that this was not true. Even if you plan to keep a watch over your child, many abusers are devious and will use any opportunity to molest a child.

In the rare cases when an abuser has acknowledged the abuse, shown remorse, sought therapy, and has truly transformed his life, *carefully supervised* visits may be an option. But it's best to err on the side of caution when your child's well-being is at stake.

If you discontinue visits with a family member (or if you never allowed visits in the first place), tell your children why in a way that is appropriate for their age. And if your relatives are unsuitable as a healthy extended family, consider surrogates—friends who can be loving companions and role models for your children (see "Relating to Your Family Now—and Over Time," p. 352).

IF YOUR CHILD IS BEING ABUSED

If your child tells you he or she has been abused, believe it. If you suspect that your partner, the person who abused you, other family members, or your child's caretakers are being abusive, take action immediately. Countless women have been sure they were the only ones to be abused, only to find out years later that their own children, grandchildren, or even great-grandchildren had become victims as well.

Barbara Hamilton was in her late fifties, at the start of her own healing process, when she discovered that there had been extensive abuse in her family:

My own healing came to a screeching halt when I heard about my daughters. The pain of that whole thing, I don't know how to describe it. I just felt so much worse about them than I did about me. That's the trap you're in as a mother. I felt flattened by the news. It just knocked me out. I didn't have the *umph* left to deal with my own abuse.

These men, starting with my father, were stealing my childhood, and were stealing my children's childhood, and were stealing everything about us, even our memories. I felt like there was some big force trying to obliterate us from the earth. It was all one great big river of male abuse. We were all just tumbling down the rapids together and there was no possible way I could separate myself from them, because they were littler, and they were going to drown sooner.[*]

Even though it is devastating to find out that your children are being abused, *it is essential that you muster the strength to protect them.*[†] Take your son out of day care. Stop visiting your father. Don't let your brother babysit anymore. Don't think that the abuse was an isolated incident that won't happen again. It will.

It's essential that you break the silence and get help. Ideally, you should choose a professional who specializes in child sexual abuse, so your family can be evaluated and receive skilled, compassionate support. Counselors (as well as teachers, medical personnel, and most clergy) are mandated reporters; by law they must report suspected abuse to child protective agencies, who may also notify police. A therapist who is experienced with child sexual abuse, and who knows your local child protective agency can be an ally who helps you navigate the system. If you get your family into counseling *before* the local child protective agency is alerted, then your therapist can help you make the report, oversee the process, and hopefully minimize further trauma to your child.

While reporting the abuse may be frightening, it is important for your child, for your family, and even for the offender. Reporting makes a clear statement to the child that he or she is not to blame and deserves protection and that the abuser will be held accountable. An abuser who is in the home will be removed in many, but not all, jurisdictions. Having a case go through the criminal justice system is the only way most offenders ever get into treatment.

GETTING AWAY FROM THE ABUSER

I remember when I was a kid saying, "I'll never be like my mother. I'll never let those things happen to my kid. I'll stand up to my husband." But in retrospect, I can see that I was doing exactly the same thing. I thought I had broken away from all of them, that nothing was ever going to happen like it had to them. Yet it did.

---

[*] For more of Barbara Hamilton's story, see "It's Never Too Late: Barbara Hamilton's Story" on p. 61.

[†] *Helping Your Child Recover from Sexual Abuse* by Caren Adams is an excellent book. For this and other resources, see "If Your Child Is Abused" on p. 577 of the Resource Guide.

I was so blind. I married someone ex-actly like my father. He battered me and molested our daughter.

If you're living with a molester, it's essential that you take steps to protect your child im-mediately.

Breaking the Chain:
Dana's Story

Dana, the daughter of a survivor, the mother of a survivor, and a survivor herself, took her ex-husband to court after he molested their daughter, Christy. She talks about the resistance she met in her family and the isolation she felt when she took action to break the cycle of repeated abuse.*

My mother-in-law and I were in court one day and she said, "Dana, why are you making such a big deal out of this?"

And I said, "Do you know what he's done?"

"Look," she said, "Jack slapped me around and he slapped the kids around and I'm okay." She refused to connect the fact that her son was doing it to his wife and to his child with the fact that she had allowed it to hap-pen to her and her children.

Then when I was having dinner with my grandmother, my mother's mother, I was trying to get her to tell me more about when I was little. And she said, "Why do you have

to bring up these things? Does it really make a difference?"

And I said, "It really does make a differ-ence." And then I asked about what happened in her family when she was young. She said, "Well, my mother and father fought a lot. My mother was always antagonizing my father and he would have to hit her to make her stop. She really brought it on herself."

Those are the two women who are the matriarchs in the families that came together and created Christy. There's so much com-placency. No one is willing to look at the fact that abuse formed the way we behave now, the way we react in relationships, the way we treat our children, and the messages we give our children about their self-worth. No won-der it's going on generation after generation.

And I can't believe that I'm the only one in these two families that include my grandmother, who had nine children, and my mother-in-law, who was one of eleven children, and my father-in-law, who was one of eleven children, who is saying anything. Of all those people and all those people's children and grandchildren, I'm the only one who's saying, "Hey, you think maybe we have a problem here?" It makes me feel incredibly alone. But someone had to stop the cycle. And I did.

IF YOU'VE BEEN ABUSIVE

When I was fourteen, I was babysitting for a little girl who was around two. I was diapering her, and she was lying there were

---

* For more of Dana's story, see "When You Become a Mother" on p. 78 and "You've Got Two Choices: Dana's Story" on p. 362.

her legs spread, and I felt furious with her for how vulnerable she was. "You can't do that! You can't be a little girl in the world like that!" And what I ended up doing was touching her vagina and putting my finger inside. I did it for a minute or two, and I was furious at her the whole time. I hated her for being vulnerable. And I had this warped feeling that I was protecting her. "You can't go around being this vulnerable, so I'm going to do something to make you less vulnerable. That way, when the *real* child molesters come along, you won't be hurt by it."

I had the assumption this happened to every little girl, and that didn't stop me from hurting a child. I had to smash the vulnerability I saw in her. It frightened me. It was that simple.

Women and girls do abuse children—emotionally, sexually, and physically. When a woman's own experience of child sexual abuse remains buried, there is a chance that she will repeat the pattern:

My earliest memory of my mother is her trying to drown me when she was washing my hair. She was holding my head under the faucet, crying, saying, "I can't love you. I'm sorry. I can't love you." I have no reason to believe I received any warmth or comfort from her as an infant. She was always drunk and beat me all the time. When I was eighteen she told me she'd never loved me. My grandmother said my mother openly hated me while I was in her womb.

I got pregnant at seventeen to get away from home. I had a baby boy and settled down with my husband to raise him. Less than a year later, I got pregnant again. This time it was a daughter. And I hated her while she was in my womb. I didn't want her. I was desperately ill the whole pregnancy. I vomited all nine months. I kept trying to miscarry.

She was born and I still didn't like her. I just knew I couldn't love her. I never held her close. I wouldn't care for her. She cried constantly. I started abusing her right away. I'd take my daughter and slam her down on the sofa. The rage was uncontrollable. I never made the connection to what my mother had done to me. At that point, I hadn't even remembered it. And all the time I was abusing her, I was being a great mother to my son.

Admitting that you have abused a child is terrifying. This is why abusers almost always deny it. Yet, if you have abused a child, it is imperative that you acknowledge the seriousness of your actions, get into counseling right away, and take responsibility for the consequences of what you've done. If the child is still under your care, it's important to get that child into therapy with someone trained to work with abused children. Don't assume the abuse won't have a lasting impact. You have only to look at your own life to know that abuse keeps affecting you until you deal with it. Good early intervention can help children heal now and save them from carrying damaging effects into their adult lives.

IF YOU'RE FEELING SHAKY

If you haven't abused a child but feel you're on the verge—either sexually, physically, or emotionally—get help right away:

> One day when I was taking Jerri to her baby-sitter's, she started crying that she didn't want to go. I was already late for work. She was screaming and throwing a fit. I finally got so angry, I picked up her box of crayons and threw them at her. She was absolutely terrified.
>
> I took her to the baby-sitter and when I was about a minute away I turned back, got her, sat down with her on the step and said, "What I just did was really terrible and no mother should ever treat her daughter like that." I told her I knew I'd been mean to her for a long time, and that I was going to get help so I wouldn't do it anymore.
>
> I got in touch with a family counselor who would see Jerri alone for play therapy and then would see the two of us together. It really helped our relationship a lot. The pressure was let out.

Many communities have groups for stressed parents. Ending your isolation can dramatically improve your capacity to cope. Don't be ashamed to ask for help. Admitting your need and dealing with your problem is an honorable way to protect your child and take care of yourself.

If you feel you can't control yourself with your children, consider placing them in a temporary safe home away from you. Protecting children has to come first. As Jennierose relates:

> I left my children with my second husband when they were four and a half and eleven months old. I couldn't have taken care of them. I was extremely disturbed. Looking back, I now know why I left them when I did. Because four and a half was when the worst part of my life started. And a few days before I decided to leave, I found myself hitting my son for the first time. I was pounding on his back and I knew that I could really injure him, like my parents had injured me, if I stayed. So really, I left because I loved them and didn't want to damage them, and I would have damaged them.

IT'S NOT TOO LATE

Children challenge us to change and grow—no matter how old we are, no matter what mistakes have been made. For years after Jennierose left her children, she was full of guilt and remorse. She repeatedly tried to find them, but every time she came close, their father and stepmother moved. Finally her children came to her:

> When my eldest son was eighteen, he came looking for me. He stayed for a week. And then my younger son, who was fourteen, came and stayed for a couple of weeks.

We had years when we weren't in contact, but in the last few years we've gotten really close. My older son asked me to tell him my life history: "I just want to know about you." And I wrote him a whole series of letters. I told him everything. Since then we've developed a real closeness, because I don't have to protect what I say. They know who I am.

I've asked them if they were angry that I left them. Both of them said they were, but they're not anymore, because they understand. There was no way I could have cared for them. I left to protect them.

Their stepmother has since died. I'm grateful to her for raising my children, but her death has made it more possible for me to be their mother again. Since my first granddaughter was born, I've stayed in close contact with both my sons, and that's been really wonderful. I have my children back.

Even when children are grown, you still have an impact on their lives. The opportunity to be nurturing and supportive, to be an inspiring role model, and to contribute to your children's healing continues.

And for some survivors, healing the pain with their children is part of coming to a resolution with their own abuse:

I'm standing in the middle between the generations. I can't face my parents and heal it that way. Maybe I can turn to my children and heal it in the other direction. That would be making an end to it.

MOTHERHOOD AS A PATH TO HEALING

Even though survivors can face some specific and difficult challenges as parents, most feel that the rewards of raising children far outweigh the difficulties. And we have been impressed over and over again with the quality of parenting that many survivors have achieved. It is a testament to the commitment, dedicated work, and wisdom of survivors that so many women who have had inadequate or abusive parenting themselves have managed to be good mothers to their own children. As one survivor recalls:

I always wanted kids, but I was scared. I was in therapy for three years and my therapist helped me understand that I have choices in my life, and that one of those choices is to not repeat what my mother did to me.

Now I'm the proud mother of two daughters, aged eleven and thirteen. Motherhood has been a great healer for me—and a great source of pleasure for me. I'm not a perfect parent; none of us are. I've made mistakes with my girls, but abusing them isn't one of them. I'm proud to have broken the cycle, to give them the protection and the nurturing my mother couldn't give to me.

For another survivor, becoming a mother showed her how far she had come in her healing:

It wasn't until my late twenties that I began to think about having children. Before I could consider becoming a mother, I had to find out if I had the capacity to nurture and care for another person that deeply.

At that point, I had already started to do the hard work of healing from sexual abuse. Through that process, I realized my heart was too much of the time living behind a closed door. But thankfully the door had a small window and I could look out and even open it for some fresh air. I was moving along and had reached a place where the window stayed open longer and I could tolerate more and more precious intimacy.

But nothing prepared me for the experience of the birth of my son. When he emerged out of me and I held him in my arms, my wounded heart cracked open, entirely and completely. At that moment all I felt was the deepest love and bond that can possibly exist in this world between people. I finally had been able to reach so deep into myself that I cried not just for the obvious joy of having my son, but also for the gift of strength to throw open that door to my heart and know that I could survive loving that hard. The personal relief from that experience has been forever with me and my son, who is 20 now, is as loving and beautiful as a human being can be. Maybe he saw into me at that moment too. Who knows?

Relating to Your Family Now—and Over Time

"I wrote to my sister and I asked if I could have a party at her house when I came to visit. She said, 'Sure, send me a list of the people you want me to invite.' So I did. She wrote back and said, 'I don't think you should invite Mother, because the last time you two were together, it was very uncomfortable for me. And I think you should invite the boys.' My brothers! She knows exactly what I'm going through. She said, 'There isn't a time they don't ask after you. They love you so much. And I don't think you should invite your friends. They can see you anytime.' It was crazy. So I wrote her back and said, 'At your suggestion, I have rethought the whole visit. I am going to the country instead.'"

Your work, as a survivor in the midst of healing from child sexual abuse, is to make your healing a priority. If you are in the early stages of the process and are trying to determine how to relate to your family, the most important question you can ask yourself is: What kind of relationship with them, if any, will serve my healing right now?*

Over time, what is best for you may change,

---

* The question of whether to talk to your family about your abuse or confront your abuser, as well as extensive information about preparation, is discussed in "Disclosures and Truth-Telling" on p. 157.

so your answer may vary from month to month or year to year. By the time you are in the stage of resolution and moving on, the question itself may evolve into a broader inquiry: How do I want to act toward other people? What is most in keeping with my own values? Ultimately, your relationship with family members may transform in ways you can't anticipate. But for now, while you're in the throes the healing process, your primary focus must be on what will support *you*.

Many factors affect the dynamics you face in your family, including whether the abuser was a relative or someone outside the family, whether you've disclosed the abuse to your family, how they've reacted, and whether you've needed—and taken—a healing separation (see "The Benefits of a Healing Separation" on p. 356).

The most important factor, of course, is the nature of your family. If your family is generally critical and unkind—or cruel—your relationships are going to be very different from those in a basically healthy, supportive family. Also, alcoholism, drug addiction, violence, and other destructive behaviors are obviously going to impede a healthy connection.

Sometimes, though, you may find that things are not clear-cut, that it's difficult to categorize your family. As one survivor put it, "It's hard to speak of the violence and the tenderness in my family because there was so much of both."*

Many survivors also find that their perspective changes as they move through the healing process:

> Before I told my family about the incest, I believed they would always offer me unconditional love and nurturing. Afterwards, I had to tear down those false assumptions and replace them with reality.

> Giving up the little girl's longing for security and protection was excruciating. Stepping outside of the shared beliefs of my family system and insisting on the truth was terrifying. I felt like a speck of dust floating all alone in a big empty universe.

You may look back from your own changed point of view at a family that's still caught in the patterns that existed when you were a child:

> I saw this picture. I was standing in the sunlight and my family and ex-husband's family were all back in this dark cave. They were crowded in there, and I was in the sunlight with fresh air all around me. They wanted me to come back in and I wouldn't do it. I'd finally made it out into the sunshine and I wasn't going back. And I had no sense that they were going to come out either. I knew for the first time that I didn't have to make them come out, that I didn't have to save them.

NOT ALL FAMILY MEMBERS ARE ALIKE

The people in your family may differ greatly in how they respond to your disclosure of abuse, your healing, and your needs now. If you are fortunate, you will have at least some family members who are genuinely supportive and understanding. At the other end of the continuum, you may be coping with an entire family that is critical, withholding, hostile, or abusive. Frequently, survivors experience positive inter-

---

* Some of the quotes and stories in this chapter were originally included in *I Thought We'd Never Speak Again* and the tape set *The Last Frontier: Is Reconciliation Possible After Sexual Abuse?* Both are by Laura Davis.

actions as well as ones that feel undermining, draining, or threatening.

> My brother has completely supported me. He always has. He's the one person who's been consistent in my whole family. He's been very compassionate toward me. He's told me he loves me, and that he knows my parents have always treated me badly. He says he's sorry about that. And he's offered me a place to stay if I ever need one.
>
> My sister, on the other hand, has completely cut me out of her life. She doesn't want to talk to me. She thinks I'm nasty and I've ruined both my parents' lives by bringing this up. She says it never could have happened and that I'm crazy to say it did.

In a situation like this, it's particularly important not to relate to your family as a single unit. You can decide to build on a strong connection with one or more relatives and limit or suspend contact with the rest.

MAKING THE MOST OF THE ALLIES IN YOUR FAMILY

If there are people in your family who respect you and genuinely want to support you, they can be valuable assets in your healing. You may have a sibling who shares your feelings, validates your reality, or can fill in gaps in your memory. You may have a mother who is furious that you were abused and wants to help in any way she can. Perhaps an aunt, uncle, cousin, or grandparent is able to offer empathy and the love of someone who has known you since you were a child.

It's also important to remember that relationships with family members can change over time. What is possible now isn't necessarily what will be possible later. Sometimes things go well at first but disintegrate later on. A father sinks deeper into alcoholism; a mother's rigidity and denial deepen with age. On the other hand, things may start off poorly and gradually improve. One woman describes how her experience with her mother shifted over the years:

> When I first remembered my brother's abuse, I tried to tell my mother, but she didn't get it. She listened, but then she just shoved it back in the drawer. I felt abandoned.
>
> A couple of years later, I began to face it for real. But this time I didn't even want her to know. I blamed her for not listening, not hearing me the first time. I blamed her for not protecting me, for being unable to see what had gone on, pretty much for everything. I was so angry, I couldn't let her help me.
>
> Over time, though, my anger at her has subsided. She has made an effort to change. She used to drown out my feelings with hers. Now she concentrates on mine. She listens when I tell her what I need. And there's a lot she knows about my childhood that I don't remember. She says things that help me piece it all together.
>
> It's been a lot of work to get here, but I'm very glad to have her in my corner. Sometimes I can even ask her for a hug now.

It may take substantial effort on both sides to build a healthy relationship or to repair one that's been damaged. But if someone in your family is willing and able to do that work, it's likely to be deeply rewarding for both of you.

PROTECTING YOURSELF

If there's abusive or disrespectful behavior still going on in your family, your first job will be to set limits to protect yourself. Being with your family can throw you back into the reality you knew as a child, as though you'd traveled through a time warp. You're a forty-five-year-old adult, but when you go home for the holidays you start feeling like a powerless, frightened child. You may still be terrified of your abuser, when in reality he's a weak, seventy-year-old man. You may be plagued by nightmares or revert to patterns of coping you outgrew long ago.

One woman was so upset by seeing her parents that she became depressed and suicidal and was unable to function for weeks afterward. If you are shattered by the experience of being with your family, that's a good indication that it's time to make some changes to protect yourself.

Often, the child inside you will choose to continue a destructive relationship in the hope that things will get better. As a wise person once said, "The definition of insanity is doing the same thing over and over and expecting different results."* To avoid revictimizing yourself, it is necessary to appraise your fam-

---

* At various times, this quote has been attributed to Albert Einstein, Benjamin Franklin, Rita Mae Brown, and Representative Dick Zimmer of New Jersey!

ily with the perspective and honesty that only your adult self can provide.

ASSESSING YOUR RELATIONSHIPS WITH FAMILY MEMBERS

Begin by looking at where things stand with your family now. Realistically consider your relationship with each family member. Ask yourself:

- What is my relationship with this person like?
- How do I feel about the relationship?
- Have I told this person what happened to me? Is he or she supportive of my healing?
- How do I feel when we talk or spend time together?
- Do I take more drugs, drink more alcohol, or eat too much or too little when I'm around this person?
- Does this person criticize me, insult me, or hurt my feelings?
- How do I feel after a visit? Depressed? Angry? Like I'm crazy? Nurtured and supported? Relaxed? Basically okay but not great?
- What kind of relationship would I like to have with this person?
- What would have to happen for this relationship to improve?

As you assess each relationship, think about both the good and the bad. What are the rewards? What is the price you pay? Look at what you want from each person. Then ask yourself, "Is what I want possible? Are my expectations realistic?"

THE BENEFITS OF A HEALING SEPARATION

If your family has been unsupportive, manipulative, or hostile—or if you've been caught up in

---

BUT HONEY, I LOVE YOU

When a relative who has abused you, hasn't protected you, hasn't believed you, or still doesn't support you says, "I love you," you are apt to feel confused and disturbed:

It infuriated me that she could sit there, smile sweetly, and say, "Honey, I love you." That was her answer to everything: "But honey, I love you," in this weak, little sad voice.

You may sense that there is strong feeling behind those words but also that there are unhealthy strings attached. "Love" in your family may mean keeping silent or being bound by obligations you no longer want to meet. Many survivors were abused in the name of love.

Genuine love is a commitment to act in someone's best interests:

When my mother tells me how much she loves me, and how sorry she is, I don't want to believe it. If I believe she *does* love me, then I have to make sense of the fact that she allowed such a terrible thing to happen to someone she loved. Even though I know,

for her, that's love, I know that's not really love. When you love somebody, you'd kill for them. You do whatever's necessary. And she didn't do that. Her love is not the kind of love I can believe in. She doesn't have the instincts of the lioness for her cubs, and that's the kind of primal love I need.

This fierce, clear love is often not available to survivors from their families. Instead you may be offered love that is smothering, manipulative, controlling, or desperate. Love that doesn't take your needs into account isn't really worthwhile. And love that requires you to compromise your integrity, your values, or your healing isn't, ultimately, love.

Yet it can be terrifying to say no to any kind of love. You want it. The need for kinship and closeness is a basic human need. If the love your family has to offer is the only kind of love you've ever known, it can be hard to believe that something better will take its place. And when there are positive aspects of the relationship mixed in with the unhealthy, it can be even more difficult to turn love down. But when you start saying no to the kind of love that drains you, you open yourself up to recognize and receive nourishing love.

old family dynamics—you may find it beneficial to create a healing separation. Taking a break from your family doesn't have to be permanent. In fact, a healing separation is sometimes the first step in developing a healthier relationship.

There are many reasons why you might choose to take a time away from your family. You may not yet be prepared to talk to them about the abuse or ready to hear or respond to their reactions. You may need space to experience your own feelings without being influenced by theirs. You may find that being with your family is too upsetting during this vulnerable time. You may need distance to get a realistic perspective of your family. A time away can help you replace the child's longing with the more accurate vision of the adult:

After our split, I didn't expect to ever have much contact with my family and so I did a lot of grieving. I gave up my hope of ever having this perfect, happy family. Three years later, when we did reconnect, I no longer carried that longing. Instead, I was grateful for any contact that was sane and healthy, even if it was just a little bit. When we saw each other and it felt good, it was like this pleasant gift.

A healing separation can give you an opportunity to build your own strength and gain your own clarity. Sometimes, a period of separation helps you sort out the good from the bad to determine what, if anything, can be salvaged from the relationship:

The break really freed me. It helped me grow and learn enough skills to be able to gradually start having contact with

them again. Before the break, I was so enmeshed in family dynamics that I never could have figured out how to be with them and take care of myself at the same time.

Those years of estrangement were the best thing that ever happened to me. I explored myself. I traveled. I learned about how the rest of the world operates. I wouldn't have been able to find out who I was—or who my parents really were—if I hadn't had that time away from them.

A period of separation can give you the opportunity to explore healthier relationships:

Instead of having the really poisonous relationships I'd had in my family, I was freed up to find people who related to the world—and to each other—in a very different way. I created my own voluntary family with lots of people who I have no blood ties with but who remain to this day my real family.

Sometimes, a period of separation is something you consciously choose. Other times, you may have no choice in the matter—your family casts you out. As Diane painfully recalls:

My mother and I went shopping for my wedding dress, and over lunch she asked me if I had ever been sexually abused. I think she was searching for a reason why I'd pulled back so much. So I told her, "Yes, I was sexually abused," and initially she believed me. But when I told her it had been my father, that's when all the lights went out. I started getting threatening phone calls from my family. My father was FedExing me letters, saying, didn't I remember the good times? Then he said I'd been brainwashed and that my therapist had planted this idea in my head. My parents insisted that I was crazy. My brother threatened to come over and beat me up. My whole extended family—cousins, aunts, uncles, everybody—went on the attack against me. None of them speak to me anymore.

There are also situations in which you set off a conflict that you never intended. Ginger didn't plan to sever ties to her family, but when she spontaneously decided not to go home for Christmas, she inadvertently set off an argument that escalated into a long-term estrangement:

Five years ago, on Christmas Eve, I went to see my therapist and ended up sobbing about not wanting to go home on Christmas Day. I just dreaded going. And my therapist said to me, "What if you didn't go home? That might be the most courageous act for you—to give yourself the gift of a peaceful Christmas." So I decided not to go.

I had to call my family and tell them, and they came completely unglued on the other end of phone. They said, "How could you? You're being selfish! You're wrecking Christmas for everyone!" I kept what I said simple: that I didn't feel good and I couldn't come home.

I never intended to create a big scene or confrontation. I just didn't want to go home for Christmas. But they kept yelling and screaming at me. Finally, I said I had to go and I hung up the phone.

Despite that horrible phone call, I did have a very peaceful Christmas. Four different families invited me over, and for the first time in my life, I had a Christmas where there weren't any arguments. I cried many happy tears that day because I was with people who cared about each other and weren't fighting all the time. It made me realize how bad things had actually been in my family.

My life totally improved after that. The less I saw my family, the happier I became. I didn't see my family at all for several years. Periodically they'd call and say that I was destroying the family by refusing to come home. Each time, after listening to all their anger, I'd hang up and think, "Why would I want to go home?" I'd never intended to break off from my family or to create a full-on estrangement, but their communications were always so angry and hateful, I didn't want to see them. And years went by like that.

HEALING SEPARATIONS OVER TIME

One of the most difficult things about separations—whether you've chosen one or had one imposed on you—is that they're fraught with uncertainty. A healing separation can last a few months—to help clear the air—or thirty years. Sometimes you expect the break to be

I'M SAYING NO, MOMMA

by Laura Davis

ESTRANGE: 1. turning away in feeling, becoming distant or unfriendly; 2. to remove from customary environment or associations; 3. to arouse enmity or indifference when there had formerly been love, affection or friendliness; synonym, to wean.

WEAN: 1. to accustom (a child or young animal) to loss of mother's milk; 2. to detach affection from something long followed or desired. Wean implies separation from something having a strong hold on one.

—WEBSTER'S DICTIONARY

Paul calls from Miami. He says I should forgive you and let go. Not hold a grudge.

Dotsy sends a postcard from Idaho: Your Mom is worried about you.

Dad says you called him, cross-continental, to ask if I'd had a nervous breakdown; seems there was no other way you could explain my letter. After all, how could a daughter in her right mind say she didn't want a relationship with her mother? How could your good little girl say no, not now, I'm not ready for you in my life?

I'll tell you how, Momma, I'll tell you how. Brick by careful brick, that's how, Momma. I've built this wall between us with careful, conscious precision. It is thick, my wall. Thick and nontransparent. I stand behind it and you cannot reach me. Its walls are smooth, Momma, flattened by ancient anger; its walls are caked with memory, bound with pitch, thick, black, and alive.

I stand back, separate from you for the first time ever, and inspect my work. What is the nature of this space I've created? What

are its dimensions? What are its depths? How far can I travel inside before I come back round full face to you? What does it mean to be estranged? To take space? To create distance? What does it mean to set a boundary? To say no?

I'm saying no, Momma. I decide I like my wall.

It is not a wall of denial, of stasis, of immobility. It is a wall that grants permission. Behind its firm thick boundaries, there is movement. I stretch. I reach. I remember. What was given. What was denied. What never was there to begin with. What was good and whole and right. The lies that were told.

For twenty-eight years, I never shared my pain with you. Only my successes, only how good life was, only the happy times. Never the sadness or fear or anger. I've been trying to make up for being different, Momma. Trying to win your love, your respect, your blessing. But I'm not trying now, Momma. I'm starting to let go.

You see, I've got this wall. They call it estrangement. I call it freedom. Behind its thick surface, I can feel and do and be, and I don't have to show you anything. I know I'm not the daughter you wanted, Momma. I've always known that. But with my wall close around me, I can see you're not the mother I wanted either, all-knowing, all-giving, all-protective. From behind my wall I can see things as they are, find my courage, and grieve for what's been lost. From behind this wall, tall and smooth and straight, I can stop striving for what I'll never have, and find room again for you in my heart.

And when I'm done, I can take it down, my wall. Brick by careful brick. So I can see you clear.

They call it estrangement. I call it loving.

temporary, but it becomes a permanent state of affairs. Other times, you think you'll never see your family again and later find yourself wanting to reengage.

If you are currently estranged from your family, your number-one task is to focus on your healing. If being separated from your family feels painful to you, as it does for many people, part of your work will include grieving for the family you wish you had. Even if you end up reconnecting with your relatives later on, your job right now is to accept the separation and create a meaningful life for yourself.

Staying Connected to My Family: Meera's Story

*Although some survivors need—and take—a healing separation, others choose to have ongoing relationships with their families throughout their healing process. Although they may set some new boundaries, they never lose the thread of their basic connection. Meera is one such survivor.**

When I was beginning my healing process, a lot of survivors around me were separating from their families in order to heal. I never did that. I needed the grounding I had with my family. I maintained my relationship with my mother the entire time I was healing, despite her reactions. There were times she told me "to get over it" and questioned whether I had really been abused by my brother. I felt sad and devastated, but I loved my mother and despite her attitude, I still saw her as my ally.

My mother had protected me from so many other things—especially the racism around us. We were living in New Orleans and my dad was a Sikh who wore a turban. In the '70s that made him the target of a lot of violence—he was followed, kicked, hit, and punched. There was surveillance of my family in 1977 by the government—everyone in those days thought you were a terrorist if you wore a turban. Our neighbors would see my brother and me playing in the front yard and call us the "N" word. Our family was under constant attack.

When I was in Indian circles, I was excluded because my skin was too light. When I was in white American spaces, I was excluded because my skin was too dark. My mom helped me see that the racism wasn't about me. She was able to do the mom thing—to be reassuring. Even though we weren't a functional family, we learned to stick together. So when I started dealing with the abuse by my brother, I couldn't just say, "Screw you. I'm out of here." There were so many other parts of my family that had to do with race, culture, and ethnicity that were a strong part of my resiliency. It wasn't an option for me to give them up. They were an incredibly important part of my identity.

RELATING ON YOUR OWN TERMS

Rethinking the nature of your family relationships—and how you want to do things dif-

---

* For more of Meera's story, see "I Was Abused By My Younger Brother: Meera's Story" on p. 125 and "My Faith Has Given Me Strength: Meera's Story" on p. 183.

ferently—is important whether you've always stayed connected to your family or are engaging again after a healing separation. Most families have habitual ways of interacting with each other in which family members fulfill particular roles and meet deeply entrenched expectations—both spoken and unspoken. Developing healthier relationships with your family often involves departing from these expectations.

As you begin building relationships that make sense for you and for your healing, you don't have to continue doing things the way you always have in the past:

The first time I didn't send my mother a Mother's Day card, I thought for sure the sky would open up and God would strike me dead. Yet I couldn't maintain the facade. So I didn't send the card, and God didn't come to get me.

When you don't meet habitual expectations or when you set new limits, it's natural to feel shaky, guilty, or terrified. It may be the first time you have ever said no to your family. It may be the first time *anyone* in your family has said no. If this is the case, you may be met with shock, disrespect, resistance, or animosity. But it is important to start interacting with your family in a way that is in alignment with what you need today and who you are becoming.

Discovering how to take care of yourself around your family is an ongoing process, one that usually involves some mistakes and trial and error. Ginger recalls the steps she took when she began visiting her family after a period of separation:

I made two promises to myself when I first started to see my family again. First, I was going to take care of myself—if things started to look like people were going to argue or get verbally abusive, I gave myself permission to get out of there. If I needed to leave a situation, if I needed to screen my phone calls, if I needed to only communicate through letters, I would do that. I made my mental health the first priority. And the second promise I made to myself was that I was no longer going to deny my past. If they didn't want to talk about it, that was fine, but I wasn't going to pretend it didn't exist. I wasn't going to force them to talk about it, but I wasn't going to edit out my childhood to protect them anymore.

I have this mantra I use when I go to visit my parents. It's an old Kenny Rogers song: "You gotta know when to hold 'em, know when to fold 'em, know when to walk away, and know when to run." If I'm not in touch with all of those things, I don't go home to visit. But when I am and I'm feeling strong, then I do go home, and my visits are fairly successful. And if at any time I feel the need to walk away or to run, I honor that. The two times I didn't were big mistakes.

For me, going home is always a gamble, because if I don't play my cards right and I don't honor those things, it can turn into a big emotional confrontation. When I'm not grounded, I can't take care of myself. And when I don't take care of myself, I can't handle being around my family.

SETTING GROUND RULES

When you decide to alter the dynamics of a difficult relationship, it is helpful to put forward some ground rules for interaction. You can communicate these conditions either in person or in writing:

"I don't want you to drop in without calling first."

"I don't want to hear any more critical comments about my parenting."

"I'd love to see you, but I'm not going out to lunch with Dad anymore."

"I'm coming to Trina and Greg's wedding, but I'm not going to sit at the same table with Mom or pose for any family pictures."

There is no guarantee that your decisions will be respected or that your boundaries will be honored, but it is still worthwhile to ask for what you want. Your family's response will give you information that can be useful in evaluating how involved you want to be with them.

You've Got Two Choices: Dana's Story

Dana is a survivor whose mother and daughter were both molested. In this story, she stands up for her daughter and sets clear expectations with her mother about honesty and facing the truth about the past.*

---

* For more of Dana's story, see "When You Become a Mother" on p. 78 and "Breaking the Chain: Dana's Story" on p. 347.

When my daughter, Christy, was five years old, she started asking, "Why did Daddy do these bad things to me? Nobody else has this kind of daddy." I explained that other people do have that kind of daddy, and that in fact, my own daddy did those kinds of things to me when I was little.

Soon after, Christy was visiting my mother. With a five-year-old's candor, she turned to her grandma and said, "My mommy said that her daddy did those same things to her that my daddy did to me."

To which her grandmother promptly replied, "What? *No!* Your mommy and her daddy never did any of those things! Oh no! *No!* Your mother's daddy loved her and he would have *never* done any of those bad things to her. You must be mistaken."

The next morning Christy reported the conversation to me. Angry and hurt, she said, "Your mommy said that your daddy didn't do those things."

I immediately called my mother: "Look, you've got two choices. You can come back here and tell Christy the truth or you can just not see us anymore, because that's exactly the kind of lying that's gotten us into this situation. That's why it happened to you, that's why it happened to me, and that's why it happened to Christy. And I'll be damned if it's going to happen again."

My mother and I were both shocked by what I'd done. I'd never talked to her that way before. But that night my mother came over. We went out for tacos and while I went up to order the food, she talked to Christy. She said that sometimes when you remember things that really hurt a lot, it's easier just to pretend they didn't happen. And she said she was sorry she lied.

VISITS WITH YOUR FAMILY

When you're actively in the process of healing from child sexual abuse, decisions about family visits should be made consciously and deliberately. It's wise to ask yourself, "Will this visit support my healing?" If the answer is no, then you may want to postpone the visit—or structure it very carefully so you don't derail your healing. If the answer is yes, think through what might increase the odds of a positive experience.

You might want to get together at a neutral time, instead of at a traditional holiday. You can invite your family to your home if you feel safer there. You can stay in a motel instead of sleeping at your sister's house, bring a friend along for supper, or stop by for an afternoon instead of a week:

> I only see my parents for small amounts of time. That way, I feel like I get the best of them. When we get together, they try to put their best foot forward, and I get to enjoy the best strengths they have.

However, there are often factors you can't anticipate or control. Visits may be precipitated by a specific event—a wedding, a birth, an accident, a serious illness, a death. Although you may have to make a quick decision, you can still weigh the risks and benefits of the trip—and take the best care of yourself that you can.

Sheila O'Connell, who was abused by her uncle, recalls:

> When my grandmother died, I knew my uncle was going to be at the funeral, so I had to figure out whether or not I was going to go. My siblings rallied around me. My sister invited me to stay at her house after the wake. My brothers were like, "If he tries to say anything to you, we're going to punch him."
>
> After the funeral, everyone went to my aunt's house. My uncle tried to shake hands with one of my brothers, "Oh Jeff, it's good to see you." And my brother just shook his head and said, "I don't think so," and walked away.
>
> My aunt and uncle stayed clear of me. The idea that my brothers would need to stand around me to keep my uncle away from me was completely unnecessary. My uncle didn't come anywhere near me. But my dad's other sister came up to me and said, "I understand what you're going through and I'm really glad you're here," and the way she looked at me when she said it let me know that she was on my side. I felt really supported.*

Sometimes a visit is a way to strengthen ties with the allies in your family. Or it can be the first step in rebuilding broken relationships. Being with your family gives you the chance to see what's possible in each relationship now. Sadly, it can also validate that, yes, it really was (and still is) as bad as you remembered. Painful as it is to recognize that your family can't give you what you need, facing reality is an important part in healing.

---

* For more of Sheila's story, see "Sheila O'Connell" on p. 510 in "Courageous Women."

HOLIDAYS

Traditionally, holidays are a time for families to come together and celebrate. If your relationship with your family is strained or if you are not seeing them at all, you may feel the loss acutely on holidays. (The same can be true of birthdays or significant days of any kind.) You may feel lonely and sad. You may be jealous that your friends are able to enjoy their families and you can't. If you don't have close friends to be with, you may feel unloved and lonely. You may be drawn to spend time with your family even though you have an intuition—or know for sure—that it's not in your best interests.

It's especially important to take care of yourself during holidays. Do everything you can to be good to yourself—whether you spend time with your family or not.

If you're not celebrating holidays with your family of origin, you can start new traditions of your own. Think back to your childhood. Were there holidays you especially liked? Are there parts of those holidays that you could incorporate as you create your own traditions? Are there ways you've seen other people celebrate that you'd like to try? Holidays are rituals in which we affirm our values and our relationships. Although most people follow customs established by their families, religion, or culture, it's possible for you to modify these or to invent new ones with people of your own choosing:

Passover has always been an important holiday for me. My grandfather, the patriarch of the family, presided over Sed-

CATCHING ONE LITTLE FISH: EDITH'S STORY

Edith Horning is a forty-seven-year-old personnel director who lives on a farm and raises horses. She's the mother of three grown children. Over the years, Edith has made many changes in the way she's related to her parents regarding her father's incest.

I love my parents. And they love me. They love me the best they can. I happen to be a lot more fortunate than both my parents, in that my capacity for loving is far greater than theirs. They just don't have it.

For a long time I had more anger at my mother than I did toward my father. I felt the same way a lot of women do—you somehow always forgive the man because he's "weaker" and "can't help himself." But I expected my mother to be much stronger and to protect me.

As I got older and became a mother myself, I found out how little an ability to protect I had. I changed my feelings and became more compassionate toward my mother.

In the last couple of years, she has finally begun to acknowledge that there was incest. She's started to remember little pieces. A few years ago, she totally denied that it had ever happened. I told her, "You didn't listen to me any more this time than you did when I was nine."

And she said, "You never told me. You've never spoken to me about this."

And I said, "When I was nine years

old, I came to you and said, 'Mom, Dad's coming into my bedroom, and he pulled down my pajamas.' And you said, 'How did you know it was a man?' And I said, 'Because I felt his whiskers on my leg.' And you said, 'No. That's a dream.' And Mother, that was no dream. I was nine and I remember."

She said, "No, you never talked to me about this."

That was in November. In January, she called me on the phone and she said, "I remembered something. I remembered holding you by the hand and walking out of the house and walking all the way down the road, and getting clear down past the end of the corner, and realizing I had nowhere to go. And so I turned around and walked you back home again."

I said, "I'm glad to see that you can remember these things. Now you understand how I felt. Now you understand how it happened. You can't blame yourself. You just do the best you can at the time, Mom. When you're trapped, you're trapped." I really heard her. I could very easily see just how powerless my mother had been.

When I decided to go on television to talk about the incest, I went to my parents and told them. I didn't ask their permission. I just told them so they'd be aware of it. I told them I was going to be using my own name. And my mother said, "Aren't you going to turn your face or anything?"

And I said, "No, I'm not going to turn my face! What's the matter with you?"

"Well, people will *know!*"

"That's right. They sure will."

"Well, what will they think of me?" That was the first thing my Mom said. "What will people think of me?"

"They'll think you made a mistake, probably."

"Well, I don't know how you can do this."

And I said, "It won't be easy, but I'm going to do it."

When I told my father I was going on TV, he couldn't even get close to me, he was so scared. It just terrifies my father that I'm not weak anymore. Once it registered with him that I had taken charge, my dad became scared to death of me. All because I didn't ask him. I *told* him what I was going to do. I watched him get little. But I think it also registered that I wasn't out to beat him, to destroy him. I said, "Dad, this is going to be hard for you. It's going to be hard for me. But I don't want it to continue. If I can talk to people and I can stop one person, it's worth it."

When I went on TV, I wasn't concerned with protecting my family. Why should I be? They never protected me. What the hell did they need protection for? They're all adults.

My kids knew. They weren't embarrassed for me. In fact they encouraged me to do it. I talked to the man who owns the business I work for and told him what I was going to do. And he said, "Edie, if you throw out a net and you catch one little fish, it's worth it. Do it!"

And I did. And I'm glad I did.

ers. He also molested me. I stopped going to family Seders because I couldn't stand the idea of all my relatives sitting around talking about what a great man he was. So I make my own Seder instead.

I always invite the same close friends—my chosen family. We eat the traditional foods—matzoh, hard-boiled eggs, bitter herbs—and sing the traditional songs, but instead of using the customary service, we write our own each year. Since Passover commemorates the Jews' struggle for freedom, each of us talks about what the struggle for freedom means to

us today. For me as a survivor, escaping from bondage has taken on a whole new meaning. Combining the old and the new feels liberating, which is what Passover is all about.

DEALING WITH THE PERSON WHO ABUSED YOU

The same issues you need to consider in relating to your family are also important if you choose to interact with a former abuser. Of course, in many cases, you may not want any relationship at all. The abuser may have been a stranger or someone with whom you don't feel a connection. The abuser may be someone you dislike or hate—or a person who is still so violent, manipulative, or hostile that you are safer and smarter to stay away. Diane remembers the day she called it quits with her father:

> My father wanted a chance to defend himself to me, to prove that the incest never happened. So I agreed to meet him in a restaurant. I met with him not in anger but in sadness. I remember initially hoping we were going to get somewhere, but he immediately started accusing me of being brainwashed, and that was the only place he would go with it. He'd joined the False Memory Syndrome Foundation. He'd gone to meetings, so he had all these arguments prepared. I just got very quiet inside and thought, "This isn't

---

DO I WANT TO SEE MY FAMILY NOW?

The following questions can help you evaluate the merits of a particular visit:

- Why do I want to be with my family now?

- What do I hope to get out of it?

- Are my expectations realistic?

- Is this the right time for me to get together with my family? Is this what I need at this point in my healing process?

- How do I usually feel during and after spending time with my family? Do I have reason to believe I'll feel the same or different this time?

going to work. I have to accept that I'm never going to get through to my father. We are never going to speak the truth about this."

I let him talk for half an hour, and then I said, "Now you have to let me talk." He tried to cut me off, but I was very calm and I said, "You have to let me say what I need to say." And the main thing I wanted to say to him was that he had hurt me very badly.

At one point, I said to him, "I'm willing to accept that we have different memories about my childhood. Can we move forward and have a relationship?"

And he replied, "No."

We were there for forty-five minutes. If you were a patron in the restaurant you would have thought, "Oh how nice. A father and daughter meeting having a nice Sunday-morning coffee." You would never have known what we were discussing.

When I got up to leave, I put my hand on his shoulder and said, "I feel very sad because I believe the next time I see you will be at your funeral." I did not say it as a threat. I said it as a very sad thing. Then I said I hoped he stayed well. Then I walked out of the restaurant and that was it.

For Diane, continuing to see her father at all was impossible. But many survivors want to find a way to maintain some connection with the person who abused them. If this is important to you, it will take careful work to discover what kind of relationship, if any, is possible.

Setting appropriate boundaries is absolutely essential if you choose to continue a relationship with a former abuser. You must be explicitly clear about what is and isn't acceptable. You will need to specify your expectations and ground rules. For example, you might have a list of unacceptable behavior, including dirty jokes, any discussion of sex, or comments about looks or cleavage. At least for a time, you may decide to avoid any physical contact, including hello hugs, good-bye kisses, or slaps on the back. And you may need to spell out whether and under what conditions you're willing to talk about the abuse—or other difficult subjects. These are choices you are entitled to make.

If you do want a relationship, the possibility of building a healthy one will depend on how well you can navigate the complex terrain of taking care of yourself while reaching out.[*] It will also depend on how much the abuser is able or willing to acknowledge responsibility, to change, to make amends, and to contribute to your healing.

Deep healing with someone who has sexually abused you is rare but not impossible.[†] It is much more common for survivors to achieve a minimal or conditional relationship. And for some survivors, ending the relationship is the healthiest option.

---

[*] See "Pauline Szumska" on p. 502 in "Courageous Women" for an example of a woman who is learning to keep her equilibrium while relating to her former abuser.

[†] For an example of a woman who was able to rebuild a worthwhile relationship with her father once he acknowledged the abuse, see "Vicki Malloy" on p. 487 of "Courageous Women."

I Wanted to Get My Father
Out of My Life:
Judy's Story

Judy Gold came from an upper middle class Jewish family and describes her father as "Dr. Jekyll and Mr. Hyde." To the outside world, he was a respected philanthropist; at home, he was a violent man who regularly abused her in her bed.

After Judy grew up and left home, her husband, Howard, joined her father's business, and Judy spent years pretending all was well. When she finally decided to sever all ties with her father, it wasn't easy.*

I'd thought about it for a year. My father was in the hospital. Fittingly, he had something wrong with his pecker. I thought, "Maybe they'll cut it off."

We went to visit him. He had on one of those hospital gowns with the back cut out. He purposely stood up and exposed himself to me. Then he said, "Judy darling, would you help me with this?"

I said, "For Christ's sake, can't you put a bathrobe on?" and I walked out. That was the beginning of the end.

But still, it wasn't easy getting my father out of my life. My husband was in business with him. And I was still scared of him. I made a list of all the times I had to have contact with him, whether it was by phone or in person. And I thought, "What is one thing I could cut out? Is it maybe calling him on his birthday?

Could I not have him come to my house for Thanksgiving dinner?" Well, I couldn't do that the first year, but I didn't call him on New Year's Eve to wish him a Happy New Year.

Every time I was able to cross something off the list, I'd feel terrific. The first time I didn't call him on his birthday, I cannot tell you my sense of elation. But it was very hard. I lived in fear that that phone was going to ring and he was going to yell, "Why didn't you call me on my birthday?"

I would rehearse—"If he does call me, what am I going to say?" I would act it out with Howard. He would play my father, and I would practice what to say. I wrote out scripts and carried them in my wallet.

And finally my father did call, and he said, "What is going on between us? You never call me back. Do you have any intentions of calling me back?"

And I said, "No." That was the end of it. I never said why.

Then his wife called and asked what was going on. She said, "He's so upset. He doesn't understand. Is it because he took you out of temple when you were nine years old and made you go home?" Can you believe this?

And I said, "You know, I'm not prepared to discuss this with you right now." She kept saying, "What did he ever do?" And I just repeated, "I have no intention of discussing this with you. Now if you want to talk about something else, I'd be more than happy to talk to you. But otherwise, we have nothing more to say to one another." And that was the end of it.

Do you know how long it took me to rehearse that? But when I could do it, what

---

* You can read more of Judy Gold's story on p. 411 of "Courageous Women."

a victory! When I got him out of my life, the rest of the healing just fell into place. That was the moment when I knew that I really was in control of my life.

NOW THAT YOU'VE DONE ALL THAT

Ultimately, no matter what steps you take to try to create a workable connection with your family, you can control only your side of the relationship. There comes a point where you have to stop pushing against the current and let go of the things you cannot change. For Laura, this couldn't happen until she was finally ready to relinquish the fantasy of the mother she would never have. The process was excruciating.

Giving Up the Fantasy: Laura's Story

After a six-month estrangement, my mother came to visit me. I sat across from her and read her a letter I had written in her voice. It was the letter I wished I'd received from her during this heart-wrenching period.

Dearest Laurie:

I received your letter today. I'm so sorry you are in so much pain. It has been very difficult for me to believe what you've told me—until now—because I did not want to face the fact that my father could have hurt you that way. Frankly, for me, denial has been the easiest way to deal with the unpleasant things in life. But now that I see how deeply this has affected you, I realize that I must step past my own denial and support you. I believe what you have told me. What my father did to you was an atrocity. No wonder it has so deeply affected your life. I know sometimes it must seem like it would have been better never to have remembered at all, but now that you have, you at least can put to rest some of the deep questions you've had about your life.

Laurie, I am so sorry it happened to you. I am sorry I didn't see it, sorry I didn't stop it, and I am sorry you are living with it still. My biggest regret is that I didn't protect you, but you have to remember, such things were not even thought of then.

Unfortunately for both of us, nothing can be done about that now. Yet here we are in the present, two adult women. As your mother, I want to give you whatever love and nurturing I can to help you get through this thing. I'm not saying this to rush you. I know it will take time for you to heal from the effect this has had on your life. You've lived with this secret festering inside of you for more than twenty years, and that's got to have taken its toll. I want you to know, Laurie, that you have my full support for as long as it takes for us to lick this thing. He's not going to win. You're not going to let him and neither am I. Whatever I can do for you, just let me know.

I also want to tell you that this last year has been one of the hardest years of my life. It has been hell for me to come to accept this about my father, to shatter the picture I had so carefully constructed of the man who raised me.

At times I hated you for bringing this horror into my life, but now I realize that it's not your fault—it's his. He's the one who did this to us. Now that I understand that, I've been able to let go of my anger and put myself in your shoes a little more. I never thought the day would come when I would say this to you, but I'm actually glad you told me. You've given me a chance to give you the kind of love and support I wish I could have given you then, when you couldn't fight back for yourself.

Laurie, I think you are incredibly brave to do this work. I am proud of you. Your willingness to face the truth of your life is an inspiration to me. I only hope I can face my own life with as much grit and determination. For a while, I was convinced that this incest thing would tear us apart and destroy all love between us. But now I know it is only with this kind of truth that we can forge the kind of healthy mother–daughter relationship that we have both always wanted. I truly believe this healing can bring us together.

All my love,
Mom

I had to stop many times as I read, I was crying so hard. When I finished, there was a long silence in the room. Then my mother turned to me and said she couldn't give that to me.

She said, "It's like the Laurie I love so much and want to comfort is sitting right there. And there's this other horrible monster next to her, who's making these accusations about my father."

I told her, "They're just one person, Mom. They're all me. It's a package deal. It's taken me over a year to accept and love that monster and I can't afford to split her off from me anymore, not even for you."

That exchange said it pretty clearly. I was not going to get what I wanted from my mother. She was not going to get what she wanted from me. I had to live my own life.*

COMING TO RESOLUTION OVER TIME

Eventually you will need to come to some kind of resolution with your family. For some survivors, deep healing takes place and family relationships are restored. For others, a permanent separation is what will enable you to live a saner life. Most people fall somewhere in the middle, with a level of involvement ranging from satisfying to minimal.†

---

* Ultimately, after years of estrangement, Laura and her mother were able to reconcile. Today, they enjoy a positive, loving relationship. You can read about their process of reconciliation in *I Thought We'd Never Speak Again.*

† Laura Davis discusses different types of reconciliation in great depth in *I Thought We'd Never Speak Again* and

DEEP HEALING

Deep healing, of course, is the resolution most of us hope for. When such a reconciliation occurs, it is a true gift. You feel that you now understand and accept each other, old wounds are healed, and there is real warmth, intimacy, and safety between you.

One survivor told her cousin that their grandfather had molested her. Her cousin abruptly broke off their relationship:

> She left me when I needed her most. I was furious. I felt abandoned and betrayed. We had no contact for many months, when I received a letter from her explaining that she hadn't been able to listen because she had been molested by him, too. She said she was sorry and we met for lunch. Over Chinese food, she was ready to hear about everything that had happened to me—and about how angry I had been with her for leaving. She talked about her own fears and pain. And we recemented our bond more solidly than ever.

Sometimes deep reconciliations come about naturally with the passage of time. More commonly, they are precipitated by conscious work by everyone involved.

Healing With My Siblings: Patricia's Story

Patricia came from a prominent, wealthy family in which her father and one of her brothers sexually abused her. After decades of estrangement from her siblings, and some years of tentative reaching out, they came together for a group therapy session. Patricia believes such a session was finally possible because both of her parents were dead.[*]

The main topic was my father. My sister said she had memories of him feeling her up. My brother seemed to have more issues with my mother. All of us had a different take on our childhood, but the fact that we were all able to sit together and talk about what happened represented a major healing.

At one point, our therapist pointed out that all of us had been working on issues from our childhood for some time, but we'd been doing it in isolation. We'd never sat down and talked openly about what had happened. I don't think any of us realized how much the others were suffering.

When I used to confront my siblings with our history, it was all about them hearing me. After the group session, I realized that the communication needed to go both ways—that I wasn't the only one involved in this. A lot of stuff went on for them, too. And so I'm teaching myself to listen. As a result, we are growing to be more and more of a support for each other.

---

in *The Last Frontier: Is Reconciliation Possible After Sexual Abuse?* (an audiotape/workbook available at www.lauradavis.net).

---

* For more of Patricia's story, see "I Had Been Silent For So Long: Patricia's Story" on p. 164 and "You May Feel Compassion or Forgiveness" on p. 173.

My relationship with my siblings is budding—kind of like a rose that's coming into full bloom. You have to treat it carefully and water it a lot. But it feels like there's a closeness and a real mutual respect now. We're all honoring each other's experience. Love is growing between us. There's still more work to do, but I can say stuff now and everyone's not going to scatter to the winds.

There was a time in my life when I was looking everywhere for what I didn't get as a child. I would latch on to people and on to things—drugs, alcohol, working, fame, money, clothes, friends, men—looking for what I missed. After the group session, it felt like part of me was given back to me and that that hole I was trying to fill was no longer there.

SHIFTING YOUR PERSPECTIVE

Sometimes a relationship improves because your perspective shifts, even though the other person hasn't made significant changes. Though on the surface, much may look the same, you experience the relationship in a different way.

Molly Fisk, a poet, was abused by several members of her family. Her mother, whom she'd been close to, refused to believe her. Molly found her mother's denial so painful that she didn't speak to her for seven years. During that time, Molly grieved the loss of her mother and didn't know if they would speak again. She describes this time as excruciating, "not quite as bad as being killed." Yet Molly knew she was not ready to reengage:

I would have wanted to argue about exactly what happened—what I remembered and what she remembered. And in our case, that would have been a totally useless pursuit. My mother gloms onto logic and would have been arguing about dates and times and places. It would have been like getting into a legal argument about something that happened when I was three and she was twenty-six. And I had no desire to do that anymore.

It wasn't until I no longer needed my mother to believe me that I could get back in contact with her. And that couldn't happen until I believed myself. Now I know what happened, and I don't need proof or external validation. The proof is in my body. I live with it every day.

When I got to the place where I no longer needed to convince her, I could start being myself around her. And that's really helped me to see her as a person, too—a person from whom I no longer expect acknowledgment or an apology.

Molly's choice to reunite with her mother arose from her ability to accept dual realities: that she wasn't going to get what she wanted from her mother *and* that there was still a connection she valued:

In the process of writing poetry, I started to realize how much of my ability to look at the world was formed by my mother. My mother is a painter, and she taught me to look underneath leaves to see how the colors were different from those on the top of the leaf. She taught me to study the refraction of light. My powers of observation were very much trained by her. I use those abilities all the time in my work, and I enjoy them immensely. I started to feel grateful to her for giving me that. That was when I began thinking, "Maybe I ought to get in touch with my mother. Maybe I ought to reconnect with her."*

If you're at the beginning of the healing process, it might be hard to understand why anyone would choose to continue a relationship with someone who doesn't validate her deepest reality. It might seem like capitulation, caving in, and in some cases, it would be. But for some survivors, accepting this kind of paradox makes sense. Kathleen, who worked out a limited reconciliation with her parents after a long, bitter estrangement, explains:

My reconciliation hasn't been a giving in. It's very important to say that. I haven't victimized myself by giving in to the perpetrator's control or knuckling under his denial. I'm standing firm and strong: "Dad abused me, and he's abused others." I don't care how crazy they think I am, and how many people they tell I'm crazy, because I've finally attained that inner strength inside of me. I know the truth, and I don't have to prove it to them, or to myself. And that enables me to accept them as they are.

---

* Molly Fisk's poem "Surrender" appears on p. 89.

AGREEING TO DISAGREE

Many survivors, once they've moved past the intensity of the active healing process, choose to stay somewhat connected with their families despite shortcomings in the relationships. Colleen is one such survivor. She and her father have agreed to accept their differences and focus on what is possible between them.

I Realized I Couldn't Change Him: Colleen's Story

Colleen grew up in a middle-class family. Her mother, an elementary-school teacher, was extremely abusive, both emotionally and physically. Her father loved Colleen and her sister but never took a step to protect them from their mother's wrath.

Colleen's mother and sister have both died. Colleen is a single mother, and the relationship she has with her father today is extremely limited. It is not a connection everyone would choose to maintain, but it is something Colleen continues to want in her life. It feels important to her to stay connected with the last surviving member of her family.

My father was basically nice, but he always made excuses for my mother. In his eyes, she was wonderful. So if there was something wrong, it was wrong with me. I remember one time he told me he didn't feel safe leaving the knives on a magnetic rack in the kitchen because she threw one once. It was crazy.

I remember thinking, "He doesn't want to leave the knives on the wall, but he's willing to leave his small children with her?"

For years, I was angry with my dad. After my mother's death and my sister's suicide, I confronted him again and again. He would always say, "Your mother was a good mother. We were good parents." Repeatedly, we came to these impasses about what my childhood had been like.

Finally at age 43, after years of therapy, I realized that if my sister's suicide and my mother's death didn't change him, he wasn't going to change. For my dad to acknowledge what had happened, he would not only have to look at his role in what happened, and alter his view of himself, but he would also have to look at his family of origin, and what happened there. And there was no way he was going to do that. He was in his late sixties, he had this circle of protection around himself, and he wasn't going to let go of it. It became clear to me that what my father thought wasn't in my control.

So I said to him, "Let's agree to disagree. If you change your mind, you can let me know. Otherwise, I'm going to assume that yours has stayed the same. And the same goes for me. If I change my mind, I will let you know. Let's no longer try to convince each other that our version of history is right."

Since we've made this truce, my father feels less under attack, and so do I. A lot of the tension between us is gone. There's an acceptance of "We're the last two people left in this family. Let's try to make the best of these years."

Three or four times a month, my son and I go out to brunch with my father. That's what we do together. My father doesn't babysit. We don't take walks or call each other up to chat. I don't call to let him know that I made it safely home from a trip or that something special is happening at my son's school. We call to make arrangements for brunch or if someone has died.

For me, the change has been on the inside. Now when we meet for brunch, I hug my dad and tell him I love him. And he now says those things to me. Those are not words he ever used before.

You could never call our relationship warm or close, but it is respectful. We will never be intimate, but I will always love him, and in his own limited way, he loves me.

A VERY LIMITED CONNECTION

Though continuing a relationship with your family is not right for everyone, many survivors eventually choose to maintain some kind of connection. Once they have moved through the intensity of the healing process, including healing separations, disclosures, and truth-telling, and have done all they can to work through the issues involved, it seems that most survivors would rather have some tie—even if it's extremely flawed and limited—than none at all.

One survivor spent years trying to have decent visits with her mother. Each time the visit would fail, she'd berate herself: "Why can't I work it out with my mother?" Then she'd try again, always prepared with phone numbers of friends she could call for support. Again the visit would fail.

Finally she decided to stop seeing her mother: "I was sick of repeatedly putting myself in a situation in which I needed backup reinforcements just to get through. I thought, 'Why am I doing this to myself?' And I decided to give myself a break. I started doing more of what I liked to do, instead of always picking the hardest thing and forcing myself to do it."

This woman stopped torturing herself when she accepted the reality of her situation. "The best relationship I have with my mother is through letters. We write nice letters to each other. We cannot be in the same room, but at least I have a mother in letters."

Another survivor, who visited her parents after an estrangement of thirty years, expects that she may see them again, but only rarely:

I don't feel a personal need to have my parents in my life on any kind of day-to-day basis. These are not people who've shown me that they can nurture me or care about me. They're not people who are willing to look at things with much scrutiny. I prefer to spend my time with a different group of people. That's not saying I'm going to shut them out the same way I did before; I'm just not going to choose to put much of my energy there.

LETTING GO

Sometimes it's not possible to salvage anything from your relationship with your family. Contact with them may leave you feeling too upset, depressed, or unstable. Or you may have family members who are violent, dangerous, or overtly aggressive. They might have tried to have you committed, sued you (or your therapist), been abusive to your children, or threatened you with violence or vengeful acts. In circumstances like these, separating from your family is a matter or self-preservation and common sense—and the most responsible decision you can make.

One survivor, after years of going back and forth, finally came to the conclusion that she had "evolved past" her family altogether. "I have no family. They're still relating in that old destructive way, and I don't want anything to do with that. Life is too short."

Yet the decision to break off all contact with your family is a serious life choice, one that has consequences in many areas of your life. In addition to love and personal connection, families provide a link to the culture you grew up in and a sense of rootedness. Severing ties with your family can also mean forfeiting material support. Depending on your age and your family's economic situation, this can be a significant price to pay. Whether it's help with doctors' bills, someone to fill out financial aid forms or pay for college, money for a deposit on your first apartment, or an inheritance that might help you buy a home or start your own business, survivors who have broken all ties with their families often feel the loss acutely:

My husband and I just bought our first house and there were things that were wrong with it. We had no one to consult about a mortgage. Our circle is very small, and that makes the world feel unsafe. If anything terrible ever happened to me, there's no one besides my husband who would help me. There's no source of money that would come in. There's nothing, and that makes me feel very unattached. And the fact that I'm infertile and can't have children means I don't feel attached at either end of life. I have no ancestors and I'm not going to have any children to carry on who I am in the world. When I die, that's it, and it's a very lonely feeling. I just feel so incredibly alone.

Sometimes, an estrangement solidifies into a permanent break not because you choose it but because your relatives are unwilling to see you:

> I have no grandparents for my children. My mother is alive. My father is alive. I have grandparents who are alive, and they won't see me. I have aunts and uncles in the same town who won't see me. My sister won't see me. And it's all because of the incest. I ache for an extended family.

She Chose My Father Over Me: Diane's Story

Diane's family cast her out after she disclosed her father's abuse. Two years after their estrangement began, Diane reached out to her mother in hopes of reconciling.

I sent my mother a note that said, "I'd really like to see you. I've been having some really hard times in my life," and she said, "Okay,

let's meet for lunch." And we did meet for lunch. In fact, my father dropped her off at the restaurant because my mother doesn't drive. But he didn't come in.

My mother and I had a tearful lunch. We cried and we hugged and we said how sorry we were that things had turned out the way they had turned out in our family. We never really addressed the incest and whether or not it was true, but we both expressed how sad we were that we couldn't be together. I started feeling very close to her, and I remember we were in the middle of Lord & Taylor and we were saying good-bye, and I didn't know if I was ever going to see her again, and I just started crying hysterically. All these people were looking at us. The woman spritzing perfume was staring at us. And we were just hugging each other and crying, both of us. Then my mother disentangled herself and said, "Well, I'll talk to you soon," and we went our separate ways.

That afternoon I got a call that they had found a suspicious growth on my kidney. They thought I had kidney cancer. And since I had already opened the door to my mother, I called and told her. She said, "I'm sure you're going to be fine, but let me know what happens." Then she offered to come with me to get the CAT scan. I felt like I had a mother again.

When the results came back, it turned out I didn't have cancer, and everything settled back down again. My mother and I continued to see each other on and off throughout that fall. By Christmas, she was starting to act very strange with me. She was starting to be very withdrawn again. We met right before

Christmas. She had walked a mile in very cold weather to meet me, because my father refused to drive her to meet me anymore. At the time, I remember thinking, "My mother must really love me to have walked all this way."

But as soon as we got to the restaurant, she told me that my father and brother had told her that she couldn't see me anymore. That was pretty much it. I haven't seen her since.

I feel very hurt about it to this day. It's incomprehensible to me that my mother would choose my father over me. I can't believe that she could choose not to have a relationship with me ever again. But that's exactly what she did.

FINDING YOUR OWN RESOLUTION

Although you may wish that more was possible, eventually you have to accept the reality of your situation:

We all long for that moment where the people who have harmed us say, "I'm sorry," and we say, "I'm sorry for the harm I've done you," and everyone comes together in a big group hug, but that hasn't been an option for me. I've had to reconcile myself to the fact that my parents are not going to be able to acknowledge what they did. They're not going to ask for forgiveness and I'm not going to be able to say, "I forgive you." What happened is larger than that and my parents were simply incapable of doing that kind of work.

When there's no possibility of healing with your family, it's necessary to find resolution within yourself, to come to a place of acceptance and your own inner peace. For some survivors, this is quite separate from any thoughts about their families. For others, it includes compassion for them, even though there will be no relationship. Pam's journey ultimately led her to pray for the healing of the people who had hurt her so badly.

Finding Peace with Parents I Will Never See Again: Pam's Story

Pam Leeds's parents sexually abused her when she was a child, and then when she had children, they sexually abused them as well. Pam wanted nothing to do with her parents, and for years she was consumed with rage. After a long and active healing process, Pam has found a place of peace in her relationship with her parents, not with them, but inside of herself.

I needed to see my parents for who they were—damaged people rather than terrible monsters controlling my life. They had been huge and powerful to me when I was a child, but that they were no longer huge and powerful.

From an adult perspective, I could see that their lives were limited by the choices they had made, and they made some terrible choices. Instead of nurturing their children, they exploited us. They used us sexually instead of loving us and helping us grow up.

My parents were spiritually deprived people. They operated from such a sad and damaged place. They had a sort of greedy dragon quality. I don't think my parents could have done what they did if they had been happy and connected people. And because of that, they lost out. They were surrounded by potentially loving relationships and they missed out on them. I wish they could have experienced a tenth of the happiness that I have in my life today.

I began to see this huge gap between the kind of life that I was leading and the impoverished lives they had led. And I began to feel a great sadness that they had experienced so few of the things that make life rich and give it meaning.

At the same time I felt this sadness for them, I came to realize that it was unhealthy and unsafe for me to have them in my life. I needed to focus on my healing, and I could not do that when I was in touch with them. And so eight years ago I told them, "I don't want you in my life. I don't want you to contact me in any way."

Still, I sincerely desired healing for my family. Praying for them was something I could do, and it gave me a place to sort out my feelings about them.

I prayed for healing for each member of my family. I consciously thought of each of them and what they had done. I described the sadness I felt about their separation from the most important things in life—connection and love. I prayed that the damage that they had done not be continued, and not be passed on, and that they be healed.

A friend taught me a wonderful meditation I sometimes use. It goes, "May you be free of suffering. May you be healed deep inside.

May you dwell in open heart. May you be at peace." When I say that for the people who have hurt me, it puts me in an open-hearted place in the world. I can be a loving person, even though bad things happened to me.

Praying for them allowed me to step back and see my parents as people who needed greater help than I could give them. I realized that I didn't have the power to heal them, and that I don't have to do this all by myself. Prayerful meditation has helped me feel connected to a much larger network of compassionate beings, and I laid my parents in their hands.

CHANGES OVER TIME

For some survivors, very little ever alters in their relationships with their families. A bad situation never gets better. Cassondra recalls:

> When my mother died, I hadn't seen her in ten years. I stayed at her funeral to make sure she was in the casket. I made sure that that same casket got put into that hole in the wall. I waited until they screwed the monument in place. Then I said, "She's not coming back anymore. Now I can breathe.*

But for many survivors, change does take place, unlikely as it once might have seemed.

---

* For more of Cassondra's story see "Cassondra Espinoza" on p. 492 in "Courageous Women."

One survivor, who'd worked through several decades of healing, put it this way:

> I've learned that it is possible to go through the most intense amount of hell and come out of it accepting things you never thought you could accept and loving people that you never thought you could love. It's amazing to me how much we all have gone through—and how much healing we've done. It's amazing to me—the strength of the human spirit.

Another survivor describes the changes in her family:

> I've come to see that family relationships evolve. When I was younger, I thought you have a confrontation with your parents and the relationship is over. It cannot be repaired. When I cut off from my family, I thought that if I wanted to stay healthy, I'd never be able to see them again. Now I realize that all of us have changed enough to make seeing them a possibility.

Sometimes the relationships that are restored are not the ones you would have anticipated:

> When my father pistol-whipped me at fourteen, I had to be hospitalized and the bruises and damage took more than six months to heal. It was my mother's choice whether or not to prosecute my father. She chose not to.

It's worth noting that today, after many honest conversations and confrontations with my father, that he and I have an open and loving relationship. I have no contact at all with my mother and I intend to keep it that way.

There's an important distinction between remaining in a perpetual state of longing and staying open to change. If your relationship with your family is unhealthy for you, it's necessary to make peace with your losses. But even after you've accepted the rift in your family, over time you may still be surprised. For Molly Fisk, one of the greatest benefits of reconciling with her mother was learning that the future is an open door:

> If you had told me anytime in the process of going through this estrangement that I would get back in touch with my mother, and that I would be doing her laundry and making her dinner and brushing what's left of her hair, I would have laughed. I would have vehemently protested, and said that it was impossible. I couldn't imagine growing so much that I could accept what she did and who she is now, and actually spend time with her. Knowing that I don't know what's going to happen is a wonderful thing. It's a great gift to finally realize that you can't predict the future.

WRITING EXERCISE: YOUR FAMILY NOW

(See the basic method for writing exercises on p. xxix.)

What are the positive aspects of relating to your family of origin now? What do you like? Who are your supporters? Whom do you enjoy being with? What is nurturing or satisfying for you in your contact with them?

What isn't okay for you? What is destructive, irritating, infuriating, frightening, threatening, painful? Whom do you feel bad being with? What are the disadvantages of being with your family?

Lucky

BY TONY HOAGLAND

If you are lucky in this life,
you will get to help your enemy
the way I got to help my mother
when she was weakened past the point of
     saying no.

Into the big enamel tub
half-filled with water
which I had made just right,
I lowered the childish skeleton
she had become.

Her eyelids fluttered as I soaped and rinsed
her belly and her chest,
the sorry ruin of her flanks
and the frayed gray cloud
between her legs.

Some nights, sitting by her bed
book open in my lap
while I listened to the air
move thickly in and out of her dark lungs,
my mind filled up with praise
as lush as music,

amazed at the symmetry and luck
that would offer me the chance to pay
my heavy debt of punishment and love
with love and punishment.

And once I held her dripping wet
in the uncomfortable air
between the wheelchair and the tub,
until she begged me like a child

to stop,
an act of cruelty which we both understood
was the ancient irresistible rejoicing
of power over weakness.

If you are lucky in this life,
you will get to raise the spoon
of pristine, frosty ice cream
to the trusting creature mouth
of your old enemy

because the tastebuds at least are not broken
because there is a bond between you
and sweet is sweet in any language.

Tony Hoagland, *Donkey Gospel* (Saint Paul, Minnesota: Graywolf, 1998).

PART FOUR

For Supporters of Survivors

The Basics

"When we honestly ask ourselves which people in our lives mean the most to us, we often find that it is those who, instead of giving advice, solutions, or cures, have chosen rather to share our pain and touch our wounds with a warm and tender hand."

–HENRI NOUWEN*

Being a close supporter of a woman actively healing from child sexual abuse can be both challenging and rewarding. Being part of a deep healing process holds the potential for tremendous growth and intimacy, but it can also leave you feeling conflicted, overwhelmed, or resentful. You may be frightened or confused, unsure what to do, how to feel, or what to expect. These are natural responses to a complex and trying human situation.

This is a time when it's important for you to take care of yourself as well as offer support to the survivor. It's essential that you honor your own needs. If the survivor wants more than you are able to give, admit your limits. Encourage her to call on other resources. Take some breaks. Get help for yourself. Dealing with such raw pain is difficult, and you need a place where you can express your own fears and frustrations.

If you find yourself feeling extremely defensive or upset when the survivor talks about her abuse, you may be reacting from experiences you've repressed from your own past. This is very common. One person's pain frequently brings up grief for another. Seek support in dealing with your own unresolved feelings. You are important, too.

---

* Henri Nouwen was a Dutch Catholic priest who spent his life helping people respond to the universal "yearning for love, unity, and communion that doesn't go away."

HOW TO HELP

When a survivor tells you that she was sexually abused as a child, she is entrusting you with a part of her life that is painful, frightening, and vulnerable. These guidelines can help you honor that trust and assist her healing:

- **Be willing to listen.** Let her know that you are open to hearing anything she wishes to share and that although it's painful and upsetting, you are willing to enter those difficult places with her and to receive her words with respect.

- **Join with the survivor in validating the damage.** All abuse is harmful. Even if it's not violent, overtly physical, or repeated, all abuse has serious consequences. There is no positive or neutral experience of sexual abuse.

- **Be clear that abuse is never the child's fault.** No child seduces an abuser. Children ask for affection and attention, not for sexual abuse. Even if a child responds sexually, even if she wasn't forced or didn't protest, it is still never the child's fault. It is always the responsibility of the adult not to be sexual with a child.

- **Educate yourself about sexual abuse and the healing process.** If you have a basic idea of what the survivor is going through, it will help

you to be supportive. Read this book and see the Resource Guide (p. 521) for other suggested reading.

- **Don't sympathize with the abuser.** The survivor needs your absolute loyalty.

- **Validate the survivor's feelings: her anger, pain, and fear.** These are natural, healthy responses. She needs to feel them, express them, and be heard.

- **Express your compassion.** If you have feelings of outrage, compassion, empathy for her pain, do share them. There is probably nothing more comforting than a genuine human response. Just make sure your feelings don't overwhelm hers.

- **Respect the time and space it takes to heal.** Healing is a slow process that can't be hurried.

- **Encourage the survivor to get support.** In addition to offering your own caring, encourage her to reach out to others. (See "Working with a Counselor," p. 45.)

- **Get help if the survivor is suicidal.** Most survivors are not suicidal, but sometimes the pain of childhood abuse is so devastating that women want to kill themselves. If you are close to a survivor who is suicidal, get help immediately (see "Dealing with Her Pain, Grief, and Depression," p. 396 and "If Your Partner Is Suicidal or You're Afraid She Might Be" on p. 397).

- **Accept that there will very likely be major changes in your relationship with the survivor as she heals.** She is changing, and as she does, you may need to change in response.

- **Resist seeing the survivor as a victim.** Continue to see her as a strong, courageous woman who is reclaiming her own life.

All intimate relationships—friends, couples, or family—have a lot in common. The next chapter, "For Partners," offers specific suggestions that will help even if you're not in a partnered relationship with the survivor.

For Partners

"Unless you have your own psychological house in order, relating to a survivor opens up old wounds and challenges every facet of the way you live. My feelings toward Barb run the whole gamut from 'What did I do to deserve a relationship with a screwed-up person like you?' to 'If we can hang on and lick this, my life will be rich beyond measure.'"

—PHIL TEMPLES, HUSBAND OF A SURVIVOR

The information in this chapter pertains to all couples—married and unmarried, heterosexual and lesbian. Although there are significant differences in cultural conditioning, power dynamics, and role expectations between heterosexual and lesbian couples, these differences are far outweighed by the common problems all couples face when one or both partners are survivors.

This chapter addresses the partners of survivors, but many of the suggestions will be equally useful to other family members and to survivors themselves.

Allies in Healing: When the Person You Love Was Sexually Abused as a Child, provides more in-depth information (see p. 569 of the Resource Guide).

Being the partner of someone actively healing from child sexual abuse has both problems and rewards, although the problems are sometimes more obvious than the rewards.

Survivors commonly have difficulties with trust, intimacy, and sex, all of which have a direct impact on your relationship. Often, at least for a time, the survivor's problems and healing dominate your time together. Depending on the stage of the healing process the survivor is in, she may be angry, depressed, or totally preoccupied. She may be self-destructive or suicidal (see "Dealing with Her Pain, Grief, and Depression" on p. 396 and "If Your Partner Is Suicidal or You're Afraid She Might Be" on p. 397).

She may need to maintain a great deal of control in her life. Sometimes the abusive patterns from her original family are acted out with you or your children.

As a partner, you may not understand what is going on. You may feel inadequate because you can't fix things, guilty if you aren't 100 percent supportive. You may be isolated, with no one to talk to. Partners often feel frustrated at the extensive time healing takes. Sometimes you will have to continue to deal with the survivor's abusive family members. Other times, your own family history will be reawakened, accompanied by painful emotions. And all the while, your own needs may not be getting met.

If both you and your partner are survivors, your relationship is likely to be affected in complex ways. Depending on how far along you are in the healing process, you may be able to offer each other tremendous support, reassurance, and understanding. On the other hand, you may intensify each other's struggles, trigger memories and old patterns, and otherwise get entangled in painful dynamics.

Since so many women have been abused, lesbian couples often find themselves in this situation. So do an increasing number of heterosexual couples, as more men identify their childhood abuse. If both you and your partner are survivors, this will create both liabilities and opportunities. Be especially patient and compassionate with yourselves and each other and consider couples counseling with an experienced therapist.

THE BENEFITS

There are powerful positive elements to being in a close relationship with someone healing from childhood sexual abuse, but sometimes these may be hard to see. At a workshop for partners of survivors, Ellen suggested that the participants write about the ways they could benefit from being in a relationship with a survivor—what were the opportunities for them? One man sat through the fifteen minutes allotted for this exercise, looking perplexed. At the end he said, "I'm really confused. I came here to learn how to help my wife with her problems and now I'm supposed to be finding my opportunities?"

It may seem crazy to look for what is positive for you, personally, in a situation that causes you—and the survivor—a lot of pain and stress. But there are valuable aspects to being the partner of a survivor.

Being with someone actively engaged in the healing process means that you are in a growing relationship, not a stagnant one. One partner, Roger, explained:

People unconsciously pick a mate where your meeting point is where you both need to grow, and that's definitely true for us. Around this issue of sexuality is where we're both wounded and we're both the most deaf to each other. There's no way I would dredge through my own shit as deep as I have if I didn't have to relate to Karen. If we each didn't have this problem, we wouldn't each be confronting our own shadow.

One partner found that her own problem area was learning to be separate:

> She's good at autonomy. She knows how to take care of herself. She's not so good at intimacy. I'm good at intimacy. Give me a person and I'll merge. Being with her, I've had to learn to be independent.

Another partner grew in his capacity to express feelings:

> As I look back over the last six months, I realize the tremendous personal growth we've both undergone. I've always lagged a bit behind in the communications department. But I'm now expressing feelings and allowing myself to experience emotions that never before would have been possible. At the height of an argument I can now recognize when I'm no longer mad, but instead very sad—and then I can cry.

If you haven't been used to thinking about your own feelings, your own fears, or the ways you were influenced by your childhood, you may initially feel uncomfortable with such a major focus on self-exploration. But even if this is unfamiliar to you, the emphasis on growth can provide you with valuable opportunities. And working together can bring you closer to your partner and build a more solid foundation:

> When we've come through the rocky points, we were able to look at each other with pride and say, "We did it!" It was a sense of mutual accomplishment. That's been a real special thing in our relationship.

Taking part in a deep healing process is a miracle and an inspiration. Although it's demanding, it is also a privilege. There are rewards both in the giving and in the receiving.

DON'T TAKE IT PERSONALLY

Intimacy is paradoxical in relationships with survivors, especially if someone they were close to abused them. Their love and trust were met with betrayal. Now, the more intimate a relationship becomes, the more it feels like "family," the scarier it is for the survivor. If you're unaware of this dynamic, the whole thing can seem incomprehensible.

Some survivors have had more superficial relationships in the past and have handled them relatively well. They may have managed short-term relationships, or even long-term ones, before they began to deal actively with the abuse. They kept their coping mechanisms intact and though some depth was sacrificed, they functioned well enough.

If the two of you really love each other and yet the relationship is rocky, this does not mean that something is wrong. It's more likely to mean there's something very right—so right, in fact, that she's threatened. If both of you know that it is frightening for her to get close—and for good reason—then it's less likely you'll be diverted into dwelling on rejection, fighting, or breaking up.

Survivors always tell their partners, "Don't take it personally." This is extremely difficult because so much of it *is* personal. Roger recalls:

A lot of my fears sexually have always had to do with rejection. I'm a very threatening size and part of me has internalized those threatening pictures as who I am: "Okay, I'm a real monster." I began to believe that all the things that are frightening and injurious about maleness were embodied in me. Having Karen withdraw brought all those feelings right to the surface.

If the survivor withdraws, is angry, is sad, needs time alone, doesn't want to make love, all this affects you personally. And yet her behavior does not necessarily reflect her feelings for your or for your relationship. In reality, your partner is either repeating coping behaviors from years before you ever met her or she is doing what she needs to do to heal. It often has very little to do with you.

Maintaining a balance between sharing wholeheartedly in the process and keeping an appropriate sense of independence and separateness is one of the challenges of supporting a woman who is actively healing from child sexual abuse. Throughout, you will be trying to encourage her, nurture yourself, and create healthy patterns for a relationship that will serve you not only during this crisis but also into the future.

OVERCOMING SHAME

One man at a workshop for partners asked Ellen, "Could you talk about shame?" So Ellen went on at length about survivors' shame for having been abused, for having experienced sexual arousal, for having needed attention, for the ways in which they coped. When she finally stopped, the partner looked at her blankly. "Am I getting to what you want?" Ellen asked.

"No," he said. "I mean the kind I felt today when I was coming to this workshop and I had to tell my coworkers where I was going. I didn't tell them. I made up something."

Yes. You too may be ashamed. You're not supposed to have problems. Your sex life is supposed to be terrific, your relationship perfect. You're not supposed to need counseling, workshops, or help.

Partners, as well as survivors, find obstacles that keep them from reaching out for support. Shame is one of them. But you have nothing to be ashamed of. There is nothing dishonorable about loving a woman who is working to heal from trauma. There is nothing wrong with you for struggling with the problems that result from such abuse. There is nothing shameful about your own pain, anger, or fear.

GETTING SUPPORT

Just as survivors need support through the healing process, you need support as well. Some of this can come from the survivor, but the demands on her own healing are often too great for her to have much energy left over to support you. Nor should you expect it. As one survivor put it: "If someone has a heart attack, you don't go into the hospital and go on and on about how upset *you* are about *their* heart attack. You talk about your concerns with other people. And while you're with the patient you act confident about their ability to heal. You have to approach survivors the same way."

Yet you need someone to listen to your pain, your fears, your frustrations, and your confusion. You need compassion, too.

For the partner, it's bewildering. There's no way to cope with what seems like rejection. I would not have been able to do it, as dedicated as I was to making this relationship work, without knowledge of what was happening. I had a friend who was an incest survivor, too. Talking to her about her feelings helped me understand what the impact of abuse can be.

It is essential that you have a place where it's safe to express your feelings bluntly. You need to air your anger, frustration, and despair. Sometimes you need to just stomp around and yell, "I can't take it anymore!" The survivor needs to know how you feel, but she doesn't need to hear it in the direct, unfiltered way you may need to talk about it.

- **Talk to a counselor.** Couples counseling or individual therapy can provide you with essential support.
- **Seek out friends who are good listeners.** Before you do this, clarify with your partner the specifics of what she's willing for you to share and with whom. But within these guidelines, do talk to at least one friend. It's not healthy to be isolated with your feelings.
- **Find other partners of survivors.** Other partners can be a tremendous source of support. If there are no workshops specifically for partners in your area, your partner may know other survivors who have partners. Try calling a local counseling center for leads. If you're already in counseling, ask your counselor about starting a group for partners.

There still aren't many resources for partners, but it's worth the effort to build a support network. The chance to talk and to listen can be an incredible relief. As one man put it, "You think there's something wrong with you—that you're too demanding, too impatient—and then you hear everybody else feels that too. It's like the burden drops. You can stop thinking of yourself as a rapist just because you want sex. You can stop feeling so bad about yourself."

TAKING CARE OF YOURSELF

Although any caring person feels the pain of a loved one, excessive identification with the survivor's pain is not healthy. Some partners are more comfortable attending to the survivor's problems than to their own. If this has been your pattern, it will be a difficult but necessary change in perspective to make a distinction between your partner's feelings, wants, or needs and your own. Do whatever it takes to get some time alone for yourself, to get to know yourself separately from your partner and her problems.*

DO THINGS THAT MAKE YOU FEEL GOOD

Many, if not most, people look to their partners for their primary emotional contact and companionship. But while your partner is immersed in her own healing, she may not have the time, energy, ability, or desire to meet your needs. It's essential that as the partner of a survivor and also as an autonomous person, you not be totally dependent on your lover and your family for all your nurturance.

Start to make meaningful connections with people outside your relationship, and find fulfilling activities that are your own. Think about the things that make you feel good, and do these things regularly. If you have previously relied on shared experiences for pleasure, you may have to change your patterns to avoid feeling deprived and annoyed.

One partner said that she and her lover had always gone backpacking together, but recently her lover had been so involved with other sur-

vivors and support groups that she didn't want to go away with her. The partner was disappointed but decided to go backpacking with a friend. Although she missed her lover and felt some sadness that they weren't together, she was a lot happier backpacking with her friend than she would have been sitting home idle and lonely.

BECOMING ALLIES

One of the important realities to keep in mind is that your partner did not create the difficulties you are both facing. One man said:

> I've never blamed her for making the relationship difficult because of the incest. That seemed like such an obvious trap. It would just be terribly rude for me to think that. She didn't do it. It was her father who did it. Not her. She didn't have this little qualifications list when we got together. Neither of us knew this was coming. To me, it's just part of growing and trusting and opening doors, and that was what was behind one of them. That was just part of the package.

Although the abuse happened to the survivor, it affects your life and becomes your concern as well. Many partners get angry when they realize that they have to deal with the abuse, yet they may be reluctant to admit to those feelings. Although it's not appropriate to direct your anger at the survivor, you may need her to acknowledge that you're upset about the

---

* Al-Anon (the support group for partners of alcoholics) and ACA (Adult Children of Alcoholics) can be useful resources. Many partners have benefited from attending these meetings, even if alcohol wasn't a problem in their families, because many of the dynamics of dependence and caretaking apply to a broad range of relationships.

situation—and to show her concern over the impact sexual abuse is having on your life.

Both you and your partner have valid feelings and needs. Neither of you is wrong or to blame. If you can see yourselves as allies with a common problem, rather than as adversaries in combat, it becomes possible to find ways to reconcile your differing needs.

On Communication: Roger's Story

We got into this situation where the communication between us was getting more and more closed. Karen had been seeing a therapist for some time. She'd come back from therapy and I'd ask her how it went, and she'd say, "It's too painful to deal with. It's too much work. I don't want to talk about it." That keyed me into my stuff about feeling rejected: If she couldn't trust me, then I must really be a monster.

I needed her to communicate with me more. I needed her to pay more attention to what I needed. I needed just as much support and nurturing as I gave. I finally came to a point where I exploded. We call it the dynamite incident. I said to her, "General information isn't enough for me. I need you to tell me what you're going through. And you have to deal with what's happening to me too! I want communication and I'm not going to settle for no!" I knew I had to break through. It really caused fireworks because Karen felt threatened, but I couldn't keep letting the gap widen.

Things did change after that. We started talking more. And since then, I feel much more hopeful. I have some idea where she is and where she's going, and where we are in the process.

LEARNING TO ASK

Even with a good support system and other friends to talk with, there will be times when you want and need attention from your partner and no one else will do. You may want time together, reassurance that you're loved, or help with some problem of your own. Whatever it is, you need to ask.

For many partners this is difficult. You may be afraid of making demands. You may feel the survivor is too fragile. But stating a need is not the same as making a demand. Stating your needs directly is the most effective way to communicate. But as one man explains, it's not always easy:

My habitual way of asking was to complain: "You haven't told me you loved me for ages," or "It's been four days since you've even wanted to make love. Monday night you were at class. Tuesday you went to the movies. . . ." Immediately my wife became defensive. She wanted to protect herself, not open up.

It felt too vulnerable for me to say, "I really need to be close to you" or "I'd like it if you'd rub my back" or "I've been feeling insecure. Would you tell me that you love me?" Coming forward with criticism was easier for me than exposing my simple need.

Even though you can't always get what you want, you increase your odds by asking clearly in a nonthreatening way. If, for example, you're not getting the attention you want, you might ask your partner to set aside one night a week to be together—an evening to *not* talk about sexual abuse, to just have a relaxed time together. The rest of the week, you won't expect her to really be with you. If she feels able, she may agree. If not, you can ask if an hour might be possible or even ten minutes. The bottom line might be, "Are you able to give *anything* at this point?" Although at some critical times the answer may be no, it's likely that most of the time she will be able to agree to some minimal togetherness.

As a bonus, sometimes just talking about a difficulty goes a long way toward dissolving it.

SETTING LIMITS

If you're committed to supporting your partner, that doesn't mean you're required to be available for every crisis or to take care of every need. Everyone has limits, and you need to be responsive to your own. When you try to extend beyond your capacity, there's usually a backlash of resentment that undercuts the value of what you've given. It's far better to admit honestly that you can't be there, to tell her that you love her and have faith in her, and then go on with your own life.

It's not realistic to expect yourself to be able to handle everything just because the survivor is healing from a major trauma. A relationship, even when one person is in crisis, involves two people, and you can't obscure yourself totally without damage to both of you.

You may not want to hear every detail of her healing process. Or you might not want to hear every detail every time. One woman said, "She had some horrible things happen to her and sometimes I don't even want to know." This partner felt guilty, but no one is superhuman. You do your best to be empathetic, but you also have the right to say no.

Everyone has different limits. Don't wait until you're past yours to you speak up. If you do, you're apt to be resentful, and it will make your communication less effective. Instead, speak up before you've reached your limits.

COPING WITH HER NEED FOR CONTROL

Survivors often have difficulty compromising or relinquishing control. It may seem to you that the survivor needs to control everything: when and if you have sex, how you should raise the children, even down to details of everyday life—when and where you go out to eat, which movie to see, where to hang a picture on the wall. Sometimes this control will be straightforward. Other times it will be indirect—for example, maintaining control through moodiness or preoccupation.

What you are up against is a survival mechanism that has been absolutely essential to her. By now it is a firmly entrenched habit. If you want to work toward balancing the power in your relationship, start by appreciating how fundamental her need for control is. She grew up being abused by an adult who was out of control. Now she feels that it is crucial to stay in charge of her life. It's only when the survivor knows that you understand the depth of her need for control that she will be able, gradually, to give it up.

Expect changes to go slowly, but do express your needs. For example, you can make it clear that you want this dynamic to begin to shift but don't expect to set all the terms. If you want to spend more time with your partner, try saying, "I need more time with you. How can we do that?" instead of "You've got to quit your yoga class. You're spending too many nights away from home."

If your partner is being particularly controlling, it may also help to ask if she wants to talk about what's going on. If she's feeling powerless in another area of her life, if something is frightening her, or if there's a crisis, her need for control may flare up. Often it helps just to recognize and talk about her fears.

TRUST

When children are sexually abused, their capacity to trust is shattered. Now this trust has to be consciously rebuilt. You can't just say, "Trust me—come on and trust me already," and expect your partner to leap into the land of the trusting. If she could do it that easily, she would have done it already. To make the shift from not trusting to trusting, she must go step by step. (Read "Learning to Trust" on p. 277.)

At the same time, *you* need to be conscious of just how trustworthy you are. Be scrupu-

lously honest with yourself: In what ways can she trust you safely? In what ways are you careless or undependable? Inconsiderate, preoccupied, or scared? Is there an arena in which you feel confident that you can absolutely be trusted, where you can commit yourself to come through no matter what? For example, if you're supposed to be on time, would you be willing to get there ten minutes early rather than be five minutes late?

To establish trust, you must work together. Try making a specific offer: "I'll water your plants while you're on vacation. You can tell me in detail just what each plant requires and I'll do it carefully." Or "Please trust me that if I offer to give you a massage, I won't try to seduce you into sex." Or "I'd like to make a commitment to you to cook dinner on Mondays and Wednesdays, since those are the days you work late. It won't always be a big deal, but there'll be something ready by the time you get home." You can add, "I really am reliable about this. Please risk it and trust me."

If you do come through, that will make an impression. And if you do this over and over, you will definitely build trust.

WILL THE REAL ABUSER PLEASE STAND UP?

It is common for survivors to see the person they're relating to as the abuser. Various things can trigger this identification: a similar gesture, an increase in closeness, sexual passion, anger. If you start to feel that the survivor isn't relating to you anymore but rather to the abuser from her past, you need to stop and check. Ask her, "What's happening? Did something scare you? Are you reminded of something?" Or more simply, "Where are you?"

Getting to know what the issues are, naming them, and tracing them back to their source will help differentiate the present from the past. One partner, Phil, describes a unique way he was able to do this for his wife:

> For a long time Barb had asked me to grow a beard. She kept telling me how attractive it would look. I wasn't very keen about the prospects of a scraggly-looking face, but I started growing it.
>
> About six months later, I told Barb I was thinking of whacking it off. She suddenly burst into tears. She told me that the hair on my face allowed her to maintain a reality check during certain times when flashbacks of her father molesting her interfered with our love-making. Barb's father was always clean-shaven.
>
> I don't believe Barb fully understood the importance of my having a beard until that conversation. Certainly I didn't. And keeping my hair took on a totally different perspective for me. I now take a certain delight in experimenting with various cuts and trims. More importantly, I've found yet another way I can be there for Barb.

This determination to distinguish her husband, whom she loved and wanted to make love with, from her father, who had molested her, appeared in a guise neither of them consciously recognized at first.

IF THE SHOE FITS

At one workshop for partners, Ellen explained that survivors often identified their partner with the abuser, and one man said that yes, that was happening in his relationship. Ellen went on to talk about not taking it personally and supporting the survivor in differentiating between the two, but she failed to mention the fact that sometimes partners *are* abusive.

About a year after that workshop, the survivor who was married to this man told Ellen that every time she had tried to get him to see that he was being abusive, he referred back to Ellen's statement that survivors often identify their partners with their abuser. And that became his excuse for not changing. Eventually, though, he was able to hear her and did join a group of men who batter. Their relationship improved dramatically after that.

This man, like many others, was not blatantly violent, but in subtle ways his behavior was threatening, and the power he wielded was destructive to their relationship.*

---

* If there is battering or violence in your relationship now, it's essential that you get help right away. Call the domestic violence hotline at (800) 799-SAFE. Also see "Learning to Live Without Violence" on p. 232 and "Domestic Violence, Rape, and Sexual Harassment" on p. 563 of the Resource Guide.

DEALING WITH HER PAIN, GRIEF, AND DEPRESSION

Recovering from child sexual abuse entails feeling the pain and grief of early wounding. This can be very difficult. As one partner put it, "It's hard to witness so much pain and be so helpless."

People tend to think they have to *do* something to help a person get over pain, but often there's not a lot you can do. Your place is not to make it better—your place is to be a loving partner through hard times.

CRISIS PERIODS

For many survivors, there is a time when pain eclipses every other feeling. These crisis periods often come when a survivor gets her first memories, initially faces the long-term effects of her abuse, or confronts the people who hurt her. If your partner is in a crisis stage of her healing, you will have your hands full. (See "The Emergency Stage" on p. 64.) She may be unable to meet any of your needs and few of her own.

It is extremely stressful to love someone who is in deep pain. Even if you're good at taking care of yourself, being with someone who's suffering inevitably affects you. On top of that, the survivor may be angry. She may blame you or pick fights. You may feel overwhelmed by the extras duties you've had to take on—paying for therapy, increased obligations with your children, assuming responsi-

Basket of Figs
BY ELLEN BASS

Bring me your pain, love. Spread
it out like fine rugs, silk sashes,
warm eggs, cinnamon
and cloves in burlap sacks. Show me

the detail, the intricate embroidery
on the collar, tiny shell buttons,
the hem stitched the way you were taught,
pricking just a thread, almost invisible.
Unclasp it like jewels, the gold
still hot from your body. Empty
your basket of figs. Spill your wine.

That hard nugget of pain, I would suck it,
cradling it on my tongue like the slick
seed of pomegranate. I would lift it

tenderly, as a great animal might
carry a small one in the private
cave of the mouth.

Ellen Bass, *Mules of Love* (Rochester, New York: BOA Editions, 2002).

bility for myriad tasks the survivor had always done before. And you may be frightened, unsure of what to do.

At one workshop, a man described his conflict and guilt as he was torn between taking care of his wife and taking care of his child during a crisis: "It'll be in the middle of a Saturday afternoon and my wife will be totally hysterical. I want to comfort her, but our four-year-old daughter is there and she's affected by all of this. So I take my daughter out—to a shopping mall or something—but I feel so guilty. I'm not there supporting my wife. But I can't just leave the child."

Everyone in the group hastened to assure this man that he had done the right thing. It was essential that he take care of his child and give his wife the space to be with her feelings. The partner was reassured, but their lives were still in tumult. "It can happen anytime, any day," he said.

"I know what you mean," another man said. "When I walk into the house I never know what I'll find. It's totally unpredictable."

And another: "I thought I had a reasonable relationship with a reasonable person."

Periods of intensity like this are hard on you, as well as on the survivor. Make sure you both have the support you need, take care of yourself as best you can, and try to remember, "This too shall pass."

IF YOUR PARTNER IS SUICIDAL OR YOU'RE AFRAID SHE MIGHT BE

If the survivor is talking about suicide or has attempted suicide, do not try to deal with this alone. Get help.

Call suicide prevention. Make sure you have the phone numbers of the survivor's therapist. Call her or him. If the survivor is isolated, take an active role in helping her find skilled support. Have her make a no-suicide agreement. (For information on no-suicide contracts, see p. 37.)

While it's impossible to stop a person from killing herself if she is truly determined to do so, these measures can help sustain the survivor through a time of acute despair. (For more on preventing suicide, see "Don't Kill Yourself," p. 36.)

RELATING TO HER FAMILY

Survivors usually have complicated feelings about their families. The mother who didn't protect her also tucked her in at night and sang lullabies. The brother who raped her was a victim of their parent's abuse, too. Her feelings may be complex and difficult to sort out, and they may change over the course of her healing.

Your feelings may be complicated, too. You may feel loyalty to or love for her family. If the abuser is someone you've respected, you may find it hard to see him now as the perpetrator of a terrible violation. You may not want to believe it's true. Or you may want the survivor to forgive the abuser or other relatives. You may want relations to go on as they always have.

But this is not possible. It is essential that you not defend the abuser for past or present actions. It is up to the survivor to determine what kind of relationship she wants to have with the abuser, with the people who didn't protect her, or with anyone in her family who doesn't respect her healing now.

If you feel an allegiance to the abuser, you need a place to talk about your feelings, but the survivor is not the one to whom you should turn. She should not have to convince you that the abuser is to blame or that she has a right to be angry. And if she wants to sever relations with the abuser or her family, you will have to go along with that decision even if it's not what you want. To insist on remaining on friendly terms with someone who abused your partner, or who denies or minimizes the abuse, is a betrayal in itself.

If, on the other hand, you're so raging mad that you want to kill the abuser, it may be difficult to allow the survivor the room to sort through her own mixed feelings. Although it's essential that she not minimize what was done to her, it frequently takes some time for women to feel the full range and depth of their feelings.

Sometimes partners of survivors think that they shouldn't get angry with abusers or family members, especially if the survivor isn't angry yet. But your anger can be a helpful catalyst in awakening her own. She needs to hear that she has a right to her anger, that it's safe to be angry, and that you're angry that she was hurt.

Although it's important not to overwhelm her with your own reactions, your anger is appropriate, justified, and ultimately in her best interests. If she tells you that she doesn't want to hear it, respect her request, but find other people to talk to. You wouldn't be angry if you didn't care about her. It's part of love.

ACTIVE SUPPORT

There are many things you can do to actively support the survivor in dealing with her family. One partner reads the letters that come from her lover's relatives. She passes on any important information and then throws out the letter. Others field phone calls or screen e-mails.

Phil regularly composes letters to his wife's parents and relatives:

One of my coping mechanisms for my anger and frustration is writing confrontational letters to Barb's parents and other relatives. In fact, I have spent hours and hours in front of the word processor with a letter—polishing every insignificant word and phrase.

You can accompany the survivor when she visits her family or support her during disclosures or truth-telling conversations. When one survivor went to therapy with her parents, her partner sat in on the session. Although he said very little, his presence was enormously reassuring.

If there's a way you'd like to offer support, ask the survivor first. If it's not what she wants, you don't have to feel hurt or rejected. You're a caring person who is willing to try, and she'll probably appreciate your intentions.

SEXUALITY

For most couples in which one or both partners are healing from child sexual abuse, sex is particularly difficult. Since the means by which the survivor was abused were sexual, it makes sense that this would be an arena charged with problems.

It will help you to be allied with the survivor if you understand the process of healing sexually. Many survivors have been split sexually—what they felt inside didn't match the way they acted on the outside. To heal, the survivor must stop doing anything she doesn't genuinely feel.

Healing sexually takes conscious time and attention. It requires stopping, slowing down, and reexamining everything, so that she has time to integrate the feelings, memories, and associations that emerge.

This process will probably have a radical effect on your sex life. The survivor may want no sex at all for a while. She may want sex only under very controlled circumstances. She may want only certain sexual activities. She may want only to touch you and not be touched herself, or vice versa. She may want sex only if she initiates, only if you massage each other first, only if you have time to talk before or afterward. Sometimes it may seem to you that she wants sex only if the moon is new, it's snowing, *and* the kids are at summer camp.

The survivor may have difficulty staying present when you make love. One partner explained, "We'll be kissing and making out and then I get this eerie feeling that I'm all alone." She may have flashbacks to her original abuse.

She may have to stop suddenly. She may go numb or have no desire whatsoever. If your partner has had orgasms, she may stop having them. Or she may cry hysterically when she comes, as she connects with powerful feelings of rage, horror, or sadness. She may become afraid of or disgusted by sex. Or she may vacillate. As one partner put it, "I feel like this oven getting turned on and off, but I don't know which way to turn."

Frustration: Roger's Story

There was a long time when we shuffled around to find out what was safe sexually. Karen set the standards. She began orchestrating what our lovemaking would involve, and I went along with that because I wanted to support the growth she needed.

It felt to me like there was this stone wall with this one little box in it where we could make love according to certain rules. Then, and only then, was it okay. For a while it felt real hopeless. The box kept getting smaller and smaller. It was very difficult for me to be patient when I had no idea whether she was in the first 10 percent or the last 10 percent of working this out. I felt like she was saying, "I'm going to work on this stuff. You're just going to have to forget all about sex until I'm done. I'll call you and tell you when I'm through." I knew it could take years. It felt like it could take forever.

It seemed like my only options were either to shut down or to leave. I didn't want to leave. And the problem with shutting down was this: She finally gets through her stuff and there I would be, all shut down, and how do you break through the ice then?

In the beginning I just stuffed down my needs and said, "I'll wait my turn," but then I realized I had always put someone else in front of me, and my turn never came. I finally got to the point where I realized I couldn't keep sitting around patiently waiting, slam my dick into a drawer until she was through, and just forget it.

THE VALUE OF COMMUNICATION

When couples first admit that they have sexual difficulties, they often see only two options when sex isn't going well: pretend and continue to make love or be honest and stop completely. Once the survivor is committed to honesty, she stops. At this point the partner is usually hurt or angry and withdraws more or less. The survivor is left feeling guilty and ashamed of her failure. And both people are isolated.

This is a time for communication. Talk to each other. Ask questions. What's happening that is upsetting her? When did she go numb? When did she get scared? Did she have a flashback? But don't barrage her with questions. The survivor may not be ready to talk right away. She may need time to stay quiet with her feelings. She may want to wait a day or two. Or she may want to spill everything out immediately. The important thing is that the two of you stay engaged through the process.

(See "Working with Triggers" on p. 312 for a thorough discussion of how to stay engaged when difficulties arise during sex.)

One partner described the process with her lover, Jesse, this way:

> Eventually Jesse told me that she didn't want me to just turn away if she didn't want to make love, or if she spaced out while we were making love. She asked me to talk to her, to help her identify her feelings and to express them. We discovered that this communication right on the spot really helped.
>
> Jesse began to identify her feelings more precisely. Rather than say "I'm not sure if I want to make love," she'd say "I feel very closed right now. I'm afraid to open up and let you in." Often she discovered that it wasn't so much the sex that scared her, but the intimacy, the trusting.

If the survivor hasn't explained what she wants from you, ask. If she doesn't know, experiment together. For every survivor, what is frightening will be somewhat different. By communicating, you can explore the threatening aspects and find ways to move through them.

CREATIVE INTIMACY

Many of us are accustomed to getting our needs for intimacy met through sex. Sex is the only way we really feel loved. When sex is not an option, we're stymied. Yet there are times when simple holding or tender words can bring comfort and closeness. Soothing, rather than forced passion, may be more appropriate when you are ragged from a difficult day or are overly tired. As you begin to explore a variety of avenues for intimacy, you will feel less compulsive, freer, and more satisfied.

Look at the needs you meet through sex. We all need intimacy, touch, validation, companionship, affection, nurturing, pleasure, intensity, love, passion, release. See which of these needs you can meet in other ways.

OKAY, I'VE DONE ALL THAT

Some needs simply can't be met in nonsexual ways. Some of what you want is sex, making love—that specific combination of you and your lover coming together with all your body parts engaged. Foot rubs aren't going to do it. You're frustrated and angry. Okay. Allow yourself to be frustrated and angry.

It's important to be clear about what you need even if you're not getting it at the time. Don't pretend to yourself that you're satisfied if you're not. Don't be dishonest with yourself about what you want or need. One partner, whose wife hadn't yet remembered her abuse, tells the following story:

There was a time early on in my marriage when my wife wanted to be permanently celibate, like Gandhi. Because I didn't know myself very well, I decided that if she wanted to be celibate, I would accept that. The way I put it to myself was that I loved *her*, that she was more

important to me than the nature of our relationship.

This was very noble. It was also a complete failure. I was hurt, angry, and frustrated with myself and with her. It would have been far better if I could have been honest with both of us and said that although I loved her, I didn't want a celibate marriage. But I didn't know then that I was entitled to want or to need.

Your partner is trying to learn about herself, to learn what she does and doesn't want. This is an excellent time for you to explore what *you* need in a relationship. Keep in mind your image of the satisfying relationship you're working toward, even if you can't realize it in the present.

Healing sexually is usually a slow process, but as one partner said, "Going slow is a lot faster than not going at all."

MUTUAL HEALING

Few of us feel totally healthy, joyous, integrated, and free. When one person in a relationship is dealing with sex in such a conscious way, both partners have the opportunity to heal sexually. One partner explains:

The quality of my own experience of sexuality has improved dramatically since my lover and I began to work together on her healing. I can't ever just go through the motions anymore. Both of us are more present than ever. The sexual inhibitions and tense, blocked places I used to experience are much less present because I have had to become aware of myself. I've had to face my own fears and vulnerabilities. So, although I've assisted her, she's assisted me as well. Even speaking selfishly, it's been more than worth it.

DO I WANT TO BE IN THIS RELATIONSHIP?

Being the partner of a survivor can be extremely challenging, and the issues you are dealing with are not ones that will be resolved quickly or easily. Therefore, it's important to be realistic about your commitment to the relationship. Are you willing to hang in through some rough times? For how long? Is your bond strong enough to withstand the problems you're facing? One partner put it this way:

> If someone came to me and said, "I just found out my partner's dealing with incest. What should I do?" I'd say, "Seriously evaluate your relationship and how much you're willing to put out when you may not get much back in return. After that, make sure your partner gets professional help, and consider therapy for yourself, too. It'll bring up a lot for you. But first, evaluate the relationship, because it's hell. You've got to be strong. You've got to be patient. You're going to get angry."

Another partner recalled:

> During the period where I felt a widening chasm, a lot of what I went on was just faith and commitment: "I promised to hang in with this no matter what, and damn it, I'm going to make it work." Our wedding vows said we would be together "through all the changes of our lives." I often remembered those exact words. Either I was going to eat those words or I was going to back them up.

And a third confessed:

> If someone had shown me the job description for being the partner of an incest survivor, I never would have signed up for the job.

ACKNOWLEDGING DOUBT

Most partners go through periods when they wonder whether they are doing the right thing, doubt their capacity to help the survivor, or question their overall commitment to the relationship. You may wonder if the survivor will heal or if the relationship will stabilize. Partners often question their capacity to deal with the deep pain that accompanies healing. One partner explained that her lover, a survivor, kept a journal where she wrote about all that she was going through: "She says if I knew what was in those notebooks, I'd leave her. Sometimes I wonder myself."

You may worry whether you're repeating a self-destructive pattern of your own. This might mean remaining in a situation where your needs aren't getting met, staying in crisis, or concentrating on someone else's problems instead of your own. One partner, the child of an alcoholic, said, "I just don't think it's healthy for me to be waiting around for someone to change. That's what my childhood was all about."

When you have doubts, it's important to accept them and to talk about them. While it's good to let the survivor know what you're thinking, it's also important not to burden her excessively. Find other people to talk to.

Even if you're married or are in a committed relationship, you still have a right to express your feelings and make choices about staying together. You can decide that you will remain in the relationship no matter what. Or you can choose to reassess an earlier commitment. But if you consistently feel trapped, your feelings of resentment are likely to poison the relationship. On the other hand, making a conscious choice to stay together can be empowering for both of you. Going through a difficult time is much more bearable when it's something you are choosing to do.

IF YOU'RE THINKING OF LEAVING

Partners often feel guilty if they think of leaving. At one partners' workshop, a woman told Ellen, "I want to leave but I feel like I shouldn't. She's trying so hard."

Ellen replied, "Just because someone is trying doesn't mean you have to make a commitment to go on the journey with her. You can leave and wish her well. The only good reason to do this is because you really want to. It doesn't help her if you stay only because she needs somebody."

You're not necessarily a better person if you stay. You're not selfish or cruel if you decide to leave. The essential thing is to be honest. It's very useful to be honest with someone who's been abused, even if the truth is blunt and miserable. Most survivors have had to deal with too many lies already.

Admitting what you can handle and the extent of your commitment is essential. It gives you both the best chance of growing together through this challenge. And if it becomes clear that you are not able or willing to meet each other's needs, you then can separate in a way that's respectful, even with its pain.

SEPARATING

Sometimes you have both tried your best and it still isn't working out. Your needs are incompatible. You're fighting all the time. You keep going around on the same loops and you're stuck.

It's common to get bogged down temporarily. No couples glide through the healing process smoothly. But if the bitter times are outweighing the progress, and if you feel that you're in each other's way more than you're being helpful friends, then you may want to consider a separation.

Separations need not be permanent. A separation of a week, a month, six months, or a year can sometimes give you both some room to disentangle and actually prevent the need for permanent separation. Although separations are usually painful, there is often a good deal of relief as well. Both people get the opportunity to try to meet their own needs and live their own lives without tripping over each other.

Separations, like most major decisions, work best when there is mutual agreement. Leaving the survivor in the middle of a crisis is not going to be beneficial for her. If she's just recovering memories, inundated with flashbacks, and terrified of being alone, she's not going to appreciate your rational words in favor of time apart. But if you both agree that you've tried everything else and it's time for space apart, that can be a positive step, not only for each of you individually but for the relationship as well.

If you don't want to separate but need some way to make room for your vastly differing needs during this crisis, an amended living-together agreement can help. You might come up with something like this: "For the next four months, we'll live together but we will be like two ships that pass in the night. That way you'll have space to concentrate on healing and I won't be hanging on your every step. This is different from our regular relationship."

PERMANENT SEPARATIONS

Working through the difficulties of healing from child sexual abuse sometimes causes more stress than a relationship can bear. A new relationship may not have enough foundation to hold up under the pressure. The coping patterns of both people may have dovetailed for so long that there's no way to sort them out. And one or both of you may have changed to the point where you no longer want to be together. Although a permanent separation or divorce is painful, staying together when you truly can't support each other, can't grow, and can't make peace is worse for both of you.

IF YOU STAY

There are no guarantees about the length of time healing will take for any survivor. But if your partner is actively working—and you are too—you can be assured that things will change. The problems you're confronting now won't be exactly the same as the ones you'll be dealing with six months or a year from now. You are not in a static situation. There will be transformation. Of course, she's not going to be perfectly healed at some specific moment in time. But then again, neither are you.

It's difficult to be patient when you're under stress. You're trying to work, keep a roof over your head, cope with her problems, cope with your own, change, and keep it all together without going crazy. But she needs to pace her own healing. You can encourage, but you can't rush her. You can say what you need and negotiate what's possible, but sometimes you're just going to have to wait.

And of course it helps to take breaks. One husband of a survivor said, "I'd be happy if I never heard the word 'growth' again." If you feel like this, it's time for a break. The survivor may not need one, but you do. Take a weekend off and go fishing. Take the kids and visit your family. Or just get out more on your own in ways that give you relaxation, enjoyment, and a break from the healing process.

IT'S WORTH IT

Moving together through the tight places, learning about each other's fears and insecurities, becoming more sensitive to each other and to yourself, is a lifelong process. If you consider this a long-term partnership, a few years of struggle is worth it:

> It feels to me right now that what's coming through on the other side is a much more fulfilling and exciting relationship than the one we started with. It's made us close. I mean, you don't get close living in a bowl of cherries. It's coming through stuff together that makes the bond stronger. When you're not dealing with it, it seems like a mountain. In reality, it comes down to a smaller scale when you take it apart and work with it. In retrospect, it really is not a very long process. I mean, what's a couple of years?

And as one partner makes clear, things do change:

> Being sexually abused isn't that unusual. The shocking thing is that it's so common that it almost isn't an appropriate way to delineate people anymore. What's important isn't that it happened to her, it's how she's dealt with it in her life. She's not a victim anymore. She's a survivor. I'm coming to her years after she's delved into all this. She's a well woman. I'm happy with her just the way she is.

ALL THAT IS FINE AND STRONG BETWEEN YOU

When there are serious problems, it's easy to concentrate so much on the difficulties that you lose sight of all that is fine and strong between you. Make time to enjoy what you really like in your relationship right now. Affirm those aspects to each other. In the midst of all this growth and change, remember to celebrate what you've got.

In the meantime, expect her to be powerful. Don't think of her as a victim. Don't see her as weak, sick, or permanently damaged. Instead, hold the attitude that she's a whole human being going through some difficult struggles. See her as courageous and determined. Concentrate on her strength and her spirit.

Reflecting the survivor's strengths back to her is a gift you can give throughout the healing process. Even if it's a time when she doesn't want your direct help, even if you're separated by distance or differing feelings, you can always hold in your mind the image of her as a healthy, vibrant person. Healing from child sexual abuse is a heroic feat. She deserves your respect, confidence, and admiration.

PART FIVE

Courageous Women

Introduction

"Until lions start writing down their own stories, tales of the hunt shall always glorify the hunter."

– AFRICAN PROVERB

The seventeen stories of these courageous women represent a broad range of experience and highlight particular aspects of the healing process. You will probably see parts of your own life reflected in them. We hope you will find at least one woman with whom you can identify.

The stories are not finished, because the lives are not finished. Each represents one fixed moment in time—the day the interview took place. Often when we sent copies of the interviews back to the survivors, they'd say, "But that's not me. So much has happened since then!" Like all of us, these women have continued to grow.

Some of the women whose stories you are about to read were interviewed more than twenty years ago; others were interviewed in preparation for this edition. As a result, their stories may reflect different perspectives, different stages of the healing process, and access to different resources for healing.*

We interviewed women near the beginning of the healing process and others who have been healing for more than twenty years. We have chosen stories at both ends of this continuum to give you a sense of the immediacy and intensity of the early stages, as well as the wisdom gleaned by women who have been healing much longer.

---

* We indicate which women were interviewed for the twentieth-anniversary edition in the footnotes that accompany each story.

To make room for the new stories, we have had to edit down some of the original ones, as well as delete some entirely. This has been a difficult process since we are aware of the immense value of every story. It was hard to let any of them go. But we think the final result is a collection of stories with both range and depth.

Take your time reading these stories. Give yourself a chance to digest each one, rather than reading them all at once. Let yourself feel. They are meant to be an inspiration, a touchstone, a reminder that healing is truly possible.

NAMES OR PSEUDONYMS: THE RIGHT TO CHOOSE

It's such a disappointment not to be able to use my own name. I've earned the right to own my words, my journey. I feel angry at the situation, denied what is mine by birthright—my name connected with my truth. Strange, so much of the journey has been a "naming" of shadows. And now I must place my own name back in the shadows . . .

—GIZELLE

Most of the women who share their stories here chose to use pseudonyms to maintain their privacy. But there were a number of women who wanted to use their own names. They saw identifying themselves as a way to end the secrecy and shame that burden survivors of child sexual abuse. They also wanted, quite simply, to tell their story honestly—to name themselves, their abuser, the place where they lived, the facts of their lives.

As authors, we were committed to respecting each woman's decision. We wanted each woman's participation to be an empowering experience for her. However, it is not legally possible for a publisher to print a survivor's story with actual names and places if the abuser (and possibly other family members) is alive and identifiable (except in cases where the abuse has already been made public—for example, through a trial).

Regrettably, this situation perpetuates the very hiding and silence that we are working to end. We discussed this problem with the women who wanted to use their own names and together decided that we'd rather use the stories with pseudonyms and changes in identifying details than not include them at all. We all felt their value to survivors was so great that it was worth compromise.

Judy Gold

"There's nothing as wonderful as starting to heal, waking up in the morning and knowing that nobody can hurt you if you don't let them."

Judy Gold is forty-five years old.* She is a musician and lives with her husband, Howard, in an upper-middle-class, predominantly Jewish suburb of New York. Howard is a businessman and works for his father-in-law in the garment industry. Judy and Howard have been married for twenty-five years and have four children, the eldest of whom is nineteen.

Of her childhood, Judy says: "My father's sister died in an insane asylum and I was named for her. I was always told I was going to end up just like her—bad and crazy. We were upper middle class. My mother was addicted to prescription drugs. She was always hazy. Before she married my father, she had been a published author. It's

too bad because she could have had a successful life and it ended up being a real zero. She's dead now.

"My father was a very violent man. He was like Dr. Jekyll and Mr. Hyde. He was loving toward us whenever our family was portrayed to the outside world. He used to march us out every Sunday night to a fancy restaurant for dinner. It was like Make Way for Ducklings. But what went on before we got into the car was a horror show.

"The world loved him. He set up scholarships; he helped build the local temple. He's given buildings to universities and hospitals. So no one would ever suspect what went on in that house.

"The only time I can remember him being loving was when he was in my bed. He would batter

---

* Judy Gold chose to use a pseudonym.

me at night and after he'd beat me up, he'd make me take his shoes off and kiss him good night. And then in the morning he'd climb in my bed and molest me. There was never any intercourse, but there was everything else.

"My first memories of being abused are tied in to my sister's birth, when I was six. The beatings continued till I went away to college, but the incest stopped when I was about twelve, when my baby sister turned six. That's always made me wonder if he moved on to her.

"Even though the actual abuse stopped when I reached puberty, the sexual innuendos never stopped. He's just sleazy, horrible. You wouldn't want to meet him. Yet, as I say, the whole world loves him."

How did the incest affect me? I've never really been in touch with me or my feelings. I was always real tough. If I ran fast enough and far enough, then I wouldn't have to think. I did a lot of drinking, a lot of drugs, a lot of fast living. I would drive at high speeds. I would think nothing of walking out at three in the morning in a deserted area. It was almost like I was tempting fate.

I had learned to tune out when my father beat me as a child. I never physically felt any pain. I used to say, "You'll never make me cry." And I never did. I allowed myself to feel anger, but never sadness or pain. It's what saved me, but it got out of control, the living out of my body. Spacing out was a very common thing for me. It wasn't until about a year and a half ago that I stopped doing that. I would be sitting talking to you, and I wouldn't be in my body. I used to say, "I turn into foam rubber."

Everything went numb. My whole body would tingle, like your fingers going to sleep. Or my hearing would go off.

A dread that something bad was waiting for me has followed me most of my life. I have a morbid fear of the dark. I will never close my eyes in the shower. There are parts of my own house I am just beginning to go into.

There Was Always a Wall Around Me

I could go anywhere and make friends, but I allowed people to get only so close. The minute you got closer, I turned you off. I felt I was filled with something evil, and that evil rubbed off on anyone I came into contact with.

Then I met Howard, who was my knight in shining armor. I was twenty-three. He was going to save me from all this craziness. Howard is the antithesis of my father. My survivor self knew I could not get into a relationship that would be a repeat of what I'd had with my father. Yet I know I've tried to goad him. I would test him. I'd say, "Go on, I know you want to hit me." And he never did. When I look back, I marvel at the composure he had.

Howard put such order into my life. And I really believed he was going to save me from the insane asylum. That's how the relationship began. Of course, things have changed. Things are much more realistic. As I began to work on this stuff, I was strong enough to say to Howard, "You know, I'm never again going to hold you accountable for my failures, but I'm never going to give you credit for my successes either." That was the beginning of the eroding of the white knight.

My sexuality has definitely been affected by the incest. I was uncomfortable having sex, but I never knew why. Every time Howard and I had sex in our marriage, I would wake him up and tell him I was sure someone was breaking into our house. And afterwards, I would get up out of bed, go to the kitchen and eat, and make like it had never happened: "Who me? Have sex?" And the strange thing is I enjoyed the sex! It was hard to get started, but once I got into it, I really enjoyed it. There were parts of the incest I enjoyed too, and that has been a really heavy trip for me. I mean, my body responded. It had to. But I'm not so quick to forgive that part of me.

I've never been able to have sex in the morning, obviously. Howard wouldn't dare touch me in the morning. We've had a lot of fights, mostly over sex. As much as I loved him and looked at him like he was going to save me, I never trusted him.

It was also very hard for me to hold my kids. They suffered because of what happened to me. I was not a nurturing mother. People see me as a wonderful mother. They marvel at how laid back I am in my parenting, but what they don't understand is that I was afraid to get close to those kids because I felt that I would infect them. So what they interpreted as giving my children independence was me being scared to death of them. I was scared to touch them.

If you asked people, they would tell you I was the most self-assured, self-confident, commanding, imposing woman. Once I started therapy, I would always complain, "I don't know who I am. People tell me I'm one thing, but I feel like I'm another." They see me as

someone who has her whole life in order, because I never talked to anybody about what I really felt.

Come On, Ask Me

When I stopped smoking, I gained thirty pounds in four months. Somebody gave me the name of this therapist who did hypnosis for overeating. I really believe that there are no accidents. I think I ate myself up to those thirty pounds for the purpose of seeking therapy. It was right there on the surface, waiting to come out.

I was almost provocative in the kinds of things I said to my therapist, like "Oh, you should know my family." In other words, "Ask me. Come on. I'll tell you if you ask me."

What was going to be five sessions has now become over four years. A couple of months into the therapy, he asked me to tell him about my father. I said he used to beat me up. And he said, "What else did he do to you?" And I said, "Nothing." And he said, again, "What else did he do to you?" And I said, "Oh, well, he crawled into my bed." And he said, "What else?" And I kept insisting there was nothing. And then he just asked me point-blank, "Did he ever touch you?" That started the whole thing. I finally admitted, "Yes, he touched me."

When we started using hypnosis, I got to the first memory. Then I started to remember incidents without the hypnosis. I got to the point where I could remember my father's precise smell. It took me two years to clearly remember what had happened.

The one thing that brought it all into focus—and it was the hardest thing—was a memory that I had always wet my pants. I used to hide all these sticky underpants in my closet as a little girl. And now I know I didn't pee in my pants at all. My father had ejaculated on me when I had them on, and I had saved all those underpants on the floor of my closet. My grandmother found piles of them in the closet and she showed them to my mother, who accused me of wetting my pants. I told her I hadn't done it, but she wouldn't believe me. She punished me for denying it, and he beat me for lying later the same night. As I pieced this together in therapy, I realized she had to have known the difference between urine and semen. It was the worst memory I had. But it made it all very real.

My mother's death freed me up to remember all of this. I remember when my mother was dying, I talked about the beatings. I said, "Why didn't you stop him? How could you allow him to do those things to us?" And her answer was "What could I do?"

I had always adored my mother because she was so talented. And I felt such pity for her. But when I realized that she had known what was going on, I hated her. I even went to her grave and stomped on it. I was screaming at her. They could have locked me up then if they had seen me.

After I got through all the anger, I realized that she really was helpless. I'm sure that she had been a victim herself. And she sacrificed me so that she could live.

If for No Other Reason Than Spite, I Forced Myself to Get Better

When I first started remembering, I was very scattered. I was totally depressed. I gained a tremendous amount of weight. I didn't go out of the house. I became very solitary. I couldn't stop crying for a long time. I was making up for forty years of not crying. I could have been hospitalized at points. It was an effort to get out of bed in the morning. It was an effort to decide what to put on. I would go through periods of that and then periods of feverish activity. I would play the piano for hours on end, and then I wouldn't sit down at it again for months.

I didn't want anyone touching me. There was no sex. I had a tremendous amount of back pain. The psoriasis I'd always had got worse.

But the worst part was the terrible despair. I just felt like I was down in the sewer and I was never going to see daylight again. And I kept saying, "Why did I do this? Why did I open up Pandora's box?" I cursed myself because I could see no end in sight. I remember saying to my therapist, "Am I ever going to smile again?"

I felt like I was being battered from the inside. It was like a parade of demons, only the parade never stopped. I'd no sooner put one to bed than another one would come out to haunt me. There were a lot of nightmares; I was always being chased by an unknown male.

I felt so close to crazy, but I kept saying to myself, "Are you going to let him win out? How can you let that prophecy come true?" If for no other reason than spite, I forced myself to get better. I was hell-bent on surviving, if only to show him that I was going to outlast him.

If I were to name one particular reason I got through it, it would be the anger. I was angry at myself first, for having delved into the subject. What did I need it for? I was angry at myself for having put on so much weight, for doing all those drugs. And then suddenly the anger starting being directed where it should have gone all along. And that anger—at him—is what fueled me to get well. When I would be raging, my therapist would say to me, "Hold on to that anger. That's your best friend." And he was right.

Then I had to grieve. That came toward the end of the process. I grieved for that little girl who never was. I never had a childhood, and I think that's what I mourned more than anything. For the longest time, I never understood what my therapist meant when he said, "Get in touch with the little girl. Feel her. Forgive her."

It took me a long time to understand that I hadn't done anything to cause the molestation. The little girl was not to blame. Even if I had lain there spread-eagled, naked, he was the adult, and I was the child, and not accountable. I finally believe that now. I've been able to forgive her.

I Found Out I Wasn't Alone

Along the way, there were little tiny victories that got me through the next day: like getting up, like getting out of bed, like saying, "I'm going to go to an exercise class today." It was a victory to be able to make dinner for my fam-ily, to be able to be out there in the market with people.

Another thing that helped me was reading articles, books, anything I could get my hands on. I watched every program about incest. I kept saying, "It's got to get better, because other people have lived through this and survived." It helped to know I was not alone.

I have a very dear friend from my college days who I've kept in touch with all these years. She knew I was in therapy for eating, and she could see that I was gaining weight. About a year into my therapy we went out to lunch, and she said to me, "I have to ask you a question. Were you ever sexually abused? You don't have to answer if you don't want to. I'm asking you because I was, and you sound just like me." You could have knocked me over. I couldn't even get the word *yes* out. I just nodded my head and started sobbing. And that has been one of the greatest sources of healing for me.

It's Our Problem, Howard

It was two years into my therapy before I told Howard what was going on. I never told him before because I thought he would be repulsed by me. It never occurred to me that he might be angry with my father instead. Until that point, I'd just said to him, "I'm dealing with some very heavy issues, and I just don't feel free to discuss them with you." I let him know I was in trouble, but I wasn't going to tell him why. It was a nightmare. The fact that we're still married is amazing.

In order to tell Howard, I had to get drunk and drugged and angry. I just spit it all out:

"Oh, yeah, let me tell you something. . . ." He was numb. He never said a word. I picked something up and I threw it at him. And I said, "Damn you, you give me a reaction. Do you hate me? Do you think I'm terrible? Do you think I'm dirty?" I was filling in the blanks. Everything I thought he should think of me, I told him.

He admits now that for a whole year he never really integrated the information. I don't think he believed a lot of it. He'd seen my father get violent, so he believed that part. But he didn't want to talk about the incest. I think he operated on the premise "If I don't talk about it, then it doesn't exist."

But I would force him to talk about it. I said, "Didn't you ever wonder why I always fooled around for hours to avoid coming to bed? Didn't you ever wonder why you couldn't touch me in the morning?"

I remember one time Howard said to me something about "my problem." And I said to him, "You don't understand. The minute I told you about this, it became our problem." It took him a long time to realize it was a problem we shared now. It was very hard for him. It still is. And it's doubly hard because he works with my father.

Once we started to talk about it, we talked all the time. I would sometimes say, "I can't talk about it anymore." Or "Let's promise that on Tuesday and Thursday night we won't discuss it." We actually had to make appointments not to talk about it. Your brain can only absorb so much.

I still have battles with Howard over the incest because he is embarrassed by it. He would say things like "Be careful who you tell." And I would say, "Look, I don't care who knows. As long as I'm the one who tells them." And he would say, "You'd better be careful who you tell. Some people would love to get some dirt on you." He's ashamed. He'd rather I kept it a secret.

Howard is thrilled about the changes in me—that I'm off the drugs and off the cigarettes—but it's hard for him to give up control. He's been used to having the control in our relationship. And now he's had to give a lot of it up. He's given up all control in terms of sex.

Now it's when I want it and that's been very hard for him, but he's been wonderful about it. I've finally been honest. A lot of these problems came up because I was so dishonest. Now I can say to him, "I don't want you to touch me." I don't have to hang out in the bathroom for half an hour or get busy doing something. I used to say my greatest creative time was at night. That was just so I didn't have to go to bed.

I am just starting to realize that I am a very sexual human being. It's such a nice feeling to know that after I have sex I can go to sleep. I don't have to go in that kitchen and eat and pretend that it didn't happen, that it was somebody else in that bedroom responding.

It's taken a lot of hard work for us to stay together. There have been some real rough times. My way of dealing with most problems was to run away from them. And in a marriage, you just can't do that. Gradually we've learned to deal with problems right when they happen. And that's making us closer than ever.

It Was Time to Rebuild

Over time, I've come to accept what happened to me. I don't think there's any more to remember. And even if there is, so what? It can't be any worse than what I've already remembered. So what am I going to remember, one more night?

The incest happened. I can't change that. But I have the rest of my life ahead of me. I'm not going to live the way I lived the first forty years, because they weren't fun-filled years. But I don't have to. And that's what I've worked so hard for. I can change.

There was a point where I felt like I had gotten all the poison out and it was time to rebuild. It was a different pain. Now the healing has to do with dealing with my life: What do I do from here on in? How do I set things up that I'm not so rigid in what I expect from myself?

I finally know that I'm a nice person. I'm not that sleazy, slimy black goo I thought I was. It's nice to look in the mirror and say, "You're not ugly. You're not crazy." And I like myself. I never liked myself before. I always thought that what they'd told me was true, that I was bad. But I wasn't bad. I was screaming for help and nobody heard.

Eva Smith

"You get tired of dealing with incest all the time. There's an ending point to everything. There's an ending point to life. Why can't there be an ending point to dealing with this shit?"

Eva Smith is an African-American woman in her early thirties who lives in California.* She is a therapist and an artist. She lives with her two teenage children. "I share this information with you as a gift of healing for other women. I am truly living my life now, after just surviving for so many years."

Between the ages of three and eight, I was molested by my great-uncle. From nine to fifteen, my stepfather molested me. I grew up just trying to live from day to day and survive, wishing the whole thing would be over and stop. I used to pray my stepfather would get struck by lightning. I wasn't above making a pact with

the devil to get rid of him. Anything. And anything happened. I got pregnant.

I had always been a fat child. When I was thirteen, I weighed 188 pounds. And then I lost weight. So when I got pregnant, everybody just thought I was getting fat again. I'll never forget—I was going into my junior year in high school and my mother and I went shopping for clothes, and my mother came into the dressing room with me. She really was looking at me and she was saying, "You look different." And I said, "I'm just getting fat again." And she said, "I'm taking you to the doctor." That was in September and considering that my son was born in November, I must have been at least seven months pregnant, but all this was brand new to me.

When the doctor told my mother I was pregnant, she asked me who the father was,

---

* Eva Smith chose to use a pseudonym.

and I told her. She confronted my stepfather and he claimed that he knew nothing about it. Within a week we left him and went down South.

When I first realized I was pregnant, I attempted suicide. It was a hard time for me. I knew I needed therapy. I wish somebody else had realized it at the time!

My mother told me I didn't have to keep the child, that I could put it up for adoption or that she would raise it as her own. I chose to keep that child because it was the first thing that was ever mine.

I created a cover story about who the father was. I said he was some boy I'd been going with. I had to deal with a lot of put-downs from people, you know, 'cause I was fifteen and having this baby.

Because of all the things that happened to me, there was this question that used to haunt me, you know, "Why me?" Those were the years I call my trauma years. And I went out of the trauma years into being a battered wife.

I got married at seventeen. I was already pregnant with my daughter. My husband and I were the same age. I told my husband about my stepfather and that he was my son's father. If only I knew then what I know now! I would have never told him. Because he got jealous. Every time we argued, he'd bring that up. I was different kinds of whores and sluts and this and that.

We were into it before we ever got married. We used to argue once a week when we were going together, but not real physical kind of stuff. But after we were married, he had the license. You know, they pronounce you man and wife, not man and woman. To my way of thinking it gives men a free ticket to do whatever they want. So the battering started and increased till I couldn't take it anymore.

I left him after he'd taken a branch off a tree and beat me with it, but then I came back and went through what I call my three months of hell. I was making $1.79 an hour. I was paying all the bills; I paid the rent. I was buying all the food, all the clothes, even renting him a television. I got off work at 4:30. I was expected to catch the bus at 4:35, hit downtown at 5:00, change buses, and walk in the door at 5:20. If I walked in the door at 5:30, I got my ass kicked.

So in essence, he held my children hostage. He did lots of sadistic things to me during that time. I was on a large dose of Librium. My nerves were so bad, I was going through bouts of temporary blindness.

I was twenty then, and I tried to kill myself. I had gotten my prescription filled. I came home and I took about half the bottle. He found the bottle and he woke me up 'cause I was going off to la-la land. And he got me up and went and got my son, who was about four then. He sprayed Raid in his hair, then he took a lighter and held it over his head and said, "If you don't wake up, I'm gonna light his hair." I mean I was going through it. We didn't have a phone or anything. There's that isolation thing.

I decided to kill him.

It was a question of survival. I knew we couldn't live together without one of us killing the other. So I was going to kill him. We had this argument on a Monday and I had planned that Friday that when I got paid, I'd pay the rent, the water bill, buy a gun, go home, walk in the door, scream, and kill him. Even now, I can say with conviction I was going to kill him.

And this woman who was like my second mother said, "You don't want that on your conscience the rest of your life." So I turned him over to the military because he'd gone AWOL. They took him to jail. I took my children to safety and moved out of the house in four days. I started divorce proceedings immediately.

When I got rid of my husband, all that weird stuff went away. I didn't have to take Librium any more. The blindness went away. The shaking went away. All of that went away.

So by the time I was twenty-one, I had been married, divorced, and had two children. When I moved to California, I had seven suitcases, two kids, and one hundred dollars. And Lord, I've come a long way from there.

I Have Told My Son

My son will be eighteen this fall, and when he was thirteen, I told him who his father was. He had been asking questions on a regular basis. He wanted to know who he was, where did he come from, what was he about.

When he was younger, I'd told him my cover story—that his father was a teenager I had sex with. That was okay then, but as he got older, when he'd ask questions about his father, there'd be a hush in the whole room or people would change the subject. So he got the feeling there was this secret, and there were a number of people who were in on the secret, and he wasn't one of them. There's no father

listed on his birth certificate, so there was always this air of mystery. And at thirteen he just asked me in a much more straightforward way than he ever asked me before, so I told him.

Ahmal, the man I was involved with at that time, who was a father figure for my children, and I got together and discussed it very thoroughly. And then the three of us went into my bedroom. My son was trying to be grown up, wanting to have a cigarette. Everybody was cool, you know. I think it's important to say how I told it to him because I didn't make it a real heavy-duty kind of thing.

I'm a storyteller, and I just told it like you'd tell any kind of story to a child. I had parts in it that made him laugh. I told it in a way that wasn't condemning about my stepfather, because no matter how much pain he had brought into my life, the bottom line to this whole thing was this: This man was my son's biological father and whatever I told him was going to mold a certain part of him for the rest of his life. So it was important to me to not make my stepfather an ogre, to tell my son about it in such a way that he would not become as devastated as I was by it. Your children are more important than anything that may hurt you or the hate that you feel.

And so I dredged up every good memory about my stepfather that I could find. I really worked at making him very human. I talked about his shortcomings and the good things about him. I talked about his smile, 'cause he had a wonderful smile. I didn't go into the sexual abuse real heavy because that was not the important thing at that point. I talked about what he did to me and how young I was. I put a little drama in, 'cause there was plenty of drama in what happened, but I didn't make it a great big thing. And I talked about what it was like being pregnant with him. How I felt. I was fifteen. How that felt.

My son's first reaction was, "Wow, all of that happened to me!"

And Ahmal said, "Hey, blood, check this out. None of that happened to you. It happened to your mother."

And so my son had to deal with that. He had to weigh how this affected who he was as a person. He had to make sure he was never that type of male himself. It was a very difficult time for him. And it was a very, very hard time for me because he was trying to punish me for who his father was.

Slowly it has healed for my son. Now it's just a fact of being. I don't think he resents me for it. If anything, I think maybe he loves me a little more. He was a spirit that had to come here and that was the way he came.

It's Made Me More Courageous As a Parent

Because of the things that happened to me, I was very open with my children about sex. I've always told them the truth. My children did not grow up talking about dick and pussy. They grew up talking about penis and vagina, you know, and had a very clear understanding about what sex was all about. I didn't want them to be in the dark about what happens when you stick a penis in a vagina.

My son was talking to this woman and he said, "My momma would beat me to death if I hit a woman." Oh good, he knows. He's going to have to have a certain amount of respect toward women. That's how he's been raised.

I Used to Call Myself the Thirty-to-Ninety-Day Wonder

I was only involved in relationships that lasted thirty to ninety days. On the ninety-first day the relationship would be over, you could give it up. And this went on for many, many years, until I met Ahmal, who was willing to really put in some time.

After I'd been involved with him for ninety days, I began to end the relationship. On the ninety-first day I was suddenly pissed off and acting different. And he said, "Okay, what's going on? I woke up this morning and you've changed, you know. What's happening?"

I can remember saying to him, "Hey! After ninety days I don't know what to do! We're into the ninety-sixth day and I don't know how to relate to you." And you know, we worked to stay together. And I give him a lot of credit for that.

He was a very compassionate man. I could come home from group and share what I had done and what had come up for me and he wouldn't browbeat me about it. If he felt there was something more that I needed to explore, he'd help bring that out for me.

But I think when you go through sexual abuse you almost become a bottomless pit—this is what he used to say—of need. And that's what he became upset with, became frustrated with. After a year we broke up and that was a part of it. He's still very close to me, though.

He's still an integral part of my life and the lives of my children.

What's important to me now is to be in a relationship with someone who has a certain amount of tenderness and compassion toward me, you know. I am a very strong sister. I admit it. But by the same token, I got this other little part that's kind of, you know, soft, and you know, like lace, and most people don't see it. Most men don't see it. So when I meet a man who sees that, I'm very drawn to him.

"Okay, Body, Feel!"

I have always enjoyed my sexuality. But there have been these "little" issues that come up from time to time.

I'd be out of my body and not even aware of it. Tactilely, I was very numb. I had one lover who used to pinch me all the time, just so I could feel. He recognized how numb I was.

When I began to make love or masturbate, these pictures from my past would come up and that was a trip. It was erotic and it wasn't. It was my orientation to sex, so it got me off, but I always felt bad. I had a lot of guilt and shame about it. So when I began to have sex and these scenes would begin to bleed through, it would make me numb out. I could be with somebody I really cared for and liked. I could be having a real good time, and all of a sudden I'd just numb out.

I'd never tell my partners what was going on. I'd just continue what I was doing and lay up there and say, "Okay, body, feel! Toes, I want you to feel. Let's feel in the toes now.

Okay, let's bring it up to the ankles." I used to do this, you know. I'd bring the feeling up. "Okay, fingers, let's feel. That's the way. C'mon, arms, we're feeling now!" I used to do this so that I could be able to have some kind of feeling.

Most of the time I did have orgasms, but how far I would let the orgasms go was another thing. I could feel sexual pleasure to a certain extent, but I was afraid that it would make me crazy, so I would feel a little bit and then I would cut if off—you know, put on the brakes. Then there would be no more feeling.

I've worked on it metaphysically. I took out those pictures and I destroyed them. As I eliminated the pictures, so went the guilt and the shame. And I'm very happy about that. It's a miracle that I am a sexually active woman today and that I enjoy sex as much as I do. And I do!

I Needed to Scream and Holler and Yell

Confronting, dealing with, and releasing anger has been the hardest part of healing for me. In a survivors' group that I was in, all this anger came up. I needed to scream and holler and yell, but I didn't feel safe in the group. So what happened was, I didn't express it.

You know how women talk about falling apart and crying all the time? They're going from crying to anger and all that. Well, I did that in three days. It came close to breaking me 'cause I'd never realized the depth of that anger. I realized why I'd never let myself feel it either, 'cause it was so debilitating. All I could feel was this raging. I probably could have torn up sheets with my fingers. And to go between this anger and this crying. I had to leave work because I was always breaking into tears. But I couldn't stay at home either.

I went to a movie. I watched the movie with tears just streaming down. In the theater I could be out of control and no one would pay attention to me. I felt like there were little pieces of me all over the theater. I called this man who was like a brother to me. He picked me up and took me to the beach. I lay down in the sand and cried. I made these mounds of sand and pounded them. My head was hurting terribly. I couldn't take it anymore. So he took me to the hospital and they gave me a shot, something to relax me. I was okay after that—physically.

My advice to someone working on this stuff is to find working therapy as opposed to talking therapy. Talking doesn't truly release it. That's why people can be in therapy for twenty years, you know—because they just talk about it. Express it and release. If you need to scream and holler, that's what you need to do. So do it.

A Trip Back Home

Recently I made a trip back home, and a lot of that had to do with making peace with all of that old bull, 'cause that's where the original sexual abuse began. I went down to look at the house where it all began. The house isn't there anymore because it burned down. I went there and thought about some of the things that had happened to me there, and I was able to leave it and not feel that I had to carry it anymore, like "Hey, that was then!"

I went to complete one cycle and to begin a new cycle for myself—making peace and coming to terms with what that whole area means to me. Before, whenever I went into that area, I don't care how sunny it was, it was cloudy for me. One of the things that happened on this trip was that this was erased. All of that for me has been lifted and it's gone. It was really quite wonderful that I could be there and not be upset.

Anna Stevens

Q: How did dealing with incest affect the rest of your life?

A: What rest of my life?

Anna Stevens was born in Taiwan.* A diplomat's daughter, she grew up in ports around the world. Her background is a cross between English and Irish. Anna's family was well off and kept up appearances. Her mother was an alcoholic and a pill addict—there is extensive alcoholism on both sides of the family. Anna has one brother.

Anna says: "Everything in my house was designed to keep conflict from surfacing. No one ever admitted my mother was crazy, of course. No one ever raised their voice. Nothing was discussed. Everything was shrouded in denial and secrecy."

Anna was physically abused by a nanny when she was three. Her mother sexually abused her repeatedly from the age of two until she was eleven. She masturbated Anna and used Anna's body to masturbate with. After her mother reached orgasm, she'd put Anna in a scalding bath or beat her. Anna learned to leave her body when the incest happened: "I watched it all through a kind of yellow fog.

"I forgot what happened to me as I grew up, but I hated my mother with a poisonous hatred. I was completely nauseated by my mother's smell. And as an adolescent, if she touched me, I'd throw up. The flip side of my physical revulsion was some kind of sexual feelings."

Anna now lives in New York City and works as a carpenter. She writes poetry and is working on a novel. She is twenty-six and has been in recovery for alcoholism for the last year and a half.

* Anna Stevens wanted to use her own name but couldn't for legal reasons.

The bottom-line effect of the incest for me was trust and not-trust. I felt zip trust for anybody. When I reached a certain level of closeness, I'd have anxiety attacks so bad I couldn't breathe. But I'd also flip to the opposite extreme. I'd just throw my trust at people—because it became so intolerable not to trust. That got me into dangerous situations, including getting raped. I had no blueprint for knowing who or how to trust. I only knew the extremes.

It's only been in the last couple of years that I've even been able to admit I wanted human company. From the age of four, my strongest fantasy was to go live on a desert island by myself and to be absolutely self-sufficient. My basic attitude toward life had always been that I'd be happier alone. And if I was kindly permitting you to be in my life, I wanted you to know it was only on probation.

The ironic thing is, I tell people incredibly intimate things very quickly. It's an appearance of intimacy. I'd hear myself saying these "really honest things." But I said them so many times that they were just blunt instruments. The other person would react like I was taking them into my confidence, but I knew it was all fake. It was just an appearance of belonging to the human race.

I didn't have any self-esteem. I had a mixture of arrogance and fear. I always felt I was dirty. Part of me believed I must have asked for it. I had responded physically. I was sure people could see it on me.

Adolescence was particularly terrible. I was growing breasts and becoming like my mother. I felt puberty was a direct consequence of what had happened with her. It was as if she was pulling it out of me, making me like her. I loathed any resemblance between us. I remember when I was fourteen, looking in the mirror and seeing her face in my face, and wanting to tear the skin off my face. I felt an incredible sense of vulnerability and exposure. I disguised myself as best I could in men's clothes.

I was always acting out. I was a kleptomaniac. I stole from the time I was eleven until I was caught shoplifting booze when I was fifteen. When I was caught having a lesbian affair with a married teacher, I was expelled from boarding school.

I lied all the time. I didn't tell lies to get out of trouble. I told them to erase difference, because I felt so weird. I'd lie so I could make connections with people. It was a case of having to invent circumstances because my own truths weren't good enough.

I Started Drinking When I Was Twelve

I was an alcoholic drinker from the start. I drank alone. I kept a supply of booze I didn't like, in case I ever ran out. When I was sixteen, I was told I was an alcoholic. I thought that was ridiculous. After all, I only drank like my parents. But really I did it more drastically. I drank not to feel, and then when that became intolerable, I'd drink to feel. I did that for thirteen years.

I was always as rigidly controlled about my drinking as I was about everything in my life. But you can't control alcoholism in the long run. By the end I had such an incredible thirst for alcohol, it had become the most important thing in my life. I was terribly lonely and frightened. The thing that had helped me to control things was finally out of control. So I had to stop.

I'd always been sure I'd be dead by the time I reached twenty-five. Instead, that's when I went to AA and got sober. Going to AA was terrifying. My specialness was being taken away. My specialness had been being crazy. But there was also this tremendous relief. I don't think about my drinking in terms of wasted time. Partly that's because I got in fairly young. I'm actually very grateful that I'm an alcoholic because it got me into AA and that's been the basis for real growth.

Truths I Didn't Know Yet

When I put down drinking, the connection to the abuse was almost immediate. There'd been this black hole I'd inhabited at various points in my childhood. Once I got sober, that image began to obsess me again. I started to paint it. I drew all these strange pictures of children being pulled back into the womb.

I had this recurring dream when I was a child. I had it again when I first got sober. It was of a happy family on a speedboat, smiling in the sun. They all had on bright new clothes. I wanted to scream and I wasn't able to. There was a monster that was coming up under the water. And everyone was immobilized with these smiles on their faces. Everybody knew that the monster was there, but nobody could react at all.

After a month, I went to see a therapist. The third session, I went into that black hole and remembered being abused by my nanny. I saw

someone pushing a hairbrush into my vagina. Then I became the three-year-old. It was terrifying.

I knew the memories were true because I was remembering in German, and that was what the woman spoke. I only spoke German until I was six. I was completely bilingual. Then I forgot it all. My therapist said, "What's she saying to you?" And I said, "I don't know. I can't translate it."

That was the beginning. My therapist asked me if I thought there might have been any incest. She said lots of people make up stories like this because it's safer to say it's somebody outside of the family. And I said, "No." What I kept thinking was, "Not my father. Not with my father." I had never heard anything about incest with your mother. A part of me knew it, but it seemed so outlandish. And I was very practiced at denial.

When I first starting having actual memories of incest with my mother, I had a hard time believing them. It was over a year before I believed that it was my mother who raped me. But increasingly, and mostly through my writing, so many involuntary things I'd always said and done just suddenly fit into place. It was like writing a story. You know things are right when they start falling into place. I knew this story was right. Everywhere I turned with it, something just went, "Yes. Uh-huh. Yes."

There were so many things that I thought were lies, and I couldn't understand why I kept telling them. I would think, "That's a lie. Why do you say that?" Things like telling people, "I don't know who I lost my virginity to." I knew perfectly well the first boy I had fucked, but I kept saying this other thing. Everything I habitually said has a story inside of it. Part of me was always telling the truth. I realize now that some of the lies I told weren't lies, they were just truths I didn't know yet.

There Was Nowhere to Hide

When I talk to incest survivors who've been abused by men, I'm always relieved that the effects are the same. I need to talk to other women who've been abused by their mothers in order to see what the differences are. But there hasn't been much opportunity. I've come across little snippets, mostly by women who were abused by both parents.

I didn't want my mother to know anything about me. I had the feeling that if she knew me, she'd be able to dismantle me and turn me into someone else. I was fighting for my right to exist at all as a separate self. My gut feeling about my mother was that she had reached so far inside my body that there was nowhere to hide.

I also had to accept that I was turned on by my mother. I had wanted contact with her—even if it was sexual contact. For a long time I felt like a collaborator. It was very hard to untangle my need for closeness from "I wanted it. I deserved it. I seduced her." I tried to protect her by taking on the blame myself.

I have had to accept that my mother is a part of me. Because she violated me when I was that young, my boundaries got fucked. Literally, they got fucked.

Because she was my mother and not my father, I think the separation issue is stronger. Even though other survivors talk about being colonized by their fathers, or that they were his toy or his doll, or that they can't get the dirt off, I haven't heard many people talk about the feeling of actually *being* their abuser, or just having them inside you. And that, I think, is really tied up with it being my mother. I mean I get really nauseous if I think about being born, because being born has sexual connotations for me.

It brings up such wells of self-destructiveness. I feel her in my throat. I feel I have to give birth to her, which means giving birth to the anger. There's a scream inside me that I've wanted to scream forever. Just saying that is making my skin crawl right now. I feel revolted.

Incest Was Stamped in Every Yard of My Cloth

During the first stage of dealing with incest, I was in shock. I fought for a long time about how much it was inside everything. I'd scream, "Enough already! Why the fuck doesn't it just get fixed?"

Eventually I had to accept that incest was stamped in absolutely every yard of my cloth. I had to understand that it was a part of my life, not just something to fix and get over. What happened gave me strengths as well as incapacities, and I am learning from it. It was only when I reached that level of acceptance that I could be patient with myself.

The second stage was developing enough trust in myself and in other people to put down the survival mechanisms that didn't work any longer. It's about not repeating the same patterns in relationships. It's about taking risks I wouldn't have taken before. It's not quite so backward looking. I also feel strongly that part of the second stage is beginning to reach out to other people, to pass the strength on. That's what saves me from hopelessness.

Healing Sexually

My pattern was to get intensely involved sexually with someone for a few months. Then the intimacy would have built up to the point where it started to bring up real problems. Then I would cut off. I would decide the sex was no good, and I would leave the relationship. It never occurred to me that you could negotiate a sexual relationship, that you could take it apart and change it. It was either there or it wasn't. And if it wasn't there, I left.

When I first got sober, I realized that since I wasn't going to get involved with anyone for a while, I was going to get sexually frustrated if I didn't deal with masturbation. I had always felt that my masturbation was very ugly, and so in limited doses, I started to allow myself to touch parts of my body and just feel them. That was very difficult because I felt safer with other people touching me than I did with myself. I did not trust my own hands not to hurt me. I would masturbate in a sensual way, and then, all of a sudden, I would start thinking, "I have to orgasm now. I have to orgasm now!" And I would rev into these old fantasies that actually bored me, that actually took away from the pleasure but helped me orgasm fast. It was a feeling that I had to orgasm fast or I would hurt myself.

There were certain things I didn't want to do because they had happened with my mother. I didn't want anything to do with oral sex. I detested the nice romantic practice of bathing after sex. And before I could change any of those things, I had to accept that it was okay to have limits: "It's okay. Not everybody in the world likes oral sex."

I had to be clear with anyone I slept with: "These are things that I don't like, and they are in the course of changing. I will let you know what's okay and what isn't. My commitment to you is that I will let you know if something is upsetting, so you don't have to worry about it. And if you do freak me out inadvertently, I won't hate you forever."

Then I had to pay attention to times when I really did want to do those things. Doing them once didn't mean I always had to do them. And there are a whole lot of behaviors I use now which let me know I am not with my mother anymore. I can't orgasm if I can't make noise, because I had to be silent with her. I always call out the name of the person I'm with when I orgasm, because I need to know it's them and not her.

It's difficult for me to feel sexual when my partner isn't. As soon as my desire makes someone else feel uneasy, I want to crawl right back in my shell. I'm sure that has to do with my fear of being abusive. Not that I'm going to throw them down and rape them, but simply that my desire for them is abusive. And that's pretty obvious in its origins.

Surprisingly, I'm fairly accepting of my sexuality. Sex is something that I enjoy. All the exploration I've done, I figured out on my own. And I feel proud of that. My experience of masturbation has really changed. It's much more sensual. The orgasms have grown. They're no longer just like a sneeze.

You Don't Graduate

Healing is not a finite thing. You don't graduate. It's been a lot of work. The beginning of the healing process was a sequence of choosing not to kill myself, then beginning to write and let things through, and then getting sober. Next I came to understand that I only got what I could handle. And that was the beginning of a spiritual connection, the feeling that I am on a path and that I am being looked after. All I have to do is be with whatever is happening in the moment.

Sachiko O'Brien

"There was a time I felt defeated. But I found support, connection, and ways to channel my sadness and anger into change. And this gave me a sense of hope. Over time I learned organizing skills and strengthened my resilience so I could talk in front of groups, say my name, and declare, "I am an organizer with the movement to end child sexual abuse." That was a huge step in my journey, but I was still afraid, and for a long time, I didn't fully believe that our vision was really possible. Yet slowly over time, with each action I took, my fear and despair was transformed into hope."

Sachiko O'Brien is a thirty-five-year-old mixed-race woman of Japanese, Irish, and English descent who lives with her partner and their six-month-old daughter.* Sachiko's mother has just moved in downstairs. Sachiko has a master's degree in public health. Most of her work focuses on public health strategies to prevent violence.

My mother came from a very traditional merchant family in Japan with a business that has been passed down from eldest son to eldest son for the last 300 years. She was the first daughter to attend an academic university. It was while she was a student in Spain that she met my father, a white American. My mother got pregnant while my parents were still in Spain, but my two brothers and I were all born in the United States.

When I think back on my childhood, I remember happy times and a lot of love. I also remember a lot of conflict and stifled affection. My parents carried their own wounds and communication was really a struggle. There were things that were hard to talk about and other things that weren't talked about at all. All of this made it difficult for us to have a sense of connection as a family.

---

* Sachiko O'Brien was interviewed for the twentieth-anniversary edition of *The Courage to Heal*. She chose to use a pseudonym.

During my early years, we lived in a small town in Pennsylvania in a neighborhood where there were ample opportunities for bad things to happen. I'd be at the park with my friend and a man would show us pornography. Or we'd be playing and a man would masturbate in front of us. These things happened more than once.

When I was seven, a neighborhood teenager lured me to the back of the park and tried to rape me. I was able to get away, but the experience was traumatic. Later that same day, I was playing with my brothers and their friends. I told my brothers I thought I might be pregnant and they told all their friends. It was embarrassing and I ran away. After that, I never tried to tell anyone again.

Moving to Japan

When I was ten, we moved to Japan. My mother wanted her children to grow up there, and my father agreed. After we moved, my middle brother Tom started sexually abusing me when I was asleep. He would be touching my genitals. I'd wake up and he would leave the room. Then I'd be in shock and not know what to do. I'd say to myself, "I can't believe what just happened." Then it wouldn't happen for a little while. Then it would happen again. Needless to say, I developed a lot of issues around falling asleep.

Early on, I told my mother what my brother was doing, and she asked him about it. He denied it, and she believed him. She came back and told me, "He said he didn't do anything." My mother doesn't remember ever having those conversations.

At the time, I felt devastated. I felt hatred toward my brother because I thought he had more power with my mother than I did. A part of me gave up; I felt there was nothing I could do if she wasn't going to believe me. I had to figure out how to defend myself or stop the situation on my own.

My solution was to stop going to sleep at night. Or I'd sleep in the closet. I'd rig up booby traps where something would fall down if someone opened the door. Bells would ring. Chimes would get set off. To this day, I keep bells on doors; they still feel like protection.

The trouble is none of it really worked. Inevitably, I would fall asleep. And the booby traps never stopped him. I'd wake up with my brother hanging over me with his hands under my blanket as I slept.

Night after night, I rehearsed responses in my mind. I'd tell myself that I had to wake up, grab him, and say, "What are you doing? You can't do this." I wanted to confront him, but I just couldn't pull all the pieces together at one time. I'd wake up and I'd be in shock. Or I'd be too scared. Or I'd question whether what was going on was really going on.

But then one night, when I was eleven, I did confront him, and he scurried away, very scared. He never came back to my futon again. At the time I remember thinking, "Was that all I had to do?" I was angry with myself for not confronting him sooner. Now, I have a lot of compassion for myself at that age, but at the time I didn't.

My parents divorced when I was fourteen and we moved back to the States. My brother went to live with my mother. I split my time between my parents. When we were in the same house, I avoided my brother whenever possible. We barely spoke or acknowledged each other.

It Happened Again

One day during my first year of college when I was studying in my dorm, I fell asleep on a couch. A guy I took classes with came in and tried to rape me while I was asleep. When I woke up, he stopped. I confronted him, and we argued about it. I didn't really have words for what had happened. He didn't think what he had done was wrong.

I had a really difficult time after that. This guy and I were both economics majors and we had lots of classes together. As much as possible I tried to avoid him. I withdrew quite a bit from my classes and friends. Two years later, I found out that he had assaulted and raped numerous women. Two other women and I filed charges against him and he was expelled.

Becoming an Activist

During my college years, and into my early twenties, I suffered from chronic low-level depression. There were a few times I'd be so depressed I had a hard time getting out of bed and functioning. I had difficulties with relationships. I was friendly and outgoing and able to make friends, but I had a hard time forging or sustaining intimate relationships. My emotional struggles during that time took away a lot of energy that I wish I could have devoted to developing my skills and talents.

Eventually I joined a support group on campus and really began my healing process. I became part of a wonderful community of people who gave me a sense that healing was possible. I felt so blessed to find other women—and a few men—who embraced personal growth and social change and had great resources to share.

When a woman was raped on campus, a group of us sponsored a campus-wide protest because the college's response was inadequate. We started a student organization called Sexual Assault Survivor Advocates that helped create new policies to stop sexual violence and make the campus safer. We were trained by the local rape crisis center; I became a peer counselor and a trainer. Becoming an activist gave me a place to channel my anger and sadness into change.

My Brother Told the Truth This Time

Before I came home on my next school break, I called my mother and talked to her again about what had happened with my brother. I specifically asked her not to talk to him about it because I wasn't ready to confront him, but she did anyway. Just like the first time, she went to my brother and asked, "Is this true?"

This time, Tom said yes. He told her he'd spent years feeling terrible. He said he was really sorry and agreed not to be around when I came home.

After that, my brother wrote me a letter and apologized. He said he had blocked the whole thing out but was relieved to finally face up to it. He said he felt incredible sorrow and regret, that the things he did were inexcusable, and that he hoped that something he or someone else could do could help heal the wounds he inflicted.

At first it was hard for me to accept his letter, because I wasn't ready to confront him at the time, but it meant a lot to me that he acknowledged what he had done and apologized for it. The struggle of being believed had finally been won.

Right now I have a mix of feelings about Tom. We haven't fully reconciled, but I don't want him to feel horrible or guilty. I also have compassion for him. I can see how, as a child himself, Tom didn't always have the support and guidance he needed to grow up healthy, and that the ways he harmed me have ultimately also harmed him.

My Mother and I Have Significant Cultural Differences

The second time I told my mother about the abuse, I was disappointed and angry at her response. She had a really hard time with my anger. Part of our struggle was cultural; as much as we have cultural commonalities, my mother and I also have significant generational and cultural differences.

Japanese culture is, as most cultures are, a male-dominated society where men are more entitled in every area of life. And as is the case in most cultures, not talking about bad things is considered more desirable, or more protective.

There's a word in Japanese that comes to mind when I think about my mother's approach to pain: *gaman*. When I try to translate it into English, the two phrases that come to mind are, "to be resilient" and "to suck it up." Basically *gaman* means to endure pain. I think, that to my mom, seeking support or feeling vulnerable or sad are signs that you're not being strong, that you're not enduring.

My healing, on the other hand, was influenced by my largely white group of activist friends, and I had more liberal and "American" expectations of what my healing process should be and what my mother's response was supposed to be. And she had more "Japanese" expectations of what I, as her daughter, should be like. The way I expressed my feelings about the abuse didn't make a lot of sense to her. She suggested we not talk about it anymore. Because of this and other issues, we became estranged and we didn't talk for several years.

The Whole Thing Is So Intergenerational

I can't think about the abuse without thinking about it being intergenerational. There are other perpetrators and survivors in my parents' and grandparents' generations—at least two in each that I know of. I imagine, sadly, there are probably others. Knowing this really changes my perspective; I can see how all of our lives have been shaped by sexual abuse—as survivors, bystanders and/or perpetrators.

I still struggle with feeling angry and disappointed in my parents, but I also feel a lot of compassion for them. Their lives have been shaped by sexual abuse, just as mine has, and I know they did the best they could.

I sometimes struggle with feeling guilty that I have found so much healing. I don't know if others in my family have experienced as much profound transformation as I have. I want them to be happy. I want to support their happiness without trying to fix anyone. This is something I am trying to learn—how to have close relationships with my family members without feeling that I am responsible for helping to heal anyone's wounds.

Now that I have a daughter, being responsible for her, and learning compassion for myself as a parent, has given me a whole new perspective and has been a huge source of motivation. I won't be able to prevent all bad things from happening to her. But I can do my best to protect her and be present with her.

Where I Am Today

I grew up being told by my mother that I would take care of her when she became old. I always wanted that to happen, but there were a few years when I worried it wouldn't because of our estrangement.

Over the last decade, my mother and I have slowly moved back into our relationship. In the past few years, we've had to learn how to get along, and how to not be angry or defensive around each other. I always have cherished and admired my mother and I continue to do so more and more deeply.

Now, my mother is moving in downstairs. I feel blessed and happy about it, but it's also kicked up a lot for me. My mother and I are learning to be more present with each other. In many ways, we're building a whole new rela-

tionship, creating a foundation that will allow us to talk about more things. Eventually, I want to be able to talk to her again about what happened to me. My approach this time will be to have more compassion for both of us, to see things more from her experience and perspective, and to take things one step at a time.

I've tried in small ways to break the silence that has surrounded these issues in my family. My older brother and I have talked about child sexual abuse and the things he can do to protect his children. But other than that, it feels like the abuse still creates a barrier in our family. I love, respect, and appreciate all of my family members, each in their own unique ways. As we all grow older and my brothers and I raise our own children, I have more compassion for each of us, a greater ability to assert my own boundaries and needs, and I hope, a greater ability to offer support and encouragement to them.

My greatest wish is that eventually there will be a sense of family solidarity where we all say, "This is a bad thing. We want to heal from it and we want to prevent it from happening." In the meantime, thankfully, I have a wonderful partner and community of friends who are striving to foster healing, health, and adult responsibility for protecting children, who are committed to supporting our own children and teaching them healthy sexual behavior.

And things are slowly starting to change in our communities. Through my activist work with Generation Five,* I've done trainings

---

* Generation Five is an organization that pledges to stop child sexual abuse within five generations. See p. 528 of the Resource Guide for more information.

about child sexual abuse with Asian-American community groups. People often say things like, "Kids won't remember" or "Some kinds of abuse are not that bad." But when I talk about the reality that sexual abuse causes a lot of harm and can have long-term detrimental effects and suggest that there are a lot of things communities can do to prevent it, there is often a switch and people get it: "Oh, this really is harmful" and "Oh, this is about protecting our children and strengthening our community—we really need to take action." Seeing this kind of change at the community level gives me hope.

Embracing Transformation

Several years ago I had a dream. In the dream, I went to my doctor and said: "I think I need to have exploratory surgery on my heart because there's something wrong with it." He told me that the surgery was very dangerous, so he would only do if I had support people with me.

I knew immediately who I wanted to support me—a childhood friend in Japan and my deceased aunt who had committed suicide after having been abused by her husband. In the dream, I went to Japan and talked to my friend, who agreed to come to the U.S. for the surgery. Then I went to the spirit world and asked my aunt. She said, "You're asking a lot of me. It's very difficult to travel from the spirit world to the material world." But she agreed, on the condition that I make a pact with her. She said, "Since I am no longer alive, there is

little I can do for children. I will accompany you, if you agree to do whatever you can to look after children." I made the agreement.

My friend and my aunt came with me and the doctor opened up my chest. He exclaimed, "Oh my God!" I asked what it was and he gave me a mirror. Inside my chest were all these lacerations and the lacerations were full of little white pearl-like balls. It was as if the wound was trying to heal, but the white things were in the way. I asked the doctor what they were and he said, "They're fear molecules."

I asked, "Well, what do I do with them?" And I said it so loudly in the dream, I woke myself up. So the doctor never did tell me what to do with them.

The dream affirmed how important it is to for me have support in my healing. It also revealed the fear inside my heart in a way that somehow made it seem more manageable. Those fear molecules became something symbolic to focus on. I came to the conclusion that the fear molecules were part of me. I couldn't get rid of them; instead I had to absorb them, transform them, and release their energy. And that helped me realize more than ever that I didn't want to hide from the painful parts of my life. I realized I would be happier and more whole if I fully embraced all of my struggles. Now, I try not to see fear or most kinds of pain as liabilities. Rather than resisting them, I try to see them as opportunities for greater consciousness and transformation. Letting go of some of my resistance has helped me to develop greater compassion, resilience, and emotional presence. Now that I'm a parent, these are gifts I particularly appreciate.

Soledad

"When it happened, I couldn't name it. And then when I got the words to be able to name it, I forgot. All I was left with was hatred for my father. For a long time, I thought that people were born hating their fathers."

Soledad is a twenty-eight-year-old Chicana who was severely abused by her father throughout her childhood.* For the past eleven years she has lived in Sonoma County, California. Today she is a high school counselor.

Soledad writes, "In this interview, I have spoken more of my biological parents (due to my feelings of betrayal and violation) than of my tias and tio, who were very much my parents, in the true sense of the word. Without them, I am convinced that my ultimate survival would not have been a reality, for I am certain that my life would have been beaten or suffocated out of me. To them I owe my life. And because of them, I will struggle to keep it.

"I once read that we can give two things to children—one is a sense of roots and the other is a sense of wings. I now know my roots, my history. Now I am ready to fly towards the sun."

As was sometimes true for other women of color, it was particularly difficult for Soledad to entrust us—two white women—with her story. Because much of white America holds the stereotype that abuse happens only to "others," many women of color are reluctant to disclose their abuse for fear that it will reinforce existing prejudices. Still others come from cultures that have a strong taboo against exposing "private" experiences. Pushing past these barriers to speak out is courageous.

---

* Soledad chose to use a pseudonym.

Being Latina is real precious to me. However, part of the culture that I hate is the silence. As beautiful as our language is, we don't have words for this. Our history is passed orally, yet there's such silence in Latino families about this.

There was no talk of sex in the house, ever. It was all out on the streets. And how can you go to a woman you haven't been able to talk to about your damn period and tell her that her husband is raping you?

I think this kind of silence might be common, but I think it's especially true because my people feel so powerless in this culture, fearing authorities outside of the family. We had to stick together and protect each other from the system, and from the white people who control it. What other option did we have? We just had to keep it in. Admitting any problem would reflect badly on our whole culture.

And that's why it's still hard for me to talk about it. I don't want anyone to use this against people of color, because there are so many negative stereotypes of Latinos already. People are already more willing to trust white men than they are men of color. And I don't want to promote more mistrust of men of color. But this is how it happened for me and I feel I need to break the silence.

My Father Was Like a Volcanic Eruption

I was raised in an extended family in Los Angeles, in a hard-core ghetto. I'm the oldest of three kids. My dad worked on and off in factories. My mom worked in sweatshops until she became disabled. We not only lived in poverty, we were poverty.

I was beaten at least every other day for years. I hated that my parents beat us, but everybody around us got whipped, so that was just the way it was. At least when my mother beat us, we still had a feeling she loved us. And it hurt less.

My father was like a volcanic eruption. You wouldn't know when it was going to happen, but when it did, there was no stopping what was happening. He wore these steel-toed shoes for work, and he'd kick us everywhere, including the head. You could get arrested for kicking a dog like that.

When people smack you around the way my father did, it's hard to decide which is worse—that or the sexual abuse.

My father not only molested me, he molested all my cousins and all the girls in the neighborhood. The ones that I know, there are at least twenty-four. There are others I've thought about. People really trusted him with their kids. He was a great social manipulator and he knew how kids thought. It's amazing how one person can mess with so many kids.

From what I can tell, the sexual abuse with me started right when I was brought home from the hospital. I found out from another relative that for a long time he didn't even sleep with my mother. He slept with me when I was a little baby.

In the beginning there was a lot of fondling. He could be what you would call "gentle," but I would interpret that as being sneaky, because I knew that he could kill me, too. If you already know that this man can kill you so easily, you're not going to say anything. And so I would just be frozen, with the feeling "Soon it will be over." But it got worse and worse.

The peak of it all was at about eight. That's when he first raped me. It was pretty regular after that, at least three times a week. It happened in a lot of different places. We lived in really small quarters. There was no privacy. So he'd tell me we had to go out for milk, or that we needed to go for a ride in the car. He really loved to take all the girls out for a ride. Most of this stuff happened in the car, a lot of it in the dark, so this left a blank for me because a lot of it I didn't see.

A lot of the raping happened from behind. When he abused me, he would talk to me in Spanish, threatening to cut my throat or cut my tongue out. So now, telling you my story in English is easier. Telling you in English keeps more emotional distance. I probably would be sobbing by now if I was describing what he had done in Spanish.

When I was thirteen, the sexual abuse stopped. I had gotten more streetwise than ever, and he started to be fearful of me. He knew I was ready to die, that I would fight him to our graves if I had to.

I Lived on the Streets

I was very self-destructive in terms of drugs and fighting. I started taking drugs at nine. I started hustling. I did just about everything. I would do drugs and at the time I wouldn't even know what the hell it was that I was using. I didn't care. That went on until I was sixteen.

Fighting was an everyday occurrence on the streets. As we got bigger, the toys got more dangerous. I carried knives. I got into fights with people who carried knives. And some

with guns. They would be tripping, too. You would never know if you would come out of there alive. I thought this was just the way it was, and it was fine if I died with it.

Between what was happening to me at home with him and having to fight and live on the streets too, I always thought the only freedom would be to go to prison. Then I would be "free."

I always dealt with my life on an hour-by-hour basis. For a long time, I never did want to live. I'd be five and I'd think, "Maybe I won't live until I'm ten," and I would hope that that would be true. Or I'd get to be ten, and I'd think, "Okay, fifteen, max. That's as long as I'm going to live."

What other choices did I have? I grew up poor. I didn't know there were other worlds outside of this. I still have a hard time with the whole concept that you have control over your own destiny. Life was just the way it was, and the only way out of it was to kill myself or destroy myself or become like a vegetable. I never knew there was a way out.

I didn't have much self-esteem. Self-esteem wasn't a concept I learned till I went to college. With Chicanos, that can get confused with being pompous, and if you're being pompous, you're forgetting who you are and where you're from. I just didn't think too much about myself.

There Was More to Life Than What I Knew

How I got out of that whole drug and fighting scene was that there was a teacher who took an interest in me when I was sixteen. I was always in and out of school and I was illiterate. And this woman did care about me. She thought that I had a good mind. She was scared of me, but she wanted to find out why I was the way I was. And I trusted her. I didn't tell her anything about the abuse, just that it was a bad situation at home. I think she knew what I was not telling her.

She started talking to me and just spending time with me. It mattered to her that I didn't destroy myself. And that made all the difference. There wasn't anyone before who had ever spent that kind of time with me.

Learning to read helped me see there was more to life than what I knew, and that in fact, this was not life. That was the beginning of my healing. It was the first time I thought that maybe I could survive without hustling. Maybe I could learn something from some magazine or some book and get some power from it. Get some options.

I was lucky. I got into an Upward Bound program. She helped me get into college. College was a real culture shock. I hadn't ever been around that many white people. I still couldn't read enough to understand the menus in the cafeteria. And I didn't know what any of the foods were. I not only didn't know what it was, I'd never heard the words "eggplant parmesan" before. But I stuck it out. I had to make it work for me.

I Was Barely Keeping Myself Alive

Even though I succeeded in going to school and getting a job, I knew things weren't right inside. For a long time all I was doing was com-ing home and laying in my bed. Sometimes I'd turn the TV on, sometimes not. My dinner would be a bottle of Coke. Maybe I'd decide to have a real dinner, and I'd have a pint of ice cream. And that was my life. I'd never open these drapes, never would answer my phone. If anyone knocked on the door, I wouldn't even look to see who was there. I could care less who it was. I was barely keeping myself alive.

Because I wouldn't let anyone take care of me, I ate to comfort myself. I gained a lot of weight. I drank a lot. I remember one time in particular when I had no intention to fuck my-self up, but that's just what I did. I drank shot after shot of tequila. I finished off half a bottle, and then I went for another. I think I would have died if my girlfriend hadn't found me on the floor and gotten help.

I never really believed that anyone loved me, so I felt kind of orphaned. I was self-sufficient. If I hadn't been, that would have been the end of me. It's prevented me from ever want-ing anyone to take care of me. I will take care of myself and that's it. And if anyone needs to be taken care of, I will take care of them, but I will never let them take care of me. And that's kind of hard, 'cause I get sick too and I'll grow old.

I Knew I Wasn't Crazy and That I Needed Help

This whole thing got triggered by talking to a cousin of mine who had also been molested by my father. She called me up a year and a half ago and said, "Did you know that your dad molested my sisters?"

I said, "I never really thought about him that way. But it doesn't surprise me." I went to visit her to find out what had happened. We stayed up the whole night and the whole day to talk about it. It was painful, but I felt so vindicated the whole time. I knew I wasn't crazy. I knew there were reasons why I was destroying myself and why I hated him so much.

It was validating to know it happened to all of my cousins, too. It's sad that it did. But if it had only just happened to me, I'd probably still be questioning it. If you're told you're crazy enough times, you really start to believe it.

From then on I couldn't stop thinking about what I knew. I started getting really obsessed. And I started to understand all these things. I started to wake up feeling powerful. I'd always had to carry a knife or be hustling to feel powerful before. All of a sudden, I had a belief in myself.

But at the same time, I got very depressed. It just seemed like one more heavy thing to cope with. It felt like another death. I needed help dealing with it. So I went to a Chicana therapist that I knew. I said, "God! I found this out. I talked to my cousin and then I remembered." I told her this had happened twenty years ago, that there were no kids around him now. Right while I was talking to her, she gets up and goes to the phone, and starts to call Child Protective Services.

Now that is my ultimate fear. First, I was just learning about this thing. And second of all, he has that fear about outside authorities, and if that car pulled up to his house, he would never live through that. And not that I especially wanted him to live, but I wouldn't want him to die in the hands of the system.

So she picked up the phone and she started saying, "Well, I have this situation here . . ." And I started saying, "What the hell are you doing? I swear to you there are no kids . . ."

And she said, "I need to talk to a supervisor." She just kept on. She asked how she was supposed to report this. And I was just shitting. Give me a break! What the hell are you fucking doing? I knew that they had to assess if there was someone in danger now.

What this person finally told her was that what she was reporting had happened twenty years ago, that there were no children in the home, and that they were overloaded and couldn't deal with situations that weren't definitely happening now.

That scared the shit out of me, but I still needed help. I couldn't handle what I was feeling. I had a definite picture in mind of the kind of person that could help me. I wanted a Chicana. I wanted a lesbian. I wanted this and that. I spent months and months looking, and I really couldn't find anyone who lived near me. And I didn't want to commute.

I could have been so damn picky that I never would have done it. That was my pattern. I would never have to be vulnerable and could just keep it in. And I couldn't do that anymore. Finally, I had to ask myself how much of this was my defenses in being scared to work on the molest issue. So finally I decided she had to be someone who had dealt with abuse. She couldn't be homophobic or racist, but I had to get started.

So finally I found this woman who's straight, middle class, white, but she's been good. She's been fucking good. I can't say a bad thing about her. I still wish I could have the other, but this is working for now.

I'm Trying to Learn to Be a Little Girl Again

To be a healthy adult, I think you need to have been a child at one time. And I wasn't. I was always trying to be an adult. So now I'm an adult, and I'm trying to redo my childhood. It's totally reversed.

I'm trying to learn to be a little girl again. I have to find that softness that I lost or never was able to deal with. I have to cry those little girl tears. I have to feel what happened.

It's been painful. At first the only way I could relate to the little girl was by drawing pictures. Since I could always deal better with other people's problems than my own, she always came out looking really different from me. I'd think about the terrible things that had happened to her, and I would feel bad for the little girl in the picture, but I would separate her from me.

I've had to get under her skin, and that's when the process started getting hard. I've almost had to make myself regress. I've had to remember what it felt like to have a little body, to wear those little clothes.

I've Had to Change Patterns Around Sex

I've always been more content being alone than with a lover, but I have had lovers since I was twelve, thirteen. I never felt I had the right to say, "No, I'm not interested in you. I don't want to be sexual with you." But they weren't relationships. They were just people to fill time with. I didn't know there was more to being a lover than just the sexual part.

It's always been important for me to control the whole sexual thing and to be really detached. I thought being soft was the same as being weak. When you're from the streets, you're just not vulnerable like that. You don't submit yourself to those feelings. At least you never let people know you have those feelings. I'd be hard and distant and cold, and now I can't even imagine why people wanted to be sexual and intimate with me.

A lot of times when I would have sex with someone and they would be coming, maybe they'd be making noise or breathing hard, I'd think to myself, "Oh, just get over it. How weak you are!" Because that's what I'd thought of my father.

I always made sure when I was sexual that I was really quiet. I was not having an orgasm because of anybody else. To me, having an orgasm was just like my body reacting to something. It had nothing to do with emotions. You know how you smack your knees to test how fast your reflexes are? Well, that's how I felt about sex. It's a crass way to describe it, but that's what coming was like for me. It was easy to be quiet. Some people call it being butch; I call it being really repressed. And that just came from that frozen little girl who was being molested and raped, waiting for it to be over soon.

The most important thing I've realized is that relationships can be different from how they have been for me. I'm really trying to turn that around, to let people in on an emotional level. I've been plenty in people's bodies, but not in their souls. I've finally been able to realize that just because you're being sexual with someone doesn't mean that you're being close.

I Didn't Want to Hurt the People I Love

Another area that's been hard for me is dealing with my anger. Anger was always really easy access for me. It would come out like that! [She snaps her fingers.] But now that I have more information about why I'm angry, it's better. When I didn't have any information, the anger was explosive, just like my father's.

But I didn't want to hurt people I loved. I didn't even want to hurt people I didn't like. But it was hard to break that pattern. Whenever I started to have those feelings, I'd stop and say, "I just want to beat the shit out of you right now!" It was hard to admit it. But it was a start. I'd be able to talk about the feelings of wanting to punch her out rather than doing it. It was a matter of starting to live my life watching what I did, because for a long time I hadn't ever watched any of it. Now I try to be more aware of where that behavior came from. I don't want to repeat what they did to me.

I think there's a lot of anger still pinned inside me, but I'm getting it out in better ways. I use my voice, and if the neighbors hear us, then fine. At least I'm not using my fists. I also have a couple of friends that I wrestle with. It's terrifying to be pinned, but it's an outlet for the rage. I've done weight lifting too. That really helped a lot.

I Expect to Confront My Father by the End of the Year

Sometimes I think I'd like to confront him right in the middle of a party, right in front of all his friends. Other times I think I'll call him out to a park. I want to get it through his head that he really lost something and someone special. A lot of people who were really special. He lost the opportunity to even be a father to me and to my sister or to be a trusted uncle to my cousins. I want him to know he has no claims on me as a daughter.

I also want to tell him that he was the one who gave me reason to hate him, and that I do not love him. That I never loved him. And whether he loves me or not doesn't matter. If he does love me in his own sick way, he can just stick it somewhere else. And I also want to tell him that I think he is a really sick man. This thing he probably figured didn't hurt anybody, hurt plenty.

Some people don't deserve a chance. I'd like to put my hands around his neck and say, "Remember, you used to do this to me?" I really want that opportunity to deal with him in the way he deserves to be dealt with. I have fantasies of mutilating him in the ways he threatened to do to us, beating him in the ways he used to beat us. I'd like to cut off his little huevos. I've had offers from people who said they'd go with me. But I've learned to respect life more than he ever did.

I've Come Out of My Shell Stronger Than I've Ever Been

I feel lighter, like a real burden has come off me. I literally felt less pressure in my chest and in my shoulders. I felt like I'd been walking around with twenty pounds of cement on my chest all my life. If I had run away from the pain, I don't think I'd ever have been able to shed that weight. I would still be destroying myself in some way.

It's a small thing, but I never had plants before. It's just my way of trying to keep something other than me alive. It gives me a lot of pleasure. I grew up where there weren't too many flowers, right in the middle of the damn city.

I got my first plant about six months ago. Now I have all sorts of flowers on my porch. I have big bushes with purple flowers. I have big round pots with different flowers in them. I wanted color around me. It's real Latina, all these colors. It reminds me a lot of my aunts.

It's a reason to live, really. I was scared about it at first. But now I know I can nurture them and keep them healthy. I make sure they don't have bugs. After I've been so rough in my life, I can still take care of something so delicate. Even though I've been knocked around, I can still keep them alive.

Janel Robinson

"If I was talking to another teenager in my situation, I'd say, 'Hang in there. It's tough, but it gets better. It may not seem like it, but it does. It's a process you have to go through.'"

*J*anel Robinson is nineteen years old.* She lives with her mother, stepfather, and fourteen-year-old brother, works part-time selling newspaper ads, and is completing her AS degree at her local community college. Janel studies computer science and would someday like to have a career helping other survivors of sexual abuse.

I was molested by two of my grandfathers. The first time, it started when I was two and went on until I was six. The only reason anybody found out was that I kept having bladder infections. The doctor found bruises in my vulva. That's how everything came out.

---

* Janel chose to use a pseudonym.

I remember being questioned with anatomical dolls, but I didn't really know what was going on. My mom stuck me into counseling for a little while, but I didn't like it. There was this big dark hallway we had to go through and it scared me, so after a while we stopped going.

My family handled the first molestation fairly well. My grandmother was shocked, but she helped with the prosecution. She said, "This is what we have to do. This is what's right." The whole family helped out. My grandfather was convicted and sent to jail.

When I was nine or ten, my cousin told me my other grandfather had been molesting her for years. At first, I didn't believe her. It was too shocking. I'd blocked out the earlier molest. But after she told me, I stopped and said, "Wait a minute! That happened to me before!"

My cousin went to my grandfather and said, "Tell her it's true."

He said, "Okay. We're going to play a little game. Take off all your clothes." I just stood there in shock.

My grandfathers knew each other and they talked about the molestation. I guess he figured since it had happened to me already, it was okay to do it again.

He molested us for the next year. I kept telling my cousin, "We need to say something." Finally we made a plan to tell our parents the same weekend. I went home and told and she went home and didn't. Our grandfather was convicted and went to jail. And that whole side of the family resented me.

The hardest thing for me was that my parents wanted to stay on good terms with my grandfather and that side of the family. They pushed me to go over there for holidays and then I'd get shunned. It was awful.

My relatives hated me because I had put him in jail. One even implied I was the one who had initiated the molestation. He told me, "From now on, you'd better mind your parents and be a good little girl."

That was the last time I went over there. I started staying home by myself on holidays. That's what started the healing process for me—taking a stance and saying, "I'm not going to put myself through that."

Everyone protected my grandfather. The family kept sweeping it under the rug. Even my cousin protected him. When he got out of jail, she and my brother continued to go to his house. He started molesting both of them again. And he was sent back to jail.

After he was convicted the second time, my parents finally came to the conclusion, "This is not right." They only have minimal contact with my grandfather now.

How the Abuse Affected Me

I started acting out some time after the second molestation. I didn't know why. I didn't connect it to the molestation. I just thought I was a bad person who was going in the wrong direction.

I did drugs, marijuana, and LSD. I carved on myself. I was promiscuous. I didn't get along with anybody. I hated myself.

I remember being in the fifth grade and thinking of suicide.

By my freshman year in high school, I was doing a lot of cocaine. I did it to feel better about myself. I also thought I was fat and wanted to lose weight. But I was really skinny. That was another reason. When you do cocaine, you feel great. You're on top of the world. But when you come down, you feel awful, like you're the lowest person in the world.

When I was thirteen and coming down from cocaine, I tried to kill myself.

My mother and I had been arguing. I wanted to go out and she didn't want to let me. I was wearing a miniskirt, and she said I looked like a slut. Something clicked in my brain. I said to myself, "Even my mom thinks I'm a slut. Everyone thinks I'm a slut because I was abused. So it's all my fault." Boom. I ran into the bathroom and slit my wrists. I didn't really realize what I was doing till I started bleeding all over the place. I didn't feel anything.

My mom didn't know what to do with me. She put me in bed and watched me all night long. Two days later, she took me to the emergency room and I was hospitalized.

Starting to Heal

Being in the hospital was comforting. I'd hit such a bottom, I didn't resist it. It was a women's hospital. There were adults and teenagers there. The majority of women had been sexually abused. Sharing with them was really helpful. I was able to say, "Here's my story. This is what happened to me." That was a real turning point for me. I learned that I was not the only one. I started realizing I had a lot of problems and that they were related to the molestation.

It was almost like a type of school. All I did there was learn. I learned a lot about me. It was wonderful. I was still feeling confused and introverted and not so hot about myself, but at least I had some insight to work with.

After a month, my insurance ran out. My psychiatrist went on vacation and the person who took his place said, "You're out of here."

My psychiatrist came back and said, "Where is she?" I wasn't supposed to be released, but they released me anyhow.

When I went home, I was really depressed. I wasn't eating or sleeping. I wasn't functioning. My mom said, "I don't know how to deal with this," and she put me in a group home. She said, "They can deal with you."

Initially we were going to do a six-week trial period—a kind of assessment. I thought,

"Six weeks, no problem. That's half my summer vacation—I can deal with that." Six weeks passed and I said, "Okay, Mom. I'm ready to come home."

And she said, "No, you're not. We really aren't ready to deal with you."

So I said, "Screw you," and stayed in the group home.

Three or four times we made a date for me to come home, and that day would roll around and pass. She kept saying I wasn't ready, that she didn't think she was ready. Looking back, I realize she didn't feel capable of dealing with me. She didn't think she could handle it if I had a really bad day and felt suicidal. I don't really blame her. Now. But at the time, I really resented it. It was really disappointing. I had to separate myself from my mom and say, "I'm my own person. I don't need to be so attached to you."

I was in a group home for a year. There were meetings twice a week. We saw psychologists and counselors and social workers. It was very structured and I think that was helpful. Looking back, I'm extremely thankful I was there.

After a year, I finally went home. At first my parents tried to structure everything—they overstructured it for the first couple of months. We argued a lot. My mom threatened to send me back to the group home. But after that, we laid out everything straight and said, "Here's your space. This is ours." We worked it out. I'm still living with them, and it's great.

Confronting My Grandfathers

While I was in the hospital, I decided I wanted to confront my first grandfather. He molested me from the time I was two until I was six, yet I only remembered three incidents. Obviously I'd repressed a lot because I lived with him for quite a while, and this was a regular thing that went on, probably every day. But I couldn't remember it, and that really scared me.

I found out he had cancer. I decided to confront him before he died. I wanted some closure. I wanted to find out what happened to me rather than spending lots of money on a hypnotist. So we had a confrontation. I talked to him for an hour. It was really scary. He told me just about everything that he had done to me. He said, "I didn't do anything bad to you. You liked it. You kept coming back. I just gave you what you wanted."*

I said, "A two-year-old doesn't know what's right and wrong." He couldn't really say anything to that. When he died a couple of years ago, I was really glad I'd talked to him.

We sued my second grandfather. It wasn't my idea, but I felt good about it. My mother called me while I was in the hospital and said, "Guess what? We're suing your grandfather." She said, "If you can't get them to stay in jail long enough, the best way you can get them is where it really hurts—in their pocketbook." I knew the hospital was really expensive. I thought, "If this is going to put my parents in a financial bind, maybe this is what we should do."

It was a really long process. He made me go through a deposition. It lasted two or three hours. He had three different lawyers there. They didn't even want to let my mom in with me. It was really scary. I was only thirteen.

The deposition was almost like a court trial, the kind you see on TV. It was awful. They asked everything. I've blocked out a lot of it, but I remember them asking me if I was a virgin. He began to explain to me the process of losing your virginity and what happens with the breaking of the hymen. I was shocked. I thought, "How could this pertain to my grandfather molesting me?" I just looked at him and said, "That's none of your damn business." He asked me again, and the lawyers got into an argument.

They asked me every personal question in the book: what boyfriends I had, how my other grandfather molested me. They asked me more questions about my personal life than they did about the molestation. They tried to minimize the molestation, saying, "Isn't it true he only did this to you?" They made me feel really bad. When I walked out of there, I felt really small, like I was the bad person.

It's awful how the justice system makes victims feel that way. I think people being accused of the crime should go through that—not the victim. If the victim says, "This happened to me," why should they be questioned and bugged about it? It's just a tactic lawyers use to scare the victim. I don't think they should be allowed to do it.

---

* Janel's experience with her grandfather is unusual. Most perpetrators deny the abuse and aren't reliable sources for finding out what happened to you.

I Think the System Is Really Screwy

The system—the criminal justice system, the social workers, the police—handle these things terribly. A lot of kids are abused, and the system says, "Okay, we're going to take you out of your home." Why do they have to take the kids out of the home? Why can't they put the abuser somewhere else? Why do they have to disrupt the child's life? While I was in the group home, there were two or three girls I knew personally who had been in ten foster homes, two or three group homes, different shelters, juvenile hall, out on the street, thrown here, there, and everywhere. Personally, I don't think it's good for kids to be shuffled around like that.

When I was in the group home, I met this girl who was my age. We had the same status; we'd gone through a lot of the same stuff. Both of us had been abused. Neither of us had ever broken any laws. By the time she left the group home, she had a police record. She ended up killing herself.

That was really hard on me. She was a good friend. We were in exactly the same boat. She went in one direction and I went in the other. She came to the group home to get therapy and become more stable. I believe the system made her worse. She fell through the cracks. A lot of kids do.

Where I Am Today

Once I figured out that a lot of my problems stemmed from the abuse, I knew I needed to deal with them. I had a lot of determination. I wasn't going to let anybody or anything stop me.

I'm still healing. I'm not in as intense therapy as I was, but it still affects me. I still have trouble trusting people and trusting my own judgment.

For a while I had trouble being sexual. I'd look at my boyfriend's face and all of a sudden it would be my grandfather. It was awful. My boyfriend and I worked through that. It took quite a while, but he has a lot of patience. He listened. He went to counseling with me. We read books together. Anytime I'd have a memory or flashback, he'd be there. He'd listen and comfort me. Now my sex life is great.

I'm proud of coming as far as I have. I can say to myself, "Hey I survived that, and I'm still here."

Going through what I've gone through has made me a stronger person. I've converted the pain into tools and knowledge that I can apply to problems that come up now. I'm proud of that.

Evie Malcolm

"Face a fear, and the death of that fear is certain."

*E**vie Malcolm is thirty-eight years old.* She lives in Boston, works as a secretary, and lives with her partner of thirteen years, Faith. She has spent eight years recovering from agoraphobia, which resulted from her experiences being molested by strangers in New York City.*

"When people hear my story they say, 'Oh that happens to everyone who grows up in New York. What's the big deal?' It's so common, they accept it. When I was in eighth grade, the teacher asked all the girls if it ever happened to them, and every single girl raised her hand. Were we given any advice on how to deal with it? Were we told we could yell or kick or even say 'Stop'? No. It was totally expected and totally normalized. We learned that nothing could be done about it.

"But that doesn't make it tolerable for a child.

That doesn't make it any less devastating. People say, 'That's just part of living in New York,' as though it's not bad if it happens to everyone. But the fact that it's so widespread makes it worse, not better."

I grew up in the suburbs of New York. My mother was a secretary who worked her way up to an administrative assistant position. My father is a businessman. They both grew up poor, leaving high school before they graduated, but they strove hard to be educated. Intelligence and scholastic ability were highly valued in my household. We were working class in reality but rose through determination.

My family was very old-fashioned. I was extremely protected. I was raised to be polite and respectful of authority. The abuse took

---

* Evie Malcolm chose to use a pseudonym.

place at a time when no young girl was encouraged to defend herself or be strong.

The first time, I was ten years old. I had taken my little brother to a children's matinee on a Saturday. A man sat down next to us, threw his coat on my lap, and started feeling me up. I said to my brother, "We've got to move." My brother complained, but we got up and switched seats. As soon as we were settled, it happened again. I didn't know if it was someone else or the same man, but we got up again. The theater was crowded and I couldn't find any empty seats. By that time, my brother was screaming. The usher told us we'd have to go back to our same seats or leave. So we left.

My brother screamed all the way home on the subway. I said, "I can't explain it, but when we get home, Mom and Dad will explain it to you." When we got home, I immediately told my parents. My mother turned away in disgust. My father started intellectualizing about the whole thing. They didn't do anything. They didn't explain it to my brother. They didn't say I was right to leave. They didn't offer to take us back to the movies the next day. I saw they were powerless against that man. And I learned I could never look to them for help. Somewhere inside, I gave up.

Shortly after that, I passed the test to get into a public school for intellectually gifted girls. My new school started with seventh grade, so I was eleven when I began.

I lived in Brooklyn and my new school was in Manhattan. In order to get there, I had to ride three different subways. And that's where the rest of the abuse happened. It started the second day of school, during rush hour. I got on the train. I sat across from an old man. He was staring at me. And then I realized that he was exposing himself and masturbating. I thought he was crazy and insane and I was afraid that he was going to kill me. In my mind, only a lunatic would do something like that.

For the next six years, that kind of incident and much more—the grabbing and being molested in a crowd, the being followed from car to car—kept happening to me. I was very tall for my age, five foot nine. Yet I was childlike in appearance—no makeup, plain and childish clothes. I made an easy target.

Something happened almost every day. It was inevitable. And then after it happens a few times, it doesn't matter whether it happens or whether it doesn't—you have to get back into the exact same situation, and you think about it happening all the time. I had to get on that train five days a week for six years.

Quite a few of the incidents are burned into my brain. I call it being raped standing up in a crowd. It was as much rape as if there'd been actual penetration. And sometimes they got awfully close. One man stood near me masturbating with a vacant look on his face. He was smiling and his penis was completely out of his pants. With his free hand he took my arm, linking it in his—like friends walking down the street together. Just then the train got stuck in the tunnel. I felt completely trapped. In my head I was screaming, "Oh God, get me out of here." My whole self went up into my head. I felt completely disembodied.

Have you ever heard of deer who get on the road and get blinded by the headlights and they stop, and stand there, and the car hits them? What, is the deer wrong? That's what happened to me in the subway. I'd never seen these things before. I just thought, "Oh my God," and froze. And it ran over me like a two-ton truck.

I doubt it was ever the same person. There are a million nasty men in the subways of New York. The majority were well dressed; they were coming from good neighborhoods, they were carrying briefcases. It was never a Black or Hispanic man or a man of any other race but white. It wasn't poor old bums. It was all so-called normal men on their way to work, who casually took advantage of the opportunity. It was just like "Here's this young flesh. Reach out and grab it." You can molest a child so easily.

I never told anyone. I knew it was useless to tell my parents. Besides, my mother would have taken me out of my school, and I wanted to keep going. It was a tremendous honor. And I had every right to go. And I love the kid that kept going to that school. She didn't let those fuckers stop her.

A Full-Blown Panic Attack

I graduated when I was seventeen. I left the city and for five years I didn't come back. When I did, I started riding the subway again, and I started having panic attacks. I'd go down to the platform to wait for the train, and as soon as the doors to the subway would open, I'd have a full-blown panic attack with all the physical symptoms—I'd feel like I was going to die.

It's the kind of terror anyone would experience if they were being kidnapped, if they were about to be murdered. I don't know how to make it strong enough that it's about the worst feeling you can have. Every single body part feels threatened, and the adrenaline is pumping in your body, and you feel like a trapped rat. You want to run. You want to scream. You want to get out. And so I'd run out of the subway.

At that point I had no idea what was happening. I was twenty-two years old and I had no memory of what had happened to me as a kid riding the trains to school. It seemed like a panic that came out of the blue.

Over a period of years, I ended up not being able to ride the subways, then not being able to ride buses, then not being able to take cabs, then not being able to walk anywhere but to my college, ten blocks away. I could function at school and I could function at home, but I couldn't even go across the street for a cup of coffee.

Agoraphobia is like a mental cancer—it extends into everything. At my worst, the panic attacks came on no matter what. I'd have several a day. And they're really debilitating. There's a lot of fatigue connected with agoraphobia. I was worried all the time. I developed a nervous bladder and a spastic colon. I have high blood pressure, and there's no history of that in my family. There isn't a part of my life it hasn't affected.

I Went to All Kinds of Therapists to Get Help

No one ever told me what was going on. No one ever told me I had agoraphobia. The therapists I went to didn't talk. You spill your guts and they never say anything. I just got worse and worse. I'd say, "I can't take trains anymore. Now I'm taking buses." And then a year later, it was "Dr. Horowitz, I can't get on the bus anymore. I'm too frightened. What's happening?"

One doctor told me I was obsessive-compulsive and that he had a new medicine he wanted to give me for free, which means they don't know what it's going to do yet. I had to sign a release to take it. Not only couldn't I get out of my house on that medicine, I couldn't get off my couch. I was like a cucumber or a head of cauliflower. I got so depressed from that medication. I called Faith at work and I said, "You better come home. I'm thinking razor blades here. I don't want to kill myself, but it's all I can think of."

I finally self-diagnosed myself as agoraphobic after seeing a woman on the Tom Snyder show describe exactly what I experienced. I said, "Oh my God! That's me!" I called the station to get the number of one of the doctors who had been on the air with her. I ended up going to the Roosevelt clinic and getting help from some of the top people in New York.

I Wasn't Alone

I went to phobic therapy three times a week for two and a half years. It was important for me to know there were other people suffering what I was suffering, that I wasn't alone. All my friends were phobics. Those women were very important to me. I worked on a phobic newsletter.

They teach you that fears don't come without thoughts. People usually say, "I was just in the supermarket and suddenly it hit me." It feels like it comes from nowhere, but there's always a trigger. It's your own thoughts. It's a command you're giving.

What you need to learn is, "What are the thoughts?" Then you can stop them. Then your body doesn't pump the adrenaline, your throat doesn't close up, your palms don't sweat, your legs don't get shaky, you don't feel like you're going to vomit.

I was lucky enough to hook up with a wonderful phobic therapist, who's called a "helper." We did what's called contextual therapy. The purpose of contextual therapy is to get frightened, so you can feel the fear with another person who can help you reinterpret it and teach you to cope with it. You literally find the places where you're going to be afraid. If you're afraid of restaurants, you go to a restaurant.

You don't try to figure out why. You need to be able to function. If you can't get out of your house, a phobic therapist will come to your house, because obviously, how does the person get better if they can't get to the therapist's office?

My therapist's name was Sandy. We worked together for four years. She was completely fearless and warm. I owe most of my life to her.

Sandy got me out of my house again. She'd come over and walk out a little bit with me, walk me to the corner, go out to a restaurant. She asked me where I had the very worst panic attacks. I said, "On the subway." She said, "That's where we should start."

So we'd buy the tokens and go down there. We did it in small increments. It's sort of like someone who has a stroke and can't speak. They have the kind of therapist who teaches them how to speak again. Sandy taught me to be on the subway again.

At first we'd sit on the bench and watch the trains go by. That was all I could do. And she'd have me quantify the fear level from zero to ten. It would go up to an eight or nine, at which point my neck was stretched, my heart was pounding, I'd want to run. She would help me feel those feelings and not run. Then we'd get on the subway and ride one stop. And if I wanted to get out after one stop, I could. The important thing was for me to be in control.

When we got in a subway car and the doors shut—and that's a frightening moment for me—she would say, "Now what are you feeling?" And we would talk about it. Then she would say, "What are you thinking?" And I would say, "I'm not thinking anything. I'm just getting scared." And she would say again, "What are you thinking?" And it would be the same thing, over and over, until I could hear the thoughts. And the thoughts were saying, "You're trapped and you're going to die."

And she would say, "Look around. There are other people on the train. They're not trapped. You're not either. We can get off at the next stop. Whatever you want." She always restored the control to me, allowing me to break down in small pieces this huge problem of being unable to function in the world. Sandy made me feel there was no pressure or right timetable to get better. I was calling the shots. She was just there to help me.

And after an hour of working with her, I could come home just as proud from being able to ride the subway a couple of stops as someone who accomplished something at a high professional level at work. And I probably was using as much energy, intelligence, and commitment in what I was doing with Sandy as they did in their jobs.

The Ghosts of the Men

After I'd worked with Sandy for a year and a half, I was able to get on the subways when I wasn't with her. On Thanksgiving that year, Faith and I were going to my parents' house for dinner. We had to ride the exact same route I had used when I was a kid coming home from school. When we got on the train, I had to ride in the first car, because my head was racing ahead to be on the other side of the tunnel. And she was saying, "Are you going to make it?" I was using every phobic technique they had taught me. I felt I was really driving that subway train with this incredibly powerful fear.

When we got to Brooklyn, the doors opened and I got off. I went up to a pillar, leaned against it, and I burst into tears. All of a sudden I was eleven years old. It wasn't a memory. It was a reexperiencing. The ghosts of all those men who molested me came around, and I sobbed and sobbed. Faith held me. I couldn't have cared less what people thought. It had taken a year and a half of healing for me to have the strength to remember.

I'm Very Proud of What I've Done

Remembering the molestation and connecting it to the agoraphobia didn't suddenly cure me, but it did allow me to know it wasn't all coming out of the blue. I don't think anyone develops agoraphobia for no reason. I mean you don't just develop a fear of pigeons for nothing. Something happened to you with pigeons. Agoraphobia is so complex, it's hard to figure out exactly where it started, but I think it often has to do with sexual abuse.

Phobias are coping mechanisms, and though they limited me, I found I was sad to give them up. The day I could get on the bus without any phobic feelings, I felt really weird. It's like when a refrigerator goes off and you realize it's always been on. It was disorienting, and it was a loss. But the gains were so much bigger.

All my symptoms have gotten less, but they haven't gone away entirely. I liken it to turning the volume down on a radio. If the radio is blasting, then you can't function. If you turn the radio down to a moderate level, you can still hear it, but you can function. There are times when that panicky feeling in me is very low and I can ignore it. Other times it's stronger but I can push myself to ignore it. And then there are times when it overwhelms me.

I'm rebuilding my confidence slowly. The damage that's done to you when you're a kid, I don't know how much you get over it. I'm strong in my conviction that I want to be cured, but I'm not looking for a miracle. At the same time, I don't want to see a therapist who says, "You have to live with this." Maybe I will have to live with some of it, but I want to break through those limits as much as I can. I've worked very hard to do that, and I'm very proud of what I've done.

I Fought Back and I Feel Great About It

There was a man who exposed himself to me, my mother, and my aunt in front of Korvette in New York a couple of years ago at Christmastime. A Salvation Army Santa Claus was standing right next to us. My aunt and my mother were talking about where to go to lunch. I was looking around, and out of the corner of my eye I saw this guy's face, and I just knew this man was exposing himself. He had the same spacey, faraway look on his face that the molesters in the subway had. I thought, "I can't believe this. This guy's jerking off in the middle of a Christmas crowd, in front of Santa Claus, no less!"

The man was standing very close to me, and the look on his face was getting more and more urgent. He was beating off to beat the band. I had a shoulder bag, and it was heavy, and I swung it at him, hitting him really hard in the head. He started hopping and jumping everywhere, trying to protect himself from the blows and trying to zip up his pants and trying to run, all at the same time. I screamed at him and ran after him, and I said very loudly, very publicly to my mother and my aunt, "That man was exposing himself to us, right here in front of Santa Claus!"

They were very supportive. They said, "That's awful! Good for you for chasing him away!" Their response was wonderful. I didn't feel the shame or the humiliation I'd felt in the subway. Because this time, I fought back. And this time I wasn't alone.

Diane Hugs

"One of the major aspects of healing from childhood abuse is to begin to love yourself. With multiple personalities, this task is much more difficult, because I have to love parts of myself that have been so walled off that I don't even know them."

Diane Hugs is a thirty-two-year-old writer who has been struggling with memories of her childhood abuse for ten years.* She's had multiple sclerosis for twelve. MS is a degenerative condition of the central nervous system, with symptoms that vary greatly from person to person. In Diane's case, she has been paraplegic for six years and legally blind for one year. Diane connects her disease with the severe abuse she experienced, starting in infancy.

In the past two and a half years, Diane has become aware that she has multiple personalities—more than thirty of them, ranging in age from three to thirty. As she eloquently expresses, women with multiple personalities can heal.

---

* Diane Hugs is using her own name.

From the time I was a very young child, I had experiences that were so traumatic, they split my personality wide open. There was no way for my young mind to cope with the brutality and random acts of sadism that I experienced. Instead, I completely forgot the incidents and created a totally new personality. Within two years, I went in and out of three such changes: from being an introverted, shy pacifist, to being the leader of a girls' gang that went after known rapists and child molesters, to becoming an academic scholar. Each of these personalities began without the old scars, without the old terror, without the anger. Each had her own coping mechanisms, approaching the world in a completely different way. I, as the core personality, was totally unaware of their existence. Every time I wiped the slate clean, a new and different personality would come out to take over so I might survive. There were many times as a child when I questioned whether I would survive. The ultimate threat was always "I will kill you if you tell, if you . . . if you . . ."

It wasn't until I was much older that I realized I had multiple personalities—more than thirty of them. I also realized that I had blocks of time that I did not remember. I had always accepted that as being normal. I thought everyone occasionally spaced out and found themselves in another city or in the midst of a conversation with no idea what was being talked about.

Accepting each of these parts of myself, and then integrating them into my personality, is a long process. And it's often very painful, as each of these splits, each of these personalities, has memories and feelings separate from my own experience. So to integrate means to accept those feelings and to accept those memories that I have successfully blocked since I was a child. Sometimes, accepting how I coped in order to survive is extremely painful. Imagine integrating an eighteen-year-old part who is a prostitute when you've been a lesbian for over ten years.

Usually, when one of these personalities takes control, so to speak, I lose time. It seems to me as if seconds have gone by, when in reality minutes, hours, or a day has gone by with this other personality functioning in my place. As I begin to accept the feelings and the parts of me that have split off, instead of losing time with that particular personality, I hear a voice in my head which is that other personality talking. Sometimes it's totally against what I'm thinking or feeling, so I have a lot of inner arguments as part of the process of integration.

After the arguments comes a blending where I not only accept those parts of me, but am also strengthened by the knowledge, the courage, whatever it is that each part holds. It's as if each personality holds a special part of my life, not only a painful part of my life. And each time I integrate one, I'm integrating another part of myself that adds to my understanding.

One of the major aspects of healing from childhood abuse is to begin to love yourself. With multiple personalities, this task is much more difficult, because I have to love parts of myself that have been so walled off, so blocked from the conscious personality, that I don't even know them. Over and over, I have to figure out ways to get through those walls so I can know other parts of me. Before I can love myself, I have to know myself.

Kyos Featherdancing

"What do you feel there is left for you to do?"

"Heal the earth. My mission in life is to heal the earth and all living things."

"Yeah, but is there anything left for you to do for your own healing?"

"That is for myself. I don't see my healing as separate from that."

Kyos Featherdancing is a thirty-four-year-old Native American woman, born and raised in a rural town in California's San Joaquin Valley.* She now lives in the San Francisco Bay Area. Kyos works odd jobs as a landscaper and as a chef, but primarily she is a healer.

Her father was of the Caddo tribe, her mother a mixture of Choctaw and German. Kyos grew up poor. Her family picked cotton. Later her father became a welder and a plumber, and eventually he went to work for the nuclear industry. Kyos says, "He sold his soul and stopped being an Indian."

Kyos has two brothers and two sisters, all of whom were abused by her father.

The most sustaining influence in Kyos's childhood was her grandmother. From her, Kyos learned the "old ways," which have remained the source of her survival and healing.

I Thought It Was a Gentle and Very Loving Relationship

From the time I was a baby until I was nine, I loved my father more than anything in the entire world. No one could say anything bad about him to me. His favorite thing was to suck my cunt when I was a baby. When I was three years old, I first remember him actually putting his prick into my vagina. That was something that we had between each other.

---

* Kyos Featherdancing is using her own name.

He made me believe that every father did that with their daughter. So I believed that. And I became that. And I loved it, too.

My parents didn't let me go to other people's houses very much. I know now my father didn't want them knowing what he was doing. But when I was nine, I went to stay with a friend, and when it was time to go to bed, her father and mother tucked us in and gave us a kiss on the forehead and said, "Good night." I thought that was real strange. I kept wondering if anything else was going to happen. And finally I nudged my friend and said, "Hey, does your father come in and give you nookie?"

And she was like, "What? What are you talking about?" She told her parents about it, and they said we couldn't be friends anymore after that. That was the first time I realized not everybody had a father like that.

You Do What You Have to Do to Get Through It

I became the woman my dad wanted me to be. I dressed how he told me to dress. I never went out of the house without makeup. I always shaved my legs. I shaved my underarms. I shaved my eyebrows and my legs around my cunt so I wouldn't look hairy. I shaved hair on my stomach. My dad taught me women were put here to be fucked by men, so that's the way I was. I began to be that to men in the neighborhood, to men in the streets, to the men in the office in that town. I had routes. I made money.

And my father sold me to his friends. I couldn't bring my friends to the house because they would end up in bed with him. He'd manipulate that somehow.

From nine to eighteen, I hated my father's guts and did every conniving thing I could think of, every conniving thing he taught me, and turned it around on him. I used his money. Made him buy me cars. Made him buy me good clothes. I got hooked on drugs, made him pay for it. I was strung out on junk by the time I was sixteen. I did speed. I dealt drugs to some of my teachers. I made grades that way. Some of them passed me to get rid of me. They didn't want to get hit or kicked in the balls. I was mean. No one could control me.

I hated myself completely. It was, "Okay, this is who you are. This is who he wants you to be. This is what you have to do, so just do it to get by." To me, that's what surviving is about. You do what you have to do until you can get out of it.

"You're Going to Find Out You Have a Path"

When I was thirteen, I had an abortion. It was my father's child. He made it look like I was lying, and I was really angry. I started going to this Pentecostal church with my aunt. It was a place where I could go to scream and shout out my anger. She told me, "Give it all to the Lord." And that's what I did.

When I was fourteen or fifteen, I started hanging out with this black woman. She was my best friend. The woman took me in and mothered me like I'd never been mothered before. She'd take me down to the church and she'd jam on her piano. She gave me singing lessons, and the first thing she said to me was, "Sistah, you're gonna hafta open up your mouth and get ugly!" And from that point on, I just let it roar. I sang it out. Singing has been one of the most healing things for me. Singing and shouting and dancing in the spirit.

My father would forbid me to go to church. He was into all kinds of ugly spiritual things—black magic and all kinds of sorcery. That was one of the things that he put on me at a very young age. Different tribes do their own sorcery, their own ceremonials, but my dad used magic in very dark ways that are not to be done. I was into those things too, but I began breaking away from them.

My grandmother had taught me healing ways. She taught me a lot about my own self and about healing, about how to cook, how to clean. My grandmother lived the old ways. She had her blackberry bush. She did her rituals. She burned sage. She burned cedar. She had her path. I never forgot those ways. My dad forbade me to do them. He tried to keep me away from her. But she's alive in me. She always told me, "You're going to find out that you have a path and it's going to be different from who your father is." He tried to kill that, but he couldn't.

Some Hard and Heavy Things Came Down on Me

I left home at eighteen. I'd run away before, but every time they'd pick me up and take me right back. I hung out with bikers and rowdies from the time I was twelve, and my father always made it look like I was the bad one and he was respectable. He had cousins and uncles that were pigs in that town and he did deals with one judge there. I learned real fast that he could get me locked up for a long time.

The day I turned eighteen, I split. It was about a month before I was going to graduate from high school. I was going to go to college and get into home economics. Being Indian, the government was going to pay for the whole thing. But a close friend of mine came home from Vietnam and committed suicide and I couldn't go through with it. So I left with just the clothes on my back and an overnight change. I sold some dope and hitched to Chicago. I stayed in an all-night laundromat the first two weeks.

The next years were rowdy. I got into a biker's club. I was heavily into drugs. I didn't take a bath. I wore Levi's for months on end. I was mean. Always drinking, always fighting, always in gang fights—rowdy.

After I left the bikers, I joined a Christian band. They were doing heroin addict programs, and I ended up in a halfway house. Christians is the biggest way to get out of tight situations. I learned how to use it for my benefit. I got myself clean and stayed with the halfway house for quite a while. Then they sent me to do a street ministry in Boulder, Colorado. I was living with three other single Christian women. I fell in love with one of them, and we got caught having an affair. I felt guilty and I started getting back on drugs again. And they kicked me out of the house.

I Wanted to Love Women

I moved to Denver to this boardinghouse. Ended up meeting all these lesbians, women who were into all kinds of healing. At that point, I was an alcoholic. I was back on drugs. I was just sick. I felt I was dying. I didn't want to be a Christian anymore, but I didn't know what direction to take.

I met this woman, and we hitched to the Michigan Womyn's Music Festival. I'd never met so many healers in my life. I learned that being a lesbian is not just about sexuality. It has to do with healing power. It was the first time I was allowed to be a real woman, because churches do not allow this. I became aware of who I really was. Then I had a real clear picture of why my father wanted to destroy me. But it hadn't worked. I had survived.

Your Heart Will Never Lie to You

At that point I started healing on a different level than I had ever known before. I started cooking healthy foods. I was stretching. I was running. I was riding a ten-speed. I didn't do any more prescription drugs. I didn't do any more speed. I didn't do any more cocaine. I didn't go back to junk. For a while I kept drinking, then I quit. I had a lot of support. It was a good time for me. I was very impressed with the changes that I was making.

Then I met a woman who became my mentor. She taught me about group therapy, primal screaming, and co-counseling. I added this to everything I knew from my grandmother, everything I had picked up from the earth.

This woman helped me to realize that I needed to have a relationship with myself before I could have a positive relationship with anyone else. So I became celibate for quite a long time, about nine years. I chose to be celibate because I didn't know how I wanted to be touched, or whether I wanted to be touched.

When I was younger I had relationships I would just call fucking relationships. I didn't know or care who I was fucking or who was fucking me. I had practiced this one pattern my whole life, that I had to be fucked in order to be loved. And that was a hard pattern to break.

I spent a lot of time alone, loving myself, touching myself in loving ways. I spent a lot of time hugging myself. Getting feelings back of sensuality rather than sexuality. Just lots of real comforting times with myself. Hot tubs. And sweating. I like to do sweat lodges with sage.

It was a time for my own personal therapy. I lived in the mountains for a while. I rented a room in the city for a while. I beat drums. I chanted. I wrote. I did anger work. I went to the woods and shouted and beat and screamed and cried and gave it to the wind. I did rituals for turning myself around and letting the earth heal me. I did rituals in the sun to burn the poisons out of me. I fasted. I drank spring water.

I had collected a lot of ideas about how to heal myself and I needed to be alone to do that healing. That time was really important. I learned how to have a relationship not only with myself but also with the earth I love so dearly. When I need to be alone, I need to be alone with the earth. I get my energy and my answers from her.

I have everything I need to heal myself. That's what my grandmother taught me. She taught me how to follow my heart and my intuition. I have always had a vision of my grandmother's brown crinkly hand coming toward me to walk with me in that blackberry patch. She is my protector and has always been my protector. She taught me, "Trust your heart. Your heart will never lie to you."

That's one of the reasons I've never really been able to get therapy, because I don't believe therapists can give me the answers. I have everything I need to heal myself because no one knows my experience like I know it. I've turned myself around and nobody else could.

I Don't Need to Forgive That Bastard

A lot of people believe forgiveness is the ultimate healing. And to me, that's bullshit. The man doesn't deserve my forgiveness. *I* deserve my forgiveness. What I need to do is get right the fuck on with being right where I'm at with my anger. If you're looking to forgiveness as this goal, then you're still believing that lie that keeps you under control. That's what Christianity is about—keeping you under control.

And as far as freeing myself, I freed myself by saying, "Get out. I don't want you and I will not be ruled by you, and I will not let you overwhelm my life."

And I don't have to get any revenge, because the way he's done his magic, he's brought it back on himself. He avoided the earth and who he is, so now he's dying. He's got cancer. They've cut half of his stomach out and his genitals. That's where it all started. And that's where it's all ending for him.

Giving It to the Wind

I sometimes wonder when the work is going to be finished. I don't think it ever really is. It doesn't overwhelm me as much as it used to. I used to cry and cry about it. It felt like everything inside me was collapsing. I don't feel that way now. Some subjects about this, I'm cried out. I've let it go and given it to the wind, and let the wind heal it.

I'm excited about my life now. I'm excited about the healing I'm going to do next, because it's going to be the ultimate freedom that I've been wanting—the healing of my spiritual life. I know now that I can truly be a healer and that what I've lived through doesn't have to hold me back. When it does, I can control it. I can tell it to leave me alone. I can spend time with it. Whatever I choose. It doesn't have to hinder my walk with the spirit.

Randi Taylor

"I never saw anyone like me in the incest books. I never saw anyone who said she had a good relationship with her father. All the perpetrators looked like angry, ugly, mean people, and yet my father appeared to be a loving, charming, wonderful man. I loved and adored him. He treasured me. That made the whole thing even more insidious. My story needs to be told because women need to know their experience counts. There's no such thing as mild abuse."

Randi Taylor is thirty years old.* She is single, lives alone, and works as a restaurant manager in Seattle. Randi was raised in an upper-middle-class family. Her parents were English, Scottish, and German. Randi's father was an accountant; her mother, a housewife. She has two sisters and two brothers.

Randi's parents were very liberal. She called them by their first names. They were "cool." They knew their children were smoking pot but never reprimanded them. They kept a keg of beer in the garage so the kids could invite their friends over to drink. There were no limits, no boundaries.

Randi was always Daddy's girl. She idolized him. The molestation occurred when Randi was twelve to fourteen, just as she was going through puberty. It was always in the guise of playing games and laughing.

My father and I would do a lot of ruckus, fun things together. I'd pour a glass of water on his head, and he'd pour a glass of water on mine. We'd be tickling and wrestling and chasing each other around the house. A lot of times while he was tickling me, he'd reach his hand around and cup my breast. I'd always scream at him not to do that, but my screams would get mixed up with all the laughter and hilarity and screaming that was already going on. I'd

---

* Randi Taylor wanted to use her own name but couldn't for legal reasons.

tell him to stop, and he'd say, "Oh gee, did I slip? I didn't mean to." It was in the same tone as someone who just poured a glass of water on you and said, "Oops! I didn't mean to do that." He made a mockery of it.

Whenever we rode in the car, I'd sit in the middle of the front seat. When we went around a sharp turn, my father would elbow my boobs. He'd do it on purpose, always with an exaggerated gesture. My sisters and I had a name for it. We said my father was "boobing" me.

Then there was a routine we went through every morning. I'd get up to brush my teeth, and when I came back to my room, I'd have to search in my closet and under my bed, because my father would be hiding there, waiting for me to undress. I knew he wanted to see me naked, so I'd have to chase him out before I changed my clothes. I had to protect myself from this Peeping Tom who was my father, but it was made into a game. It was just part of the Taylor family morning routine.

At one point my father took up a sudden interest in photography, but the only thing he wanted to photograph were his daughters. He made me wear a thin T-shirt and he shined a light from behind my boobs. He wanted a picture of my boobs showing through a filmy T-shirt. That one never quite came out right, so he talked me into taking off my shirt. He promised he wouldn't photograph my breasts—only my chest and shoulders above my breasts. But they were definitely erotic photos.

While he was doing the photos, his hands would get shaky. His breath would be louder than normal. He would be excited. It was very scary for me to see him that way. Here was

this man I adored and something happened to him. He was out of control and I never knew how far he would go.

One time my mother was going to be away all day. I was home sick from school. And in the middle of the day, my father came home from work. I was very frightened. I said, "What are you doing here?" He was joking and smiling and happy. "Oh, I thought I'd come home to see you. I knew you were here by yourself not feeling good. I thought I'd spend a little time with you."

He'd brought home some felt-tipped pens, and the game he had in mind was to decorate my breasts. He made me pull up my nightgown and he drew on my body. He made my two breasts into eyes, and then he drew a nose and mouth below it. His hands were shaking and his breath was really hot while he was doing that. And all the time, he was joking and teasing. It was horrible for me. Yet it was the one experience that allowed me to feel anger at him later on. All the rest of it, I said to myself, "Oh, he just slipped accidentally." But this was clearly thought out ahead of time. It was the only time he ever did anything that no one else saw him do. The rest of it was all out in the open.

Soon after, when I was fourteen, he complained that I was never home anymore, that I was always off with my friends. I turned to him with anger and said, "Why do you think I never spend time at home anymore? It's because I'm always afraid of what you're going to do to me." That stopped him cold, and he didn't touch me again after that. But an atmosphere of sexual jokes and innuendos continued.

I Didn't Know How to Say No

Before he molested me, I was a happy child, a normal child. But after it happened, I started seeking out friends from the other side of town. I hung out with guys with motorcycles, the kind of guys who drank a lot, who had tattoos and dropped out of school. We stole cars and went joy-riding. I had a boyfriend who was a year older than me. I got pregnant the first time we had sex, when I was thirteen. He dumped me, and I was afraid to tell my parents. I wore a lot of baggy clothes. It was the style at the time. I was six months pregnant before they figured it out. It shows how little parenting was going on.

My mother and I went shopping for a new bra because my breasts were swelling. When she saw me nude in the dressing room, she knew, but she didn't say anything to me. Instead she came home and told my father. That night when I was in bed, he came into my room and said my mother had told him I might have a problem. He asked if I was pregnant. I said I was. He asked me when I'd had my last period. I said six months ago. He was shocked. He told me my mother had known I was pregnant because my breasts had changed, that the nipples were larger and the brown area around the nipples had gotten bigger and browner. Then he said he wanted to see. I protested. He said he wouldn't touch me, and then he insisted I pull up my shirt. He stared at my breasts for a few minutes, and then let me pull my shirt down. I felt invaded and ashamed.

My parents never got angry at me for the pregnancy. They asked me what I wanted to do. I said I just wanted to get rid of it. I flew to New York with my mother to some sleazy hospital for a saline abortion. They injected saline to kill the baby and then they gave me a drug to induce labor. It was extremely painful. I gave birth to the baby more than twenty-four hours later. I had no idea what was happening. I remember the water broke and I thought that was it. I yelled for the nurses and told them it was over. I had no idea there would actually be a baby, or that it would be so big. I only knew that the abortion would get rid of this problem.

The nurses had me give birth into a bedpan. It was only then that I realized it was a baby. It wasn't just a thing. Then they took it away. I never found out if it was a girl or boy.

My mother visited me a couple of times, but she only sat there crying. She was frightened and didn't nurture me at all. She hadn't brought enough cash and her main concern was that she might have to spend the night in the hospital waiting room. I ended up feeling guilty that I'd caused her all this pain. I felt like a horrible person. And once we got home, it was never mentioned again.

I now see how the pregnancy was a direct result of being molested. I didn't know how to say no. My boyfriend told me he had biological needs and that all the other boys were getting it, that if I didn't give it to him, he was going to have to go somewhere else. And I didn't think enough of myself to let him go. Having had the experience of my father being sexually out of control made me believe that boys had this need that had to be filled. And of course I had to fill it.

Self-Abuse and Anxiety Attacks

As a teenager, I smoked a lot of pot and took a lot of acid. I went through a period in my early twenties of eating compulsively and making myself throw up. I finally quit overeating when I started doing cocaine. I no longer had any desire for food. The cocaine addiction only lasted a few months. I spent all kinds of money, and then I knew I had to stop. Then I started drinking too much.

But nothing worked to keep away the fear. I'd started having anxiety attacks when I was a teenager, but they got really bad when I was in my twenties. When I was twenty-four I had a nervous breakdown. I thought I was going crazy. I said to myself, "This is it. I'm over the edge. I need to be taken to the mental ward." I went to see a psychiatrist, but I couldn't afford to keep it up. Besides, it didn't seem to be helping.

The panic attacks kept increasing. They seemed to come from out of the blue. They were crippling. Adrenaline would rush through my whole system. My muscles would pump up, my arms would tighten, my whole body would start to sweat and shake. I'd feel like I was about to blank out. My vision would change. It's like looking at an overexposed photo. The world becomes this foreign place where everything is just whitewashed.

The panic attacks happened most frequently when I was in the car. I'd be driving on the freeway and I'd feel like I was being forced to go faster than I wanted to go. When I had to pull up at a stop light, I'd feel completely trapped. I'd want to run the red light.

Sometimes I got the feeling that the sky was just too big. I wouldn't see it as blue sky but as infinity, as something that went on forever, that really had no boundaries. For me that had a lot to do with the lack of boundaries when I was growing up. I'd feel like I was going to be swallowed up by that vast, limitless sky. If I was walking in a field, I'd cover my head and crawl on the ground so I didn't float away into this limitless space. It was terrifying.

"It Was Molestation"

One of my sisters is an alcoholic. When I was twenty-five, she got into AA. As part of her 12-step recovery program, she did an inventory of her life and had to tell someone about it. Part of her story dealt with our father. He'd never touched her when she was a teenager, aside from the photo sessions. But when she was twenty-two, they went on a trip together. They'd gotten drunk and had sex. Because of her age, my sister had always blamed herself.

When she talked about it in her inventory, the other person said, "My God, you were molested. That was incest. It wasn't your fault." My sister started reading books about incest, and then she came to me and said, "What Dad did to us was incest."

I said, "Maybe for you, but not for me. I love my father. He loves me. He never did anything to hurt me." But she gave me a bunch of books to read. And I started to think about it. I went back into counseling.

It took the longest time for me to wholeheartedly believe that my experience counted.

I felt like what happened to me was minor compared to what happened to other women. Molestation sounded like something horrible, and what happened to me didn't seem that horrible. My father just slipped once in a while.

I think it was the panic attacks—the fact that there was a direct result I could point to—that made me start to believe that he had done something wrong. They pushed me to break through that barrier of protecting my father, to face how terrified and angry I had been.

One day when I was driving, I started to panic. I was trying to talk myself down by saying, "You don't have to scare yourself this way." And all of a sudden this thought popped into my brain: "You don't have to frighten yourself the way he frightened you the day he came home from work."

That's when I finally made the connection. I realized the phobias were the fears I had to suppress. It was like a suspense thriller, where the girl has trusted someone to protect her from the killer who's after her, and all of a sudden she finds out he is the killer. That's the kind of fear that was going on for me. My father, who was supposed to keep me safe from harm, was the harm.

I finally realized there had been damage done. For the first time in my life, I got angry at my father. He lost his hero status.

For a long time I stayed in the grief of having lost him. Looking at the reality of what happened meant losing the fond relationship I had with my father, and I wanted to hang on to that desperately.

At First I Felt Sorry for My Father

My sister confronted my father a couple of years ago. She told him we were both in therapy. When she told me she'd talked to him, all I could think was "How is he going to handle it?" I felt sorry for him. I felt it was such a big burden for him to shoulder—that two of his daughters were in therapy. I thought the guilt would crush him. I'd taken care of my father's emotional needs for so long that it was hard for me to recognize that he was a sick person who did bad things.

My father's admitted to me that what he did was wrong. He knows there's nothing he can do to make it better, but says if there was, he'd do it. He says I'm still special to him, and that the only important thing is that I get better. For a while he called me quite regularly. I'd get angry at him over the phone and he'd apologize. But it wasn't really helping me. Finally I told him I didn't want to do that anymore. Just recently I wrote him a letter and said I didn't want to have contact with him for the time being. I was crying, but it felt terrific to write. It's hard because I don't know what kind of relationship I will have with my father when this is all over. I don't know what will be left. But at least I know I'm getting healthy.

Michelle and Artemis

"Because we're sisters, I think we blared through everything at an incredibly high intensity and speed. Having each other to bounce off of has really catalyzed things. As each one of us broke a barrier for ourselves, we broke a barrier for the other person."

Michelle Thomas is thirty-one years old.[*] *She is a counselor and lives with her husband of four years, David, in Boulder, Colorado. Her sister Artemis is thirty-seven. She is a nurse and was recently divorced after a twelve-year marriage.*

Michelle and Artemis grew up in Denver. They lived with their mother, their stepfather, and their younger sister, who is now twenty-five. Their stepfather worked for the military and earned a good income, but they lived in poverty because he gambled. Frequently there was no food in the house.

Both parents were violent alcoholics, and both sexually abused the girls. Their mother abused them mostly in the context of "preparing" them for Ben, their stepfather. She was totally unpredictable—kind one minute and sadistic the next. He was particularly brutal in his abuse, often torturing the girls.

MICHELLE: When we were children, we never talked about the abuse. It was almost as if we couldn't stand to look at each other—you know, the victim-hating-the-other-victim syndrome.

ARTEMIS: You never knew what you were going to get from who, when. There was never a feeling of safety. When I was eleven, I had an abortion with my stepfather's child and almost died. Michelle was five years old and she was told to take care of me.

---

* Michelle Thomas and Artemis wanted to use their own names but couldn't for legal reasons.

MICHELLE: My stepfather had my mom committed to a number of mental facilities. The message was, if you said anything or you crossed him in any way, it would be very easy for him to institutionalize any of us. And so it was progressively impressed upon us to not go to the outside.

ARTEMIS: And even when we did tell, no one believed us. Michelle told the principal in fifth grade. And I used to draw pictures of what was happening to me and leave them places. I got in a lot of trouble for drawing dirty pictures. I told people I baby-sat for. They'd just go on with their conversation as if I'd never said anything. I remember my exact thought: "I must be telling a lie. Why am I telling a lie?"

MICHELLE: I was just on a straight survival mode. I never did anything that would be your normal teenage routine. Life was very serious. I put myself through school. I worked; I crammed my life as full as I possibly could with outside stimulus. I was a zombie, just going through the motions of being alive.

And then there was my tough guy. We grew up in a tough neighborhood. I always used that as a cover: "I was just a hard kid because of where I grew up." Yet I never got into dope. I needed control much too much to allow myself to get stoned or drunk.

I was very withdrawn. I made sure that nobody knew me. And at the same time, I bounced around in a lot of relationships. There was a revolving door on my bedroom. That lasted until I met David.

ARTEMIS: My coping was very different. I learned the tremendous capabilities of the mind. I could keep myself from feeling pain. I took a lot of drugs. Nothing that addicted me—just so I stayed in the ozone. I screwed around. I hated men. I hated myself.

As an adult, I was either docile and helpless or I would fly into violent rages and get ugly as hell. I'd fix the house up very nice, and I'd try so hard to do things beautiful for myself and for my husband. But I couldn't handle it for long. He'd come home and the house would be in shambles. I would have demolished it. And my husband would say, "Why did you do it?" And I'd say, "I don't know why."

Things would trigger me off and I'd run down the street just screaming. Or I'd be in a car and kick the windshield in or try to jump out. At this point I hadn't remembered anything about the abuse.

Looking back, I have no idea how I was able to function as a nurse for all those years.

Don't You Know I'm Poison?

MICHELLE: In sex I was always the controller and there was always a very fine knife edge between pain and pleasure. I would say where it was going to go, and when it was going to go, and how far.

I had an almost sadistic desire to watch the other person come to a point of pain. I knew how to string it out to a fine degree where they weren't sure if they were in pain or whether it was just slightly pleasurable. I would toy with other people to the point of being cruel. I had been extremely well trained. I was very adept at it.

I had lots of denial about being vulnerable and feminine. It wasn't until I came into a soft relationship with a strong woman that I learned not to be in that dominant role in sex. From her I learned to touch and to feel because it was safe.

ARTEMIS: I was never cruel or sadistic sexually. I was always just the victim. I would seduce a lot of people into bed, and then I'd disappear and not feel anything. I also had a big appetite for sex, a lot of actual physical desire, which confused me, and I hated it. It was the most disgusting, degrading thing to actually want sex.

With my husband, who was a very gentle man, I got more destructive. It was like, "Don't love me. Don't you know I'm poison?" I would often get hysterical and start beating at him, screaming, "I'm a whore. I'm a whore. Can't you see how ugly I am?"

And then he'd say, "Artemis, no." Because he loved me, he sincerely loved me. He'd say that and I'd go into absolute hysteria. I'd go about definitely proving to him how evil I was. I'd start smashing everything in the room or cut myself with a knife or everything in the room with a knife. It would then be a matter of him trying to save us both.

He'd say, "Artemis, don't close off to me. I'll stay right here till you're ready, but don't close off." And then he'd say, "Okay, can I reach out to you?" And he'd gradually reach out to me, and then slowly I'd be able to climb out of this hole I was in and reach out to him.

MICHELLE: When I first remembered the abuse, I went through long periods of "Don't touch me." Then when I started feeling sexual again, I tried to go back and do the same kind of sexual controlling I had always done with David, and it didn't work. I'd crack up laughing in the middle of it.

My domination and cruelty had been connected to my fear of feeling. People set up scenarios to keep from feeling particular things. If you're going to go to that elaborate way of making sure that you don't feel something soft, something's going on.

ARTEMIS: I remember coming to a place where I let myself admit that I loved my husband. That was a big taboo. I mean, you can let a man beat you, you can let him rape you, you can hate him, but you can't love a man. Sincerely care for a man? That was against all the rules of the universe, and God was going to strike me down for sure. It's almost like that was more humiliating than being raped and being beaten and tortured. That fresh, wonderful feeling of just loving him. And I did love him.

If I Had Been Alone, I Would Never Have Believed It

ARTEMIS: Before I even began remembering the abuse, I had a dream in which a friend stood at my bedroom window with a long scroll and said, "You have to remember, Artemis. You have to remember." And I had no idea what I was supposed to remember.

MICHELLE: I always remembered the alcohol and the neglect. But I didn't remember anything about the sexual abuse until I was in a very safe relationship. David and I were driving from Boulder to Denver. All of a sudden I saw my stepfather's face and knew what had happened. His face just kind of hung outside the window, and when I turned to look at David, he was Ben. I remember going very white and afraid, and throughout the rest of that night, I progressively became more conscious of what that fear and those feelings were. I knew why I hated him so much.

ARTEMIS: I was the opposite of Michelle. I didn't start remembering until everything that was secure around me left. My husband and I separated.

Our youngest sister got married. Michelle and I were driving home from the wedding. I don't remember what led up to it, but Michelle looked at me and said, "Did anything happen to you?"

And I said, "No, nothing ever happened to me. But I always had these dreams." And so I told her the dreams, and she looked me straight in the face and said, "Those were not dreams, Artemis." And it just cracked. It was like a lightning bolt hit me and my head opened up. And I knew. My God, they were not dreams.

That night I did not sleep. I kept the light on all night, and just remembered. I had no control over the memories. But I had done a lot of meditation, so I knew there was some part of my brain where I could sit in a calm and neutral place. In the midst of experiencing it very intensely, I climbed into that one little corner of myself that could view it neutrally.

MICHELLE: You get to the point where you realize that the memory is only a memory. You already lived through it the first time, and it can't hurt you anymore. And if you can just take the observer role and watch it, then the fear of going crazy goes away. But that fear was there for the longest time.

I remember coming up against a picture and fighting it for days: "No, I'm not going to see this. Because if I see this, I'll go crazy. If I see this, I'll disappear." And finally I came to a place where I knew I needed to see the pictures, and I would actually chase after them.

I believed the memories right away, but believing another human being could do those things to a child was where the doubt came in.

ARTEMIS: I never would have believed the memories if I hadn't been able to call Michelle and tell her, "This is what happened." And she'd say, "Yes, it did happen. And here's the other part of it." Between the two of us we were able to put the puzzle pieces together.

MICHELLE: For a long time, I didn't realize how bad these things were. It had been such a way of life that I just accepted it. It wasn't until I could bounce it off somebody else and see their reaction that it sank in.

ARTEMIS: There were times I felt I was going to go under with the memories. The agony was so awful, and the aloneness. The feeling was, nobody loves someone who needs. Everyone is afraid of the rawness of pure human need, so don't let anybody see.

But finally I said, "Fuck it! I'm going to look myself and I'm not going to be afraid to let anyone else see." Because everybody's human. So I just dove into that aloneness completely, and dove all the way through it until I was no longer afraid of the intensity of my need as a human being.

Facing the Shame

ARTEMIS: I've done everything in the damn book that's wrong, or had it done to me. And I realize the integrity of who I am in the face of all that. I'd worn that cloak of shame and it branded itself into my skin. But I found out that I could take it off, even if it meant taking my skin off along with it. I could grow back new skin that was healthy and good.

What helped me do that was allowing myself to be deeply loved. I allowed myself to be loved in the places where I felt the ugliest and most ashamed of myself. And I don't mean physical places.

MICHELLE: I'm in a marriage where there's total, unconditional love—to do the most horrible rotten things you can do to a person and to have them be accepting of you, and love that ugliness in you, until you yourself can love that ugliness. And that ugliness and that shame turns into something very soft and very warm and very beautiful inside of yourself.

The particular incident I'm thinking of is the time I was staying at Artemis's house. I remember reading, for the third time, *If I Die Before I Wake*. I was by myself. And I was in a total state of agony and numbness at the same time, if you can do that. The world could have disappeared and I wouldn't have known it. I was feeling the shame and the ugliness that had surrounded my life so intensely, and feeling horribly alone, like I had no right to be alive because I was the carrier of all this horrendous atrocity. And that day, I dove into that self-destructiveness because I knew I had to or I would never get to the other side.

There were knives in the house, which were my favorite tool as a child. As a kid I would sit and carve and just watch the blood to know I was alive. There are scars on my body and I have no idea where they came from. I couldn't tell you which ones I inflicted and which ones were inflicted upon me. When I was twelve, I realized I could kill myself, so I quit. This was the first time since then that I'd had that feeling again. And so I got myself out of the house.

I walked to the top of a steep cliff, watching the ocean and thinking about different ways that I could kill myself. I thought about jumping off the cliff. I thought of this whole series of things, one, to intensify the pain, and two, to get away from it. And I looked down and I happened to be sitting right in the middle of poison oak.

I remember very vividly thinking about my mother, thinking that staying alive didn't matter because she never loved me. She never cared. I finally faced that I'd never had a mother, and I never would.

And so, sobbing, I just picked up handfuls of poison oak and rubbed it into my skin from head to toe. After doing that I felt better. There was always a release with the carving—and this time with the poison oak—because somebody on the outside could see the pain that was a constant on the inside.

And then I went and sat on the steps outside Artemis's house and waited until somebody came home. And I told both David and Artemis what I had done.

ARTEMIS: You risked being vulnerable and we both were there for you. I think that was the day you lost your hard guy.

MICHELLE: Yeah. I did. You just loved me. Even with what I had done. So to heal shame, you just dive right into that shame and you risk letting somebody love you inside of that.

We Literally Reraised Ourselves

ARTEMIS: Bringing my selves together was a long, slow process. There was a time when I had to go back to being a young child. I had to learn to feel and reach out and touch the world. For a while I went around and touched everything. It was so magical just to feel things that were soft, to feel my feet in shoes, my legs in my pants, how the cloth felt on my body. And be able to say, "It's safe to feel."

MICHELLE: That's the intense integration process that happens. You raise that two-year-old to a five-year-old and then you bring the five-year-old up. You have to function in the outside world as an adult, but part of you inside is growing up. Remember the little notes we'd write and leave around the house?

ARTEMIS: Oh, yeah: "It's okay to feel safe in my room. It's okay to feel safe in my house." All these little reminders. I also remember when I became aware that I took up space. I had volume. I was not just a thought. I was not just flat; there was a behind to me, a side to me. And other people took up space too, and there was space between us through which we could reach. At first that was extremely threatening because that also meant there was a space between us that they could hurt me in.

No Longer Would Abuse Be the Cause and My Life the Effect

MICHELLE: I had always considered myself a chalkboard that somebody erased really fast. And there was a little scratch of a piece of chalk here, and here. If you've ever had a sloppy teacher, you know what that looks like. And I was angry about that. I wanted to know where I'd been in this life. Yet there was a fear. What if it's just too horrible? And it was horrible. It was pretty damn close.

And then you get to the point of "Well, I lived through it once and it didn't kill me. Somehow I managed to survive it that time and I had a hell of lot less resources than I do now. It's time to face it."

So you face, and you face, and you face, and you continue to face each aspect of yourself. You have to remember and claim each individual experience. Acknowledge that it happened. Acknowledge that you lived through it.

I realized why I would always position my bed in a particular part of the room. I realized there wasn't an aspect of my life that wasn't somehow a response to the abuse. The way I walked. The way I breathed. There was nothing about me, at some point during this healing process, that I haven't confronted and changed. I have totally metamorphosed.

And then I had to face that person who was my mother. And there was a period of "I hate you because you did that." And "Why did you do that?" You ask, "Was there some way as a child I unknowingly invited all of that?" And you come up with the answer, "No, there's no way."

And then I blamed my mother for being in her own agony so much that she wasn't willing to challenge herself, if for no other reason than to save her kids.

And you hate. And you hurt. And you hate yourself. And you hate the mess that you're in. And you'd love to run away. And I think as the stages progress, there are parts of the cycle that recur. Each time it looks like you're going through the same thing, but it's elevated just a little bit. And you have to come to a position of trust that "Okay, I'm facing this thing again. There's a reason I need to face it from this particular position. There's something I didn't learn before."

Then I stepped out of my own life to see where my stepfather was coming from. He had also been sexually and physically abused by his parents. My mother told me that. And I know that she had been abused. I slowly started to see the other people's positions in the whole play. And once I did that, I was able to make that quantum leap of no longer identifying with my past.

ARTEMIS: For me the decision not to identify with the past was a decision, not just a change I went through in the healing process. I had to make a quantum leap that I was no longer going to have the abuse be the cause and my life be the effect. And to say, "I am me, whole and complete." I'm able to do that because now I do have an identity, a whole person that I have given birth to, that the people who love me have given birth to.

MICHELLE: The identification as an abused person can be a prison in itself. I had to say, "I'm just going to risk who I am here and now, without that identity." It's almost a rebirthing. You change your birthright.

ARTEMIS: It's like, "Where are you now? Right now you have to choose what standpoint you are going to live life from." And it's a constant choice. Every time I'm in a situation where I start acting in those same patterns and my mind says, "I need this security, I need these ways of manipulation, and it's because of what happened to me," I have to say, "No! No!" Sometimes I'll be in a state of terrible limbo because I'm not sure what to do instead.

For me the hardest part was letting go of the right to hate. It was letting go of the right to be confused and messed up because of what had happened to me. Because I did have a right to those things. And they were treasures, but if I wanted to heal all the way, I had to give them up.

I mean I grew up waking up in the morning in a pool of my own vomit and my own blood. And I grew up having to wake myself up in the morning, having to clean myself up and get ready for school alone. I lived it. I grew up being raped at knifepoint by somebody I was supposed to be able to trust. I had a right to hate. I had a right to get even. And I did!

Until finally I realized, "I'm destroying myself because of this. As long as I hold on to my right to hate, I am limiting myself. I'm the only one who's putting the prison walls around me now. Because there's no one raping me anymore. There's nobody torturing me anymore. I am surrounded now by nothing but loving people." I realized I loved myself too much to keep myself in that prison, and so I let go of my hate for me. It was a real inside job.

I experienced some damn heavy things and I've come through it. I've come through with an intense love for myself and an intense amount of love even for that man who was called my stepfather. I have struggled intensely, and I have come into a state of real forgiveness, to the point where I feel love for him. I have never seen him again, but I don't feel fear anymore. It goes all the way straight through me, clean.

MICHELLE: But you can't fake it. There's a fine line between denial and moving on. You can't forgive someone until you're ready. I went through a phase of trying to be magnanimous and forgive before I was ready, and I got smacked right in the face with it. It was like a boomerang.

There is no way to move on without total acceptance of each place where you are. You have to accept yourself as the awakener, as the victim, as not wanting to be the victim, and then as the survivor. And you have to go through all the pain and agony and pride of being that survivor before you can move beyond that to warrior status.

Each step becomes a sweater that you wear and it keeps you warm and it keeps you safe until you grow out of it. Then the sweater gets tight and starts pinching you. You say, "I'm never going to let go of this sweater." And it's not until that sweater becomes so outrageously uncomfortable that you just have to take it off that you take a chance that maybe you'll find something else to take its place. You have to be willing to accept the next void, at any given point in time, in order to be able to fill it.

ARTEMIS: I had a sense, even when I was in the deepest hell, of something that said, "I'll get you out of this. Don't worry. Trust me." I don't know what to call it. I don't know if that's called spiritual awakening. But I trusted it. And that for me is where the healing really happened. When I felt connected to that part of myself, it healed the rest of me.

MICHELLE: I didn't go to much therapy. I wasn't inclined that way, to be honest, because I haven't found anybody who could stay ahead of me. "How am I going to give my trust over to somebody to guide me when I don't feel they're any more capable than I am?" Mostly I've utilized my own resources. I can process and analyze things up one side and down the other. And my stubbornness really helped.

ARTEMIS: I didn't go to therapy either. Because as a teenager it meant someone trying to throw me in the hospital and put me on drugs. And when I did try counseling they identified me so much as a victim that I could hardly get past their image of me.

But even though I didn't go to therapy, I did not do it alone. I had people around me who had deep insights into me as a person, who knew the reality of my intrinsic self, who were able to hold it for me even when I couldn't hold it for myself. Their belief in me was like a magnet that pulled me through.

I realized I didn't want to be loved because I had survived these things. I want to be loved and cared for who I am. And it's a fine line. I'm not ashamed of what happened to me. But I don't want that to be an excuse through which someone loves me. Or the only reason I can say, "I need."

When I need, I immediately lapse into that person who was desperately needy and could not have any of those needs filled. I want to be able to say, "I need" because I'm a woman alive today, without having to throw myself back into being the victim. I want to risk coming as a person needing now because I'm a human being, not because of what happened to me.

Coming Over the Rise

MICHELLE: I think when I learned that I could have a sense of humor, that it was okay to laugh at things, that it was okay to be joyful in the world, was when I started having hope.

Now there's amusement in my life. I realized there were things in life that were actually designed to be enjoyable, that I didn't always have to struggle at being alive. It's like coming over a rise and all of a sudden you see in the horizon a world that you've never experienced before. You have no idea what's going to happen to you. It's all brand new. The world starts opening up. You slow down enough to feel the trees. To notice light and shade and shadow. To notice sounds. And to start expanding your life in other ways. And that's an even bigger challenge than the one you just came from.

Rifat Masoud

"My parents had never talked to us about sex or sexual violence—as many families do not. So I was more vulnerable to what happened than I might have been."

Rifat Masoud is a twenty-eight-year-old Bangladeshi-American woman who lives in a large East Coast city. She was abused by her hoozoor, or religious tutor, as a child in Bangladesh. As an activist in a social justice organization, Rifat does community organizing around child sexual abuse. She also studies bodywork and is starting a wellness business that combines yoga and holistic health counseling.

As an immigrant and a Muslim, and as a woman straddling two cultures, Rifat found it particularly challenging to tell her story. As she explains, "In these times of rampant religious discrimination and violence against immigrants, telling my story is a tremendous struggle not only because I am speaking as a survivor but also because much of my abuse occurred within a Muslim household, while much of my coming out as a survivor occurred in the United States as an immigrant. I fear that some readers might find it easy to stereotype Muslims and immigrants and fail to see the universality of the social conditions that uphold child sexual abuse. As a survivor, I often feel split. I'm caught in the sticky situation of holding multiple identities, survivor being only one of them."*

I was born in Bangladesh, the third child of four. We moved to the United States when I was in third grade, and I've been here ever since.

---

* Rifat Masoud was interviewed for the twentieth-anniversary edition of *The Courage to Heal*. She chose to use a pseudonym.

Back when we were in Bangladesh, we lived in an extended family with my grandmother and my father's sister and her family. My mom was always crying about the way they treated her. They'd complain about her to my father and then he'd come after my mom. There was a lot of yelling and screaming. My father would curse at my mother in Bengali. He was always degrading her and blaming her family for his problems. He'd swear on the name of her parents. He'd slap her or pick up a shoe and beat her.

One night, after we moved to the United States, my dad came home late after we were all asleep. He started fighting with my mom and gave her a black eye. That incident led her to seek shelter and press charges.

My mother went through the court system, but once she realized she couldn't take care of us on her own, she dropped the charges and went back to him. After that, my father was affectionate and bought her gifts. But within a year, he poured a hot saucepan of water on her arm. She got third-degree burns and still has the scars today.

No matter what happened in our household, no one ever intervened. My aunts and uncles all knew there was violence, but it was just something to accept. People did say things behind doors, like, "Oh, that's so bad," but no one ever did anything about it.

My Father Held Complete Control Over Our Lives

My father held a huge level of control over my mother's life. When her father died, she didn't know for months, because my father never told her. My father became a U.S. citizen, but my mother didn't because he never finished the paperwork for her green card. He didn't complete it on purpose so he would have total legal control over her. He told her if she ever said anything about the abuse again, she'd be sent back to Bangladesh and would never see us again.

We were totally dependent on my father. He provided very well for the household; he made sure we always had food on the table and the best education. But he maintained authority over every aspect of our lives—our friends, every penny we spent, which relatives we got to visit—or didn't. There was always a tremendous sense of fear inside our house. We had to obey him and do as he said. At times, I felt like I was being blackmailed.

Growing up, I avoided drawing attention to myself. I believed I had to blend in, to not make waves, to be in the backdrop. I couldn't create any commotion; I didn't want to make more problems in the household. What I felt had to be shoved to the side. I remember thinking, "If I say what I'm feeling, they'll see me as a horrible girl instead of a good girl." It was very important for me to be a good girl. As a result, I learned silence.

It Happened in Front of Them

The sexual abuse occurred before we came to the States. In a culturally Muslim country, many kids are expected to learn the Koran from the moment they can read. Education was very important to my father, so from the time I was five, I was taught to read the Arabic alphabet. My father hired a series of tutors to teach us at home. My older brother and sister and I were tutored by an imam, or prayer leader, from the local mosque, who became our *hoozoor* (teacher).

Our study sessions took place on the weekend. The room had a large table and four chairs. I wore a skirt to lessons because when you read anything Koranic, you're encouraged to wear a dress and cover your hair. I was seven years old at the time; my brother and sister were four or five years older. Because I was the youngest, I sat next to the imam. My brother and sister sat across the table. But some days they couldn't make it to our lesson.

The first few times the imam molested me were on days my siblings couldn't come. He touched my legs and then moved up my skirt, working his way up my leg until he was inside my underwear. Then he stuck his finger in my vagina. I froze and pretended nothing was happening. I just kept reading my lessons from the Arabic alphabet book.

After that, he molested me every time. It happened when we were alone; it happened when my brother and sister were sitting right across the table. I remember feeling powerless and terrified that they would find out.

The imam told me that what he was doing to me was a secret and that I shouldn't tell anybody. He said, "Good girls don't talk about such things." I had always been taught to obey my elders. I saw him as an absolute figure of authority, a man of God who was teaching us the Koran. At the time, I remember thinking, "I must be bad. That's why this is happening to me." I decided to be a good girl and never tell.

The abuse continued until we moved to the States.

I'd Never Told Anyone Before

I never told anyone what had happened for years, until my sister approached me one afternoon when I was in junior high. She said, "Do you remember when we studied with those *hoozoors*? Did they ever touch you?"

I was totally thrown off guard. I was quiet at first, but then said, "Yeah."

My sister told me that the first *hoozoor* had fondled her. He had taken her up to the rooftop and laid her down. The next thing she remembered was getting up.

My sister asked me where the *hoozoor* touched me. I didn't know what to say. I didn't know why she was asking or what she was going to do if I told her. I worried what my parents would think about me if they found out. Just the idea of talking about it made me feel ashamed. So I didn't answer and ran upstairs. My sister and I didn't talk about it again for many years, until recently.

Last year, my older brother, his wife, and I were at the dinner table and my brother started talking about the same imam. He'd also been fondled by him. It was the first time the issue had been discussed in my mom's presence. My brother and I both talked about what had happened to us. My brother laughed when he told his part of the story. Then my mother started laughing. She sat there cracking up. It was really disheartening and hurtful that my mom minimized the whole thing and didn't take it seriously. I said, "It wasn't funny. This has happened to all your kids." She tried to tone down her laughter, but she was still smiling. I didn't appreciate it, but I'm still glad the conversation happened. I know a lot of people laugh when they're uncomfortable, but I wish we could talk about it more seriously. But I'm grateful the issue has surfaced—and the silence broken.

Redefining My Relationship to Islam

I came from a Muslim family, but the way Islam was introduced was superficial. It was about going through the rituals without knowing why. It was reading the Koran without knowing the meaning of the words. I was taught to pray five times a day, but no one ever taught me why. Because of this and the way I saw Islam practiced, being a Muslim never made sense to me. I never connected to it as a child. I never understood the deftness of its teaching or practices.

When I thought of Islam as a teenager, I'd think, "How messed up is this?" My father, who preaches Islam and is teaching us to read the Koran, is abusing my mom. And here's the imam and he's molesting me. Yet I knew intellectually that wasn't what Islam stood for. Just because these men weren't practicing what they preached didn't mean the whole religion was bad. But still, part of me wanted to see Islam in a bad way. When I was in ninth or tenth grade I denounced Islam. I wanted nothing to do with it because I needed to disown the part of me that I related to the abuse.

During my high school years and in college, I was drawn to metaphysics and Buddhist texts. I read the writings of Thich Nhat Hanh and studied yoga and Native American teachings. And I started to see the common thread in all these teachings. Love is the thread that unites all spiritual practices. I realized that was my reason to get up each day, to be more compassionate toward the people around me.

Even though I grew up with Islam, it wasn't until I was exposed to these other teachings that I could come back to it and embrace it as part of my identity. Three years ago, I started studying Islamic texts, prophets, and stories.

That's when I realized that love and compassion also lie at the root of Islam. I started meeting people who were practicing and teaching Islam in a much more just manner. The true teachings of Islam are about offering love, gratitude, and compassion to those around us and into the world. For me, being a Muslim is about sharing my humanity and being there for those in need.

Now, spirituality is central to my healing—and everything else in my life. How I move through the world, how I see myself in relationship to my environment is because of my spiritual outlook. The divine energy and Allah Subhanath'allah, the Omnipresent, and all the titles by which we call it, is what sustains me and keeps me going through all struggles. It is what keeps me centered and grounded in this space, time, and existence. I don't know how else to survive.

Where I Am Today

One big way the abuse impacted me is in my dating life. It's been hard for me to develop intimacy. When someone is really there for me emotionally, I have a strong need not to get any closer. I always have to maintain a bit of distance in order to feel safe. I'm not able to trust completely. When I'm presented with lots of love, I don't fully let it in. I always have this level of detachment, and I don't think it's healthy for me. I wish I could be in a receptive mode, but if I succumb to receiving, all kinds of fear come up. I'm aware of it now. I observe the way these patterns show up in my relationships again and again. I keep working on it.

I'm also having to unlearn all the messages about being quiet and good. I'm in a very confident place, but there are still moments where a lot of those old familiar feelings come up. It's still a deep struggle for me today.

Where I Am With My Family Today

My relationship with my siblings and my mother continues to improve. I'm learning to hold my ground in a powerful way I couldn't before. We still can't talk about everything, but I'm starting to be able to voice what I've experienced in the past and share my perspective on our family.

We're coming to see that there's another way to be together without all the blaming and shaming that were so typical for our family. We don't yet have all the skills, but we're learning how to support each other in an emotional capacity. As a result, I'm more invested in being a part of the family, because I can be more of me. But there are still times when it's too hard, when I totally need to be on my own.

I rarely talk to my father, just a few times a year for five minutes, and it's not a conversation, it's him going off about his finances and whatever is stressing him out in the moment. My father still tries to tell me what to do, from a place of demands. The last couple of years, I've started talking back to him. As a daughter, I'm not supposed to do that, so he just escalates more. He talks over me or gets louder. He mocks me or invalidates me. Sometimes I hang up on him. Or I hand the phone to my brother or sister or mom. I find it difficult to keep talking with him. While I'm grateful for the financial support my father has provided over the years, what I really wish for is accountability and a truly loving relationship.

Becoming an Activist

When I was in high school, my inner voice told me to study psychology so I could learn how to create healthier families. Taking psychology classes in college led me to learn more about family violence. At the same time, I got involved in activist work for women's rights. Being an activist gave me the language and knowledge to understand sexual violence and the dynamics around it. Learning about social conditions and social constructs gave me the ability to recognize why abuse happens. It gave me the language to describe how I saw and related to the world and what I was feeling. It gave me ways to talk about something about which I'd been silent for years.

Recently, I completed a two-year leadership development fellowship with a group that addresses sexual abuse specific to the South Asian community. Being an activist is an integral part of my healing. It empowers me as a survivor and has helped me let go of any shame or stigma I was still carrying. My work with the group has given me more of a holistic, conscious, and political perspective, along with concrete tools that I find empowering. My activism helps me see that my experiences are not just my individual experiences; I see now how they fit into a broader context of social conditions. There are reasons abuse happens to women and kids. And that oppression is ultimately connected to greater systems of oppression that are constantly influencing how people treat each other and relate to one another.

Because I'm able to share my experiences now, I don't feel trapped by them. I don't feel like I used to—that there's a part of me that has to be buried. I can be my whole self now, and that feels totally healing. I feel free.

Lorraine Williams

Q: *Was there any time in the process of healing that you lost hope that life was worth living?*

A: *Oh, about once a week.*

Lorraine Williams is a twenty-two-year-old albino African-American woman.* She is legally blind, and her disability makes her extremely sensitive to the sun. Lorraine is a sociology student at a large eastern university.

Lorraine was the second child of five in an upper-class home. Her family was a religious one. Several of her relatives are ministers and missionaries.

Lorraine was abused by a brother and a cousin, though her primary abuser was her maternal grandfather. The incest with him started when Lorraine was fourteen and lasted until she left home at eighteen.

On being abused as a teenager, Lorraine says, "Being fourteen or fifteen years old had nothing to do with it. I could have been three for all the power I had." At fifteen, Lorraine became pregnant with her grandfather's child, and a quiet abortion was arranged. Everyone denied he was the father.

In the course of confronting her grandfather and talking to other relatives, Lorraine learned that he also had sexually abused her mother, a sister, and a niece.

I was twenty years old when I actively started to deal with the incest. The first year there was a lot of groundbreaking, actually facing and pinpointing instances, saying, "Yes, I am an

---

* Lorraine Williams wanted to use her own name but couldn't for legal reasons.

incest survivor." Before that time, those words did not exist. Yet deep down I knew: "This happened to you, Lorraine." Once I admitted that to myself, everything came caving in. Life was therapy. I couldn't focus on anything else. I felt like I was going insane. But after the first six months, I realized I would live. I still didn't want to deal with all of this, but I knew I had to.

I Confronted My Grandfather

In the second six months, I confronted my grandfather. I didn't plan to confront him. I was going to visit my mother and I had taken my friend, Debra, with me. My brother picked us up at the train station and then proceeded to drive to my grandfather's house "to get a few things."

I felt really set up. Debra said, "I won't let that bastard touch you." When I saw him, I was instantly repulsed. He was up to his old tricks, guilt-tripping me for not visiting him. I stood there, listening quietly. All of a sudden I started screaming at him, "Who do you think you are? Who do you think you are, trying to make me feel guilty? You, of all people! You who hurt me, who abused me, who molested me? Don't you think that's sick? Don't you think you've done anything wrong?"

He just laughed. He said he hadn't done anything wrong, but that it had been, as he called it, his right to "educate his girls." This angered me even more, because I realized he was probably going to die thinking he'd done nothing wrong. He didn't deny it at all! He called it "educating his girls"!

My Mother Was the Most Difficult Person to Confront

I wrote my mother a letter and was absolutely crazed on the day I knew she was going to receive it. I was so overwrought I got on the wrong bus.

The letter was direct. It said that my grandfather had molested me for years because she hadn't done anything about it. That I was in therapy now to recover. It was a very detailed letter with lots of different instances spelled out. I told her that she was a fool if she couldn't believe me. Why the hell would I be going through therapy if nothing had happened? And I said that she was partly responsible.

I had always been the good girl in my family, the one that didn't cause any trouble. This is not what a good girl does. So I was terrified. She had denied it when I was a teenager. She was his daughter. I didn't know how she was going to react. I could only go by how she reacted previously. So I unplugged my phone.

When I finally plugged the phone back in, she called right away. It was six in the morning. I knew it was her. I just picked up the phone and said, "Yes, mother?"

I think the letter really got to her. My sister disclosed to her, too, so she was getting it from both of us. She was very sympathetic, and she cried. She didn't get angry. I was prepared for her to be angry, and I was unprepared when she wasn't. She believed me. She said she was so sorry she hadn't believed me before. Then she told me he had molested her, too. She was very angry with him. She actually wanted to go kill her father. I remember saying, "It's not worth it, Mama. He's already dead as far as we're concerned."

Since then, she's been a good ally when I've confronted other family members. She and I have done a lot of work getting to know each other.

I'm Not Being Silent

My grandmother didn't believe anything had happened and said that I had an overactive imagination. And if anything had happened, I should be over it by now. My sister, who's also a survivor, doesn't talk about it. She won't see my grandfather and won't let her child see him, but she won't talk about it either. My brother, who molested me when I was younger, blames me and sides with my grandfather. He feels nothing wrong happened.

Last Thanksgiving, I went to Pennsylvania to visit my mother. The family has a weeklong celebration every time there's a holiday. Different people in the family have different creative pursuits. Some dance, some sing, some play an instrument. I'm the writer. I was to bring up some of my writings and read them.

I have a very large family. There were thirty people there. Only two of them—my mother and my brother—knew anything at that point. So there were twenty-eight people who knew nothing. Included among them were two of his other daughters.

I thought I had brought only "safe" pieces, and then I realized I had brought very volatile pieces. One of these dealt with the incest. I wavered back and forth about whether I should read it. I really didn't know if I would until the actual moment I got up there. I pulled it out and was trying to decide. And then I realized that I had brought that story for the specific purpose of reading it. I just said to myself, "Yes. These people need to know he's not the angel they've painted wings on."

So I said, "There really isn't anything that I can tell you to preface this story, except that by the time I finish reading it you'll know why I wrote it." I was scared. I was shaking and sweaty on the inside, saying, "You really can't do this!" But on the outside, all appearances were intact. And I read it:

November

BY LORRAINE WILLIAMS

It was November, the month each year that Grandmother went away. She took a week off from the family to attend the annual church convention in Memphis. It was my job to stay at the house that she and my grandfather shared, to cook and clean. The two operated a board and care home for emotionally disturbed men.

The year that I was seventeen I especially resented having to stay at the house. I fussed, fumed, and fought, trying to find a way out. I tried endlessly to convince my mother that she should be the one to stay at the house. I mean, they were her parents. I did not want to be alone with my grandfather. Finally defeated, I gave in. I created what I thought was an elaborate plan. I'd make my younger brother, then eight, sleep in the bed with me. For him, it was a way to stay up late and watch TV. For me, it was a small act of defense.

My grandmother always departed at night, because she said the flights were cheaper. I sat on her bed as she packed the last few things in her overnight case. We sat and talked as we waited for her sister's arrival. She, too, was a missionary.

"You'll take care of everything, won't you?" Grandmother asked, as she stood adjusting her hat in the mirror.

"Of course," I told her. I wondered if she knew just how well things would be cared for.

"If anyone calls, tell them that I'll be back next Wednesday."

"But that's ten days!" I said in shock. Usually she was only gone for a week.

"Three more days won't kill you."

"No, I suppose it won't." Inside however, I was already dead.

That night, after I'd gone to bed, my body jolted awake, feeling another next to it. Immediately I knew it was him. I tried to pretend I was asleep as his hands invaded me, probing. Inside I felt nauseous, sick, repulsed.

"Get up and come into my room," he demanded. I ignored him, refused to move.

"Dammit, get up or I'll do it here." I didn't want my little brother to see anything, so I rose and did as he said.

I followed him into his bedroom, separate from that of my grandmother,

slid into the bed, and went back to sleep. I hoped that he would feel sorry for waking me and thus leave me alone.

I awoke once again to his hand pawing my body, trying intently to gain access. I fought him by clamping my legs shut and wearing flannel pajamas, my only defenses. I didn't want to be there, didn't want any of it to be happening. Silently, I began to cry. Anger, agony, and shame filtered through me, lingering. He continued in an attempt to force an entrance. I crying, he pushing, me feeling totally helpless.

"Open your legs," he whispered angrily.

"No," I said, knowing already that I was powerless.

"Well then, I'll just take what I want."

He pushed against me, pumping hard and harder again. My skin felt as if it were being bludgeoned, beaten. His body slapped against my own, making it feel like it was being stoned. Heavy breathing filled the room as he panted and exclaimed obscenities. His moans and words filled my ears, though I attempted to block them.

"I'm coming, baby. Please, please never leave me," I heard.

My only thoughts were that it was almost over. The steamy, slick semen contaminated me. It burned the insides of my vagina, reaching, it felt, far into my uterus. My tears lay in a puddle on each side of my head.

I rose like a zombie as he rolled off of me, leaving the room quickly, quietly. I went straight to the bathroom adjacent to my room, sat on the toilet, and sobbed uncontrollably. I sat there, still like a mannequin, for an endless amount of time. Finally I turned on the water in the tub. I made it hot, steamy hot, as hot as I could bear. I needed to cleanse the infection from my system. I scrubbed and rubbed, making my white skin pink. Afterward, exhausted, I returned to bed. I changed the sheets, making the bed clean once more.

Sleep did not come. I lay there motionless, awake, afraid to return to slumber. I listened to my brother's breathing, deciding it was easier being a boy. I watched as dawn crept into the deep blue sky. Watching until my eyes closed in some deep sleep.

Time came for me to get up and prepare for school. I dressed carefully, finding soft clothes to hug my body, for it still hurt. I saw my image in the mirror, very pale. I knew it was going to be a bad day. I went downstairs to breakfast, my brother and my grandfather already there. Grandfather had a smile on his face that read, "I got what I wanted from you. HA, HA, HA."

We said not a word to each other until I started to leave, when, as I was exiting the door, he said to me, "Have a good day."

I read the story. Everyone just sat there and didn't say anything. I looked up occasionally. Some of their faces were blank. Some were horrified. Others were just awed. There was dead silence.

I followed it with a light poem, and they all discussed the poem, but no one said a word about the story. Afterwards, various individuals came up to me. One of my aunts was angry at him. My other aunt was furious at me, saying I had written a bunch of lies: "My father couldn't have done anything like that. My father is a good person." I was the bad person. A couple of my male cousins and uncles were very angry at him and supportive of me. I was really shaken up.

And then during the course of my visit there, my twelve-year-old cousin told me that after I'd done the reading, she had had a dream that he had molested her, too. She remembered everything and was very upset, very afraid to tell her mother. So I did it with her. The three of us sat down and talked. We all ended up sitting there crying together.

It was an overwhelming visit.

But I'm glad I told in the manner I did, because it destroyed their image of me as the good one, as the one who was always nice. Having that spot in the family meant I couldn't be me, couldn't be independent. And I feel better about myself.

We have to speak out and break the silence, especially in our own families. I know I have been able to heal because I'm not being silent.

Vicki Malloy

"For a number of years, my father and I struggled to have some kind of relationship. I kept trying because I've always felt close to my father, and I wasn't ready to say good-bye to him. I wanted to give him the chance to do right by me; I offered that to him, and he took it. And I was shocked. He must have really loved me to put himself through that kind of agony."

*V*icki Malloy, whose father molested her once, shared her story for the first edition of The Courage to Heal, *to demonstrate that sexual abuse did not have to be severe or protracted to have a profound impact on a child's life. At that time, Vicki was thirty years old and completely estranged from her father. Now Vicki is forty-five and her father is seventy-nine, and they have worked their way back into a caring, honest relationship.*

---

* Vicki Malloy chose to use a pseudonym. Other segments of her story were first published in 1988 in the first edition of *The Courage to Heal* and appear also in the current edition on pp. 97, 166, and 487. Almost twenty years have passed between her first interview and this current one, showing how her perspective has shifted over time. A longer version of the story given here was first published in *I Thought We'd Never Speak Again* by Laura Davis.

My father and I were always very close. We had a strong bond. Growing up, we were like kindred spirits. We understood each other. But there was always something inappropriate about the way he was with me. He was too affectionate, too close. His kisses would last too long. I could never put my finger on it, but things just didn't feel right.

When I was twelve, my father sexually molested me. I was asleep in bed. He came into my room and lay down next to me. He put his hand down my pajamas and started playing with my vagina. It woke me up. I turned away from him. I pretended I was turning over in my sleep. He must have gotten frightened that I would wake up, and he left. I remember watching his shadow outside the door. He never did it again.

I never told anyone about it, but I got much more distant from my father. I talked to him, but I shied away from any physical contact. I felt really icky if he hugged me. I went through my teens feeling very depressed. It was as if all my vitality had been sucked out of me.

I basically buried the incest until my early twenties when it resurfaced. It came up in different relationships, usually around sexuality. I'd start to have trouble, and often the relationship would end.

Sixteen years ago, I met my life partner, Gayle. A couple of years into our relationship, I really started struggling with intimacy and being close. I knew it traced back to what my father had done, and I resented it. I decided I was going to confront him about it, something I had never done before.

Up until this point, my relationship with my father had been very cold. My parents got divorced, and I didn't talk to my father in six years. That period of estrangement wasn't planned or premeditated; it just kind of happened.

I had grown up. I wasn't a kid anymore. I didn't need my father anymore. So I never called him, and he never called me. Looking back now, I realize that I couldn't get back in touch with him until I had dealt with what had happened between us.

It Was Like a Poison in His Soul

I called my father and said I wanted to see him. He came down, and I confronted him. I said, "You molested me."

He didn't say he didn't do it, but he said, "I don't remember anything like that." He had amnesia about the whole thing. Then he left and went home. It was very tense and sad and painful.

At that point, I think my father realized that he was going to lose me if he didn't pull his shit together. Once I gave him the information about why we were estranged, it was like a poison inside of his soul. Either he was going to get it out or he was going to be like the living dead. So he woke up and decided to face it.

Several months after our confrontation, my father contacted me and said he wanted to talk. He said, "I did do that." And he told me he had started doing some counseling on his own.

From that point on, we struggled to have some kind of relationship, but our attempts to reconcile on our own didn't go very well. We wrote letters back and forth. He would repeatedly ask for forgiveness. He was full of guilt, and it was extremely important to him that I forgive him. And I said, "I'm not ready to forgive you, and I don't know if I ever will forgive you." I didn't say it in a mean way. I just wanted him to know: "That's not what's happening right now."

He wrote back and said, "My father was cruel to me and I forgave him. Why can't you forgive me?" We went back and forth like that for quite a while.

Finally, I said, "This is not going anywhere. Would you be willing to go to my counselor with me?" And he said he would.

My Father Was Open and Vulnerable

Ten years ago, my father traveled to Phoenix so we could do several marathon therapy sessions. My father stayed in a hotel and met me each day at my therapist's office. Those sessions really opened things up between us. My father was as open and vulnerable as he could possibly be, and that's what led to us being able to have the relationship we have today.

One of the first things my father and I worked on was establishing boundaries. The critical thing about incest and sexual abuse is boundaries, and I had never set any boundaries with my father. So I had to figure out what I needed to feel comfortable and safe with him again, and that took a long time. By the time we had our first big session together, I had gotten clear on what I needed from him. I wasn't wishy-washy at all, and I think that helped him a lot.

The first thing I said was, "If you want to have a relationship with me, you're not allowed to touch me. We don't see each other often, and when you see me, you can't hug me until I say it's okay to hug me." He hated that and said it was absolutely ridiculous. But we worked on it. I said, "That's it. I need the control. I need the power to say, 'Okay, now you can touch me.'"

Slowly, he started to get it. He didn't like it, and he made it clear he didn't like it, but he agreed to do it for me. It was extremely difficult for him. And for a couple of years, when I saw him, I'd say, "Hi, Dad," and he'd say, "Hi," and we wouldn't touch.

Another thing I told him was that he wasn't allowed to mention how I looked. He couldn't say, "Oh, you look really good," or "You've gained a little weight." He could not talk to me about my appearance, because it felt to me like he was checking me out, and I did not like it.

The third thing I wanted was to be able to talk to my father about the incest whenever I felt the need to do so. I wanted him to know that it wasn't a done deal just because we'd talked about it in therapy. I needed permission to be able to explore it further. He didn't like that either. He really wanted us to put this behind us, but he accepted my terms.

I didn't take advantage of that. I knew how hard it was for him, and it wasn't easy for me either, so I didn't go out of my way to bring things up. But once in a while, I felt I needed to. Once I asked him, "Dad, what was going on in your life that you would do something like that? What was wrong?" I remember being worried about his answer, because I really didn't want to hear about his sex life with my mother. But he responded in a way that was very mature and respectful; he really tried to give me the information I needed.

My Father's Been Able to Come Through for Me

My relationship with my father has continued to evolve. Over time, things have gotten increasingly comfortable. I no longer worry about my father being inappropriate. That feels totally in the past. I've really been able to relax and open up around him.

Over the years, we've developed our own rhythm for staying in touch. My father isn't much of a phone person, so we don't talk on the phone much. I try to go see him every six to eight weeks.

As my father gets older, we've reached an understanding that allows our communication to be a little more real. He's started to show me more need than he has in the past—he's asked me to call him and he's sought my advice about decisions he has to make about his health.

He's also come through for me. I have asked my father for things, and he's given them to me. I asked him to tell me that he loved me and to show a little more emotion. He's really done both of those things. He tells me he loves me and it's sincere. He expresses more love for me now than he ever did when I was a kid.

My father still yields to my cues physically. He still holds himself back until I initiate contact. I hug him now, but we're really not too physical. I still don't really want to be very close to him physically, and I think that's okay.

My relationship with my father is forever damaged on some level, and that's gonna be. I feel like we've patched it up the best we can, but it is patched.

People Make Mistakes and It Doesn't Mean They're Evil

Reconciling with my father has taught me a great deal. I've learned that people make mistakes, and it doesn't mean they're evil. My father is not an evil person; it's his own frailties, confusion, and pain that led him to do what he did.

I've learned that it's important to give people the chance to make right what they've screwed up. My father was able to do right by me. He is the person who molested me, but I really respect him for the hard work he's been willing to do to keep me in his life.

I've also learned that reconciliation is ongoing. Just because you get past the most difficult part of the conflict does not mean "We're reconciled now." The big secret is out, but I'm still thinking and feeling and wondering and processing my relationship with my father. It's not a done deal.

The Question of Forgiveness

I don't broach the subject of incest with my father anymore. My father is seventy-nine. He's an old man. He's declining, and I'm not interested in confronting him anymore. Even though there are times I would like to talk to him about it, I'm choosing not to. Part of it is not knowing how much I'd get out of it, and part of it is not wanting to put him through it again. He's old, and I'm trying to care about him now. I want to love him for the remaining time he has. I'm acutely aware that he's going to die soon, and I'm not the kind of person that needs to keep pushing at things. I'm ready to let it go, but that doesn't mean I've forgiven him.

Forgiveness has never been part of our reconciliation. Somehow I knew that I didn't want it to be part of the healing between us. If I didn't have to forgive, it felt to me like I still had some power in the situation, and I was so completely powerless as a child.

My intensity around it has faded over the years, and it's been a long time since he asked me if I'd forgive him, so I haven't had to actively think about it. But if he did, I'd probably say, "No, I don't. I see you as a human being who has problems like everyone else, but I don't forgive you for molesting me." I wouldn't say it to be mean or to punish him, but simply because I haven't forgiven him. It's just the way I feel.

I forgive my father for other mistakes he's made, but not for that. There are some mistakes you don't get to wash your hands of, and incest is one. It's the absolute worst thing you can do to your child, and he did that to me. It's not something I can forgive.

The Turning of the Tides

It's been ten years since we started to reconcile, and now my father's mortality is shaking things up for me. I know my time with him is running out. It's a real time of change for us. I can feel him depending on me and needing me more. I'm just entering that world of having an aging, ill father. I feel sad, and I'm wondering what his last years are going to be like, and what role I'm going to play in his life. He's got a younger wife who's very healthy, and I imagine he'll die before her. But I also feel a real pull to see him more because I don't know when he'll die.

I feel at peace with my father now. What he did can't be undone, and our relationship has limitations, but I am grateful for the reconciliation we have achieved. My father defied all the odds. The percentage of fathers who are willing to admit what they did and go through what I made him go through, is very, very low. Given that he was willing to do that says something about the kind of person he is. He was willing to go through hell to save his relationship with his daughter. I really admire him for that. I know I'm really lucky.

Cassondra Espinoza

"I took an art history class where they turn out the lights and show slides. I loved it; I cried through the class. I had grown up in a house where everything you did was to survive. I didn't know there was art in the world. I didn't know there was beauty.

"I loved the Impressionists. I loved Rubens's big, voluptuous women. They were naked, and it wasn't shameful. And nobody was being hurt. Seeing all that beauty, I remembered the resolution I made as a child to survive. I thought, 'This is why I lived.' I'd always known there was another side to life, and this was it."

Cassondra Espinoza is a forty-six-year-old medical technician and mother of two, who she says she has a great life now.* But the road she's had to travel to get there has been long and arduous: "I've worked damn hard to get where I am today. From the abuse I had and where I came from, I should have been dead. I should have been a drug user or a prostitute. I should have been hateful and bitter. And I'm not. I'm a law-abiding citizen whose life is full of love, whose main goal in life is to do no harm."

---

* Cassondra Espinoza was interviewed for the twentieth-anniversary edition of *The Courage to Heal*. She chose to use a pseudonym.

My parents both grew up poor. My father didn't finish high school; he went to ninth grade, then left school to work in the fields. My mother worked in a cannery.

My parents were fifteen when they met. She was the love of my father's life. They married at seventeen; my brother and I were their only kids.

We lived in San Jose, but my mother wanted to be in Los Angeles with her family. There were lots of emotional scenes about that when I was growing up. My father was a quiet man; my mother was a screamer. She constantly held it over my father's head: "You promised me I could go home whenever I wanted to." She'd say our house was not her home.

My parents were very hurtful to each other. She'd yell at him, and then they would hit each other. My brother and I got really close because of what was happening. He would take me to another room while they were screaming and yelling at each other. He was only four years older, but he became my protector.

My mother always adored my brother. She didn't hit him; she didn't scream and yell at him. Just at me. I had screaming, yelling spankings with a belt and my bottom exposed. My mother shook me a lot. She told me I was not supposed to have been born. She'd say things like, "Be good because I could have flushed you down the toilet."

When I was growing up, I knew my family was crazy. I'd see *The Brady Bunch* on TV and think, "This can't be my family. I must have been adopted. My real family is out there someplace. Someday, they'll come and get me." But they never did, so I learned to accept. But deep inside, I knew there was a different way to live—and that if I could only grow up and get out of the house, I'd find out what that different was.

No One Will Believe You If You Tell

My parents were both functional alcoholics. They drank when our families got together; they drank on Fridays; they drank if they had a hard day. But they weren't what my father's father was—a drunk laying on the ground on a street corner. My father went to work, the bills got paid; my parents were always able to function, but they liked to go drinking and dancing on Friday and Saturday nights. They'd

leave me in my brother's care. And that's when the sexual abuse began.

We had a rocking chair that was nasty green. My brother and I used to make forts out of it. When I was eleven, I made the fort, and my brother came in and raped me. I was in the fifth grade and had just started my period. I had just gotten one of those little bras you start out with. Everything happened at the same time.

From then on, whenever my brother made a fort, I knew what he wanted. Whenever he felt safe enough that he wasn't going to get caught, my brother was on me. I'd wake up in the middle of the night, and he'd be on top of me.

Over time, my brother got more violent. He used Coke bottles on me. He used a gun. I remember cold metal against my head, inside my vagina, in my mouth. He'd say, "All I have to do is pull this trigger."

All of this was with the mantra, "If you tell, I'll find you and I'll kill you." He'd choke me and say, "If you tell, they're not going to believe you." I knew he was right.

Once, when I was twelve, my parents went to get groceries on a Saturday. I knew that as soon as my parents left, my brother was going to abuse me. He dragged me out into the hallway and raped me. My parents came back for something. We could hear the garage door opening. My brother got up and started putting on his clothes. He was yelling at me when my mom walked in, and then she started yelling at me, too: "What are you doing?" She saw what was happening and she blamed me. That was the moment when I gave up.

When I was thirteen, I miscarried my brother's child. I stayed home from school that day because I had really bad cramps. I went to the bathroom and I passed a lot of clots. One of them had a fetus in it. It was tiny; it was pale white and I could see the great big eyeball and the fins for the hands. I buried it in the backyard. I wasn't going to flush it down the toilet, since that's what my mother had always threatened me with.

I remember pressing the earth down after and smelling the lilacs. That's how I know it was late spring. Then I went back in bed and put my pajamas on. Everybody came home and I pretended everything was fine.

After the miscarriage, I tried to commit suicide. The pain of being abused, of living in a house with all that screaming was too strong. My dad had a razor that unscrewed. I took out the blade and tried to cut my wrists in the shower, but I couldn't do it. I couldn't even kill myself; I had to live with the pain.

School Was an Escape for Me

I loved school because it was away from home. I had always escaped into books. I was good at math, and in seventh grade, I had a really cool algebra teacher. She was young and motivated. I ate lunch in her classroom and we were close.

My sophomore year of high school, I went back to visit her and she asked me how I was. I said I wasn't so good. She sat me down and said, "Cassondra, what's wrong? Really, what's wrong?" And I told her I didn't want to go home because my brother was going to abuse me. And she said to me, "What do you mean, abuse you?"

I said, "My brother makes me do things I don't want to do and he hurts me. He makes me have sex with him." I said it, and she didn't jump up and run out of the room. She didn't say, "You're lying."

She said, "Cassondra, what do you want me to do?"* I didn't know that there was anything she could do. This was my life, what I was used to, so I didn't know what to tell her.

She said, "You have to tell him to stop. You have to tell him no more. Tell him that you told me and that I believe you. Tell him that if he touches you again, we're going to the police."

I freaked. "We can't do that. They're not going to believe me; they're going to believe him. I'll get in trouble at home. We can't go to the police!"

"Okay," my teacher said, "But tell your brother that I know and that if he touches you again, we're going to do something."

The next time my brother put a hand on me, I told him I'd told my teacher and that if he did it again, we would take him to the cops. You don't know how much strength that took, for a Hispanic female to tell a male, who has more authority, not to touch her. You just don't do that. But I did, and he stopped. It was amazing. I was sixteen years old, and I got my brother to stop.

Don't get me wrong. He was still emotionally abusive after that. He'd make suggestive remarks. "One of these days, I'm going to come across you and I'm just going to fuck

---

* Cassondra's abuse took place before mandatory reporting laws were in place. Now, her teacher would be legally bound to report her abuse.

you." Or "When you least expect it, I'll come find you and kill you." I was just waiting for him to do it.

I Realized There Was Beauty in the World

I met my husband when I was a junior in high school. He was a senior, a quiet, unassuming, polite, soft man who made me feel special. I got pregnant and we got married January of my senior year. I had so many credits that I was able to graduate early. Our daughter, Sandra, was born that spring.

My husband and I were married for eighteen years. We were poor; the first six months we were together, we lived with his family. Then we lived with my family. Here I was thinking I was going to get away from my abusive family, but it didn't happen. My brother was still part of our family unit. Finally, when Sandra was two, we moved into our first duplex.

I stayed home with my daughter. My husband worked swing shift as a machinist. When Sandra was in kindergarten, I went to college. I didn't know what I wanted to be, but I wanted to have a career.

I was very focused on what I needed to do for my education. To fulfill my humanities requirement, I took an art history class where they turn out the lights and show slides. I loved it; I cried through the class. I had grown up in a house where everything you did was to survive. There was never any excess money for anything. I got yelled at when I needed to go to the doctor. I didn't know there was art in the world. I didn't know there was beauty.

I loved the Impressionists. I loved Rubens's big, voluptuous women. They were naked, and it wasn't shameful. And nobody was being hurt. Seeing all that beauty, I remembered the resolution I made as a child to survive. I thought, "This is why I lived—to realize there was beauty in the world. I'd always known there was another side to life, and this was it."

I knew then that I had to find a way to work past being so broken, dirty, and used. I didn't want to feel unworthy of having that kind of beauty in my life. I wanted to feel I deserved it.

It's Not Right to Want to Leave Your Family

When my daughter was seven, I got pregnant again. I was using birth control, so I was in shock. When Hector was born, I felt disconnected from him. I didn't want another baby. I didn't want to have a boy who would grow up to become a molester. Finally, one day, when he was four months old, I looked at him and thought, "It's not his fault." That's when I fell in love with my son.

My mother loved her grandchildren to excess. When I went to school, I'd take the kids over to her house and I'd hear what a bad parent I was. They were convinced I wasn't feeding my son. They were always shoving food down his throat. She'd say to me, "I don't know why you had children. You're such a bad parent. Why don't you feed this child?" That's all I heard. And she'd tell the kids not to listen to me.

I was so connected to my mother's way of seeing me, I didn't know there was a way out.

I didn't know I could have a life away from my family. I never thought, "If I move to another city, I can pick and choose when I see my folks, if ever." That just wasn't an option. You went and had dinner with your parents on Saturdays and Sundays. You came over during the week. That's what Hispanic families do. They stick together.

I Stopped Feeling Connected to My Daughter

When Sandra turned eleven, I stopped feeling emotionally connected to her. I didn't feel comfortable touching her or when she hugged me. She looked just like I had at eleven, and that's when my abuse began.

I wanted to be a better parent, so I went to my family doctor and said, "Something's wrong with me. I don't feel comfortable with my daughter." She gave me a referral to a counselor.

At first, our focus was on parenting skills. Then the counselor asked about my family, and I told him about the alcoholism and the physical abuse. He asked if there had ever been any sexual abuse. I went out on a limb and told him about my brother. He said the incest might have something to do with the distance I was feeling from my daughter.

That's when I thought, "I need to educate myself." I had been a reader my whole life, so I went to the library and read everything I could about sexual abuse. My kids would be in the children's section, and I'd be reading books about incest. I never checked the books out. My kids were reading by then,

and I couldn't let them see me with those books. But just the fact that there was a section in the library with books about incest taught me that what had happened to me was real. I started healing in the library—it was a safe place, and everyone can afford a library card.

I kept going to therapy until my insurance ran out. After my eighth session, the therapist offered me some medication and gave me a referral to my first 12-step meeting. He said, "This is a place where you can go and talk."

It took me three months to go to my first meeting. I was convinced that no one would believe me and terrified that my brother would find me and kill me. But finally, I went. The meeting was warm and nurturing. It took me a while to be able to say, "I was an incest survivor."

I kept going back, but I felt guilty about it. I felt selfish because I was taking time for myself, away from my family. Hispanic females don't do that. But I wanted my kids to have a mom who was half there emotionally. I went to meetings so I could have a better family.

I went every week, but I never told my family where I was going. My husband was at work and my kids thought mom was in school, taking another class.

What's Wrong With Me, Mom?

When my daughter was in seventh grade, she started doing the Goth thing—the black hair, the black nails, the black clothes. Then one night she was in her room and she couldn't stop crying. She said, "What's wrong with me,

Mom?" and "I don't want to kill myself." She wouldn't tell me anything else. She was inconsolable.

We took her to Kaiser and they put a seventy-two-hour hold on her. Then they transferred her to their residential facility. She was there for almost a month. During that time, it came out that she was doing major drugs—marijuana, cocaine, crystal meth—and that she had tried to commit suicide before.

We also found out that Sandra had been abused by her cousin—my brother's son—for a year. I had no clue. His abuse of her was so horrendous that they took him to court even though the two of them grew up together and their ages were so close. The abuse was so bad, they were able to make the case stick.

My husband was devastated that his nephew had done this. I had never told him what his brother-in-law had done to me. I did tell my daughter's therapist in the intake, because he asked if there was a history of abuse in the family. A couple of weeks later, the therapist let it slip in front of my husband, who had an anxiety attack when he found out. I had to take him to the emergency room so they could see if he'd had a heart attack.

My husband was completely blindsided by the whole thing; it was the worst thing that had ever happened to him. I blamed myself because I was the one who had continued to see my family. If I had just said no in the very beginning, none of this would have happened. I felt guilty because all the filth and ugliness of my life was coming out. I was the one who had brought this into our lives.

So I had a suicidal daughter in lockup and my husband in the emergency room. And Hector was only three years old. It was a horrible time in my life. And the next thing I knew, my marriage was falling apart.

I Just Couldn't Hide It Anymore

Right after I first took Sandra to the hospital, I went to my best friend's house, told her what was happening, and asked her to come with me to my parents' house. I brought her with me because I was afraid I'd never walk out if I went there alone. I told my friend, "If things start getting ugly, make sure I leave."

I knocked on my parents' door, and we walked in. They were sitting in the front room watching TV, and I told them straight out, "I just had to lock Sandra in a psychiatric facility so she wouldn't kill herself. I want you to know that your son's son abused my daughter so badly that she wanted to kill herself, and your son abused me for years and years, and I never said anything."

My father sat there, silent. My mother started yelling, "That's not true. That can't be true. My son didn't do that!"

I said, "Mom, your only granddaughter just tried to kill herself. Why would she do that? Why would she lie?" I just couldn't hide it anymore. How could I, with my daughter in lockup?

My mother just kept yelling, "I don't believe this! It never could have happened." She started really getting in my face. That's when my friend pulled me out of there.

I Became the Black Sheep of the Family

Even after all of that, I kept bringing Hector over to see my parents—not very often, but every now and then. Each time, they'd say things to me like, "You're such a bad parent. No wonder Sandra is in the hospital."

At that point, I didn't have the backbone to say, "You're being abusive to me by saying this in front of my child." I just went less often. But then my mother would harass me about keeping her from her grandson, so I'd take him over there.

Finally, my daughter's therapist said to me, "If you continue to see your family, they can take your son away because your parents are emotionally abusive to your son and to you, and you're letting him be in that situation."

That's what gave me the strength to stop seeing my family. I did it for my son. If it had just been me, I don't think I could have done it.

Now I look back and say, "How stupid! Why did you want to set yourself up like that again and again?" The truth is I didn't know a way out. People in my culture don't walk away from their family; it just isn't done.

I come from a huge family. There's my parents, my aunts and uncles, my brother and his family and tons of cousins—forty or fifty of them within seventy miles. None of them believed me. Even though my nephew went to court and had to go to treatment, everyone sided with my brother.

I became the black sheep of the family. No one called to see how I was. No one invited us to family gatherings. I'd rocked the boat by opening my mouth.

As a Hispanic female, you're taught from the time you're little that your role is to cook, clean, and raise the kids. The male can come in, be drunk, beat up his wife, have sex, and leave again. My grandmother raised thirteen children by herself, with an alcoholic husband who'd come back for a while, then leave again. That's why she had all those children; there was no birth control and she couldn't say no. You martyred yourself for your man and your family. I said no to that. I told the truth, and I lost my family because of it. There's a real hole there. It still tears at my heart.

My Daughter Has Never Been Able to Deal With the Abuse

My daughter is twenty-seven now, and she's never been able to deal with the abuse. As a teenager, we took her to family therapy. We took her to individual therapy. But we never found an answer for her.

We tried to get the right help for Sandra, but we weren't rich. We didn't own a house; we didn't have new cars or go on vacations. There were no lockup facilities for kids her age that were affordable.

Sandra kept doing drugs and running away. Then the cops would bring her back. She'd be home for a little while, eat, clean up, and then she'd run again.

After the court case, we did get some victim witness money from the state, and we used it to send her to a residential treatment center, but she ran away from there, too. She was sixteen at the time, and for a year, I didn't know where she was. I remember my son and I going to our neighborhood 7-Eleven and seeing her face on a poster for missing children.

Sandra doesn't do drugs anymore, but she likes to drink. She never finished high school and works as a manager in a retail store. She sabotages herself but always manages to land on her feet. She never talks about the abuse and insists there's nothing wrong with her. It's something she's going to have to come to in her own time.

More than anything else in the world, I wish it hadn't happened to her, but it did. I can't be in charge of the time frame of her healing, but I can be there as much as she will allow me to be. Someday I hope I can hold her hand and say, "I believe you." If I can do that for my daughter, if I can be there at the time she needs that from me, all the years of work I've done on my incest will have been worth it.

Nothing Too Heavy to Share

I've been doing 12-step on and off for sixteen years. The first three years, I did a 12-step women's group. It was really nurturing, like a nice, soft, warm egg that felt comfortable and safe. But I got to a point where I felt like there was work I had to do that I couldn't do there. It felt too safe. It was okay to say you were an abuse survivor, but it wasn't a place where I felt I could say, "You know what? I don't feel connected to my kids." No one in that group ever really talked about the ugliness of child sexual abuse. Nobody ever went too heavy into the details of what had happened.

One of the ladies there told me about the Monday-night Nothing Too Heavy to Share group, and I started going to it. People in that group talked about horrendous things; they were honest about their incest at a deeper level. And everyone was believed; no one ever said, "You're just blowing smoke out of your ass."

The whole first year I went to that group, I lay on the windowsill and slept. I slept through every meeting because it was a safe place to sleep. At the time I was waking up at night with memories of my brother putting the gun in my vagina and in my mouth. I could taste the metal. I was convinced my brother was going to come to my room at night and kill me. I was exhausted all the time. So I slept on the windowsill, and everybody was fine with it. As long as I wasn't hurting anybody. You do what you need to do.

My second year in that group, I'd come in, sit in the corner, and cry. They'd ask, "Do you want to share?" And I'd say no. I just needed to cry, and it was a safe place for me to cry.

After my year of sleeping and my year of crying, my daughter came home. I started working on my stuff really hard because I wanted her to have a role model for the day when she was finally going to be ready to work on her stuff. And at some point, it switched over from doing it for her to doing it for me. My revenge on my brother was that I was going to have a damn good life.

I stayed in the Nothing Too Heavy to Share group for ten years. I still go back every six months or so, just to check in. It was in that group that I was finally able to say, "The crap that I went through—it was real." I was able to own the worst of what had happened to me. I don't think I could have said, "I buried a baby" anywhere else.

A deeper healing comes from being able to be that brutally honest. And hearing other people's stories, I could say, "They went through that, and they're still good people. Maybe I'm not so bad after all."

I've Worked Hard to Get Where I Am

My healing has been an interplay of individual therapy, 12-step, and group. If I hadn't slept when I'd slept, cried when I'd cried, or heard the stories I heard in 12-step, I never would have known I was part of a tribe of people who survived and thrived through hardship. If I hadn't done individual therapy, I wouldn't have learned to honor the truth of my feelings or get to the core of how deeply I was affected by the abuse.

Then I found a healing group for Latinas. I've been doing that for five years. I grew up in a house without sisters, and we're a group of *hermanas*. I didn't know what sisterly love was, and now I do. And because I have limited contact with my extended family, they have become my family.

These women know, down and dirty, what I'm dealing with. They understand where I come from when I say, "I'm feeling bad be-cause I'm here instead of at home where I should be."

Seeing people of my own ethnicity deal with their guilt about opening their mouths, not being good daughters, and not conform-ing to our culture is incredibly empowering. We support each other in becoming stronger females even though our culture tells us we're supposed to be suppressed. We support each other in not being martyrs anymore. That's the biggest thing I get from my group—that it's okay to be a strong Hispanic woman.

And now we are taking it back out into the community. We're reaching out to at-risk families and doing outreach about incest. Just recently, we had a panel with a mediator and translators and questions and answers, where we told our stories. Forty Hispanic females showed up that night. Forty women took time away from their families to come to an evening presentation about incest. That in itself was a major achievement. I'm a firm believer in giv-ing back, in putting a hand out for someone behind me.

Every Morning I Practice Gratitude

I didn't have my own life until I was thirty-three years old. I was a daughter and a mother. I got pregnant young and got married—the His-panic way. And then I got divorced and I had to ask myself, "What do I want to do with the rest of my life?" I'm still answering that question.

Every morning, when I get up, I practice gratitude. There's not a day I don't wake up and say, "My Higher Power, this is a beautiful day. I can get out of my bed. I can wipe my own ass. I have a job and a roof over my head. I have a family that loves me. Life is really, really good, and I should have been dead. This is all icing on the cake."

I'm grateful that I am alive to see it, that somewhere inside of me I found the courage to keep moving forward and to live. Everything else—all the petty stuff—is meaningless, although a good pair of shoes every now and then doesn't hurt.

Pauline Szumska

"After a while, I began to miss my family. I wanted to reestablish a relationship with my mother and with my sister, and maybe my brothers. I thought about it literally for years—about whether it was worth what it would take to make that happen."

Pauline Szumska is a fifty-two-year-old nurse.* She grew up in the Midwest, the eldest of five children born into a Catholic, working-class family. Pauline's father was an orphan, a World War II veteran, and a prisoner of war in Germany. Her mother was an only child raised in a large extended family of Polish-American immigrants. Pauline's father physically and sexually abused her and all of her siblings from earliest childhood. The incest didn't end for Pauline until she moved out at eighteen.

Once Pauline left home, she focused her energy on building a life that was safe. During the next ten years, she maintained a limited, cordial relationship with her family. The abuse was never

discussed or acknowledged. As she put it, "We never talked about anything that might cause a problem."

Then in 1983, her brother shot himself in the head. His suicide attempt motivated Pauline to speak candidly about the abuse. Because she insisted on telling the truth about what had happened, neither her parents nor her siblings would speak to her for ten years. As Pauline recalls, "The silence was deafening."

Although she didn't choose it, at least not initially, Pauline benefited from this decade of estrangement. She needed time away to establish herself as a separate person and to focus on her healing. But as the years wore on, she began to long for her sister and tentatively reached out to her. Her contact with the rest of her family, including both her parents, grew from there.

---

* Pauline Szumska chose to use a pseudonym.

Pauline is a good example of a survivor in the latter stages of healing whose reconciliation with family members—limited in some cases and more significant in others—has been an integral part of her process.*

The relationship with my family was always very complicated. No one was allowed to do anything that might upset the stability of the family. My siblings and I just did what we could to make it through the days. Everyone lived in his or her own bubble. I was closer to people at school than I was to anyone in my family. That was very sad.

Each of my siblings responded very differently to the incest. My response was to wait. It never occurred to me to do anything other than wait until I was eighteen and then leave home.

Once I was physically out of the house, I had even less contact with my siblings. Basically, we were strangers. I was busy building a life that was safe, and they were still in the house, trying to survive. I had felt guilty when I was living with them because I was the oldest and wasn't able to stop the abuse. I felt guilty when I left because I had gotten away. It took years of therapy to let go of that guilt, to understand that we were all children. None of

us could have done anything to protect one another.

For the first ten years after I left the house, we had what looked like a normal family from the outside. I came to the house for Christmas and for major holidays. My mother and I sometimes went to a movie. We were cordial, and I knew not to raise certain subjects. My father, I just avoided.

Over the years, we became more and more estranged. At one point, my sister and I stopped talking to each other for many years. My mother and I continued to have infrequent contact on major holidays, but I never went home. During those years, I considered myself to be without a biological family.

Confronting My Family

I was in therapy off and on for years, but I never confronted my father about the abuse. I never talked to my mother about it. But then, in 1983, my brother shot himself in the head. I was the one who had to tell my parents, and I didn't want my mother to walk into the hospital unprepared. As an emergency room nurse, I know some of the things people write in notes when they take a step like the one my brother had taken. I didn't want my mother to learn about what my father had done in front of a bunch of strangers.

So I sat with her in the car and said, "I want you to understand what you're walking into when you go to that hospital." I didn't know how to say it, so I was very blunt. I said, "You need to know that your husband molested me

---

* A longer version of this story, and other stories of family healing and reconciliation after sexual abuse, can be found in a workbook and series of taped interviews done by Laura Davis called *The Last Frontier: Is Reconciliation Possible After Sexual Abuse?* For information, visit www.lauradavis.net. Laura's book, *I Thought We'd Never Speak Again: The Road from Estrangement to Reconciliation*, is also full of stories and information about the process of reconciliation from rifts caused by many events, among them, sexual abuse.

and all of us. It went on for years, and I think Frank shot himself because of that."

My mother was stunned, but she didn't question what I told her. Both my parents went to the hospital, and my brother survived the attempt, but after that, we didn't even pretend we had a relationship anymore. I was no longer ever invited home. It was pretty clear that I just wasn't welcome in the family.

Seeds of Reconciliation

Over the next ten years, while we were estranged, I felt so many things. I was angry because I was the one who had to tell. I felt guilty because I had told. It was painful and it was sordid. I didn't want anything to do with them. I just wanted a life where I could have a job and some friends and not have to come home and deal with everything that had happened to me.

I really needed healing time. I read every book on sexual abuse that was ever written. I worked with a therapist individually and in a group. I journaled. There were years where I slept, ate, drank, dreamed incest. Then I started working my way out to the other side. It took a lot of work. And time. I needed time to recuperate.

But after a while, I began to miss my family. I wanted to reestablish a relationship with my mother and I wanted to see if I could have a relationship with my sister, and maybe my brothers. I thought about it literally for years—about whether it was worth what it would take to make that happen.

I knew my family and the dynamics well enough to know that any movement that was going to occur was going to have to be mine. Everyone was so entrenched in their position. No one in my family was capable of changing their feelings or attitudes about me, so I was going to have to be the one to make the change.

I had to reach a point where that didn't feel like I was capitulating, where I could accept them without absolving them. That took a tremendous amount of work and the help of a gifted therapist.

I Sewed Love Into Every Stitch

During the time I was thinking about reconnecting with my mother, I embroidered a wall hanging for her. I wanted to do something that would communicate to her that I was thinking about her and that I cared about her, in a way that couldn't be misunderstood.

I didn't want to reach out to her with words. In our family, words just get in the way. We don't have a lot of experience communicating. We exchange information: "The groceries are on the table. It's time to go to school." We don't discuss things. My mother doesn't know how.

But my mother really likes needlework, and I love doing it. So I found a pattern for a cross-stitch sampler that had her favorite psalm on it. Making it for her was like a six-month meditation. I was careful to only work on it when I was in the right space; I didn't work on it when I was angry with her. While I sewed it, I thought about the positive things I was hoping she would hear when I sent it. I thought about my mother, about where she came from, and what she'd been through. I sewed compassion and understanding into that sampler. I made it with intention. I had it nicely framed and I sent it to her for Christmas, and she was very pleased.

Some time after that, my mother invited me home for a family reunion. My first thought was, "No way!" I could imagine meeting one-on-one with my mother or my sister, but meeting with them all there seemed overwhelming. But I have a dear friend who is an attorney, and he specializes in mediation. He offered to come with me. He said, "Look, we'll take our own car. If it goes well, we'll stay. If it doesn't, we'll leave." And I agreed. I needed an advocate, someone who would be on my side if things went badly.

The visit went amazingly well. My friend knows how to be with people, so they were comfortable with him. But my sister and I were still not talking. We were doing this interesting little dance: I would enter a room, and she would leave. She would enter the room, and I would leave. We never sat close to one another.

But both of us do needlework; I embroider, and she quilts. I finally sat myself down in the living room, which is the same place my mother had hung the sampler I had made. I was working on some needlework, and my sister walked in and sat in a chair near me with her quilting. We were sitting there in complete silence, doing our needlework. She looked over at my needlework and said, "That's nice."

And I said, "Thank you."

And she looked up at the sampler on the wall and said, "That's really nice."

And I said, "Thank you. Your quilting is very nice, too."

Everything else came from that. It didn't get better overnight, but two pigheaded Polacks started talking again. Tentatively, we began rebuilding a relationship.

It's been a gradual thing. We started off slowly. We never sat down and processed what happened. We started off with phone calls. She lives halfway across the country, and I made a point of visiting her. Gradually over time, the frequency and the duration of the contact got better. The content got deeper. We've reached the point where we actually talk about what happened to us now. We talk about pretty much anything. We've spent over ten years rebuilding, and it's really good.

Still, I'm careful with my sister. I'm careful the way you tend a garden you really care about. I try to be conscious of being the kind of sister I want to be, and I think she does the same thing.

I'd Never Seen My Mother Happy Before

My mother and I have had a parallel process to what's happening with my sister and me, although we don't have the same depth. I'm very aware that there are barriers. My mother can go so far, and she really can't go any further. She doesn't deny that the incest happened, but she just can't go there. She hits a wall where she just shuts down and goes away, not physically, but emotionally. I don't think that's ever going to change.

My relationship with my mother takes constant maintenance. There's this part of me that thinks if I could just get over this wall that our relationship could have some more depth, that we could be closer. It makes me sad, but I try to remember that she's doing the best she can. I authentically believe that. Given when she was born and how she was raised and what she's had to deal with, she's come a really long way.

I've been through a lot of phases with my mother. I was angry and frustrated with her. I've felt hurt by her. One thing that's helped me understand why she can't really talk about the sexual abuse is "There but for the grace of God go I." I could have ended up married to a man who abused my children. I could have responded to what happened to me the same way she did.

My mother, even though she was not a nurturing woman, taught me to be strong. That strength helped me turn out healthy. That's a real gift, because I could have turned out a lot of other ways. For that I am very grateful—and I've tried to tell my mother that.

I've also realized that there are whole parts of my mother I know nothing about. Once, when my sister brought my mother to visit me, I found out that she had always wanted to ride a boat on San Francisco Bay. So my sister and I took her out on one of the ferries. And she had the best time. It was a side of her I had never seen. She went out to the bow and leaned on the railing. To this day, I'm sad I didn't have a camera, because there's this image I have of my mother leaning against the railing with the wind in her hair, looking at the ocean. She was so happy. I had never seen my mother happy before. As a woman and as a daughter, it was very powerful.

Thinking about it makes me cry. It's sad to be fifty-three years old and to have never seen your mother happy. I've had many, many opportunities to be joyful in my life, and it's sad to think that that boat trip may have been it for my mother. Every woman is entitled to that kind of joy more than once in her life.

Adding to Their Pain Isn't Going to Diminish Mine

There were five children in my family, and we all grew up in the same house. We were all exposed to the same abuse from the same person, yet each of us responded very differently. I feel lucky because I came out of it in pretty good shape. When all is said and done, I'm healthy physically and emotionally. I have a good life. Some of it is because of what happened to me, not just in spite of it. I have strength and insight and empathy that not everybody has. Would I wish for this? No. But because of what happened, I'm a stronger and wiser person.

My brothers and my sister all responded to the abuse differently, and each of them has to process it in their own time and their way. I wouldn't have wanted anyone to rush or force me, so I try not to do that to them. I'm on my own path; it's only fair to recognize that they're on theirs. Adding to their pain isn't going to diminish mine.

There was a time I just had to say it out loud and I wanted to force them to listen. But I no longer need them to hear me. I know what happened to me. I understand what happened to me. I accept what happened to me. What we went through was bad enough in itself without me trying to impose my time frame on them.

My Relationship With My Father Is Really Complicated

On several occasions, I confronted my father about what happened. The first time I talked to him, it boiled down to me saying, "You know I'm seeing a therapist and it's because of you," and he said, "I know." That's all I could do. And that took several years of therapy.

A couple of times, my father has tried to say he's sorry. I don't accept his apology. I feel that what's he looking for from me is absolution, and I'm not willing to grant absolution. I have an understanding of how he got to where he is and how he turned into a man who sexually abused his children, but I don't feel he's ever really accepted responsibility for it. He's sorry. I know he's sorry, but he's sorry about the pain it's bringing *him*. He's sorry because he doesn't have the old age he'd like to have. And part of him is sorry because he doesn't understand how he got there. How did his life turn out this way?

If anybody but my father had sexually assaulted me, no one would expect me to understand. No one would expect me to forgive. No one would expect me to have any insight into him. It would be okay just to be mad and to hate, or just to erase it. But this man is my father, and in addition to sexually abusing me, he did some good things for me. My love of music comes from my father. My compassion for other people's difficult lives comes from him.

So this person that did unspeakable things to me also gave me some great gifts. That's what makes incest so terrible. You can't just hate the man, because he also is your father.

I Don't Want My Father to Define My Life

I try to be conscious of how I behave towards my father because there's this part of me that still wants to hurt him, be unkind to him, and treat him badly, but that doesn't leave me feeling good about myself. I want to treat him respectfully and to maintain some dignity in myself. Otherwise, he's running my life again.

My mother taught me that when I react to someone, or against someone, they're running my life as surely as if I was following their direct orders. So I've needed to be clear with myself that the way I interact with my father is right for me. I want to behave in such a way that I can look in the mirror and be happy with what I'm seeing. I don't want to feel ugly because of how I'm treating another human being, even a child molester. So I treat my father respectfully. I try not to do things to add to his pain because I don't feel it's my job or my right to judge him. I used to feel it was. Now I feel that what he needs to do is between him and his God. I wish him well in that, but it's not my job to fix it.

Part of it is my own recovery—getting over my own pain. Part of it is living long enough to understand that people live their lives and sometimes they make terrible, terrible mistakes that they can't change. Sometimes people do things because they're desperately afraid. I've done things I'm not proud of because I was afraid or because I was lonely. I have compassion for how he ended up doing something he would have considered unthinkable. But on the other hand, I spent years in a situation that I almost died from because it was so unbearable. Each time he abused me, he had a choice. He could confront his own fears and stop doing it—he could have gone to jail, gone to therapy, or gone away—or he could choose to abuse me. And not once but countless times he made a choice to continue abusing me and my siblings. He gave in to the impulse every single time. For that reason, I can't say, "Yes, I forgive you." I understand. I have compassion. I don't want to add to his pain. But he had a choice, and each time, the choice was to hurt me and my sister and my brothers rather than face his own fear. He and his God have to work that out, not me.

I don't want to be defined by my father's needs, whether it's his need to abuse or his need for me to forgive him. I have a responsibility to take care of myself. He has a responsibility to take care of himself.

Right now, I can only be with my father in small doses. It's not easy, and I always have to be conscious of how I respond to him. It's like standing up in a rowboat. You can do it, but you have to be very careful about balance and perspective. You have to think about each step. That's what my relationship with my father is like. It's never

relaxed. It's never unconscious. If we had another fifty years, maybe we could get there, but we don't. I think this is as good as it's ever going to get.

My father's in his early eighties, and he's in poor health. Out of self-preservation, I'm looking carefully at the decisions I'm making about him. This work is a lot harder to do after they die. So I've been asking myself, "Is there something more I need to do to take care of me?"

I've thought a lot about how I'm going to feel when my father dies. Part of it is self-protective. I don't want to have a lot of unresolved issues gush up when he dies. I want to be done with this. When he dies, I think I'll feel many things. I think I'll be sad. I think I'm going to be relieved. And I think the proportions of those will vary from day to day for a long time.

Just recently, I was having a phone conversation with my father. He was being authentic with me in a way that is rare in our family. I can't remember what the conversation was about. It wasn't about the abuse. I think we were talking about his health and his day. It was an ordinary conversation. It was not profound, but there was a quality to it that was different—an openness, an honesty. I felt I was talking to a human being. I know my father really cares whether or not I love him, and because he was being authentic, I felt I could say I loved him, and I did. I hadn't said it to him in many, many years, but I felt very clean about saying, "I love you," to him. I could say it because it was true. I could say it and not have it damage me.

What I've Learned About Reconciliation

I've learned that it takes time. I've learned to really think about my motives before proceeding. I've had some false starts. I've made some mistakes. I've learned not to make assumptions about what is going on in someone else's head or heart, because there are whole buckets of information I don't have.

The other thing that's really helped me is something my mother told me when we were beginning to reconcile. She said, "You know it's just as far from me to you as it is from you to me. I'm willing to do some of the work, but this is a stretch for me, too. You have to cut me a little slack." That was good advice, and I try to keep it in mind. The outcome may not always be what I want, but they're working at it, too.

Every time I took a new step on this journey, I'd ask myself, "What's the worst thing that could happen?" If I could deal with that, I'd go ahead. And if I couldn't, I didn't. But by and large, I'm really glad I took the risks I took. The risk to reconcile is worth it.

Sheila O'Connell

"What happened feels bigger than just my story. This happens. This happens in many times and places. This is part of being human—facing it, overcoming it and being caught in it, being undone by it, helping people through it. All the facets are part of being human."

*S*heila O'Connell is a forty-eight-year-old massage therapist from Boulder, Colorado. She enjoys a close relationship with her grown son. Sheila was raised in a large working-class Irish Catholic family and has been actively healing for more than twenty years from the abuse she suffered as a child.*

I grew up outside Boston in the suburbs. My father was a plumber. My mother stayed home with the kids. I was the fifth of six siblings. We grew up in a little ranch house. My parents still live in the same house today.

Our family was Catholic. My parents are very spiritual people, but they aren't dogmatic, so we went through all of the Catholic rituals, but not in a harsh way. We would come home and talk about what the sisters said at school and my mother would counter it with a different way of thinking. She softened the rigid, "You're evil. You're bad" kind of thinking we were exposed to at school. She was much more open-minded.

The religion I experienced as a child gave me a template to look for a deeper life. I was raised to believe that the material world isn't all there is. I really clung to that. It got me through everything that happened later on.

Even though I'm not a practicing Catholic today, I have a real respect for it. There's something I learned about the aliveness of a

---

* Sheila O'Connell was interviewed for the twentieth-anniversary edition of *The Courage to Heal*. She chose to use a pseudonym.

spiritual path that I've been able to take other places in my life.

It Was My Uncles

My father's brother-in-law started molesting me when I was two-and-a-half. My first memory of it was at my brother's christening. His abuse went on for five or six years. He usually did it at family parties.

My mother's brother also molested me, and there were some occasions where they molested me together in the back room.

Their abuse was very different. My father's brother-in-law's attitude was "I'm doing something nice for you," but then he silenced me by saying, "If you tell, your parents won't love you and they'll send you away." His abuse was really confusing. He acted loving, but he was harming me.

My other uncle was cold, sadistic, and violent. There was a sense of hatred that came through everything he did. It was clear that he *wanted* to harm me. He would get me aroused and then ridicule me. He blamed me in a creepy, dark way. It was a real mind-fuck. The cruelty that came with his abuse was conscious, and as a result, it was more devastating. It's not that my other uncle was innocent or that what he did felt good or okay, but I don't think he had any idea how much he was harming me. Clearly, this uncle did. And he enjoyed it.

My second uncle was a part-time police officer and he was involved in a cult. He would pick me up in his police car and take me to the police station, where they did rituals in the basement.

The men in the cult did sick and twisted things and then they'd mess with my mind, saying things like, "You really like that." They used guns and rifles and crucifixes to enter me. They put plastic over my face or held me under water until I was at the edge of death, and then brought me back.

There were four or five rituals a year. I was in first grade when it started; the last memories I have are when I was nine or ten. As I got older, the rituals changed. Toward the end, they had more to do with indoctrinating us into their group. There was much more emphasis on, "You're one of us."

Each time, when the rituals were over, my uncle would clean me up and take me home. He'd scrub me with a brush and cold water, and when he did that, there would always be a sense of relief: "Okay, it's over now." I would start feeling my body again.

When I got home, I would sit in the closet for a while so I could get myself together. I can remember my body calming down. Then I would act like nothing happened. I tried not to think about it.

Who Will Be Chosen?

The leader of the group was the chief of police. His daughter was a year older than me. They'd lock us up in jail cells naked and then come get us for the ritual. One day they came to get us and I was really scared. She took my hand and whispered, "We'll be okay. Let's keep holding hands." We went down this corridor into the room, and they asked, "Who will be chosen?" Whoever was "chosen" would be the one something would happen to. The rest of us would be left alone in the jail cells, naked and cold for hours at a time. Or we'd be forced to watch. There was this ambivalence: You wanted to be chosen and you didn't want to be chosen. So when they asked that question, I said, "Choose her," not knowing what would happen. And that was the day they killed her. And they put my hand on the knife.

This is still the hardest part of everything that happened: how I said, "Choose her," how my hand was on the knife, how she died and I had to keep living. The sense of guilt and shame has been very severe. Even today I find myself working extra hard simply to justify the fact that I survived when she did not. I dream about her, sometimes about her death; other times, she comes to me like an angel, a benevolent loving presence who comforts me.

I Made Sure I Didn't Stand Out in Any Way

I never told anyone about the abuse. It made me feel separate from my family, like I didn't fit in. I think I was actually loved a lot more than I could afford to take in. There was a sense that whatever love and goodness there was in my family wasn't for me.

I soothed and cared for myself by hiding in my closet all the time. I'd lie on the floor and stare at the ceilings and imagine walking up there, having to step over all the thresholds. Or I'd lie out in the grass and look up at the sky. I missed out on a lot of my childhood. I was in another world.

My parents were oblivious to what was going on. Their overriding attitude was that we were okay, so I learned to fake being okay. I didn't show my hurt, sadness, or disappointment. I was a good student; I made sure I didn't stand out in any way.

Yet I kept trying to find meaning. As a teenager, I read Ram Dass's books. In college, I took a yoga class and learned meditation. Meditation gave me a way to slow down, feel my body, and pay attention to what was happening. I was able to create a bigger sense of sense of myself than all the emotional turmoil I was going through. I began to connect with my own heart and my own ability to love. I was able to feel like part of the goodness in the world. It felt like a true spiritual path for me; by that point, I was already alienated from Catholicism and all the baggage of the church.

I felt a little more stable at that point, but I was basically just falling into things. After I graduated from college, I thought about going to graduate school, but I ended up moving in with some hippies I met at the Renaissance Fair.

I married at 25. My husband and I had a sweet, spiritual connection. We read Khalil Gibran together. He was gentle and I felt safe with him. We had a son, Alex, when I was 27. Having a baby motivated me to get my shit together; I didn't want to raise my son in a hippie school bus, driving around the country.

When Alex was still a baby, I went to massage school. It gave me my first real sense of having a grounded, steady life. Massage felt like a way I could help people and be of service. That was a great comfort to me because I'd always had the prevailing feeling that I was bad at my core and that something disastrous would happen when people found out who I really was. I needed to make up for all that badness and helping people was one way.

I Couldn't Get Over It

One day, when Alex was a few months old, my husband wanted to have sex and I didn't. I went along with it, but I wasn't really there. My husband knew I wasn't there, but went ahead anyway. We both felt bad about it afterwards, but I felt horrible. From that point on, I shut my husband out. I was able to be open and connected with my son, but I couldn't let my husband get close to me.

I talked about it with Kate, a woman we'd done some premarital counseling with, and she asked if I had ever felt this way before. I had completely repressed all memory of the abuse, but at that moment, I had the bizarre sensation of my body shrinking into a child's body. Then I had a memory of my uncle pressing me up against the toy box and molesting me. I remember thinking, "Holy shit, this can't be possible." But the memory came back in such a physical way I couldn't deny it. It explained why I'd shut my husband out so completely. It explained a lot of things I hadn't understood before.

I continued working with Kate, and things kept coming up in a very visceral way. She helped me make sense of the memories and the emotional aftermath of the abuse, but she never pushed me. Kate helped me harness my spiritual practice for my healing. My

work with her enabled me to repair that really broken sense of "There's something bad about me." She created a loving and safe place for me, and I felt held by her.

My marriage fell apart during this time. My husband and I were able to end things on good terms and Kate helped me gather the strength to stand on my own.

Getting Back in My Body

The next person I worked with was Sharon, a dance-movement therapist who had training in Hakomi.* We didn't meet in an office; we met in a big room with lots of space to move around in. We did not sit in chairs.

Up until this point, I was always tripping and falling and walking into things. I had no sense of my body in space. There'd be a lamppost, and I'd walk right into it. I was always twisting my ankles.

Sharon helped me come into my body and find my skin and bones and muscles. She did it through doing very specific exercises of tensing and relaxing or moving.

Sharon believed in letting the body lead. She would say, "Just feel your body and begin to move." She had me start with whatever was going on. If I felt tension, she would have me go with that tension, feel it, and exaggerate it. Or make it smaller. Then she would mirror me and help me identify the feelings and underlying beliefs that went with the emotions. If

---

* Hakomi is a psychotherapy based in nonviolence, being connected in the body, and mindfulness—bringing a loving presence to whatever is happening.

I started moving in a way that seemed child-like, she would say, "It seems like you got really little here."

Sharon helped me translate the language of the body into meaning. Rather than analyze something, she'd ask, "If this movement could speak in words, what would it say?"

Sharon also taught me grounding exercises to get in my body—a lot of patting and tapping and grinding my feet into the ground, anchoring myself in a way I had never been anchored before. With her, I learned to move my anger out, find my natural authority and seat of personal power. When memories came up, she kept me from going into a trauma state by having me feel the muscles of my body, stamp my feet, and shout no. Sometimes, we did boundary exercises where she would slowly bring her hand toward me and have me sense when I didn't want her to come any closer. Then I'd use my hand to stop her.

In the year we worked together, a lot of memories came up, but I was still only dealing with the memories about my first uncle.

Telling My Family

Six months into my work with Sharon, I brought my mother into therapy to tell her about my first uncle. I was going through all this intense emotional work, then I'd see my mother and the family and say, "I'm fine." It was getting harder and harder for me to play that game.

My mom was shocked and appalled, but she was really supportive. Her response let me have her love in a really fresh way. There was never any question in her mind about whether it had happened, because my uncle always had such creepy, slimy behavior. I could see that it broke her heart.

My dad didn't like to talk about feelings much; it made him really uncomfortable, so I let my mom tell him about the abuse. Later he told me he was so mad he just wanted to go and beat the crap out of my uncle. I was lucky. I could tell then how much they really loved me.

My parents responded so positively, I decided to tell my siblings. They were like, "Ewww, gross!" The first thing my sister said was how she remembered my uncle flirting with my mother and how much she hated that. My sisters-in-law told me he had tried to feel them up at family weddings.

My mother and I kept up an ongoing conversation about the abuse. At one point, I brought up the possibility of confronting my uncle. My mom called one day and said, "I don't know if you're ready to do this or not, but I just got word that James and Maggie are coming through town. If you want, we could invite them over and not tell them what's going on. If you want to confront him, we can arrange it and support you."

I was amazed my parents volunteered to do that. And then we did it.

My aunt and uncle were shocked to see me. I said to my uncle, "I remember what you did to me." Right after I said it, there was this split-second look between my aunt and my mother, where a moment of recognition passed over my aunt's face. She knew it was true. It happened really fast, and then the denial came up. But my mother saw it, too.

Then my aunt and uncle went into complete denial and said all these mean, nasty things like "You'd better stay in therapy. You really need it. You're really sick" and "How dare you accuse me?" and "I never touched anyone."

And I said, "Well, we know you felt up my sisters-in-law in recent times." The lie was really obvious.

There was one point where my uncle looked at my father and said, "Well, what do you think about all of this?"

My dad had been silent up until this point. He started squirming and was really uncomfortable. Then he got quiet, looked at my uncle and said, "I have no reason not to believe my daughter. My daughter would never make up something like this."

It was amazing. And at that point, my uncle said, "I've had just about enough of this," and they stormed off.

Afterwards my dad said, "Well, that went pretty well. I'm really proud of you. Let's go out to dinner and celebrate." And that's what we did. We went out to Chi-Chi's and had margaritas and dinner.

The Next Layer

Soon after the confrontation, the memories of my sadistic uncle started to come back. A few things led up to it. The first was the safety created when my family believed me. The second was that my son was approaching the age I had been when the worst abuse began. And the third was having to deal with two male authority figures in my work life who crossed boundaries inappropriately. It was yet another betrayal—and the fact that there were two of them reminded me of my uncles.

I began to remember them molesting me together and the twisted verbal abuse that accompanied the sexual abuse. I remembered my sadistic uncle laughing at me.

Each time I had a new memory, I'd go into an altered state. I could feel it coming on, so I'd know something was about to come up. My nervous system would get activated; I'd feel shaky in my body. I'd get spacey. Little things would freak me out. If I was driving, I'd see something out of the corner of my eye and my startle response would be extreme. I'd feel extremely anxious and I'd start to eat, because I tried to regulate my nervous system by stuffing everything down with food. All of a sudden I'd have finished a bag of cookies and I wouldn't even realize I'd eaten them. I'd think, "Oh my God, this is a bad sign."

I started having nightmares about being stalked, and faces I hadn't yet recognized in black robes would be chasing me. They pervaded my dreams for a couple of months, and I'd wake up terrified. I didn't know the meaning yet.

During this time, I upped my self-care. I was a single mother, and I was friends with several mothers who had kids Alex's age. They were really good friends; I could just show up at their house with extra groceries—or not—and cook dinner with them. I did that several times a week. If I needed extra care for Alex when I was feeling triggered, they would show up and take him. Or they'd come over and keep us company until he went to bed and then help me process a little. I had a great support system.

The Worst of the Memories Started Breaking Through

My memories came back in stages. Right before the ritual abuse memories broke through, I felt like a volcano was about to explode inside me. I had been doing this work long enough to know this was not good news.

I remembered my uncle taking me to the police station and being abused by four cops. Their abuse was very sadistic, and there were ritual qualities to it. I had to say to each of them, "I belong to you." And the face of one of the men was the same face that had been haunting me in my dreams. It was Frank, the man who ultimately murdered his daughter and put the knife in my hand.

At the time I started remembering all of this, I was working with a terrific therapist. Al and I met twice a week, and he'd schedule me as his last appointment and stay with me as long as I needed. Sometimes I was there for two hours. It gave me the chance to connect with him, to go into my body and let whatever needed to emerge, process it through, and then calm down a little afterwards. Then I'd go back home and be a mom again.

Some of what I was remembering was hard to believe. The first memories about the police station made sense to me; I knew my uncle was a cop, and I knew how sadistic he could be. The other stuff, I thought, "No way."

But Al was great. He had excellent training, a lot of experience, and a strong spiritual practice. In the most unbelievable moments he'd say, "Right now you're finding this hard to believe. Maybe it didn't happen, but it's here and we need to deal with it. We can worry about figuring it out later." He didn't get in a cognitive argument with me. He gave me a framework within which I could believe, not believe, believe, not believe.

When I was uncertain about a particular memory, Al would say, "I don't have any reason to disbelieve it, and we don't have any concrete proof to prove it. But regardless of whether it actually happened the way you are remembering it or not, you're having these feelings and images and memories, and we need to address them so you can move through them and be free of them." He was good at not taking a stand one way or the other. He let me have my uncertainty and didn't behave in any way, even subtly, that would take one side or the other away from me.

When I would say, "This is impossible; people can't do this," he'd respond, "As hard as it is to believe, people do these things. We don't know whether this actually happened to you, but this has happened."

At the other extreme, he also held the door open: "People are looking at this in lots of different ways." He would talk about what infants experience with blood and feces in the birth process, and he'd say, "It's possible you're actually having a birth memory—that the blood and feces you're feeling on your skin doesn't go with this story. But right now it doesn't matter, because they're here together. Let's see where this wants to take you."

A couple of the events I remembered during that time have come back so many times in exactly the same way that I feel pretty certain they happened that way. There are other things that came back in a more amorphous way and I don't know if they happened the way I remembered them. It doesn't feel like it matters whether those particular incidents happened, because everything else I went through was horrible enough. So much of what happened to me goes to the extreme of the horrible things human beings can do to each other: the torture I experienced, the mind control, the manipulation, seeing a child murdered. It doesn't get worse than that. So the details I'm not sure about don't seem very important.

I'd Rather Be Crazy Than Evil

When I brought the ritual abuse to my parents' attention, I was hoping their response would prove that I was crazy and that none of it ever could have happened. But when I told them, my father responded, "Yeah, they were all part-time police officers. Frank was the chief of police, and he lived across the street from your uncle. He was crazy enough to be mixed up in something like this."

I hadn't expected my parents to believe me, and the first thing out of my father's mouth was to name the one man I remembered and to locate him as my uncle's neighbor. The name matched the face.

When I told him about the girl who was murdered, my father said he remembered Frank's daughter dying in some weird accident—like a toaster falling in the bathtub. That was the explanation that had been given for her death. Shortly thereafter, her mother hung herself in the garage. The fact that my father provided those corroborating details shocked me.

My father's affirmation let the bottom fall out. This was real; it had happened to me. I

found it really threatening. It brought up an existential crisis about humanity—that people were capable of doing these things to children. I couldn't accept the kind of world that implied.

It was all tied to the death of that girl. I was the one who said, "Choose her." I participated. My hand was on the knife. I killed her. I felt responsible and guilty. Cognitively, I could say, "I was six years old. I couldn't possibly be responsible for her death." But then I'd think, "If this really happened, I'm part of this evil and I'd rather be crazy than evil. I'd rather live in a world where crazy people make up these things than in a world where people actually commit these kinds of acts, and do so consciously."

During the year I was flooded by ritual abuse memories, I had lots of suicidal thoughts and feelings. I wasn't actively suicidal, but I couldn't keep sharp knives in the house. There were times I didn't feel safe driving because they had programmed me: "If I remember, kill myself." "If I remember, drive into a tree." And I did have a cousin who died driving into a tree. I think he was a part of this, too.

I Had to Forgive Myself

I had grown up as a Catholic where it was a mortal sin to kill someone. I knew I would go straight to hell for what I had done. I also grew up in a Satanic world where sacrifice and murder occurred. The fact that they were overlaid on top of each other was extremely disturbing.

I went to talk to a minister about it. She said: "These events happened. You were a child. You have done enough penance." The fact that she used religious language helped me free myself from that bind for the first time.

I realized that I needed to come to peace with my Catholic upbringing and honor it. I needed to forgive myself and let myself feel forgiven.

I found a beautiful church where all the Catholic mystical symbols were painted in frescoes on the ceiling, and I went there for an entire Lent and Easter season. During the holy week of Easter, I attended all the services and did all the rituals: from Palm Sunday through the Last Supper and Good Friday and Holy Saturday and then the Coming of the Light and the Resurrection. Doing the rituals helped me go through that process within myself: atonement, purification, forgiveness, and resurrection. I felt a real sense of cleansing.

Letting the History Be the History

Soon afterward, a friend invited me to a Buddhist silent meditation retreat. It was the first time I ever understood: "Oh, you *stay* in your body while you're meditating. You don't try to transcend the body."

Buddhist mindfulness affected me deeply. It helped me integrate what I was going through in a new way. I felt connected to something much larger than the story or the moment-to-moment experience of reliving it. It created room for me to let the history be the history, for the thoughts and feelings and memories to be the thoughts and feelings and memories. It helped me recognize what I was going through as temporary, to see that it was always changing, that trauma was not who I am.

When really strong feelings came up, I was able to say to myself, "I'm going through this now, but this isn't who I am. This is going to pass. In twenty minutes or an hour, I'm not going to be sobbing anymore." And because of that, I experienced much less turmoil. I was able to calm down afterwards in a way I had never calmed down before. And I learned to ease my own suffering by not adding on to what I was going through by being judgmental or harsh or critical of myself. I began to have more compassion for myself.

As my Buddhist practice deepened, I became more grounded and relaxed. I felt more warmth and ease in my life. I felt happy. The ritual abuse wasn't as immediate; I was no longer walking around in trauma. I felt intact. The things I was going through seemed more like the normal issues people deal with. They didn't have such a catastrophic feel to them. I no longer felt on the edge of life and death all the time.

The mindfulness practice helped me get out of those really extreme states of mind. It gave me the tools to connect in a deeper way to my own basic goodness and helped me find a quiet stillness inside that's connected with everything. It's a deep ability to love.*

Psychological Healing, Spiritual Healing

I took Buddhist refuge vows in the summer of 1994. For me, the vows are about choos-

---

* For basic mindfulness meditation instruction, see p. 180.

ing compassion for myself and for others as my practice. This has been profound for me, but I couldn't have taken vows if I hadn't done the psychological work first.

A meditation teacher once said, "You have to be somebody before you can be nobody." That's the simplest way to put it. Psychological work is essential to healing the harm that happens when trust is broken. Yet there's a way that most psychotherapeutic approaches stop at repairing the ego. The goals of psychotherapy are to have a positive sense of self, to be able to function in the world, and to have good relationships. That's where meditation practice and spiritual practice come in, because our trajectory as human beings is much greater than just having a healthy ego.

Mindfulness meditation is an incredible technology for building presence—for discovering what you're actually experiencing and developing the capacity to stay with it and let it change on its own. It's a process that's very different from "understanding." A friend of mind used to say, "A well-analyzed problem is just that."

For me, sitting meditation—watching the stories and thoughts cycle around and around— has allowed something new to emerge: a deep quiet, calmness, and clarity. I feel a friendly warmth toward myself and don't take things so seriously. What extends out from that connection, warmth, and spaciousness is a connection to all other people going through the same thing. I have developed a deep appreciation of being human. I feel the suffering exquisitely, but I also feel love in a way I never did before.

For me, the psychological and the spiritual have complemented and deepened each other. With the kind of wounding I experienced, I don't think I could have healed without both of them.

The Most Important Truth

I've realized that the most important truth is that I'm bearing witness to the horror and tragedy of what happened. I am bearing witness to the sacrifice of it, not just for the victims but the harm it caused the perpetrators as well. The incredible loss. And the incredible victory of not having become part of it and not passing it on to my son.

What happened feels bigger than just my story. This happens. This happens in many times and places. This is part of being human— facing it, overcoming it and being caught in it, being undone by it, helping people through it. All the facets are part of being human. It's also not all there is. There is the truth of the tragedy, but there is also the truth of the goodness that has run through it.

I often think of the girl who was murdered and how precious she was. How in the midst of this horrible environment, she reached out her hand to me. That seems extraordinary. It was a moment of kindness in the midst of the horror. There's something in that about being able to gather the light and the dark together. They didn't exist separately from each other even in that horrendous environment. That truth feels really important to me.

Resource Guide

Dear Readers:

We've once again revised the Resource Guide, adding many new books, videos, organizations, and online resources. We've also reorganized the listings so that they're easier to find. However, since many bridge more than one category, skim through other related sections if you don't find what you're looking for right away.

There are new sections on the body's role in healing, on trauma, memory, and the brain; on addiction, recovery, and eating disorders; and on family healing. We've highlighted our favorite spiritual books, expanded the section on creativity, and added listings for poetry, films, and documentaries. We are particularly pleased with the number of excellent new resources for young people that are now available.

Books, organizations, or resources we have found to be especially valuable or unique are noted with an asterisk (*).

Many of the books listed here are new, but others are old classics that are still the best resources available in a given subject area. Most of the books are currently in print, but we've retained some excellent out-of-print titles because they can still be found in libraries and used copies can be ordered online. Also, many independent bookstores will find used books for you.

The listings for national organizations are intended as suggestions about where to look for help, not endorsements. Although we've contacted every organization personally to assess the reliability of their information and the responsiveness of their staff, changes inevitably occur: organizations shift focus and staff members come and go. Also, what's useful to one survivor won't necessarily benefit another. Therefore, it's essential that you use your own judgment.

For the online resources, we've chosen Web sites that have been stable, reliable sources of information, but the Internet is fluid and sites come and go. Also, there are no guarantees of truth on the Internet. Occasionally there are pornographic and anti-survivor sites that masquerade as sites that can help you. So use caution as you search for online resources.

Many survivors, particularly those who are isolated, have found companionship and built strong online support communities through the use of chat rooms and bulletin boards. Although the sharing that takes place can be empowering, these venues are not supervised, screened, or protected. The advice or information that is given is not always helpful or accurate. And not everyone you meet is who he or she claims to be. If at any time you feel uncomfortable, unsafe, or invalidated or sense that something isn't right, trust your gut feelings and don't continue on. It's also a good idea to report abuses you find online to the sites hosting the discussion board or chat room in question.

It's our hope that you'll find the information, connections, and support you need in the pages of this guide.

Ellen Bass and Laura Davis, March 2008

ACKNOWLEDGMENTS

This twentieth-anniversary edition of the Resource Guide has been in the capable hands of Cynthia Lamb. She had the primary responsibility for soliciting and assessing resources, reorganizing the guide, and discerning what would be most useful. We are grateful to her for her insight, unflagging optimism, impeccable organizational skills, excellent judgment, good humor, and diligence. Her deep commitment to survivors is evident in the care she took with every detail. We are honored to have had her as an integral part of our team.

Cynthia would especially like to thank Carolyn Lehman, author of *Strong at the Heart,* for her excellent resources for young people; Suzette Rochat (aka Cybele), originator of "Breath and Body" groups for survivors; Eileen King of Justice for Children; Betsy Salkind; Matthew Hadden; Dana Scruggs; Jojo Hill; Pamela Pine of Stop the Silence; Jean Riseman of Survivorship; Jim Van Buskirk; Connie Valentine of California Protective Parents Association; Staci Haines of Generation Five; Barbara Dorris of SNAP; Wendy Maltz; Susan Brady, and Peter Pollard of Stop It Now!

We greatly appreciate the many survivors, counselors, authors, publishers, and others who have helped us update this Resource Guide over the years. For help with earlier editions, we'd like to thank Euan Bear, Joyce Boaz, Donna Covello, Marge Eide, Kerry Ellison, Anne-Marie Eriksson, Molly Fisk, Eileen King, Mike Lew, Anita Montero, Marcia Cohen Spiegel, and the women who worked at Full Circle and Herland Books, two great independent stores that are no longer with us. Teri Cosentino put in endless hours inputting text on her computer. The staff at Bookshop Santa Cruz generously provided us with countless biographical details. And our fabulous researcher, Shana Ross, made earlier updates possible with her intelligence, persistence, and marvelous sense of humor.

CONTENTS

FINDING HELP, BUILDING COMMUNITY

HOTLINES

Childhelp National Child Abuse Hotline
800-4-A-CHILD
800-422-4453
www.childhelp.org
> Counselors are available 24 hours a day and offer crisis intervention, information regarding child abuse, resources for adult and child survivors, help with parenting, and referrals to agencies across North America.

Love Is Respect National Teen Dating Abuse Helpline
1-866-331-9474
1-866-331-8453 TTY
www.loveisrespect.org
> A national Web-based and telephone helpline for teens who are experiencing dating abuse. Trained volunteers offer one-on-one support and referrals for girls and boys, friends, parents, and other concerned adults. The phone helpline is available 24 hours a day; the online peer-to-peer chat is available 4 PM to midnight Central time.

National Domestic Violence Hotline
800-799-SAFE, 800-799-7233
800-787-3224 TTY
www.ndvh.org
> The hotline is staffed 24 hours every day by advocates who listen and offer support, education, and information to help callers make the best choices for themselves, which may include how to leave, how to be safe, where to find a shelter and other services, and how to file a report, find a counselor, or interact with the court system. Assistance is available in English and Spanish, and they have access to translators for more than 140 languages.

National Suicide Prevention Lifeline
800-273-TALK (8255)
in Spanish: 888-628-9454
TTY: 800-799-4TTY (4889)
www.suicidepreventionlifeline.org
> The toll-free hotline operates 24 hours a day. Callers are routed to local trained crisis counselors who will listen and offer help and referrals. A call to them can save your life.

RAINN
800-656-HOPE
www.rainn.org
> The Rape, Abuse and Incest National Network (RAINN) operates a free 24-hour-a-day hotline for survivors of all kinds of sexual assault, including sexual abuse, rape, and domestic violence. When you call RAINN, a computer instantly connects you to the nearest rape crisis center. At least 1,000 trained counselors are available to answer calls. All calls are confidential and will not show up on your phone bill.

ORGANIZATIONS THAT PROVIDE RESOURCES OR DIRECT SERVICES TO SURVIVORS

There are more organizations listed in the "Activism and Public Policy" section (p. 528) as well as under other specific topics.

Darkness to Light, 7 Radcliffe St., Suite 200, Charleston, SC 29403; help line: 866-FORLIGHT/866-367-5444; www.darkness2light.org

Nonprofit organization whose mission is to reduce the incidence of child sexual abuse by shifting the responsibility from children to adults. Their Stewards of Children child sexual abuse prevention training is available online and through workshops. Their *7 Steps to Protecting Our Children from Child Sexual Abuse* booklet is free from their Web site. Callers to their helpline are routed to a representative in their state who can refer them to sexual abuse resources in their community.

Gift From Within, 16 Cobb Hill Rd., Camden, ME 04843; 207-236-8858; e-mail: joyceb3955@aol.com; www.giftfromwithin.org

This nonprofit group produces high-quality educational materials for people suffering from post-traumatic stress disorder and those who care for them. Among others, see the excellent videos/DVDs *Recovering from Traumatic Events: The Healing Process*, which has both a survivor and professional version; *Living With PTSD: Lessons for Partners, Friends & Supporters*; and *When Helping Hurts: Preventing & Treating Compassion Fatigue*. Also offers an online support pal network for isolated female trauma survivors, articles, inspirational stories, and a poetry and art gallery.

Incest Resources Inc., c/o The Women's Center, 46 Pleasant St., Cambridge, MA 02139; www.incestresourcesinc.org

Founded in 1980 by and for adult survivors of incest. This nonprofit offers educational resources and recovery items by mail order on topics of interest to survivors, partners, and allies, such as *Starting from Scratch*, a manual for organizing survivor support groups. They also have resource lists for male survivors, survivors abused by women, ritual abuse survivors, nonoffending parents, and more.

*KIDPOWER TEENPOWER FULLPOWER International; 831-426-4407; safety@kidpower.org; www.kidpower.org

Ellen Bass is the founding board president of KIDPOWER, a nonprofit that teaches people of all ages and abilities to stay safe, act wisely, and believe in themselves. Services include publications; a free e-newsletter and articles, including "How to Pick a Good Self-Defense Program"; and workshops for children, teens, adults, families, and schools in personal safety, boundary-setting, advocacy, and physical self-defense skills, including full-force self-defense with a head-to-toe padded instructor. These skills prepare people to protect themselves from most bullying, molestation, relationship violence, assault, and abduction.

*King County Sexual Assault Resource Center, P.O. Box 300, Renton, WA 98057; 425-226-5062; www.kcsarc.org

This politically sensitive, groundbreaking agency provides free publications, programs, and counseling for sexual assault prevention and treatment. They are the source of many excellent resources in this field; see their listing under "Resources for Teenagers" (p. 573) and "Prevention Resources for Parents" (p. 576).

*The Lionheart Foundation, P.O. Box 194, Back Bay, Boston, MA 02117; 781-444-6667; questions@lionheart.org; www.lionheart.org

This pioneering organization helps incarcerated men and women recognize, acknowledge, and heal from the childhood trauma that is often at the root of the violence and addictions that led them to prison in the first place. At a time when rehabilitation is being shelved in favor of bigger prisons, the work of the Lionheart Foundation is essential. The foundation also runs the National Emotional Literacy Project for Youth-at-Risk.

National Center for Victims of Crime, 2000 M Street, NW, suite 480, Washington, D.C. 20036; 800-FYI-CALL (394-2255), Monday–Friday, 8:30 AM to 8:30 PM EST; TTY: 800-211-7996; gethelp@ ncvc.org; www.ncvc.org

Nonprofit resource and advocacy organization for crime victims. Offers information, resources, and referrals; advocates for passage of laws and public policies that benefit victims of crime; and provides training. The Web site offers a wealth of information about dating violence, stalking, resilience, and more.

National Organization for Victim Assistance (NOVA); 510 King Street, suite 424, Alexandria, VA 22314; 800-879-6682 (24-hour line), 703-535-NOVA; www.trynova.org

NOVA is an advocacy organization for crime victims. Sponsors training seminars, educational programs, and conferences; provides a 24-hour information and referral line.

PANdora's Box, www.prevent-abuse-now.com.

Information about child abuse prevention, child protection, resources for protective parents, and more.

*The Safer Society Foundation, Inc. (SSFI), P.O. Box 340, Brandon, VT 05733; 802-247-3132; referral line, 802-247-5141; www.safersociety.org

National research, advocacy, and referral center for the prevention and treatment of sexual abuse. Publishes excellent groundbreaking literature, including resources for youthful sex offenders. Maintains a computerized nationwide directory

of agencies, institutions, and individuals who provide specialized assessment and treatment for youthful and adult sex offenders.

*Sidran Institute, 200 East Joppa Rd., suite 207, Baltimore, MD 21286; 410-825-8888; to reach the help desk, call 410-825-8888, ext. 203, or e-mail help@sidran.org; www.sidran.org

International nonprofit that helps people understand, treat, and recover from trauma, dissociation, and related issues, such as addictions and self-injury. They offer training; excellent resources, including many free articles on their website; and a help desk that will aid callers in finding a therapist, reading material, and other resources. The Sidran Institute also develops collaborative projects to foster multidisciplinary, community-based responses to the emotional, physical, social, and spiritual impacts of traumatic stress. Sidran Press publishes high-quality books for professionals, paraprofessionals, survivors, and their friends.

*Stop It Now! 351 Pleasant St., suite 319, Northampton, MA 01060; office: 413-587-3500; help line: 888-PREVENT, available 9 AM–6 PM EST; info@ stopitnow.org; www.stopitnow.org

Founded in 1992 by a survivor, Stop It Now! provides support, information, resources, and referrals that enable individuals and families to keep children safe and create healthier communities. Stop It Now! reaches out to adults who are concerned about their own or others' sexualized behavior toward children and offers adults the tools they need to prevent sexual abuse. Their confidential, toll-free help line is available to any adult with questions about sexual abuse, including those who have sexually offended or feel at risk to offend and who want help to stop.

Survivors of Incest Anonymous (SIA), P.O. Box 190, Benson, MD 21018; 410-893-3322; www.siawso .org

A 12-step self-help peer program for incest survivors and supporters. They offer extensive literature—the newcomer packet is free if you can't afford it—and have a pen pal program. To locate groups in your area, visit the Web site or write to them and include a SASE (self-addressed stamped envelope) with two first-class stamps.

Survivor Connections Inc., 52 Lyndon Rd., Cranston, RI 02905-1121; www.survivorconnections.net
Started by Frank Fitzpatrick, a survivor of clergy abuse, this nonprofit activist organization is for all survivors of sexual abuse and rape. Maintains a database of perpetrators and sponsors the annual To Tell the Truth events.

*Survivors Healing Center (SHC), 2301 Mission St., suite C-1, Santa Cruz, CA 95060; 831-423-7601; www.survivorshealingcenter.org
Survivors Healing Center was founded by Ellen Bass and Amy Pine in 1987. Provides education, information and referrals, a local lending library, and support to survivors and their allies. Their primary goals are to empower survivors and to prevent sexual abuse. The center offers therapy groups for survivors and workshops and training for service providers and sponsors the Annual Art of Healing Event.

ACTIVISM AND PUBLIC POLICY

Organizations and Web Sites

For advocacy organizations that deal specifically with custody and issues regarding children who are currently being abused, see "If Your Child Is Abused" on p. 577.

ECPAT International, www.ecpat.net; ECPAT-USA, 157 Montague St., Brooklyn, NY 11201; 718-935-9192; www.ecpatusa.org

ECPAT started in Thailand in 1991 to combat the child sex tourism trade and has expanded its mission to eliminate the sexual exploitation of children, including child prostitution and pornography. Seventy countries have chapters. The U.S. chapter focuses on children brought here from other countries for sexual slavery, American children prostituted in the United States, and American sex tourists who exploit children in other countries. ECPAT-USA does advocacy research, training, and public policy advocacy. Their Web site includes a wealth of information, articles, and resources, as well as links to local groups.

*Generation Five, 3288 21st St., #171, San Francisco, CA 94110; 415-861-6658; info@generationfive.org; www.generationfive.org
This nonprofit organization has a mission to end child sexual abuse within five generations. They work in collaboration with service providers to ensure that affordable, culturally relevant support is available to survivors, offenders, and affected families. They provide leadership training to community members, activists, and agency professionals and foster national strategy and information exchange on child sexual abuse.

Institute on Violence, Abuse and Trauma (IVAT), at Alliant International University, 6160 Cornerstone Ct. East, San Diego, CA 92121; 858-623-2777, ext. 416; www.ivatcenters.org
Provides information on many areas of violence, abuse, and trauma. Conducts workshops and trainings, sponsors international conferences that address cutting edge issues, and provides consulting and program evaluation. Their online bookstore is an excellent resource.

*Justice for Children, 2600 Southwest Freeway, suite 806, Houston, Texas 77098; 800-733-0059; info @justiceforchildren.org; www.justiceforchildren.org.
With chapters in four states, Justice for Children advocates and intervenes on behalf of abused and

neglected children in child abuse cases. They provide guidance through a complex child protective system, legal advocacy, professional referrals, public policy monitoring, mental health services, court watch, research, education, and emotional support. They also provide attorney referrals for adult survivors.

Prevent Child Abuse America, 500 N. Michigan Ave. #200, Chicago, IL 60611; 312-663-3520; www .preventchildabuse.org

National organization committed to preventing child abuse in all its forms through education, research, public awareness, and advocacy. With a network of more than forty state chapters, they provide grassroots leadership on the local level. Their Healthy Families America program promotes positive parenting, child development, and health. Web site includes parenting tips, child abuse facts, and excellent links on adult survivor issues, children's legal rights, parenting, adoption, and more.

PROTECT, the National Association to PROTECT Children, 46 Haywood St., suite 315, Asheville, NC 28801; 828-350-9350; www.protect.org

America's first political lobby for child protection. This nonpartisan, pro-child, anticrime association has successfully used its national membership to force the passage of state-level legislation that protects children from abuse, exploitation, and neglect. The organization is now moving toward federal legislation.

Stop the Silence: Stop Child Sexual Abuse, Inc., P.O. Box 127, Glenn Dale, MD 20769; www.stopcsa .org.

Stop the Silence aims to prevent and treat child sexual abuse as well as address the relationship between sexual abuse and broader societal violence. The organization's approach includes support for direct services, advocacy, training of service providers, community education and outreach, policy

development, and research. It hosts the annual International Race to Stop the Silence.

LEGAL RESOURCES FOR SURVIVORS OF CHILD SEXUAL ABUSE

Organizations and Web Sites

Child Sexual Abuse Lawsuit Information, http:// csfwlaw.com/child-sexual-abuse-lawsuit.php

Web site of attorney G. Dana Scruggs includes the article "Should I Sue My Perpetrator?" It's a concise yet thorough discussion of the issues to consider, such as "Am I ready?" and "How will the process affect me?" as well as pertinent information about the law.

Legal Resources for Survivors of Sexual Abuse and Their Lawyers, www.smith-lawfirm.com

An impressive, comprehensive collection of information for survivors considering civil action against their perpetrators. Also very useful for attorneys.

Martindale-Hubbell Peer Review Ratings, www .martindale.com

National system by which lawyers and judges rate other lawyers on legal ability and professional ethics. While not all good attorneys are included or receive the highest rating, Martindale is still an established way to assess the ability and experience of a given attorney.

*National Crime Victim Bar Association, 2000 M St., NW, suite 480, Washington, D.C. 20036; for referral to an attorney, call 800-FYI-CALL; victim bar@ncvc.org; www.victimbar.org.

Provides free attorney referrals to crime victims in civil suits against perpetrators and other responsible parties. This network of attorneys, affiliated with the National Center for Victims of Crime, also provides technical support to attorneys who are representing crime victims in civil actions. Their booklet *Civil Justice for Victims of Crime*, available free on their Web site, provides a clear overview of the civil process.

Books

Crnich, Joseph and Kimberly. *Shifting the Burden of Truth: Suing Child Sexual Abusers: A Legal Guide for Survivors and Their Supporters,* Lake Oswego, OR: Recollex, 1992.

> This carefully compiled, user-friendly guide for adult survivors considering suing their perpetrators was published in 1992, so much of the technical information is outdated—although it still contains some useful information. Currently out of print but available.

Rix, Rebecca, ed. *Sexual Abuse Litigation: A Practical Resource for Attorneys, Clinicians, and Advocates.* Binghampton, NY: Haworth, 2000.

> Experienced child sexual abuse attorneys share their knowledge of all phases of the legal process, including tested strategies for dealing with expert witnesses and sustaining the admissibility of the survivor's testimony. Primarily for professionals.

Sanchez, Nora, ed. *The Bench Book for Judges.* Glenn Dale, MD: Stop the Silence, 2007. Available through www.stopcsa.org

> Landmark book written for the judicial and legal community addresses how the courts can best help children who have been physically or sexually abused by a family member. Abusive parents are frequently granted custody or visitation rights, which leads to further abuse. Since children's fates are often left to judges, they are in need of this kind of information to make the best decisions for the child.

SEXUAL ABUSE AND HEALING

SURVIVORS SPEAK OUT

This section includes memoirs and first-person accounts from both female and male survivors of child sexual abuse, as well as a few books written by people who have survived other traumas, such as war and imprisonment.

Alleyne, Vanessa. *There Were Times I Thought I Was Crazy: A Black Woman's Story of Incest.* Toronto: Sister Vision, 1997.

> A painfully honest memoir that tells how the denial of her family and community almost made her believe she was crazy, and ultimately, how she began to heal.

Angelou, Maya. *I Know Why the Caged Bird Sings.* New York: Bantam, 1980.

> A moving memoir of incest and its effects. A wonderful autobiography that celebrates life.

Aptheker, Bettina. *Intimate Politics: How I Grew Up Red, Fought for Free Speech, and Became a Feminist Rebel.* Emeryville, CA: Seal, 2006.

> A courageous story of one woman's struggle to speak her truth, no matter what the cost. Everyone interested in the ongoing work for peace, justice, and human rights will want to read this thoughtful memoir.

Armstrong, Louise. *Kiss Daddy Goodnight: Ten Years Later.* New York: Pocket, 1987.

> An updated version of the classic speak-out on father–daughter incest. Challenges us to consider why incest is still going on.

*Bass, Ellen, and Louise Thornton, eds. *I Never Told Anyone: Writings by Women Survivors of Child Sexual Abuse,* 2nd ed. New York: HarperCollins, 1991.

These personal accounts of childhood abuse will let you know you're not alone.

Berendzen, Richard. *Come Here: A Man Overcomes the Tragic Aftermath of Childhood Sexual Abuse.* New York: Villard Books, 1993.

A famous astronomer and academician tells the story of sexual abuse at the hands of his mother. He repressed all memory of the abuse for more than fifty years.

Brown, Cupcake. *A Piece of Cake: A Memoir.* New York: Three Rivers, 2007.

With strength and clarity, Brown shares the details of her harrowing childhood of abandonment, physical abuse, and rape; then later, prostitution, gangbanging, and drug addiction; and then eventual recovery and success. Inspiring and hopeful.

Camille, Pamela. *Step on a Crack, You Break Your Father's Back.* Pagosa Springs, CO: Freedom Lights, 1988.

A tough, funny, down-to-earth account of a young girl's journey from abuse to healing—and happiness. Good advice to survivors throughout.

Claman, Elizabeth, ed. *Writing Our Way Out of the Dark: An Anthology by Child Abuse Survivors.* Eugene, OR: Queen of Swords, 1995.

This strong collection of poems, stories, and essays is by women and men who are survivors of all kinds of abuse. Many fine writers are included.

*Cutting, Linda Katherine. *Memory Slips: A Memoir of Music and Healing.* New York: HarperCollins, 1997.

Cutting, a concert pianist, lost her ability to remember her music when she recovered memories of abuse. This book chronicles her struggle to regain herself and her music. A gripping, beautifully written memoir. Because music is so integral to this story, the audio version is particularly compelling.

Danica, Elly. *Don't: A Woman's Word.* Toronto: Ragweed, 1988.

A gripping account from a survivor of sexual abuse and child pornography. A very hard book to read. The sequel, *Beyond Don't: Dreaming Past the Dark* (1996) talks about what happened to Danica once she published *Don't* and became a public incest survivor. Includes a response to the backlash and an eloquent call to activism.

de Milly, Walter A. *In My Father's Arms: A True Story of Incest.* Madison: University of Wisconsin Press, 1999.

Sensitive, brave, and unforgettable memoir about de Milly's abuse by his prominent father, whom he confronts when his father is caught molesting a neighbor boy.

Doubiago, Sharon. *My Father's Love: Portrait of the Poet as a Girl.* Granada Hills, CA: Red Hen Press, 2008.

William Carlos Williams said, "Memory is accomplishment," and *My Father's Love*, is an accomplishment of memory, courage, and healing. Doubiago brings her poet's sensibility to the task of discovering and establishing her history. A powerful, heartbreaking book. See also her stunning poetry, *Love on the Streets: Selected and New Poems* (2008).

Fisher, Antwone. *Finding Fish: A Memoir.* New York: William Morrow, 2001.

Fisher's remarkable resilience inspires throughout this memoir of sexual and physical abuse in a foster home, homelessness, a tour in the navy, and success as a screenwriter.

Fraser, Sylvia. *My Father's House: A Memoir of Incest and Healing.* New York: Houghton Mifflin, 1988.

A stunning memoir—beautifully written, heartwrenching, and ultimately healing.

Goff-LaFontaine, Jan. *Women in Light and Shadow: Journeys from Abuse to Healing.* Reno: Creative Minds Press, 2005.

Intimate, beautiful photographs along with stories of forty survivors create a powerful portrait of healing from abuse in this coffee table–style book.

Hamilton, Barbara Small. *The Hidden Legacy: Uncovering, Confronting, and Healing Three Generations of Incest.* Fort Bragg, CA: Cypress House, 1993.
From the vantage point of her early seventies, Hamilton focuses an unflinching eye on the abuse that marred her childhood and the horrifying discovery that the tragic pattern was repeating for her children and grandchildren. Also available in audio.

Harrison, Kathryn. *The Kiss.* New York: Random House, 1997.
A memoir of Harrison's incestuous relationship with her father that led her to the brink of insanity.

*Hoffman, Richard. *Half the House: A Memoir*, 10th anniv. ed. Moorhead, MN: New Rivers, 2005.
Beautifully written memoir about a working-class childhood that included sexual abuse by a coach as well as other family tragedies. This memoir led to the arrest of his perpetrator thirty years later.

Holiman, Marjorie. *From Violence Toward Love: One Therapist's Journey.* New York: W.W. Norton, 1997.
A courageous, fascinating memoir by a therapist about her personal and professional experiences with interpersonal violence.

Holloway, Monica. *Driving with Dead People: A Memoir.* New York: Simon & Schuster, 2007.
Moving, wry, and authentic memoir about growing up in a family obsessed with death, sexual abuse by her father, and throughout it all a shining resilience that inspires hope.

Jacobs, Harriet. *Incidents in the Life of a Slave Girl.* Clayton, DE, Prestwick House, 2006. Originally published in 1861.

Jacobs's classic account of her life as a slave, the horrors she suffered, her escape and seven years in hiding, and ultimate freedom.

*King, Neal. *Speaking Our Truth: Voices of Courage and Healing for Male Survivors of Childhood Sexual Abuse.* New York: HarperCollins, 1995.
A moving collection of first-person testimonies. Currently out of print but available.

Lauck, Jennifer. *Still Waters.* New York: Pocket, 2001.
This second volume of Lauck's memoirs, is a riveting and inspiring account of survival and resilience. The first volume, *Blackbird*, is equally strong.

Matilda, Matt Bernstein Sycamore. *Dangerous Families: Queer Writing on Surviving.* New York: Harrington Park, 2004.
A gritty, provocative, diverse, and graphic anthology. There is much pain in these stories but also much courage and resilience. The authors' fierce determination to claim their own lives inspires confidence that we can do it, too.

*McLennan, Karen Jacobsen. *Nature's Ban: Women's Incest Literature.* Boston: Northeastern University Press, 1996.
An eloquent anthology from the twelfth century to the present. In an era in which women's writing about incest is still often trivialized by the literary establishment, this is a powerful achievement.

Mirikitani, Janice, ed. *Watch Out! We're Talking: Speaking Out About Incest and Abuse.* San Francisco: Glide Word Press, 1993.
Essays, poems, and life stories from women and men who've been sexually abused. Because many of the contributors, who were poor, homeless, or in recovery, were not comfortable with writing, their first-person accounts were drawn from a careful process of interview, transcription, and approval.

As a result, there are many important voices we usually don't hear.

Moran, Martin. *The Tricky Part: A Boy's Story of Sexual Trespass, a Man's Journey to Forgiveness.* Boston: Beacon, 2005.

Tender, powerful, and beautifully written memoir that centers around Moran's confrontation of his perpetrator thirty years later.

O'Brien, Tim. *The Things They Carried.* New York: Houghton-Mifflin, 1990.

This beautifully written memoir by a Vietnam veteran is a remarkable journey through post-traumatic stress disorder and the long-term impact of trauma. An excellent portrayal of how trauma is remembered and what healing requires.

Oufkir, Malika. *Stolen Lives: Twenty Years in a Desert Jail.* New York: Hyperion, 2002.

An amazing triumph-over-adversity memoir about the 20-year imprisonment of Oufkir's upper-class Moroccan family following the coup attempt by her father against King Hassan II.

*Perin, Margo, ed. *Only the Dead Can Kill: Stories from Jail.* Berkeley, CA: Community Works, 2006. Includes an audio CD. Available at www.margoperin.com; margo@margoperin.com.

Powerful, raw, and ultimately inspiring stories and poems by women and men incarcerated at the San Francisco County Jail. Edited by their writing teacher, the stories of sexual and other abuse reveal the courage of those facing their shame and pain for the first time. Don't miss the terrific CD of the contributors reading, rapping, and singing.

Peterson, Betsy. *Dancing with Daddy.* New York: Bantam, 1991.

A moving memoir of incest and recovery.

Portwood, Pamela, Michele Gorcey, and Peggy Sanders, eds. *Rebirth of Power: Overcoming the Effects of Sexual Abuse Through the Experiences of Others.* Racine, WI: Mother Courage, 1987.

A wonderfully creative collection of writings by sexual abuse survivors.

Ramsey, Martha. *Where I Stopped: Remembering Rape at Thirteen.* New York: Putnam, 1995.

Ramsey unravels and attempts to understand the impact of the rape she suffered as a teenager.

Randall, Margaret. *This Is About Incest.* Ithaca, NY: Firebrand, 1987.

Well known as a witness to Latin American progressive movements, Margaret Randall documents through words and photographs her own healing from her grandfather's incestuous assaults. *Memory Says Yes* follows with more poetry.

*Rhodes, Richard. *A Hole in the World: An American Boyhood,* 10th anniv. ed. Lawrence, KS: University Press of Kansas, 2000. First published in 1990 by Simon & Schuster.

A magnificent autobiography by a renowned scientist about horrible abuse in his childhood.

Silverman, Sue William. *Because I Remember Terror, Father, I Remember You.* Athens, GA: University of Georgia Press, 1996.

Award-winning memoir. Terrifying and heartening.

*Smith, Holly A. *Fire of the Five Hearts: A Memoir of Treating Incest.* New York: Brunner-Routledge, 2002.

Unflinchingly honest, heartbreaking, and ultimately inspiring memoir by the veteran leader of a Colorado sexual abuse task force that rescues abused children. It's also a beautiful book about the toll of one's calling and how we persevere, even minute by minute, when we want to give up.

Thomas, T. *Men Surviving Incest: A Male Survivor Shares the Process of Recovery.* Walnut Creek, CA: Launch Press, 1989.

A male survivor tells his story. Focuses on 12-step recovery.

Van Derbur, Marilyn. *Miss America by Day: Lessons Learned from Ultimate Betrayals and Unconditional Love.* Denver: Oak Hill Ridge, 2004.

A healing book that normalizes the symptoms of trauma and helps survivors accept themselves and continue on the road to recovery.

Walls, Jeannette. *The Glass Castle: A Memoir.* Riverside, NJ: Scribner, 2006.

A candid story of resilience in spite of terrible parenting, poverty, and abuse.

*Wisechild, Louise. *The Obsidian Mirror: Healing from Childhood Sexual Abuse,* 3rd ed. Emeryville, CA: Seal, 2003.

A powerful description of healing from the inside out. Vividly describes the process of remembering and connecting with inner children. Graphic descriptions of abuse, however; you may need support when reading this book. Also excellent are Wisechild's *The Mother I Carry* and a fascinating book about the creative process, *She Who Was Lost Is Remembered: Healing From Incest Through Creativity.*

ABOUT SEXUAL ABUSE AND HEALING

Bloom, Sandra. *Creating Sanctuary: Toward the Evolution of Sane Societies.* New York: Routledge, 1997.

A unique psychiatric program to treat survivors that not only helps the individual but also addresses the wounds in our society. A much-needed call to action.

Briere, John. *Therapy for Adults Molested as Children: Beyond Survival,* 2nd ed. New York: Springer, 1996.

A clinically solid book that is politically sensitive and empowering. Guidelines for running groups are included.

*Butler, Sandra. *Conspiracy of Silence: The Trauma of Incest,* updated ed. Volcano, CA: Volcano Press, 1996. First published 1978.

A classic. Feminist analysis of child sexual abuse.

*Courtois, Christine. *Healing the Incest Wound: Adult Survivors in Therapy.* New York: W.W. Norton, 1996. First published 1988; new edition, 2008.

A feminist psychologist writes a top-notch guidebook for therapists on healing.

*de Becker, Gavin. *The Gift of Fear: Survival Signals That Protect Us From Violence.* Boston: Little, Brown, 1997.

Written for a general audience, this helpful and compelling text is nonetheless validating for survivors who trust, or want permission to trust, the intuition that warns them about impending danger. Also useful are techniques for distinguishing between imminent danger and triggers.

Ernst, Sheila, and Lucy Goodwin. *In Our Own Hands: A Book of Self-Help Therapy,* reissue ed. London, England: Women's Press, Limited, 1997.

Guidelines for starting a self-help group and for picking a therapist. Feminist analysis of encounter groups, bodywork, massage, dance, psychodrama, gestalt, regression, and dream work. Practical exercises for each.

*Farley, Melissa, ed. *Prostitution, Trafficking, and Traumatic Stress.* Binghamton, NY: Haworth, 2004.

Riveting and groundbreaking. Thirty-two contributors offer clinical examples, analysis, and original research that counteract common myths about the harmlessness of prostitution. Documents the violence that runs throughout all types of prostitution and shows that prostitutes often have a lengthy history of trauma, including childhood sexual abuse and rape. Farley's Web site, www.prostitutionresearch.com, lists resources for those leaving prostitution and contains articles about prostitution, trafficking, activism, and more.

Finkelhor, David. *Sexually Victimized Children*. New York: Free Press, 1979.

> Results of a landmark study on sex between adults and children. Combines survivors' accounts with data in a readable style. *Child Sexual Abuse: New Theory and Research* and *A Sourcebook on Child Sexual Abuse* are among his follow-up books.

*Fontes, Lisa Aronson. *Child Abuse and Culture: Working with Diverse Families*. New York: Guilford, 2005.

> Practical ideas for making child welfare programs, particularly child protection services, more effective and equitable in their work with families from diverse backgrounds. Fontes's *Sexual Abuse in Nine North American Cultures: Treatment and Prevention* (Sage, 1995) is a fascinating exploration of the role culture plays in allowing, preventing, and treating sexual abuse.

Friedman, Sara Ann. *Who Is There to Help Us: How the System Fails Sexually Exploited Girls in the United States*. Brooklyn, NY: ECPAT-USA, 2005.

> Impressive report by an international group that fights child trafficking that takes on the plight of American child prostitutes. Their cause still faces resistance, often by a law-enforcement system that fails to acknowledge that they are victims, not criminals. And many have a history of sexual abuse at home. Available in print or for a free viewing at www.ecpatusa.org/documents.

Gil, Eliana. *Treatment of Adult Survivors of Childhood Abuse*. Walnut Creek, CA: Launch Press, 1988.

> Excellent guidelines for therapists for working with survivors, including memory work, group therapy, dissociation, and post-traumatic stress disorder. See also Gil's other books, *Helping Abused and Traumatized Children* (2006), *Systemic Treatment of Families Who Abuse* (1995), and *Treating Abused Adolescents* (1996).

Gonsiorek, John, ed. *A Guide to Psychotherapy with Gay and Lesbian Clients*. Binghamton, NY: Haworth Press, 1985.

> A landmark work for therapists that provides insight into the special needs gay men and lesbians bring to the therapy setting.

*Herman, Judith. *Trauma and Recovery: The Aftermath of Violence—From Domestic Abuse to Political Terror*, 2nd ed. New York: Basic Books, 1997.

> A brilliant and compassionate synthesis of the impact of trauma, including the experiences of battered women, sexually abused children, war veterans, and prisoners of war. Herman's *Father–Daughter Incest* (1981) was one of the first to deal with incest from a feminist perspective.

Levenkron, Steven, with Abby Levenkron. *Stolen Tomorrows: Understanding and Treating Women's Childhood Sexual Abuse*. New York: Norton, 2007.

> Helpful, well-written text for therapists and survivors that draws the connections between childhood abuse and later behaviors, such as addictions, cutting, and anorexia.

Lightfoot-Klein, Hanny. *Children's Genitals Under the Knife: Social Imperatives, Secrecy and Shame*, 2nd ed. (Originally published as *Secret Wounds*.) North Charleston, SC: Booksurge, 2007.

> Third of a trilogy about the horrors of genital mutilation. Lightfoot-Klein's earlier books were *Prisoners of Ritual* and *A Woman's Odyssey*.

Masson, Jeffrey Moussaieff. *The Assault on Truth: Freud's Suppression of the Seduction Theory*. New York: Ballantine, 2003. First published in 1984.

> This book challenges Freud's seduction theory; it sent shock waves through the psychoanalytic community.

*Miller, Alice. *Thou Shalt Not Be Aware: Society's Betrayal of the Child*, 2nd ed. New York: Farrar, Straus and Giroux, 1998.

Miller brilliantly rips apart the Oedipal theory and shows that sexual abuse is real. Required reading for every therapist. Miller has written a number of other excellent books, including *The Drama of the Gifted Child* (1981), *The Truth Will Set You Free* (2001), *For Your Own Good* (1983), *Banished Knowledge* (1990), *The Untouched Key* (1991), and *Breaking Down the Wall of Silence* (1997).

*Mollica, Richard, M.D. *Healing Invisible Wounds: Paths to Hope and Recovery in a Violent World*. New York: Harcourt, 2006.

Drawing on thirty years of work with trauma and torture survivors from all over the world, Mollica lets their stories reveal our capacity for self-healing. An important and valuable book for the medical community as well as survivors.

*Naparstek, Belleruth. *Invisible Heroes: Survivors of Trauma and How They Heal*. New York: Bantam, 2004. www.healthjourneys.com.

A well-written, groundbreaking book about healing from trauma. Comprehensively explores the nature of trauma and its assaults on the mind, body, and spirit. Explains why and how imagery is so effective at healing trauma and offers a program of guided imagery to promote healing. Naparstek's Web site offers beautiful recordings of guided imageries for healing trauma and many other health conditions.

Oz, Sheri, and Sarah-Jane Ogiers. *Overcoming Childhood Sexual Trauma: A Guide to Breaking Through the Wall of Fear for Practitioners and Survivors*. New York: Haworth, 2006.

An engaging collaboration between a therapist and her ex-client that enables the reader to gain a sense of the experience of both.

Robinson, Lori S. *I Will Survive: The African-American Guide to Healing from Sexual Assault and Abuse*. Emeryville, CA: Seal, 2003.

An insightful, powerful book about sexual violence and healing. Explores sexual violence in the context of American violence, particularly the legacy of slavery. Addresses self-care; the legal system; spiritual, sexual, and emotional healing; and more.

*Rush, Florence. *The Best Kept Secret: Sexual Abuse of Children*. Columbus, OH: McGraw Hill Education, 1991. First published in 1980.

A lucid feminist analysis of child sexual abuse from biblical times to the present. Rush was the first to expose the Freudian cover-up.

Russell, Diana E.H. *Behind Closed Doors in White South Africa: Incest Survivors Tell Their Stories*. New York: St. Martin's Press, 1997.

Personal accounts as told by the survivors, with analyses of important incest-related issues. Compares the exploitation of girls by white male relatives with the exploitation of black people. Russell's first book, *The Secret Trauma: Incest in the Lives of Girls and Women* (1986), was the first to present extensive research on the prevalence of incest.

Salter, Anna. *Transforming Trauma: A Guide to Treating Sexual Abuse*. Newbury Park, CA: Sage, 1995.

Extremely well researched and astute. Her prior book, *Treating Child Sex Offenders and Victims* (1988), is also informative and excellent.

Sue, Derald Wing, and David Sue. *Counseling the Culturally Diverse*, 4th ed. New York: Wiley, 2003.

The new edition of this resource to help counselors overcome obstacles in treating clients from backgrounds different from their own presents a more expansive definition of mulitculturalism. Includes new chapters on biracial/multiracial populations, the elderly, gay/lesbian, the physically challenged, and more, as well as updated chapters on Native Americans, Asians, African-Americans, and Hispanics.

GUIDEBOOKS FOR HEALING

Bear, Euan, with Peter Dimock. *Adults Molested as Children: A Survivor's Manual for Women and Men.* Brandon, VT: Safer Society Press, 1988.

Excellent. A simple, straightforward approach to healing for both men and women.

Blume, E. Sue. *Secret Survivors: Uncovering Incest and Its Aftereffects in Women.* New York: Ballantine, 1998. First published in 1990 by Wiley.

Clearly delineates the long-term effects of incest. Can help survivors discover that their experiences and reactions make sense.

Carnes, Patrick. *The Betrayal Bond: Breaking Free of Exploitive Relationships.* Deerfield Beach, FL: Health Communications, 1997.

Insightful, challenging, and compassionate exploration of how the bond between victimizer and victim is formed, maintained, and replicated—and how we can break the pattern and heal. Carnes is the author of many 12-step recovery titles, including *Out of the Shadows*, *A Gentle Path Through the Twelve Steps*, and *Don't Call it Love.*

*Casarjian, Robin. *Houses of Healing: A Prisoner's Guide to Inner Power and Freedom.* Boston: Lionheart Foundation, 1995.

An excellent, helpful, and caring guidebook that offers the opportunity for survivors in prison to transform patterns of self-defeating behaviors. A follow-up, *Power Source: Taking Charge of Your Own Life*, written with child psychologist Bethany Casarjian in 2002, is an excellent book on emotional healing for at-risk youth.

Cori, Jasmin Lee. *Healing from Trauma: A Survivor's Guide to Understanding Your Symptoms and Reclaiming Your Life.* New York: Marlowe & Co., 2007.

An excellent resource written by a survivor and therapist. Clear, accessible, hopeful, and supportive.

BEGINNING BOOKS

*Bass, Ellen, and Laura Davis. *Beginning to Heal: A First Book for Men and Women Who Were Sexually Abused as Children*, revised ed. New York: HarperCollins, 2003.

An easy-to-read introduction to the healing process based on *The Courage to Heal.* Especially useful for new readers, those with limited English, teens, and anyone needing a shorter, less intensive beginning. Also on audiotape.

Daugherty, Lynn B. *Why Me? Help for Victims of Child Sexual Abuse (even if they are adults now).* 4th ed. Roswell, NM: Cleanan Press, 2007.

A good, simple beginning book for child, teen, and adult survivors.

Gil, Eliana. *Outgrowing the Pain: A Book for and About Adults Abused as Children.* New York: Dell, 1988.

A good overview of the healing process for all kinds of abuse. Cartoon illustrations and simple, clear text. A helpful place to begin. Available in Spanish through Launch Press at www.selfesteemshop.com.

*Davis, Laura. *The Courage to Heal Workbook.* New York: HarperCollins, 1990.

Diverse in-depth exercises for women and men. Designed for both individual survivors and groups. Emphasizes skills in building your support system and learning to take care of yourself. Includes exercises that correlate with the stages of healing outlined in *The Courage to Heal*, as well as sexual healing.

Engel, Beverly. *The Right to Innocence: Healing the Trauma of Child Sexual Abuse.* New York: Ballantine, 1991.

A recovery guide for adult survivors. Full of sensible, nurturing ideas for healing.

Huber, Cheri. *There Is Nothing Wrong with You: Going Beyond Self-Hate.* Murphy, CA: Keep it Simple, 2001.

Wonderful, groundbreaking book about where self-hatred comes from, its many insidious forms, and how to use meditation to manage it. The follow-up, *When You're Falling, Dive* (2003), answers questions raised by the first. Huber has written nineteen books on subjects such as depression, fear, and unconditional acceptance.

Katherine, Anne. *Boundaries: Where You End and I Begin.* New York: Simon & Schuster, 1991.

Explains what healthy boundaries are, how to recognize violations, and how to protect yourself. Straightforward and practical.

King, Ruth. *Healing Rage: Women Making Inner Peace Possible.* Berkeley, CA: Sacred Spaces Press, 2004.

Insightful, spiritually focused guidebook for recognizing and using the power of rage as a vehicle for healing.

Laidlaw, Toni Ann, Cheryl Malmo et al. *Healing Voices: Feminist Approaches to Therapy with Women.* San Francisco: Jossey-Bass, 1992.

An excellent, diverse collection of essays on a variety of empowering healing techniques, including group therapy, native storytelling, dream analysis, bodywork, imagery, and hypnosis. Strategies for working with sexual abuse, compulsive eating, violence in native communities, adult children of alcoholics, and more. Currently out of print but available.

Matsakis, Aphrodite. *I Can't Get Over It: A Handbook for Trauma Survivors*, 2nd ed. Oakland, CA: New Harbinger, 1996.

A comprehensive, step-by-step, and effective guide through the process of recovery from trauma.

Normalizes the reactions to trauma and offers real hope for healing. Matsakis is the author of many excellent books on trauma and recovery.

Miller, Dusty. *Your Surviving Spirit: A Spiritual Workbook for Coping with Trauma.* Oakland, CA: New Harbinger, 2003.

This book looks through the pain of trauma to the resilience and capacity for spiritual strength that survivors especially possess. Miller is a survivor and author of several books on trauma and recovery, including *Women Who Hurt Themselves* (1994) and *Addictions and Trauma Recovery* (2001).

Rafanello, Donna. *Can't Touch My Soul: A Guide for Lesbian Survivors of Child Sexual Abuse.* Los Angeles: Alyson, 2004.

Very useful, supportive book that shares the experience of the author and the sixty women she interviewed about every aspect of healing from child sexual abuse. Written about and for lesbians, but the insights would be helpful for all survivors. Contains a resource guide and bibliography.

*Rosenbloom, Dena, and Mary Beth Williams. *Life After Trauma: A Workbook for Healing.* New York: Guilford, 1999.

A helpful, hopeful, and healing book for survivors and those who work with them. Includes a wealth of information about sorting through beliefs and reactions, ways of coping, how to discern safety and regain control in your life, issues of trust and intimacy, and healing for the long term.

Schiraldi, Glenn. *Post-Traumatic Stress Disorder Sourcebook: A Guide to Healing, Recovery, and Growth.* New York: McGraw-Hill, 2000.

This clear, helpful guide normalizes the experience of post-traumatic stress disorder by helping trauma survivors understand their symptoms, and then offers techniques for managing them. Also includes a wide variety of treatment options.

Schmidt, K. Louise. *Transforming Abuse: Nonviolent Resistance and Recovery*. Philadelphia: New Society, 1995.

A strong, respectful stance that offers a theory and method of recovery grounded in the connections between feminism and nonviolence. A challenging, inspiring book. Currently out of print but available.

*Stone, Robin. *No Secrets, No Lies: How Black Families Can Heal from Sexual Abuse*. New York: Broadway, 2004.

An important and compassionate guide by a survivor who illuminates the cultural taboos and dynamics that have kept survivors silent—such as fear of betraying the family, distrust of police, the legacy of enslavement—and then with moving and courageous survivor stories and expert advice shows the path of healing.

*Vermilyea, Elizabeth. *Growing Beyond Survival: A Self-Help Toolkit for Managing Traumatic Stress*. Baltimore, MD: Sidran, 2000.

Encouraging and helpful workbook that provides trauma survivors with a wealth of practical coping strategies to take control of and de-escalate their trauma-related symptoms. Can be used independently or with a therapist.

Williams, Mary Beth, and Soili Poijula. *The PTSD Workbook: Simple, Effective Techniques for Overcoming Traumatic Stress Symptoms*. Oakland: New Harbinger, 2002.

Very useful, comprehensive set of exercises for survivors and professionals. Includes exercises on identifying the trauma, dealing with flashbacks, physical symptoms, dissociation, trust, self-image, finding meaning, and more.

FOR MALE SURVIVORS

Organizations and Web Sites

Hopper, Jim. Sexual Abuse of Males: Prevalence, Possible Lasting Effects & Resources. www.jimhopper.com/male-ab

A helpful and comprehensive source of information and resources for male survivors.

MaleSurvivor: The National Organization on Male Sexual Victimization (NOMSV). www.malesurvivor.org.

Organizes national conferences and, through its Web site, provides a wealth of information, resources, and support for male survivors.

Books

Memoirs and collections of stories by male survivors are listed in the "Survivors Speak Out" section (p. 530).

*Dorais, Michel. *Don't Tell: The Sexual Abuse of Boys*. Montreal, Canada: McGill-Queen's University Press, 2002.

Compassionate, comprehensive analysis alternates with extended first-person survivor stories in this helpful, powerful, and heartbreaking book. Translated from French.

Estrada, Hank. *Recovery for Male Victims of Child Abuse*. Santa Fe, NM: Red Rabbit Press, 1993.

An informative and inspiring interview with a male survivor that includes an extensive resource bibliography of articles, books, and periodicals regarding male victimization and healing.

Gartner, Richard. *Beyond Betrayal: Taking Charge of Your Life after Boyhood Sexual Abuse*. Hoboken, NJ: Wiley, 2005.

Accessible and compassionate. Clearly lays out the healing process for men, providing the necessary tools to reclaim their lives. Gartner also wrote a comprehensive guide for clinicians, *Betrayed as Boys: Psychodynamic Treatment of Sexually Abused Men* (Guilford, 1999).

Grubman-Black, Stephen. *Broken Boys/Mending Men: Recovery from Child Sexual Abuse.* Caldwell, NJ: Blackburn, 2002. First published in 1990.

> Full of firsthand accounts of men sexually abused as children, this healing book written by a survivor is simple, clear, and helpful.

Hunter, Mic. *Abused Boys: The Neglected Victims of Sexual Abuse. Healing for the Man Molested as a Child.* New York: Fawcett, 1990.

> Solid, well researched. The follow-up, *The Sexually Abused Male*, is an excellent two-volume collection of professional articles.

Isensee, Rik. *Reclaiming Your Life: The Gay Man's Guide to Recovery from Abuse, Addictions, and Self-defeating Behavior*, 3rd ed., Lincoln, NE: Backinprint.com, 2005. First published in 1991 as *Growing Up Gay in a Dysfunctional Family.*

> Validates how growing up gay in a homophobic society and being abused as a child create a double trauma and offers specific suggestions for working through the problems involved. Warm, intelligent, and sure to be of real help.

*Lew, Mike. *Victims No Longer: The Classic Guide for Men Recovering from Incest*, 2nd ed. New York: HarperCollins, 2004. First published in 1988.

> Solid, clear, warm information and encouragement for men healing from child sexual abuse. This comprehensive, groundbreaking book was the first to talk about men who were abused as survivors, not just potential perpetrators. It helped launch the male survivor movement. In his second book, *Leaping Upon the Mountain: Men Proclaiming Victory over Sexual Child Abuse* (1999), survivors share their insights about what

resources, strategies, and practices have been important to their healing.

Miletski, Hani. *Mother–Son Incest: The Unthinkable Broken Taboo.* Brandon, VT: Safer Society Press, 1995.

> This booklet presents an overview of the research on mother–son incest.

Sonkin, Daniel. *Wounded Boys, Heroic Men: A Man's Guide to Recovering from Child Abuse.* Cincinnati, OH: Adams Media, 1998.

> A simple, straightforward guide for men who were hurt as children. Especially good for men not versed in the language of feelings or recovery.

Wright, Leslie Bailey, and Mindy B. Loiselle. *Back On Track: Boys Dealing With Sexual Abuse.* Orwell, VT: Safer Society Press, 1997.

> Excellent and simply written. Helps boys (age 10 and up) recognize their feelings and take steps toward healing.

RESILIENCE

Coffey, Rebecca. *Unspeakable Truths and Happy Endings: Human Cruelty and the New Trauma Therapy.* Lutherville, MD: Sidran Press, 1998.

> An intelligent discussion of trauma therapy that focuses on facilitating a positive outcome as it explores the similarities among diverse types of traumatic experiences.

Foster, Rick, and Greg Hicks. *How We Choose to Be Happy: The 9 Choices of Extremely Happy People—Their Secrets, Their Stories.* New York: Penguin, 1999.

> Laura adores this book because it is fascinating, diverse, surprising, and inspirational. According to the people the authors interviewed, happiness does not depend on money, material possessions, an easy childhood, or a lack of adversity in life.

Grossman, Frances, Alexandra B. Cook, Selin S. Kepkep, and Karestan C. Koenen. *With the Phoenix Rising: Lessons from Ten Resilient Women Who Overcame the Trauma of Childhood Sexual Abuse.* San Francisco: Jossey-Bass, 1999.

> The authors conducted extensive interviews with ten survivors, with diverse backgrounds and abuse histories, about the "keys to resilience" that enable survivors to thrive. Written with professionals in mind.

Higgins, Gina O'Connell. *Resilient Adults: Overcoming a Cruel Past.* San Francisco: Jossey-Bass, 1996.

> An inspiring study of forty adults who came from families judged to be "severely, extremely or catastrophically stressful," who went on to have stable, successful love relationships, as well as positive experiences with work and parenting.

*Rhodes, Ginger, and Richard Rhodes. *Trying to Get Some Dignity: Stories of Triumph Over Childhood Abuse.* New York: William Morrow, 1996.

> After the publication of his gripping memoir, *A Hole in the World*, Richard Rhodes corresponded with hundreds of survivors of childhood abuse. He and his wife, Ginger, chose twenty to interview in depth. Filled with uplifting accounts of creative, original strategies for survival.

*Sanford, Linda. *Strong at the Broken Places: Building Resiliency in Survivors of Trauma.* Holyoke, MA: NEARI, 2005. First published in 1990 by Random House.

> Back in print, this classic studies transformation in the lives of twenty survivors. Focuses on the positive lives survivors can create out of the devastation of their childhoods. Empowering and empathetic.

Seligman, Martin. *Learned Optimism: How to Change Your Mind and Your Life*, reprint ed. New York: Vintage, 2006.

> Drawing on more than twenty years of clinical research to demonstrate how optimism enhances the quality of life, Seligman offers many simple techniques to show how anyone can learn the skills of optimism and undo habits of pessimism and resultant depression. Dr. Seligman also wrote *Authentic Happiness*.

THE BODY'S ROLE IN HEALING

Braddock, Carolyn J. *Body Voices: Using the Power of Breath, Sound and Movement to Heal and Create New Boundaries.* Berkeley, CA: Page Mill Press, 1997.

> An approach to integrating body, mind, and spirit for survivors. Includes guided sessions in which you learn to listen to the voices of your body to unlock feelings.

*Clarke, David. *They Can't Find Anything Wrong! 7 Keys to Understanding, Treating and Healing Stress Illness.* Boulder, CO: Sentient, 2007.

> Written by a physician, this fascinating book for physicians and patients illuminates the connections between stress and illness. Clarke's winning storytelling style provides subtle suggestions as well as concrete steps to take toward healing.

Duff, Kat. *The Alchemy of Illness.* New York: Bell Tower, 2000. First published in 1993 by Knopf.

> A brilliant, beautifully written treatise on the meaning and experience of illness. Among other things, Duff writes about the memories the body holds as well as the relationship between her diagnosis of chronic fatigue and immune dysfunction syndrome and her process of recalling the abuse she suffered as a very young child.

Eckberg, Maryanna. *Victims of Cruelty: Somatic Psychotherapy in the Treatment of Posttraumatic Stress Disorder.* Berkeley, CA: North Atlantic, 2000.

> Part personal testimony, part professional book shows how people can heal after extreme trauma. Illuminates the value of somatic therapies for sufferers of post-traumatic stress disorder.

BODY-BASED THERAPIES AND GROUPS

American Dance Therapy Association. www
.adta.org

> General information about dance/movement
> therapy, publications, and research.

Continuum. www.continuummovement.com

> Uses movement, the breath, sound, and mean-
> ing to strengthen communication within our-
> selves, with others, and with the world.

The Foundation for Human Enrichment. www
.traumahealing.com

> A nonprofit educational and research organi-
> zation dedicated to the healing and prevention
> of trauma. Provides training in Somatic Expe-
> riencing as well as outreach to underserved
> populations and victims of violence, war, and
> natural disasters.

Generative Somatics. www.somaticsandtrauma
.org

> Uses an integrative approach of somatic
> awareness, bodywork, and somatic practices
> to move from managing traumatic symptoms
> to transforming trauma and our lives.

The Hakomi Institute. www.hakomiinstitute.com

> A body-centered, somatic psychotherapy.
> Through the body's habitual patterns, uncon-
> scious core material is allowed to emerge safely
> into consciousness, where it can then be re-
> evaluated.

International Institute for Bioenergetic Analysis.
www.bioenergetic-therapy.com

> Combines work with the body and the mind to
> help people resolve their emotional problems
> and realize more of their potential for pleasure
> and joy.

**International Somatic Movement Education and
Therapy Association.** www.ismeta.org

> Through advocacy and their registry of profes-
> sional practitioners, the association promotes
> high standards and professionalism.

Jin Shin Jyutsu, Inc. www.jinshinjyutsu.com

> An ancient Asian art that was rediscovered in
> the early 1900s. The hands are placed on the
> body to redirect or unblock the flow of energy
> along its pathways.

The Lomi Foundation. www.lomi.org/founda
tion/foundation.html

> Counselors practice a somatic approach to
> psychotherapy by focusing on the body, mind,
> and spirit of the person.

The Rosen Institute. www.rosenmethod.org

> Practitioners use hands that listen rather than
> manipulate and focus on chronic muscle ten-
> sion. As relaxation occurs and the breath
> deepens, unconscious feelings, attitudes, and
> memories may emerge.

**Women of Courage Program, Outward Bound
Wilderness Group Programs,** 910 Jackson St.,
Golden, CO 80401; 888-837-5211; www.outward
boundwilderness.org

**Women of Courage Program, Canadian Out-
ward Bound,** 996 Chetwynd Rd., RR #2, Burk's
Falls, ON P0A 1C0; 888-688-9273, 705-382-5454;
www.outwardbound.ca

> These wilderness courses for survivors of sexual
> assault, incest, and domestic violence provide
> opportunities for survivors to build self-confi-
> dence and self-esteem, practice safe risk-tak-
> ing, get in touch with their bodies, and develop
> trust and support within a group. Financial as-
> sistance available. The U.S. Women of Courage
> Program isn't on their Web site, so call or write
> for information.

Hunter, Mic, and Jim Struve. *The Ethical Use of Touch in Psychotherapy*. Thousand Oaks, CA: Sage, 1998.

> Hunter argues that touch—a basic human need—is intrinsic to the healing process. He asks therapists to reexamine prohibitions against touch and offers guidelines for its integration into talk therapy.

Levine, Peter. *Healing Trauma: A Pioneering Program for Restoring the Wisdom of Your Body*. Boulder, CO: Sounds True, 2005. Book with CD.

> Integrated book and CD present insightful, compassionate exercises for healing trauma. Levine believes that human beings, like all animals, have a deep and instinctual capacity to overcome traumatic experiences and that our body holds the key. *Sexual Healing: Transforming the Sacred Wound* is an earlier audio that is not only about sex but also about body-based healing in general. By the author of *Waking the Tiger, Healing Trauma*, and *It Won't Hurt Forever*.

Miller, Alice. *The Body Never Lies: The Lingering Effects of Hurtful Parenting*. New York: Norton, 2005.

> A fascinating book that shows how the denial of our true emotional reactions to parental mistreatment leads to illness in adulthood. Also argues that widely held beliefs in the necessity of forgiveness and honoring our parents continue the harm.

Palmer, Wendy. *The Intuitive Body: Aikido as a Clairsentient Practice*. Berkeley, CA: North Atlantic, 1994.

> Valuable, insightful, and practical guide. Teaches how to become more aware of the body and trust its wisdom.

Radomsky, Nellie A. *Lost Voices: Women, Chronic Pain, and Abuse*. Binghamton, NY: Haworth Press, 1995.

> An enlightening exploration into the roots of chronic pain and healing by a family physician. Should be required reading for every doctor and a valuable resource for sufferers of chronic pain.

Rothschild, Babette. *The Body Remembers: The Psychophysiology of Trauma and Trauma Treatment*. New York: Norton, 2000.

> This important book bridges the gap between verbal and body-oriented therapies. Explains the importance of "body memories" in processing trauma and discusses many ways professionals can help clients process them. Rothschild also wrote *The Body Remembers Casebook* (2003).

Scaer, Robert. *The Body Bears the Burden: Trauma, Dissociation, and Disease*. Binghamton, NY: Haworth, 2001.

> Explains the way trauma impacts the brain and can affect muscles, digestion, and other bodily systems. The medical language may be a barrier, but the information is empowering to survivors with unusual physical symptoms no one can explain. Scaer extends this work into a broader definition of trauma in *The Trauma Spectrum: Hidden Wounds and Human Resiliency* (2005).

Shapiro, Francine, and Margot Silk Forrest. *EMDR: The Breakthrough Therapy for Overcoming Anxiety, Stress, and Trauma*. New York: Basic, 2004. First published 1997 by HarperCollins.

> A fascinating book of case studies that illustrate the transformations made possible by EMDR (eye movement desensitization and reprocessing). See also Shapiro's *Eye Movement Desensitization and Reprocessing (EMDR): Basic Principles, Protocols, and Procedures*, 2nd ed. (Guilford, 2001) and *Handbook of EMDR and Family Therapy Processes* (Wiley, 2007).

HEALING THROUGH CREATIVITY: WRITING, ART, AND MORE

*Adams, Kathleen. *Journal to the Self: Twenty-Two Paths to Personal Growth*. New York: Warner Books, 1990.

> A gem for those of us who "get it out on paper" when we're searching to find our heart. Her excel-

lent follow-up, *The Way of the Journal: A Journal Therapy Workbook for Healing*, 2nd ed. (1998), is specifically designed for sexual abuse survivors and for people diagnosed with dissociative disorders.

Cameron, Julia. *The Artist's Way: A Spiritual Path to Higher Creativity*, 10th anniv. ed. New York: J.P. Tarcher, 2002.

This practical, personal guide offers a simple twelve-week program to recover your creative energy, even if it's long lost.

Capacchione, Lucia. *The Art of Emotional Healing*. Boston: Shambhala, 2001.

A comprehensive, inspiring guide for exploring emotions through the arts of drawing, dancing, writing, collage-making, drumming, and more. Capacchione has a number of other excellent books, including *The Picture of Health, Recovery of Your Inner Child, The Power of Your Other Hand, The Creative Journal for Parents*, and more.

The Clothesline Project, c/o 138 Tubman Road, Brewster, MA 02631; www.clotheslineproject.org.

A display of shirts created by survivors of violence or their loved ones. Each shirt tells a woman's story through words, pictures, and other decorative art, bearing witness to violence against women and its impact on society. Simply seeing the Clothesline can be validating for a woman who feels isolated and ashamed. More than 750 Clothesline projects now stretch from its birthplace in Hyannis, MA, across the United States and Canada to England, Taiwan, Germany, and Australia.

*Cohen, Barry M., Mary-Michola Barnes, and Anita B. Rankin. *Managing Traumatic Stress Through Art: Drawing From the Center*. Lutherville, MD: Sidran Press, 1995.

Accessible art exercises that can help with an array of issues such as self-care, emotional health, and present-day life skills. Excellent for survivors and therapists.

E., Nancy. *Once I Was a Child and There Was Much Pain: A Glimpse into the Soul of an Incest Survivor*. San Francisco: Frog in the Well Press, 1988.

A breathtaking collection of drawings by a survivor.

Edwards, Betty. *The New Drawing on the Right Side of the Brain*, 2nd. ed. New York: Tarcher/Putnam, 1999. First published in 1979.

A classic on developing your creativity. A friendly, readable companion. *Drawing on the Artist Within: A Guide to Innovation, Imagination, and Creativity* (1987) is equally worthwhile.

Goldberg, Natalie. *Wild Mind*. New York: Bantam, 1990.

A remarkably wise and lovely follow-up to her underground Zen writing classic, *Writing Down the Bones. Living Color: A Writer Paints Her World* (1997) is a beautifully illustrated, inspiring book about Goldberg's development as a painter.

Hopkins, Khristine. *SURVIVORS: Experiences of Childhood Sexual Abuse and Healing*. Berkeley, CA: Celestial Arts, 1994.

This award-winning exhibit of hand-colored photographs and text consists of visual metaphors that express the experiences of women members of a survivors' group. Currently out of print but available.

*Metzger, Deena. *Writing for Your Life: A Guide and Companion to the Inner Worlds*. San Francisco: HarperSanFrancisco, 1992.

A deep and valuable book by an extraordinary life teacher.

Mines, Stephanie. *Sexual Abuse/Sacred Wound: Transforming Deep Trauma*. Barrytown, NY: Barrytown Ltd., 1996.

A rich guide for healing through the expressive arts. Abounds with creative suggestions and a wonderful sense of possibility.

Pennebaker, James W. *Writing to Heal: A Guided Journal for Recovering from Trauma & Emotional Upheaval.* Oakland, CA: New Harbinger, 2004.

> A truly hopeful book that makes a strong case for the power of expressive writing to heal, and then guides the way.

*Reis, Patricia, and Susan Snow. *The Dreaming Way: Dreamwork and Art for Remembering and Recovery.* Wilmette, IL: Chiron, 2000.

> Gorgeous, unique two-year collaboration between a therapist and her client, both of whom are artists. The images are beautiful, the dreamwork powerful, as they plumb the landscape of trauma, memory, and healing.

SARK. *Succulent Wild Woman: Dancing With Your Wonder-Full Self!,* New York: Simon & Schuster, 1997.

> SARK's books invite you to celebrate yourself, to enjoy and experience the woman you are right now, with no improvements. Delightful. See also *Living Juicy* (1994), *Inspiration Sandwich* (1992), and *SARK's New Creative Companion* (2005).

Simonds, Susan L. *Bridging the Silence: Nonverbal Modalities in the Treatment of Adult Survivors of Childhood Sexual Abuse.* New York: W.W. Norton, 1994.

> A wealth of practical and theoretical information on integrating creative art therapies into healing. Currently out of print but available.

*Wisechild, Louise. *She Who Was Lost Is Remembered: Healing from Incest Through Creativity.* Emeryville, CA: Seal, 1991.

> A wonderful, inspiring anthology that presents the work of more than thirty visual artists, musicians, and writers, along with essays by each contributor on how she used creativity to heal.

HEALING MUSIC

*Baez, Joan. *Play Me Backwards.* Virgin Records. www.joanbaez.com

> The title song—about sadistic ritual abuse—is stunning. Joan Baez at her best.

Day, Nancy. *Survivor.* www.nancydaymusic.com

> Honest songs about abuse and recovery. Also, listen to "Memory Lane" on her new CD *Born to Live*—a laugh-out-loud spoof on the False Memory Syndrome Foundation (FMS).

Fix, Amy. *Spoon.* The Orchard. www.amyfix.com

> Songs about healing from sexual trauma are mixed with romps. Especially like the haunting, moving "Who Will Hold Me" and the hilarious "Closet."

Huber, Ruth, and Kate McLennan. *Trailblazers.* www.katemclennan.com

> Uplifting songs for adult children.

Hunter, Tom. *Bits and Pieces.* The Song Growing Co. www.tomhunter.com

> Includes a lullaby for grown-ups, "Rock Me to Sleep," that survivors love (and love to have sung to them).

*Ian, Janis. *Breaking Silence.* Columbia Records. www.janisian.com

> Title cut is one of the best on the subject. Inspiring.

May, Judith. *Heal the Broken Wing.* Yes You May! Music, P.O. Box 31539, San Francisco, CA 94131-0539.

> Deep emotion and beautiful music. Also, *Rising Again*, a celebration of the Divine.

*Mountain Goats, the. "The Sunset Tree." 4AD.

> With a humor born of pain, and a rage born of healing, these cathartic, danceable songs are about making it out alive. The lead singer, John Darn-

ielle, is a survivor of physical abuse by his stepfather. See also "Get Lonely" and "We Shall All Be Healed."

Noll, Shaina. *Bread For the Journey*. Sing Heart Productions. www.shainanoll.com

A well-chosen collection of beautiful songs, including our personal favorite, "How Could Anyone" (How could anyone ever tell you that you're anything less than beautiful?).

Porter, CiCi. "Emergence." www.wholenessproject .com

Hopeful, inspiring songs about healing. The only thing better than buying this lovely album, is hearing her perform live.

*Small, Fred. *I Will Stand Fast*. Rounder Records. www.rounder.com

Title song is the theme song for partners everywhere. Small's album *Jaguar* features a powerful, evocative song about incest, "Light in the Hall."

Weiss, Jim. *Good Night*. Greathall Productions. www .greathall.com

Jim Weiss is a fabulous storyteller. These stories are soothing, comforting, and dreamy visualizations. They put us to sleep every time.

TRAUMA, MEMORY, AND THE BRAIN

[See also "Dissociative Identity Disorder (Multiple Personalities)" on p. 558.]

Clear, thoughtful information about traumatic amnesia, dissociation, and the complexity of memory can be gleaned from the resources below. Many are written with therapists in mind but can be useful and informative for survivors as well.

Organizations and Web Sites

AAA: Accuracy About Abuse. www.accuracy aboutabuse.org

An archive of the 1994–2001 newsletter published by activist Marjorie Orr. *Accuracy About Abuse* documented events about the backlash against survivors and the controversy about survivors' memories in Great Britain, the United States, and elsewhere in the world.

David Baldwin's Trauma Information Pages. www.trauma-pages.com

An excellent source of information about emotional trauma and traumatic stress, post-traumatic stress disorder, and dissociation. Primarily for clinicians and researchers.

International Society for the Study of Trauma and Dissociation (ISSTD), 8201 Greensboro Dr., suite 300, McLean, VA 22102; 703-610-9037; info@isst-d .org; www.isst-d.org

For professionals studying trauma and dissociative disorders. Web site includes information of interest to survivors, including frequently asked questions, links, and guidance in finding a therapist. Also publishes *The Journal of Trauma and Dissociation*.

The Leadership Council, 191 Presidential Blvd., suite C-132, Bala Cynwyd, PA 19004; 610-664-5007; www.leadershipcouncil.org

Excellent source of information on the impact of trauma on the brain and memory.

Recovered Memories of Sexual Abuse: Scientific Research & Scholarly Resources. www.jimhopper .com/memory

A comprehensive and accessible source of information about recovered memory.

The Recovered Memory Project: Case Information and Scholarly Resources. www.brown.edu/ Departments/Taubman_Center/Recovmem

A survivor and scholar's impressive collection of the extensive and growing evidence of recovered memory.

Trauma Center. www.traumacenter.org
The Web site of this acclaimed Massachusetts center features the latest research about trauma and its treatment by Bessel van der Kolk and others.

Books

Briere, John. *Principles of Trauma Therapy: A Guide to Symptoms, Evaluation, and Treatment.* Thousand Oaks, CA: Sage, 2006.
Very thorough discussion of trauma, its effects, and treatment. Primarily for professionals. See also *Child Abuse Trauma: Theory and Treatment of the Lasting Effects* (1992) and *Assessing and Treating Victims of Violence* (1994).

*Brown, Daniel James, Alan W. Scheflin, and D. Corydon Hammond. *Memory, Trauma, Treatment, and the Law.* New York: Norton, 1998.
Comprehensive examination of the scientific evidence that traumatic memories are often forgotten.

Carter, Rita, with Christopher Frith. *Mapping the Mind.* Berkeley: CA, University of California Press, 1998.
One of the most accessible books about the brain and the physical underpinnings of mental illness, compulsions, addictions, and more. Terrific graphics illustrate how human behavior and culture have been molded by the brain's topography.

Contratto, Susan, and M. Janice Gutfreund, eds. *A Feminist Clinician's Guide to the Memory Debate.* Binghamton, NY: Haworth Press, 1996.
A collection of articles integrating clinical, political, legal, and ethical issues. Informative and intelligent.

*Courtois, Christine. *Recollections of Sexual Abuse: Treatment Principles and Guidelines.* New York: Norton, 1999.
A valuable guide for clinicians that stakes out the middle ground in dealing with the exploration of memories and the possibility of past abuse.

Foa, Edna, Terence Keane, and Matthew Friedman, eds. *Effective Treatments for PTSD.* New York: Guilford, 2000.
Leading experts in the field evaluate established and emerging treatments in this comprehensive collection.

Fredrickson, Renee. *Repressed Memories: A Journey to Recovery from Sexual Abuse.* New York: Simon & Schuster, 1992.
Clinical expertise combined with good storytelling. Lots of valuable, practical information about recovering memories of sexual abuse.

Freyd, Jennifer. *Betrayal Trauma: The Logic of Forgetting Childhood Abuse.* Cambridge, MA: Harvard University Press, 1996.
Explores the issues of memory and amnesia when children are sexually abused by a trusted adult. Includes a careful review of research and a discussion of the social, historic, and linguistic context.

Freyd, Jennifer, and Anne DePrince, eds. *Trauma and Cognitive Science: A Meeting of Minds, Science, and Human Experience.* New York: Haworth, 2001. http://dynamic.uoregon.edu/~jjf
Collection of papers from experts in the field that addresses traumatic memories and recovered memories of abuse.

Goodwin, Jean, and Reina Attias, eds. *Splintered Reflections: Images of the Body in Trauma.* New York: Basic Books, 1999.
Thirteen essays cover how memories are stored, how we forget and reexperience trauma, trauma's

impact on the body, and body-image distortion. Primarily for professionals.

Knopp, Fay Honey, and Anna Rose Benson. *A Primer on the Complexities of Traumatic Memory of Childhood Sexual Abuse: A Psychobiological Approach*. Brandon, VT: Safer Society Press, 1996.

This well-written book examines the physiological processes of the brain in storing, retaining, and remembering traumatic experience. Makes very complex material clear.

*Perry, Bruce. *The Boy Who Was Raised As a Dog And Other Stories from a Child Psychiatrist's Notebook: What Traumatized Children Can Teach Us About Loss, Love, and Healing*. New York: Basic Books, 2007.

A heart-breaking and compassionate book that uses Perry's case studies as a child trauma therapist to educate about trauma's impact on the developing mind and how children can begin to heal. Perry makes neuroscience accessible, and his humility and candor are especially winning.

Pope, Kenneth S., and Laura S. Brown. *Recovered Memories of Abuse: Assessment, Therapy, Forensics*. Washington, D.C.: American Psychological Association, 1996.

Brings together a review of the research, pragmatic guidelines for clinicians, and guidance on forensic issues. Sane and practical.

Revera, Margo, ed. *Fragment by Fragment: Feminist Perspectives on Memory and Child Sexual Abuse*. Charlottetown, Prince Edward Island, Canada: Gynergy, 1999.

Seventeen essays take on the organized campaign to silence survivors with claims of false memory.

Rogers, Annie G. *The Unsayable: The Hidden Language of Trauma*. New York: Random House, 2006.

A lyrical blend of personal memory of her own breakdown and professional insight as a clinical psychologist. Rogers illuminates the silent language of girls who can't speak about their sexual trauma but who communicate all the same in symptoms and code that conventional therapy can miss. Rogers also wrote *A Shining Affliction: A Story of Harm and Healing in Psychotherapy* (1996).

Siegel, Daniel. *The Developing Mind: How Relationships and the Brain Interact to Shape Who We Are*. New York: Guilford, 2001.

A groundbreaking book that explains links between neurobiology, personal experience, and human relationships, exploring how our relationships forge key connections in the brain.

*Stout, Martha. *The Myth of Sanity: Divided Consciousness and the Promise of Awareness*. New York: Viking, 2001.

A fascinating exploration of the spectrum of dissociation. Stout maintains that we all dissociate to some degree. An important read that enhances our understanding of the way survivors' minds had to function to survive trauma.

van der Hart, Onno, Ellert Nijenhius, and Kathy Steele. The *Haunted Self: Structural Dissociation and the Treatment of Chronic Traumatization*. New York: Norton, 2006.

A dense but satisfying read for anyone who wants to understand more about dissociation and the brain.

van der Kolk, Bessel A., Alexander C. McFarlane, and Lars Weisaeth, eds. *Traumatic Stress: The Effects of Overwhelming Experience on Mind, Body, and Society*. New York: Guilford, 2006. First published in 1996.

Comprehensive summary of knowledge from leading authorities around the world. An education in itself, this influential work laid the foundation for continuing advances in the field. Includes a new preface by the publisher.

Whitfield, Charles. *Memory and Abuse: Remembering and Healing the Effects of Trauma*. Deerfield Beach, FL: Health Communications, 1995.

> Written for both survivors and professionals, this clearly written book explains what we know about traumatic memory, discusses the factors involved in remembering and forgetting personal history, substantiates the existence of delayed memory, and suggests ways to sort out true from untrue memory.

Whitfield, Charles, Joyanna Silberg, and Paul Jay Fink, eds. *Misinformation Concerning Child Sexual Abuse and Adult Survivors*. Binghampton, NY: Haworth, 2002.

> Exposes and corrects the junk science and misinformation that too often passes muster in and out of the courts. Provides up-to-date science on such myths as "false memory syndrome" and "lack of harm."

SPECIAL TOPICS

ABUSE BY WOMEN

*Crockett, Linda C. *The Deepest Wound: How a Journey to El Salvador Led to Healing from Mother–Daughter Incest*. Lincoln, NE: Writer's Showcase, 2001.

> Disturbing, challenging, and important book about facing evil and surviving it. While working with a religious group among victims of torture in Central America in the 1980s, Crockett confronts memories of sadistic, ritual sexual abuse by her mother.

Diski, Jenny. *Skating to Antarctica: A Journey to the End of the World*. New York: Ecco, 1998.

> An unusual and ultimately healing blend of travel essay about Antarctica and memoir about sexual abuse by both parents.

Elliott, Michele, ed. *Female Sexual Abuse of Children*. New York: Guilford Press, 1994.

> This important and challenging collection of articles includes men and women survivors' accounts of their experiences, as well as chapters for professionals working with both survivors and offenders.

*Evert, Kathy, and Inie Bijerk. *When You're Ready: A Woman's Guide to Healing from Childhood Physical and Sexual Abuse by Her Mother*. Walnut Creek, CA: Launch Press, 1988.

> This story of a woman sexually abused by her mother may have been the first one ever published. A powerful resource for women molested by their mothers.

Ford, Hannah. *Women Who Sexually Abuse Children*. Chichester, England: Wiley, 2006.

> A review of the literature on female offenders that looks also at how the facts are interpreted and distorted in a culture that minimizes and denies female sexual abuse.

Harrison, Kathryn. *Thicker Than Water*. New York: Random House, 1991.

> A beautifully written novel about a girl molested and neglected by her mother and raped by her father. Full of truth, vivid detail, and unforgettable images. Although some things are disturbing— the girl blames herself for "allowing" her father's abuse—this is still a haunting story. Currently out of print but available.

Pearson, Patricia. *When She Was Bad: Violent Women and the Myth of Innocence*. New York: Viking, 1997.

> A feminist examines female aggression, making the case that until we acknowledge women's capacity for brutality, we cannot understand the true nature of violence or its root causes.

Rosencrans, Bobbie. *The Last Secret: Daughters Sexually Abused by Mothers*. Brandon, VT: Safer Society Press, 1997.

550 | Resource Guide

Groundbreaking research, including testimony from ninety-three women. A significant and insightful work.

Sexton, Linda Gray. *Searching for Mercy Street: My Journey Back to My Mother, Anne Sexton.* New York: Little Brown, 1996.

In this beautifully written memoir, Sexton explores and attempts to reconcile the love she felt from and for her famous mother, poet Anne Sexton, with the sexual abuse she experienced at her hands. Sexton's novel *Mirror Images* (Knightsbridge, 1990) centers on the healing of a teenage victim of mother–daughter incest.

*Wisechild, Louise. *The Mother I Carry: A Memoir of Healing from Emotional Abuse.* Emeryville, CA: Seal, 1993.

Powerful, honest, beautifully written look at emotional abuse by a mother.

ABUSE BY SIBLINGS

Organization

SASIAN: Sibling Abuse Survivors' Information & Advocacy Network. www.sasian.org

This Web site hasn't been updated in several years, but it includes a helpful parents' guide to sibling abuse, a book list, and other information.

Books

Barnes, Liz. *Hand Me Downs.* Victoria, British Columbia, Canada: Trafford, 2006. First published in 1985 by Spinsters/Aunt Lute. Available on demand at www.trafford.com.

A delightful autobiographical novel written from the point of view of a spunky five-year-old who is abused by her brother.

Caffaro, John, and Allison Conn-Caffaro. *Sibling Abuse Trauma: Assessment and Intervention Strategies for Children, Families, and Adults.* Binghampton, NY: Haworth, 1998.

A much-needed, comprehensive guide that explores sibling incest and assault in all the gender combinations, discusses risk factors, points out the need for more research, and offers helpful assessment and intervention strategies.

Fleming, Kathleen. *Lovers in the Present Afternoon.* Tallahassee, FL: Naiad Press, 1984. Available through www.bellabooks.com

Well-written lesbian novel deals with incest by a brother.

Shaw, Risa. *Not Child's Play: An Anthology on Brother–Sister Incest.* Takoma Park, MD: Lunchbox Press, 2000.

Artwork, poetry, letters, and stories by dozens of female survivors of incest perpetrated by their brothers. These are unmediated, sometimes graphic, individual survivor voices. Despite one contributor's troubling suggestion that perpetrators suffer more than their victims, this is a valuable collection that helps fill the gap in the literature on sibling abuse. The Incest Survivor Action Girl figures, pictured in the book, have taken on a life of their own; see them at www .lunchboxpress.org.

*Wiehe, Vernon. *The Brother/Sister Hurt: Recognizing the Effects of Sibling Abuse.* Brandon, VT: Safer Society Press, 1997.

A guide to acknowledging and healing from sibling abuse, with a chapter on sexual abuse. Also see Wiehe's other books, *What Parents Need to Know About Sibling Abuse: Breaking the Cycle of Violence* (2002), *Perilous Rivalry: When Siblings Become Abusive* (1991), and *Sibling Abuse: Hidden Physical, Emotional, and Sexual Trauma,* 2nd ed. (1997).

Video

Once Can Hurt a Lifetime. One Voice. Available through www.missamericabyday.com

This excellent video by Marilyn Van Derbur focuses on the damage that results when a sibling or trusted teen sexually violates a child. It is intended for both children and adults, victims and offenders, for the purpose of education and prevention.

ABUSE BY THERAPISTS AND HELPING PROFESSIONALS

Organizations

Advocate Web: Helping Overcome Professional Exploitation. http://advocateweb.org

A nonprofit that provides free online information resources for people who have been emotionally and/or sexually exploited or abused by someone in a trusted helping profession.

BASTA! Boston Associates to Stop Treatment Abuse, 528 Franklin St., Cambridge, MA 02139; 617-277-8066; 617-661-4667; www.advocateweb.org/basta

Offers consultation and advocacy for people sexually abused by professionals as well as training for professionals about appropriate boundaries. The Web site includes an extensive checklist of boundary issues that frequently occur during poor or abusive treatment by a therapist or health-care practitioner.

TELL: Therapy Exploitation Link Line; info@ therapyabuse.org; www.therapyabuse.org

TELL is an excellent Web- and e-mail–based resource, referral, and networking organization run exclusively by victim/survivor volunteers. It helps people exploited by psychotherapists and other health-care providers find the support and resources needed to understand what has happened to them, to take action, and to heal.

Books

Bates, Carolyn, and Annette Brodsky. *Sex in the Therapy Hour: A Case of Professional Incest.* New York: Guilford Press, 1993.

A woman tells the story of abuse by her therapist and the frustrating experience of suing for malpractice. Currently out of print but available.

Chesler, Phyllis. *Women and Madness,* revised ed. New York: Palgrave Macmillan, 2005. First published in 1972.

A classic, revised and updated for the first time in thirty years.

Gabbard, Glen, ed. *Sexual Exploitation in Professional Relationships.* Washington, D.C.: American Psychiatric Press, 1989.

An excellent collection of articles that deal with sexual misconduct by social workers, counselors, sex therapists, doctors, teachers, hospital staff, lawyers, and clergy. Guidelines for healing victims of abuse by professionals.

Gonsiorek, John C., ed. *Breach of Trust: Sexual Exploitation by Health Care Professionals and Clergy.* Thousand Oaks, CA: Sage, 1995.

An important collection of articles, including research, accounts by victims, legal perspectives, and prevention training.

Peterson, Marilyn. *At Personal Risk: Boundary Violations in Professional–Client Relationships.* New York: W.W. Norton, 1992.

A fascinating book that explores the dynamics of professional boundary violations. Examines the obstacles faced by both clients and professionals in coming to a responsible, healthy resolution of such violations.

Rutter, Peter. *Sex in the Forbidden Zone.* New York: Ballantine, 1997. First published in 1989 by Tarcher.

A psychiatrist analyzes why so many men in power sexually exploit the women they're entrusted to help. See also *Understanding and Preventing Sexual Harassment* (1997).

Siegel, Shirley. *What to Do When Psychotherapy Goes Wrong.* Tukwila, WA: Stop Abuse by Counselors Publishing, 1991.

A straightforward, powerful advocacy guide for clients hurt in therapeutic relationships. Defines therapist abuse and suggests ways to fight back. Includes a client's bill of rights. Currently out of print but available.

ABUSE BY TEACHERS

S.E.S.A.M.E.: Stop Educator Sexual Abuse, Misconduct, and Exploitation, P.O. Box 94601, Las Vegas, NV 89193; 702-371-1290; www.sesamenet.org

SESAME's goals are to increase public awareness, to foster the recovery of victims and survivors, to encourage the reporting of offenders, to insist on child-centered sexual harassment policies, and to promote a professional code of ethics. Offers support, information, and referrals.

ABUSE BY CLERGY

Organization

*Survivors Network of Those Abused by Priests (SNAP), P.O. Box 6416, Chicago, IL 60680; 877-762-7432; www.snapnetwork.org

A volunteer self-help organization of survivors of clergy sexual abuse and their supporters. They work to end the cycle of abuse by supporting one another in healing and by pursuing justice and institutional change by holding individual perpetrators responsible and the church accountable. Provides valuable information, resources, and referrals. The group's Web site provides links to other organizations.

Books

Burkett, Elinor, and Frank Bruni. *A Gospel of Shame: Child Sexual Abuse and the Catholic Church,* 2nd ed. New York: HarperPerenniel, 2002.

A well-documented look at child sexual abuse by priests within the Catholic Church and the unwillingness of church officials to deal with it.

*Doyle, Thomas P., A.W.R Sipe, and Patrick Wall. *Sex, Priests and Secret Codes: The Catholic Church's 2000-Year Paper Trail of Sexual Abuse.* Los Angeles: Volt Press, 2006.

Definitive and comprehensive. Written by three of the foremost experts on child sexual abuse in the Catholic Church, with documents dating back 2000 years, this book reveals that the sexual abuse of minors by priests has been well known and protected by the church hierarchy for centuries. Sipe is also the author of *Sex, Priests, and Power: Anatomy of a Crisis* (Brunner/Mazel, 1996).

Flynn, Kathryn. *The Sexual Abuse of Women by Members of the Clergy.* Jefferson, NC: McFarland, 2003. Available though www.mcfarlandpub.com, 800-253-2187.

The results of Flynn's extensive survey of twenty-five women abused by clergy in eleven states. Examines the abuse of power as well as the many traumatic impacts on survivors. Primarily for professionals.

Fortune, Marie. *Is Nothing Sacred? The Story of a Pastor, the Women He Sexually Abused, and the Congregation He Nearly Destroyed,* 2nd ed. Cleveland, OH: United Church Press, 1999. First published in 1989 by HarperSanFrancisco.

Case study of sexual abuse by a pastoral counselor.

France, David. *Our Fathers: The Secret Life of the Catholic Church in an Age of Scandal.* New York: Broadway Books, 2004.

Compelling narrative account by the senior editor at *Newsweek* who covered the sexual abuse crisis in the Catholic Church.

Frawley-O'Dea, Mary Gail. *Perversion of Power: Sexual Abuse in the Catholic Church.* Nashville, TN: Vanderbilt University Press, 2007.

A far-reaching examination of the Catholic sexual abuse crisis by a clinical psychologist and coauthor of *Treating the Adult Survivor of Childhood Sexual Abuse* (1994). Frawley-O'Dea is also coeditor of *Predatory Priests, Silenced Victims: The Sexual Abuse Crisis and the Catholic Church* (2007).

Fribert, Nils C. *Before the Fall: Preventing Pastoral Sexual Abuse.* Collegeville, MN: Liturgical Press, 1998.

Addressed to church and seminary leaders, this book presents strategies for preventing sexual abuse by priests and other church workers.

Heggen, Carolyn Holderread. *Sexual Abuse in Christian Homes and Churches.* Eugene, OR: Wipf & Stock, 2006.

This searing and insightful book provides valuable support for Christian women. Foreword by Marie Fortune.

Poling, Nancy Werking, ed. *Victim to Survivor: Women Recovering from Clergy Sexual Abuse.* Cleveland, OH: United Church Press, 1999.

Six women who were abused by their pastors tell the story of their abuse and what they did about it in this courageous, moving, and valuable collection. Foreword by Marie Fortune.

RELIGIOUS ISSUES

Organization

*FaithTrust Institute, 2400 N 45th St., #10, Seattle, WA 98103; 206-634-1903; info@faithtrustinstitute. org; www.faithtrustinstitute.org

Founded by the Rev. Marie Fortune, FaithTrust Institute is a national, multifaith organization that has been doing groundbreaking work on the religious issues related to sexual and domestic violence for decades. It provides religious leaders and advocates with the tools and knowledge they need to address religious and cultural issues related to child abuse, domestic violence, sexual assault, and sexual abuse by clergy. Offers excellent training, consultation, and multimedia educational materials. It also has produced many fine DVDs, including the following classics:

Hear Their Cries: Religious Responses to Child Abuse.

A training program for clergy of all faiths, lay leaders, educators, seminary students, and child welfare agencies.

Not In My Congregation.

The story of one congregation faced with sexual misconduct by its religious leader.

FOR CHRISTIAN WOMEN

*Fortune, Marie M. *Sexual Violence: The Sin Revisited.* Cleveland, OH: Pilgrim Press, 2005.

When Fortune's *Sexual Violence: The Unmentionable Sin* was published in 1981, sexual abuse in church had been unmentionable. The new subtitle reflects some of the progress that has been made. Fortune writes from a Christian and feminist point of view, challenging preconceptions about sexual violence, asking hard questions, and providing important guidance to religious communities. Fortune also has an excellent curriculum for running church-based family violence workshops, *Violence in the Family: A Workshop Curriculum for Clergy and Other Helpers* (1991), and a book for battered women, *Keeping the Faith: Guidance for Christian Women Facing Abuse* (1995).

Leehan, James. *Pastoral Care for Survivors of Family Abuse.* Louisville, KY: Westminster/John Knox Press, 1989.

A Christian educator and counselor addresses the role religious leaders can play in dealing with family violence. Effectively analyzes biblical prescriptions such as "Spare the rod and spoil the child" that are sometimes used to rationalize child abuse. *A Defiant Hope: Spirituality for Survivors of Family Abuse* looks at religious and spiritual resources for healing from family violence.

Reid, Kathryn Goering, with Marie Fortune. *Preventing Child Sexual Abuse: A Curriculum for Children Ages Nine Through Twelve.* Cleveland, OH: United Church Press, 1989.

An excellent resource that interweaves secular materials with biblical resources. Ideal for use in Sunday school or other religious education programs. Reid's comprehensive course for younger kids, *Preventing Child Sexual Abuse: A Curriculum for Children Ages Five Through Eight* (1994), is also superb.

Reilly, Patricia Lynn. *A God Who Looks Like Me: Discovering a Woman-Affirming Spirituality.* New York: Ballantine, 1995.

Personal accounts interwoven with the collective history of how women's stories have been buried in the Hebrew scriptures and the Christian Bible. Filled with inspiring exercises and practical suggestions.

Rossetti, Stephen J. *A Tragic Grace: The Catholic Church and Child Sexual Abuse.* Collegeville, MN: Liturgical Press, 1996.

An honest, direct discussion that offers concrete suggestions for how to understand and deal with the subject.

Voelkel-Haugen, Rebecca, and Marie Fortune. *Sexual Abuse Prevention: A Course of Study for Teenagers,* revised ed. Cleveland, OH: United Church Press, 1996.

Impressive curriculum for churches. Designed to help teens distinguish between healthy sexuality and sexual violence/abuse. Addresses power, pornography, sexist imagery, date rape, and more.

Volcano Press Staff/David Charlsen, eds. *Family Violence and Religion: An Interfaith Resource Guide.* Volcano, CA: Volcano Press, 1995. An updated paperback edition is forthcoming.

An excellent collection of articles that deal with battering from a religious perspective. Also discusses domestic violence in African-American, Hispanic, and Asian families. Includes valuable material on elder abuse.

FOR MORMON WOMEN

Beck, Martha. *Leaving the Saints: How I Lost the Mormons and Found My Faith.* New York: Crown, 2005.

A brave and riveting spiritual memoir by a woman sexually abused in a ritualized context by her powerful Mormon father. Beck has also written a wonderful memoir about having a baby with Down syndrome—and the catalyst for healing that he becomes in their lives.

Daniels, April, and Carol Scott. *Paperdolls: Healing from Sexual Abuse in Mormon Neighborhoods.* Curtis, WA: RPI Publishing, 1992.

A compelling, inspiring story of sexual abuse, sex rings, and healing in a Mormon context. Currently out of print but available.

FOR JEWISH WOMEN

Organizations

The Awareness Center, Inc. (Jewish Coalition Against Sexual Abuse/Assault, [JCASA]), P.O. Box 65273, Baltimore, MD 21209; 443-857-5560; www.theawarenesscenter.org

International nonprofit organization dedicated to ending sexual violence in Jewish communities around the world. Offers a clearinghouse of information and resources, a speakers' bureau, a certification program for rabbis and community leaders, and self-help groups.

*Shalom Task Force, Domestic Abuse Hotline, P.O. Box 137, Bowling Green Station, New York, NY 10274;1-888-883-2323; www.shalomtaskforce.org

Trained volunteers offer confidential, toll-free support and referrals for anyone concerned about domestic violence, including Jewish survivors of domestic violence, their families, and professionals. Support is available in English, Hebrew, Yiddish, Russian, Spanish, and Hungarian.

Books

Green, Lilian. *Ordinary Wonders: Living Recovery from Sexual Abuse.* Toronto: Women's Press, 1992.

An intimate story of sexual abuse and healing in a "nice Jewish family." Told through journal entries in both poetry and prose.

*Lev, Rachel. *Shine the Light: Sexual Abuse and Healing in the Jewish Community.* Boston: Northeastern University Press, 2003.

Insightful and inspiring. Lev weaves her story with those of 100 other Jewish survivors in this important resource that emphasizes healing and encourages self-expression, creativity, and community. This book inspires hope.

"Roundtable: Jewish Women Talk About Surviving Incest," in *Bridges: A Journal for Jewish Feminists and Our Friends* (spring 1991). http://bridgesjournal.org.

An excellent discussion by Jewish survivors of sexual abuse. *Bridges* deals thoughtfully with politics, religion, and Jewish women's lives. This back issue is available from *Bridges*, which is now published biannually by Indiana University Press.

FOR MUSLIM WOMEN

Organization

Peaceful Families Project, P.O. Box 771, Great Falls, VA 22066; 703-474-6870; www.peacefulfamilies.org.

Facilitates Islamically grounded nationwide workshops for Muslim leaders and communities, provides cultural sensitivity trainings for service providers who work with Muslims, and develops resources regarding abuse in Muslim families. Their programs promote peaceful family dynamics and raise awareness regarding the nature and impact of abuse. Though Peaceful Families Project does not offer direct services, it does maintain a national directory of Muslim organizations on its Web site that provide direct services.

Book

Alkhateeb, Maha B., and Salma Elkadi Abugideiri, eds. *Change From Within: Diverse Perspectives on Domestic Violence in Muslim Communities.* Great Falls, VA: Peaceful Families Project, 2007.

This unique volume brings together the experiences of diverse domestic violence advocates, including religious leaders, service providers, and researchers, as well as four survivors.

SPIRITUALITY

These are a few titles that Ellen and Laura have found to be personally inspiring and instructive.

Beck, Charlotte Joko. *Nothing Special.* San Francisco: HarperSanFrancisco, 1994. Many other titles are also available by Beck.

> This book spoke to me at a time when nothing else made sense. I found consolation in the basic, irrefutable wisdom that "what is, is."
> —Ellen

Brach, Tara. *Radical Self-Acceptance: Embracing Your Life with the Heart of a Buddha.* New York: Bantam, 2004.

> Psychotherapist and meditation teacher Tara Brach weaves stories from her life, her psychotherapy practice, and her experiences as a Buddhist meditation teacher into a powerful guide for overcoming shame and self-hatred. I love Tara's voice and am particularly fond of the audio version. [Audio is published by Sounds True, 2005.]
> —Laura

Chödrön, Pema. *When Things Fall Apart*, and many other books and CDs available from www.shambhala.com.

> Pema is my primary teacher. Again and again she guides me to open my heart to my experience, rather than trying to deny, escape, or transcend it. I rely on her every day, and especially during the hardest times. I especially love the CDs of her teachings.
> —Ellen

Gottlieb, Daniel. *Letters to Sam: A Grandfather's Lessons on Love, Loss, and the Gifts of Life.* New York: Sterling Publishing, 2006.

> Dan is my oldest childhood friend, a psychologist, quadriplegic, and my other spiritual teacher. He has the authority of living through the extremities of pain and loss, so when you bite down on his wisdom, it's gold.
> —Ellen

Katie, Byron, with Stephen Mitchell. *Loving What Is: Four Questions That Can Change Your Life.* New York: Three Rivers Press, 2002.

> Byron Katie's revolutionary work encourages us to challenge our assumptions about who we are and "how life is" by asking ourselves four simple, powerful questions. I recommend the audio version of this book, since hearing Katie's interactions with real people is more powerful than the transcriptions. [CD published by Audio Literature, 2002.]
> —Laura

Kornfield, Jack. *A Path With Heart: A Guide Through the Perils and Promises of Spiritual Life.* New York: Bantam. 1993.

> Vipassana meditation teacher Jack Kornfield is a gifted writer and storyteller who has made Buddhism accessible for thousands of Western readers. I also love his 2001 book, *After the Ecstasy, the Laundry: How the Heart Grows Wise on the Spiritual Path.* Tapes of Kornfield's talks are available at www.dharmaseed.org/dharmaseed.htm and www.soundstrue.org.
> —Laura

Muller, Wayne. *Sabbath: Finding Rest, Renewal, and Delight in Our Busy Lives.* New York: Bantam, 1999.

> Everyone who has ever felt overwhelmed by the pace of life or said, "I'm too busy," should read this comforting, insightful, beautifully written book. I read it over and over.
> —Laura

Salzberg, Sharon, and Joseph Goldstein. *Insight Meditation: An In-Depth Correspondence Course.* Boulder, Colorado: Sounds True, 1998. Available through: www.soundstrue.org

> These cofounders of the Insight Meditation Society put together this course for people who want to learn the basics of meditation. It consists of a workbook and beautifully paced instructional audio. Each CD contains a talk about a specific aspect of meditation practice, followed by a guided meditation. The course comes with a year of guidance and support from a personal meditation instructor. I corresponded with my (wonderful) teacher via e-mail (though regular mail is also an option). Terrific for people without access to a meditation center.
> —Laura

RITUALIZED ABUSE AND TORTURE

Organizations and Web Sites

Ritual Abuse, Ritual Crime and Healing; www
.ra-info.org

This well-designed, comprehensive site for ritual
abuse survivors includes extensive resources, art
and poetry, healing advice, and an e-mail newsletter.

SMART, P.O. Box 1295, Easthampton, MA 01027;
smartnews@aol.com; http://members.aol.com/smart
news/index2.html

A bimonthly newsletter, e-mail discussion list, and
annual conferences about the connections among
ritualized abuse, mind control, and secret societies.

*Survivorship, 3181 Mission St. PMB 139, San
Francisco, CA 94110; info@survivorship.org; www
.survivorship.org

Provides resources, healing, and community for
survivors of sadistic sexual abuse, ritualistic abuse,
mind control, and torture. Also provides training
and education for professionals and support for
partners and other allies, raises awareness through
community outreach and training, and publishes
an e-mail newsletter.

Books

Adams, Jeanne. *Drawn Swords: My Victory Over
Childhood Ritual Abuse.* Ogden, UT: 1999.

A personal, religious memoir that also contains
information about ritualized abuse and recovery.
Adams is the founder of Mr. Light & Associates,
www.mrlight.org, a nonprofit that advocates for
survivors of severe childhood trauma and educates
professionals about ritualized abuse.

*Beckylane. *Where the Rivers Join: A Personal Account
of Healing from Ritual Abuse.* Vancouver: Press Gang,
1995.

A poetic journal of extreme violence and healing.
Painful to read, yet a testament to courage and
hope. Currently out of print but available.

Jadelinn. *Spirit Alive: A Woman's Healing from Cult
Ritual Abuse.* Toronto: Women's Press, 1997.

Beautifully written memoir about healing from
cult ritual abuse.

Karriker, Wanda. *Morning, Come Quickly.* Catawba,
NC: Sandime, 2003.

Compelling novel by a therapist who drew on the
experiences of her ritual abuse clients in writing
the book.

Lorena, Jeanne Marie, and Paula Levy. *Breaking
Ritual Silence: An Anthology of Ritual Abuse Survivors'
Stories.* Gardnerville, NV: Trout & Sons, 1998.

A courageous collection of accounts by dozens of
ritual abuse survivors.

*Noblitt, James Randall, and Pamela Sue Perskin.
*Cult and Ritual Abuse: Its History, Anthropology and
Recent Discovery in Contemporary America,* revised ed.
Westport, CT: Praeger, 2000.

An important addition to the literature on ritualized abuse that was written by a therapist who takes
an anthropological view but never loses touch with
survivors. Well-researched, original, accessible.

*Oksana, Chrystine. *Safe Passage to Healing: A Guide
for Survivors of Ritual Abuse.* Lincoln, NE: Backin-
print.com, 2001. First published in 1994 by Harper-
Collins.

A comprehensive, compassionate, practical guide
to healing written by a survivor. Still widely re-
garded as the best.

Rose, Emilie. *Reaching for the Light: A Guide for Ritual Abuse Survivors and Their Therapists.* Cleveland,
OH: Pilgrim Press, 1996.

A helpful, sensitive, well-organized guide written
by a survivor of ritual abuse.

Sakheim, David, and Susan Devine. *Out of Darkness: Exploring Satanism and Ritual Abuse.* San Francisco: Jossey-Bass, 1997.

> A balanced, thorough perspective that shares the views of professionals and two survivors to assist therapists and law enforcement. Currently out of print but available.

Scarry, Elaine. *The Body in Pain: The Making and Unmaking of the World.* New York: Oxford University Press, 1986.

> Explains the experience of being tortured. Although it focuses on political torture, it clearly reflects the experience of survivors who have been tortured in sadistic or ritualized abuse.

*Scott, Sara. *The Politics and Experience of Ritual Abuse: Beyond Disbelief.* Buckingham, UK: Open University Press, 2001.

> An important contribution by a sociologist whose foster daughter is a survivor of ritualized abuse. Provides interviews with thirteen survivors and insightful analysis of ritually abusive groups. Scott also examines the backlash against ritual and sexual abuse.

Spencer, Judith. *Suffer the Child.* Lincoln, NE: backinprint.com, 2001. First published in 1989 by Pocket Books.

> A powerful firsthand account of sadistic ritual abuse and resulting multiple personalities. Her 1997 book, *Satan's High Priest: A True Story*, is a gripping case history of a cult that shows the way dissociation and amnesia is created in child victims.

DISSOCIATIVE IDENTITY DISORDER (MULTIPLE PERSONALITIES)

(See also "Trauma, Memory, and the Brain" on p. 546.)

Organization

Mosaic Minds, P.O. Box 26361, Colorado Springs, CO 80936; www.mosaicminds.org

> A nonprofit, Web-based group founded in 1999 by a group of dissociative survivors of childhood trauma and their loved ones. Includes interactive community forums, a reading room, links, and more.

Books

Alderman, Tracy, and Karen Marshall. *Amongst Ourselves: A Self-Help Guide to Living with Dissociative Identity Disorder.* Oakland, CA: New Harbinger, 1998.

> Written by two therapists, one of whom has dissociative identity disorder (DID), this book is a very clear and practical guide for accepting and coping with DID. Includes a discussion of DID's positive aspects as well as support for family, partners, and therapists.

Bryant, Doris, Judy Kessler, Linda Shirar. *The Family Inside: Working with the Multiple.* New York: Norton, 1992.

> An inspiring, helpful book by a client and two cotherapists that conveys both the complexity of dissociation as well as the therapeutic healing process. Currently out of print but available.

Cameron, Marcia. *Broken Child.* New York: Kensington, 1995.

> Cameron's heartbreaking, powerful, horrifying story of sadistic abuse by her mother, rape, and dissociative identity disorder, as well as her lifelong journey toward healing.

Casey, Joan Francis, and Lynn Wilson. *The Flock: The Autobiography of a Multiple Personality.* New York: Fawcett, 1991.

> A knockout of a memoir. Beautifully written, gripping, yet not sensationalized. Casey's recollections

are juxtaposed with her therapist's notes on their sessions together.

Cohen, Barry, Esther Giller, and Lynn W., eds. *Multiple Personality Disorder from the Inside Out*. Lutherville, MD: Sidran Press, 1991.

Compiled by a therapist, a survivor, and a family member, this unique book talks about dissociative identity disorder (DID) from the perspective of those who live with it. Includes contributions from 150 people diagnosed with DID, as well as their significant others. Helpful, hopeful, and practical.

Gil, Eliana. *United We Stand: A Book for People with Multiple Personalities*. Walnut Creek, CA: Launch Press, 1990.

A wonderful simple cartoon book that explains multiple personalities and dissociation.

*Haddock, Deborah Bray. *The Dissociative Identity Disorder Sourcebook*. New York, McGraw-Hill, 2001.

A sensitive and helpful guide for people with dissociative identity disorder (DID), their families, and therapists. Includes an excellent discussion of dissociation, tools for identifying DID, how to find and work with a therapist, and various self-help coping strategies.

Hocking, Phoenix J. (formerly Sandra J. Hocking). *37 to One: Living as an Integrated Multiple*. Brandon, VT: Safer Society Press, 1996.

Inspiring for survivors facing the possibility of integration. Her earlier book, *Living With Your Selves: A Survivor Manual for People with Multiple Personalities* (1992), is short, clear and full of useful information—and even a little humor. Also see *Someone I Know Has Multiple Personalities* (1994).

Ross, Colin. *Dissociative Identity Disorder: Diagnosis, Clinical Features and Treatment of Multiple Personality*, 2nd ed. New York: John Wiley, 1997. www.rossinst.com

An excellent resource for professionals. *The Osiris Complex: Case-Studies in Multiple Personality Disorder* (1994) demonstrates, through engaging stories from treatment, how virtually all psychiatric symptoms are a result of trauma.

*Schwartz, Harvey. *Dialogues with Forgotten Voices: Relational Perspectives on Child Abuse Trauma and the Treatment of Severe Dissociative Disorders*. New York: Basic Books, 2001.

An important read for therapists that provides impressive insight and compassionate guidance for working with clients. Also documents evidence of ritualized abuse by groups of pedophiles and discusses the complicity of society in the sexual abuse of children.

Steinberg, Marlene, and Maxine Schnall. *The Stranger in the Mirror: Dissociation—the Hidden Epidemic*. New York: Cliff Street, 2001.

An interesting, accessible discussion of the prevalence of dissociation. Includes questionnaires and guidelines for identifying dissociation symptoms.

*The Troops for Truddi Chase. *When Rabbit Howls*. New York: Berkley Trade, 2002. First published 1987.

Truddi Chase first developed multiple personalities when her stepfather raped her at age two. Written by her numerous selves during therapy, this book intimately shows how the mind works to cope with the horror of sexual abuse. This book can be very hard to read.

Wasnak, Lynn, ed. *Mending Ourselves: Expressions of Healing and Self-Integration*. Cincinnati: Many Voices Press, 1993. www.manyvoicespress.com

An anthology of writings about the experience of integration by the readers of the newsletter *Many Voices*. A second volume, *Poems to Our Therapists*, includes poetry and art about survivors' relationships with their therapists.

TAKING CARE OF YOURSELF NOW

HEALTH

There are also relevant titles under "The Body's Role in Healing" (p. 541).

*The Boston Women's Health Book Collective. *Our Bodies, Ourselves: A New Edition for a New Era*, 35th anniv. ed. New York: Touchstone Books, 2005.

New and expanded. The complete sourcebook on women's health-care issues, from birthing to aging, from gender identity and sexual orientation to how to evaluate health information on the Internet. A second excellent resource: *Our Bodies, Ourselves: Menopause* explains menopause, discusses mainstream and alternative therapies, and includes women's stories.

*Burns, A. August, Ronnie Lovich, Jane Maxwell, and Katharine Shapiro. *Where Women Have No Doctor: A Health Guide for Women*, revised ed. Berkeley, CA: Hesperian, 2006. www.hesperian.org

Published by a nonprofit that produces free online versions of its titles, this valuable, accessible, and comprehensive guide combines self-help medical information with an understanding of the ways that poverty, discrimination, and cultural beliefs limit women's health and access to care. Developed with community-based groups and medical experts from more than thirty countries. Available in Spanish.

Davis, Martha, Elizabeth Robins Eshelman, and Matthew McKay. *The Relaxation and Stress Reduction Workbook*, 5th ed. Oakland, CA: New Harbinger Publications, 2000.

Practical step-by-step guidebook includes relaxation, self-hypnosis, meditation, visualization, worry control, nutrition, coping skills, assertiveness, time management, exercise, and more.

Doress-Worter, Paula, and Diana Siegal. *The New Ourselves, Growing Older*, revised ed. Magnolia, MA: Peter Smith Publishers, 1996.

Comprehensive health guide for women over 40. Includes information on relationships, pregnancy, birth control, advances in breast cancer research, nutrition, menopause, and health-care reform.

*Health Journeys: Resources for Mind, Body, and Spirit, www.healthjourneys.com.

Therapist and author Belleruth Naparstek's Web site offers powerful, effective guided imagery recordings (with music) for healing trauma and many other health conditions. Laura has personally found them to be fabulous healing tools.

Hutchinson, Marcia Germaine. *Transforming Body Image: Love the Body You Have*. Freedom, CA: Crossing Press, 1985.

Every woman should read this book. Step-by-step exercises to help you integrate your body, mind, and self-image and to begin to love and accept yourself just the way you are. Also see the follow-up *200 Ways to Love the Body You Have* (1999).

Johnson, Carol A. *Self-Esteem Comes in All Sizes: How to Be Happy and Healthy at Your Natural Weight*, revised ed. Carlsbad, CA: Gurze Designs & Books, 2001. First published in 1995 by Doubleday.

A gift for women who want to feel good about themselves the way they are.

Remen, Rachel Naomi. *My Grandfather's Blessings: Stories of Strength, Refuge, and Belonging*. New York: Riverhead, 2000.

Moving collection of stories with the power to heal the heart and spirit.

Villarosa, Linda, ed. *Body and Soul: The Black Women's Guide to Physical and Emotional Well-Being*. New York: HarperCollins, 1994.

Clear, straight-from-the-heart self-help book addressing such issues as how black women feel about their bodies, how to deal with doctors, the role of spirituality in well-being, the role of black history and politics, facing abortion, sexual abuse, AIDS, loving black men and black women, coping with violence, and raising children.

*White, Evelyn C. *The Black Women's Health Book: Speaking for Ourselves*, revised ed. Emeryville, CA: Seal, 1994.

This diverse range of essays give a comprehensive picture of health issues faced by black women. Essential reading.

ADDICTION AND RECOVERY

Organizations

Alcoholics Anonymous; www.aa.org (or look in your local telephone book).
Narcotics Anonymous; www.na.org
12-Step Programs; www.12step.org

Alcoholics Anonymous (AA) and Narcotics Anonymous (NA) are extremely effective in helping people break their addictions to alcohol and drugs. They have 24-hour hotlines in almost every city in the country (and the world), many meetings at a wide variety of places and times, and people (recovering addicts and alcoholics) who will help anyone who picks up the phone or goes to a meeting. Both AA and NA are nonjudgmental and completely free. Twelve-step programs have helped millions become clean and sober and reclaim their lives. There are

also 12-step programs for many other addictions, including overeating, gambling, and debt.

Harm Reduction Coalition; www.harmreduction .org

Harm reduction works to minimize the harmful effects of drug use on individuals and communities. Needle-exchange programs—in which addicts are given clean needles to help prevent the spread of HIV—are a powerful example of harm-reduction principles at work.

SLAA, Sex and Love Addicts Anonymous, 1550 NE Loop 410, suite 118, San Antonio, TX 78209; 210-828-7900; info@slaafws.org; www.slaafws.org

Twelve-step program based on the model pioneered by Alcoholics Anonymous. Members share a willingness to stop acting out in their own personal bottom-line addictive behavior. This is done through support of each other in meetings, practice of the 12 steps and 12 traditions, and a relationship with a higher power.

Books

Black, Claudia. *It Will Never Happen to Me: Growing Up With Addiction As Youngsters, Adolescents, Adults*, 2nd ed. Center City, MN: Hazelden, 2002. First published in 1981 by MAC Publishing.

A groundbreaking book. Black has also published a workbook for adults, *Repeat After Me*, and *Double Duty*, which examines the struggles of adult children from homes where chemical dependency and another factor—such as physical disability, sexual abuse, or being gay or lesbian—make recovery more complex.

Caldwell, Christine. *Getting Our Bodies Back: Recovery, Healing, and Transformation through Body-Centered Psychotherapy*. Boston, MA: Shambhala, 1996.

An accessible and fascinating body-centered exploration of addiction and recovery by the founder of the somatic psychology program at Naropa Institute.

Carnes, Patrick. *Out of the Shadows: Understanding Sexual Addiction*, 3rd ed. Center City, MN: Hazelden, 2001.

Accessible and helpful guidebook from a pioneer in the field of sex addiction. Focuses on the 12-step approach as the path to recovery.

Hunter, Mic. *Adult Survivors of Sexual Abuse: Treatment Innovations*. Thousand Oaks, CA: Sage, 1995.

A collection of thoughtful articles on sexual dysfunction and compulsivity, partners of survivors, and chemical dependency.

Isensee, Rik. *Reclaiming Your Life: The Gay Man's Guide to Recovery from Abuse, Addictions, and Self-Defeating Behavior*, 3rd ed. Lincoln, NE: Backinprint.com, 2005. First published in 1991 as *Growing Up Gay in a Dysfunctional Family*.

Validates ways in which growing up gay in a homophobic society and being abused as a child create a double trauma and offers specific suggestions for understanding and working through the problems involved. Warm, intelligent, sure to be of real help.

Kasl, Charlotte Advise. *Women, Sex, and Addiction: A Search for Love and Power*. New York: HarperCollins, 1990.

Well documented and politically astute. Kasl speaks with depth and compassion. *Many Roads, One Journey* (1993) presents a feminist alternative to the 12-step model for women in recovery. Her books, *Finding Joy: 101 Ways to Free Your Spirit and Dance with Life* (1994) and *A Home for the Heart: Creating Intimacy and Community in Our Everyday Lives* (1997), are gems of inspiration.

Maltz, Wendy, and Larry Maltz. *The Porn Trap: The Essential Guide to Overcoming Problems Caused by Pornography: Strategies for Recovery & Relationship Healing*. New York: HarperCollins, 2008. www .healthysex.com

This clear and compassionate guide by experts in the intimacy field takes on pornography's harmful impact on sexuality and relationships. Discusses how people become involved with porn, the serious problems it creates, and the steps a person can take to quit using porn for good. Includes stories and insights from recovering addicts, their intimate partners, and other experts.

Silverman, Sue William. *Love Sick: One Woman's Journey through Sexual Addiction*. New York: Norton, 2001.

This candid story of recovery in an inpatient clinic for sex addicts will resonate deeply with anyone who's sought treatment for addiction.

Weiss, Robert, and Jennifer Schneider. *Untangling the Web: Sex, Porn, and Fantasy Obsession in the Internet Age*. New York: Alyson, 2006.

An update of *CyberSex Exposed* (2001). Examines the harmful impact of Internet pornography and sex addiction.

EATING DISORDERS

Organization

National Association of Anorexia and Associated Disorders (ANAD), P.O. Box 7, Highland Park, IL 60035; hotline 847-831-3438; anad20@aol.com; www.anad.org

Nonprofit dedicated to alleviating the problems of eating disorders, especially anorexia and bulimia, through education, research, treatment, and prevention. Offers a wealth of support and assistance, including referrals and information through its hotline, more than 250 free support groups around the United States, candlelight vigils, a free education and early intervention program for teachers, a message board and chat room, a quarterly newsletter, and much more.

Books

Chernin, Kim. *The Obsession: Reflections on the Tyranny of Slenderness*. New York: HarperPerennial, 1994. First published in 1981.

An incisive, well-researched analysis of women's obsession with weight and body size. Also see *The Hungry Self: Women, Eating and Identity*.

Hanauer, Cathi. *My Sister's Bones*. New York: Doubleday, 1996.

Well-written novel about a young woman dealing with anorexia.

Knapp, Caroline. *Appetites*. New York: Counterpoint, 2003.

Knapp uses her own battle with anorexia to brilliantly explore the broader issue of how a woman can know and honor her own desires in a culture bent on controlling them. An important, honest, and piercing read.

Kolodny, Nancy. *The Beginner's Guide to Eating Disorders Recovery*. Carlsbad, CA: Gürze Books, 2004.

Covers basic information, including the first steps to recovery, choosing a therapist, working with a nutritionist, and more. Practical and clear.

Levenkron, Steven. *Anatomy of Anorexia*. New York: Norton, 2001.

A clear and insightful examination of anorexia by a therapist and expert in the field. Addresses the causes, progression, and impact of anorexia, as well as several treatment options.

Natenshon, Abigail. *When Your Child Has an Eating Disorder: A Step-By-Step Workbook for Parents and Other Caregivers*. San Francisco: Jossey-Bass, 1999.

Encouraging, informative, clear, and supportive for parents.

Pipher, Mary. *Hunger Pains: The Modern Woman's Tragic Quest for Thinness*. New York: Ballantine, 1997.

Clear, helpful, and enlightening look at anorexia, bulimia, dieting, obesity, and our hunger for love. Pipher also wrote the groundbreaking *Reviving Ophelia: Saving the Selves of Adolescent Girls* (1994).

Roth, Geneen. *Feeding the Hungry Heart: The Experience of Compulsive Eating*. New York: Plume, 1993. First published in 1982 by Bobbs-Merrill.

Explores hunger, body image, bingeing, and nourishment as issues far deeper than food. Her second book, retitled *Breaking Free from Emotional Eating*, offers practical guidelines for stopping compulsive eating. Also see the self-help workbook *Why Weight?* and *When Food Is Love*, on intimacy.

Schwartz, Mark F., and Leigh Cohn. *Sexual Abuse and Eating Disorders*. New York: Brunner/Mazel, 1996.

A collection of academic articles that include prevalence data, treatment ideas, and an analysis of the reluctance many professionals have in recognizing the commonness of sexual abuse in women with eating disorders.

Zerbe, Kathryn. *The Body Betrayed: A Deeper Understanding of Women, Eating Disorders, and Treatment*. Carlsbad, CA: Gürze Books, 1995.

A thorough discussion of eating disorders, including their relationship to sexual abuse. Primarily for professionals, yet its elegant writing makes it more accessible than most texts.

DOMESTIC VIOLENCE, RAPE, AND SEXUAL HARASSMENT

For domestic violence hotlines see p. 525. There are also excellent resources listed under "Religious Issues" (p. 553).

SELF-INJURY

*Alderman, Tracy. *The Scarred Soul: Understanding & Ending Self-Inflicted Violence.* Oakland, CA: New Harbinger, 1997.

> A clear, comprehensive, and important book for those who practice self-injury and the people who care for them. Each chapter also includes several helpful exercises.

The Cutting Edge: A Newsletter for People Living with Self-Inflicted Violence. Edited by Ruta Mazelis. Baltimore, MD: Sidran Institute Press. www.healing selfinjury.org

> This valuable resource switched to a Web format in 2007. The site includes past issues of *The Cutting Edge*; articles and other resources for survivors, parents, family, friends, and service providers; book reviews; columns; and a blog by Ruta Mazelis and guest editors.

Levenkron, Steven. *Cutting: Understanding and Overcoming Self-Mutilation,* New York: Norton, 1998.

> Insightful, accessible, and well-written book about the causes of self-injury and methods for treating the disorder.

McCormick, Patricia. *Cut.* Asheville, North Carolina: Front Street, 2000.

> A vivid, authentic novel about a fifteen-year-old girl in treatment for self-injury at a residential facility. Written for a teen audience.

McVey-Noble, Merry, Sony Khemlani-Patel, and Fugen Neziroglu. *When Your Child Is Cutting: A Parent's Guide to Helping Children Overcome Self-Injury.* Oakland, CA: New Harbinger, 2006.

> A clear and thoughtful guide to help parents identify the warning signs of self-injury, learn about its causes and effects, communicate effectively with their child, choose professional help, and support their recovery.

Trautmann, Kristy, and Robin Connors. *Understanding Self-Injury: A Workbook for Adults.* Pittsburgh: Pittsburgh Action Against Rape, 1994.

> Honest, nonblaming, and informative. Helps self-injurers understand their behavior and underlying issues. Also offers alternatives for changing or stopping the injuring behavior.

Understanding Self-Injury. Cavalcade Productions, P.O. Box 2480, Nevada City, CA 95959; 800-345-5530; www.cavalcadeproductions.com

> Geared toward survivors, this 30-minute video discusses the forms and functions of self-harm; includes interviews with trauma survivors who have self-injured.

Organizations

National Coalition Against Domestic Violence (NCADV), 1120 Lincoln St., suite 1603, Denver, CO 80203; referrals and technical assistance, 303-839-1852; facial plastic surgery, 800-842-4546; dentistry, 800-773-4227; skin injuries, 888-892-6702; www.ncadv.org

> A national information and referral center for battered women and their children, the public, and agencies. Since 1995 they have offered cosmetic and reconstructive surgery for injuries caused by an intimate partner or spouse.

National Resource Center on Domestic Violence (NRCDV), 6400 Flank Dr., suite 1300, Harrisburg, PA 17112-2778; 800-537-2238, TTY 800-553-2508; www.nrcdv.org; National Online Resource Center on Violence Against Women: www.vawnet.org

> Provides information and referrals, does training and research, and sponsors projects, such as the Women of Color Network. Its National Online

Resource Center on Violence Against Women offers information and publications about domestic and sexual violence.

National Sexual Violence Resource Center, 123 North Enola Dr., Enola, PA 17025; 877-739-3895, 717-909.0715 (TTY); www.nsvrc.org

A national information and resource hub for all aspects of sexual violence. The center develops, collects, and disseminates resources on sexual violence and assists coalitions, rape crisis centers, agencies, and others interested in eliminating sexual violence. It publishes the newsletter *The Resource* and coordinates an annual national sexual assault awareness campaign in April. Callers seeking direct services are referred to programs in their area.

Books

Brewster, Susan. *To Be an Anchor in the Storm: A Guide for Families and Friends of Abused Women.* Emeryville, CA: Seal, 2000. First published in 1997 by Ballantine.

Written by a psychotherapist who was stalked and battered by an ex-boyfriend, this book offers support and guidance for family and friends who want to help.

Brownmiller, Susan. *Against Our Will: Men, Women and Rape.* New York: Ballantine, 1993. First published in 1975.

A comprehensive history and analysis of rape. A classic.

Carosella, Cynthia. *Who's Afraid of the Dark? A Forum of Truth, Support, and Assurance for Those Affected by Rape.* New York: HarperCollins, 1995.

Thirty rape survivors share the ways they cope with the long-term effects. Together, they are powerful proof that it is possible to regain trust, hope, and self-esteem. Currently out of print but available.

Goldstein, Harvey. *Scared to Leave, Afraid to Stay: Paths from Family Violence to Safety.* San Francisco: Robert Reed Publishers, 2002.

By showing how ten women left their abusers—what they did before, during, and after—this book offers hope to women that they can successfully leave too. Written by an attorney who specializes in domestic violence, the book contains practical strategies, advice, and resources.

*Griffin, Susan. *Pornography and Silence: Culture's Revenge Against Nature.* New York: HarperCollins, 1981.

Explores the ways pornography is woven through the texture of our society and the role it plays in undermining our basic humanity. Her earlier book, *Woman and Nature*, a gorgeously written classic, parallels the violation of women with the continuing violation of the earth. (*Woman and Nature* is on Ellen's list in *Poet's Bookshelf: Contemporary Poets on Books That Shaped Their Art.*) Griffin's *Rape: The Power of Consciousness* is a series of powerful essays. Both books are currently out of print but available.

Island, David, and Patrick Letellier. *Men Who Beat the Men Who Love Them: Battered Gay Men and Domestic Violence.* Binghamton, NY: Haworth, 1991.

An important silence broken. Includes both theory and practical help.

Ledray, Linda. *Recovering from Rape,* 2nd ed. New York: Henry Holt, 1994.

A compassionate book that addresses the immediate aftermath, as well as the long-term effects. The second edition includes information about changes in the law, DNA testing, and health issues. Recommended by rape crisis centers.

Lobel, Kerry, ed. *Naming the Violence: Speaking Out About Lesbian Battering.* Emeryville, CA: Seal, 1986.

Includes personal stories, a look at the homophobia that has kept lesbians from seeking help, and suggestions for services.

Martin, Del. *Battered Wives*, revised ed. Volcano, CA: Volcano Press, 1981. First published in 1976.

The pioneering book that first framed the problem of wife-beating. Still a great overview.

Matsakis, Aphrodite. *The Rape Recovery Handbook: Step-by-Step Help for Survivors of Sexual Assault*. Oakland, CA: New Harbinger, 2003.

Full of helpful exercises and insights. Compassionate and clear guide for rape survivors.

McAllister, Pam, ed. *Reweaving the Web of Life: Feminism and Nonviolence*. Philadelphia: New Society, 1982.

A well-written and challenging collection of writings by feminists on nonviolence.

*NiCarthy, Ginny. *Getting Free: You Can End Abuse and Take Back Your Life*, 4th ed. Emeryville, CA: Seal, 2004.

A must for any woman wanting to leave an abusive partner. Valuable information on both practical and emotional issues. Has sections on lesbian abuse, teen abuse, and emotional abuse. The new edition includes information about children's reactions to battering, issues relevant to immigrant women, and how religious beliefs and communities affect the choices of women facing violence. Also adapted into an easy-to-read edition, *You Can Be Free* (2005). NiCarthy's *The Ones Who Got Away: Women Who Left Abusive Partners* (1987) is a powerful chronicle of battered women who've left abusive spouses.

Parrot, Andrea. *Coping with Date Rape and Acquaintance Rape*, revised ed. New York: Rosen, 1995.

Helpful book about date rape that focuses strongly on prevention.

*Pierce-Baker, Charlotte. *Surviving the Silence: Black Women's Stories of Rape*. New York: Norton, 1998.

Pierce-Baker carefully and powerfully weaves her story with those of other survivors and supportive men in this important anthology that rings with urgency, offering strength and hope to survivors who also face racism's ugly hand.

*Raine, Nancy Venable. *After Silence: Rape and My Journey Back*. New York: Three Rivers, 1999.

A remarkable book that skillfully integrates Raine's healing journey with information, insight, and research about rape and its traumatic impact.

Sonkin, Daniel Jay, and Michael Durphy. *Learning to Live Without Violence*, updated ed. Volcano, CA: Volcano Press, 1997.

Designed as a handbook for men who batter women, this excellent, practical guide can help anyone who wants to deal with anger more effectively. Also available in audio.

Sumrall, Amber Coverdale, and Dena Taylor. *Sexual Harassment: Women Speak Out*. Freedom, CA: Crossing Press, 1992.

A collection of personal testimonies compiled as a response to Anita Hill's ordeal during the 1991 confirmation hearings for U.S. Supreme Court Justice Clarence Thomas. Many excellent writers and inspiring stories.

West, Carolyn. *Violence in the Lives of Black Women: Battered, Black, and Blue*. Binghampton, NY: Haworth, 2002.

Therapists, activists, survivors, and researchers explore the impact of violence on black women in this important collection. Addresses domestic violence, sexual harassment, rape, and sexual abuse.

White, Evelyn C. *Chain Chain Change: For Black Women Dealing with Physical and Emotional Abuse*, 2nd ed. Emeryville, CA: Seal, 1994.

A direct, clearly written, valuable resource.

Zambrano, Myrna M. *Mejor Sola Que Mal Acompañada: Para la Mujer Golpeada/For the Latina in an Abusive Relationship*. Emeryville, CA: Seal, 1985.

Bilingual. Excellent sections on institutionalized racism and the barriers that Latinas face in getting help.

SEXUALITY

There are also relevant books in the section "For Partners and Couples" (p. 569).

Blank, Joani. *The Playbook for Women About Sex*, revised ed. San Francisco: Down There Press, 2000.

A nonthreatening, fun place to start a loving relationship with yourself. There is also a *Playbook for Men About Sex*. Blank's book *Femalia* (1993), features color photographs of women's genitals. If you've ever wondered if yours are "normal," here's beautiful reassurance.

Dodson, Betty. *Sex for One*. New York: Crown, 1996. First published in 1986.

A beautifully illustrated sex-positive guide to masturbation. Dodson's DVD, *Celebrating Orgasm: Women's Private Selfloving Sessions*, shows five women (ages twenty-six to sixty-two) practice and achieve orgasm through a step-by-step process.

Engel, Beverly. *Raising Your Sexual Self-Esteem: How to Feel Better About Your Sexuality and Yourself*. New York: Fawcett, 1995.

A clear, compassionate book that helps you gain confidence, enjoyment, and pleasure in your sex life.

Fortune, Marie M. *Love Does No Harm: Sexual Ethics for the Rest of Us*. New York: Continuum, 1998.

A straightforward guide to ethical decision making in intimate relationships for people of all ages and sexual orientations. Grounded in religious values, but applicable for everyone, with an intelligent social and political understanding.

WOMEN, WORK, AND ABUSE

*Brook, Nancy, and Cynthia Krainin. *Thriving at Work: A Guidebook for Survivors of Childhood Abuse*, 2nd ed. Brookline, MA: Career Resources, 2006. Available through guidebook@thrivingatwork.net or 617-732-1200; www.thrivingatwork.net

An important book every working survivor should read. Explores the negative impact that abuse has on work and career and also the *strengths* that survivors bring to the workplace. Assists with finding healthy work environments, choosing work that matches your phase of healing, creating safety, handling difficult situations, and much more.

Murphy, Patricia A. *A Career and Life Planning Guide for Women Survivors: Making the Connections Workbook*. Boca Raton, FL: St. Lucie Press, 1996.

A well-designed empowering tool for any woman who wants to understand the connections between her abuse, her problems with work, and her future vocational goals. Its predecessor, *Making the Connections: Women, Work and Abuse* (1993), is a groundbreaking book that explores specialized vocational rehabilitation counseling as part of the healing process.

---

*Haines, Staci. *Healing Sex: A Mind–Body Approach to Healing Sexual Trauma*. Originally published as *The Survivor's Guide to Sex*. San Francisco: Cleis, 2007.

An encouraging and important book for every survivor. This down-to-earth guide helps survivors attain the joy of freely chosen, healthy sexual pleasure. The new edition integrates Haines' mind-body approach to healing from sexual trauma.

Loulan, JoAnn. *Lesbian Sex*. San Francisco: Spinsters Ink, 1984.

A good read about sexuality, sexual problems, and healing for *all* women, not just lesbians. Sections on sex and disability, sobriety, sexual abuse, motherhood, aging, and youth. The follow-up, *Lesbian Passion*, has a chapter for partners.

*Maltz, Wendy. *The Sexual Healing Journey: A Guide for Survivors of Sexual Abuse*, revised ed. New York: Quill, 2001. www.healthysex.com

This comprehensive resource helps survivors understand the impact of sexual abuse on sexuality and learn how to create a new approach to intimate touch and sexual sharing. Maltz's first book (with Beverly Holman), *Incest and Sexuality* (1987), is also excellent. Maltz's Web site is full of helpful resources.

Maltz, Wendy, and Suzie Boss. *Private Thoughts: Exploring the Power of Women's Sexual Fantasies*. Novato, CA: New World Library, 2001. Originally published as *In the Garden of Desire*. www.healthysex.com

An informative and often entertaining look at where sexual fantasies come from, how they function, and what they mean. Special chapters devoted to understanding and healing unwanted fantasies caused by abuse.

Mariechild, Diane, and Marcelina Martin. *Lesbian Sacred Sexuality*. Oakland: Wingbow Press, 1995.

A beautiful exploration of opening to the sacred—and healing—in sexuality, in text and photographs.

Newman, Felice. *The Whole Lesbian Sex Book: A Passionate Guide for All of Us*, 2nd ed. San Francisco: Cleis, 2004.

Definitive, thorough, and inclusive how-to guide that explores all aspects of lesbian sexuality, in-

---

MAIL-ORDER SOURCES FOR VIBRATORS, SEX TOYS, AND BOOKS ON SEX

Eve's Garden, 119 West 57th St., #1201, New York, NY 10019; 800-848-3837; www.evesgarden.com

"Where pleasure blooms." Books, sex toys, DVDs, product reviews, and more.

Good Vibrations, 938 Howard St., San Francisco, CA 94103; 800-289-8423; customer service@goodvibes.com; www.goodvibes.com.

This popular store for sex toys and books also offers free written and video information about sex on its Web site.

---

cluding support for bisexual, transgendered, and sexually inexperienced women.

Ogden, Gina. *The Heart and Soul of Sex: Making the ISIS Connection*. Boston: Shambhala, 2006.

Shaped by Ogden's massive sex survey that asked women what they experience in sex and what it meant to them, *Heart and Soul* is a well-written and inspiring exploration of the spiritual and sexual connection that two-thirds of the women said was vital to their satisfaction. Ogden also wrote *Women Who Love Sex* (1995).

Westerlund, Elaine. *Women's Sexuality After Childhood Incest*. New York: Norton, 1992.

A therapist's study on the sexual attitudes and experiences of women who've been sexually abused. Through statistics and first-person accounts, Westerlund explores issues of body image, reproduction, sexual orientation, and sexual functioning. Includes a treatment model for healing that enables counselors and survivors to address sexuality issues as a team.

Winks, Cathy, and Ann Semans. *The New Good Vibrations Guide to Sex: How to Have Fun, Safe Sex*, 2nd ed. San Francisco: Cleis, 1997.

This comprehensive manual is by the woman-owned store that makes shopping for sex toys non-threatening and safe. Covers sexual self-image and anatomy, masturbation and vibrators, S/M, safer sex, censorship, and more.

DVD

Healing Sex: The Complete Guide to Sexual Wholeness. Staci Haines. 112 minutes. Available through www.healingsexthemovie.com

Moving, encouraging, and important film that every survivor and partner of a survivor should see. Features a diverse cast of women and men, hetero- and homosexual, who have put into practice Haines's step-by-step lead toward freeing sexuality from the effects of trauma.

FOR SUPPORTERS OF SURVIVORS

FOR PARTNERS AND COUPLES

There are also relevant books listed in "Sexuality," (p. 567).

Cameron, Grant. *What About Me? A Guide for Men Helping Female Partners Deal with Childhood Sexual Abuse.* Carp, Ontario, Canada: Creative Bound, 1994.

A distillation of what Cameron learned while helping his wife recover from abuse. Talks openly about sex, suicide, anger, nightmares, and gaining trust. Supportive and honest.

*Davis, Laura. *Allies in Healing: When the Person You Love Was Sexually Abused as a Child.* New York: HarperCollins, 1991.

A clear, supportive, and comprehensive guide for partners who are struggling to take care of themselves and the survivors they love. Full of helpful anecdotes, useful suggestions, and powerful first-hand stories. Also available on cassette.

Engel, Beverly. *Partners in Recovery: How Mates, Lovers & Other Prosurvivors Can Learn to Support and Cope with Adult Survivors of Childhood Sexual Abuse.* New York: Fawcett, 1993. First published in 1991 by Lowell House.

Good advice on how to be supportive to survivors as well as how to take care of yourself.

Gil, Eliana. *Outgrowing the Pain Together: A Book for Partners and Spouses of Adults Abused as Children.* New York: Dell, 1992.

An eloquent, optimistic introduction to issues for partners of survivors.

*Hendrix, Harville. *Getting the Love You Want: A Guide for Couples.* New York: Owl, 2001. First published in 1988.

Beginning with the premise that we all choose partners with whom we can work through our childhood pain, this excellent guide helps couples create a conscious partnership in which both partners can heal from old hurts. See also the accompanying *Getting the Love You Want Workbook* (2003).

Matsakis, Aphrodite. *Trust After Trauma: A Guide to Relationships for Survivors and Those Who Love Them.* Oakland, CA: New Harbinger, 1998.

A caring and practical guide that helps survivors understand, accept, and cope with their common reactions to childhood trauma. Also very helpful for loved ones of survivors.

Strong, Maggie. *Mainstay: For the Well Spouse of the Chronically Ill*, 3rd ed. Northampton, MA: Bradford, 1997.

Written by a woman whose husband has multiple sclerosis, this powerful, practical, and beautifully written book raises many issues and feelings that will ring true for partners of survivors as well.

DVD

Relearning Touch: Healing Techniques for Couples. Wendy Maltz, Steve Christiansen, and Gerald Joffee. 45 minutes. DVD/VHS. Distributed by Independent Video Services: 800-678-3455.

Moderated by veteran sex expert Wendy Maltz, this helpful DVD demonstrates the relearning of touch techniques and interviews three couples who have used it to improve their relationship and foster positive sexual experiences. *Partners in Healing: Couples Overcoming the Sexual Repercussions of Incest* is a valuable resource for survivors, their partners, and therapists. Three couples, including a male survivor, discuss healing their sexuality. Helps partners become allies by explaining the impact of abuse and showing how they can assist their survivor partner in healing.

FAMILY HEALING

Organization

*The Family Dialogue Project, The Center for Contextual Change,** 9239 Gross Point Rd., Skokie, IL 60077; 847-676-4447; www.centerforcontextual change.org

The Family Dialogue Project, founded by Mary Jo Barrett, is a national resource center for families seeking mediation in response to sexual abuse. The center provides resources for families in which abuse allegations are disputed, as well as those in which the abuse is acknowledged. Family dialogue is an alternative to legal confrontation and stalemate that helps families find common ground from which they can grapple with—and sometimes resolve—these difficult issues.

Books and Audio Programs

*Davis, Laura. *I Thought We'd Never Speak Again: The Road from Estrangement to Reconciliation.* New York: HarperCollins, 2002.

A gradual reconciliation with her mother, after a long estrangement, led Laura to research and write this book about the process of healing damaged relationships. The book covers a wide variety of circumstances, including sexual abuse. This book does not advocate one particular course but uses teaching stories to explore four pathways to resolve difficult relationships and make peace with the outcome.

*Davis, Laura. *The Last Frontier: Is Reconciliation Possible After Sexual Abuse?* Self-published, 2004.

This audio series features 15 interviews with survivors, parents, and several former perpetrators about the possibility of healing family relationships after sexual abuse has occurred. *The Last Frontier* does not advocate a particular point of view; rather, it lets the interviewees tell their stories in their own words. Outcomes range from finding peace on the inside to deep mutual healing and everything in between. Includes a dozen cassettes and an accompanying workbook to help you chart your own path through challenging family relationships. Available only at www.lauradavis .net

Engel, Beverly. *Families in Recovery: Working Together to Heal the Damage of Childhood Sexual Abuse,* 2nd ed. New York: McGraw-Hill, 2000.

A straightforward guidebook for family members of survivors, intended to bring families together and help them recover from the devastation of abuse. Frank, sensible advice.

Landry, Dorothy Beaulieu. *Family Fallout: A Handbook for Families of Adult Sexual Abuse Survivors.* Brandon, VT: Safer Society Press, 1991.

A clear, comforting, and useful book for parents, siblings, partners, and children of adult survivors.

Smith, Shauna. *Making Peace with Your Adult Child.* New York: HarperCollins, 1993.

A recovery book that encourages cross-generational healing. Written for parents who are struggling to heal painful rifts with their adult children. Wise, compassionate, and accessible.

SAFE, STRONG, AND FREE

PARENTING

*Davis, Laura, and Janis Keyser. *Becoming the Parent You Want to Be: A Sourcebook of Strategies for the First Five Years.* New York: Broadway Books, 1997.

A comprehensive sourcebook that respects parents and kids. Helps you conceive and embody your own vision of parenting. Realistic, inspiring, multicultural.

Faber, Adele, and Elaine Mazlish. *How to Talk So Kids Will Listen and Listen So Kids Will Talk*, 20th anniv. ed. New York: Avon, 1999.

Excellent, respectful, intelligent. Will bring about more cooperation from children than all the yelling and pleading in the world. Also available in audio. See also *How to Talk So Teens Will Listen and Listen So Teens Will Talk* (HarperCollins, 2005), *Siblings Without Rivalry*, revised ed. (1998), and *Liberated Parents, Liberated Children* (1990).

*Kabat-Zinn, Myla, and Jon. *Everyday Blessings: The Inner Work of Mindful Parenting.* New York: Hyperion, 1997.

A practical, poetic, and spiritual guide. Inspiration for being in the moment, fully present with our children.

Kurcinka, Mary. *Raising Your Spirited Child*, revised ed. New York: HarperCollins, 2006.

An invaluable resource for parents who have a child who is more active, emotional, or otherwise intense than others. One reading can shift your perspective on your challenging child forever. Highly recommended.

Siegel, Daniel, and Mary Hartzell. *Parenting from the Inside Out: How a Deeper Self-Understanding Can Help You Raise Children Who Thrive.* New York: Tarcher/Putnam, 2003.

The authors present research in neurobiology to help parents who have experienced trauma become better parents. Siegel wrote *The Developing Mind* (2001) and *The Mindful Brain* (2007).

*Simkin, Penny, and Phyllis Klaus. *When Survivors Give Birth: Understanding and Healing the Effects of Early Sexual Abuse on Childbearing Women.* Seattle: Classic Day, 2004.

Unique, compassionate, and extremely thorough guide through the birth experience for survivors. Important reading for every birth professional, paraprofessional, and survivor who is pregnant or considering pregnancy. Foreword by E. Sue Blume.

Sperlich, Mickey, and Julia Seng. *Survivor Moms: Women's Stories of Birthing, Mothering, and Healing after Sexual Abuse.* Eugene, OR: Motherbaby Press, 2008

An excellent resource for survivors who are pregnant or considering pregnancy—and for the professionals who work with them. The birth process can be retraumatizing for some survivors, but this much-needed contribution includes eighty survivor voices providing information that can help to transform the process into an opportunity for healing.

ESPECIALLY FOR CHILDREN

Bass, Ellen. *I Like You to Make Jokes with Me, But I Don't Want You to Touch Me.* Durham, NC: Lollipop Power Books, 1993. First published in 1981.

A gentle picture book. Sara is a little girl who learns to tell a clerk in the grocery store that though she wants to be his friend, she doesn't want him to touch her. Bilingual in Spanish and English.

Freeman, Lory. *It's MY Body.* Seattle, WA: Parenting Press, 1984.

A picture book for preschoolers with an accompanying parent's discussion guide. Also available in Spanish.

*Hansen, Diane. *Those are MY Private Parts*, 2nd ed. Redondo Beach, CA: Empowerment Productions, 2007.

This effective, easy to read book for preschoolers is filled with catchy rhymes to make it easier for children to learn that no one has the right to touch them in a way that makes them feel uncomfortable. You may find yourself joining in: Those are *my* private parts.

*Harris, Robie, with illustrations by Michael Emberley. *It's Perfectly Normal*, 10th anniv. ed. Cambridge, MA: Candlewick Press, 2004.

A clear, user-friendly book on bodies, growing up, sex, and sexual health. Fabulous cartoon illustrations. For preadolescents or anyone who wants accessible information about how our bodies work. Not to be missed. See also the sequels, *It's So Amazing! A Book about Eggs, Sperm, Birth, Babies, and Families* (1999) and *It's Not the Stork! A Book About Girls, Boys, Babies, Bodies, Families, and Friends* (2006).

Jukes, Mavis. *It's a Girl Thing: How to Stay Healthy, Safe and In Charge.* New York: Knopf, 1996.

A kid-friendly guide to puberty and early adolescence. Talks about getting your period, physical and mental health, diet and eating disorders, drinking, drugs, crushes, dating, sex, birth control, sexual abuse, and more.

Loulan, JoAnn, and Bonnie Worthen. *Period: A Girl's Guide*, 4th ed. Hopkins, MN: Book Peddlers, 2001. First published in 1979 by Volcano.

Clear, well-illustrated information for girls. A book that will give girls a strong, self-confident feeling about menstruation and their bodies. Includes a chapter for parents.

Madaras, Lynda. *Ready, Set, Grow! A "What's Happening to My Body?" Book for Younger Girls.* New York: Newmarket, 2003.

Warm, funny, and easy-to-read journey through the physical changes of puberty. Terrific illustrations.

Marvel Comics and Prevent Child Abuse America. *The Amazing Spider-Man on Bullying Prevention.* New York: Marvel Comics, 2003. To order, call 1-800-835-2671, e-mail pcaamerica@channing-bete .com, or visit www.channing-bete.com

Abuse prevention in a comic-book form. There are comics on emotional abuse, violence prevention, physical abuse, and fatherhood. Marvel stopped producing this long-running series, but copies are available until they run out.

New Moon: The Magazine for Girls and Their Dreams. 800-381-4743; www.newmoon.org

A fabulous alternative to traditional "teen" magazines. Full of relevant information, great stories, women's history, and stories of girls' lives around the world. A must for girls age 8 and up.

Polese, Carolyn. *Promise Not to Tell.* New York: HarperCollins, 1993.

A book for eight- to twelve-year-olds. This moving, beautifully illustrated story encourages children to tell if they are being abused. Currently out of print but available.

RESOURCES FOR TEENAGERS

Andersen, Laurie Halse. *Speak*. New York: Puffin, 1999.

Raw, authentic novel about a ninth-grader who struggles to survive date rape and simultaneously cope with the loss of her friends. Intense.

*Bass, Ellen, and Kate Kaufman. *Free Your Mind: The Book for Gay, Lesbian, and Bisexual Youth—and Their Allies*. New York: HarperCollins, 1996.

A refreshing change from the barrage of books focusing on the despair and suffering of lesbian, gay, and bisexual youth. This comprehensive, practical guide supports youth to stand up, speak out, and know their own worth.

Bell, Ruth. *Changing Bodies, Changing Lives: A Book for Teens About Sex and Relationships*, 3rd ed. New York: Times Books, 1998.

An antisexism, no-nonsense guide for teens, updated and expanded in a third edition. Clear definitions of sexual violence. An all-around reference book that every teen should have access to.

Berg, Elizabeth. *Durable Goods*. New York: Avon, 1993.

A beautifully written coming-of-age novel. Twelve-year-old Katie is facing her growing up crisis on a Texas army base after her mother has died.

Coman, Carolyn. *What Jamie Saw*. Volcano, CA: Volcano, 1996.

A gripping young adult novella about a nine-year-old boy who witnesses family violence. Dramatically portrays the impact of violence and documents what it takes to start a new life.

Editors at Fairview Press. *Teens Write Through It: Essays from Teens Who Have Triumphed Over Trouble*. Minneapolis: Fairview, 1998.

Bold and brutally honest essays from teens who have experienced sexual abuse and assault, drug addiction, racism, illness, disability, and more. Through their courage, wisdom, and willingness to survive, the teens offer hope and healing.

Foltz, Linda Lee. *Kids Helping Kids (Break the Silence of Sexual Abuse)*. Pittsburgh, PA: Lighthouse Point, 2003.

Young survivors will find hope and encouragement in these first-person accounts by young people abused as kids.

Goobie, Beth. *The Dream Where the Losers Go*. Custer, WA: Orca, 2006.

Haunting, brilliant, poignant novel about a teenager hospitalized for self-injury who finds refuge in dreams where she meets a boy who seeks also to "feel his way through pain."

Gravelle, Karen, and Jennifer. *The Period Book: Everything You Don't Want to Ask (but Need to Know)*, revised ed. New York: Walker, 2006.

Presented in a light and interesting way, this book educates girls and their parents about the changes that occur around puberty and beyond.

Harper, Suzanne, ed. *Hands On! 33 More Things Every Girl Should Know: Skills for Living Your Life from 33 Extraordinary Women*. New York: Crown, 2001.

Lively, eclectic, sometimes moving, sometimes hilarious collection of essays for girls. Its predecessor, *33 Things Every Girl Should Know* (1998), edited by Tonya Bolden, is also worthwhile.

Hughes, K. Wind, and Linda Wolf. *Daughters of the Moon, Sisters of the Sun*. Stony Creek, CT: New Society Publishers, 1997.

Vivid, real stories from forty teenage girls about their coming of age, accompanied by interviews with accomplished women mentors, including poet Maya Angelou, the Indigo Girls, Native American leader Wilma Mankiller, activist Angela Advise, and others.

*King County Sexual Assault Resource Center, P.O. Box 300, Renton, WA 98057; 425-226-5062; www.kcsarc.org.

King County has a wealth of fine material for teens about sexual violence, sexual harassment, dating, relationships, and more. All are free on the center's Web site.

Kuklin, Susan. *Speaking Out: Teenagers Take On Race, Sex, and Identity*. New York: Putnam, 1993.

This book of first-person stories documents the feelings and experiences of teenagers at a large multicultural high school in New York City.

Lee, Sharice A. *The Survivor's Guide*. Thousand Oaks, CA: Sage, 1995.

Written to educate adolescent girls about the effects of abuse, this small book will help young survivors understand that their reactions and difficulties are normal and that they're not alone.

*Lehman, Carolyn. *Strong at the Heart: How It Feels to Heal from Sexual Abuse*. New York: Farrar, Straus and Giroux, 2005.

A gentle, powerful journey through the healing process with nine diverse survivors, most still in their teens, who have made the passage. Their moving, personal stories and wonderful photographs touch the heart and inspire hope. Includes a resource guide kept up-to-date at the excellent Web site www.strongattheheart.com. For adults as well as teens.

*Levy, Barrie. *In Love and In Danger: A Teen's Guide to Breaking Free of Abusive Relationships*, 3rd ed. Emeryville, CA: Seal, 2006.

A wonderful, effective guide that motivates through encouragement and respect—using the experience of teens who have been there to show others how to make the best choices for themselves. *Dating Violence: Young Women in Danger* (1998) is an excellent anthology of firsthand accounts and essays about the emotional, physical, and sexual violence facing young women.

*Lorig, Steffanie, and Jeanean Jacobs. *Chill & Spill: A Place to Put It Down and Work It Out*. Seattle: Art with Heart, 2005. www.artwithheart.org

This beautifully designed guided journal features twenty activities that combine creative writing and expressive art to help adolescents cope with trauma, post-traumatic stress disorder, depression, self-harm issues, and more. Created by Art with Heart, a nonprofit organization that helps kids deal with crisis through publications and programs that foster self-expression.

Lynch, Chris. *Inexcusable*. Atheneum, 2005.

Compelling novel about a date rape told from the offender's point of view as he's confronted by the girl he raped. Lynch's *Sins of the Fathers* (Harper, 2006) is a wonderfully written story of three boys who stand up for themselves and each other against three priests in a Boston Catholic school.

Madaras, Lynda, with Area Madaras. *The "What's Happening to My Body?" Book for Girls: A Growing Up Guide for Preteens and Teens*, 3rd ed. New York: Newmarket, 2000.

This lively and comprehensive primer on puberty includes sections on breasts, periods, pubic hair, girls' and boys' sexual organs, romantic and sexual feelings, and much more. Includes an introduction for parents.

Mather, Cynthia, with Kristina Debye. *How Long Does It Hurt?: A Guide to Recovering from Incest and Sexual Abuse for Teenagers, Their Friends, and Their Families*, revised ed. San Francisco: Jossey-Bass, 2004.

A careful guide through the healing process for teens.

McCormick, Patricia. *Sold*. New York: Hyperion, 2006.

An important, heartbreaking, and beautifully written novel about a brave and resilient fourteen-year-old Nepali girl sold into sexual slavery.

Mufson, Susan, and Rachel Kranz. *Straight Talk About Date Rape*. New York: Facts on File, 1997.

Provides information about sexual assault by acquaintances and friends and offers ways to avoid, and, if necessary, deal with unwanted sexual encounters. The *Straight Talk* series has other good books for young people, including *Straight Talk About Post-Traumatic Stress Disorder*.

Pledge, Deanna. *When Something Feels Wrong: A Survival Guide About Abuse for Young People*. Minneapolis: Free Spirit, 2003.

Helpful guide that answers hundreds of questions that teens and children have about abuse. Addresses sexual, physical, and emotional abuse as well as neglect, bullying, and more. Includes resources.

*Rubin, Nancy, and a cast of hundreds. *Ask Me If I Care: Voices from an American High School*. Berkeley, CA: Ten Speed Press, 1994.

A remarkable teacher from Berkeley High School gets students to write about their real lives—on topics ranging from racial identity to death, from sexual orientation to sexual abuse. Outstanding.

Shandler, Sara. *Ophelia Speaks: Adolescent Girls Write About Their Search for Self*. New York: HarperCollins, 1999.

With poignant, piercing honesty, teenage girls speak for themselves about their experiences of sexual abuse and rape, self-injury, depression, breakups, body image, independence, and much more.

Shimko, Bonnie. *Kat's Promise*. New York: Harcourt, 2006.

Beautifully written novel about a resilient thirteen-year-old girl adopted by her cruel aunt after her mother dies.

Turner, Ann. *Learning to Swim*. New York: Scholastic, 2000.

A beautifully written memoir in narrative poetry about the importance of breaking silence about abuse. Deeply encouraging to young survivors. Authentically depicts the anguish caused by silence and the healing that begins when you tell and the abuse is finally stopped.

Voight, Cynthia. *When She Hollers*. New York: Scholastic, 1994.

Emotionally brutal portrait of one day in the life of a teenager who fights back against her adoptive father's abuse. It's an intense book—not for all young survivors, but excellent.

Weeks, Sarah. *Jumping the Scratch*. New York: HarperCollins, 2006.

Beautiful, chilling, and ultimately inspiring novel about an eleven-year-old boy who copes with emerging memories of abuse while contending with a bully, the loss of his beloved cat, and a loving, ailing aunt with a head injury.

*Wright, Leslie Bailey, and Mindy B. Loiselle. *Shining Through: Pulling It Together*, 2nd ed. Orwell, VT: Safer Society Press, 1997.

An excellent, empowering book and workbook written especially for teenage survivors. The revised edition adds material about self-esteem, body image, relationships, sexuality, therapy, and life. *Back On Track: Boys Dealing With Sexual Abuse* (1997) is excellent and simply written. Helps boys (age 10 and up) recognize their feelings and take steps toward healing.

PREVENTION RESOURCES FOR PARENTS

*King County Sexual Assault Resource Center, P.O. Box 300, Renton, WA 98057; 425-226-5062; www.kcsarc.org.

King County has many fine publications about sexual abuse and prevention for parents and teens—available free from the center's Web site or by mail. Be sure to get *Especially for Parents of Adolescents* and *ACT for Your Kids*. King County is currently translating all of their publications into other languages, including Spanish, Chinese, and Vietnamese.

Books

Adams, Caren, and Jennifer Fay. *No More Secrets: Protecting Your Child from Sexual Assault*. San Luis Obispo, CA: Impact Publishers, 1981.

A fine practical guide. Currently out of print but available.

Fay, Jennifer, et al. *He Told Me Not to Tell*, 2nd ed. Renton, WA: King County Sexual Assault Resource Center, 1991. www.kcsarc.org

A parents' guide for talking to children about sexual assault. This clear, direct book is also available in Spanish.

Krazier, Sheryll Kerns. *The Safe Child Book*, revised ed. New York: Fireside, 1996.

This is a clear, practical guide for teaching children skills to protect themselves. Reassuring, direct language.

Levy, Barrie, and Patricia Occhiuzzo Giggans. *What Parents Need to Know About Dating Violence*. Emeryville, CA: Seal, 1995.

Drawing on real-life experiences, this book offers straightforward advice to parents who are concerned about teenagers in abusive dating relationships.

Reeves, Claire. *Childhood: It Should Not Hurt! A Guide for Those Concerned with Our Children's Health and Welfare*. Huntersville, NC: LTI, 2003.

A call-to-arms discussion of frontline issues in the effort to protect children. Written by the founder of Mothers Against Sexual Abuse, the book covers child custody cases against abusers, cybermolesters, clergy abuse, and more.

Salter, Anna. *Predators, Pedophiles, Rapists, and Other Sex Offenders: Who They Are, How They Operate, and How We Can Protect Our Children*. New York: Basic Books, 2003.

An important book for parents and educators that dispels common and dangerous myths about sex offenders. Salter is also the author of *Transforming Trauma* and *Treating Child Sex Offenders and Victims*.

Sanford, Linda. *The Silent Children: A Parent's Guide to the Prevention of Child Sexual Abuse*. New York: McGraw-Hill, 1985.

Detailed and practical. Resources for single parents, parents of children with disabilities, and parents who are Asian, Native American, African-American, and Hispanic. A comprehensive guide. Currently out of print but available.

*van der Zande, Irene. *The KIDPOWER™ Book for Caring Adults: How to Teach Self-Protection and Confidence Skills to Young People*. Santa Cruz, CA: KIDPOWER, 2007. Available at www.kidpower.org

Teaches adults how to teach personal safety skills to children in an empowering, fun, and effective way. Includes building a foundation of emotional safety, keys to preventing trouble, protecting children from sexual abuse and bullying, and much more. With a Foreword by Ellen Bass, KIDPOWER founding board president.

IF YOUR CHILD IS ABUSED

Organizations and Web Sites

See "Activism and Public Policy" (p. 528) for additional organizations that address political, legal, and other advocacy issues.

Bikers Against Child Abuse (BACA); 866-71-ABUSE; www.bacausa.com

BACA's intent is to provide aid, comfort, safety, and support for children who have been sexually, physically, and emotionally abused. Founded by a therapist, many members are professionals who are frustrated at the limits of the system to fully protect and empower children. After a threat of harm to a child has been verified and is in the system, BACA will, as needed, ride out as a group to meet the child, let them know that they won't let anyone hurt them; camp out 24/7 in front of the child's home until the threat is over; write a letter to the perpetrator; and ride out to the perpetrator's neighborhood, handing out pamphlets door-to-door. They also accompany children to court when they have to testify. Currently there are chapters in twenty-seven U.S. states and in Australia.

California Protective Parents Association, P.O. Box 15284, Sacramento, CA 95851-0284; 866-874-9815; www.protectiveparents.com; and their subsidiary Courageous Kids Network, P.O. Box 1903, Davis, CA 95617; www.courageouskids.net

Nonprofit organization formed by nonabusive parents whose children were abused, then placed in the custody of their identified abusers by family courts. The association works to protect children from further harm through education, research, and advocacy. Also provides support and networking among protective parents nationally. The Courageous Kids Network is a growing group of young people who were placed in the custody of their abusers by family courts. They are speaking

out to educate the public about this violation of their human rights. Their web site, www.courageouskids.net, offers an array of online resources, support, and tools for kids who are currently trapped with abusive parents.

Justice for Children, 2600 Southwest Freeway, suite 806, Houston, TX 77098; 800-733-0059; info@justiceforchildren.org; www.justiceforchildren.org

With chapters in four states, Justice for Children advocates and intervenes on behalf of abused and neglected children in ongoing child abuse cases. They provide a full range of services that include guidance through a complex child protective system, legal advocacy, professional referrals, public policy monitoring, mental health services, court watch, research, education, and emotional support.

The Leadership Council, 191 Presidential Blvd., suite C-132, Bala Cynwyd, PA 19004; 610-664-5007; www.leadershipcouncil.org

A nonprofit scientific organization composed of respected scientists, clinicians, educators, legal scholars, and public-policy analysts whose mission is to promote the ethical application of psychological science. One of their goals is to provide clear, accurate scientific information to halt the practice of children being placed in the custody of abusers after they or a parent make a claim of abuse.

Mothers Against Sexual Abuse (MASA), P.O. Box 371, Huntersville, NC 28070; 704-895-0489; claire masa@aol.com; www.againstsexualabuse.org

Mothers Against Sexual Abuse works to prevent child sexual abuse through public education, support of legislation that protects children, and referrals for protective parents and adult survivors.

SOC-UM (Safeguarding Our Children United Mothers); www.soc-um.com

Dedicated to public awareness, children's education, and assistance to children who've been abused.

They distribute an elementary-school curriculum that can be downloaded from their Web site.

Books

*Adams, Caren, and Jennifer Fay. *Helping Your Child Recover from Sexual Abuse*, 3rd ed. Seattle: University of Washington Press, 1998.

Practical guidance for parents in the days and months after a child is abused. Information for parents is on one side of the page and sample conversations and activities for parents and kids to do together are on the other. Invaluable.

Ashley, Sandi. *The Missing Voice: Writings by Mothers of Incest Victims*. Dubuque, IA: Kendall-Hunt, 1992.

Twelve women tell their stories. Currently out of print but available.

Brohl, Kathryn, with Joyce Case Potter. *When Your Child Has Been Molested*, revised ed. San Francisco: Jossey-Bass, 2004.

Simple, clear, and helpful.

Johnson, Janis Tyler. *Mothers of Incest Survivors: Another Side of the Story*. Bloomington, IN: Indiana University Press, 1992.

A study based on firsthand accounts of six mothers whose daughters were abused by their fathers or stepfathers. Gives mothers a voice and challenges the stereotype of the collusive mother.

Matsakis, Aphrodite. *When the Bough Breaks: A Helping Guide for Parents of Sexually Abused Children*. Oakland: New Harbinger Publications, 1991.

A compassionate guide full of exercises, examples, and strategies for helping children. Written by a therapist whose daughter was sexually abused. Currently out of print but available.

Myers, John. *A Mother's Nightmare—Incest: A Practical Legal Guide for Parents and Professionals*. Thousand Oaks, CA: Sage, 1997.

Written by a law professor, this book is a valuable resource for mothers who are trying to protect their kids. Discusses the ways the legal system sometimes fails and explores the complexities of taking child sexual abuse cases to court.

*Ogawa, Brian. *To Tell the Truth*. Volcano, CA: Volcano Press, 1997.

A full-color illustrated book for children eight years and older to help guide them through the criminal justice system. Excellent resource for children who have to testify in court.

WHEN CHILDREN MOLEST

These resources can be helpful to both parents and counselors.

Organizations

*The Safer Society Foundation, Inc., P.O. Box 340, Brandon, VT 05733; 802-247-3132; referral line 802-247-5141; www.safersociety.org

The foundation maintains a computerized nationwide directory of agencies, institutions, and individuals who provide specialized assessment and treatment for youthful and adult sex offenders. It also publishes many useful resources for helping young sex offenders.

*Stop It Now! 351 Pleasant St., suite 319, Northampton, MA 01060; office, 413-587-3500; help line: 888-PREVENT, available 9 AM–6 PM EST; info@stopitnow.org; www.stopitnow.org

The Web site of Stop It Now! and its toll-free confidential help line offer adult support, information, and resources to adults who are concerned about adolescents and children engaging in harmful sexual interactions with other children.

Books

*Abel, Gene, and Nora Harlow. *The Stop Child Molestation Book: What Ordinary People Can Do in Their Everyday Lives to Save Three Million Children.* Xlibris, 2001. www.xlibris.com.

A clear, hopeful book that focuses strongly on prevention, encouraging parents to intervene to prevent abuse by their adolescents before it happens. Includes stories of parents who took steps to get help for their children who were acting out sexually.

*Allred, Terri, and Gary Burns. *Stop! Just for Kids: For Kids with Sexual Touching Problems by Kids with Sexual Touching Problems.* Brandon, VT: Safer Society Press, 1999.

Written by a group of boys in a treatment program for young offenders. Faces the hard issues with candor and hope. Easy to read.

Araji, Sharon. *Sexually Aggressive Children: Coming to Understand Them.* Thousand Oaks, CA: Sage, 1997.

A comprehensive overview of sexual abuse perpetrated by children. Araji explores the causes of such abuse and identifies nine treatment models for dealing with sexually aggressive kids. Written for professionals.

Cunningham, Carolyn, and Kee McFarlane. *When Children Abuse: Group Treatment Strategies for Children with Impulse Control Problems,* revised ed. Brandon, VT: Safer Society Press, 1996.

Valuable compilation of therapeutic exercises and activities. Useful also for teachers and school counselors. A follow-up by this same team, *Steps to Healthy Touching: A Treatment Workbook for Kids Who Have Problems with Sexually Inappropriate Behavior,* 2nd ed. (JIST, 2003), is a 12-step workbook designed to help kids ages five through twelve who have acted out sexually with younger children.

*Gil, Eliana. *A Guide for Parents of Children Who Molest,* 2nd ed. Rockville, MD: Launch Press, 1995. Available at www.selfesteemshop.com

Clear, simple, and compassionate. A must.

Gil, Eliana, and Toni Cavanagh Johnson. *Sexualized Children: Assessment and Treatment of Sexualized Children and Children Who Molest.* Rockville, MD: Launch Press, 1993. Available at www.selfesteemshop.com

A comprehensive look at the problem of sexually aggressive children. Clearly differentiates between age-appropriate sex play and molesting behaviors.

Hunter, Mic. *Child Survivors and Perpetrators of Sexual Abuse: Treatment Innovations.* Thousand Oaks, CA: Sage, 1995.

The first half of this book for professionals deals with treatment of sexually abused boys, inpatient treatment of adolescent survivors, and ritual abuse. The second half presents treatment strategies for abuse-reactive kids and their parents.

*Johnson, Toni Cavanagh. *Helping Children with Sexual Behavior Problems: A Guidebook for Professionals and Caregivers,* 3rd ed. San Diego, CA: IVAT, 2007. Available through www.tcavjohn.com

This often-recommended, thorough guide offers a wealth of support and information. Includes creating healthy boundaries, how to make the home safe for all children, developing a plan to decrease the behaviors, and more.

Pithers, William, Alison Gray, Carolyn Cunningham, and Sandy Lane. *From Trauma to Understanding: A Guide for Parents of Children with Sexual Behavior Problems.* Brandon, VT: Safer Society Press, 1993.

This pamphlet informs, reassures, and gives hope to parents.

*Stop It Now! *Do Children Sexually Abuse Other Children? Preventing Sexual Abuse Among Children and Youth.* Brandon, VT: Safer Society Press, 2007.

This expanded and updated booklet provides a clear, positive discussion about actions adults can take to prevent harmful sexual interactions between children, general information about children and sexuality, a description of behaviors that may suggest a risk of sexual abuse, and effective responses when concerns arise or harmful sexual behaviors are disclosed. Available in print or for free viewing at www.stopitnow.org/pubs.

FOR PEOPLE WITH DISABILITIES

Garbarino, James, Patrick Brookhouser, and Karen Authier. *Special Children Special Risks. The Maltreatment of Children with Disabilities*. New York: Aldine de Gruyter, 1987.

A collection of clinical essays on a critical topic.

Maxwell, Jane, Julia Watts Belser, and Darlena David. *A Health Handbook for Women with Disabilities*. Berkeley, CA: Hesperian, 2007. www.hesperian.org

A wonderful, comprehensive and compassionate guide that addresses everything from taking care of your body and pregnancy to self-defense and preventing abuse. See also *Helping Children Who Are Blind* (2000), in Spanish *Ayudar a los niños ciegos*, and *Helping Children Who Are Deaf* (2004). Hesperian is a nonprofit that publishes free online versions of all its titles.

Plummer, Carol. *Preventing Sexual Abuse: Curriculum Guides for K–6, 7–12, and Special Populations*, 2nd ed. Holmes Beach, FL: Learning Publications, 1997.

Includes sections on parent education and teacher training, role-plays, other suggested activities, and guidelines for working with developmentally disabled children.

Rappaport, Sol, Sandra Burkhardt, and Anthony Rotatori. *Child Sexual Abuse Curriculum for the Developmentally Disabled*. Springfield, IL: Charles C Thomas, 1997.

A comprehensive discussion about sexual abuse and treatment of sexually abused developmentally disabled children, followed by a curriculum that teaches abuse-prevention skills at the children's reasoning level.

Sgroi, Suzanne. *Vulnerable Populations: Sexual Abuse Treatment for Children, Adult Survivors, Offenders and Persons with Mental Retardation, Vol. 2*. New York: Lexington, 1989.

A helpful manual for professionals, teachers, and caregivers that includes a curriculum, information on sexual abuse avoidance training, and evaluation and treatment of sexual offense behavior.

DVD

Charting New Waters: Violence Against Women with Disabilities. National Clearinghouse on Family Violence. Distributed by the Justice Institute of British Columbia. VHS/DVD. cfcs@jibc.ca; www.jibc.ca/cfcs/CustSol/Publications.html

Explores the issue of violence in disabled women's lives. A useful resource for teaching caregivers, social workers, advocates, and criminal justice personnel how to deal with these situations in a respectful, appropriate manner.

FILMS AND DOCUMENTARIES

Films and documentaries are also listed in individual subject areas of the Resource Guide.

An increasing number of mainstream feature films address child sexual abuse as well. Depending on where you are in your healing process, some of these may be triggering.

Abuse: Part 1. The Loss of Abundance, Part 2. The Art of Healing. Brazen Video, available from Wisconsin Committee to Prevent Child Abuse; 608-256-3374; www.preventchildabusewi.org

TRAINING FILMS

*Cavalcade Productions, P.O. Box 2480, Nevada City, CA 95959; 800-345-5530; www.cavalcadeproductions.com

Producers of more than fifty fine films for professionals about psychological trauma. Topics include self-injury, trauma and eating disorders, successful trauma therapies, dissociation, legal issues, boundary issues, vicarious traumatization, trauma and memory, and more. They also produce films for survivors. See their online catalog for titles.

This special film combines a social and political awareness with artistic expression. Part 1 explores the roots of abuse through interviews, art, song, and performance. Part 2 documents a project of healing through art. Both men and women survivors of many races and cultures are included.

Breaking Silence. Theresa Tollini. Future Educational Films. Distributed by New Day Films; www.newday.com

One of the first documentaries to address incest and child sexual abuse. Celebrates survivors who find the courage to break silence, claim their self-worth, and regain their lives. In *Still Missing*, four parents of children who were taken from their families share their stories and provide concrete ways to protect children from predators.

Downpour Resurfacing. Frances Nkara. Available at www.downpourresurfacing.com

A brilliant, experimental documentary and must-see for what it says about memory, attachment, the effects of trauma, and healing. A masterful combination of eclectic imagery, survivor story, and healing guide. The subject of the film is Robert

Hall, a survivor, bodyworker, and leader in the somatic healing movement.

Hand of God. Joe Cultrera. www.handofgodfilm.com. Powerful, beautifully done feature-length documentary about sexual abuse in the Catholic church.

The Healing Years: Surviving Incest and Sexual Abuse. Kathy Barbini. KB Films/Big Voice Pictures. www.bigvoicepictures.com

This powerhouse of a film profiles three strong, vibrant survivors of child sexual abuse who convincingly tell us—once and for all—that we must take back our lives. Banishes shame and celebrates women's power.

Hollow Water. Bonnie Dickie. National Film Board of Canada. www.nfb.ca

This documentary features an isolated Ojibway community that uses traditional Aboriginal approaches to heal its history of sexual abuse, violence, suicide, and addiction.

Locked. Juli Lasselle. Mardorla Pictures.

Authentic and painful portrayal of a woman trapped inside the hell of her silence and her pain. Follows her attempts to break free and tell her sister the truth about the abuse she suffered as a girl.

Narrow Bridge. Israel Moskovits. IzzyComm Motion Pictures. www.narrowbridgefilm.com.

A young Orthodox Jew faces the truth of having been sexually abused by his rabbi when he was twelve.

Searching for Angela Shelton. Angela Shelton. Hillhopper Productions. Available at www.searchingforangelashelton.com

An inspiring, heartbreaking, and powerful cross-country journey by a survivor and filmmaker who set out to survey American women through the lens of every woman she could find who shared her name. She found that seventy percent had been raped, molested, or beaten. In the film she confronts her own father. Also see her memoir, *Finding Angela Shelton: The True Story of One Woman's Triumph Over Sexual Abuse*, 2008.

To a Safer Place. National Film Board of Canada; 800-542-2164; www.nfb.ca

This award-winning hour-long film shows one survivor's path toward healing. It follows Shirley Turcotte, a survivor of father–daughter incest, as she returns to her hometown and confronts her family.

A Story of Hope. Marilyn Van Derbur. Available through www.missamericabyday.com

Marilyn's first public presentation of her story of childhood incest and her victorious road to healing and recovery.

FICTION FOR INSPIRATION

Allison, Dorothy. *Bastard Out of Carolina*. New York: Plume, 1992.

A powerhouse of a book. A beautifully written, painfully gripping story of poverty and abuse in rural North Carolina. May be triggering for some survivors.

Berg, Elizabeth. *Talk Before Sleep*. New York: Random House, 1997.

A moving story about two women's friendship while one dies from breast cancer.

Danticat, Edwidge. *Breath, Eyes, Memory*. New York: Soho, 1994.

All of Danticat's novels are stunning and often-tragic glimpses into the Haitian experience. In *Breath*, her first, a twelve-year-old girl, who was born after her mother was raped, leaves Haiti to rejoin her mother in New York. Accurate and artful portrayal of trauma. Also read *The Dew Breaker* (2004), *The Farming of Bones* (1998), *and Krik Krak* (1999).

Flagg, Fannie. *Fried Green Tomatoes at the Whistle Stop Cafe*. New York: Fawcett, 1988.

A funny and wise book about the things that are important in life. Every woman we know who's read this book—from twelve to sixty-five—has loved it.

Garden, Nancy. *Lark in the Morning*. New York: Farrar, Straus and Giroux, 1991.

A fine young adult novel about two abused children who run away and the young woman who finds them. The children are brave and resourceful.

Gibbons, Kaye. *Ellen Foster*. New York: Vintage Books. 1988.

The story of a young girl who overcomes adversity with considerable spunk.

Harrison, Kathryn. *Exposure*. New York: Warner, 1993.

A well-written and disturbing novel about a woman violated by her father's erotic photographs of her.

Haruf, Kent. *Plainsong*. New York: Knopf, 1999.

A quiet, beautifully executed, character-driven novel that evokes small town life on the American Plains. Kent also wrote *Eventide* (2006), *Where You Once Belonged* (2004), and *The Tie that Binds* (2002).

Hosseini, Khaled. *The Kite Runner*. New York: Penguin, 2003.

This novel about class divisions, war, the rape of a child, the price of silence, healing, and redemption is set in Afghanistan and the United States. His second novel, *A Thousand Splendid Suns* (2007), juxtaposes the brutality of domestic violence with the power of women's friendship.

Karr, Mary. *The Liar's Club: A Memoir*. New York: Viking, 1995.

> A vivid, intense memoir. Exceptionally well written, full of grit, humor, and love.

Kingsolver, Barbara. *The Bean Trees*. HarperCollins, 1988.

> A wonderful novel about finding yourself, healing an abused child, and the power of love in a new "found" family. Her other fiction includes *Prodigal Summer* (2000), *The Poisonwood Bible* (1998), *Pigs In Heaven* (1993), and *Animal Dreams* (1990).

LeGuin, Ursula. *A Wizard of Earthsea*. New York: Bantam, 1975.

> Compelling fantasy about a young man's quest to seek out and conquer the frightening shadows that chase him. Survivors of sexual abuse will have no trouble identifying with his denial, his search, and his recovery.

Luders, Lesa. *Lady God*. Norwich, VT: New Victoria, 1995.

> An achingly real novel about healing from mother–daughter incest.

McKinley, Robin. *Deerskin*. New York: Ace Books, 1993.

> A fierce and beautiful tale of sexual abuse and healing told in the fantasy genre—complete with princess, prince, castles, and even a dragon.

Morrison, Toni. *The Bluest Eye*. New York: Plume, 1970.

> A beautiful novel about a young survivor from an extraordinary writer. Ellen considers her novel *Beloved* the finest of any living author.

O'Brien, Edna. *Down By the River*. New York: Farrar, Straus and Giroux, 1997.

> Moving, lyrical novel about a young Irish girl who seeks an abortion after finding herself pregnant through incest. Based on an actual 1992 case that came before Ireland's Supreme Court.

Palwick, Susan. *Flying in Place*. New York: Tor, 1992.

> Twelve-year-old Emma learned to leave her body when her father molested her, and now does it often, meeting the sister who died before Emma was born.

Quindlen, Anna. *Black and Blue*. New York: Delta, 1998.

> A disturbing novel about domestic violence as an abused woman and her son start over in a new city.

Salkind, Betsy. *More than Once Upon a Time*. Self-published, 2006. Available through www.betsysalkind.com.

> Written and illustrated in a children's picture-book format, this deceptively simple, thirty-one-page, full-color book for adults portrays abuse and healing. Salkind is a stand-up comedian by night and sexual abuse activist by day.

Salter, Anna. *Shiny Water*. New York: Pocket Books, 1997.

> Written by a prominent therapist with long experience with both victims and offenders, this is a fine mystery about a child sexual assault custody case. See also *Truth Catcher* (2006); *Fault Lines* (1998), about a sadistic sex offender and a victim with post-traumatic stress disorder; *Prison Blues* (2002); and *White Lies* (2002).

Sapphire. *Push*. New York: Knopf, 1996.

> A powerful portrayal of resilience and determination as an illiterate incest survivor learns to read.

Sebold, Alice. *The Lovely Bones*. New York: Little, Brown, 2002.

> Haunting novel about a raped and murdered girl who keeps watch over her grieving family and

friends, her killer, and the detective working on her case, from heaven. Sebold also wrote *Lucky*, a memoir about her recovery from a violent rape. *Lucky* is graphic and can be disturbing, though the resolution is ultimately positive.

Smiley, Jane. *A Thousand Acres*. New York: Fawcett, 1992.

A finely written story of complex people in a family whose foundation was undermined by sexual abuse.

Walker, Alice. *The Color Purple*. New York: Washington Square Press, 1982.

A young woman's letters to God. A passionate human story of triumph through adversity.

Watson, Larry. *Montana 1948*. New York: Simon & Schuster, 1993.

Told from the point of view of an adolescent boy, this well-written novel portrays a family's struggle when it is discovered that one of its members is guilty of sexual abuse. Shows small-town life and the tensions of class and race between whites and Native Americans.

Williams, Reverend Cecil, and Janice Mirikitani. *I've Got Something to Say About This Big Trouble: Children of the Tenderloin Speak Out*. Glide Word Press, 1989.

Drawings, poetry, rap poems, and stories by children from the Tenderloin district of San Francisco. Children speak for themselves about crack, homelessness, and being poor.

Winterson, Jeannette. *The Passion*. New York: Vintage, 1989.

Unforgettable, brilliant, and beautifully written novel about a woman and the woman she loves.

POETRY

Anderson, Alice. *Human Nature*. New York: NYU Press, 1994.

In haunting, elegant verse, these poems rise out of childhood suffering, danger, and darkness, to affirm survival and life.

Bass, Ellen. *The Human Line*. Port Townsend, WA: Copper Canyon Press, 2007.

Ellen Bass sees into the life of things, creating a poetry that goes straight to the heart. See also Ellen's previous book, *Mules of Love* (2002).

Brown, Nickole. *Sister*. Granada Hills, CA: Red Hen Press, 2007.

When there is sexual abuse in a family, all the relationships are affected. In this compelling book, Brown explores her relationships with her sister and mother, focusing especially on the impact her own leaving home had on her sister.

Cartier, Marie. *I Am Your Daughter, Not Your Lover*. San Diego: Clothespin Fever Press, 1994.

A brave document—poetry of resilience, perseverance, and renewal.

Derricotte, Toi. *Tender*. Pittsburgh, PA: University of Pittsburgh Press, 1997.

In all Toi Derricotte's work, there is an astounding honesty. She digs down so deep she actually arrives at saying the unspeakable. See also *Captivity* (1989), *The Empress of the Death House* (1978), and *Natural Birth*, 2nd ed. (2000), as well as her brilliant memoir *The Black Notebooks* (1999).

Duhamel, Denise. *Two and Two*. Pittsburgh, PA: University of Pittsburgh Press, 2005.

Smart and unpretentious, Duhamel's poetry takes on a wide variety of subjects, including a brilliant sestina, "Incest Taboo," that's a must-read.

Fisk, Molly. *Listening to Winter*. Berkeley, CA: Roundhouse, 1999.

> Molly Fisk writes about love, sex, small towns, child abuse, and the solace of the natural world. See also the letterpress collection *Salt Water Poems* (1994).

Howe, Marie. *What the Living Do*. New York: Norton, 1999.

> With enormous clarity, grace, and compassion, these poems tell us about abuse, pain, death, and the preciousness of life. Marie Howe's poetry is luminous and unforgettable. See also *The Kingdom of Ordinary Time* (2008) and *The Good Thief* (1988).

Laux, Dorianne. *Facts About the Moon*. New York: Norton, 2005.

Lindsay, Frannie. *Lamb*. Florence, MA: Perugia, 2006.

> These poems about abuse, trauma, and healing transcend their subjects. They are hymns of praise for the love we are able to wrest from our flawed lives.

Maltz, Wendy, ed. *Passionate Hearts: The Poetry of Sexual Love*, 2nd ed. Novato, CA: New World Library, 2006.

> Celebrates sexual intimacy based on caring, safety, and respect. See also *Intimate Kisses: The Poetry of Sexual Pleasure* (2001).

Whether she is writing about incest, sex, or the life of trees, these poems are astonishing, full of courage and clarity, precision and beauty. A brilliant poet with heartbreaking, heart-mending poems. See also *Awake* (1990, 2007), *What We Carry* (1994), and *Smoke* (2000).

Olds, Sharon. *The Gold Cell*. New York: Knopf, 1987.

> One of the finest poets writing today, Sharon Olds captures the range of feelings in complex family relationships. See also *Strike Sparks: Selected Poems, 1980–2002* (2004); *The Unswept Room* (2002); *Blood, Tin, Straw* (1999); *The Wellspring* (1996); *The Father* (1992); *The Dead and the Living* (1984); and *Satan Says* (1980).

Sachs, Carly, ed. *the why and later: an anthology of poems about rape and sexual abuse*. Cleveland, OH: Deep Cleveland Press, 2007.

> A compelling and crucial anthology that explores heartache, rage, devastation, and healing. It's amazing that it's taken so long for an anthology like this to be published, but we're fortunate to have this excellent collection that includes poems by some of the best poets of our time, as well as strong work from new poets.

Acknowledgments

ACKNOWLEDGMENTS FOR THE TWENTIETH-ANNIVERSARY EDITION

We have a host of people to whom we're grateful for help with this new edition of *The Courage to Heal*:

First and foremost, we'd like to thank our inestimable researcher, Cynthia Lamb, who is truly the third member of our team. Cynthia was responsible for revising and updating the Resource Guide, she provided additional assistance with research for the footnotes and text, and handled all the permissions. Cynthia's intelligence, hard work, compassion, insight, good humor, and good sense have been a joy to us throughout the year we've worked together.

Amy Pine helped us begin work on this new edition by offering her perspective on how best to revise and update the book, as well as providing exercises, resources, and other assistance along the way. Karen Olio generously read large sections of the book and helped us shape our approach to this new edition. Staci K. Haines read several chapters of the book and allowed us to draw heavily from her work in the field of trauma, the role of the body, and sexuality. Belleruth Naparstek helped us understand new developments in trauma and healing, read portions of the book, and shared powerful guided imagery from her book, *Invisible Heroes*. Mary Jo Barrett read sections of the book and helped us clarify and shape our perspective on family issues. Wendy Maltz allowed us to include significant excerpts from her work in the field of sexuality.

For their careful and generous reading and critique of the book, we have many people to thank. Jackie Sheeler provided a poet's ear with her detailed line editing. Pam Mitchell read every word of this book, as she has for past editions, and offered invaluable critique and insight every step of the way. Lucy Diggs also read every word and once again gave us terrific line editing and critique.

Donna Henderson, Rob and Deb Longo, Doug Sawin, Christine Courtois, Laurel Andrew-Salvay, Charlotte Kasl, and Nancy London all read sections of the book and offered helpful feedback and further perspective.

Among the survivors we'd like to thank for their contributions are Pauline Eanlai Cronin, Donna, Molly Fisk, Margot Silk Forrest, G. Herbkersman, Deborah Hirsch, Terresa Lauer, Dorianne Laux, Carolyn Lehman, Rae Luskin, Carole McPherson, Sandra Paiva, Lisa Fujie Parks, Jeanann Power, Linda S., S. Sonali Sadequee, Beverly Sky, Carol Steele, Maureen Stone, and Evie Thompson (Evie T.).

Other people whose contributions have helped along the way: Janet Bryer, Sigrid Erro, Linda Goode, Leslie Crowell Ingram, Jeanne Lenzer, Pamela Pine, Anneliese Singh, Shalom Victor, and Robyn Clare Wesley.

We'd also like to thank our agent, Charlotte Raymond, for her encouragement and dedication from the very beginning and our editor, Toni Sciarra, for her support of this new edition. Thanks also to Anne Cole who graciously stepped in and saw the book to completion.

A NOTE FROM LAURA

Two months before the revisions for the twentieth-anniversary edition of *The Courage to Heal* were due, I was diagnosed with breast cancer. During the final weeks in which we were sup-

posed to be completely engrossed in finishing the book, I was getting lab tests, meeting with surgeons, oncologists, and radiation therapists; reading everything I could about breast cancer; and trying to grapple with the new terrain I had suddenly been thrust into. With incredible grace, generosity, and love, Ellen shouldered the challenge of finishing the book without me. She is a colleague and a friend beyond measure. I feel an incredible depth of gratitude to her and to all the angels who appeared at the zero hour so that this twentieth-anniversary edition could make its way into your hands.

A NOTE FROM BOTH OF US

We are grateful for the help we've been given all along the way—with every edition of *The Courage to Heal*. We'd like to add our special thanks to the last-lap angels. Pam Mitchell and Lucy Diggs kindly offered their help with numerous late-stage decisions when Laura was unavailable. And Cynthia Lamb graciously took over an unexpected load of exacting tasks, including research, correspondence, permissions, proofreading, and final manuscript preparation. We are both immensely grateful not only for their time and work but also for their open-hearted willingness to help.

AND A P.S. FROM LAURA AS WE GO TO PRESS

I'm happy to report that I have completed my treatment for breast cancer and am regaining my strength and vitality. As I reflect on the challenges I have faced in the past year, it is absolutely clear to me that the lessons I learned as a survivor of child sexual abuse are what enabled me to respond to my diagnosis and the trauma of treatment with courage, resilience, and an open heart. Because it was not the first time I had faced great adversity, I brought to my illness an unshakable confidence in myself. As I commented to a friend one day, "I was already a well-seasoned human being." I knew how to breathe through hard times, gather the resources I needed, build a supportive community around me, and successfully advocate for myself. Most importantly, I trusted my own deep intuition about the steps I needed to take in order to heal. All of this was possible because of the life lessons I learned as a survivor. For those lessons—and for my life now—I am extremely grateful.

ACKNOWLEDGMENTS FOR THE FIRST EDITION (1988)

We would like to thank the hundreds of survivors and partners who answered our ads, returned our calls, and shared their stories with us. We are also grateful to the participants in Ellen's workshops who generously allowed us to tell their stories and describe their struggles. Their courage and determination inspired us and deepened our own commitment. This book would not exist without them.

There are many people who've provided invaluable assistance to us in completing this project. Together, we'd like to thank:

Janet Goldstein, our editor at Harper & Row, for her incredible support, brilliance, dedication, and her unwavering belief in this book from the beginning.

Katherine Ness, production editor extraordinaire, whose care, thoughtfulness, and attention went beyond the call of duty; Laura Hough, whose creative attention to design made for a beautiful book; and to our literary agent, Charlotte Raymond, for her ongoing encouragement and support.

Sandra Butler, Lucy Diggs, Jeanne Mayer Freebody, Dorothy Morales, Nona Olivia, Kay Slagle, and Daniel Sonkin for their invaluable criticism of the manuscript as a whole. And Lucy Diggs for extensive line editing, and for cooking a fine Christmas dinner.

Lola Atkins, Janet Bryer, Jesse Burgess, Mariah Burton-Nelson, Pandora Carpenter, Lauren Crux, Carol Anne Dwight, Rashama Khalethia, Edith Kieffer, Ellen Lacroix, Donna Maimes, Wendy Maryott-Wilhelms, Rose Z. Moonwater, Pat Pavlat, Amy Pine, Robin Roberts, Helen Resneck-Sannes, Ariel Ellen Shayn, Roger Slagle, Deborah Stone, and Karen Zelin for their careful reading of portions of the manuscript.

Kristina Peterson, Margaret Hill, Pat Saliba, and Emily Joy Hixson, Laura's housemates, for love and patience all those days when Ellen slept in the living room and the dining room table was piled with papers.

Among the survivors we'd like to thank for their contributions are Janice Avila, Rachel Bat Or, Shelley Bennet, Eileen Daly, Natalie Devora, Martha Elliott, Jill Fainberg, Ely Fuller, Ann Marie Godwin, Jayne Lacey, Barbara Hamilton, Margaret Hawthorn,

Rashama Khalethia, Edith Kieffer, Krishna-bai, Dorianne Laux, Jennierose Lavender, Suzanne Leib, Cristin Lindstrom, Julie Martchenke, Erin May, Sharrin Michael, Janet Hanks Morehouse, Nina Newington, Kathleen O'Bannon and her daughter Maureen Davidson, Lynn Slade, Kay Slagle, Catherine Stifter, Teresa Strong, Josie Villalpando, and Diana Wood.

Others whose contributions have helped along the way: Jane Ariel, Beth Beurkens, Diana Bryce, Judy Butler, Don Cotton, Gabby Donnell, Linda Eberth, Sandi Gallant, Diane Hugs, Adrianne Chang Kwong, Julie Robbins, Kathleen Rose, Sue Saperstein, Theresa Tollini, Donna Warnock, Mary Williams, and Linda Wilson.

The Fessenden Educational Fund, for help with expenses.

Florence Howe, for teaching me the basics of facilitating groups: respect for each person's feelings and thoughts. And for opening so many doors.

Marty Bridges, for promoting the first I Never Told Anyone workshops; Pam Mitchell, for bringing them to Boston; and Becky Northcutt, for bringing it all back home.

Susan Bass, for vigorously encouraging me to write this book, against all my protestations.

Laura Davis, for pushing me past what I thought were my limits.

Saraswati Bryer-Bass, for making me care so much.

And Janet Bryer, for loving my eccentricities instead of my virtues and for teaching me to fool around.

ELLEN BASS

I have received such abundant encouragement and support that I can't name everyone, but I would particularly like to thank:

All the workshop participants who taught me what survivors need in order to heal.

Mildred Bass, my mother, for giving me the wholehearted love and commitment every child deserves. And Sarah Wolpert, her mother, for giving that to her. So much of what I have to give to survivors I received from them.

Josephine Clayton, for being a second mother to me.

Pat Pavlat, my therapist, for being a model of excellence. And for inspiring me to climb Angel's Landing.

LAURA DAVIS

Writing my first book on an issue of such deep and personal significance has been possible only because of the tremendous love and support I have received. I'd like to thank:

Karen Zelin for being everything a best friend should be; Natalie Devora for many kinds of sustenance; Barbara Cymrot, Dafna Wu, and Ruby for being family; Nona Olivia for humor, encouragement, and wisdom; Aurora Levins Morales for cooking me duck and telling me to write; Roberta Rutkin for teaching me to honor my creativity.

Janet Bryer and Saraswati Bryer-Bass for patience, love, countless wonderful meals, and always making me feel at home.

Abe Davis, my father, for creative inspiration, his quick wit, and most of all his unyielding faith in me.

Linda Eberth for teaching me that healing was possible, even for me.

Dagny Adamson, Marcy Alancraig, Ophelia Balderrama, Theresa Carilli, Kimberly Jane Carter, Lynn Chadwick, Diane Costa, Carol Anne Dwight, Brandy Eiger, Toke Hoppenbrouwers, Diane Hugs, Shama Khalethia, Wendy Maryott-Wilhelms, Helen Mayer, Jennifer Meyer, Nina Newington, Kathleen Rose, Paula Ross, Jane Scolieri, Ray Gwyn Smith, Catherine Stifter, Deborah Stone, and Cheryl Wade for friendship, encouragement, and belief in this project.

Irena Klepfisz, Sandy Boucher, and Tillie Olsen for inspiration, wisdom, and encouraging me to write.

Rick Eckel, Alan Burton, and all the reporters at *Youth News* for patience and flexibility.

Dorothy Morales for wisdom and generosity.

Melanie Joshua for helping me stay in my body.

And finally my coauthor, Ellen Bass, for a million things, but mostly for changing her mind and saying yes.

ACKNOWLEDGMENTS FOR THE THIRD EDITION (1994)

This third edition of *The Courage to Heal* would not have been possible without the generous help of the following people:

Our irreplaceable and irreverent research assistant, Shana Ross, for whom no job was too big—or too small.

Our editor, Janet Goldstein, for her commitment to ensuring that *The Courage to Heal* continues to address the needs of survivors with integrity.

Our agent, Charlotte Raymond, for her encouragement, advocacy, and dedication.

Our colleagues at *Moving Forward*, Lana Lawrence, Linda Palmer, and Susan Neill, for their hard work and willingness to make "Honoring the Truth" available prior to its publication here.

Our readers, whose careful critique of "Honoring the Truth" informed our thinking and infused our work with their collective wisdom: Sherry Anderson, Kathy Barbini, Sandra Butler, Christine Courtois, Abram Davis, Jill Freeland, Denise Gaul, Evelyn Hall, Mary Harvey, Judith Herman, Leslie Ingram, Jaimee Karroll, Richard Kluft, Dan Lobovits, Teri Ray, Shauna Smith, Maxine Stein, Mary Tash, Ellie Waxman, and Judy Wilbur-Albertson. Special thanks to the Dayenu Club—Lucy Diggs, Jennifer Freyd, Barb Jackson, Lana Lawrence, Susan Frankel, Larry Klein, Karen Olio, Nona Olivia, Anna Salter, Margot Silk Forrest, and Roland Summit—who not only read the manuscript but shared their time and knowledge in countless other ways.

Many others contributed time, information, and resources: Brian Abbott, Patricia Alexander Weston, John Backus, Mary Jo Barrett, Pamela Birrell, Laurie Braga, John Briere, Jennifer Carnes, Teri Cosentino, Renee Fredrickson, Gail Gans, Faye Gorman, Jaime Guerrero, Cory Hammond, Val Hartouni, Lisa Lipshires, Elizabeth Loftus, Màiri McFall, Chrystine

McCracken, Kee McFarlane, Rebecca North-cutt, Jackie Ortega, Sherri Paris, Judith Peterson, John Rhead, Margo Ross, Lynne Sansevero, Mark Schwartz, Jane Sinclair, Gary Stickel, Gayle Stringer, Patricia Toth, Heidi Vanderbilt, Charlotte Watson, and Linda Meyer Williams.

We also thank our partners, Janet Bryer and Karyn Bristol, for their love and moral support.

For the math we couldn't do ourselves, we thank Saraswati Bryer-Bass and Chantalle von der Zande.

And for loving care of baby Eli so Laura could go back to work, Laurel Wanner.

Grateful acknowledgment is made to the following for permission to reprint copyrighted material:

"What My Father Told Me" and "Two Pictures of My Sister" by Dorianne Laux. Copyright © 1987 by Dorianne Laux. Published with the permission of the author.

"to my friend, jerina" from *Quilting: Poems 1987–1990* by Lucille Clifton. Copyright © 1991 by Lucille Clifton. Reprinted with the permission of BOA Editions, Ltd., www.boaeditions.org

"The Thing Is," "Bearing Witness," and "Basket of Figs" from *Mules of Love* by Ellen Bass. Copyright © 2002 by Ellen Bass. Reprinted with the permission of BOA Editions, Ltd., www.boa editions.org

"There is a pain so utter" reprinted by permission of the publishers and the Trustees of Amherst College from *The Poems of Emily Dickinson*, Thomas H. Johnson, ed., Cambridge, MA: The Belknap Press of Harvard University Press. Copyright © 1951, 1955, 1979, 1983 by the President and Fellows of Harvard College.

"Surrender" (published subsequently in *Listening to Winter*) by Molly Fisk. Copyright © 1992 by Molly Fisk. Published by permission of the author.

"Putting Away My Bras" from *Lamb* by Frannie Lindsay. Copyright © 2006 by Frannie Lindsay. Reprinted with the permission of Perugia Press, www.perugia-press.com.

"Bubba Esther, 1888" from *Permanent Address: New Poems 1973–1980* by Ruth Whitman. Copyright © 1980. Reprinted by permission of the author.

"The Minks" from *Captivity* by Toi Derricotte. Copyright © 1989. Reprinted by permission of the University of Pittsburgh Press.

"Girl Child" from *Facts About the Moon* by Dorianne Laux. Copyright © 2006 by Dorianne Laux. Used by permission of W.W. Norton & Company, Inc.

"Moon" from *Picnic, Lightning* by Billy Collins. Copyright © 1998. Reprinted by permission of the University of Pittsburgh Press.

"When My Father Was Beating Me" from *Tender* by Toi Derricotte. Copyright © 1997. Reprinted by permission of the University of Pittsburgh Press.

Material excerpted from *Radical Acceptance: Embracing Your Life with the Heart of a Buddha* by Tara Brach, Ph.D. Copyright © 2003 by Tara Brach. Used by permission of Bantam Books, a division of Random House, Inc.

"Morning Meditation" by Lee Whitman-Raymond. Copyright 1990 © by Lee Whitman-Raymond. Published with the permission of the author.

"Reconciliation" by Cheryl Marie Wade. Copyright © 1987 by Cheryl Marie Wade. Published with the permission of the author.

"Little Things" from *The Gold Cell* by Sharon Olds. Copyright © 1987 by Sharon Olds. Use by permission of Alfred A. Knopf, a division of Random House, Inc.

"Autobiography in Five Short Chapters" from *There's a Hole in My Sidewalk: The Romance of Self-Discovery* by Portia Nelson. Copyright © 1994 by Portia Nelson. Reprinted with the permission of Beyond Words Publishing.

"The Guest House" from *The Essential Rumi*, translated by Coleman Barks. Copyright © 1997 by Coleman Barks. Reprinted with the permission of Coleman Barks.

Material excerpted from *Invisible Heroes: Survivors of Trauma and How They Heal* by Belleruth Naparstek. Copyright © 2004 by Belleruth Naparstek. Used by permission of Bantam Dell.

Material excerpted from *Healing Sex: A Mind-Body Approach to Healing Sexual Trauma* (originally published as *The Survivor's Guide to Sex*) by Staci K. Haines. Copyright © 2007 by Staci K. Haines. Reprinted with the permission of Cleis Press.

"The Attic" from *What the Living Do* by Marie Howe. Copyright © 1997 by Marie Howe. Used by permission of W.W. Norton & Company, Inc.

"Uses of the Erotic" from *Sister Outsider* by Audre Lorde. Copyright © 1984 by Audre Lorde. Reprinted by permission of Crossing Press, a division of Ten Speed Press, Berkeley, CA, www.tenspeed.com.

"The Split" from *Human Nature* by Alice Anderson. Copyright © 1994 by Alice Anderson. Reprinted by permission of the author.

Material excerpted from *The Sexual Healing Journey: A Guide for Survivors of Sexual Abuse*, revised edition, by Wendy Maltz. Copyright © 2001 by Wendy Maltz. Reprinted with the permission of the author.

"The Lovers" from *What We Carry* by Dorianne Laux. Copyright © 1994 by Dorianne Laux. Reprinted with the permission of BOA Editions, Ltd., www.boaeditions.org.

"Lucky" from *Donkey Gospel* by Tony Hoagland. Copyright © 1998 by Tony Hoagland. Reprinted with the permission of Graywolf Press, Saint Paul, Minnesota.

List of Poems

Index